Wisdom of Communities

Wisdom of Communities

Volume 3
Communication in Community

Published by
The Fellowship for Intentional Community
Rutledge, Missouri

The Fellowship for Intentional Community, Rutledge, MO 63563

Printed in the United States of America

ISBN: 978-0-9995885-4-3
Printed by CreateSpace.

Cover design: Megan Cranford, www.megancranforddesign.com

Layout design: Marty Klaif

Project managers: Chris Roth, Christopher Kindig

COMMUNICATION IN COMMUNITY

(Wisdom of Communities, Volume 3)

CONTENTS

II. DECISION-MAKING AND GOVERNANCE

II. POWER, GENDER, CLASS, AND RACE

V. RELATIONSHIPS AND INTIMACY

Introduction

Volumes 1 and 2 in this series address how to find your place in intentional community by either creating or joining one. But how can this experience—and communities themselves—last past the "honeymoon" phase? How can groups turn long-term ideals into reality within their lives together?

A combination of "soft" and "hard" skills and systems must be present for intentional communities and their members to endure, evolve, and thrive. Sustainability in both human and ecological relationships is key to developing a cooperative culture that lasts—and is the focus of *Wisdom of Communities* Volumes 3 and 4.

The stories in this third volume focus on the "soft" skills and approaches—the human dimension of community living. Authors share experiences, tools, advice, and perspectives that will benefit anyone who wants to help their community function well and support members' well-being.

Articles explore the nuts and bolts of living together in community: creating and sustaining a cooperative group culture; decision-making and governance (including extensive reflections on consensus as well as Diana Leafe Christian's complete series on sociocracy); power, gender, class, and race; relationships and intimacy; politics and neighbor relations. These are all essential areas that communities need to address if they are to retain members and develop strong and healthy group connection.

Communitarians often discover that the quality of life they experience has much more to do with the quality of their interactions with each other than with physical amenities. Systems, structures, agreements, understandings, awareness, cultural practices, and self-education can all contribute to increasing that quality of life. Learning about these "soft skills" from others engaged in similar work can help communities immeasurably.

All articles are drawn from the past decade of Communities magazine. Every issue of Communities contains further treatments of these and similar themes, so we hope that you'll not only learn from these past stories, but also keep up with new ones by subscribing to the magazine (ic.org/subscribe).

Thanks for making use of these resources, and good luck on your community journey!

Chris Roth
Editor, Communities
May 2018

I

COOPERATIVE GROUP CULTURE

Good Meetings:

Business & Well-Being

How do you suggest keeping business decision-making, on the one hand, and community well-being issues, on the other, both healthily separate and integrated?

Q Historically, our group has felt fairly unified in our core values. Our business discussions and decisions rested on certain basic assumptions and expectations, including the importance of respecting others, welcoming feedback, accepting personal responsibility for feelings and actions, avoiding blame, and—to the best of our abilities—communicating openly, nonviolently, and compassionately. We held both regular business meetings and regular well-being meetings, so that business discussions could flow more efficiently and interpersonal and emotional issues could have their own forum. This arrangement allowed us to "call vibes" during a business meeting and channel an obvious well-being issue into another setting, untangling it from the matter at hand; it also gave us circles in which we could focus exclusively on nurturing individual and group well-being, resolving conflicts, and becoming more connected as a community.

More recently, our group grew in size and it became more difficult for everyone to attend regular well-being circles. Some people tired of the structure, while others got intensively involved in a different well-being circle instead, separate from the whole community. We scheduled less-frequent community well-being circles, and attendance even at those slowly declined. Some newer arrivals turned out to be resistant to or rebellious about "dealing with feelings" and elected not to participate in well-being circles. Concurrently, there was an increase in focus on certain business issues, and more talk about the importance of "separating business and community."

Unfortunately, "separating business and community" now seems to mean, for some people, that we each have a choice whether or not to deal with well-being issues or feelings when they impact business issues. Our old practice, with a balance of business and well-being circles, gave equal importance to the two areas, and included everyone in both. Now, it seems that well-being issues can affect our business circles more than they ever did before—through cynicism, unresolved interpersonal conflicts, and negativity—while some of the most outspoken people apparently do not share the core values and understandings that allowed us to deal with these issues in a separate well-being forum, in which they often resist or avoid participation.

How do you suggest keeping business decision-making, on the one hand, and community well-being issues, on the other, both healthily separate and integrated? How can our community return to better balance, more effective decision-making, and greater connection?

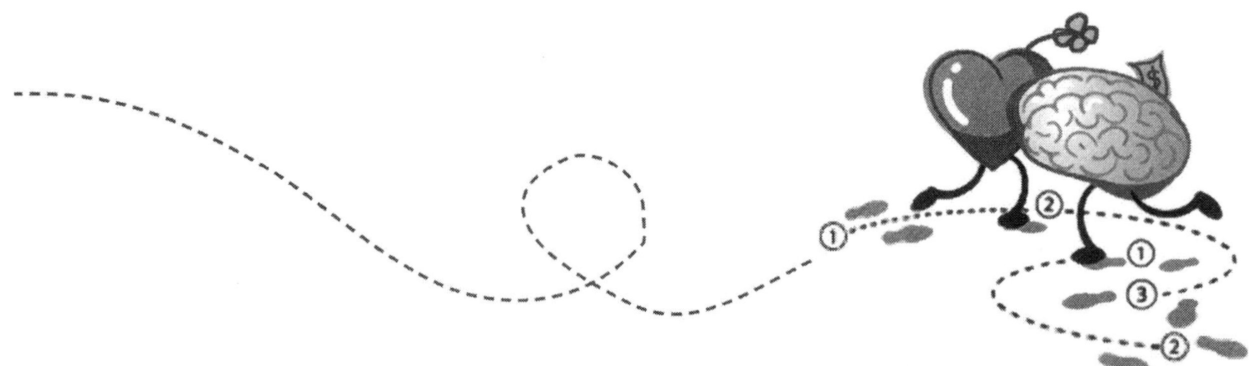

Tree Bressen responds:

I have to say, i feel for you and your community. This sounds like a tough one. While it might have been better if the group had done more effective membership screening up front or taken other steps to prevent the shift in core values, telling you that probably doesn't feel like much help now. So what are your options? Because the group is not on board with what you are wanting to see happen, my response focuses on what you as one individual can attempt.

1. Do whatever you can to make whatever remains of the well-being forum keep healthy and happening. Put positive energy into it. Help make it a fulfilling experience for whoever is there. Good energy will make it attractive to others to join.

> *Be a role model yourself in how you relate with others.*
>
> — Tree Bressen

2. Assuming the sessions are flowing well, approach members who haven't been coming one-on-one to invite them to attend. Tell them you would love to see them there. If you can't make the approach without a judgmental tone, recruit someone else to have the conversation instead. Or split up the membership list, with each regular attendee committing to talk with a few other people who they have a good relationship with.

3. Be a role model yourself in how you relate with others. If you have a conflict with someone, don't wait for them to approach you (which they may never do), take the initiative to work it out.

4. When you notice emotions coming up at business meetings, you can help create safe space to bring them out, whether or not you are the official facilitator. Statements like, "Wait a moment, i'd like to hear more from Sam about why he supports the proposal," or "Jo, it sounds like your concerns are X, Y, & Z, is that right?" can potentially get at feelings without necessarily using explicitly emotional language. Because they are clearly based in an effort to be productive on the issues at hand, even people who are "anti-touchy-feely" are likely to respond well and appreciate these efforts.

5. Does your group do evaluations at the end of meetings? That might be an appropriate time to bring up observations of how conflicts are getting in the way of communication. Or if it's really obvious that this is happening in the middle of an agenda item, you might choose to be bold and call it in the moment. If you take that route, try to express yourself in a compassionate way if you can.

6. To the extent possible, avoid polarizing the issue. Find the part of yourself that appreciates an emphasis on task, and express that to the more business-oriented members. Look for how you can be their ally. State things in terms they can relate to. For example, "I really think that in order to move forward effectively with this proposal, Wilma and McKenzie need to sit down and discuss the reasons for their differing viewpoints." (As opposed to something like, "The bad vibes in here are driving me crazy—can't you two work out your stuff?")

7. Recruit more members who share values of communication, dealing with emotions, and personal growth. Over time you may be able to reverse the shift.

Tree Bressen is a group process consultant based in Eugene, Oregon, who works with intentional communities and other organizations on how to have meetings that are lively, productive, and connecting. Her website, www.treegroup.info, offers extensive free resources on consensus, facilitation, and more. (Tree uses a lower-case "i" in her articles as an expression of egalitarian values.)

Laird Schaub responds:

This is a great question, touching on a number of important topics.

First, what does it mean to be a member of the community? Apparently, at first there was a clear value around working through interpersonal tensions and then, for some reason, you ceased screening new members for a fit with that value. Unless that shift was consciously made, that's

a guaranteed train wreck. The old timers will lament the "heartless" newcomers, and the newbies will feel blindsided by the old fogies' hidden agenda.

The solution to this is being as intentional as possible about matching prospective members with community values. If you intend that working through emotional issues is group work, make sure incoming folks know what they're signing up for (and have sufficient social skills to get the job done).

> *I am not a fan of automatically separating business and heart (isn't the new culture we're trying to create essentially about the sensitive integration of the two?)*
>
> — **Laird Schaub**

Second, I am not a fan of automatically separating business and heart (isn't the new culture we're trying to create essentially about the sensitive integration of the two?). Please don't misread what I've just said. I am not saying it's never appropriate to hold well-being circles. Rather, I advocate the community choosing, case by case, whether to work emotions that surface in general meeting in the moment or in a different setting (which could include one-on-one with facilitation, a well-being meeting of the whole group, work with outside counseling—really anything that the participants are willing to try).

Sometimes productive work on a particular issue is simply not possible until and unless the distress arising in the examination is resolved first. In such situations, tabling the interpersonal work for the next well-being meeting effectively means that the topic is held hostage to the distress. It's reasonable for the group to be able to ask if it can afford that. By extension, if the answer is "no," then it needs to be possible to work tensions on the spot.

Digging deeper, this is not likely to succeed unless the group has a clear understanding of how to work constructively with emotions. The art here is understanding when distress has risen to the level that it's starting to cause non-trivial distortion of information. It is highly helpful for the group to have an agreement about checking this out whenever it is perceived to be happening (I phrase it this way because people often project distress onto others by assuming, erroneously, that everyone evidences distress the same way)—even in business meetings.

The idea here is to acknowledge the distress for the purpose of addressing the distortion—not to "fix" someone, or heal them. This is a meeting (of caring people), not therapy. Done well, the group need not be reactive to the fact that someone was reactive. They can simply validate what has occurred, counteract the tendency of distressed people to feel isolated and misunderstood, and return to the discussion of the issue. This last is key. It is the attempt to balance heart and business in the moment.

By assiduously separating business and heart into two different forums, it is predictable that you'll get the result you've described: the "product" people will focus more on the business meetings, and the "process" people will attend more to the well-being sessions. Instead of enhancing integration, you'll be inadvertently reinforcing the differences and accelerating a schism. In my book, offering "full-service" meetings where business and heart are both in play is the surest path to sound decisions and a cohesive group.

Laird Schaub, a member of Sandhill Farm community in Missouri, has been doing consulting work on group process since 1987. A longtime activist in community networking, he has lived in community since 1974 and been involved with the Fellowship for Intentional Community (FIC) since 1986; he is currently its Executive Secretary. laird@ic.org; 660-883-5545. Laird authors a blog which can be read at communityandconsensus.blogspot.com.

Beatrice Briggs responds:

"Business" and "well-being" are not two separate categories. Like thinking and feeling, they go together. Business decisions affect the lives of community members and vice versa. Efforts to suppress interpersonal conflicts and emotions in business meetings and divert them to another forum are counter-productive, as this case shows. So the question becomes how to find more productive ways to integrate the information contained in emotional and interpersonal material into the "business" discussions—without turning the meetings into group therapy sessions. The best way I know to do this is to use Roger Schwarz's "Ground Rules for Effective Groups":

1) Test assumptions and inferences.
2) Share all relevant information.
3) Use specific examples and agree on what important words mean.
4) Explain your reasoning and intent.
5) Focus on interests, not positions.
6) Combine advocacy and inquiry.
7) Jointly design next steps and ways to test disagreements.
8) Discuss undiscussable issues.

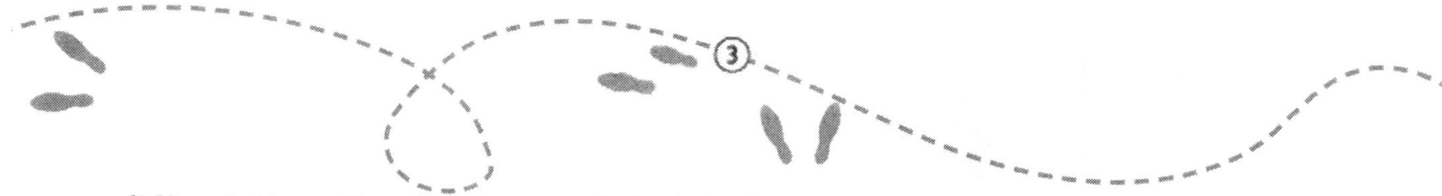

9) Use a decision-making rule that generates the level of commitment needed.

In order for these rules to work, they need to be applied in combination with the following core values:

- Valid information
- Free and informed choice
- Internal commitment
- Compassion.

In a community context, compassion is essential.

— Beatrice Briggs

In a community context, compassion is essential. Group members need to cultivate the ability to temporarily suspend judgment and really listen to what they are saying (and not saying) to each other, be concerned for each other and recognize each others' suffering. Business meetings are as good a place as any to put compassion to work.

Successfully applying these principles takes training and practice, as well as skillful facilitation. To get started, visit www.schwarzassociates.com, where you will find a lot of helpful articles and other information.

In short, my recommendation is to eliminate the practice of automatically sending emotional and interpersonal material to the "well-being ghetto." Both your business meetings and community life will benefit.

Beatrice Briggs is the founding director of the International Institute for Facilitation and Change (IIFAC), a Mexico-based consulting group that specializes in participatory processes. The author of the manual Introduction to Consensus *and many articles about group dynamics, Beatrice travels around the world, giving workshops and providing facilitation services in both English and Spanish. Home is Ecovillage Huehuecoyotl, near Tepoztlán, Mexico, where she has lived since 1998. bbriggs@iifac.org; www.iifac.org.*

Caroline Estes responds:

There are a few parameters missing from this question, so I will make some assumptions and hope that it is helpful.

It is not unusual for communities that have been around for some time to become lax in their inquiry on new members. The passage of time often blurs the original commitment and intent of the forming individuals. It would seem that there has been a lack of understanding by some of the newer members as to the basic values and commitments that the original members had.

The only "out" at this point seems to be a process of recommitment. That is not to say that some of the original values and processes may not have matured into other forms, other than those at the beginning. However, from my perspective, the balance that you put in place at the beginning seems very mature and important.

It is not clear to me if the incoming new members understood and accepted the original process. If they did not or were not informed, then it is important to return to the original meaning and organizational expectation of the founders.

As I said, I don't know under what circumstances you take new individuals, but it seems wise to be sure they understand the process they are accepting.

It is not unusual for communities that have been around for some time to become lax in their inquiry on new members. The passage of time often blurs the original commitment and intent of the forming individuals.

— Caroline Estes

The larger the community gets without a clear understanding of the original purposes and values, the more diffused will be the acceptance of those purposes and values.

Native Americans hold with a basic number of 25 for a cohesive community. If you have gone beyond this number, it might be well to have separate circles to take care of emotional and deeper issues of your community. It would seem that the situation you find yourself in cannot lead to cooperative harmony at present.

It may also be a situation in which you need to divide the community between a core group that holds to the original vision and a support group that is in general agreement but not interested in the process of the community. ❁

Caroline Estes, cofounder of Alpha Farm community in Oregon and Alpha Institute, which teaches consensus and offers facilitation services, has been teaching and facilitating consensus for more than 40 years. Caroline has taught consensus to most intentional-community-based facilitators in North America, and works with Hewlett-Packard, University of Massachusetts, the US Green Party, the Association of Waldorf Schools of North America, and many other organizations. caroline@ic.org.

Communities Editorial Policy

Communities is a forum for exploring intentional communities, cooperative living, and ways our readers can bring a sense of community into their daily lives. Contributors include people who live or have lived in community, and anyone with insights relevant to cooperative living or shared projects.

Through fact, fiction, and opinion, we offer fresh ideas about how to live and work cooperatively, how to solve problems peacefully, and how individual lives can be enhanced by living purposefully with others. We seek contributions that profile community living and why people choose it, descriptions of what's difficult and what works well, news about existing and forming communities, or articles that illuminate community experiences—past and present—offering insights into mainstream cultural issues. We also seek articles about cooperative ventures of all sorts—in workplaces, in neighborhoods, among people sharing common interests—and about "creating community where you are."

We do not intend to promote one kind of group over another, and take no official position on a community's economic structure, political agenda, spiritual beliefs, environmental issues, or decision-making style. As long as submitted articles are related thematically to community living and/or cooperation, we will consider them for publication. However, we do not publish articles that 1) advocate violent practices, or 2) advocate that a community interfere with its members' right to leave.

Our aim is to be as balanced in our reporting as possible, and whenever we print an article critical of a particular community, we invite that community to respond with its own perspective.

Submissions Policy

To submit an article, please first request Writers' Guidelines: Communities, 81868 Lost Valley Ln, Dexter OR 97431; 541-937-2567 x116; editor@ic.org. To obtain Photo Guidelines, email: layout@ic.org. Both are also available online at communities.ic.org.

Advertising Policy

We accept paid advertising in Communities because our mission is to provide our readers with helpful and inspiring information—and because advertising revenues help pay the bills.

We handpick our advertisers, selecting only those whose products and services we believe will be helpful to people interested in community living, cooperation, and sustainability. We hope you find this service useful, and we encourage your feedback. As in the Communities Directory, we edit our REACH listings only for clarity and length, and can't guarantee that all community information contained in them is accurate—we encourage you to verify it as you pursue your interest in any group.

John Stroup, Advertising Manager, 10385 Magnolia Rd, Sullivan MO 63080; 573-468-8822; ads@ic.org.

What is an "Intentional Community"?

An "intentional community" is a group of people who have chosen to live or work together in pursuit of a common ideal or vision. Most, though not all, share land or housing. Intentional communities come in all shapes and sizes, and display amazing diversity in their common values, which may be social, economic, spiritual, political, and/or ecological. Some are rural; some urban. Some live all in a single residence; some in separate households. Some raise children; some don't. Some are secular, some are spiritually based; others are both. For all their variety, though, the communities featured in our magazine hold a common commitment to living cooperatively, to solving problems nonviolently, and to sharing their experiences with others.

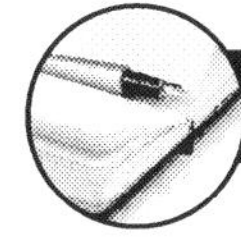

PUBLISHER'S NOTE BY LAIRD SCHAUB

Technology Doesn't Change Just the Answers

Sometimes It Changes the Questions as Well

I have a three-lettered acronym that comes in handy as a process consultant: OBE. (No, it doesn't mean Order of the British Empire, though that's a useful bit of crossword trivia.) In my argot, it means "overtaken by events." I use it to describe challenges that become moot with shifting circumstances.

For example, learning how to type accurately was an important secretarial skill when people relied on the technology of mimeograph machines to create inexpensive copies (it was an absolute booger correcting mistakes on a stencil, necessitating costly delays). Today, in the era of high-speed photocopiers, no one uses stencils. With computer word processing and inexpensive printers, it's no big deal to rework a document and crank out a fresh original if someone discovers a typo. Although it's more important today that everyone learns to type—it's hard to imagine functioning without email or access to the Web—the need to type accurately is largely OBE.

In general, people live in intentional communities with the purpose of altering their lifestyles to something more in line with their values than they can readily find among mainstream options. It's what makes them "intentional." While communities vary substantially in where they draw their lines, for the purpose of this article I want to focus on the history of television at Twin Oaks, which is a well-established income-sharing community in central Virginia that will celebrate its 42nd anniversary in June. Twin Oakers have a history of being deliberate about how much they let outside culture seep into their environment, and yet the floodgates are never closed completely. They are not trying to be isolationist; they are striving simply to moderate their exposure to mainstream cultural influences—an effort I applaud.

Last August I was at the community to participate in their annual Communities Conference, affording me an occasion to visit with long-time friends around the edges of conference activities. In one such conversation I got a thoughtful reply about the community's evolving relationship with outside media.

Like a number of communities trying to create alternative culture, there has traditionally been a lively debate at Twin Oaks about the evils of television. In its early years, the community simply didn't allow one on the property—it was viewed as too large a conduit for promotion of the kind of values the community was trying to be an alternative to, such as manufactured demand, violence, vapid dialog, materialism, and social isolation (ever try to have a meaningful conversation in the same room with an active television?). While most people will admit that television occasionally offers programs of value, on the whole this was felt to happen not nearly enough to justify all the other crap that would come over the transom. It was an interesting line to draw. While magazine subscriptions went uncensored and there was no attempt to limit radio reception, TV was banned as too insidious.

[As a long-time member of Sandhill

Farm, another egalitarian community, I am highly sympathetic to this debate. We're a 34-year-old group and have never owned a television. Just ask my kids how weird that was. Now both adults, they were careful when growing up about how much they shared of their Sandhill upbringing with their peers. How would they explain no TV? And while I have an excellent relationship with both of my kids today, and visit them frequently, both also own large, flat-screen TVs and subscribe to cable.]

Sometime in the '80s—when Twin Oaks had about two decades under its belt—the community was anonymously gifted a large-screen television, and the community accepted. (There was an intriguing rumor that the donor was none other than B.F. Skinner, the Harvard psychologist whose Utopian novel *Walden Two* inspired the creation of Twin Oaks. It was purported that Skinner offered the television as an educational enhancement, and I never learned if this story were true or apocryphal.) While some Cassandras decried it as a Trojan Horse, the community (after considerable debate) decided it could benefit from the television recreationally. It cleverly disabled the tuner, rendering the unit useful only for showing videocassettes. These had become popular by that time and it helped keep members home, as they weren't inclined to frequent area cinemas as much when movies were coming to them.

The movies shown on campus had to be vetted for acceptable values, and viewings took place only on certain evenings. For the most part, this middle-ground position has worked well and the practice continues today. Technology, however, as it is wont to do, kept evolving and the equation got considerably more complex with the advent of personal computers, miniature televisions, and cell phones.

While the community kept pace with the Information Age by providing an increasing number of desktop computers available for member use in public space, it was perhaps inevitable that machines would start moving into people's private rooms. When the community committed to providing wireless hubs and DSL service, anyone with a computer in their bedroom had unfettered access to the cornucopia of information and visual stimulation of the world wide web. (Sandhill has DSL and wireless service as well, and I am not criticizing that choice; I am only trying to point out how the questions change with the technology.)

Laptops kept getting cheaper, and new, younger members started arriving already owning them and having grown up with the baseline expectation of internet access. Several years ago the community made a conscious effort to recruit and retain younger members, and the decision to support high-speed internet in particular (and modern electronic technology in general) has aided that campaign. Today,

"And this is our community room where we socialize"

Ethan Hughes

publicly shown movies are still screened for appropriateness, yet there is no control whatsoever about what members are watching in their own rooms. While the community is pleased with its success in attracting a younger population, my friend at the Communities Conference related her uneasiness with this shift to wide open video access—be it DVDs, something from Netflix, or whatever catches your fancy on the web—having taken place as a result of cultural drift, rather than as the outcome of conscious choice.

A particularly poignant event occurred at Twin Oaks in the late '90s that highlights the emotional flaring that's possible when values and technology collide. I want to tell the story of my pseudonymous friends Dale and Fulano.

[While "Fulano" is not in my normal pantheon of androgynous pseudonyms, I've selected it here because it was a distinctive favorite of my recently deceased friend and Twin Oaks founder, Kat Kinkade. Kat, this bud's for you!]

Though neither lives in the community today, they were both well-established members at the time of this incident. Dale was mild-mannered, yet highly principled. Fulano was creative and fun-loving.

It happened one day that Fulano was discovered to have smuggled a small television into his bedroom. While clearly against the community norms, he figured no one would notice and what harm was he causing anyway? He was just quietly watching movies in his own room. Dale was pissed by this flaunting of community norms and Fulano's apparent insensitivity to the community's carefully worked position regarding how much mainstream culture was allowed to permeate the community's cultural membrane.

While Fulano was promptly asked to remove the television (and did so), Dale still seethed and was contemplating what he felt might be appropriate consequences for this flagrant violation of agreements. At this critical juncture (are there ever any accidents?), it came out that Dale, a devoted Trekkie, had occasionally been secretly entering the community's public television space after hours and privately watching videos of Star Trek, the Next Generation. Oops. You might say Dale was hoisted by his own Picard.

In the ensuing decade, personal computers have gradually become a normal feature in members' rooms at Twin Oaks. It's a done deal. While private televisions are still outlawed, who cares? It was this back-door development that my friend was unhappy about. However, I am not writing this article to say that technology is bad or that Twin Oaks has sold out. I don't think either thing.

Twin Oaks is living in the same world as the rest of us and we all have to face the challenge of deciding which aspects of modern technology to embrace and which to set aside.

Twin Oaks is living in the same world as the rest of us and we all have to face the challenge of deciding which aspects of modern technology to embrace and which to set aside—typically before we can see clearly the full ramifications of our choice. I am writing this article to point out that as technology changes, so do the questions. I'm imagining, for instance, that Twin Oaks today is more concerned with whether its acceptance of modern electronic technology enhances the quality and frequency of social connections among members. Twenty years ago with television, the answer was "no." In the current world of iPhones and YouTube, the answer is not so clear.

Today, Twin Oakers, like a lot of us, still wrestle with questions about what constitutes healthy culture and how to manifest it. That said, concerns over how much someone is watching Jean Luc outwit aliens is OBE. Just do it in your own room. ❋

Laird Schaub is executive secretary of the Fellowship for Intentional Community (FIC), publisher of this magazine, and cofounder of Sandhill Farm community in Missouri, where he lives. He authors a blog which can be read at communityandconsensus.blogspot.com.

COOPERATIVE GROUP SOLUTIONS Advice About How to Handle Challenging Dynamics

Cigarettes, Alcohol, Visitors, and Events

Ethan Hughes

Q: *Our intentional community hosts many outside events and ongoing programs with residential students. Some of the policies regarding substance use that we instituted for ourselves as members don't seem to "cross over" very well when applied to visitors and event attendees.*

For example, we originally had a "no alcohol" policy on the property, since we wanted to create as clear a space as possible for exploration of feelings and for personal and spiritual growth, but we changed that policy to allow alcohol consumption in private residences, as long as it was done in moderation and without obvious adverse effects on work performance, community life, etc. The reality was that some members who'd joined after the community's founding enjoyed very moderate amounts of alcohol, and it seemed reasonable to make our policies match our practices rather than forcing those members to lie. Since then, alcohol has become more common in private residences, as witnessed by the piles of bottles and cans in our recycling area.

One difficulty has come in deciding what to tell program and event attendees about alcohol. Some of our literature tells them that alcohol is not allowed, but when they arrive here, they inevitably discover that it is in fact present. Some then start to use it in their own and others' "private spaces"—which, because of the nature of our guest accommodations, often turn out to be rather public spaces. Others, who had been looking forward to an alcohol-free environment, are confused and disappointed. Alcohol consumption was manageable and caused no problems when it was confined to just some of the residents, who did it in private, but when our many additional visitors start to get involved, it can escalate into a part of the shared culture, which is not what we ever intended it to be.

Similarly, in years past, we often had one or two smokers, usually new or exploring members, who smoked in the single "smoking allowed" area. This had some impact on others in the community, especially those very allergic, but it was a compromise that allowed smokers to be here instead of excluding them out of hand. Usually our shared goal was for the person to kick the habit. We also kept that smoking area open for conference guests—we figured we couldn't afford to lose business by making our site completely non-smoking. The problem has come with more and more people arriving at our community, both for short- and long-term stays, who are not necessarily aiming to quit and who quickly seem to use smoking as a way of socializing and hanging out. Suddenly, we have way more smokers and way more smoke fumes in the environment than any of us—even the resident smokers—had anticipated or wanted.

In both cases, guidelines that were tenable when applied to a smaller group of longer-term residents, all of whom shared a common desire to not make substances a big part of their lives, seem to be untenable when applied to a larger group of visitors and shorter-term residents. Community members themselves seem to have contributed to the drift. Do we need to become more rigid? Or do those who are most negatively impacted by alcohol consumption and smoking simply need to accept the situation, or leave? How can we as a community establish healthy boundaries in relation to event and program attendees? Is it fair to have two sets of standards, one for community members and one everyone else? And how can we discuss this in a way that brings the community together rather than tearing it apart?

Beatrice Briggs responds:

It sounds as if your business model is affecting the quality of life of the community members. To minimize the danger of "tearing the group apart" over this issue, I suggest convening a process divided into three parts: analysis, reflection, and decision. Make sure that all members understand which phase of the process they are in, and limit discussion to topics relevant to that phase. Properly facilitated, this should cut down on the amount of self-serving drama, foster a learning environment, and lead to a decision that everyone can support.

1. First, analyze the business aspect.

a. Assemble as many verifiable facts as possible. The kind of data needed could include: How much income came from visitors and shorter-term residents in the past two years (or whatever period makes sense in your context)? What percentage of total income does this amount represent? How many community members earn all or part of their income from the visitor programs? How many visitors and shorter-term residents came to the community in this period? What percentage of them smoked or drank during their stay? How many complaints were received? How many days or weeks per year is the community open to visitors and shorter-term residents? After digesting the facts, reflect on how these numbers affect the members and their quality of life.

b. Conduct a survey of past visitors and shorter-term residents, asking questions such as: How important is a smoke- and/or alcohol-free atmosphere is to you? To what degree were you bothered by the presence of smoke/alcohol at the community? Would you come to the community if you knew there was a strictly enforced no smoking/alcohol policy?

c. Research the market. Find out what alcohol/smoking policies other retreat and conference centers have.

2. Then revisit the community's vision and mission. Are they still relevant in the current context? If so, what do they tell you about the alcohol/smoking policies as they relate to members and visitors? If not, how should they be changed?

3. Finally, jointly construct a proposal for a new alcohol/smoking policy—or affirm the existing one. Weigh the options and make a decision.

This process could take some time to complete. Meanwhile, I suggest modifying your literature to convey a more accurate picture of the current community policies regarding alcohol and cigarettes—even if this involves admitting to a certain amount of ambivalence around these issues.

Beatrice Briggs is the founding director of the International Institute for Facilitation and Change (IIFAC), a Mexico-based consulting group that specializes in participatory processes. The author of the manual Introduction to Consensus *and many articles about group dynamics, Beatrice travels around the world, giving workshops and providing facilitation services in both English and Spanish. Home is Ecovillage Huehuecoyotl, near Tepoztlán, Mexico, where she has lived since 1998. bbriggs@iifac.org; www.iifac.org.*

Tree Bressen responds:

I'm starting from the assumptions that any of the outcomes mentioned here are potentially fine, and that it's not up to me to tell your community what its substance use policy should be. Therefore i'm going to focus here on how to have a good conversation about these charged topics.

The most common problem with lifestyle discussions of this nature is if a group falls into blame and defensiveness. One good way to avoid that is to keep the discussion personal at first, before getting into solutions. Have people share stories from their own life experience—no one can argue with another person's life. Or start the discussion in small to mid-sized groups, either before a full-group discussion or early on in a meeting on the topic. These tactics invite compassion over judgment.

What you want is to fill out the complexity of perspectives, and then create a dynamic of the whole group against the problem instead of people in the group feeling at odds with each other. Another method for doing this might be to explore each viewpoint in turn. For example, ask everyone to step into the role of smoker/drinker and talk about how the world looks from that perspective; then invite everyone to step into the role of someone concerned about substance use and say what that's like for them. Next invite everyone into the role of resident member, and then ask everyone to remember back to when they were a visitor or guest. Have everyone brainstorm reasons for a firmer guideline, and then have everyone list what's good about keeping things more loose. And so on. That way each role is de-personalized.

Once a diversity of feelings and viewpoints have been explored, look for areas of agreement...such as your statement that even the smokers are currently wishing for less smoke in the living areas. Then problem-solve together on how those joint desires could be fulfilled. As an example from another arena, abortion foes and pro-choice activists have sometimes found common ground in working on programs to prevent unwanted pregnancies. If you can hold a constructive discussion on the whole subject, my experience is that people will naturally generate good solutions and gravitate to them together.

Tree Bressen is a group process consultant based in Eugene, Oregon, who works with intentional communities and other organizations on how to have meetings that are lively, productive, and connecting. Her website, www.treegroup.info, offers extensive free resources on consensus, facilitation, and more. (Tree uses a lower-case "i" in her writing as an expression of egalitarian values.)

Caroline Estes responds:

It is an interesting phenomenon that oftentimes the values a group of people start a community with get diluted as the community ages. Such is the case with us. However, when we began most people smoked, and within a year everyone stopped. We thought the reason was that we were in control of our own lives to a large extent and did not need the release that smoking seemed to give. However, I have seen a resurgence of the need to smoke within the last few years. We too have an outside smoking area (no smoking inside any of our houses).

Our situation is a bit different in that we don't have events, but we do have many visitors. Our visitors are informed of our smoking policy and are welcome in the smoking area.

However, the alcohol problem is different. We take up this issue at least once every year or so, and have actually denied internship to some because of the excessive use of alcohol. It would seem that you need to decide as a group what you want to do. It would seem wise to segregate the two groups when making this decision—members or visitors/event participants. Members have an ongoing commitment to each other. If someone got to drinking to excess it could be taken up within the membership. However, with visitors to your community it seems within your responsibility to have a "no alcohol" policy for them.

We are wrestling with the same problem since our residents interact with our visitors and the use of alcohol is apparent. We are in the midst of another round of discussions on the alcohol problem.

Caroline Estes, cofounder of Alpha Farm community in Oregon and Alpha Institute, which teaches consensus and offers facilitation services, has been teaching and facilitating consensus for more than 40 years. Caroline has taught consensus to most intentional-community-based facilitators in North America, and works with Hewlett-Packard, University of Massachusetts, the US Green Party, the Association of Waldorf Schools of North America, and many other organizations. caroline@ic.org.

Laird Schaub responds:

This is a great example of clashing values. On the one hand your group likely has a value of supporting individual choice, so long as the exercise of it doesn't harm others and is otherwise consistent with your other values. As it does not appear that you have a group value against smoking or against alcohol consumption, you probably want to support the right of individual members to choose their own path with respect to substance use.

On the other hand, you probably also have a value of being a conference center that conducts its business with integrity—by which I mean you practice what you espouse—and you may have a commitment to providing a healthy, safe environment for guests and visitors using your facilities.

Assuming I am right about your core values, your challenge is to figure out how to balance these values appropriately on the issue of how smoking and alcohol consumption are practiced among consenting members and guests. The key to this going well is being able to talk about what's happening accurately and without judgment. If there are unresolved tensions around this topic (which there probably are), then you'll need to clear those before attempting the balancing process.

I am reasonably confident that you'll want a solution that you can openly share with potential clients, and which will accurately reflect your actual practices. You don't want either members or guests sneaking off to smoke or drink, nor do you want them shunned or embarrassed when enjoying their habits within the boundaries everyone agreed with.

In the end, your group will be watched more closely for how well you deal with tough issues than how purely you lead your lives. ❋

Laird Schaub, a member of Sandhill Farm community in Missouri, has been doing consulting work on group process since 1987. A longtime activist in community networking, he has lived in community since 1974 and been involved with the Fellowship for Intentional Community (FIC) since 1986; he is currently its Executive Secretary. laird@ic.org; 660-883-5545. Laird authors a blog which can be read at communityandconsensus.blogspot.com.

Do you have a question for our Cooperative Group Solutions panelists? Please send it to editor@ic.org.

COOPERATIVE GROUP SOLUTIONS ADVICE ABOUT HOW TO HANDLE CHALLENGING DYNAMICS

Balancing Outer and Inner Ecology

Ethan Hughes

Q: *Our community is dedicated to a wide range of goals, from ecological responsibility and sustainability to healthy interpersonal relationships and personal and spiritual growth. We strive for a holistic integration of them all, but in reality people who come here have varying priorities. Some interns and members focus intently on living lightly, eating locally, assessing the impacts of every potential purchase, becoming "native to this place," and educating others about permaculture, environmental issues, and responsible global citizenship. Others find the natural world, environmental issues, and sustainability skills relatively unexciting, and focus much more on human relationships, personal evolution, individual choice, and freedom from strict guidelines, categories, judgments, and right/wrong dichotomies (like "sustainable"/"unsustainable"). On a bad day, the eco-oriented group perceives this inward-focused, relativistic attitude as a frustrating obstacle to making necessary changes in the way we live, and sees the others as clueless about the natural world and the global situation. The relationship-focused group, in turn, can experience the eco-group as overly judgmental, dogmatic, afraid of feelings (other than those they project onto external situations), clueless about healthy communication, and no fun. When issues come up, each group seems to provoke defensiveness in the other, and those of us caught in between are not sure what to do.*

How can all of us come together to support one integrated vision? How can we learn from one another rather than see each other as threats?

Tree Bressen responds:

From the outside, it seems obvious that each side is holding an important part of the truth. But from the inside, the group is getting caught in an archetypal polarization.

Ideally, everyone's consciousness would be raised so that in the future when this conflict emerges, people would recognize it for what it is and keep the polarity in check (by actions such as kindly challenging each other on blaming or stereotypes, reminding each other that both sides are important to the well-being of the whole, and so on). There are a bunch of methods for raising consciousness, many of which involve the use of meeting formats that move well beyond general discussion. For example:

1. Present a roleplay with exaggerated versions of both sides having an argument. Use techniques from "Theater of the Oppressed" (Paulo Freire) to freeze-frame, replace actors, and otherwise explore possible outcomes.

2. Ask people on each side to take structured turns answering questions, perhaps in small groups. The following sample questions draw from the work of the Public Conversation Project:

a. Please share something about your life experience that you think may have shaped your perspective on this issue.

b. What is at the heart of the matter for you?

c. Within your thinking about this issue, are there any dilemmas, value conflicts, or gray areas you'd be willing to share? Where is it that you question or don't fit the ideology of your side?

d. What beliefs about your side do you experience from others as hurtful? What is it about who you are and what you care about that makes those beliefs upsetting?

e. Are there some stereotypes of your own side that you feel are somewhat deserved, even if they are not fully true?

f. In your highest ideals, how would the group deal with this conflict? What is one step you could take toward making that happen?

3. Ask everyone on one side to come into the middle for a "fishbowl," while the other side sits silently outside witnessing the conversation. Invite them to answer questions, such as those listed above. Then switch. And switch a few more times, so that each side is in the middle at least twice. Then have everyone go into pairs across sides for ten minutes, and then all join in one group conversation to talk about what they learned.

A proposal for an activity like this that is co-presented by someone from each perceived side is especially likely to be well-received. Once you've conducted such an activity, the challenge is to keep that learning alive and act on it. If you see a member fall into old habits, you can invite them to share about what's important to them, gently drawing attention away from their negative feelings toward others and instead focusing on their hopes and dreams.

See if your group can learn to make friends with the conflict, and laugh together when it comes up again. Then you'll have more bonded relationships, and rich stories to share with new community members about how you learned to treat each other with affectionate respect.

Tree Bressen is a group process consultant based in Eugene, Oregon, who works with intentional communities and other organizations on how to have meetings that are lively, productive, and connecting. Her website, www.treegroup.info, offers extensive free resources on consensus, facilitation, and more. (Tree uses a lower-case "i" in her writing as an expression of egalitarian values.)

Beatrice Briggs responds:

Part of what I see here is common confusion between "vision," "values," and "mission." I find it helpful to define vision as a desired future for the community, a dream that motivates the members. Values are what guide us in our day-to-day decision-making. Mission is the action plan we adopt to move us toward the vision.

While all three elements (vision, values, and mission) are important, I suggest starting with values clarification to overcome false dichotomies and establish common frame of reference for addressing the other issues. Here is a process that might help.

1. Hire an outside facilitator to lead the process so all the community members can participate. The facilitator should be comfortable with conflict and skilled in multi-stakeholder negotiation.

2. Pose the question "What are the values that should guide this community?"

3. Generate hot debate. Encourage people to state their views strongly, take sides, get emotional. Ask them to go stand with those who most closely articulate their position on the values question. (A third group is likely to emerge who do not identify strongly with either side and just want everyone to get along.)

4. Pause. Reflect. Ask the group if this is a familiar, community dynamic? How does it feel to be so polarized? Then suggest that there is a solution "out there" that is neither of the two existing positions nor a false compromise (a solution that everyone can agree to but no one is happy with).

5. Move from positions to interests. Form two groups, one for each side of the debate. (Divide the non-aligned between the two groups or let them form their own group.) Ask each group to draft a list of their interests in relation to the community's values. Define "interest" as bedrock necessity, what the participants need in order to remain members of the community. Distinguish interests from positions, defined as solutions to problems. (For example, "Respect the Earth" is an interest and "Create a car collective" is a position.) Clarify that interests are NOT a wish list of things that would be "nice to have," nor are they proposed solutions to specific problems. The interests are those needs that must be met in order for a solution to be acceptable.

6. Review the interests. Each group brings an easel sheet with its list of interests back to the plenary. Review the lists and eliminate any items that are positions (solutions). Merge the remaining needs into one list.

7. Seek solutions. Create teams comprising members of both (or all) groups. Working with the "merged" list, seek a solution that could meet all the identified needs. The facilitator moves between the groups, coaching as needed. After a specified period of time, the groups reconvene and present their proposed solutions. Depending on the degree of similarity in the proposals and the energy of the group, it may be possible to agree on a draft list of community values. If exhaustion has set in, decide on next steps for moving the discussion forward.

The key to this process is to allow the polarization to manifest and then require both sides to work together to find a solution.

Beatrice Briggs is the founding director of the International Institute for Facilitation and Change (IIFAC), a Mexico-based consulting group that specializes in participatory processes. The author of the manual Introduction to Consensus *and many articles about group dynamics, Beatrice travels around the world, giving workshops and providing facilitation services in both English and Spanish. Home is Ecovillage Huehuecoyotl, near Tepoztlán, Mexico, where she has lived since 1998. bbriggs@iifac.org; www.iifac.org.*

Laird Schaub responds:

I think the key here is in the opening statement about goals. If it's accurate that the group embraces values that range "from ecological responsibility and sustainability to healthy interpersonal relationships and personal and spiritual growth" then the question I'd pose to both factions is what each is doing to make room for the *other*, which is also an express value of the community?

The key here is asking each side to talk *first* about how they're honoring (both in their hearts and in their behavior) members who are focusing on different community values than they are. The answers here should be an olive branch. *Then* you can discuss how difficult it's being that everyone doesn't see things the same way. If you do it the other way around, the olive branches become kindling for the fires of resentment on the altars of righteousness.

The key here is asking each side to talk first about how they're honoring (both in their hearts and in their behavior) members who are focusing on different community values than they are.

Assuming you can get buy-in with the notion that it's unreasonable to expect everyone to be the same and that it's appropriate to honor different ways of being in the world, let me walk you through a constructive sequence for accomplishing de-escalation. I'd set aside all requests that others make changes until the following four steps have been taken:

1. For everyone who reports feeling *currently* upset in connection with this dynamic (as opposed to *remembering* being upset in the past), I'd give room for each person—one at a time, please!—to fully express what their feelings are and what actions or statements they're connected with. To satisfy this step, you're only making sure that everyone feels heard; you're not trying to problem solve (yet).

2. Next I'd ask what's at stake for each person in connection with this dynamic. In other words, how much does it matter, and why? Again, you're just listening. You might point out how some answers are similar and some different, yet you're not trying to determine right or wrong, or get commitments about anything.

3. Check with the group to see what aspects of everyone's answer to #2 are recognized as a reasonable expectation of what the group can provide. **Hint:** you're looking for what expectations are widely recognized as being associated with explicit common values. **Caution:** if someone's response to #2 is that they want to *feel* good about what others are doing, it's OK to point out that the group can be responsible for actions and statements done in its name, but feelings are totally the responsibility of each individual.

At the end of this you should have identified a composite of the factors that a good response to this issue will need to address.

4. Last, invite everyone (not just those who spoke up in response to #1) to answer this question: "After hearing all the responses, what can *you* do that you are currently not doing that would help balance the factors vetted in #3?" **Note:** what you are *not* looking for here is advocacy; you're looking for bridging.

If you go through this whole sequence, I guarantee you'll have new material to work with and hard edges will have softened. While I'm not promising that you'll have everyone singing Kumbayah, you should have entered an authentic and constructive space for dealing with this dynamic.

Laird Schaub, a member of Sandhill Farm community in Missouri, has been doing consulting work on group process since 1987. A longtime activist in community networking, he has lived in community since 1974 and been involved with the Fellowship for Intentional Community (FIC) since 1986; he is currently its Executive Secretary. laird@ic.org; 660-883-5545. Laird authors a blog which can be read at communityandconsensus.blogspot.com.

Paul DeLapa responds:

The issues here touch on three maintenance aspects of every group gathering: content, process, and relationships. At the content level, and speaking to the first question, is the critical need for shared vision and values (priorities being another lens on values), without which truly collaborative effort becomes an exercise in mutual frustration. If we aren't clear what we're co-laboring toward, and how we want to be with each other in that working together, we're likely to experience a lot of tearing and bumping as we pull and push in opposing directions.

It's not unusual for groups to avoid the difficult conversations needed to create clear shared prioritized values during their initial and ongoing visioning. A resulting "wide range of goals" invites conflict later on when choices or trade-offs are needed between values. An ideal like "holistic integration" (itself an abstract value), while sounding good, may be a set-up for conflict in daily life; what does it really mean and look like in action?

"How can all of us come together to support one integrated vision?" First, take adequate time to clarify what that integrated vision is, what it means individually and as a collective, and what it looks like in action. Presently you may have several visions operating, one of being a model community for a local living economy, and another a community experiment in freedom and personal choice. A healthy in-depth dialog on these visions may lead you to some shared discovery (e.g., are they two sides of the same coin?).

Often groups encounter differences in interpretation and execution regardless of how clear and well prioritized their vision and values. This leads me to the process level of group life. How do we work with differences? What tools and processes do we have to support and guide us when our energy rises? "On a bad day" we stereotype others, generalize their intentions, and either victimize or play victim. Any of these approaches leads to defensiveness since most of us dislike feeling judged or marginalized, or having our intentions questioned.

A first step out of a "threat and defend" spiral is being able to see what's happening in the moment or circumstance. Many groups have little awareness of what's happening because they're mesmerized by the content (and the accompanying drama as well). Individuals in groups can learn process awareness skills by practicing more objective participation through leadership, facilitation, and process-observer roles.

A second step out of paralysis is offering process observations to the group for their verification, interpretation, and choice of action. Process observations give us the opportunity to choose course and effectively reclaim our ability to respond to what's happening rather than being swept away or dumbfounded. Often what's needed isn't so much knowing what to do, but simply being willing to name what's happening without judgment and suggest optional process pathways in search for what helps. A large "process toolkit" of different approaches to dialog and engagement can be very helpful for finding a way through; what works in one moment may not be effective in another.

"How can we learn from one another rather than see each other as threats?" The ability to learn from one another rests on several things including collective intention (vision, values, aspirations, and ground-rules), a shared commitment to healthy relationships, and individual skills like self-awareness and managing emotions. People rarely consciously choose to create disharmony and conflict, and yet it happens all the time. Why? In addition to structural conflict influences (like unclear vision or values), often we don't see the connection between our actions and their impacts on others and the situation. In short, we lose our sense of responsibility and hence our ability to constructively respond.

The sense of "threat" implies a fear of losing something, and what feels at stake is often influence or power. Power issues can be explored in a variety of ways including: using meeting processes to help balance power and influence (e.g., go-'rounds, talking circles, paired conversations); taking physical positions in the room relative to your sense of power (or fear of its loss), speaking from those positions, and shifting to feel other positions as well; and individuals can explore their own issues around power and share (or not share) those with the group. In these ways (and others) we can take more responsibility for how we experience others, learn to see each other with less distortion or projection, learn new options for responding when we feel fear without attacking and provoking defensiveness, and genuinely experience others as more like us (less threatening).

Finally, a few thoughts about the unavoidable task of maintaining healthy relationships. Each of us comes to groups and community living with a particular (limited) set of skills for collaboration. What seems to be required and may be most important for successful collaboration is a shared commitment to learning through relationship—that learning being personal development to some degree. Without this, we're stuck in old patterns and unsatisfying results. Learning through relationship (the community crucible) requires a healthy dose of humility, which is fostered by an equal measure of compassion for our selves and for each other. Practicing these two keys, humility and compassion, is perhaps a short answer to both your questions.

Paul DeLapa is a community and organizational development facilitator with extensive experience supporting groups at all stages of their work together. He resides in the San Francisco Bay Area, travels, and offers facilitation services for meetings and retreats, leadership coaching, and workshops in consensus agreement building, facilitation skills, and teambuilding. He can be reached at 707-645-8886.

Do you have a question for our Cooperative Group Solutions panelists? Please send it to editor@ic.org.

Communities Editorial Policy

Communities is a forum for exploring intentional communities, cooperative living, and ways our readers can bring a sense of community into their daily lives. Contributors include people who live or have lived in community, and anyone with insights relevant to cooperative living or shared projects.

Through fact, fiction, and opinion, we offer fresh ideas about how to live and work cooperatively, how to solve problems peacefully, and how individual lives can be enhanced by living purposefully with others. We seek contributions that profile community living and why people choose it, descriptions of what's difficult and what works well, news about existing and forming communities, or articles that illuminate community experiences—past and present—offering insights into mainstream cultural issues. We also seek articles about cooperative ventures of all sorts—in workplaces, in neighborhoods, among people sharing common interests—and about "creating community where you are."

We do not intend to promote one kind of group over another, and take no official position on a community's economic structure, political agenda, spiritual beliefs, environmental issues, or decision-making style. As long as submitted articles are related thematically to community living and/or cooperation, we will consider them for publication. However, we do not publish articles that 1) advocate violent practices, or 2) advocate that a community interfere with its members' right to leave.

Our aim is to be as balanced in our reporting as possible, and whenever we print an article critical of a particular community, we invite that community to respond with its own perspective.

Submissions Policy

To submit an article, please first request Writers' Guidelines: Communities, 81868 Lost Valley Ln, Dexter OR 97431; 541-937-2567 x116; editor@ic.org. To obtain Photo Guidelines, email: layout@ic.org. Both are also available online at communities.ic.org.

Advertising Policy

We accept paid advertising in Communities because our mission is to provide our readers with helpful and inspiring information—and because advertising revenues help pay the bills.

We handpick our advertisers, selecting only those whose products and services we believe will be helpful to our readers. That said, we are not in a position to verify the accuracy or fairness of statements made in advertisements—unless they are FIC ads—nor in REACH listings, and publication of ads should not be considered an FIC endorsement.

If you experience a problem with an advertisement or listing, we invite you to call this to our attention and we'll look into it. Our first priority in such instances is to make a good-faith attempt to resolve any differences by working directly with the advertiser/lister and complainant. If, as someone raising a concern, you are not willing to attempt this, we cannot promise that any action will be taken.

John Stroup, Advertising Manager, 10385 Magnolia Rd, Sullivan MO 63080; 573-468-8822; ads@ic.org.

What is an "Intentional Community"?

An "intentional community" is a group of people who have chosen to live or work together in pursuit of a common ideal or vision. Most, though not all, share land or housing. Intentional communities come in all shapes and sizes, and display amazing diversity in their common values, which may be social, economic, spiritual, political, and/or ecological. Some are rural; some urban. Some live all in a single residence; some in separate households. Some raise children; some don't. Some are secular, some are spiritually based; others are both. For all their variety, though, the communities featured in our magazine hold a common commitment to living cooperatively, to solving problems nonviolently, and to sharing their experiences with others.

How Collaboration Falls Short

With Hints About How to Help It Go Long

The theme of this issue is Community in Hard Times. Could there ever be a moment when information about how to collaborate is more critically needed? If income is down, what are our options for keeping quality of life up? Sharing—of all stripes—provides terrific leverage on this issue. If you have *access* to a thing, do you really need to *own* it? To be sure, sharing means you have to work out with others who gets to use a thing when, how it will get stored and maintained, and how to sort out hurt feelings when any of these arrangements go awry.

These pitfalls notwithstanding (think of them as opportunities to get to better know your friends and neighbors), collaboration offers tremendous potential for achieving or maintaining a standard of living with fewer dollars. What's more, if you're not so busy chasing dollars, you'll have more time to pursue less remunerative passions, and isn't that what you *really* meant to be doing with your life anyway?

If you have less money, will you be less secure? Not necessarily. It's been my experience that a life built more explicitly around stable relationships (paying at least as much attention to who you're doing things with as what you're doing) pays off in the long run as well as the short. While conventional wisdom equates security with net financial assets, after 35 years of community living I've come to understand that one's ultimate security is in relationships—the people who will be there for you in time of need. And stable relationships go hand-in-glove with successful collaboration.

• • •

Collaboration was on my mind when I attended Green Business Camp in South San Francisco at the beginning of May. I was curious what interest existed among self-identified green entrepreneurs for enhancing workplace social skills. I figured that "green" implied sustainable, and sustainable has a social component. Were my fellow campers thinking along those same lines?

In a keynote talk, Paul Hawken (who characterized himself as a "change slut") emphasized how much our future will be impacted by jumps in energy costs that are outside our frame of reference. He called it "civilizational" change, to distinguish it from the cyclical change that most economists think in terms of. To my delight, he also emphasized the increasing need for collaborative savvy.

So when I attended the first breakout session—on the topic of teamwork, partnering, and cooperation—I was curious to see what the pressing needs were. Though I had my chance to pitch the relevance of what's being learned about cooperative dynamics in intentional communities, there wasn't much grab in the room. Instead, there was a lot of attention given to why collaboration—for all its sex appeal—wasn't easy to pull off. (There was also frustration expressed about how there was much more talk about collaboration than there was actual collaborating—which phenomenon we then promptly recapitulated by spending the bulk of our 45 minutes cataloging shortcomings, and marveling at how similar our stories were.)

To be fair, it probably wasn't realistic to expect this audience to be able to see the immediate application of the intentional community experience to their desire for collaboration. (For many folks—espe-

Ethan Hughes

cially political activists and social change advocates—intentional communities are a middle class indulgence, not a serious choice for those who are ready to roll up their sleeves and get into the trenches to battle hierarchy, oppression, and social injustice.) Rather than criticizing others for a lack of sophistication about how 0.03 percent of North Americans live, I think it's more productive to look at how we communitarians are failing to tell our story of what we're learning about how to make collaboration work—in the crucible and complexities of community living—that is readily applicable to the wider culture.

In any event, I listened to the laments and figured it would be instructive to round them up in a single list. While 45 minutes wasn't long enough for us campers to start turning our attention to solutions, I have tried to lay out the issues in such a way that pathways to solutions are implied, figuring that if you've properly described an issue, then you're most of the way toward knowing what to do about it.

1. Shallow agreement

This is where people feel good about reaching an agreement to collaborate, but the basis for it hasn't been fully explored and the buy-in is weak. Typically people are "making nice" and avoiding the hard questions. The fragile seedling withers from neglect.

2. Unclear implementation

The collaborators didn't go far enough to create a solid plan for who would do what, when, and with what resources. At worst, there may be no implementation plan at all. However, a vague or incomplete plan may be enough to strangle an initiative.

3. No accountability

When different entities are attempting to collaborate, it can often be tricky navigating who will monitor progress and handle task follow-up. This tends to be viewed as a position of authority and coalitions may inappropriately shy away from that assignment for fear of establishing a hierarchy among "equals." Lacking clarity about who's moving things along, it tends to be that no one does and momentum dies.

4. Poor leadership models

This is a continuation of the previous point, broadened beyond task monitoring. We need leaders to motivate, organize, and think strategically. Yet we've not done a good job of coming up with good models for working in a healthy way with power and leadership in cooperative situations. Mostly we look at current situations through the lens of prior damage and are far more critical of leaders than supportive. Leader bashing in cooperative groups is an art form, yet we have to learn to stop eating our own if we're going to create viable alternatives to traditional business models.

5. Wrong people at the table

For coalitions to be effective, it's important that all the key stakeholders are at the table. You can run into problems with this in two ways: either by leaving out one or more key stakeholders, or by the right groups sending the wrong people—those who either don't grasp the issues and or don't have the authority to commit their group to agreements and actions. This gets to be a chicken-and-egg dilemma in that key people tend to be busy people who don't have time to attend meetings that aren't going to get things done. However, if they don't attend a meeting and send an underling with no authority, it may guarantee that the outcome will be weak.

6. Not carefully vetting implementors

One of the keys to effectiveness is having the right people doing the right jobs. Thus, even if there's solid agreement and a good implementation plan, coalitions can shoot themselves in the foot by being sloppy about who's assigned tasks. Often, groups do little more than ask for volunteers and happily accept whoever puts their hand in the air. I think of this as Implementation Roulette, and it's a poor way to run a railroad. If the task is important and takes certain skills, take the time to identify the qualities needed and evaluate candidates deliberately.

7. Process too slow

Meetings need to produce results. If it takes too long to reach agreement, or there's no identifiable product from each investment of time, people lose heart and put their attention elsewhere. There are subtleties that underlay this, such as not having too many people in the room (the flip side of point 5 above), having good facilitation (to make sure that meetings stay on task and don't duck the tough topics), and having good minutes that are promptly posted.

8. Culture clash

When two or more entities attempt collaboration, they may not have similar cultures, or ways of doing business. When that happens and is not addressed, it's a sure path to misunderstanding and an erosion of trust.

9. Constricted information flow

Often collaborations result in a mushrooming expectation of who should receive updates on what's happening, and it's relatively easy to drop a ball or two. When people are left out of the loop, even inadvertently, this also will erode trust and undercut the good will needed for a collaboration to remain robust.

• • •

OK, so collaboration isn't easy. The good news is that it's *possible*, and that intentional communities have learned a lot about it. The Fellowship wants people to have a realistic picture of the challenges ahead, yet we also want readers to be optimistic.

Though this short article can't do more than point you in the right direction, this magazine is devoted to cooperative living, and you'll find on our pages a wealth of practical advice about how to make collaboration work. The FIC believes it's the responsibility of the Communities Movement to help the wider culture learn how to better navigate the pitfalls outlined above, and we're dedicated to spreading the word about successes wherever they occur—especially now, when the need is so great. ❋

Laird Schaub is executive secretary of the Fellowship for Intentional Community (FIC), publisher of this magazine, and cofounder of Sandhill Farm community in Missouri, where he lives. He authors a blog that can be read at communityandconsensus.blogspot.com; this article is adapted from his blog post of May 2, 2009.

Communities Editorial Policy

Communities is a forum for exploring intentional communities, cooperative living, and ways our readers can bring a sense of community into their daily lives. Contributors include people who live or have lived in community, and anyone with insights relevant to cooperative living or shared projects.

Through fact, fiction, and opinion, we offer fresh ideas about how to live and work cooperatively, how to solve problems peacefully, and how individual lives can be enhanced by living purposefully with others. We seek contributions that profile community living and why people choose it, descriptions of what's difficult and what works well, news about existing and forming communities, or articles that illuminate community experiences—past and present—offering insights into mainstream cultural issues. We also seek articles about cooperative ventures of all sorts—in workplaces, in neighborhoods, among people sharing common interests—and about "creating community where you are."

We do not intend to promote one kind of group over another, and take no official position on a community's economic structure, political agenda, spiritual beliefs, environmental issues, or decision-making style. As long as submitted articles are related thematically to community living and/or cooperation, we will consider them for publication. However, we do not publish articles that 1) advocate violent practices, or 2) advocate that a community interfere with its members' right to leave.

Our aim is to be as balanced in our reporting as possible, and whenever we print an article critical of a particular community, we invite that community to respond with its own perspective.

Submissions Policy

To submit an article, please first request Writers' Guidelines: Communities, Rt 1 Box 156 Rutledge, MO 63563-9720; 660-883-5545; editor@ic.org. To obtain Photo Guidelines, email: layout@ic.org. Both are also available online at communities.ic.org.

Advertising Policy

We accept paid advertising in Communities because our mission is to provide our readers with helpful and inspiring information—and because advertising revenues help pay the bills.

We handpick our advertisers, selecting only those whose products and services we believe will be helpful to our readers. That said, we are not in a position to verify the accuracy or fairness of statements made in advertisements—unless they are FIC ads—nor in REACH listings, and publication of ads should not be considered an FIC endorsement.

If you experience a problem with an advertisement or listing, we invite you to call this to our attention and we'll look into it. Our first priority in such instances is to make a good-faith attempt to resolve any differences by working directly with the advertiser/lister and complainant. If, as someone raising a concern, you are not willing to attempt this, we cannot promise that any action will be taken.

John Stroup, Advertising Manager, 10385 Magnolia Rd, Sullivan MO 63080; 573-468-8822; ads@ic.org.

What is an "Intentional Community"?

An "intentional community" is a group of people who have chosen to live or work together in pursuit of a common ideal or vision. Most, though not all, share land or housing. Intentional communities come in all shapes and sizes, and display amazing diversity in their common values, which may be social, economic, spiritual, political, and/or ecological. Some are rural; some urban. Some live all in a single residence; some in separate households. Some raise children; some don't. Some are secular, some are spiritually based; others are both. For all their variety, though, the communities featured in our magazine hold a common commitment to living cooperatively, to solving problems nonviolently, and to sharing their experiences with others.

PUBLISHER'S NOTE BY LAIRD SCHAUB

Ethan Hughes

Problem Solving in Community

How a Group Addresses Issues Says a *Lot* about Its Cohesion... and Vice Versa

As the FIC's main administrator, I do a fair number of press interviews—about two or three per month. Thus, I get a lot of practice coming up with sound bites that nuggetize the essence of community living. Up until recently, my favorite had been:

The essential challenge of cooperative living is learning how to disagree about non-trivial matters and have that be a unifying experience.

While I still like that one, lately I've been test driving a newer model:

Intentional community is about learning how to solve problems without running anyone over or leaving anyone behind—which is fundamentally different *from the way problems are typically addressed in the mainstream culture.*

While I reckon these two aphorisms are roughly equivalent, I like how the latter suggests culture shift (where the former has a whiff about it of mental jujitsu and sleight of hand).

As most people know, community comes in a kaleidoscope of sizes and flavors: from so big that you don't know everyone's name, to so few that there's nothing that you *don't* know about each other; from the isolation of rural Wyoming to the urban density of Manhattan; from the sacred to the secular; from celibate to no-holds-barred-among-consenting-adults sexuality. In short, the range is very wide.

A Family Affair

Because this issue of Communities is focused on Family, I want to shine the spotlight on one of the lesser appreciated spectra into which intentional communities sort: Degree of Engagement. To be sure, this is somewhat a matter of size. At my community, Sandhill Farm, our five adult members eat dinner together almost every evening; at nearby Dancing Rabbit there aren't more than a handful of days in the year when all 45 members are on the property at the same time, which means that daily contact among members is necessarily more diffuse. Where Sandhill is striving to be an intentional family, Dancing Rabbit is aiming to be a village, which, in turn, is comprised of many household units—some of which are families about the size of Sandhill.

While you have no choice about the family you are born into (or, depending on your views about reincarnation, maybe you *do*, but that's beyond the scope of this exploration), you have considerable latitude when it comes to a chosen (or intentional) family, and that's one of the main motivations for people seeking community: to create a feeling of family in the context of living with people with whom you're aligned in values.

In the case of smaller communities (like Sandhill), the aim is typically for the entire group to have a family quality. In the case of larger communities (like Dancing Rabbit), the idea is to create an environment that will support multiple family units—including both biological and chosen. In larger groups, individual members may feel affinity with the whole community, with one or more subgroups that identify as families, or with both. In this sense, independent of the size of the group, the family is one of the fundamental social building blocks of community.

While one's family experience growing up tends to be a hit or miss proposition when it comes to psychological health and functionality, whenever people aspire to create family as adults—whether through mating and raising children of one's own, or through joining a chosen family—people invariably hold the expectation (or at least the hope) of creating a family that functions well. Unfortunately, we don't all mean the same thing by "functioning well," and good intentions are not nearly enough to ensure success.

Many groups don't know what to do with emotions when they enter the room, and take the ostrich approach—hoping they'll go away if the group pretends they're not there.

Beyond intention, the degree of cohesion that a group achieves is also a matter of how much time the members regularly spend together, how aligned members are on the community's common values, how central the common values are to what each member values in life, and how the group solves problems. It's this last yardstick that I want to focus on in this essay.

Here's a set of questions I've distilled from 22 years as a group process consultant. The answers, I believe, will be highly predictive of where a group lands on the Degree of Engagement scale.

Checklist for How Cooperatively Your Group Solves Problems

1. To what extent does the group welcome emotional input on problems?

As a species, we're hard-wired to have emotional responses. I don't mean we have strong emotional responses all the time; I'm only saying that they're not rare. Yet many groups don't know what to do with emotions when they enter the room, and basically take the ostrich approach—hoping they'll go away if the group pretends they're not there. Most groups have a meeting culture that says, in effect, that expressing strong emotions is immature and inappropriate. In consequence, most groups have brittle conversations about problems, because they're ever vigilant about suppressing strong feelings. Instead of figuring out how to harness passion, they harass it.

For those with high emotional intelligence (by which I mean they know things and respond more accurately in the emotional realm than rationally), meetings are stressful because these folks are not generally allowed to use their best language. If it's bad enough (maybe they're not bilingual), they'll stop coming to meetings. Worse, the group might take comfort in that outcome.

2. How dedicated is the group to hearing from everyone before entertaining proposed solutions?

Problem solving will be both more inclusive and more effective if the group develops the habit of making sure that everyone who wants to has had the chance to help define the problem before the group starts batting around potential solutions. When proposals are allowed to enter the conversation at any time (or worse, are encouraged at the outset as part of the introduction of the topic), those members who are slower to organize their thoughts or who struggle to get air space may give up. To them, they face a Hobson's choice of either betraying their nature by pushing into the conversation, or giving up and trusting that the quicker and more assertive will take their unvoiced considerations into account. Good luck with that.

3. To what extent has the group been successful in creating an atmosphere of curiosity in the face of disagreement?

The essence of cooperative culture is encouraging a full expression of viewpoints (under the assumption that if everything is out on the table, then it will be easier to weigh and balance factors appropriately). If, however, opposing opinions are met with resistance or hostility—rather than curiosity—then the speaker must gird their loins in preparation for an onslaught. Sometimes it won't be worth it, and alternate viewpoints will not surface.

4. How often do you hear "But..." as a person's first word in response to another's statement?

In the mainstream culture, we're used to doing battle when someone disagrees with our position (the most appalling tactics can be euphemistically labeled "healthy debate"), either through a vigorous defense or an aggressive counterattack, challenging their premises or the flow of their logic. The key to inclusivity is responding to alternate opinions with openness and interest, with the possibility in view that your mind might be changed (rather than fear that you'll be publicly humiliated as a consequence of another's idea being found superior to yours). Does the group understand the importance of creating and fostering a culture of curiosity in those moments?

5. Does the group have facilitators capable of consistently bridging between conflicted parties?

In the heat of the moment, we tend to revert to our deepest conditioning, rather than responding from our loftiest ideals. Thus, if it appears that some matter close to the bone is not going our way, we tend to fight rather than cooperate, and it can make all the difference whether you have the capacity among your in-house facilitators to bridge between conflicted parties and help guide everyone back—with honor—from the brink of a fight that no one really wants.

6. How frequently does the community meet?

This is a loaded question. The facile answer should be, "as often as needed," yet the question beneath this is whether the group is avoiding meetings because they have no confidence in their going well. The group may be ducking issues, or loathe to tackle them with everyone in the room. If so, this is not a good sign and will surely indicate weakness in the group's cohesion.

7. Does the community regularly evaluate managers and committees?

While it may not be obvious why this indicator is on the list, many groups fall into a trap of allowing long-term members to remain in the same position of responsibility for years at a time without examination. While this is not inherently bad, it can be trouble if there is no way to discuss dissatisfaction with performance, or to review what the community really wants out of that position. When people become entrenched in positions of power and create fiefdoms, it leads to demoralization and undercuts the will to engage.

8. What effort is made to integrate new members into the community's culture?

Over time, communities inevitably create their own idiosyncratic culture. There becomes a "normal way things are done around here." For long-term members, this become second nature and is the air they breathe. For new folks this is all very mysterious, and it can be exhausting worrying over the possibility of committing a social faux pas that was never explained ahead of time. It's like walking through a minefield blind. If new members are obliged to walk through that field alone, it takes an exceptionally tough person to weather more than a few explosions and keep putting one foot in front of the other. Many will tend to get less venturesome. At best, this retards the integration process and prolongs the power gap between old and new. At worst, you'll lose the new person.

• • •

How did your group measure up? While it's up to the members of each group to decide for themselves how much they want to be in each other's lives, I've offered the Checklist above as an aid for groups to be able to achieve the level they want, rather than the best they can stumble into, guided only by good intentions.

Think of it as a way to solve problems about how you solve problems. ❁

Laird Schaub is Executive Secretary of the Fellowship for Intentional Community (FIC), publisher of this magazine, and cofounder of Sandhill Farm, an egalitarian community in northeast Missouri, where he lives. His blog that can be read at communityandconsensus.blogspot.com. An earlier version of this essay first appeared as the December 2, 2009 entry in Laird's blog.

Communities Editorial Policy

Communities is a forum for exploring intentional communities, cooperative living, and ways our readers can bring a sense of community into their daily lives. Contributors include people who live or have lived in community, and anyone with insights relevant to cooperative living or shared projects.

Through fact, fiction, and opinion, we offer fresh ideas about how to live and work cooperatively, how to solve problems peacefully, and how individual lives can be enhanced by living purposefully with others. We seek contributions that profile community living and why people choose it, descriptions of what's difficult and what works well, news about existing and forming communities, or articles that illuminate community experiences—past and present—offering insights into mainstream cultural issues. We also seek articles about cooperative ventures of all sorts—in workplaces, in neighborhoods, among people sharing common interests—and about "creating community where you are."

We do not intend to promote one kind of group over another, and take no official position on a community's economic structure, political agenda, spiritual beliefs, environmental issues, or decision-making style. As long as submitted articles are related thematically to community living and/or cooperation, we will consider them for publication. However, we do not publish articles that 1) advocate violent practices, or 2) advocate that a community interfere with its members' right to leave.

Our aim is to be as balanced in our reporting as possible, and whenever we print an article critical of a particular community, we invite that community to respond with its own perspective.

Submissions Policy

To submit an article, please first request Writers' Guidelines: Communities, RR 1 Box 156, Rutledge MO 63563-9720; 660-883-5545; editor@ic.org. To obtain Photo Guidelines, email: layout@ic.org. Both are also available online at communities.ic.org.

Advertising Policy

We accept paid advertising in Communities because our mission is to provide our readers with helpful and inspiring information—and because advertising revenues help pay the bills.

We handpick our advertisers, selecting only those whose products and services we believe will be helpful to our readers. That said, we are not in a position to verify the accuracy or fairness of statements made in advertisements—unless they are FIC ads—nor in REACH listings, and publication of ads should not be considered an FIC endorsement.

If you experience a problem with an advertisement or listing, we invite you to call this to our attention and we'll look into it. Our first priority in such instances is to make a good-faith attempt to resolve any differences by working directly with the advertiser/lister and complainant. If, as someone raising a concern, you are not willing to attempt this, we cannot promise that any action will be taken.

Tanya Carwyn, Advertising Manager, 7 Hut Terrace, Black Mountain NC 28711; 828-669-0997; ads@ic.org.

What is an "Intentional Community"?

An "intentional community" is a group of people who have chosen to live or work together in pursuit of a common ideal or vision. Most, though not all, share land or housing. Intentional communities come in all shapes and sizes, and display amazing diversity in their common values, which may be social, economic, spiritual, political, and/or ecological. Some are rural; some urban. Some live all in a single residence; some in separate households. Some raise children; some don't. Some are secular, some are spiritually based; others are both. For all their variety, though, the communities featured in our magazine hold a common commitment to living cooperatively, to solving problems nonviolently, and to sharing their experiences with others.

PUBLISHER'S NOTE BY LAIRD SCHAUB

Three Essential Agreements of Effective Groups

In mid-May of 2009, the FIC held a Community Building Day at Kimberton Hills (a community 30 miles west of Philadelphia) and about 56 people joined our crew of 12 presenters and support people to create a 12-hour experience devoted to the information and inspiration of community. During a general Q&A session right before dinner, one woman asked, "What are the three most critical agreements that a community should have in place in order to succeed?"

What an excellent question! Over the course of my 22 years as a process consultant I've slowly accumulated an understanding of a goodly number of key questions that healthy groups need to address, so limiting it to three was a challenge. What trio do I feel encompasses the *most* pivotal issues?

Here are my nominations:

1. Working with Emotional Input

The main model for appropriate group communication in our culture is to offer one's best thinking. While rational thought is a wonderful tool, it's hardly the only one available to us, and it really doesn't make much sense to paint with only one color. As human beings we take in, process, and communicate information in an amazing variety of ways. It's my view that groups function best when they openly embrace a wider range of input than just what's available through ideation.

In addition to rational knowing, humans can access knowing that is emotional, intuitive, instinctive, spiritual, and kinesthetic. (While I don't presume that this is a complete list of the alternate channels available to us, it's enough to make my point.) Though not everyone operates with the full bandwidth, multiple channels are nonetheless available, and groups will tend to be more sophisticated and dynamic in their examination of issues to the extent that they consciously embrace more *kinds* of information (not just more data).

For the purpose of identifying a key agreement, I will narrow my focus to a single question: how does the group work with emotional input? Sadly, most groups never explicitly ask that question and have no clear answer. In consequence, they are unsure of their footing when emotions enter the equation—and the stronger the feelings, the more unsure the footing. Mostly groups discourage the expression of strong feelings, or relegate that kind of sharing to heart circles only (where they won't "infect" the business meetings).

Strong feelings can be scary for groups because their expression is often associ-

> *The reality is that power is never flat; it's* always *distributed unevenly.*

Ziggy

ated with attacks or manipulation, and groups (understandably) want to limit both from occurring. There is fear that the expression of strong feelings may undermine safety and lead to people being afraid to share their full thinking on a topic.

Best, I think, is that groups appreciate that emotions can be distinguished from aggression, and that it's possible to welcome feelings while objecting to attacks. Emotions can be an important source of both information (people may know something more profoundly on an emotional level than on a rational level) and energy—let's bring passion into our work!

Too often groups banish feelings altogether in a baby-and-the-bath-water response to nervousness about how to handle emerging conflict. Surely we can do better.

2. Critical Feedback

In biological systems, feedback loops are crucial to survival. Think about it: if you step on a nail, it's important that it hurts, alerting you to the need to pull the damn thing out of your shoe. While you'd rather not hurt, you certainly don't want to be walking around with a nail in your foot.

I don't think it's any different in groups. If Chris and Pat are both in the same group and Chris is having trouble with something that Pat is doing as a member of the group, then there needs to be a known avenue through which Chris can communicate concerns directly with Pat. Absent a known channel, it can be hit or miss whether Pat ever hears what's going on for Chris. Not only will this mean that Pat doesn't get the chance to work with the information (which may enhance their effectiveness in the world), but it will likely lead to a degradation in trust and an erosion of relationship between Pat and Chris. This can be very expensive.

While I'm all in favor of people having choices about the timing and setting in which feedback is delivered (some prefer to get it on the spot, others prefer advance warning; some prefer that it occur one-on-one, others prefer to receive it in the whole group), it's important that everyone offers something and that that preference be known. A mysterious feedback loop is the same as no feedback loop. And no feedback loop means the flow of life-giving information has been choked off. It's hard to thrive with a poor circulation system.

3. Talking about Power

Cooperative groups tend to have trouble talking openly about power dynamics. They typically strive to flatten hierarchies and to share power as broadly as possible. While there's nothing wrong with that goal, the reality is that power is never flat; it's *always* distributed unevenly. The key question is whether the group has a clear way to discuss the perception that someone has used power in a less cooperative way (power *over* instead of power *with*) than that person thinks they have.

Healthy groups need people functioning as leaders. Leaders need to exercise power to be effective, and there needs to be a way to examine how power is being used. We tend to bring into our current cooperative realities damage from past abuses of power and we have to sort out how much of our current discomfort is projection from the past, how much is misuse of power in the current situation, and how much is a misunderstanding about what's actually happening (never mind what was intended). It can get messy in a hurry and we need a pathway through this morass.

• • •

In the end, if a group fails to address any one of these three issues, I guarantee that the ensuing ambiguity will be crippling. Though I'm not saying that this will necessarily be fatal, it will certainly be expensive, and seriously limit the group's capacity to realize its potential.

Laird Schaub is Executive Secretary of the Fellowship for Intentional Community (FIC), publisher of this magazine, and cofounder of Sandhill Farm, an FEC community in Missouri, where he lives. He authors a blog that can be read at communityandconsensus.blogspot.com. This column is adapted from his blog entry of May 19, 2009.

COOPERATIVE GROUP SOLUTIONS ADVICE ABOUT HOW TO HANDLE CHALLENGING DYNAMICS

Ethan Hughes

Call in the Experts?

Q: *Our group is very divided. We need to make major decisions regarding finances, organizational structures, and policies, at a time when interpersonal tensions have reached a boiling point. Certain individuals and factions seem to be locked in power struggles, and at this point we are almost completely paralyzed by internal conflict.*

Now we have one more source of conflict: some members want to bring in outside facilitators to help us work through our problems, and others say that we should rely on our own resources and skills, and not spend money on outside "experts" who will come and then leave (possibly stirring up more trouble in the process). Without full group agreement, we won't be able to bring in outside help. What do you suggest?

Laird Schaub responds:

This story is a cautionary tale about how problems can compound (with interest!) when not dealt with as they occur. In my experience, the first strand to pull on in unknotting this tangled skein is the one relating to unresolved interpersonal tensions. Until and unless you can make progress there, it will infect all other conversations, and render brittle and non-resilient any agreements you can forge around finances, organizational structure, policies, and power dynamics (all of which are plenty interesting topics unto themselves).

For the purposes of getting traction on the interpersonal tensions, it may make sense to work it in the context of one of your other issues (one that showcases the damaged relationships), so that your efforts are rooted in something you need to address anyway (rather than just tackling interpersonal tension

Sadly, many times groups cannot agree to bring in help because some members have no sense of how much difference it can make, and are unwilling to take a chance to find out.

in theory). For the purposes of this response, let's say the issue you decide to work is pet policy.

Then, I'd make a commitment to the group that you will not make any binding agreements about dogs until you've first handled the interpersonal tensions to everyone's satisfaction. Then you can use the ideas and concerns that surfaced in the unpacking to springboard into a constructive dialog about rogue hamsters. Successfully dealing with the tensions first should give you an energetic bounce with which to make progress on how cats and birds can coexist in trees outside the common house.

To be fair, it's much harder to successfully tackle interpersonal tensions when they've been festering for some time and there's no clear group agreement about: a) whether members are expected to make an attempt to deal with such troubles; or b) how to go about it. The good news is that it can be done. The bad news is that few of us have the skills to guide a group through it, which brings me to the delicate issue of whether or not to bring in outside help.

As a process consultant, I am hardly neutral on this question. I always think I'll be able to make a positive contribution when working with a group in trouble, and I think there are any number of occasions where a group can get stuck in a dynamic and there is no internal member with sufficient skill or neutrality to shepherd the group through it. While it's also true that outside help is not always needed (or effective), it's important to have options. Sadly, many times groups cannot agree to bring in help because some members have no sense of how much difference it can make, and are unwilling to take a chance to find out. As bad as it gets, some people have grown so inured to poor dynamics that they have no expectations of it ever getting better (so why spend time and money on a fool's errand to raise the dead?).

For what it's worth, one of the most important and helpful decisions my 36-year-old community, Sandhill Farm, ever made was to start asking in outside help on a regular basis. Though we weren't smart enough to start doing that until we were about 20 years old—we were slow learners—it made a huge difference, and now we do it one or more times a year.

With care, you should be able to find someone who can help with both agendas: get you out of the swamp you're in right now; and teach you the skills needed to get yourselves out the next time.

Laird Schaub, a member of Sandhill Farm community in Missouri, has been doing consulting work on group process since 1987. A longtime activist in community networking, he has lived in community since 1974 and been involved with the Fellowship for Intentional Community (FIC) since 1986; he is currently its Executive Secretary. laird@ic.org; 660-883-5545. Laird authors a blog which can be read at communityandconsensus.blogspot.com.

Beatrice Briggs responds:

Until the members get in touch with what brought them together in the first place, it will be hard to move on.

Assuming that there is a real desire to get beyond the paralysis, I suggest an appreciative inquiry approach. The process focuses on strengths and what the group wants more of, not the current problems. For example, a typical exercise to start the work involves group members interviewing each other about a time when they were really happy to be a member of the community. What was happening? Who was there? What made that moment or period so memorable? What was their personal role? And (without being too modest), what skills from that experience do they bring to the community now? The process moves on from there, building on this foundation. (For more on this powerful approach to positive change, consult Google or Amazon for books and other resources.)

This situation cries out for skillful, external facilitation. First of all, the entire group needs to be engaged in the process—which means that no one is left to facilitate. Secondly, as Einstein said, "We can't solve problems by using the same kind of thinking we used when we created them." The group got itself into this mess. I frankly doubt that it will be able to extract itself without some outside help. Perhaps those most opposed to bringing in an outsider could be asked to select a person they would trust. In any case, I would not try to address any of the operational and policy issues until there are some clear signs that the group wants to stay together and is ready to move past the current impasse.

Beatrice Briggs is the founding director of the International Institute for Facilitation and Change (IIFAC), a Mexico-based consulting group that specializes in participatory processes. The author of the manual Introduction to Consensus *and many articles about group dynamics, Beatrice travels around the world, giving workshops and providing facilitation services in both English and Spanish. Home is Ecovillage Huehuecoyotl, near Tepoztlán, Mexico, where she has lived since 1998. bbriggs@iifac.org; www.iifac.org.*

Tree Bressen responds:

This is a really hard situation, and i feel like i would need more context to offer useful advice. That said, here are some thoughts.

The idea that we don't need outside help was common among '70s-era communities. One might observe that most of those communities no longer exist. I'm not saying this is the sole reason of course, but it probably didn't help. Getting outside support when you need it is an investment in the well-being and future of your community. The happiest and healthiest communities i've observed have gotten lots of process training and support from **both** external and internal sources, setting a high standard for good meetings and nourishing strong friendships with each other outside the meetings too.

I lived for years at a co-op where the general process skill level was higher than most places, and we still brought in an outside facilitator about once a year either for training or to help us work through an issue. It's not just about skills, it's about being in a **role** that's neutral. I had professional-level skills, but i could only use them when: (a) i felt neutral and not charged on the issue at hand; (b) i had a decent relationship with the key people involved in the issue; and (c) other people trusted that both (a) and (b) were the case.

Part of the egalitarian culture in the secular communities movement is that outside experts typically get way more cache than a community's own members do (and the farther away they live the better, of course). As a traveling facilitator, i know this and use it to advantage in helping the communities i work with. For example, a group might be willing to try a nonverbal exercise with me that they would resist doing under the guidance of a member. I am transparent about this power and at the end of my work often encourage communities to give their own facilitators some of the support and openness to trying new things that they were willing to give me.

However, what i've said so far here is preaching to the choir, and the people you are disputing with will not necessarily be swayed by any of these points. I'm guessing you need to push harder, on one or more of the following fronts:

1. Switch the dynamic. Ask them to convince you as to why outside help is not needed. Ask for solid examples addressing questions such as:

a. Which member(s) do they imagine facilitating this process?

b. What form do they think it might take?

c. What will they do to help people they disagree with feel safe?

d. What past issues of this magnitude has the group successfully resolved without outside assistance? How was that accomplished?

If they have good answers to these, then maybe it's time to reevaluate your stance that outside support is required.

2. Include people who are distrustful of outside facilitation on the team interviewing potential candidates. Invite them to explicitly raise their concerns during interviews with both facilitators and references (past clients).

3. Give them a chance to have it their way, within limits. Set reasonable criteria for how and when the issues will be resolved internally, and agree in advance that if those benchmarks are not met then outside help will be hired. For example the group could agree to have three meetings on the big, tough issues, and at that point if half or more of the members want outside facilitation then it goes ahead.

4. Address their concerns as directly as possible. What are they scared of? What does "stirring up more trouble" really mean? (Does it mean they want certain issues or conflicts to be off-limits, and if so, does the rest of the community agree?) Is there a way to ameliorate whatever the specific concern is? Would requesting that an outside consultant include an emphasis on internal empowerment for future situations address part of it? Is barter an option to help reduce fees? If not, which budget item are they worried might get cut in order to pay for a facilitator, and if that item is a priority for others too then can the group agree to avoid that cut? What does using an outside facilitator signify to them (does it make them feel like the community has somehow failed)?

5. Tell them your legitimate concerns and request a response. "I've noticed in past meetings that this set of people often doesn't listen to each other well. I don't trust that we can handle this on our own." "I'm worried this might be an attempt to keep on avoiding the interpersonal conflict between Dakota and Cary, which i think we need to deal with to move forward." "I'm scared that a few people will blow up, others will shut down, and then we'll be even worse off than we are now." "I'm concerned that this might be an effort to hold power and avoid accountability." Name the core of your concern, whether it is personal or on behalf of the community's well-being or both, as kindly and as directly as you can. Stand up for yourself. This is particularly effective if done by multiple people who normally don't make waves.

6. Consider whether there are any middle-ground solutions. For example, inviting in a circle of friends to witness the meeting. Knowing you are being watched tends to put people on better behavior, which may address some of the need for outside facilitation, and doing this is free. What are other creative ideas? ❧

Tree Bressen is a group process consultant based in Eugene, Oregon, who works with intentional communities and other organizations on how to have meetings that are lively, productive, and connecting. See her website, www.treegroup.info. (Tree uses a lower-case "i" in her writing as an expression of egalitarian values.)

Do you have a question for our Cooperative Group Solutions panelists? Please send it to editor@ic.org.

COOPERATIVE GROUP SOLUTIONS Advice About How to Handle Challenging Dynamics

Eggshells and Stone Walls

Q: *I am new to living in community (rather than being a part of a community) and I am wondering if I can get some advice. My family and I currently rent a large house with another woman who was a colleague and friend prior to deciding to begin forming our community. I knew that she had the habit of not speaking up at work, and then making online critical comments about issues on which she had not spoken. I thought our level of friendship precluded that behavior, but we are now at the point where there are co-habitation issues to work out, and she mostly silently, but with a smile, agrees to whatever we discuss without contributing to the discussion. Not only do I feel that we are steamrolling her into doing things without her input (although she is given ample time and invitation to speak or even email about chores, time issues, and other responsibilities, and we WANT to know how we can help meet her needs), I also suspect that she is posting complaints online since I know that was her pattern at our workplace. I do not want to stalk her to find out what she is thinking; I just want to encourage her to be direct with us in the same way we are trying to be with her—constructive and non-confrontational without subsuming our own needs or discomforts. I have noticed that the advice in the magazine often addresses more aggressive meeting contributors, but what about the ones who are smilingly refusing to participate? It makes the rest of us feel as though we are walking on eggshells because we feel can never tell how she is really feeling, and that creates a discordance in our living situation.*

Tree Bressen responds:

I have been trying to wrap my head around this one. I think it's really easy for those of us who are comfortable with direct communication and formal process to think that everyone should be like us, and the reality is that they aren't. The use of strategies such as passive-aggression and gossiping signal that someone is feeling less empowered, but multiple communication cultures also exist in our diverse society, and the combination can be very difficult.

I assume that you've already tried talking with your roommate about the overall pattern (beyond any particular chore or household issue), and that that has not worked, that you've not been able to make a real connection there. If not, i suggest trying that first. If this is impacting your friendship with her—and it seems like it must be, given the loss of trust expressed in your story—be real about that. The more you can come from a place of heartfelt caring and friendship, and a genuine willingness to explore her point of view, the more likely a good outcome...but there are no guarantees.

If you've tried that and felt stonewalled, then it seems there are two main possibilities:

(1) Your family can learn to adapt to your friend's communication style, which is likely far more subtle than what you are accustomed to. Preferences may be indicated through small comments during otherwise unrelated conversations, jokes, and mostly through energy and body language, which you'll slowly get better at guessing and interpreting over time. Take this as a growth opportunity, a chance to expand your awareness and flexibility to encompass the many people who aren't jazzed by immediate direct talk on sensitive subjects and prefer a more indirect mode of working things out. Note that this choice is unlikely to succeed if it's based on avoidance of choice #2 rather than genuine desire.

(2) You can stop living together, with all the fallout that goes along with that (which apparently in this case may include the posting of complaints about you online).

What i don't recommend is trying over and over to get the other person to change, which even if well-intentioned, can be experienced by them as a form of violence. If your friend aspires to more direct communication and simply has a gap in skills, that's one thing—then you can be her ally on that journey. But if it's really not the direction she wants to go in, or if she is unwilling to back up theoretical desire with committed action, then it's unrealistic and unfair to both your family and her to expect her to become the roommate of your ideals. Better to accept her as she is and move from that base. Hopefully it's not too late to salvage a mutually respectful relationship.

Tree Bressen is a group process consultant based in Eugene, Oregon, who works with intentional communities and other organizations on how to have meetings that are lively, productive, and connecting. Her website, www.treegroup.info, offers extensive free resources on consensus, facilitation, and more. (Tree uses a lowercase "i" in her writing as an expression of egalitarian values.)

Next time, do some "trial runs" with prospective housemates. Go on a weekend trip, plan an outing, throw a party together—anything that lets you experience each other's capacity to give and receive feedback.

Beatrice Briggs responds:

I suggest that you raise your concerns directly with your housemate, explaining your dissatisfaction with the current situation and asking for her views on the situation. If she is unable or unwilling to open up, then it is time to acknowledge that you may not be compatible and that you and your family may need to start looking for another living situation—or a new housemate. Who knows, she may be relieved at the opportunity to be given a graceful way out. Or she may acquiesce and then complain bitterly online about the bad treatment she received at your hands. Or she may acknowledge how important this living situation is to her and agree to make an effort to speak up more in the future.

Next time, take the time to do some "trial runs" with prospective housemates. Go on a weekend trip, plan an outing, throw a party together—anything that lets you experience each other's capacity to engage in constructive dialog and give and receive feedback. Be explicit about the purpose of these activities and the importance that you and your family place on open communication.

Beatrice Briggs is the founding director of the International Institute for Facilitation and Change (IIFAC), a Mexico-based consulting group that specializes in participatory processes. The author of the manual Introduction to Consensus *and many articles about group dynamics, Beatrice travels around the world, giving workshops and providing facilitation services in both English and Spanish. Home is Ecovillage Huehuecoyotl, near Tepoztlán, Mexico, where she has lived since 1998. bbriggs@iifac.org; www.iifac.org.*

Laird Schaub responds:

It's a good sign that you've tuned into the subtle possible meanings of this woman's low level of input on group matters. Silence, in my view, is the hardest thing of all to interpret accurately, and I think you're right to have your eye on it.

Reading between the lines, I'm assuming that something feels off to you about her silence; that her energy is somehow out of alignment with her words. At least some of the time, you read her agreeable smile as false, and you're racking your brains for how to draw her out. While I'll address your options about that below, I want to start by looking at the possibility that she really is OK with what's been happening, and that you are misreading her. While I wholeheartedly support groups exploring the potential meanings of "off feelings," it's important to appreciate that Intuition is not necessarily Truth. It's not always simple to distinguish readily whether the observed person is in discord, or the observer is projecting discord onto them. Tread lightly here.

While I understand your frustration at this woman's lack of participation in meetings (it would certainly bother me), would it be acceptable if she were a member who makes her contributions to the group in other ways than in meetings, so long as she's not rocking the boat? My point here is that it's one thing to be quiet, happy, and productive; it's altogether different to be quiet, disgruntled, and withdrawn. This is a non-trivial question about the expectations of membership and is something for the group to talk about.

Now let's explore your choices where you suspect that she's holding relevant views that she's not sharing in meetings. My first piece of advice is to put into place (if you have not already done so) an explicit you-gotta-deal agreement whereby all members of the group are expected to make a good faith effort to hear and work constructively with questions or feedback that any other member has about their behavior as a member of the group. While it generally works best if you give members a fair amount of latitude about the timing and format for those conversations (safety and authenticity trump speed), it's my view that this kind of agreement is foundational in healthy groups.

While a fair number of groups have effectively developed a norm around this, few state it explicitly and its absence can lead to what folks at Ganas (on Staten Island) style "non-negotiable negativity," where it's possible to filibuster your way out of addressing things about your behavior that others find odious, or at least uncomfortable. Note that I am not saying that anyone has to agree with someone else's analysis that they've done something wrong, or necessarily agree to do something differently—the commitment here is only to listening to the feedback and agreeing to attempt to be constructive about what to do about it.

Assuming you have that in place, I'd then approach this quiet woman with a request to speak with her one-on-one about your concern that you're not hearing enough from her to feel confidant that her thinking and desires are adequately reflected in the group's deliberations. If she reports being mystified as to why you'd ask that, you can relate your experience with her as a co-worker where she said little in meetings and then posted criticism online. Having seen her voice concerns indirectly in the past, you're worried that she might do that again, and you're wanting direct communication.

While this gambit may open things up, let's suppose it doesn't. Suppose she denies that she's posting criticism online or that she's holding any unvoiced concerns (which, after all, may be true, as I pointed out above). If it plays out like this, I think you'll want to stay in the conversation long enough to do two more things:

Question A: First, ask her if there are things about how the group operates that inhibit her from speaking. Perhaps certain people or styles are intimidating for her. Perhaps the free-flowing dialog moves too fast for her to organize her thoughts. Maybe expressing emotional needs is too scary for her (based on how she was raised or past traumas). Rather than guess why she's generally so quiet, ask.

At the end of the day, all you can do is try, and you may ultimately be faced with the choice of either accepting that she's someone you'll rarely get input from, or asking her to leave the group.

To be fair, there's delicacy here in creating an environment for the conversation that doesn't trigger the things that shut her down. Not knowing ahead of time what those triggers are, it's not hard to imagine that you might inadvertently trip them. My advice here is to trust your instincts (watch her body language and tone of voice for cues about her level of comfort) and be cautious about projecting what you need for safety onto her.

Request B: Second, make it clear to her that it's hard for you (caution: speak only for yourself and resist the urge to arrogate to yourself the authority to speak for others) to feel that the group is on solid ground when she contributes so little to the conversation. Make a request that in the future, whenever she's asked for her opinion on group issues and she doesn't feel she has anything relevant to add, that, at a minimum, she either explains briefly how her views have already been expressed by others, or why this issue doesn't concern her and she's fine with whatever others decide.

If you can offer her reasonable assurances that you'll try to be her ally in getting whatever she asks for in response to Question A, I think there's an excellent chance that she'll agree to Request B, and that should help.

Having said all this, it's possible that none of it will succeed in drawing her out. At the end of the day, all you can do is try, and you may ultimately be faced with the choice of either accepting that she's someone you'll rarely get input from, or asking her to leave the group.

Laird Schaub, a member of Sandhill Farm community in Missouri, has been doing consulting work on group process since 1987. A longtime activist in community networking, he has lived in community since 1974 and been involved with the Fellowship for Intentional Community (FIC) since 1986; he is currently its Executive Secretary. laird@ic.org; 660-883-5545. Laird authors a blog which can be read at communityandconsensus.blogspot.com.

Do you have a question for our Cooperative Group Solutions panelists? Please send it to editor@ic.org.

Social Permaculture–What Is It?

By Starhawk

Within the permaculture movement, more and more of us have been looking at aspects of something we've come to call "social permaculture." But what is that?

People often think of permaculture as another system of gardening or land management, but it is far more. Permaculture is a system of ecological design that looks to nature as our model. It originated in the '70s with Australian ecologists Bill Mollison and David Holmgren, who were looking to create a "permanent agriculture." Now it has become a worldwide movement, and expanded to encompass "permanent culture."

Patrick Whitefield, author of *The Earthcare Manual*, called permaculture "the art of designing beneficial relationships." We look at plants in the garden not in isolation but in terms of how they affect one another, how they interact, how the pathways and beds determine the flow of our energy in caring for them, how they can provide fertility or protection for one another, how we can get multiple yields from each element.

But relationships between plants, insects, soil, water, and micro-organisms, complex as they may be, are relatively easy to deal with. Roses love garlic—or so says the title of a key book on companion planting. And pretty much they do. We don't have to worry about whether this particular rose holds a grudge against that individual garlic for something insensitive it said to her.

People are much more challenging. We each have our own needs and goals and complicated life histories and styles of communication. Our understanding of soil biology or water harvesting techniques is often far more advanced than our skills at making decisions together. Our needs and goals often clash, and we don't always have the tools we need to resolve conflicts.

According to Diana Leafe Christian, author of the key book on intentional communities, *Creating a Life Together*, 90 percent of intentional communities fail—largely because of conflict. That statistic represents an enormous amount of shattered dreams, personal pain, and wasted resources.

Why are human relationships so difficult? We each carry the imprints of our early experiences, and often respond to current situations with the negative patterns of the past. We hold onto painful memories and anticipate future hurts. When we come together in community, our own needs, goals, and communication patterns often clash.

Moreover, we are embedded in larger systems that do not encourage beneficial relationships. Our overarching economic system sacrifices the good of people and the earth to the goal of achieving short-term profits. It maintains itself by fostering systems of prejudice and exploitation—racism, sexism, classism, heterosexism, ageism, ableism—all those constructs that separate us and elevate some peoples' good over others. Those systems affect us deeply, often unconsciously, no matter how much we might deplore them and struggle against them.

People are hard to change. Religions, psychotherapy, meditation, self-help programs, diet and exercise programs, stop-smoking campaigns, 12-step programs, and the criminal justice system all attempt to change people—and when they succeed it is often only after months or years of painful effort. Most of us have experienced just how difficult it is to change ourselves!

• • •

What can permaculture—which began as a way of looking at food growing and land management—bring to this effort?

The key insight of social permaculture is that, while changing individuals is indeed difficult, we can design social structures that favor beneficial patterns of human behavior. Just as, in a garden, we might mulch to discourage weeds and favor beneficial soil bacteria, in social systems we can attempt to create conditions that favor nurturing, empowering relationships.

Permaculture's three core ethics are care for the earth, care for the people, and care for the future—that third ethic is also often framed as "fair share": share surpluses and reduce consumption. These ethics can serve as a guideline for weighing our decisions and actions. Before we build a structure or engage in a new endeavor, we ask ourselves—how will this impact the environment around us? What resources will it use? Will it provide for people and community, and further empowerment and equality, or the reverse?

Permaculture rejects the notion that people are separate from nature and inevitably destructive, or that destruction of the environ-

ment is justified in order to provide jobs or profits for people. Instead, the good of the people and the good of the earth go together. For example, Tony Rinaudo of Global Vision, an organization that has successfully reforested millions of hectares of land in Niger, Mali, and Ethiopia, found that involving farmers in regeneration efforts, teaching them simple techniques to protect and prune existing trees and plant new ones, and allowing them to benefit from the increased firewood and other products was the key to success.

An enterprise that is destructive to the environment is inevitably bad for people. Without a thriving, vibrant ecosystem around us, people cannot thrive. And without limits to exploitation and consumption, without an ethic of returning benefits to soil, to plant, animal, and human communities, balance cannot be obtained.

One aspect of social permaculture looks at how physical structures impact social interactions. This aspect of social permaculture has some key forerunners from the disciplines of city planning, economics, and architecture. Economist Jane Jacobs, in her classic book *The Death and Life of Great American Cities*, articulated patterns that make for lively and diverse urban spaces. Christopher Alexander and his group of architects, back in the '70s, compiled the groundbreaking book *A Pattern Language*, which looks at the built environment from a city scale down to the décor on your house walls in terms of the human relations that structures and spaces elicit.

Today, the group City Repair, based in Portland, Oregon, creates gathering spaces out of intersections and hosts an annual Village Building Convergence to teach natural building techniques and permaculture and collectively transform the urban environment. Founded by architect Mark Lakeman, the group models how creating inviting social spaces can influence a city, from slowing traffic to encouraging neighborhood unity and civic engagement. They have inspired similar efforts in cities all over the US and worldwide.

• • •

Permaculture has a set of principles, derived from an understanding of ecology and systems theory—guidelines for how we go about designing systems. Some translate directly into social applications. For example, in designing a garden we understand that diversity is a value. We might plant polycultures instead of monocultures, including flowers in the vegetable patch to bring in beneficial pollinators or planting multiple varieties of apples in the orchard.

In human systems, valuing diversity might lead us to value our differences instead of letting them divide us. A community that includes people of diverse ages, genders, races, sexual orientations, physical abilities, and economic backgrounds, as well as diverse ideas, cultures, and opinions, will have broader perspectives and a deeper understanding of issues and events, as well as more resilient responses. For example, in one of our recent Earth Activist Trainings—permaculture design courses with a grounding in spirit and a focus on organizing and activism—a young environmental activist ended up working on a design project with a Spanish farmer who currently uses pesticides and artificial fertilizers. Initially shocked at the farmer's use of chemicals, the activist found himself growing to understand the farmer's constraints and needs at a much deeper level, and the farmer found himself inspired and enthusiastic at the prospects for transitioning his farm to become a permaculture model.

Photos by Brooke Porter

Diversity must be functional. Planting a cactus in a redwood forest will not create more diversity—it will result in a dead cactus. A cattle rancher and a hard core vegan may never be happy farming together.

Creating meaningful diversity requires a process of self-reflection and personal growth and transformation. What are the values and practices that are deeply important to us, that we don't want to compromise? Where are there places that opening to difference might expand our horizons? Are there ways in which our community norms and assumptions are limiting our diversity? Are we responding to differences in others out of fear or prejudice, or the privileged assumption that our group norms are universal standards?

Embracing diversity also means confronting those systems of racism, sexism, ableism, ageism, heterosexism, and all the other destructive patterns of discrimination and structural oppression that keep us divided and separate. It requires us to actively engage in efforts to change those larger societal patterns.

Functional diversity might mean bringing in women and people of color at the beginning of a project, not at the end; including diversity in the organizing committee that plans a conference and determines its overarching culture, rather than inviting one black speaker at the last minute. It might mean providing facilities that allow access to diverse participants: for example, providing childcare for a conference so that parents of young children can attend; offering translation so that non-English speakers can contribute to a discussion; providing interpreters for the Deaf or wheelchair-accessible facilities for the differently-abled. It might also mean making an organizational commitment to look at issues of power and privilege, and to engage in training and education to expand our understanding of different cultures and heritages.

Earth Activist Training, the organization I direct, offers Diversity Scholarships for people of color and differently-abled people for our programs and trainings. We have found that when the composition of a group shifts so that a third or more of the group are people of color, the group culture also changes and excitement and learning radically increase. Diverse groups can be more challenging to facilitate, as differences sometimes clash, but the depth of learning that results is more than worth the efforts.

• • •

There are many other permaculture principles that can inform our social designs. The principle of edge or ecotones, for example, tells us that where two systems meet, a third system arises, dynamic and diverse. Where the ocean meets the shore, the varied conditions of tides and waves create multiple niches for various forms of life. Where two human systems meet, we can expect great creativity and possibly also tension and conflict. The meeting of European and African musical cultures produced spirituals, gospel, blues, jazz, rock-and-roll, hip-hop, and many other creative forms that arose in spite of the overarching system of oppression that also generated conflict and suffering. Systems change from the edge, and systems also resist change and try to maintain themselves. So when we set out to change a system, we can expect both resistance and opportunities for great creativity and surprises.

"Capture and store energy" is another principle, and its application to solar or wind energy is obvious. But there are also many forms of human energy and creativity we can benefit from that often go to waste—when young people, or women, or people of limited economic means are excluded from programs or projects, for example. And "obtain a yield" is a good principle for activists and communitarians to remember when we fall into the trap of exploiting ourselves out of our altruistic desires to serve a greater good. We also need to get something back, to sustain ourselves economically, emotionally, and physically with food and rest and beauty and yes, also money, if we are not to burn out and become nonfunctional.

• • •

Permaculture also looks at patterns. What are the patterns and understandings that can help us structure groups in a healthy way? What tools and techniques—from ecology, but also from psychology, social science, spirituality, and the human potential movement—can help groups communicate more clearly, resolve conflicts, and function better?

In my book, *The Empowerment Manual: A Guide for Collaborative Groups*, I examine patterns I've observed over decades of participation in groups that were organized without top-down hierarchy: spiritual groups, activist groups, living collectives, permaculture groups, and many others. Over and over again, I saw groups struggle with the same issues of power and conflict. I came to the conclusion that non-hierarchical groups are inherently different from groups with top-down authority, and need a different set of tools and understandings.

In a healthy group, power is balanced by responsibility—that is, people earn power by taking on and fulfilling responsibilities. And when people take on responsibilities, they are empowered by the group to carry them out.

But power can be many things. Power-over is command and control power, the sort we're all familiar with in top-down institutions from corporations to schools to the military. Power-from-within, or empowerment, is the personal and spiritual power we each have; creative power, skill, confidence, and courage—qualities that are not limited. If I have the power to write something inspiring, that doesn't take away from your power. In fact, it might actually encourage your creativity.

And in groups, we encounter a third type of power: social power, prestige or influence, the measure of how much each person's voice is heard. Social power can be earned, as it is by elders in tribal societies when they build a track record of good decisions and care for the community. But it can also be unearned—the privilege we might accrue from our gender or skin color or class background.

Healthy and functional groups attempt to do away with privilege, and to allow people to fairly earn social power by fulfilling responsibilities and developing a track record of commitment and service. And when people are given a responsibility, they are also given the authority—the license to use power—that they need to carry it out.

Groups fall into error when social power is hoarded—when, for example, the founders of a project cannot let go of control and new people cannot shape the group's direction. But they may also err by according power indiscriminately to anyone who shows up, at the expense of those who do have a long-standing commitment to a group. If people cannot earn power by committing to the group and fulfilling responsibilities, the most committed and responsible often become discouraged and leave; unearned power or privilege creeps in and thrives. Power may become vested in those with the loudest voice or the most ardent desire, rather than in those who truly serve the group.

Nonhierarchical groups also need good communication skills and conflict resolution tools. Many of us grew up in families where Mom or Dad would step in and say, "You kids stop fighting!" In groups with top-down authority, someone—the boss, the leader, the guru—takes that role. But in horizontally-organized groups, no one has the authority to resolve a dispute or end a conflict. If such authority exists, it is held in the group itself—but often groups have no mechanisms or agreed-upon processes to invoke that authority. So conflicts may bounce around and around, without resolution, until people get sick of it all and leave.

To prevent this, groups need to consider how to deal with conflict before it develops. They need clear agreements, conflict resolution structures, and channels of communication built into group design, as well as tools and frameworks for governance and decision-making, for group facilitation and self-care.

Many of these tools exist in other disciplines. Social permaculture draws on the work many people have done in the group dynamics, nonviolent communication, psychotherapy, self-help, and the human potential movement for skills and tools, and part of our work is to bring these more fully into the trainings, gatherings, and projects of the permaculture movement.

Many people are now engaged in bringing forward social permaculture. I regularly co-teach social permaculture and facilitation trainings with Charles Williams of Earth Activist Training and Pandora Thomas, founder of the Black Permaculture Network.

In September of 2015, I was privileged to co-teach a special course on Social Permaculture with Looby McNamara and Peter Cow from Britain, Robyn Clayfield from Australia, and Robina McCurdy of New Zealand. Looby's book *People and Permaculture* has been hugely influential in making people aware of the need for people-focused design. She and Peter Cow teach many courses together in permaculture people skills, facilitation, nature connection, and cultural design. Robin Clayfield has developed a wealth of tools for group facilitation, creative teaching methods, governance and decision-making systems. Robina McCurdy is skilled at community development, teaching environmental education and participatory decision-making. And many more teachers and leaders in the broad permaculture world are now understanding the need to strengthen the social aspect of regenerative design.

The ability of individuals and groups to collaborate successfully is one of the largest constraining factors in all forms of organizing, and as we succeed in creating more functional groups, all our work in every area of life will be strengthened.

Websites:
Starhawk: *starhawk.org*
Earth Activist Training: *earthactivisttraining.org*
Black Permaculture Network: *blackpermaculturenetwork.org*
City Repair: *www.cityrepair.org*
Pandora Thomas: *www.pandorathomas.com*
Looby MacNamara: *loobymacnamara.com/home*
Peter Cow: *www.livingincircles.com*
Robin Clayfield: *dynamicgroups.com.au*
Robina McCurdy: *earthcare-education.org/wp_earthcare/about-us/robina-mccurdy*

Starhawk is the author or coauthor of 13 books on earth-based spirituality and activism, including the classics The Spiral Dance, The Empowerment Manual: A Guide for Collaborative Groups, *her visionary novel* The Fifth Sacred Thing *and its long-awaited sequel,* City of Refuge. *Starhawk directs Earth Activist Trainings, teaching permaculture design grounded in spirit and with a focus on organizing and activism (www.earthactivisttraining.org, starhawk.org). She travels internationally, lecturing and teaching on earth-based spirituality, the tools of ritual, and the skills of activism.*

Social Permaculture: APPLYING THE PRINCIPLES

By Brush

Permaculture's 12 principles apply to human groups just as much as to any other ecological system. Here are some ways we can implement them in the social sphere:

1 **Observe and interact.** No matter how much you're "starting" something, there's an existing network of patterns. See what's already happening. Participate in similar groups or processes, or ones from which you'll be drawing participants. Write down observations day after day, and take the time to trace out patterns. You want to "nudge" the existing systems, not create new ones from whole cloth!

2 **Catch and store energy.** Sometimes, energy is high: celebrations, successes, summertime! Energy in social systems is stored when healthy, positive relations are fed with joy, supportiveness, and pleasure. It can be more deeply rooted with rituals and formalized events that memorialize the experience. Later, when times are harder, these positive resonances can be drawn on to heal and sustain the social weave.

3 **Obtain a yield.** People need to feel compensated for their participation. This can be money—$$ or local currency—but it can also be many other things. Food, services, or simple affirmation and appreciation. Observe what people currently consider a "yield" in their lives (a necessity that they do work to obtain), and find ways for your system to obtain it for them—and you.

4 **Apply self-regulation and accept feedback.** Figure out how each part of your system can have tight, well-functioning feedback cycles: each individual looking at their own actions; each group evaluating its progress; groups interacting with each other. Giving and receiving feedback well is an art: cultivate it, recognizing that each person has their own preferred ways. Mantra: "Trust <=> Accountability."

5 **Use and value renewable resources and services.** Build recharge and renewal into your social fabric. Watch out for patterns of stress and burnout, and make everyone as accountable for them as for work product. Rely on long-lasting relationships (usually local) rather than fly-by-night cheapest deals. Fair trade! Living wage! Joyful gifts!

6 **Produce no waste.** People can be wasted, too: when they're treated as unworthy of respect, when they're discarded because no longer useful or interesting or cool. Choose your relationships wisely, and then invest in them heartily. Have a clear process for determining when it's time to separate, and do so cleanly and gently. Support people with direct feedback about what worked and what didn't, and help them (within reason) find a new place to plug-in. The whole system is interdependent: there is no "away"! It's best for everyone to find the best fit.

7 **Design from patterns to details.** Every group and close formation of groups should take regular time to explore the "bigger picture." Rather than simply extrapolating the past into the future, really step back, observe your patterns again, look at what's really going on in the world around you and how best your network can support the sustainable momenta and relations. Then, having clearly identified the patterns to work with, design back towards the specific.

8 **Integrate rather than segregate.** Make space for different kinds of work, groups, and functions to interact (formally and informally). Bring diverse work processes into physical proximity. Create pathways and spaces for communication to flow about what different people/groups are doing. (Skits? Videos?) Have liaisons between all different groups that go to each other's meetings. Etc.

9 **Use small and slow solutions.** Don't try to create big, tech-heavy, shock-inducing changes to the social system! It will revolt! Look for small tools and practices that will accomplish what's needed with a minimum of bureaucracy and hassle. Build on these once the system has adjusted.

10 **Use and value diversity.** There are many different ways people influence and learn, think, and feel. We need all of them in our world systems! Valuing diversity can mean including a variety of cultures, perspectives, and attitudes in a group in order to improve its internal robustness and resilience. At the same time, true diversity requires that particular skills and perspectives be honed for their unique values: this often means a group that is very specific in at least some of its attributes. Diversity is ensured when both kinds of groups thrive, and all of them are strongly interconnected in "a world where many worlds fit"!

11 **Use edges and value the marginal.** Bring different groups together, and explore the boundaries between them. This is where exciting conflict and synergy can happen! Support isolated, unpopular perspectives in your group: they're often bringing key wisdom to the center

12 **Creatively use and respond to change.** Change creates openings for new growth. Whether this is the departure of key participants, success or defeat at some major goal, or dislocations in the social environment: notice when change is imminent, prepare the ground, and use the space proactively to build energy from new and unexpected places.

Brush is a longtime radical organizer, writer, parent, orchardist, facilitator, mediator, and legal worker; a person who walks the land in prayer and a heartfelt participant in Cedar Moon, an intentional community sharing the land with Tryon Life Community Farm in Portland, Oregon (cedarmoon.us, tryonfarm.org).

Five Tools to Help Groups Thrive

By Melanie Rios

I've noticed similar themes that underlie struggles within communities during the decades I've lived and worked in these groups. Good people get together with good intentions, and then find themselves wallowing in the doldrums of unresolved conflict, fear, isolation, and ineffective systems. Frederic Laloux's book, *Reinventing Organizations,** inspires helpful ideas for addressing the following kinds of situations:

People join an ecovillage to live in community and close to nature, and later come to learn that there is disagreement about what these words mean. Angry factions develop over what kind of nature to cultivate at the village, with one group valuing food production on-site, another group wanting to cultivate native plants, and another group advocating for growing beautiful ornamental plants. There is disagreement about the meaning of community as well. Some residents hope the village will feel like a happy family with daily authentic connection. Others are busy with their nuclear families and work, and so are content to know their neighbors' names and to lend each other items occasionally. Some village members want to welcome neighbors outside the ecovillage onto the property, while others feel nervous about opening the ecovillage doors to those who don't live there. Disappointment due to mismatched expectations abounds.

Meetings are frustrating. Some people attribute the problem to one person who complains frequently in meetings on a recurring theme.

A few community members were excited about starting a business that they believed would benefit themselves, the group, and the larger community. A couple of people blocked this proposal, and the three initiators decided to move away in order to have the freedom to pursue their dream. Over time, there were fewer people still living at the community with energy for bringing new projects and ideas to the community and the world.

I was moved by a permaculture convergence keynote address Doug Bullock gave about 10 years ago in which he said that we have the technological knowledge to solve the survival challenges humans and other beings are facing, and that what is limiting our success is our ability to work effectively with each other. I decided in that moment to be a practitioner of social permaculture, dedicated to helping groups that care about people and our planet to get more done while having fun. This article offers specific ideas for increasing joy and effectiveness in community, and focuses on an emerging approach to collaboration described by Frederic Laloux, who studied 10 financially viable businesses that serve their employees and their communities. He discovered three characteristics they all share in common:

- They each have a clearly articulated evolutionary purpose
- They welcome the whole self
- They are governed through self-management

One business Laloux studied is Buurtzorg, a Dutch health care organization in which small teams of nurses care for patients in their homes. Buurtzorg was founded with one group of 10 nurses in 2006, and had grown to 7,000 nurses by 2013, representing two thirds of all neighborhood nurses in the country. Buurtzorg has decreased the number of hours each patient needs professional care by 40 percent and decreased by one third the number of emergency hospital visits of their patients compared to the traditional care offered in the Netherlands. Patient health and satisfaction with their care increased, while absenteeism of nurses due to sickness has been cut 60 percent, and turnover is 33 percent lower. What can we who live and work within intentional communities learn from this type of organization, which Laloux calls "Teal"? How might the three characteristics Laloux observed in the businesses he studied address the community scenarios described above?

Articulating a Shared Evolutionary Purpose

An evolutionary purpose is one that seeks to contribute something of value to the world beyond the boundaries of the organization. In the first community scenario, people joined the ecovillage because they thought there was agreement about purpose, only later to discover that they meant different things by the words "community" and "nature." It's important that people who live and work closely with each other share the same goals, or at least support each other in pursuing different goals, and it's not enough to agree upon general and ambiguous terms. An ideal time to clearly articulate the group's purpose is when the group is first forming, as this helps people decide whether the community will be a good fit for them before they invest in moving in. But it's never too late to clarify purpose, and once the purpose is articulated, it should be revised periodically to keep it fresh. Here are a couple of tools that I have found useful for clarifying purpose:

Tool #1: A Question Process from *Moving Icebergs*

In this process from *Moving Icebergs: Leading People to Lasting Change*, Steve Patty offers some good questions for helping people ascertain whether they share the same purpose:

- What are your ultimate aims? By this he means, what kind of person do you want to be no matter what happens in the external world? (Honest? Kind? Compassionate? Curious?)
- What are your core convictions and as-

Mindy speaks on behalf of Mothership community children at a Worldwork session.

Lauren describes an initiative she'd love to see happen at her community.

sumptions? (Core convictions are your deepest values, for example that transparency is more important to you than confidentiality, or vice versa. Assumptions are key beliefs based on what you see in the world, such as that climate change is a serious problem that needs to be addressed.)

• What impact does your group intend to have? (There is so much to contribute to our world, and no one individual or community can do everything that is needed. What specifically will you focus on contributing as a group?)

• What are the best means to accomplish your chosen impact?

• What action steps will you take?

If there's not enough commonality in answering these questions within the forming or already existing community, a viable action step may be for some people to break off and start a different group. Or it may be that people deepen their appreciation for each other's passions through participating in this process, and graciously make more room for differences of perspectives within the community. The community that argued about what kind of plants to grow could decide to divide up the property into sections, with each group caring for part of the land held in common, or they could cultivate beautiful, native, food-producing plants.

Tool #2: Worldwork

Developed by Arny Mindell of the Process Institute, Worldwork is a useful tool for addressing conflict related to differing purpose, such as whether vegan or omnivore food will be offered for community meals, or how much and what kind of supervision children are given. Here's how to hold a Worldwork gathering:

• One person speaks something that is true for them, or they may also speak what they imagine other people or entities might say on the topic. The goal is to have every possible perspective shared, even those that aren't in the room currently.

• People place themselves physically in the room based how much they resonate with what was just said. They stand next to the speaker if they agree with what was said, and farther away if they disagree.

• Someone else expresses a different idea, and the others reposition themselves physically in relation to this speaker.

This process provides an efficient way to gauge the sense of the group on controversial topics. Participants aren't rigidly locked into their initial perspectives, as they find themselves moving close to people with different, seemingly contradictory perspectives. I have noticed that challenging issues often solve themselves after these sessions. After a worldwork session on raising children, for example, more community members engaged with the children, and parents became more consistent and clear about boundaries for their kids. Even without negotiating specific policies, safety concerns expressed in the worldwork session were addressed.

Welcoming the Whole Person

What Laloux means by the expression "welcoming the whole person" is that feelings, intuitions, expressions of vulnerability, and rational thought are all invited to be expressed. A worker might let her colleagues know about extra responsibilities that have temporarily arisen at home, for example, and the coworkers might offer to cover some of her work roles so she can spend more time at home. This form of welcoming the whole person is fairly common in intentional communities, unlike traditional businesses that limit acceptable expressions to those that are rational thought, so I would add some more ideas to this category to help stretch intentional communities.

The first idea is to warmly welcome people, beaming them energetic love, which will help in the scenario where someone repeats herself in meetings. Sometimes people show up in annoying ways because they want attention, and will seek negative attention when they don't receive the affection they long for. Affection is a basic human need, and people who don't receive enough of it tend to be anxious, which affects how they act and how people feel being around them. It's helpful to greet all community members with enthusiasm and kindness as they enter a meeting room, especially those who don't receive enough affection in their daily lives.

The second idea I would add to "welcoming the whole person" is to validate what is true and valuable in each person's sharing, publicly acknowledging the contributions they bring to the group. In one meeting where I was a guest facilitator, there was someone who was very concerned about whether the group was following their agreed upon procedures, and I sensed others felt impatient with her concerns. When I thanked her for letting me know what these procedures were and for the important role she played in reminding people of them, she relaxed and agreed along with everyone else to put aside their traditional process for a specific amount of time in order to explore a different way of doing things.

The third additional aspect of "welcoming

Welcoming the whole self means that feelings, intuitions, expressions of vulnerability, and rational thought are all invited to be expressed.

Mindy and Jesse express their enthusiasm for Lauren's idea.

Jesse asks for feedback from his community. The Advice Process can happen one-on-one, or in a group.

Photos courtesy of Melanie Rios

the whole person" I recommend is to provide support for people to consciously expand their repertoire of behavior, exploring new ways of being in the world. An example is to invite those who speak often to listen more, and for quiet folks to share more in the group. In this way, everyone experiences more of the full range of being a person.

Tool #3: The Zegg Forum

The Zegg Forum is a communication tool that encourages people to show their whole selves to their community or workplace, especially sides of themselves that others don't usually see.

- Everyone sits in a circle. People take turns walking the inside perimeter of the circle to share what is alive for them, including their joy, sadness, anger, and/or fear. The speaker may talk about other people in the room as long as they don't look at them while they are speaking about them.
- For the first part of the forum, people share for a maximum of two minutes each. The second part of forum is facilitated by a couple of people who might encourage the speaker to exaggerate something, to try on an opposite way of being, or to participate in a role play.
- After the speaker sits down, others who were listening enter the circle to offer appreciations for the speaker. They also offer "mirrors," which are reflections about what the listener thinks might be under the surface of what the speaker said
- After a few mirrors, everyone claps, and a new speaker enters the circle.

This process is helpful for airing resentments that arise in daily life, and for allowing people to see each other's personal struggles. It also offers opportunities for people to try on different ways of being in the world. One man who talked about feeling lonely accepted an invitation by the facilitators to wear a "passion man" superhero outfit with a heart attached to his chest for the next three days, while those listening were invited to offer him hugs and friendly connection. He appeared to be more socially confident and connected long after he stopped wearing the costume.

It's helpful to hold separate gatherings for the expression of feelings and decision-making because people who are comfortable expressing anger and other intense feelings can end up dominating in meetings where there are others who are less comfortable in the presence of these feelings. The folks who are not yet comfortable with the expressions of feelings tend to shut down mentally when strong feelings arise, and stop participating in the rational conversation required by effective decision-making. If the culture of the group shifts so that everyone learns to stay present in the presence of strong feelings, the two kinds of gatherings can then be combined.

Governance by Self-Management

This third characteristic of the thriving businesses Laloux studied, self-management, provides ideas for addressing the third community scenario in which a few people want to start a business but are blocked from doing so. When implemented well, self-management brings out the best in people, including their dedication and creativity.

Self-management gives more power to small, semi-autonomous teams to make decisions, and these teams give more power to individuals than I've typically seen in intentional communities. This decentralization of power only works well when certain conditions exist, including the presence of a clearly articulated and shared evolutionary purpose and a group that welcomes the whole person. Two other conditions required for successful self-management are the "advice process" and a culture which supports frequent and skilled feedback.

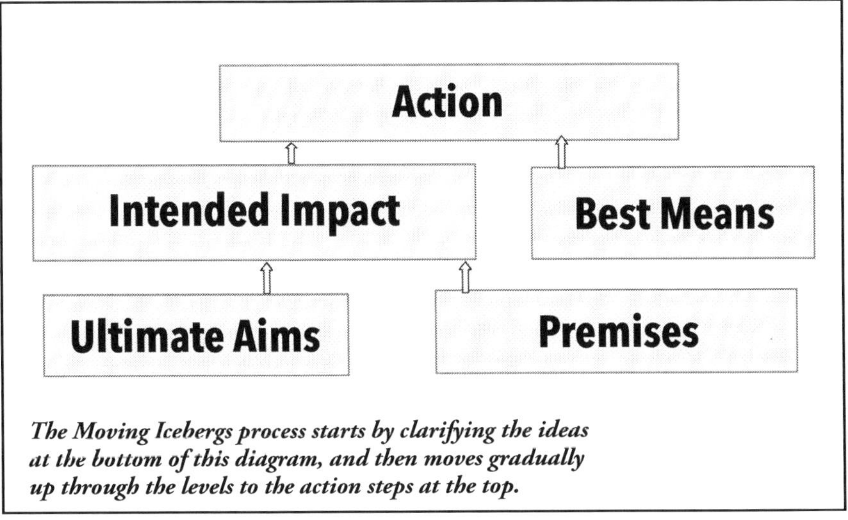

The Moving Icebergs process starts by clarifying the ideas at the bottom of this diagram, and then moves gradually up through the levels to the action steps at the top.

Tool #4: The Advice Process

One intentional community that is using this advice process is The Moss Milk Collective in Forks, Washington. Here's how they describe this on their website:

"Any person in this community can make a decision. But before making decisions that could have a significant impact on others, we ask that community members seek advice from all affected parties and people with experience or insight on the matter.... The person is under no obligation to integrate every piece of advice; the point is not to achieve a watered-down compromise that accommodates everybody's wishes. But advice is sought and taken into serious consideration. The bigger the decision, the wider the net is cast. Usually, the decision maker is the person who noticed the issue or the opportunity or the person most affected by it."

I lived in an intentional community governed by the advice process 40 years ago, and loved the freedom it offered me to explore different careers and lifestyles. I started several businesses, and built a greenhouse that was attached to our house, all without a formal proposal or meeting to approve these initiatives. This approach is a radical departure from decisions based on consensus of the whole group!

Tool #5: Frequent Feedback

Potentially destructive initiatives can be kept in check by a culture in which frequent feedback is offered between members of the community. A good resource for giving skilled feedback in delicate situations is in Susan and Peter Glaser's book *Be Quiet Be Heard*:

- Ask if it's a good time to talk
- Tell the person how you feel in response to something specific they did or said
- Acknowledge how you have contributed to the situation
- Offer something you will do, make a specific request, and then negotiate a solution.

So there are five tools for implanting what Laloux calls "Teal Organizations." I would love to hear from you about your explorations into getting more done with your groups while having more fun, as I'm in the process of creating a website with these and many more ideas. Send your experiences along to be included!

Melanie Rios consults and offers presentations on effective collaboration, including Teal Organizations, sociocracy, and emergency preparation. She loves to grow food using terra preta soil which she produces at her home in Portland, Oregon. She also enjoy singing with friends and backpacking in alpine mountains. Her email address is mel@rios.org.

**I highly recommend that you read the book, or at least watch the YouTube video about Laloux's work: www.youtube.com/watch?v=gcS04BI2sbk.*

II

DECISION-MAKING AND GOVERNANCE

BLOGGING:

Pulling Proposals out of a Hat (or Some Orifice)

By Laird Schaub

In December 2007, Communities *publisher Laird Schaub started a blog of "Commentary on Community and Consensus" at communityandconsensus.blogspot.com. As he explains, "For 20-plus years I've been a community networker and group process consultant. I believe that people today are starved for community—for a greater sense of belonging and connection—and I've dedicated my life to making available as widely as possible the tools and inspiration of cooperative living. I'm on the road half the time teaching groups consensus, meeting facilitation, and how to work with conflict. This blog is a collection of my observations and musings along the way." We asked Laird's permission to reprint his May 8, 2008 entry, which is particularly relevant to this issue's Politics theme as it plays itself out within groups.*

LESLIE MYKYTA

This is the counterpart I promised to my May 4 posting on how to get the most out of plenary Discussions. After you've flushed out all the factors that the group agrees need to be taken into account (the main objective of the Discussion phase), then it's time to start crafting solutions. Often this step is begun by a committee, but sometimes the plenary is on a roll or there's time pressure encouraging the group to proceed with all deliberate speed. In any event, I will offer here four aids for efficient and energizing Proposal Generation:

1. An Atmosphere of Curiosity, not Embattlement

The key moment is when someone says something that differs substantially from what you're thinking. How do you respond? It will make an enormous difference if your initial reply is less like, "That won't work for me... " and more like "Wow, that's really different from what I was thinking. Tell me how you got there; maybe I'm missing something... "

In the former, you're assuming a fight. In the latter, you're wondering if your mind will be changed by new information or new insights. The trick is developing the mind set that different perspectives can be a strength—they let you see the problem more completely—rather than as an occasion for a battle.

In the mainstream culture, we learn to capitulate or fight in the face of differences; in cooperative culture we need to learn wonder in the presence of differences.

2. Stretching, not Pulling

As a practical matter, the initial responses to suggestions are crucial for setting the tone. If people can learn to begin with what they like about a suggestion (rather than with "But...") there will be a lot more flexibility (and hence, creativity) with which to reach the finish line. The image I offer here is how can everyone stretch to reach what others are offering, rather than how can you pull everyone toward your position. [Remember, the object here is not how well your initial suggestions hold up; it's how efficiently the group finds the best solution.]

3. Bridging, not Advocacy

When facilitating Proposal Generation, insist (gently, yet firmly) that all suggestions be attempts to combine and balance what came out of the Discussion phase. Let's suppose that there are a list of factors labeled "x" and another list labeled "y," both of which need to be taken into account. What you don't want (now that you're in Proposal Generation) are statements in support of just "x" or just "y." Been there, done that.

So, when a person proposes something that appears to only address "x," a savvy facilitator will respond, "I get that your suggestion will satisfy 'x'; help me understand how it also satisfies 'y.'" Generating solid proposals is essentially about bridging all the factors; it is not about pushing until you get your way.

4. Build on Interests, Don't Get Stuck on Positions

For many, their nightmare dynamic (short of fulminating anger) is where the group is more or less evenly divided on some non-trivial issue: one side favors doing "Z," and the other side favors doing "not Z." That is, the positions are diametrically opposed and each side is fairly passionate about it. What to do?

(continued on p. 73)

of war, although I have written peace on my banner."

We refuse to be enemies. What are the connotations this sentence has when projected on our own life—on our own love?

An older female participant, a real veteran of the peace movement, says: "This is the first time that I have been together with a group for this long without internal fighting breaking out."

Community proves to be a real antidote to the virus of separation. An atmosphere grows in which it is possible to truly look for and think about concrete solutions.

We have planted a seed of peace from which we hope peace will germinate.

For sure, the children will throw stones again when we leave. For sure, the soldiers will take some children to jail, and settlers will attack farmers or vice versa. In other words: many impulses and heart openings which we may have induced will die away again. But a vision has been created and a core group has committed itself to a Peace Research Village in the Middle East, for which concrete preparations are under way. ❊

The next Grace pilgrimage led by Sabine Lichtenfels will take place in Colombia in October 2008. Interested people please write to info@sos-sanjose.org or visit www.sos-sanjose.org. Sabine Lichtenfels wrote a book about her experience: GRACE—Pilgrimage for a Future without War *(ISBN 978-3-927266-25-4).*

For more information about the planned Peace Research Village in the Middle East, about the next pilgrimages, about Sabine Lichtenfels, or about Tamera, see www.sabine-lichtenfels.com, www.the-grace-foundation.org, www.grace-pilgrimage.com, www.tamera.org.

Leila Dregger is an independent journalist, teacher of peace journalism, and writer, born many years ago in Germany and now based in the community of Tamera in Portugal. Her main themes are nature, international and internal peace work, and healing in the relationship of women and men. Note: We preserve the spelling of our Commonwealth country authors.

PROPOSALS

(continued from p. 53)

There's generally a way out. Almost always, "Z" (or "not Z," if you prefer to look at this the other way around) is a conclusion, and not a fundamental value. The key to getting unstuck is peeling back the deadline positions to the underlying interests. Most times, each side is looking at the same problem through a different lens, each of which is a legitimate group value. So, for example, would it be that shocking if an analysis focused on affordability came to a completely different conclusion than one emphasizing environmental impact?

The good news is that affordability and environmental impact are not sworn enemies. By identifying these two as baseline interests you now have much more room to work with. Let go of Z and not-Z; focus instead on finding proposals that do a decent job of balancing these two interests. [Hint: in the end it may turn out that Z (or not-Z) is actually a good proposal; but the energy around it will be completely different because everyone has acknowledged and honored that both core interests need to be taken into account. People can be amazingly graceful about specifics if they feel that their core interests are fully understood and will be taken care of.] ❊

Find Laird's blog at communityandconsensus.blogspot.com.

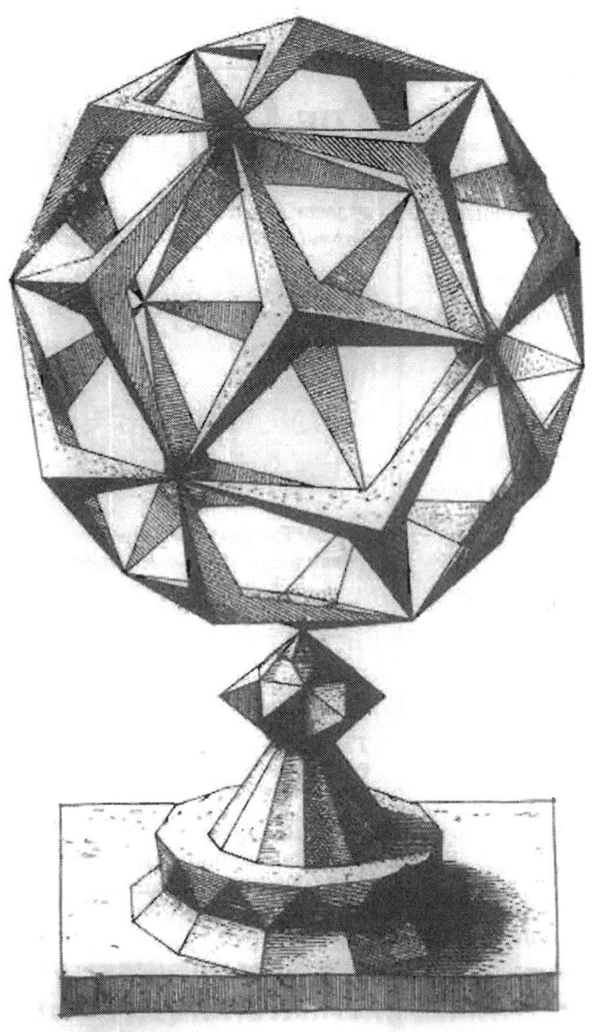

Good Meetings:

BEST

"The theme of this issue being scarcity and abundance, how about, instead of hearing yet another crisis or problem to solve, we focus on abundance as it relates to meetings? Please tell us a story of one of the best meetings you ever attended (as participant or facilitator). What was great about it? What do you think made it turn out so well?"

Tree Bressen responds:

Upon thinking this question over, i've realized that my responses fall into two categories: One is that i love it when a group that's *not* in crisis calls me for facilitation; often this happens for community visioning. The second category consists of decent outcomes to intensely challenging situations, including when the result is an amicable "divorce" between one or two members and the rest of the group. I'm writing story #1 here; perhaps a story from category #2 will appear in the future.

A few months ago a local ecovillage hired me to facilitate their visioning process. While there had been people living together on site for several years already, over time the group was gelling and becoming more intentional, and now they were ready to take the next step of drawing up vision documents together. When i met with the core team initially, they stated a clear goal of coming up with a vision statement within a one-day meeting of the full group, and filled me in on various other issues they hoped to address. I warned them that there was only so much we could accomplish in one day, and promised to do the best that i could.

Shortly before the date of the meeting itself, a dear friend with many years of group experience challenged me on the topic of visioning. "What's the point of it?" he asked. "Have you ever really seen a community use its vision statement to any real effect?" His query and our rousing conversation pushed me to clarify my own thinking. I realized that the groups i'd seen use their core documents in a way that felt alive had more than just one or two sentences; they had a set of basic principles that were meaningful to them.

On the day of the meeting, we got off to a good start. I employed an "Appreciative Inquiry" process, using a mixture of interviews, small group discussions, and other formats, and the group seemed to respond well. But as the day went on, members started approaching me one-on-one to warn that dissent was fomenting in some of the small groups. Chronic issues were reemerging during this process, and some people were starting to get triggered and upset. What to do?

MEETINGS

I was concerned that if we took the focus off visioning in order to address the upsets, the group might not meet its goal of coming up with a statement by the end of the day. At the same time, glossing over the difficulties seemed disingenuous. Thinking back to the conversation with my friend, i realized that a visioning process should include the possibility of grappling with real issues for that group, not just coming up with a glossy statement that nearly any community could sign off on. I suggested that we come back together into one big group, and give some time to the biggest controversy in the room, which turned out to be about membership standards (that is, how far did this group want to open the door to residency?).

The members were committed to listening well to each other, and each person understood that theirs was not the only viewpoint in the room and that they might not get their way. The two people holding the poles of the discussion had a friendly relationship with each other outside the context of this particular meeting. A few times while facilitating i fell into treating dissenting opinions as problems instead of as "a piece of the truth," but then caught myself and pulled back into a wider and more welcoming frame. After about an hour of discussion, all these factors resulted in an agreement to have membership standards and the beginnings of a rough outline as to what those expectations would be.

I enjoyed an "Appreciative Inquiry" process.

—Tree Bressen

After that we returned to the visioning process, and successfully passed a statement, thanks in part to the grace of one member who stood aside with some concerns, knowing he could suggest revisions later. In this particular case, we started with a statement that happened to be drafted by the community founder, but revised it substantially before the group agreed to it. There was even time for a bit of wordsmithing—in spite of the groans, i figure that one good thing about wordsmithing is that if a group reaches that stage, it means the more substantive issues have been resolved!

Furthermore, the group adopted a stepped-up schedule of meetings in order to stay connected with each other, move additional pieces of the visioning process forward, and keep addressing other community issues. All in all, i was impressed with how well the group worked together. The community founder, a builder rather than a process person who'd been skeptical of our plan for the day, was naturally quite pleased when we emerged with three key agreements (vision statement, membership, new meeting schedule). I felt deeply trusted by the group, and was able to use their faith in me to help serve them powerfully.

Tree Bressen is a group process consultant based in Eugene, Oregon, who works with intentional communities and other organizations on how to have meetings that are lively, productive, and connecting. Her website, www.treegroup.info, offers extensive free resources on consensus, facilitation, and more. (Tree uses a lowercase "i" in her articles as an expression of egalitarian values.)

Beatrice Briggs responds:

Some of the best meetings I have attended in Huehuecoyotl, the ecovillage in Mexico where I live, were planned and facilitated by a group of 10-12 visiting university students.

For the past four years, in collaboration with Living Routes (www.livingroutes.org), we have hosted a three-week course in "Leadership for Social Change." The curriculum includes training in group facilitation and consensus decision-making. Using these tools, the students research options for a community service project, prepare and present a proposal to the community and, if it is accepted, implement the plan.

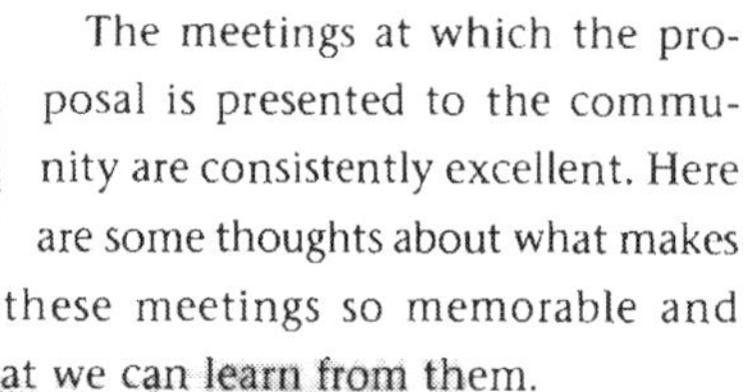

The meetings at which the proposal is presented to the community are consistently excellent. Here are some thoughts about what makes these meetings so memorable and what we can learn from them.

Beginner's mind. The meetings are 100% planned and facilitated by the students, who bring fresh energy and enthusiasm to the task. Having just learned the basics of consensus decision-making, they do not cut corners on the process. LESSON: Do not become jaded in our approach to community meetings.

Short, single-focus agenda. The meetings have only one issue on the agenda, i.e., the project proposal, and are scheduled to last 45-60 minutes. LESSON: Most of our agendas tend to be packed with a too-long list of disparate topics and go on for what seems like forever. Sometimes it is better to focus on a single issue—and then adjourn before everyone is exhausted.

By the time the meeting starts, they have explored the issue in depth and fully "own" their proposal.

—Beatrice Briggs

Clear purpose and roles. Everyone in the room knows why they are there. The community members have been interviewed by the students during the "information gathering" phase of the proposal development and are aware of their role as decision makers at this stage in the process. LESSON: Too often we arrive at meetings with no idea of what we will be asked to do or why it may be important.

Solid preparation, dynamic presentation. The students struggle among themselves to define criteria, gather information, and develop and evaluate options before reaching a decision on what they want to present. By the time the meeting starts, they have explored the issue in depth and fully "own" their proposal. The whole team works on preparing a dynamic, visual presentation that explains clearly what they propose to do, why, and how. LESSON LEARNED: Do not come to a meeting with only a vague, poorly documented idea and expect the large group to spend hours making sense of the issue in plenary. Delegate the preliminary thinking to a small group.

While none of the student proposals have ever been turned down, neither are they automatically approved. The community members ask penetrating questions, make useful suggestions, and propose modifications before reaching a decision. Nevertheless, the students' initiative, creativity, enthusiasm, and solidarity, as well as their careful attention to the norms of good participatory process, almost ensure a successful result.

Beatrice Briggs is the founding director of the International Institute for Facilitation and Change (IIFAC), a Mexico-based consulting group that specializes in participatory processes. The author of the manual Introduction to Consensus *and many articles about group dynamics, Beatrice travels around the world, giving workshops and providing facilitation services in both English and Spanish. Home is Ecovillage Huehuecoyotl, near Tepoztlán, Mexico, where she has lived since 1998. bbriggs@iifac.org; www.iifac.org.*

Laird Schaub responds:

One of the predictably difficult aspects of group dynamics is Challenging Personalities—folks whose style and behavior are frequently disruptive, or at least commonly problematic. I'm not talking about people whose views are often not aligned with the majority (though that may be in play as well); I am focusing here on those whose manner and bearing are regularly grating on the group. It's a relatively common phenomenon.

While this can manifest in more flavors than Baskin-Robbins has ice cream, one of the most prevalent is the person with high energy and a forceful delivery. They are often perceived as upset, or on the verge of it, and don't seem to mind either the tension or the chaos that typically surrounds their contributions. Their comments are not always germane, yet they are invariably delivered with conviction and high amperage.

In consequence, the group is often faced with tough choices around how to work with their input, and there tends to be a weariness and knee-jerk irritation that follows this kind of person around like a cloud of miasmic gas. Understandably, a considerable amount of resentment often builds up towards such a person, and their contributions are often marginalized (if they can't behave, then we shouldn't have to give their input as much weight). To be clear, the marginalization does not happen as a result of any explicit decision by the rest of the group; it occurs organically as everyone withdraws their support and good will in response to feeling ill-treated and disrespected. It may look like a conspiracy to the person being pushed to the side of the road, but that's rarely the case.

Dale (a pseudonym) was just such a person. I had worked with Dale's group multiple times and knew the community fairly well. I also was aware of the group's story about Dale. She was labeled "a problem," and I was cautioned (regularly) about the need to contain her behavior and not let Dale hijack the meeting.

All of this is prelude to the story of a meeting in Dale's community that I witnessed several years ago. During the prep for the meeting the facilitator fretted over how to handle a particular topic on the agenda. It had to do with how well another member (a single parent woman) was monitoring her kid's behavior in common space, a topic on which it was known that Dale was sitting on some critical feedback. The facilitator also knew that the parent was not ready to hear everyone's feedback and wanted to talk first with the group about the struggles she was going through in finding time to earn enough money and also be a hands-on parent. She was struggling.

I was coaching the facilitator (a man in this case) and he was shaky about how he'd handle Dale. To complicate matters even further, once the community meeting got underway Dale arrived late, missed the introduction of the key topic, and wasn't in a good mood. (Great start, huh?)

Sure enough, within minutes of Dale's appearance and her realization that the topic she wanted to speak to was on the table, she tried to launch into her upset (with all the subtlety of a Wagnerian opera). The facilitator took a deep breath and tried to explain to her in measured tones why the group wasn't going to tackle feedback at that meeting. Dale wasn't having any, and kept her bulldozer in gear. After a few more futile attempts at stopping Dale's gathering momentum, the facilitator turned to me with the expression of a drowning man and I stepped in.

Turning to Dale, I made sure I had eye contact, and then walked her through the sequence with a firm voice (louder than that used by the facilitator, but quieter than Dale's): "Here's where we are. The parent is not ready for feedback at this meeting. We thought she would be, but she isn't. Since having that go well is a high priority, we're accommodating her wishes. At the same time, it's important that the feedback happen and we won't leave this topic until we've agreed on a time to reschedule the feedback. As we know that you have something to say on that, we're glad you're here and can tell us when will work for you. Meanwhile, the parent wants the community's attention for discussing what she's doing to find a better balance between earning a living and time with her kid. Will this work for you?"

> *One of the predictably difficult aspects of group dynamics is Challenging Personalities— those whose manner and bearing are regularly grating on the group.*
>
> —LAIRD SCHAUB

After a moment's reflection, Dale said, "Yes," at which point I responded, "Good," and sat back down. I didn't step in again for the remainder of the meeting, and wasn't needed. Having been met energetically and acknowledged (without being chided or condescended to), Dale changed her behavior. For the rest of the meeting, her focus was good, she didn't speak off topic, and she left her bulldozer parked outside the room. In short, she behaved markedly better than you would have thought possible if the only thing you knew about Dale was the group's story about her.

It was an unusually good meeting, and the key moment was the exchange I had with Dale. Used to getting a lot of resistance to her contributions, Dale typically responded with either getting sullen or pushing harder. When she got something different from me—being heard and met—she responded in a way people weren't used to (and didn't think was possible): Dale got more flexible and listened better. Instead of focusing on Dale's bulldozing (which was absolutely no fun to be around and was potentially traumatizing for the parent), I focused on acknowledging Dale's needs and accepting her energy as not ill-intended.

Does this always work? No. Sometimes I don't hear someone accurately enough or otherwise fail to find a bridge that will connect the difficult person with the rest of the group. But if you believe it's possible and are looking for a bridge, you may be surprised how often you'll find one is there—and people can start exchanging ideas instead of salvos. ❉

Laird Schaub, a member of Sandhill Farm community in Missouri, has been doing consulting work on group process since 1987. A longtime activist in community networking, he has lived in community since 1974 and been involved with the Fellowship for Intentional Community (FIC) since 1986; he is currently its Executive Secretary. laird@ic.org; 660-883-5545. Laird authors a blog which can be read at communityandconsensus.blogspot.com.

COOPERATIVE GROUP SOLUTIONS Advice About How to Handle Challenging Dynamics

Would you trust this joker (middle) in your group meeting?

Chris Roth

Open Meetings: Worth the Risk?

Q: *Our group is committed to education and to sharing our lives in community openly with others. We frequently host visitors, and also offer regular workshops and courses. We have traditionally welcomed visitors and program participants to attend our weekly community meetings, believing it gives them even more insight into how we work as a group. We have been able to establish good boundaries about when their verbal input is welcome, and have generally encountered few problems with that. Some members have felt self-conscious in the presence of outside observers, and suggested that we not invite them to our meetings, but usually we've decided that the educational benefit of including them outweighed some of our personal preferences to have more privacy and intimacy. Members always have the option of calling for "closed session," although this has rarely been invoked.*

Recently, however, one short-term visitor used information gleaned in a community meeting to attempt to blackmail the community (on questionable grounds, but it cost us considerable time and worry), and two other disgruntled program participants started spreading damaging rumors in the local area, based on dynamics they observed while we talked as a group. These experiences have made many of us skittish about allowing outsiders to observe our meetings, and moreover we don't feel able to freely discuss this troubling dynamic in the presence of visitors. We have held one closed meeting about this issue already, and that itself had repercussions and started curious visitors talking. How can we balance these competing needs and concerns?

Beatrice Briggs responds:

Although in theory, I support the idea of open meetings, I cannot see the benefit if (1) outsiders are converting what they see and hear into grist for the local gossip mill and (2) this is causing community members to feel inhibited and uncomfortable in their own meetings. In addition, I imagine that the effort going into dealing with the situations precipitated by the open meeting policy is detracting from the time and energy available for addressing other pressing issues.

I suggest that you declare a one-year moratorium on open meetings to let things settle down. No need to explain to the outside world why this step has been taken. If asked, just smile and say, "We are on an extended retreat" or something along those lines. During this period, observe carefully whether the sensitivities uncovered by the visitors' behaviors diminish and group members begin to speak openly and honestly again in meetings. If some people are still acting inhibited, the problem probably goes beyond the visitor factor. There may be underlying issues that are not being addressed. At the end of the year, revisit the open meeting policy.

Beatrice Briggs is the founding director of the International Institute for Facilitation and Change (IIFAC), a Mexico-based consulting group that specializes in participatory processes. The author of the manual Introduction to Consensus *and many articles about group dynamics, Beatrice travels around the world, giving workshops and providing facilitation services in both English and Spanish. Home is Ecovillage Huehuecoyotl, near Tepoztlán, Mexico, where she has lived since 1998. bbriggs@iifac.org; www.iifac.org.*

Tree Bressen responds:

Have you traveled by airplane in the past decade or so? If so, you'll undoubtedly have noticed more than a few "security enhancements." Taking off your shoes, getting patted down or scanned with a metal-detecting "wand," being prevented from bringing a full water-bottle through security, that kind of thing. I personally had a small, sealed bottle of horseradish confiscated last year. Was my horseradish dangerous? Maybe if thrown at someone's head, but basically, not really. So why was it taken? Because ever since Sept. 11, 2001, the US and other countries have been making changes to airport security based on worst-case situations. At the time of this writing, banning all carry-on baggage is seriously being discussed.

If you have strong relationships with your neighbors, they'll be a lot less likely to believe any damaging rumors.

That's kinda like closing the barn doors after the cows are gone, but it happens all the time. And i've seen it a bunch in communities, where after a bad incident, legislation (policy) is passed in an effort to help everyone feel safer and more secure.

Of course groups need to learn from their mistakes, and change is not always bad. Particularly if a similar situation crops up more than once, the universe—in the form of your members (or in this case, visitors)—might be trying to tell you something, in which case it could be a good time to put those finely honed listening skills to use. And on certain occasions, even once is enough to insist that change needs to happen, like when an agricultural commune relying on visiting volunteer labor changed a few of their procedures to increase physical safety after a terrible accident. But no matter what kinds of changes you make, bad luck's still gonna crop up sometimes.

If you are unfortunately hosting the kind of person who would attempt blackmail or spread damaging rumors, they'd probably start mischief of some kind whether they attend your meetings or not. Which doesn't mean you need to make it worse by inviting them: visitors need to understand that attending community meetings is a privilege, not a right. And i think your group should feel fine about holding closed meetings to explore this particular issue if that's what you need.

However, my experience has been that the most damaging things that happen to communities happen from their own members, not from visitors. Internal lawsuits, embezzlement by a community accountant, or just really nasty interpersonal conflicts that stew for years. While many of us may have ideas on what forms of membership screening are more effective than others, i don't think any group has discovered a sure-fire method for screening.

So if you accept that bad things are going to happen occasionally, then i think the key question becomes: *How can you build and maintain resiliency?* For example, if you have strong relationships with your neighbors because you are constantly helping them out with chores, riding with the volunteer firefighting squad, or singing in the local church choir, then they'll be a lot less likely to believe any damaging rumors that might come their way. Particularly if they've known you for 20 years compared against a random newcomer who just wandered in.

In the aftermath of a negative incident, making changes like these—changes that take time for their effects to grow—might not address the part of your brain that's crying "Alarm!," but they might best serve your community's well-being in the end. If you're not sure, then it's probably a good time to invoke the Quaker practice of "seasoning" a potential decision for a month before moving ahead.

Tree Bressen is a group process consultant based in Eugene, Oregon, who works with intentional communities and other organizations on how to have meetings that are lively, productive, and connecting. Her website, www.treegroup.info, offers extensive free resources on consensus, facilitation, and more. (Tree uses a lower-case "i" in her writing as an expression of egalitarian values.)

Laird Schaub responds:

My basic advice to groups is to be as open as you can stand. There is a basic principle that applies here about how information flow is related to trust: the more information is shared (so long as it is accurate), the greater the tendency to trust; the more information is restricted, the more trust is impaired. It's that simple. Thus, I applaud the group's historic approach to open meetings. And the benefits go beyond that. In addition to trust building and the educational component named by the narrator, I have found that encouraging (not just permitting) visitors to attend meetings is a great way to assess the social skills of non-members.

Over the 35 years that my community has been around, we've found that screening prospective members for communication skills is the surest way to predict a good fit. We figure that very few people get to us without already having sorted themselves out for a reasonably good value match, and thus, when it comes to what our ongoing relationship with them might be, we look closely at things like: how well they listen; how well they can articulate their feelings; how easily they can switch perspectives to see another person's viewpoint; how well they can distinguish between personal preferences and what's good for the collective; how they work with conflict.

By having them observe a meeting (and use their judgment about if and when to speak) we get a lot of valuable information in a short time. We try to debrief with the new person right afterwards to hear their impressions and answer questions, the better to understand how they saw things, and to nip any misinterpretations in the bud. This is enormously valuable as a screening tool.

All of that said, there's no doubt that bad things can happen when you trust strangers to use appropriate discretion with privileged information. While my overwhelming experience with extending trust is that it leads to benign results, it doesn't always. Now what?

My basic advice to groups is to be as open as you can stand.

In the two examples given (one of attempted blackmail by a short-term visitor; the other of spreading negative rumors by unhappy program participants), I think it's better to focus on how the group handles conflict than on who it allows to attend meetings. The root issue is that relatively new people had a problem with something that was happening in the group and chose to act on negative conclusions outside the group rather than work it out internally. That's not good.

If, as I was suggesting above, the group was checking with non-members after meetings to see how they were doing with what they'd observed, then I think it would have been obvious that the new folks were having a bad reaction, and/or laboring under a misunderstanding. Forewarned, the group would then have had an opportunity to address this (Luke, there's a disturbance in the Force) well before it evolved into blackmail or rumor mongering.

To be fair, handling conflict effectively is a sophisticated skill, and not all attempts end well. Nonetheless, it's well worth developing that ability and I recommend that the group look first to how it can do a better job of processing tension, rather than considering structural changes (restricting access to meetings) to better contain the potential negative consequences of poorly resolved conflict.

Finally, I want to address the situation where the group feels it's necessary to hold a closed meeting. As the narrator suggested, there may be times when the members' desire for safety and full disclosure trumps the commitment to openness. While I agree that this should be an option, I think it works best (that is, minimizes negative repercussions) if the group commits to providing everyone who was excluded from the meeting with a summary of what was discussed. This offers a middle ground between full disclosure (an open meeting) and a secret meeting (where no one knows what was talked about if they weren't in the room). For this to work well, it's important that the summary be as complete as possible and delivered as shortly after the closed meeting as can be done. ❁

Laird Schaub, a member of Sandhill Farm community in Missouri, has been doing consulting work on group process since 1987. A longtime activist in community networking, he has lived in community since 1974 and been involved with the Fellowship for Intentional Community (FIC) since 1986; he is currently its Executive Secretary. laird@ic.org; 660-883-5545. Laird authors a blog which can be read at communityandconsensus.blogspot.com.

Do you have a question for our Cooperative Group Solutions panelists? Please send it to editor@ic.org.

Money, Power, and Process: How We Pulled the Plug on Consensus

By Kees Kolff

After six intense years, Helen and I did what we thought we never would: exercised our power as owners of the property and temporarily suspended our cherished consensus process. We announced that we would make all the decisions for a while, that we were going to become a homeowners' association with private lots, and that we were developing a list of required conditions if the EcoVillage were to continue. How did we get to that point?

We had searched for alternative structures and funding for six years. How could we possibly go back to a traditional homeowners' model after having tried so hard to be more innovative? Didn't our core values suggest that we don't own but rather borrow the land from future generations? That housing ownership has increased economic disparity in our society? That financial institutions are part of the problem? That intentional communities are ideal for correcting some of society's economic power imbalances? All true, but we had to face economic reality: We were out of money and needed to complete our infrastructure improvements and make mortgages available

The cutest contestant at the annual zucchini festival.

Photos courtesy of Kees Kolff

The fact that my wife Helen and I owned all 7.5 acres of the Port Townsend EcoVillage created a tremendous power imbalance with other members. We agreed to use Formal Consensus and danced with the imbalance quite successfully using Compassionate Communication and a lot of trust. But the power imbalance was always there, especially since we also had the greatest economic wealth in the group.

Terri takes the extra CSA produce to the food bank in our electric car, a ZAP.

to potential new members.

The fact that my wife Helen and I owned all 7.5 acres of the Port Townsend EcoVillage and weren't planning to move afforded us the luxury of time to explore different legal structures and different sources of funding. It also created a tremendous power imbalance with other members, since we could unilaterally pull the plug at any time. We agreed to use Formal Consensus (*à la* C.T. Butler) and danced with the imbalance quite successfully using Compassionate Communication (*à la* Marshal Rosenberg) and a lot of trust. But the power imbalance was always there, especially since we also had the greatest economic wealth in the group.

Initially we had formed a Limited Liability Company so we could share ownership, and we looked for private lenders since the banks wouldn't touch us. Then the economy crashed. We considered a limited-equity cooperative so we could still share ownership and limit profits to keep housing as affordable as possible. Then the banks crashed. National Coop Bank told us they were not offering new loans, especially to those with limited-equity constraints. We asked if a local community land trust would take the land, but they were too new and declined, and ultimately we felt it would constrain our plans for economic diversity. We considered sharing ownership as a tenancy in common, but the perceived level of liability was unacceptable. We needed more people to buy in so we could install the city-required infrastructure, and our potential new members needed loans to build their homes. We felt stuck and burned out, and that's when we pulled the plug on consensus.

It felt strange exercising our power over fellow EcoVillage members who had put in just as much time and energy and a considerable amount of cash to get us where we were. Although our consensus process might well have yielded the same decision eventually, I think we were just burned out by the almost weekly meetings and couldn't

This photo: Shae and Orion with the homeschool group that warms up in the new greenhouse, attached to the shop building. The first new cottage, with an earthen floor, is in the background.
Bottom photo: Jim and some of his professional garlic harvest.
Opposite page: A zucchini car goes for distance at the annual zucchini festival. The honey extraction house is in the background.

handle the idea of more group process. The next several meetings were very uncomfortable and then Ruth said, "So basically you and Helen are now the developers and you're just asking us for some input." Though we didn't like the title, she was right, and it did help to state the obvious. With ideas from all the members, we modified our conditions over several months and then moved back into the consensus process, but only with a smaller core group of six members who paid for lots. This left other long-term members, who either weren't ready or could not yet afford to buy in, out of the consensus process, and created a whole new power imbalance. We're still exploring different ways to include them in the discussions and in the social fabric of the EcoVillage.

With our home ownership model we hope that:

1. Options for institutional financing will be greater (and in fact we immediately had some families qualify for one-percent loans through the US Department of Agriculture),

2. We can sell or donate lots to Habitat for Humanity or a community land trust,
3. Low-income senior members can more easily get reduced city utility rates,
4. Tax credits and deductions will be available for homeowner energy-efficiency upgrades and renewable energy systems,
5. Mortgage interest payments will be tax deductible,
6. Members who need to relocate in the future may find it easier to sell their homes, and
7. Potential members may feel that their investment is safer.

We currently have eight adults, two children, four hens, and thousands of honey bees living on site. Can we inspire new members, even if we are all homeowners, to embrace our vision, including permaculture principles, living more sustainably in smaller homes, and sharing amenities like an electric car, shop, common house, and gardens? We believe we can! We published our dilemma over the LLC vs. Co-op decision back in the Winter 2006 Communities. Bucking elements of our dominant economic system had been more difficult than anticipated, yet we are still optimistic about our future as a thriving ecovillage.

Kees Kolff is cofounder of Port Townsend EcoVillage in Port Townsend, Washington.

EcoVillage Resident Reflections:

Marc Weinblatt:

Pulled the plug on consensus? I always knew that Kees and Helen could "pull the plug" at any time. When I joined six years ago I told them that the first thing I wished the group could do was to buy them out, to level the power "playing field." When they exercised their power, I mostly was grateful that they waited as long as they did and I did not mind letting two drivers take the wheel for a while.

We actually had a remarkably healthy "faux" consensus process. The Kolffs were as responsive as anyone could be under the circumstances. Members were heard and respected, and we all had a huge impact on the shaping of this community. That said, I feel great that we are on the road to *true* consensus. It takes an uncommon degree of generosity and humility, but genuine and sustainable group agreements are truly possible.

Ruth Baldwin:

Trust is what enabled me to feel secure during our recent ownership turmoil. Some might call me impetuous or even foolish since I built the first new dwelling here with no clear idea of how or when I might secure my investment. With an amendment to their wills, Kees and Helen directed their heirs to ensure I would be entitled to use and own my home should the EcoVillage fail to materialize. I definitely had my moments of fear and even a few memorable meltdowns during the non-consensus phase. I also experienced relief that our struggles over how to fit into the "dominant financial system" were coming to a close. Our community came through the power imbalance with our values and love for one another intact. Why? Because we spent so much of our time over the years building trust.

Bekka Bloom:

When Kees and Helen announced they had made some decisions about our direction and were suspending the consensus process for a while, I felt both relieved and disappointed. I didn't realize they felt so burned out by our reluctance to let go of our cherished alternative legal structure. I wish our group could have used consensus to accomplish our financial goals. At least membership now is more affordable for those like me, sharing a lot with two other adults. I had always felt awkward about operating by consensus when we hadn't purchased the existing assets from the Kolffs. By their action they clarified this—and that was a relief. Consistently Kees and Helen have proved to have only the best interests of the EcoVillage and its members in mind.

The Awesome Power of the Non-Consenting Voice

By Arjuna da Silva

I feel wonderful being admitted into a circle of consensus decision makers and participating in an egalitarian, democratic process. Here in our group, in our own small way, we can still fulfill some of the promise of empowerment that may not be achievable in our public or political lives. Consensus is so seductive, so utopian-sounding, it's hard not to feel eager for the chance to finally cast our judicious perspectives on the issues of the day.

At its core, consensus harkens from a deep spiritual understanding that there is intelligence in the mindful collective, that no one person has all the facts or has access to all pertinent information, and that contributions of genius and serendipitous solutions can come from any direction. If consensus processes are baffling and frustrating for many of us, it may be because we haven't completely given in to this spiritual underpinning.

There's a nice glow in the room until someone clears their throat and says, "I hate to tell you this, y'all, but I am opposed to this project."

At the same time that it is awesome to work with a group seeking a true consensus of its members, it can be hazardous if one's passion for participating becomes a hindrance to the group's ongoing smooth functioning. Most of us come to consensus decision making with no background in it—nor in conflict resolution—at all. Whereas the structural steps in the process are usually fairly easy to master, skill in staying on track *toward fulfillment* of others' needs or desires takes time—and sincere intention—to develop.

Dr. Dan Siegel, author of the book *Mindsight*, says research shows that children who get a lot of "no" in their upbringing have a very different kind of brain development from those who get plenty of "yes." If you think of the kinds of feelings you have when someone turns you down, how whatever you were enthusiastic about a moment ago can feel all shot to hell now, and multiply that energy into a day-in, day-out pattern, it begins to make sense that so many people in our society are so bummed out, so uninspired, so unable to be creative and encouraging to others.

Some of us were impacted by a lot of "no" energy growing up at home; some of us got it at school; and some of us got it socially from our peers. One or more of these "contributions" to our development, according to research in the Mindsight movement, affects not only our self-esteem and confidence, but our health, our intelligence, and our maturity.

If you think of your decision-making group as its members' child, at least in the sense that it's probably a tender, wobbly work-in-progress, and then think about how the atmosphere of the group shifts and changes as conversations go from ideas and proposals to opinions and approvals (or not), it's easy to see how the way a group functions—its morale, optimism, clear thinking, and cohesion—is affected by a lack of "yes." (To experiment with the power of "no" in our language, try knocking the "no's" out of your vocabulary for a while; this includes not, never, don't, can't, won't, and any other derivative of "no.")

Given the power of "no," and the way the freedom to say it can be abused, we might begin to wonder if there's a more conscious way to use our authority to dissent than we already do, both in our decision-making meetings and in the conversations that lead up to them.

There are also several ways the power of the consenting voice can be used to the group's detriment, including *hogging the mike* (power through coercion), *doubting everything* (power through stalling), *objecting without suggesting* (power through authority), and *scaring folks* (power through traumatics). Each of these produces an energetic or atmospheric disturbance in the group field. People begin to fidget, their minds wander, they

Chris Roth

lose focus—for the most part. Occasionally, groups will have at least one member who is a skilled vibeswatcher and can call the group back to focus by mentioning the shift and suggesting a conscious return to presence. If the disturbance was mild, this may be possible. If its affect was more troubling, perhaps time out to address the fractured energetics can be spent using a tool from the group's toolbox for clearing the air.*

For me, however, the most awful thing that happens to us at proposal time is the immediate response of self-protection. If, like me, you have energy you're not always aware of that's on guard about what might deter, hinder, or otherwise prevent you from realizing a dream, that might be the first filter you apply to any proposal potentially affecting you. Have you noticed yourself whether your first response is "How can this work for Jane or Harvey?" or more like "Hmm...what does this mean for me?"

One would hope, one would think, that in a consensus community, we can safely believe that others will want our needs and desires to be satisfied if possible. And yet....

There's more than one way at Earthaven to stall things. Say someone (or a small group or committee) shows up at a Council meeting with a well-prepared proposal, maybe one they've been working on a while. Then a round of comments are made, peaceably and thoughtfully, and those in the circle who find the proposal reasonable, maybe given a tweak or two, are feeling that nice feeling that comes with working together toward a useful or creative goal. There's a nice glow in the room until someone clears their throat and says, "I hate to tell you this, y'all, but I am opposed to this project. It's taking us in the wrong direction, etc., etc., etc."

Typically, if I support the proposal (or the person proposing it), I may feel defensive and on guard. Or if I also don't like it, I may feel relieved that I'm not alone in my concerns, that I may have a posse to support my objection, if it comes to that. But if I'm serious about pursuing the long-term benefits of a pure consensus, if my group is willing to struggle with differences and paradoxes and to make hard decisions about specific issues (even risking being inconsistent and "led by Spirit"), what might ensue is a marked uplift in the group's good energy.

When members of a consensus decision-making group, who are feeling well-connected and even light-hearted, can't hold on to their good vibes because someone expresses opposition during a proposal's discussion, clouds gather in the consensus sky. Without remarkable facilitation, those funky vibes can spread through the group and take its energy down. I call it The Great

(continued on p. 76)

*At Earthaven, where I live, we're collecting tools. When things get hot, either right in a meeting or when it's clear something's really up, we may use ZEGG Forum technique, or remind each other that Compassionate Communication methods for expressing (and listening to) feelings and needs work miraculously well in many, many circumstances.

THE AWESOME POWER OF THE NON-CONSENTING VOICE

(continued from p. 49)

Consensus Fumble.

Although the real beauty of consensus is in its commitment to synthesize input from the many for the benefit of the whole, staying alert to the group's energy field becomes a real challenge because it takes time away from essential business at hand or, perhaps worse, spotlights our vulnerabilities. These central features of consensus can potentially be at cross purposes if our inexperience with successful resolution presses us to cut processes short and go for the quicker solution. After a while, through moral exhaustion, a group's vision of consensus decision making can begin to feel like another day at City Hall.

The question is, what can be done differently than at City Hall? I believe the answer lies in skill-building, training, and practice. If we are given the privilege of impacting our group's development single-handedly, we need to be shown how to use that power with the highest motives. Instead of relying on familiar dysfunctional patterns, we can decide to incorporate steps and processes for working things through that leave individual integrity and confidence intact or even enhance it.

What if objectors knew that in order to stall a proposal, they had to do the following?

1. recognize feeling a sense of objection and commit to promptly:
2. examine personal emotional issues that might be feeding the objection,
3. seek to understand the value of the proposal for the proposer(s), and
4. think about ways their own concerns might be met without blocking the proposal.

How would the atmosphere of a group change under this regimen, should someone state an objection? What would it take for a group to be willing to take this process on? Try it for a year or two and see? Instead of recoiling or pouncing when objections appear, become curious, responsible, unselfish?

After 15 years of working with consensus at Earthhaven, the essential question for all of us in our Council seems to be, "How can we balance the urge to express ourselves and hone our democratic skills with appreciation and respect for the history and current time investments of an ongoing group? ❧

Arjuna da Silva is a founder and has been an officer many times of Earthaven Council. She is current president of Culture's Edge, which presents classes and trainings in permaculture, natural building, communications skills, and the healing arts. She is a consensus facilitator and trainer, as well as a counselor and hypnotherapist. She has a passion for natural building and is about to move into her earth-and-straw temple, called Leela House, at Earthaven. She can be reached at arjuna@earthaven.org.

Thanks to Our Supporters!

Special Acknowledgements are due to these supporters of our Kickstarter Campaign who made this book series possible.

$150 Series Supporters

Cohousing Coaches
Betsy Morris and Raines Cohen

Ken Schaal
Autumm Sun Community

Chong Kee Tan

Alexis Spradling

Cynthia Fisher

Liam Higgins

Susan Forkush

Laurie McMillan

Jason Ryer

Carl McDaniel

2 anonymous

$250 Series Supporter

Shabir S

$500 and up Series Supporters

Stephen Quinto

Michael Watson

Fund for Democratic Communities

The Power of Process:
How WindSong Created its Community Contribution System

By Andrea Welling

Whether you live in a small community with a few homes or a large community such as WindSong Cohousing with 34 homes and close to 100 residents, community maintenance is non-negotiable. The community needs to be cleaned and maintained, the records kept, the meetings run, minutes kept, the garden tended, and garbage removed.

WindSong (located in Langley, British Columbia) started with a voluntary community contribution system that worked well for a number of years. Over time, though, as concerns were raised and the issues became more complex, our simple discussion process didn't seem to work. We would talk in circles about a large array of topics related to contribution and then attempt to make some small changes to help the situation. While some of these changes would help, ongoing issues about fairness and burnout continued to come up again and again with increasing frustration.

Finding the way forward wasn't about jumping in and doing something quickly. Instead, it was finding a *process* that would allow honest dialogue through focused and efficient discussion to allow the group consensus to emerge. This paper explains how WindSong created its Community Contribution System (CCS) using the ***Consensus Process for Complex Topics***; a process that could be used in any community to work through a difficult and/or complex issue.

The WindSong Cohousing Community is a 34-unit strata-titled complex. Although the community opened in 1996, a group of original residents worked from 1992-1996 to design, develop, and create WindSong. I arrived at WindSong in January 1998, a year and a half after the official ribbon-cutting.

When we arrived at WindSong, the community was all abuzz with projects everywhere to complete: kitchens to be finished, dining room chairs to purchase, painting the kids room, building the community gardens…and everyone was keen and new to WindSong and the projects kept coming and getting done. Everyone was learning about consensus decision-making and discovering new things every day about their interesting neighbours.

Cleaning and maintenance and social activities happened voluntarily and almost all community members were involved. Getting WindSong completed, livable, and lovely was high on everyone's priority list because it was so obvious the projects that needed to be completed.

A couple of years later, sometime after 2000, the community changed somewhat. Residents created their own businesses, some of the couples started having children, residents were branching out into the local community to pursue their passions for

dance, music, sports, and spiritual interests. Also, for various reasons, some original members moved. Jobs moved to other cities, families needed to live elsewhere, and a few residents decided for various reasons that cohousing wasn't the right mix for them.

New residents moved in. Some residents were feeling that they barely had time to clean their own houses, let alone spend afternoons cleaning WindSong.

Initially, the voices concerned about fairness were a handful of residents. Over time, as certain issues continued to resurface, the handful turned into a third or more of the community, and one community member, out of frustration, was approaching individual members to ask them about whether they were participating or not. This questioning wasn't well received by the members and the issue of their participation remained a concern.

The Building and Maintenance coordinator at the time was feeling burnt-out and concerns were being raised about getting work done, jobs falling through the cracks, and worry about properly maintaining our community investment.

For the next three to four years, various concerns about participation would come to the community meetings. During these discussions, we created an effective team system that is part of the current CCS. Nonetheless, issues about fairness, getting work done, who is included, how many hours should residents work each month, how to address gaps, etc. kept coming up, but given the complexity of the topic, it seemed almost impossible to create consensus. There was also a strong polarity between community members who wanted a more formal system and those who wanted to keep the status quo.

Rather than focus on the issues or the solutions, a small team was formed to create an effective process to lead us through the complexity to reach full consensus.

In addition to the six steps of the ***Consensus Process for Complex Topics*** (see below), we included these important ele-

Howard and Alan C.: endurance and teamwork.

Photos courtesy of Andrea Welling

Painting mural.

Nyjal, Myra, and wood chips.

Doing dishes.

Attempts to repress or not allow certain concerns to be raised is a pitfall, because they will almost inevitably resurface later.

ments: preparedness, focused facilitation, openness, acknowledgment, allowing for authentic sharing, sticking to time and agenda agreements, and not rushing.

Consensus Process for Complex Topics

1. Scope of the topic.

- What is the scope of the topic to be addressed?
- The facilitator keeps the group focused on the scope of the topic only.
- As people wander into discussion and debate around parts of the topic, reassure them that they will have an opportunity later to get into the details.

2. Brainstorm areas of concern related to the topic.

- What are the specific areas of concern related to the topic?
- Allow the brainstorm to happen in whatever order it happens.
- The facilitator lists every concern and creates safety for people to express the breadth and depth of concerns.
- If the full range of concerns is not reached, more can be added later.
- Attempts to repress or not allow certain concerns to be raised is a pitfall, because they will almost inevitably resurface later and potentially hijack/derail or slow the process down even further.
- As people wander into discussion and debate around the specifics of the concerns, reassure them that they will have an opportunity later to get into the details.

3. Categorize the areas of concern into many small and manageable topics.

- This categorization can be done by one person or a team of persons.
- The final list should be shown to the group to ensure that nothing has been missed.

4. Discuss each area of concern on its own.

- The facilitator needs to keep the discussion focused on the area of concern only.

5. Allow consensus to emerge from the discussion of concerns.

- Resist the urge to discuss or create consensus about solutions.
- Create consensus about ***concerns*** first.
- A variety of techniques and formats can be used to facilitate the discussion of concerns, and are best tailored to the size and type of group and the topic.
- Some concerns will need more research or more time to allow the group to contemplate and consider the various options.
- If this step is not pushed through by an agenda, a group consensus will emerge.
- When consensus is hard to reach, consider asking specific individuals if they are willing to step aside, determine how personal preferences are shaping their concerns, and remind everyone to find the consensus that is the best for

the group.

6. Once consensus is reached on the concerns, appropriate solutions will follow.

Since the creation of WindSong's Community Contribution System, concerns and issues about participation have dropped dramatically and allowed us to pay for work when needed. Those individuals who wanted to keep the status quo were willing to step aside. Those individuals carrying resentment about fairness were able to let it go. Those individuals who felt guilty about not participating enough had more options to include themselves that were easy to understand and applied consistently to everyone.

In order to keep CCS working, some administrative work was needed initially to collect deposits and orient members. Ongoing CCS administration takes one to two hours per month and involves collecting reports and following up with individuals as well as creating a seasonal gap list. Once standard forms were created, this administration work was simple.

After three years, all members are in good standing and it has not yet been necessary to bring any CCS participation issues to the community. If that is ever necessary, we now have a Community Agreements Team in place to follow-up.

In conclusion, we managed to create our Community Contribution System through a strong process. This process can be used for any complex topic that your community is struggling to address. And if participation is the issue in your community, don't reinvent the wheel; try our process and watch what emerges.

Andrea Welling, B.A., M.A. is an active facilitator at WindSong Cohousing (www.windsong.bc.ca) and has been working with consensus decision making and using innovative group processes for over 10 years. Her specialty is to help groups take a "stuck" issue and create an effective process to allow the group consensus to emerge. Her diverse background includes co-owner of Ladybug Organics, Green Party candidate, personal trainer, and MomCoach.

WindSong's Community Contribution System Agreement

The following are excerpts from Windsong's CCS agreement; for the full text, email Andrea Welling at andrea@momcoach.ca.

Intention

The spirit and intent of this CCS proposal is "Not about who is watching *whom*, but about who is watching *what*."

WindSong's cleaning and maintenance is simply too big for two or three people to look out for. We need to borrow everybody's eyes to really know what needs doing to maintain the fullness of WindSong's well-being, including social connections and social events.

Some of us see "things" better than others. We see when things are "out of whack" or broken, or needs fixing. Some of us see "energy" better than others. We notice when the energy in WindSong needs tending. And some of us see social connections and disconnections better than others and can tell what needs doing. We can use everybody's different way of seeing things. All of these ways of contributing one's eyes and hands matter.

Accountability

Each household must do an amount of work based on a minimum amount of three hours/month for each adult above the age of 19, or the equivalent of $30/month (e.g., a household consisting of three adults over 19 will need to account for its minimum quota of nine hours/month total, or $90/month). If a household's CCS account is in arrears at the end of a CCS quarter, the situation will be brought to a community meeting. .

Each CCS quarter, a community-wide list of all areas and jobs getting done and not getting done will be posted for the community to view. Names of WindSongers responsible for individual areas, team coordinators responsible for larger areas, and overall admininstrative CCS coordinators, will also be posted, so that members will know with whom to communicate concerns about gaps noticed and/or appreciations for the tasks getting accomplished in these areas.

Coordination and Tracking System:

Level 1: Individuals

All WindSong adults are responsible for the ownership of a particular job and/or area that they have signed up for. That individual keeps track of how consistently the job gets done, how long it takes to do the job, and his/her own CCS hours that become a part of his/her household's total monthly CCS quota. Since the definition of CCS is broad, individuals are encouraged to find some kind of job that fits their ability. At a minimum, it is the individual's responsibility to communicate any gaps that he/she notices to the team coordinator, including if their job is not getting done.

Level 2: Team Coordinators

Each team coordinator is responsible for tracking a particular area of the current CCS job sign-up sheet. Team coordinators are also responsible for tracking their overall area with respect to minimum standards, and to communicate such standards, and can request support from the CCS coordinators. Team coordinators are also responsible for organizing blitzes periodically.

Level 3: CCS Administrative Coordinators

CCS coordinators will create and track the overall accountability system, create the communication systems that will help individual coordinators and team coordinators track gaps, support the team coordinators to help fill job gaps, orient new people to the system, and keep track of and balance the quarterly CCS household accounts. Any community member can approach the CCS admininstrative team with any questions regarding the status of any particular area or job concern in the overall maintenance, sustenance, and well-being of WindSong.

GROUP PROCESS BY LAIRD SCHAUB

The Straw Poll that Broke the Camel's Back

As a process consultant I get the chance to observe first-hand which methods consensus groups tend to use to work their way through issues. One of the most common is the straw poll, employed to determine which way and how strongly the wind is blowing part way through a discussion. As a consensus trainer I cordially detest straw polls, and I want to make the case for why this is not a good practice.

[Years ago J.R.R. Tolkien wrote that he "cordially detested" allegory when responding to a suggestion that *Lord of the Rings* was written with Hitler as the prototype for Sauron, and I've been nurturing that turn of phrase ever since, hoping that I'd eventually be able to dust it off and put it back into play. This, I think, is finally the right occasion.]

Think of me as the Big Bad Process Lupine who is going to huff and puff and attempt to blow down the house of straw... (OK, so I get carried away with metaphors.)

Consensus is a process that is altogether different from Voting. While Consensus is based on the concept that the best decisions will emerge from the full group being in alignment about how to proceed, Voting is based on the idea that the best proposal will emerge from a healthy competition.

In Consensus a proposal does not advance to acceptance if there are any principled objections—even one; in Voting it only takes a majority of votes for a proposal to succeed. Living in the US, nearly everyone has experience with parliamentary procedure and democratic decision-making that relies on majority rule. While there are a number of possible variations, in the main, Voting works like this: proposals are put forward, their merits are debated, and eventually there's a vote. If one proposal garners a majority, it passes and the matter is settled.

One of the reasons I'm uncomfortable with consensus groups using straw polls is that it's a form of voting (albeit a non-binding one), and one of the more common difficulties that groups have in fully realizing the potential of Consensus is that they struggle to create a culture of collaboration (perhaps because they don't even perceive the need for it). If a group attempts to superimpose Consensus on a culture of Voting, then you're just talking about unanimous voting, and it's no wonder that many groups report frustration and weak results (as the only proposals that can jump that high bar are typically so watered down as to have little potency for addressing issues).

> ***I'm highly concerned that if a consensus group uses straw polls, they'll be keeping alive a competitive dynamic that undercuts the attempt to build and maintain the requisite collaborative culture.***

Thus, I'm highly concerned that if a consensus group uses straw polls, they'll be keeping alive a competitive dynamic that undercuts the attempt to build and maintain the requisite collaborative culture.

The point of straw polls is to test for the presence of momentum favoring one response to an issue over another. The idea is that this will clear the fog and help the group move productively through the forest (or at least the thicket) of ideas. While there is undoubtedly a need for groups to know where they are

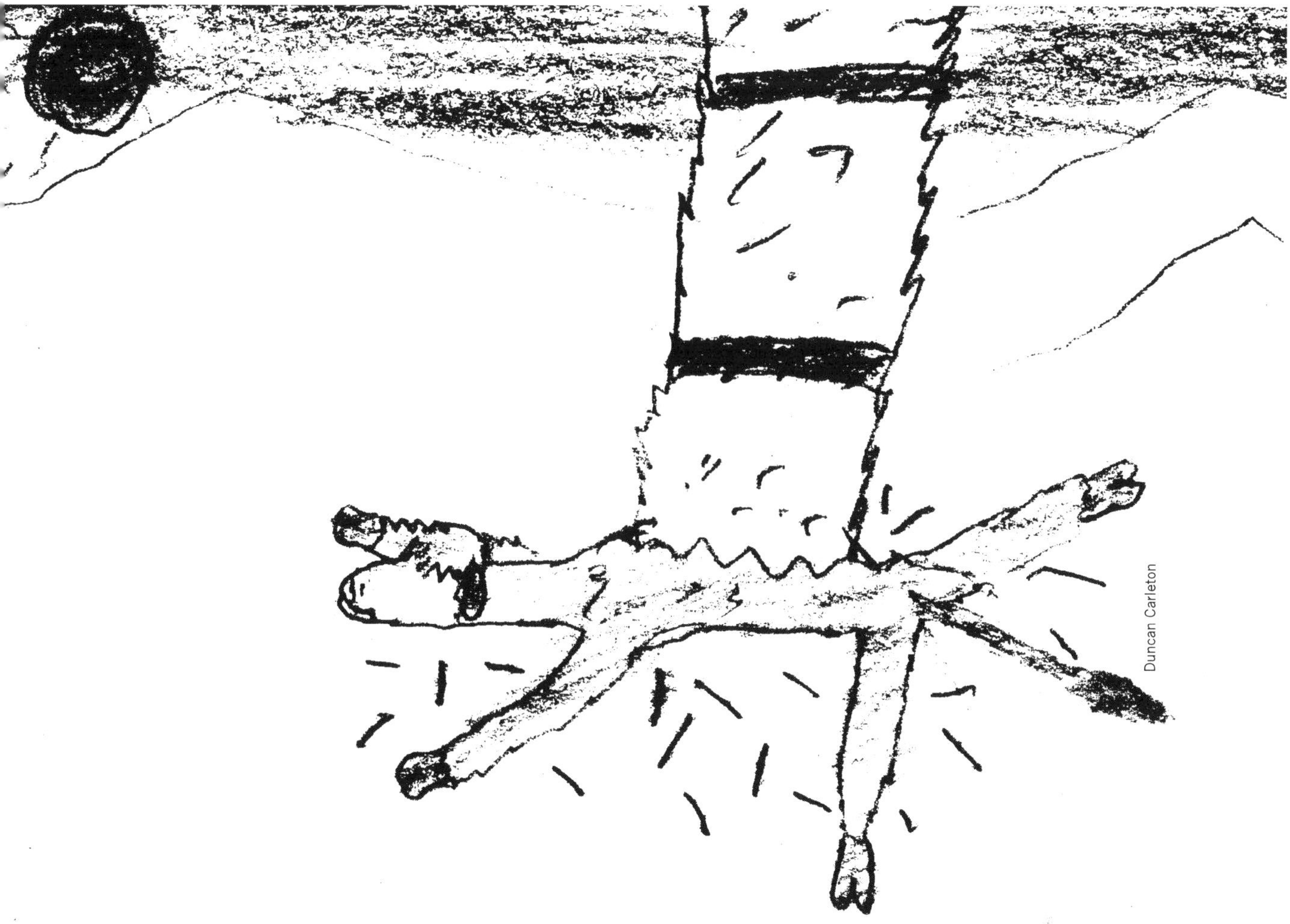

Duncan Carleton

in a conversation and what aspects hold the most promise for being a path through the woods, I think there are better ways to meet that need than with straw polls.

When a group votes, the intention is that the group will be influenced to move in the direction of the majority. (I know that's not always what happens, but that's what the people who propose straw polls are hoping will happen.) No matter how many times you insist that the straw poll is not binding and is informational only, whenever you vote you are invoking the culture of Voting, and the group can hardly help but be influenced by that dynamic. Those in the majority start to relax (after all, they're winning); those in the minority start to feel the pressure (c'mon, you're holding up progress). Some people who suspect they are in the minority may even alter their voting so as not to be singled out for this kind of attention. To the extent that the group slides back into the culture of Voting, it moves out of the collaborative environment where everyone is working purposefully and trustingly toward a we're-all-on-the-same-team solution that everyone can support.

Better, I think, is for the group (led by the facilitator) to learn to follow the energy of a discussion, diligently identifying and working all relevant ends of the discussion (not just trying to find the road where most of the traffic is). Instead of asking the group which views seem to be dominant (the point of a straw poll), you can ask instead, "What ideas do people have that will bridge the disparate concerns expressed?" In a Voting culture the conversation pivots around advocacy (of one's own position) and challenges (of differing viewpoints). In a Consensus culture, the conversation should revolve around how to develop agreements that balance and connect all the factors. You are looking for how to draw an elegant circle around all the input—not just most of it.

Take some advice from the Big Bad Wolf: if want to built an enduring collection of consensus agreements, go light on the straw. It may come at a price that's too heavy. ❧

Laird Schaub is Executive Secretary of the Fellowship for Intentional Community (FIC), publisher of this magazine, and cofounder of Sandhill Farm, an egalitarian community in northeast Missouri, where he lives. An earlier version of this essay first appeared as the January 9, 2010 entry in Laird's blog; find it at communityandconsensus.blogspot.com.

GROUP PROCESS BY BEATRICE BRIGGS

Illustration by Yulia Z.

Six Traps: How Good Meetings Go Bad

A well-planned agenda is the key to leading great meetings. Here are six common mistakes in agenda planning. (And we're not even counting the mistake of not having an agenda to begin with!)

1. Too many items on the agenda

Not everything can get covered in every meeting—prioritizing your agenda items makes your meetings more effective.

2. Unrealistic time estimates

Some agenda items can be breezed through, but many require additional clarification, questions, and discussion. Make sure you allot enough time for each agenda item.

3. Too much time spent in passive listening (reports, speeches, etc)

One word: B-O-R-I-N-G. Distribute reports in advance, and limit speechifying.

4. One person does all or most of the talking

The true purpose of a meeting is collaboration. If all of the communication is "one-way," or dominated by one individual, consider alternate communication strategies.

5. No breaks are scheduled

Bodies don't like to sit for more than 90 minutes. Regular breaks will revive your group's energy and give an appealing structure to your meeting.

6. "Miscellaneous" agenda items

Just like the "junk drawer" in your kitchen, a "miscellaneous" agenda category is sure to be a cluttered mess that contains many items of dubious value. Furthermore, because you do not know in advance what they are, they are almost sure to make the meeting run overtime.

Experienced meeting facilitators can spot these common mistakes and work with the meeting convener to plan an agenda that keeps participants engaged and serves the needs of the organization.

Beatrice Briggs is the founding director of the International Institute for Facilitation and Change (IIFAC), a Mexico-based consulting group that specializes in participatory processes. The author of the manual Introduction to Consensus *and many articles about group dynamics, Beatrice travels around the world, giving workshops and providing facilitation services in both English and Spanish. Home is Ecovillage Huehuecoyotl, near Tepoztlán, Mexico, where she has lived since 1998. bbriggs@iifac.org; www.iifac.org.*

GROUP PROCESS BY LAIRD SCHAUB

Poor Minutes Lead to Wasted Hours: Keys to Effective Notetaking

Good records of what happened at meetings are important for a variety of reasons:

• Informing members who missed the meeting what happened. The minutes should include sufficient detail that people will be able to tell if points dear to them have already surfaced in the conversation—if this is not clear, you can be certain you'll hear comments repeated the next time that topic is addressed.

• Providing a record of decisions and task assignments, which can serve to clear up ambiguities when memories fade or don't agree. This is particularly valuable for committee mandates and for explaining to prospective members what they are joining. (In a consensus group, new members must abide by the full body of agreements already in place—this generally works better if new folks are fully informed about those decisions ahead of time, rather than surprised by them afterward.)

• Helping the agenda-setting crew figure out exactly where the plenary left off and where it needs to pick up when the topic is next considered. (Re-plowing old ground can be the height of tedium.)

• Providing background on the rationale for decisions. This can be crucial in deciding whether it's relevant to reconsider a prior agreement. For my money the litmus test on whether to reconsider is "what's new?" If the minutes are good enough to spell out what factors were taken into account the last time the group grappled with that issue, you'll be in an excellent position to discern whether anything has altered enough to warrant a fresh look.

Questions to Consider

Groups can benefit enormously from discussing what they want minutes to accomplish and the standards they want to set for them. This is a plenary conversation. Questions to discuss include:

• Timeliness: how soon after a meeting should they be posted?

• How will they be disseminated? Is email to a listserv enough, or should there be a hard copy posted on a bulletin board as well—and if so, where?

• How will minutes be archived?

• Minimum standards for what content will be covered. Keep in mind the need to get enough sense of the discussion that people who missed the meeting will know whether their concerns have surfaced or not. If this is not done well enough, the next plenary will be condemned to recapitulate a conversation that's already happened.

• Process by which people can propose revisions to the minutes, and how it will be decided what changes should be incorporated if there's disagreement about it.

• Suggestions for formatting such that readers can easily scan minutes for decisions and tasks. (Do you want executive summaries of the minutes to help those with limited time get the gist?)

• What will be your standard for recording attributions (who said what)? In general, the two situations where it tends to be most valuable are when someone is expressing upset or when they are speaking in an official capacity (for example, as a board member, manager, or committee chair).

• Do you want to create an (indexed?) Agreement Log, which would provide a place for people to look up more easily what the group has agreed to?

• What compensation (if any) will notetakers get for doing minutes?

• What committee will be responsible for seeing to it that notetakers are trained, and that minute standards are being adhered to?

Not Just for Secretaries Any More

It can often be challenging for a group to find enough energy among its membership for taking, editing, and organizing minutes. Here's a hint for how this might be enhanced: *ask folks who want to learn to be better facilitators to take turns doing minutes.* The art of quickly crafting a concise yet accurate synopsis of a speaker's comments is the same as that used by facilitators to track and summarize conversations. Though the facilitator is doing it orally, while the notetaker is doing it in writing, it's still the same skill. This awareness might help generate some additional enthusiasm for practicing the noble craft of taking minutes—and doing the group a good turn into the bargain. ❧

Laird Schaub is Executive Secretary of the Fellowship for Intentional Community (FIC), publisher of this magazine, and cofounder of Sandhill Farm, an egalitarian community in Missouri, where he lives. This article is adapted from his March 23, 2010 blog post at communityandconsensus.blogspot.com.

Richard Iriga Wanyiri

The Tyranny of Structurelessness?

Q: *I'm part of a forming community. I'd like to establish operating agreements for the group, but am encountering resistance from others, including the two people who hold title to the property (until the group can get fully established and buy it from them). So far our leaders and many members tend to default into the "we-don't-need-no-stinking-agreements" point of view when I push for them, though we are creating a few. Some folks are wanting more clarity, but are not sure how to get it, and others go into hopelessness that they have no power or means to address the situation as they see it. I feel as if I am "holding the space" of possibility and optimism, as well as a sketchy vision of how to get from where we are to where we need to be, all by myself, as I am really the only one with an experience of good facilitation and good process. But frankly, it is pretty exhausting. People seem to think good process, clarity around expectations, etc. equates to a loss of personal freedom, the creation of arbitrary or onerous rules or bureaucracy, a recreation of the corporate world which we are trying to escape, etc. They get triggered into their feelings about the latter without even knowing that it's possible to have processes that are actually freeing, and that can emerge from the group, rather than be imposed from above. When I push for more "social infrastructure," I think I look like some kind of control freak to them. And the frustrating part is that as I start to freak out about the lack of clear agreements, I tend to get triggered into my own stuff, which does include a wish to control the situation. It's a vicious cycle. Any reflections or suggestions?*

Tree Bressen responds:

Here are my suggestions:

1. Provide your group with as many fabulous process occasions as you can, so they will know from personal experience that such a thing is possible.

2. Hear them out one-on-one, the ones you disagree with. How can you sympathize with their fears? What do you have in common with them? Can you engage people in a larger conversation about the archetypes of group well-being vs. individual freedom? And own it when you get triggered yourself (either in the moment, or soon afterward)?

3. Arrange for group visits to other neighboring communities, where, in front of others over a meal or consultation, you can engage established groups in conversation about clear agreements as well as other topics.

4. Get members to read Diana Leafe Christian's book *Creating a Life Together,* so they'll know it's not just you or other individuals who advocate for further clarity. You might consider actually buying every family their own copy, because frankly if the book has a positive impact regarding this issue on even one or two people, that is worth a lot.

5. Get yourself some good support personally, allies and friends outside this group—people you can lean on when things get tough.

6. Can your group do a roleplay or something to play with this issue and unlock polarization? Perhaps something including swapping roles back and forth? See #1.

At some point if the group is not prepared to undertake the basic work of creating some clarity and agreements, you may have to cut your losses and withdraw, but hopefully it won't turn out that way. Good luck.

Tree Bressen is a group process consultant based in Eugene, Oregon, who works with intentional communities and other organizations on how to have meetings that are lively, productive, and connecting. Her website, www.treegroup.info, offers extensive free resources on consensus, facilitation, and more. (Tree uses a lowercase "i" in her writing as an expression of egalitarian values.)

Laird Schaub responds:

As often occurs with interesting questions, this one breaks down into parts. So let's tackle them one at a time.

First, there's a subtle dynamic at play here about power that may or may not be something the group is aware of—I'm wondering especially about the two land owners. Ambiguity slants things toward the status quo and reinforces power gradients. If the owners take the position that no agreements are needed until and unless there's a problem ("good will will see us through"), there will be resistance to engaging in the work of clarifying that must be overcome every time. To be clear, I'm not talking about anyone having a bad heart or being purposefully manipulative; it's just the way ambiguity plays out, and people with power tend to be oblivious to it.

> ***Ambiguity slants things toward the status quo and reinforces power gradients, but people with power tend to be oblivious to this dynamic.***

Second, this is a classic manifestation of the dynamic tension between structure/no structure. Anarchy has a decent chance of working so long as everyone sits on one end of that spectrum. In a typical group though (which this one has every indication of being) the lens that the no-structure folks look through needs to be counterbalanced by the lens preferred by those who find structure clarifying and liberating (because they know where they stand and there's anxiety living in the miasma of uncertainty).

The key, in my experience, is trying to sell any structure as our structure, rather than as something imposed by others. It is not a question about right and wrong; it is a question of finding the right balance.

Third, I caution you to be patient with those who are suspicious of the benefits ascribed to spending a gob of time talking about good process. For the most part, the baseline of meeting dynamics is so poor in our culture that it's hard to fault people whose basic attitude is that group conversations are a gauntlet to survive (trial by meeting)—rather than an opportunity to build connection and solve problems. If someone has no personal experience of a thing being good, it makes a lot of sense that they learned to avoid it.

As a strategy, I suggest asking for permission to experiment with some structure and see what happens. If you can deliver productivity and connection during the experiment (rather than a sense of being hamstrung by rules and red tape), it won't be nearly as difficult to get people to make tentative agreements permanent, or to expand the experiment to additional areas. ❧

Laird Schaub, a member of Sandhill Farm community in Missouri, has been doing consulting work on group process since 1987. A longtime activist in community networking, he has lived in community since 1974 and been involved with the Fellowship for Intentional Community (FIC) since 1986; he is currently its Executive Secretary. laird@ic.org; 660-883-5545. Laird authors a blog which can be read at communityandconsensus.blogspot.com.

REVIEW BY DIANA LEAFE CHRISTIAN

We the People: Consenting to a Deeper Democracy

A Guide to Sociocratic Principles and Methods

By John Buck and Sharon Villines

Sociocracy.info, Washington D.C., 2007

I'm excited about the message *We the People* can mean for communitarians and members of other cooperative groups. As a consensus trainer and facilitator, longtime student of decision-making in communities, and community member myself, I believe using Sociocracy, or even just parts of it, could make community governance and decision-making much more effective and fulfilling. *(See "Sociocracy: A Permaculture Approach to Community Evolution," about the Lost Valley community in Oregon,* Communities *#153, pp. 20-23.)*

Sociocracy, also called "Dynamic Governance" or "Dynamic Self-Governance," is both a self-governance and decision-making method. Its decision-making process is similar to consensus in that everyone has a voice in modifying and approving proposals, and it doesn't use majority-rule or supermajority voting like 75 percent or 80 percent voting. And, as with consensus, it will work well only for groups that have a common purpose or aim, and who are trained in the method before they use it.

Sociocracy was developed in the Netherlands in the 1970s by Gerard Endenburg, an engineer who owned an electronics company. He saw that traditional business management methods did not create a harmonious, productive workplace. As an experiment, Endenburg applied the principles of cybernetics—the science of steering and control—to manage his company. The new method did in fact foster a more harmonious, productive workplace. Sociocracy is now used in businesses and nonprofits worldwide. For example, the national Center for Nonviolent Communication uses Sociocracy. Many local and regional chapters of the National Green Building Council use it. The folks protesting in the "Occupy Asheville" movement near where I live use it.

And Sociocracy is now used by a few intentional communities worldwide, including Lost Valley Educational Center in Oregon, as noted above; Champlain Valley Cohousing, Vermont; Legacy Farm Cohousing, New York; Ecovillage at Loudon County, Virginia; Cohabitat Quebec, Canada; and Sydney Coastal Ecovillage, Australia.

The governance aspect of Sociocracy includes an interconnecting stack of semi-autonomous, self-organizing circles, each of which governs a specific area of responsibility within the policies of the higher circle, and executes, measures, and controls its own processes in achieving its goals. Representatives from each circle pass information, needs, and requests between circles. Sociocratic governance also includes a circular, three-step process of planning, implementing the plan, and evaluating the plan, and then revising the plan if needed, implementing it, evaluating it, etc. But for this review I'd like to focus mainly on decision-making and how it differs from consensus.

The Facilitator of a Sociocratic meeting goes around the circle asking each person, one at a time, whether they give their consent to a proposal. To "give consent" doesn't mean the proposal must be perfect, or that you must love it. It only means you can live with it; that it's "good enough for now." This is not like consensus, in which a decision must be as good as you can make because you'll have to live with it for a long time—since it's so difficult to change a decision made by consensus once you've made it. In Sociocracy you can modify a decision easily, even the next day, if you find that it doesn't work well—your decisions only have to be good enough to try and see how it works out. This is the most significant difference I found between the decision-making aspects of Sociocracy and consensus.

As the Facilitator goes around the circle asking whether people can give their consent, people either say Yes or state a reasonable, logical "paramount objection" to the proposal. When someone has a paramount objection, it means that if the proposal were passed, it would prevent, interfere with, or reduce the person's ability to work productively in their job or role, which itself is linked to the specific purpose or aim of that circle. The group uses any paramount objections that may come up to revise the proposal at the end of the round. The person objecting must show that the objection is reasonable and logical and is about their ability to do their job or role in that circle, and not based on simply a personal preference. When one or more paramount objections are expressed in a round, either the Facilitator alone or the Facilitator and the whole circle revise the proposal to accommodate the issues raised by the objection.

The Facilitator goes around the circle a second time to ask for consent for the now-modified proposal. The Facilitator does this as many times as is necessary, seeking consent from each person. The proposal may be modified as many times as paramount objections are raised. The proposal is passed when no more paramount objections are raised to its latest version. Paramount objections are not like blocks in consensus. Rather, they are seen as ways to shine a strong light on the proposal to see where it needs improvement, and then used to improve the proposal.

Like the consensus process, this decision-making method allows everyone to have input into the modification and improvement of the proposal, and in the decision. Unlike the consensus process (as most groups practice it anyway), there is a structured, one-person-at-a-time process for this, and a clear definition of what a paramount objection can be.

Co-author John Buck, an early pioneer in computer-based instruction and former manager in the FAA, studied Sociocracy first-hand for years in The Netherlands and learned Dutch in order to read important literature on the topic not available in English, then translated much of it. Co-author Sharon Villines, a member of Takoma Village Cohousing in Washington, DC, is also a longtime *aficianado* of effective governance.

I like how the authors organized the book. They start with the scientific and philosophical ideas that influenced Endenberg and contributed to his development of Sociocracy. Next they describe how Endenburg developed Sociocracy over the years, with more detailed background on the science that supports each of its parts. Then come chapters offering a step-by-step process of how each aspect of Sociocracy works, plus a story about how doing a meeting Sociocracy-style helped a real-life situation in a school for disturbed teenagers. And many appendices at the end (essays by Ward, Boeke, and Endenburg; sample Operating Agreements and Bylaws for a Sociocratic organization; guides for circle meetings, elections, and logbooks, and more), a generous glossary, and a bibliography. The book is resource-rich.

I resisted learning about Sociocracy when I first heard about it, as its adherents always contrasted Sociocracy with improperly practiced consensus, saying how this proved Sociocracy was better. I didn't like this; it didn't seem fair to compare the incorrect practice of one method to the correct practice of another. It was only after reading *We the People*, taking several of John Buck's workshops, and talking to enthusiastic Sociocracy practitioners in intentional communities from Quebec to Sydney that I "got it." I realized, perhaps because Endenburg is an engineer, that the process doesn't actually *let* you practice it improperly. It's designed—*engineered*—to focus the group's self-governance energy through rigorous, structured channels—and this tends to consistently produce creative, fair, and beneficial results for the group.

We the People is an inspiring, empowering resource for anyone interested in an effective governance process and high-energy meetings that meet needs for both emotional satisfaction and effectiveness—and for anyone who'd like to reduce the stress and anxiety that can accompany the consensus process, as it's sometimes practiced, where chronic blocking, or the implied or veiled threat to block, can drain and demoralize a group. ❧

Diana Leafe Christian is author of Creating a Life Together *and* Finding Community *(New Society Publishers, 2003 and 2007), and publisher of* Ecovillages, *a free online newsletter about ecovillages worldwide: www.EcovillageNews.org. She leads workshops internationally on starting successful new ecovillages and on decision-making in communities. Her column on ecovillages appears on the homepage of Global Ecovillage Network (GEN), and she is former editor of this magazine. Diana lives at Earthaven Ecovillage in North Carolina. For more info. visit www.DianaLeafeChristian.org.*

Resources: About the book *We the People*: www.Sociocracy.info
SocioNet—General information and networking about Sociocracy: www.socionet.us
Governance Alive—Co-author John Buck's website: www.governancealive.com

Busting the Myth that Consensus-with-Unanimity Is Good for Communities *Part I*

By Diana Leafe Christian

"Consensus...allows each person complete power over the group."
—Caroline Estes, *Communities Directory* (FIC, 1991, 1995)

"You'd better watch out! You'd just better *watch out!*"

One community member rose from her chair as she said this, obviously distraught. She had just blocked a proposal in the business meeting of a real community I'll call "Green Meadow." The facilitator, after conducting several go-rounds about its legitimacy, declared the block invalid. "The proposal passes," he said.

The member who blocked seemed stunned. Testing for the legitimacy of a block had happened only once before in their 13 years as a community. Theoretically they had agreed in the beginning to use C.T. Butler's "Formal Consensus" process. This means the group determines whether a block is valid, based on whether the proposal violates the group's underlying principles. Unfortunately early members had failed to write down that they had decided this. So, while the community gave lip service to the idea that they used Formal Consensus, many Green Meadow members either didn't know they had the right to test a block for validity, or knew it but were afraid to try it.

This particular Green Meadow member had threatened to block numerous times over the years, which of course stopped potential proposals from being presented. It also stopped people from calling for consensus on proposals they were considering but knew she was against. And in the previous year—when they finally stopped being afraid to test for consensus when they knew someone objected—this member had gone ahead and blocked several proposals. Many people had privately expressed frustration with her power over the group, partly because of her many years of threatening to block, and also in the past year, because of her actual blocks.

The phrase *"You'd better watch out!"* was still ringing in the room.

"Excuse me, are you making a threat?" someone asked hesitantly. "What should we watch out for?"

"What should you *watch...out...for?"* the Green Meadow member asked. She paused and looked around the circle. "That you all don't trip over your own *stupidity!!"*

Hey...wait a sec. They were using consensus decision making, which is supposed to create more trust, harmony, and good will in a group—all the consensus trainers say so—but instead they had at least one member in high distress and everyone else glued to their seats in stunned silence.

Not only that—for years people had been afraid to even bring up proposals they feared this member would block.

Never again did the group test a block to see if it was valid, regardless of the belief that they use Formal Consensus. Some Green Meadow members certainly *tried* to test blocks over the next few years. But someone would always say, "But we can't prove we ever adopted it!" Or, "But we haven't agreed on what our criteria are!" So anyone who thought a block should be tested for legitimacy didn't feel enough support and ended up dropping it. Relatively frequent blocking continued.

Those who formerly made proposals stopped making them (and sometimes withdrew from community governance or left altogether). Distrust and conflict increased. Morale plummeted. Twenty-five or 30 people used to come to business meetings. Now they're lucky to get eight or nine.

Was Green Meadow an example of consensus working well?

"Consensus-with-Unanimity"

"Consensus" as described in the story above refers to what I now call consensus-with-unanimity.

The first part of consensus is the *process*—the intention to hear from everyone in the circle, asking clarifying questions, expressing concerns, and modifying and improving the proposal.

The second part is sometimes called the "decision rule"—the *percentage of agreement* needed to pass a proposal. In many communities it is 100 percent or "unanimity" or "full consent." Except for anyone standing aside, everyone in the meeting must agree to a proposal—unanimity or full consent—before the proposal can pass. Unanimity or full consent is *one possible way* to decide things after the consensus process.

(This distinction between the process and decision rule was first pointed out by Sam Kaner, et. al. in the book *Facilitator's Guide to Participatory Decision-Making*, New Society Publishers, 1996.)

In practice, consensus-with-unanimity means essentially that anyone can block a proposal for any reason, and there's no recourse—such as having criteria for a legitimate block, or requiring people who block proposals to co-create a new proposal with the advocates of the old one. (By the way, I don't think having criteria for a legitimate block works well for most communities either, as I'll explain in Part II of this article.)

In my experience, consensus-with-unanimity is what most communitarians mean when they say "consensus," and most believe it's the best thing out there.

Blocking continued. Distrust and conflict increased. Morale plummeted. Meeting attendance dwindled.

Other Decision Rules

There are certainly other decision rules groups can use with the consensus process. These include supermajority voting, with 90 percent, 80 percent, 85 percent, 75 percent, etc. agreement needed to pass the proposal, or first trying for unanimity and having a supermajority voting fallback. (Consensus-minus-one and consensus-minus-two are also decision rules. However, I believe they generate the same kinds of problems as consensus-with-unanimity.)

Using other decision rules can work very well. My friend Ronaye Matthew was the developer consultant for three cohousing communities in British Colombia, recommending consensus-with-unanimity to each group. For her fourth project, Creekside Commons Cohousing, she recommended the consensus process with a straight 80 percent supermajority vote as the decision rule.

"Creekside Commons had far less conflict than the other groups in the two years I worked as their developer consultant," Ronaye told me.

An especially effective decision rule is used in the N Street Cohousing Method, described later in this article *(see "What Works Better Instead")*.

Falling in Love with Consensus

Consensus-with-unanimity was created in the 1600s by the Quakers because of their deeply held values of equality, justice, and fairness, and thus was a reaction against autocratic rule and outright tyranny. They had the insight that anyone who saw problems in a proposal that the group couldn't see, even after much discussion, should be able to block the proposal in order to protect the group. Leftist activist groups and communitarians in the 1960s and '70s—also with deeply held values of equality, justice, and fairness—adopted consensus-with-unanimity partly because it seemed so fair and equitable—and thus partly as a reaction against not only autocracy, but also majority-rule voting, because in the latter a proposal can pass even if up to 49 percent of the group is dead-set against it.

Quakers, Leftist activists, and communitarians all understood that consensus-with-unanimity forces a group to use a participatory process that guarantees inclusion of everyone's perspectives. It was good for groups. "Consensus creates a cooperative dynamic," wrote C.T. Butler in his book *On Conflict & Consensus* (Food Not Bombs Publishing, 1987, 1991). Consensus is "a powerful tool for building group unity and strength," wrote the authors of *Building United Judgment* (Center for Conflict Resolution, 1981).

Consensus-with-unanimity was especially appealing to baby boomers hoping to change the world back in the '60s and '70s. It *empowered* us. It was as if special, magical gifts arrived just for our generation. We had sex, drugs, and rock 'n' roll. And we had consensus.

No wonder we all fell in love with it!

Appropriate Blocks, Inappropriate Blocks

One of the reasons I believe consensus-with-unanimity does not work well in most communities is that people often misunderstand and misuse the blocking privilege. As you probably know, it is appropriate (and desirable) to block if the proposal clearly violates the community's values, underlying principles, or Mission and Purpose, and one can clearly show why—or to block because implementing the proposal would harm the community in some real, demonstrable way, and the person(s) blocking can clearly show why.

Here are two examples of appropriate blocks from consensus trainer Caroline Estes. The first involves a proposal being appropriately blocked because it violated the group's underlying principles. A member of a peace organization devoted to nonviolence blocked a proposal that their organization throw chicken blood from a slaughterhouse on the wall of a building belonging to a Wall Street investment firm. The idea was to create a visual, dramatic, photo-op way to show that the Wall Street company had "blood on its hands" because of its investments in weapons manufacturers. The person blocking pointed out that passing this proposal would violate the group's basic principle of nonviolence (since defacing the wall with blood would not be a nonviolent action). The person blocking could clearly show how the proposal violated the organization's principles.

Only one community I know of that uses consensus-with-unanimity exhibits the kind of trust, cohesiveness, and well-being described in the books.

In the second example a proposal was blocked because it would cause demonstrable harm to the group. During the Vietnam War a member of a Quaker congregation in the US blocked a proposal involving civil disobedience—that the congregation send humanitarian aid (first aid supplies, food, etc.) on a chartered boat to North Vietnam, which of course was the country the US was at war with. The idea was to express the Quaker principle of being against all wars, including this war, and to literally help people in North Vietnam. The person blocking pointed out that passing this proposal would harm the Quaker congregation in general, and specifically its parents with small children. They all realized that the US government would consider their sending humanitarian aid to North Vietnam as an act of treason, and probably all members of the congregation would be arrested and jailed. The person who blocked said, essentially, if parents of young children were jailed, who would take care of their children? Again, the person blocking could clearly show how the proposal would harm the group.

I believe inappropriate blocks occur primarily for three reasons. First, because different community members interpret the community's stated purpose in completely different ways, and thus exist in different paradigms about what the community is for. When this happens, some members will be moved from the heart to make proposals to help the community (that they imagine in their minds) move forward towards its goals, and other members, equally moved from the heart, and drawing on all their courage, will block these proposals in order to protect the community (that they imagine in their minds). Nobody's right and nobody's wrong.

A second reason is because a proposal violates the community member's personal values rather than the community's shared values (and they don't realize this is not a legitimate reason to block). Or, third, they're blocking in order to receive negative group attention from a subconscious desire to satisfy unmet needs to be seen and heard.

When Consensus-with-Unanimity *Does* Work

"Granted, only a small proportion of groups have the necessary conditions to effectively use...consensus...with unanimity," wrote the Leftist activist authors of *Building United Judgment*. "Such groups are small, cohesive, and cooperative." They add, "If attempted under the wrong circumstances or without a good understanding of the technique, the consensus process can result in confusion, disruption, or unrest in a group."

Most community-based consensus trainers advise groups not to use consensus unless they meet the specific requirements for using it.

"(Consensus is) not appropriate for all situations," cautions consensus trainer Tree Bressen, but works best "for groups that have a shared purpose, explicit values, some level of trust and openness to each other, and enough time to work with material in depth." ("Consensus Basics," website: www.treegroup.info)

My teacher, Caroline Estes, said using consensus required the group to have a shared common purpose, equal access to power, and training in how to use consensus properly.

Tim Hartnett, in his book *Consensus-Oriented Decision-Making: the CODM Model for Facilitating Groups to Widespread Agreement* (New Society Publishers, 2010) is even more specific. Besides noting that the smaller and more homogeneous the group, the easier it is to reach agreement when using consensus-with-unanimity, he writes: "participants must trust each other and value their relationships highly...must be trained to participate responsibly...must put the best interests of the group before their own." And they must spend lots of group process time to keep their relationships open, clear, and healthy.

In my experience, relatively few intentional communities meet these requirements.

Some have vague, unwritten ideas about shared values rather than explicit, written-down shared values. Some communities assume they have a shared common purpose but actually have idealistic, theoretical, and vague Mission and Purpose statements that can be interpreted many different ways. Thus they experience confusion and conflict when trying to assess whether or not a proposal is aligned with their (multiply interpretable) shared common purpose. In other communities, designed primarily to be nice places to live where members can buy houses or housing units, people may not necessarily be—or care about being—cohesive and cooperative, or having sufficient trust or openness with one another, or highly valuing their relationships with one another. They just want to live in a nice place with nice neighbors (and to heck with this touchy-feely stuff). And only a handful of communities require all new incoming members to take a consensus training before they get full decision-making rights, including the blocking privilege.

Nevertheless—no matter how often consensus trainers caution against it—communities everywhere often choose consensus-with-unanimity even though they don't have even the most basic requirements in place. They choose it, apparently, because they aren't aware of these cautions or disregard them because consensus-with-unanimity appeals to their aspirations for fairness, equality, and a better world.

I have by now visited and gotten to know over a hundred communities in North America and abroad. Only one I know of that uses consensus-with-unanimity seems to exhibit the kind of trust, cohesiveness, and well-being described in the books. This community has only 11 full members with full decision-making rights, along with shorter-term residents with more limited rights. The community's Mission and Purpose statements are clear and specific. The founders and other full members are successful and effective in their chosen fields, and exhibit, most of the time, a relatively high amount of emotional well-being. They highly value their relationships with each other and are small enough for this to happen naturally. They are a tight and cohesive group.

Threatening to Block and "Premature Proposal Death"

In some communities that use consensus-with-unanimity no one has ever blocked, or blocking has occurred only rarely. Yet the problems of too-frequent blocking or personal blocking are actually there anyway. This is one of the most demoralizing unintended consequences of using consensus-with-unanimity.

This happens when people *threaten* to block a proposal, either directly ("I'd never support that," or, "I'll block that proposal!") or indirectly, by indicating disapproval, disdain, or even contempt for a proposal through facial expressions, tone of voice, and body language. This can happen even when someone is just voicing an idea that isn't even a proposal yet.

When either of these happens—threatening to block a proposal, or threatening to block an idea that isn't a proposal yet—the community suffers. People drop their ideas or proposals completely. Community members don't get to illuminate the issue through discussion and examination. An idea that could benefit the community, or could shed light on an important issue, is cast aside before it is even considered—dying before it was ever born!

In communities that no longer use consensus-with-unanimity no one has this kind of power over other people's ideas.

Denial and Disconnect

As I observed this over the years I became aware of a vague, foggy disconnect between what I believed were the benefits of consensus-with-unanimity and *what I actually experienced.* My beliefs didn't match what I was seeing and hearing. I rationalized this by assuming the community *just wasn't practicing consensus correctly.* For many years I've served as a consultant to communities seeking outside help, and six years ago began teaching consensus too. And when communities were having trouble in their meetings with consensus-with-unanimity I—of course!—thought it was just because *they probably weren't doing it right.*

It was much easier to believe what I'd been taught by my elders in the communities movement (who certainly knew more than I did) and in what I wanted to believe, rather than actually believing the evidence of my own senses!

Because, what I have seen over the years—and what many of my colleagues across North America, Europe, and Latin America have *also* seen—is that consensus-with-unanimity does *not* seem to help most communities function better.

In fact, it often seems to make things worse.

In the last few years I've been de-hypnotizing myself from the idea that this form of consensus creates more harmony, cohesiveness, and trust—that it makes groups stronger, happier, and safer from the abuses of power.

I've watched friends and colleagues in other communities who've observed the same things replace unanimity with a different decision rule, or replace consensus altogether with Sociocracy, Holacracy, or a method they created themselves.

I now believe that for many communities consensus-with-unanimity results in unintended consequences: discouragement, low morale, and diminished meeting attendance. I believe it can create a different kind of power abuse than either autocracy or majority-rule voting.

Power-Over...*Damn!*

Tim Hartnett, a community-based consensus facilitator and trainer, and licensed family therapist, is the first consensus trainer I know of to say publicly that the benefits of using consensus-with-unanimity are often outweighed by its downsides.

"Requiring unanimity," he writes in *Consensus-Oriented Decision-Making,* "is usually intended to ensure widespread agreement. When unanimity is blocked by a small number of people, however, the group actually experiences *widespread disagreement* with the result. This widespread disagreement can have very toxic effects on the group dynamic."

He observes that no matter how well and accurately a group practices consensus-with-unanimity, *doing so does not ensure unanimous approval of the final, modified proposal.* And when people block, no matter that we're supposed to assume they have a piece of the truth the rest of us don't see, we still end up with...power-over dynamics.

Tim Hartnett points out that blocking in consensus-with-unanimity is often considered a way *to equally share power* in a group. However, giving people equal rights to control the group's ability to make a decision can actually create problems with equality. "It necessitates that all group members have the ethics and maturity to use this power responsibly," he writes. "This may not be a realistic expectation." (Whew! Somebody actually said this outloud!)

"True equality may be better secured by a system that ensures *that no group member ever has the power to individually control the group,*" he continues. [Emphasis mine.]

"The process allows each person complete power over the group," Caroline Estes cautions. "(When someone blocks) they should also examine themselves closely to assure that they are not withholding consensus out of self-interest, bias, vengeance, or any other such feeling." ("Consensus Ingredients," *Communities Directory,* FIC, 1991, 1995.)

You can see the effects of this power-over dynamic clearly when committee members have worked long, hard hours on a proposal and then spent more time and energy in a series of whole-group meetings to modify and improve it, and most of the community members are looking forward to implementing it. When it is blocked by one or two people (for any of the above inappropriate-block reasons) do we feel harmony, trust, and connection? On the contrary, we often feel heartsick, even devastated. And when this kind of blocking happens often—or the threat to block, which usually has the same effect—it can result in even more unhappiness, and increased distrust, low morale, ever-dwindling meeting attendance...and people leaving the community.

Many of us chose consensus-with-unanimity in order to help our community thrive, and because we value fairness, mutual respect, trust, compassion, and equality.

But fairness, mutual respect, trust, compassion, and equality are often *not* what we get. We get conflict instead—and sometimes, gut-wrenching conflict.

This is the "shadow-side" of consensus-with-unanimity that consensus trainers don't often talk about. Yet Leftist activists and the communities movement *have* come up with a name for this: "Tyranny of the Minority."

Other Consequences of "Tyranny of the Minority"

Here are some other unintended consequences Tim Hartnett points out. I've seen each of these dynamics too.

• People able to endure more conflict may prevail, creating "decision by endurance."

Sometimes community members who can endure high amounts of conflict and for longer periods of time have a greater chance of prevailing over those who can't bear conflict for long. "OK, I give up! Do whatever you want!" When this happens, it is sometimes the ability to endure conflict, rather than the ability to seek deeper understanding and to collaborate, that determines whether or not and with which modifications a proposal may be passed.

"More obstinate participants may more frequently get their way," Tim Hartnett writes.

Consensus-with-unanimity gives exceptional power to anyone who does not want anything to change.

About two-thirds of the people in Green Meadow community—including all the young and most middle-years members—no longer attend community business meetings. Having little stomach for the intensity of the power struggles in their business meetings (which *seem* to be about proposals but may actually be about different underlying paradigms), their voices are not heard at all.

• Disproportionate power to whoever supports the status quo.

If most people in a community support a proposal to change one or more long-standing policies—the status quo—they cannot do so until they convince everyone in the group. If one or two people don't support the proposal (no matter that everyone else wants it) the original policies will remain. This gives exceptional power to anyone who does not want anything to change. At Green Meadow, most people yearn to replace consensus-with-unanimity with a decision-making process that works better, but the consistent blockers are against it. Thus they have more power than anyone else.

"This differential burden," Tim Hartnett observes, "is contrary to the principle of equality."

• The community may stagnate, unable to change or evolve.

When a community experiences conflict because people can't agree, there may be little chance of passing new proposals or revising outdated agreements, as noted above. Thus whatever the group has already put in place—the status quo—may remain in effect for years beyond its actual effectiveness for the group. As at Green Meadow, the group may be locked into their original choices for years to come.

• Power struggles may drive out some of the group's most responsible, effective members.

When people with high levels of personal effectiveness, initiative, and leadership make proposals in a community they often expect and require a timely response. If there are underlying paradigm-differences in the community, or people block for personal reasons, or for subconscious bids for group attention, these natural leaders may end up spending a lot of time in whole-group meetings processing people's reluctance or anxieties, or having long discussions outside of meetings. This kind of high-initiative person usually prefers situations in which their contributions are more easily understood, appreciated, and approved in a timely manner so they can get on with the project. When their proposed initiatives are slowed or stopped—and when this happens repeatedly—they are often too discouraged and frustrated to stay, so take their talents elsewhere.

Green Meadow used to have a relatively high number of young men with abundant creativity, initiative, and drive who founded cottage industries to provide income for themselves and jobs for other members, or created agricultural enterprises to provide organic food onsite, or both. They struggled for years making proposals which had widespread community appreciation and support, but which were blocked nevertheless. For these, and for other, more immediate reasons, most have now left.

What Works Better Instead—Three Collaborative, Win-Win Methods

What can communities do?

They can use the consensus process itself but replace unanimity with a completely different decision rule, such as the ***N Street Consensus Method***. This method, developed by Kevin Wolf, co-founder of N Street Cohousing in Davis, California, combines the usual consensus process with a decision-rule method that respects the viewpoints and intentions of both the advocates of a proposal and those who may block it. Briefly, here's how it works. Community members first seek consensus-with-unanimity. However, if one or more people block the proposal, the blocking persons organize a series of solution-oriented meetings with one or two proposal advocates to create a *new* proposal that addresses the same issues as the original proposal. The new proposal goes to the next meeting, where it probably will pass. If a new proposal is not created, the original proposal comes to the next meeting for a 75 percent supermajority vote, and it will probably pass. In 25 years at N Street Cohousing this process has happened only twice, with two solution-oriented meetings each—that is, only four of these small meetings total in 25 years.

In Sociocracy and Holacracy decisions need only be "good enough for now" and can easily be changed with experience or new information.

Or, communities can replace consensus-with-unanimity with another method altogether, such as Sociocracy or Holacracy. ***Sociocracy***, developed in the Netherlands in the 1970s, and ***Holacracy***, developed in the US in the early 2000s, are each whole-systems governance methods which include a decision-making process. (The N Street Method is a decision-making process only.)

In both Sociocracy and Holacracy everyone has a voice in modifying and approving proposals and everyone's consent is required to pass a proposal. However, unlike in consensus, decisions can be changed easily, which means there is far less pressure to make a "perfect" decision. In both Sociocracy and Holacracy decisions need only be "good enough for now" and can easily be changed again with experience or new information. This seems to liberate energy, optimism, creativity, and freedom to try new things. Both Sociocracy and Holacracy work best for communities that have a clear common purpose or aim.

While Sociocracy, Holacracy, and the N Street Method each have a collaborative, win/win decision-making process, they do not allow the kinds of power-over dynamics that can occur with consensus-with-unanimity. Communities that use these methods don't tend to have the unintended consequences that can occur when using consensus-with-unanimity. Rather, these methods tend to generate a sense of connection, trust, and well-being in the group.

Future articles in this series will describe each of these methods in more detail.

And What About Green Meadow Community?

I actually have hope for Green Meadow community. The longer their challenges continue—and especially each time a proposal is blocked that most others want—the more community-wide demoralization intensifies. Fortunately, this "fed-up" energy motivates action, and now enough community members (not just the "early adopters" who saw these problems years ago) seriously want change.

Increasing numbers of Green Meadow members are curious about other decision rules besides unanimity, as well as about other governance systems. Some are discussing radical change. For example, some are talking about using a 75 percent supermajority vote as their decision rule. Others suggest a new process for business meetings in which people would nominate themselves and be approved by most others before they could participate. Still others imagine coalescing into a loose federation of sub-committees, each with its own purpose, budget, and governance process, with a whole-community "federal" government tasked only to maintain common infrastructure and pay property taxes, etc.

And some, inspired by the Declaration of Independence—which affirms that governments can only exist by the consent of the governed—are talking about withdrawing their consent that the frequent blockers continue to have governing power over everyone else. They're considering a proposal that the frequent blocking members step out of the governance process entirely.

Several members recently presented the case to Green Meadow's steering committee that to remain healthy, intentional communities, like love relationships, must periodically "die" and be reborn. To many, Green Meadow seems to be simultaneously in the process of dying...and of being reborn—in new and far healthier ways. ❧

Diana Leafe Christian, author of the books Creating a Life Together *and* Finding Community, *is publisher of* Ecovillages, *a free online newsletter about ecovillages worldwide (EcovillageNews.org), and a columnist for Global Ecovillage Network (GEN) (gen.ecovillage.org). She is a trainer in GEN's Ecovillage Design Education (EDE) program, and speaks at conferences, offers consultations, and leads workshops internationally. See www.DianaLeafeChristian.org.*

Coming in Future Issues...

Topics in Part II of this article (in issue #156) will include: (1) Why, in my opinion, having criteria for a legitimate block and a way to test blocks against it, as several consensus trainers advise, doesn't seem to work well for most communities either. (2) More on underlying dynamics of inappropriate blocks, too-frequent blocks, and threats to block. (3) Why some idealists believe consensus-with-unanimity will work well if only people would try harder or evolve spiritually, or that the promised harmony, cohesiveness, and trust would manifest if only everyone spent more time exploring the nuances of people's different feelings about their opinions—and why baby boomers especially believe this. (4) How communities—including communities with chronic blockers, or chronic threateners-to-block—can replace consensus-with-unanimity with other, more effective methods.

Future articles in the series will describe the "N Street Consensus Method" in more detail, the "Four Decision Options/Choose Your Committee Members" method of Ecovillage Sieben Linden, Systemic Consensus, Tim Hartnett's "Consensus-Oriented Decision-Making" method, Sociocracy, and Holacracy (and why I think Sociocracy and Holacracy work especially well in intentional communities). —D.L.C.

Resources

Consensus:

- C.T. Butler's Formal Consensus process; website includes free, downloadable copy of C.T.'s book, *On Conflict and Consensus*: www.consensus.net
- *Facilitator's Guide to Participatory Decision-Making*, Sam Kaner, et. al. (New Society Publishers, 1996): www.newsociety.com
- *Building United Judgment* (Center for Conflict Resolution, 1981, now published by FIC): www.ic.org/bookshelf
- Caroline Estes, Alpha Institute: members.pioneer.net/~alpha/presenters
- Tree Bressen: www.treegroup.info
- *Consensus-Oriented Decision-Making*, Tim Hartnett (New Society Publishers, 2011): consensusbook.com

N Street Consensus Method:

- "Is Consensus Right for Your Group? Part I," in *Ecovillages* newsletter: www.ecovillagenewsletter.org (click "Articles Alphabetically" to find it)

Sociocracy:

- *We the People: Consenting to a Deeper Democracy, A Guide to Sociocratic Principles and Methods*, by John Buck and Sharon Villines (2007): www.sociocracy.info
- SocioNet online discussion: www.socionet.us
- Governance Alive, author and consultant John Buck: www.governancealive.com

Holacracy:

- *Holacracy One*: www.holacracy.org

"Busting the Myth": How Consensus *Can* Work

By Laird Schaub

Diana brings up a number of points about consensus, and I agree with many of them. With others though, I have a contrasting view.

Essential Ingredients for Consensus to Work

I agree that common values, training in the process, and commitment to relationships are all important for groups to succeed with consensus. I further agree that most groups naively agree to use consensus without knowing what they're doing and often they don't commit to training. While it creates considerable work for consultants, I'd rather they invested in deep training up front.

Diana implies that it's not easy to do consensus well and I agree with that. In my view, probably the single biggest impediment to groups succeeding with consensus is the lack of understanding that it requires a commitment to culture change: from the adversarial and competitive culture that characterizes the mainstream society—the one most of us were raised in—to the cooperative culture that we want instead. Merely agreeing that this is what we intend and having good intentions is not enough. It takes serious work to achieve this. While I think that that work is well worth the effort, it's not trivial.

Note that the challenge of creating cooperative culture will exist independently of what decision rule a group chooses. I believe consensus is a superior way to foster cooperative culture because groups need to make a good faith effort to incorporate the views of outliers. If you switch to a decision rule where outliers can be managed (essentially by outvoting them), you trade the anguish of dealing with a stubborn minority for the disgruntlement that follows from split votes.

While I think it's up to each cooperative group to make its own choice about what decision-making process to use—with options other than consensus on the menu—I have a substantially different analysis than Diana about how to interpret the pitfalls she describes in her article.

If it's important, as I suggest, to commit to culture change, there are some consequences to take into account. For one thing, it's prudent to be careful about membership selection. With each member prospect, ask yourself whether this person is

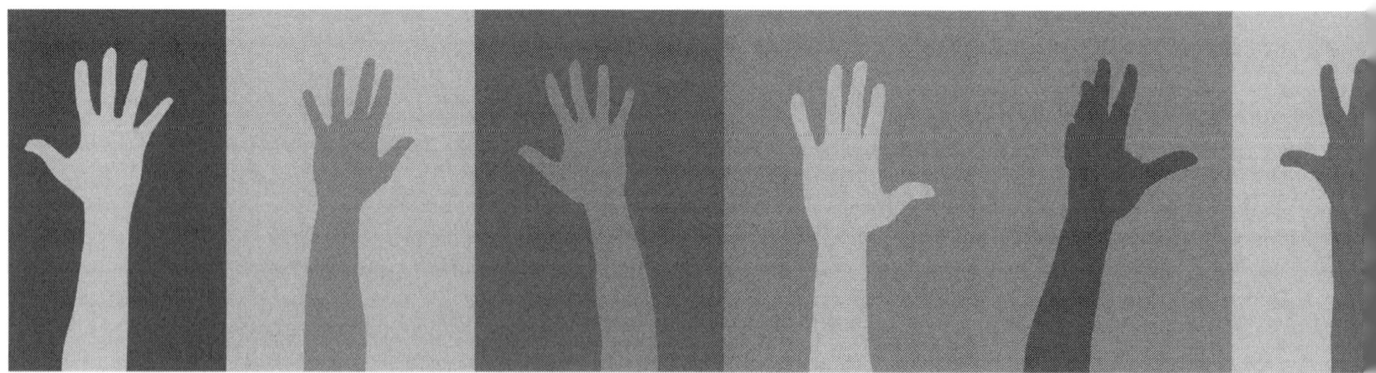

someone you believe has enough overlap in values and sufficient social skills that you feel confident you'll be able to work through disagreements with them. If you have doubts, tread carefully. If you think that a commitment to having a diverse population translates into having no standards for membership, you are sowing the whirlwind.

When a group is newly formed, and learning to use its process well (whether that process is consensus or something else that's new to the group), high quality facilitation can make a night-and-day difference. Skilled facilitators understand the process well and have the ability to redirect the group when things get hard (because of complexity, volatility, or both), reminding everyone of their commitment to respond cooperatively when the group slips off the rails in the heat of the moment. As the group gets more skilled in the process, the need for high quality facilitation will diminish, because the group will self-correct more, relying less on neutral guidance to see it through the rough patches.

In a group committed to creating cooperative culture, everyone has an active role. On any given topic, each member will either be a stakeholder or they won't be. If you are, then you'll want to be active in order to see that your input is fully expressed and because you care a lot about the outcome. If you aren't a stakeholder, then you're well positioned to safeguard the container in which the conversation happens. You can pay more attention to the quality of the engagement (how well people are hearing one another and able to bridge between positions) than the outcome.

Consensus requires a commitment to culture change: from an adversarial and competitive culture to the cooperative culture we want instead.

Blocking Dynamics

I have a different sense than Diana about both the quantity and the quality of blocking in intentional communities. In my experience (I've worked with around 75 different groups as a process consultant over a 25-year career), most consensus groups rarely experience blocks, and when they do, few groups permit them solely for personal concerns. That said, there are two aspects of blocking dynamics that Diana mentions that I agree are common and deserve attention: a) people stopping a proposal because their interpretation of group values differs significantly from that of the proposer; and b) people threatening to block and thereby quashing consideration of the proposal.

Let's look at those one at a time. Diana labeled the first one as an inappropriate block. I demur. In a healthy consensus group, a majority of plenary time should be devoted to examining how best to apply group values to the issue at hand. While a group may be solid in committing to being Green, it's impossible at the outset to anticipate all the shades that Green can come in and to determine whether all are acceptable. Expecting a group to devote serious time to theoretical conversations about how to weigh one value in relation to another is unrealistic. A more practical approach is to wait until someone proposes to buy solar panels before discussing how the group's commitment to the ecology (being Green) is in dynamic tension with the group's commitment to having a balanced budget (being not in the red). It's not that there is a "right" answer to these value questions; it's that you can't reasonably sink your teeth into them until specific issues showcase the ambiguity.

To be sure, issues can surface that reveal rifts in the group that may not be bridgeable. Not everyone is meant to live together and certain issues may expose a chasm of differences that is sufficiently broad that it will splinter the group. Before leaping to that conclusion, however, I'd test to see if the group could leap across the chasm.

Groups develop depth and nuance about what their common values mean over the course of their history, and I've

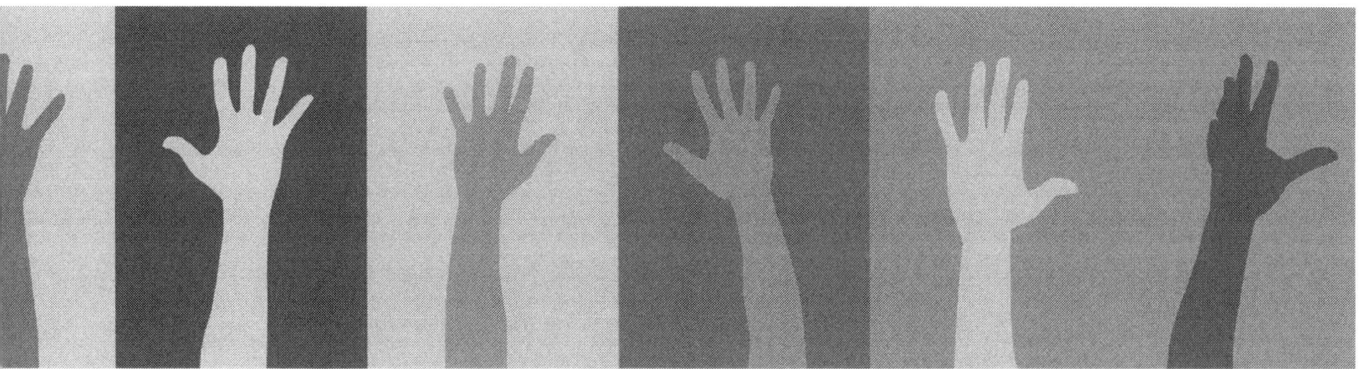

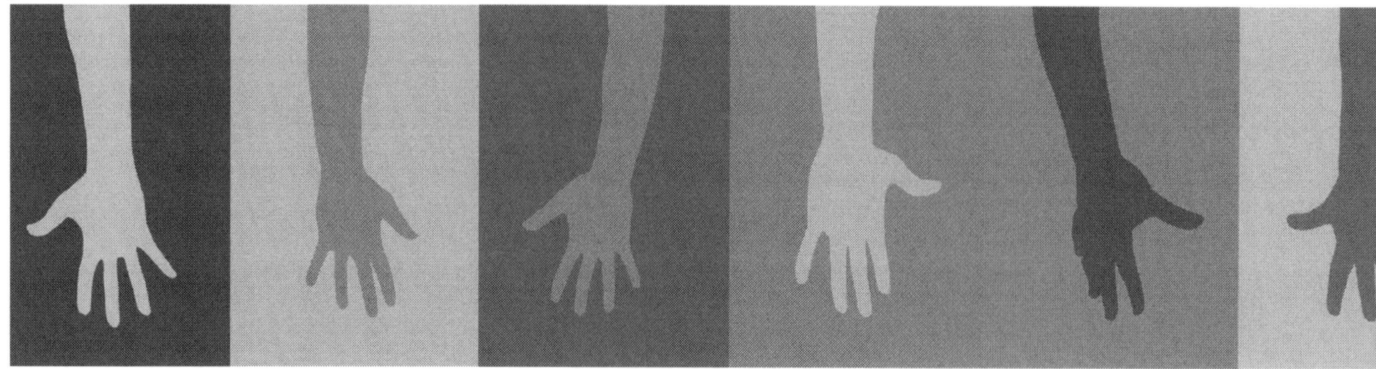

never seen a group whose common values appeared fully dressed and mature at the outset, springing like Athena from Zeus' forehead. In saying this, I am not trying to sidestep the very real anguish Diana described in groups that become paralyzed by philosophical disjuncts that appear too great to span in how members interpret key common values. I just don't agree that the answer is a different decision rule.

The fundamental challenge of cooperative groups is how to disagree about non-trivial matters and have that experience bring the group closer together. When it *really* matters, do we regress back to our deep conditioning and resort to power plays, manipulation, cajoling, back room deals, crying, parliamentary maneuvering, pouting, or just plain old shouting? Or do we respond with curiosity about how others came to weigh things differently, and arrive at a different conclusion? Can we learn to hear people disagree and not feel threatened, trusting that we need all of the input out in the open before we can assemble the best response?

Can we learn to hear people disagree and not feel threatened, trusting that we need all of the input out in the open before we can assemble the best response?

The thrust of Diana's suggestion is that groups mostly don't know how to handle that dynamic well (I agree with her on this) and when it plays out with a disgruntled and perhaps fearful, small minority, it will tend to go better if you have a process that allows the group to move forward anyway—that the benefit of not being hamstrung by a few outweighs the risk that you may move too quickly and miss a key insight that the minority is attempting to articulate.

I agree with Diana that there should be a test for validating a block—to see whether it meets the standard (that the group has established ahead of time) for what are legitimate grounds for a block. If the block fails the test, then the group can invalidate it. While this can be a heavy thing to do (as Diana eloquently described), I think it should be possible, with the process by which a block will be examined for legitimacy having been spelled out before you're there. (You don't know what hell is until you try to make up the process *after* you're already in the delicate situation where you're hoping to apply it.)

The second dynamic is the threat of a block. I agree that many groups struggle with this, and I appreciate how disruptive this can be. If the group perceives that a person is serious about blocking a proposal then it may never be tested for agreement (why bother if it's only going to be blocked?) and the person with blocking energy can retreat behind the claim that they rarely if ever block. While that may be technically true, they've unquestionably brought blocking energy into the consideration and this can be a real headache.

Rather than defanging the blocker, I have a different idea. I think N Street (as Diana describes their process) is headed in the right direction in that they expect the blocker to be actively involved in working to resolve concerns and come up with modifications that might suit everyone. While I have reservations about their method,* I like that it recognizes that the individual's right to block is paired with the responsibility to take into account the views of others and to put personal energy into attempting to close the gap.

Applying that same principle a bit earlier in the deliberation (blocks should occur only at the last minute, when you're testing for agreement; not in the discussion phase), if someone reported that they objected to what was on the table to the point of blocking (if it got that far), I would walk through a sequence like this with that person:

—Make sure I understood the basis for the objection, to the point where *the objector* reported feeling satisfied that they'd been heard.

—Establish how the objection was (or wasn't) linked to common values, or the health of the group.

—Make sure the individual under-

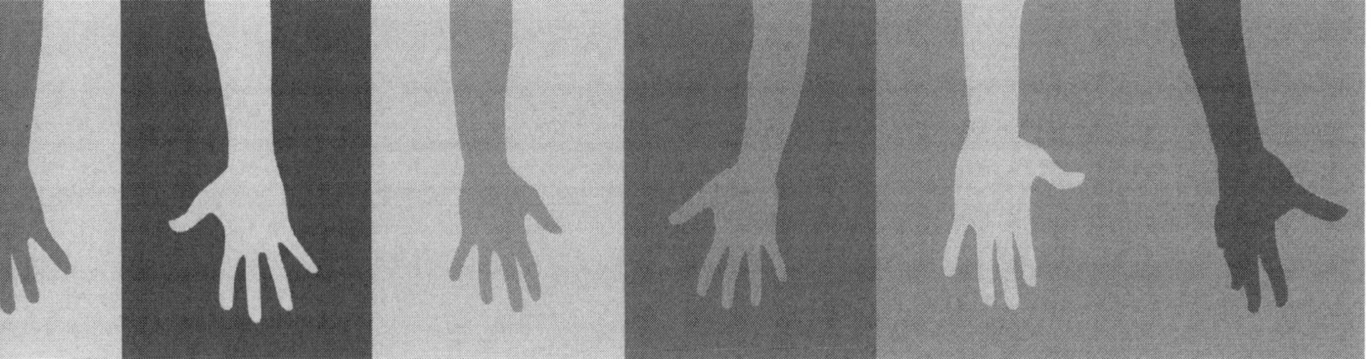

stood what others were saying.

—Labor with the objector—as well as everyone else in the group—in a collaborative search for ideas about how to address the issue effectively without leaving anyone behind.

I agree with Diana that it's not a good sign if a strongly voiced concern is allowed to simply kill a proposal, and I urge groups to expect objectors to have their oar in the water just as much as everyone else in an effort to pull the ship into a safe harbor once you've encountered rough water.

The key to doing this well is establishing a compassionate and thoughtful container, as devoid as possible from pressure and frustration. I'm not saying this is easy—especially when the stakes are high—but if you want a solution that everyone can stand behind, then you're probably going to need to work at the heart level as well as the head level. This tends to be a *very* different animal than the typical meeting culture that we've brought with us from the mainstream society. In my experience, no process does the job of rising to the challenge of melding thought and feelings better than consensus, providing only that you've created the right container.

Commitment to Relationship

Another way of expressing this is that cooperative groups hold the view that *how* you do things can matter as much as *what* you do. This tends to be a markedly different calculus than exists in the mainstream culture, where much more attention is given to the end than the means. While Diana seemed to argue that most members of intentional communities don't care *that* much about relationships—especially if groups have more than a dozen members—I don't agree with her. I think most people living in communities care a great deal about relationships. In fact, the hunger for more relationship in one's life is one of the key reasons most people are drawn to community living.

However, *wanting* more relationship is not enough to guarantee that you'll get it. Living closely with others and trying to make decisions and solve problems as a group of peers, it's inevitable that conflict and emotional distress will emerge at times. Working with conflict effectively means working with feelings. If a group struggles with that (and most do) the tendency is to back off and expect less. I can understand the line of reasoning that suggests if consensus means you're more likely to encounter conflict and you don't handle that moment well, then it makes sense to try something different. I just don't agree that this indicates that a change in the decision rule is called for. I think what needs to change is how you handle conflict.

Diana implies that there's less conflict and disharmony in groups that don't use consensus. To the extent that this claim is true (and I'm highly skeptical of it), I suspect that it's more about learning to settle for members being less involved in one another's lives. While I think it's up to the membership of each group to define how much it intends for members to lead intertwined lives, I am saddened by the choice to accept less when you'd rather have more.

The promise of community is that it can be a wellspring for getting more out of your life without ever leaving your home to get it. As a consensus consultant, whatever success I've enjoyed is directly related to working with people who want their groups to function well and are willing to put their own life force into the attempt. I find it far more inspiring to offer hope for getting both better decisions and better relationships than advising folks to downsize their dreams. ❧

Laird Schaub is Executive Secretary of the Fellowship for Intentional Community (FIC), publisher of this magazine, and cofounder of Sandhill Farm, a consensus-run egalitarian community in Missouri, where he lives. He is also a facilitation trainer and process consultant, and he authors a blog that can be read at communityandconsensus.blogspot.com.

* While I support N Street's determination to expect blockers to get involved in a good faith effort to resolve concerns, I have uneasiness with their approach in two regards. First, it puts the onus on the blocker to initiate the conversation to address the concerns. Not all people with principled concerns will have the process savvy, gumption, or energy to take the lead on this, and it sets the bar too high. I'm afraid that it will lead to people deciding not to voice their blocking concerns because it's overwhelming to contemplate what they'll be obliged to do if their block is honored. Second, if the group can override a block with a 75 percent supermajority vote at the next meeting, it puts all the pressure on the blocker to change the hearts and minds of others—in essence, the majority has already won. This is a very different atmosphere than what you'd have under consensus, where there is no agreement until all the principled objections have been resolved.

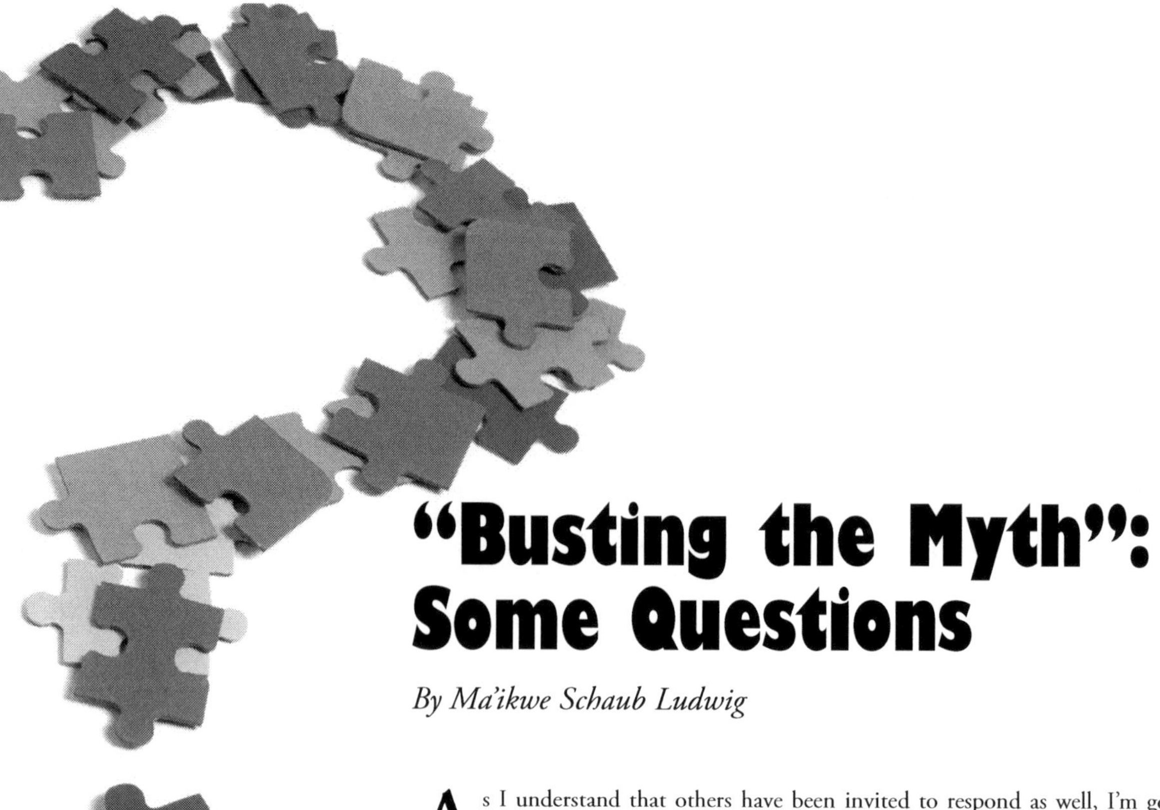

"Busting the Myth": Some Questions

By Ma'ikwe Schaub Ludwig

As I understand that others have been invited to respond as well, I'm going to limit my comments to a particular aspect of Diana's article: the opening sequence where she describes a scenario that contributes to her conclusion that consensus isn't the best option for most communities. Compelling stories are a great way to bring attention to potential problems; where it gets interesting is when we have different takes on what to do in the moment of the presenting situation. My conclusions are not the same as Diana's.

The scenario Diana describes is a complex one. You have a group committed to consensus and a member asserting their right to block. You have a general description that indicates hostility within the group. And you have a dynamic described where the blocker is challenged on their affect, and "acting out" behavior, with not a lot of attempt to connect with the person struggling. What is a process consultant to do?

The first thing I'd do is back up. I'd want to know more about the group, exhibiting a primary consensus tool of curiosity when things go awry. Here are the questions I'd ask:

- What is this group's commitment to conflict resolution?
- What is the group's commitment to training?
- If this is a pattern, when did it start, and what has happened in the interim that makes this now feel like a very uphill battle?

Let's take them one at a time.

1) What is this group's commitment to conflict resolution?

Consensus makes conflict resolution non-optional. It is simply intolerable to be in major conflict with someone with whom you have to cultivate deep listening on a regular basis. One of the gifts of consensus is that it makes us deal with our stuff. If members are blowing up at each other, threatening each other, etc., I'd say the more immediate problem isn't how you make decisions, it is how you resolve tensions. Conflict can seem worse in consensus groups not because consensus is flawed but because the stakes are higher and the need for real conflict resolution is more in your face. You simply can't blow each other off as readily: it's against the rules we've agreed on collectively.

While I'm not going to say consensus is for everyone, I am going to say that things being hard doesn't mean giving up is the right answer. Conflict in a consensus-based group is a lot like a cultural healing crisis in natural healing: you've applied a remedy to the illness and as it starts working, things can get dramatic and intense for a while, and it looks for a time like the remedy is making things worse rather than better. It's like a detox period. If the group can get through this period and stick with it, what you get on the other side is a significant gain in how you relate as fellow human beings. For people interested in cultural change, this is the real, juicy stuff.

2) What is the group's commitment to training?

I generally say that while I'm an advocate of consensus, I don't think that it is possible to do it while running default patterns we all carry from the wider culture. Reworking patterns on a personal level can require personal growth, spiritual work, therapy, etc. Reworking them on a group level requires training. Often, groups are too proud to get trained. We think we are pioneers (and of course we are), we have a commitment to self-sufficiency (which is a great thing), we are too busy for our own good (welcome to modern American life), or we are suffering from simple ego (who among us isn't). And so we don't get trained. And then the fireworks start.

I wondered as I read this opening sequence if maybe the group in question hadn't fallen into one of these traps.

The most critical thing a group learns in good consensus training isn't mechanics (which I'd say systems like sociocracy and N Street's approach address) but about the spirit of consensus: understanding that we each have a piece of the truth. Bridging between these pieces of the truth to find what is best for the group is a lot more central to having functional consensus than any particular procedure you might use.

3) If this is a pattern, when did it start, and what has happened in the interim that makes this now feel like a very uphill battle?

When I hear a story like this, I always want to understand the context. It sounds awful, right? Some characters sound completely irrational, while others come across as guardian heroes upholding a community virtue of some sort. But I think this is rarely the whole truth, and the stories we tell almost always capture as much about the person telling the tale as they do about the nature of the problems the group is facing. (I don't just mean Diana in this article; I mean all of us.) I'd assume that this group of people got on trajectories a long time ago that have landed them where they are, and also assume that getting back to a stable, respectful environment is going to take some serious backing away from current positions.

Once a group has gotten to this painful place, changing the mechanics of their specific consensus process, or even scrapping consensus completely, isn't going to fix it. You'll have the patterns in place no matter how you decide to move forward. The work at this point is facing down the patterns and recommitting to relationship. I'd advise this group to not head directly for the exit, but first attend to relationship.

At its heart, consensus is about getting the full picture and being able to hold others' perspectives as important, and other people as worthy of care and consideration. Rather than playing up the drama of a moment and drawing conclusions based on that moment, I'd want to understand how the moment was arrived at. ❧

Ma'ikwe Schaub Ludwig has lived in intentional community for 16 years, and is currently a member of Dancing Rabbit Ecovillage in Rutledge, Missouri, where she has organized its five-week Ecovillage Design Education course starting in 2012. She is former manager of FIC's Community Bookshelf and author of Passion as Big as a Planet, *which looks at the relationship between self-awareness and effective earth activism. Ma'ikwe teaches facilitation and consensus with her husband, Laird Schaub, and offers workshops on starting communities, leadership, and spiritual activism.*

Busting the Myth, or Changing the Terms?

By Tree Bressen

In the opening story of "Busting the Myth," the facilitator at Green Meadow tests a block for legitimacy. When the block is found invalid, then the proposal goes through and is adopted. Here's the curious thing: Diana says this group had tried that only once before and never did it again. When i read this, i wanted to know: Why not?

Let's leave aside for a moment the questions of consensus process and decision rules. As a community consultant, i often hear from groups who are struggling with a perceived problem member, someone who acts out in a way that others find abusive or over the line. Someone from the committee who's been assigned to find a way out calls me on the phone and tells me their tale of woe. I duly sympathize (hey, i've been there too, i know how hard it is). And then, after they hopefully feel heard by me, i ask: "So when this person does these problematic behaviors, how does the rest of the group respond?" The answer is inevitably some type of conflict avoidance...which generally makes it clear that the community is co-creating the problem.

Want that person to behave differently? Give a different response.

The response i've seen succeed most in shifting these dynamics is both compassionate and direct. It takes multiple members offering honest feedback, so don't give up when the first try does not have a perceived effect, as you are laying the groundwork for later shift. Your group needs to back each other up on this, standing up for the kind of community you want to live in, and refusing to allow yourselves to be bullied or intimidated.

If the more sensitive or vocal people who tend to step forward first get blown off by the problem member, then other people need to engage. Often the most successful interventions are by more middle-of-the-road members, perhaps a few people who are typically a bit quieter, well-respected, or hold some eldering energy in the group. Unfortunately, many groups allow their fear of being a lynch mob to divide them—and lose good members in the process—before arriving at unity on this and eventually taking appropriate action.

Returning to Diana's concerns regarding consensus practice, i agree that for groups who are struggling with dysfunctional consensus process, the biggest culprit is usually inappropriate blocking. This problem is pervasive enough that it gives consensus overall a bad rep. That's unfortunate, because the heart of the process is not about blocking, it's about listening to each other well and finding the best path forward together. Nonetheless, given that we come from a culture glorifying individualism instead of teaching us to collaborate well, it's essential that every consensus system include a way to rein in inappropriate blocks. Blocking potentially gives tremendous power to one or a few individuals, and the only way for that to function successfully is with a check and balance.

I advocate for doing this through the cultivation of both culture and procedures. The culture piece is conveyed, for example, through the shared mantra, "If you've blocked consensus half a dozen times for all the groups you've been a member of, you've used up your lifetime quota." If you provide a good orientation to the decision-making process for all incoming members (including how a constructive culture is fostered at meetings), the results will pay you back a hundredfold.

The procedural piece can take a variety of forms, depending on the system. Diana cites at least three examples: the Formal Consensus method of asking a group whether a block is legitimate, N Street's requirement that blockers convene meetings to work out an alternative, and the institution of a supermajority voting fallback. Although there are plenty of earlier examples, Quakers are thought of by many as originators of consensus practice and have been quite influential. What many people don't realize is that Quakers also give their facilitators the power to overrule any block perceived as inappropriate, even if it comes from two or three members (see, for example, Pacific Yearly Meeting's *Faith and Practice* book).

The response that succeeds most in shifting "problem member" blocking dynamics is both compassionate and direct.

Rather than giving unanimity or consensus without recourse its own name as Diana does, i simply assume that in order for consensus to function well there must be a robust response to bad blocks. When the cohousing movement started in the 1990s, in order to access conventional lending their communities put supermajority fallbacks into their bylaws to satisfy bankers. As a consensus practitioner i worried about this at first: with a voting option in place, would these groups still do the patient work of sorting through differences to arrive at genuine consensus? More than a decade later, experience has shown me that cohousing groups work just as much as other groups at coming to decisions everyone can support or at least live with, and their voting fallbacks are typically invoked only rarely in the course of years. Nonetheless, they are there if needed.

I agree with Diana that consensus-based groups can also have other problems, like stagnation, power struggles, decision by endurance, and premature proposal death. I'm not sure those problems are necessarily worse in consensus groups than groups with other decision rules (goodness knows we see enough bad examples in society of poor decision-making process regardless of whether majority vote, consensus, or some other system is used). But let's acknowledge that these are real concerns, and pledge to make improvement.

Healthy groups build a spirit and culture that honors new ideas and alternatives rather than shooting them down. Power struggles and other differences can benefit from being acknowledged and skillfully worked with. Agendas should be created mindfully and time limits honored sufficiently so that people can give thoughtful consideration to the issue at hand. And when groups tell me they are struggling with meeting attendance, i have a standard answer: If you want people to show up at meetings, then talk about things that matter and talk about them well. ❧

Tree Bressen is a group process consultant based in Eugene, Oregon, who works with intentional communities and other organizations on how to have meetings that are lively, productive, and connecting. Her website, www.treegroup.info, offers extensive free resources on consensus, facilitation, and more. (Tree uses a lower-case "i" in her writing as an expression of egalitarian values.)

Busting the Myth that Consensus-with-Unanimity Is Good for Communities *Part II*

By Diana Leafe Christian

"We're all sitting here in a cold sweat," exclaimed one member.

Most people in the room felt apprehensive. The atmosphere was grim.

The conflict in this real community I'll call "Green Meadow" (first described in Part I of this article, COMMUNITIES #155, Summer 2012) was between two community members who had frequently blocked proposals and a roomful of people who wanted to pass an Agriculture (Ag) Committee proposal about a community site plan for future farms, pastures, and orchards. Passing the proposal would mean clearing more of their forest. The two frequently blocking members were committed to protecting the community's land—to protecting the Earth—from the human impact of clearing more forest and implementing the proposed agricultural site plans.

Community meetings had been increasingly characterized by tension, frustration, and over-the-top behavior on both sides of the agriculture issue ever since the committee proposed their ag site plan six weeks earlier.

The frequently blocking members seemed desperate, apparently feeling a heartfelt obligation to, once again, protect the Earth from fellow community members. Those who supported the proposed ag site plan seemed desperate too, including committee members who'd spent months assessing and categorizing the community's potential agricultural sites for their probable best agricultural use.

People's demeanor in meetings was at the high-stress end of everyone's spectrum. Courtesy had given way to intensity; easy discussion to speaking through gritted teeth.

A few months later, during the three-week, post-meeting review period for committee decisions, one of the two chronic blockers retroactively blocked four out of five of the Ag Committee's decisions. And while this member later rescinded her blocks, the relatively frequent blocks of both of these members had a devastating effect on the committee. Discouraged and demoralized, they stopped meeting for over a year.

It's been three years since Green Meadow's "cold sweat" meeting and the subsequent blocks of four Agriculture Committee proposals. Growing and raising on-site organic food is one of Green Meadow's explicit goals in its online Mission Statement. Yet as a result of these blocks—and because other members didn't know how to respond effectively—the community has never reconsidered the proposed agricultural site plan, and no new small agricultural projects, pastures, or orchards have been proposed since then.

This kind of no-win situation is why I no longer think that consensus-with-unanimity is not only not helpful for most communities, but actually harmful. It's harmful when it results in deadlocks, desperation, and heartbreak; in low morale and dwindling meeting attendance; and sometimes, in people just giving up and moving away.

"Consensus-with-Unanimity"

As noted in Part I of this article, I use the term "consensus-with-unanimity" for the usual consensus *process* (agenda, proposals, facilitator, the group modifying and improving proposal), coupled with the *"decision rule"* of 100 percent or unanimous agreement required to pass a proposal, not counting stand-asides. (The "decision rule" is the percentage of agreement needed to pass a proposal.)

When a community has no criteria for what constitutes a legitimate block *(see below)*, nor a requirement that those who block a proposal must work with its advocates to collaboratively create a new proposal that addresses the same issues as the first one, then it has no recourse if someone blocks a proposal. With a decision-making method like this, anyone can block a proposal any time for any reason.

Consensus advocates say that because in consensus everyone's agreement is required to pass a proposal, the process naturally results in widespread agreement, harmony, trust, and a sense of connection among members.

Consider the 15-year-old community without a pet policy because a dog-owning member blocks any proposal to create a pet policy committee.

Yet consider the 15-year-old community that still doesn't have a pet policy because a member who has several dogs blocks any proposal to even create an ad hoc pet policy committee to draft a proposal. Or the 18-year-old group still with no community building because several members blocked a proposal to build it due to their personal abhorrence of being in debt—even though the community borrowed money to buy their property in the first place. Or the cohousing community that has no community labor requirement, no matter that most people want it, because a member blocks every proposal to create one, believing that if it's a *real* community people would contribute voluntarily from the heart.

These communities don't only have no pet policy, community building, or labor requirements. They also have the demoralization and discouragement that results when their vision of a congenial, collaborative community is destroyed, over and over, as they finally realize that some of their fellow community members have the power to stop what everyone else wants, or nearly everyone else wants, without the requisite personal maturity and responsibility to handle that power wisely—and there's nothing they can do about it.

Appropriate Blocks

As noted in Part I, there certainly are appropriate blocks (also sometimes called "principled" blocks, "valid" blocks, or "legitimate" blocks). Appropriate blocks are usually described by community-based consensus trainers as those in which the blocker can clearly demonstrate that if the proposal passed it would violate the group's deeply held values or shared purpose, or would otherwise harm the community. *(See "Criteria for a Principled Block," next page.)* Yet at many communities, members have never been taught the difference between appropriate and inappropriate blocks, or they have learned this but no community member has the courage to point out that someone's latest block isn't actually legitimate, but is based on his or her personal preferences or values. Thus the group meekly acquiesces to the block—even though many consensus trainers caution that blocking is so extreme, and such a nearly "sacred" privilege, that it should be used rarely.

Type One Errors and "Work-Arounds"

I believe consensus-with-unanimity as practiced in most communities is itself what Permaculturists call a "Type One Design Error." And having criteria for a principled block, as C.T. Butler recommends in his Formal Consensus process, is just another ineffective "work-around."

A Type One Error, as it's known informally in Permaculture circles, is a basic design flaw so fundamental to the whole system that it unleashes a cascade of subsequent, smaller errors downstream. My greenhouse was built with a Type One Error. With small, ineffectual vents in its end walls, it didn't have enough ventilation, and was far too hot for either plants or people. I couldn't create a new vent across the apex of the roof where greenhouse vents are usually located, as this was where the rafters were braced, and doing so would mean rebuilding the roof.

I use the term "work-around" to describe the attempts people make to compensate for such basic, foundational errors. I tried work-arounds for my greenhouse. I kept the door open all day. I cut a long, wide vent along the bottom of the front wall. I covered the roof with a tarp in summer. I tried to grow kiwis across the roof. Nothing worked: the place was still hotter than Hades. Using a vent fan would violate everything I know about Permaculture—using limited off-grid power to run a motor to cool a greenhouse that should have been cooled naturally by convection. But I could find no inexpensive structural or horticultural solution to my Type One Error. I should have just built the greenhouse with appropriately sized, properly located vents in the first place! (I finally installed a fan, and it's still too hot.)

Likewise, the Type One Error of using consensus-with-unanimity causes many communities to have ongoing, seemingly irresolvable problems.

Many communities attempt various work-arounds to deal with the unintended consequences of consensus-with-unanimity. They bring in outside consultants or get more or better consensus training. They try to create more effective agendas or better proposals. They introduce "process time" in meetings to deal with emotional upsets. I think these work-arounds work no better than mine did.

"Criteria for a Principled Block"—Just Another Work-Around

I believe having criteria for a principled block can work well for one-issue environmental or political activist groups. Shut down a nuclear power plant in your county. Get your local schools to serve organic lunches. Save the redwoods.

However, intentional communities—whether ecovillages, cohousing neighborhoods, or other kinds of communities—are *not* simple one-issue organizations. On the contrary, they are complex entities with multiple purposes and needs, both physical and non-physical. These include shelter, private or shared ownership of land and/or equipment, a place to raise children safely, a place to live one's values, collaborative decision making, problem solving, and conflict resolution. If the community has an educational mission, it's also a place to offer classes and workshops for others. And if it's rural, it can also be a place to grow and raise food, and create member-owned or community-owned cottage industries.

For these reasons, I believe intentional communities are much too complex for people to easily see whether a block meets any chosen criteria for legitimacy. In an entity as multi-faceted as an intentional community, it's much more difficult to know whether a proposal does or doesn't violate its mission and purpose, because there's so much room for interpretation. Trying to test whether a block is valid or not—trying to determine whether a proposal meets the test for harming the community, or not being aligned with its purpose—is too murky. And if the community has no agreed-upon criteria for a legitimate block, the process of testing the block *itself* could trigger conflict.

What's the Problem at Green Meadow?

One of the requirements for a group to use consensus at all—*especially* when practiced as consensus-with-unanimity, and especially when there no is recourse—is to have a clearly agreed-upon shared purpose. This is the first thing I learned in my first consensus workshop years ago. Yet, most communities' Mission and Purpose documents are vague, ambiguous, and likely to be interpreted multiple different ways.

I have observed, and Tim Hartnett (author of *Consensus-Oriented Decision-Making*) has also observed, at least three reasons people may block proposals inappropriately: (1) the blocking person interprets the community's stated purpose differently than many, or most, other community members; (2) a proposal violates a member's personal values rather than the community's agreed-upon

Four to Six Blocks in a Lifetime

• Only block a few times in one's lifetime at most, and "only after a sleepless night and the shedding of tears."—*Quakers, cited in a handout on the website of consensus trainer Tree Bressen*

• Community-based consensus trainer Caroline Estes recommends only three to four blocks in a lifetime. She says that in her 50+ years of facilitating she has seen legitimate blocks less than a dozen times.

• Community-based consensus trainer Bea Briggs recommends only three to six blocks in a lifetime. She says that her 20+ years of facilitating she has seen only one legitimate block.

—D.L.C.

shared values; (3) the blocker has a (subconscious) wish to gain attention, or otherwise to express some painful-but-suppressed emotional issue.

To me, Green Meadow's situation demonstrates all three reasons for inappropriate blocks. First, it seems as if three different sets of members live in three different paradigms about what the community is *for*.

(A) Some members seem to believe Green Meadow's purpose is to create a rural agrarian village in which some members grow and raise much of the community's food or create cottage industries providing jobs on-site. *(They don't mind that others organize emotional processing meetings, but don't tend to participate in them.)*

(B) Others seem to believe the purpose is to be a spiritually and emotionally rich group that practices whole-community emotional processing. *(They don't mind that some members want to grow and raise food and start cottage industries.)*

(C) A few members seem to believe the purpose is to protect the Earth from human impact *(and so must monitor carefully any proposals about village-building or food-growing in terms of the degree of their potential human impact).*

Second, it seems that there is little knowledge at Green Meadow that it's not a legitimate consensus practice to block because of personal, rather than community-held values. Members have blocked because of someone's personal distaste for the insurance industry, devotion to ecofeminism, abhorrence for borrowing money, or disdain for on-site small cottage industries and their need to expand enough to stay in business.

Third, blocking at Green Meadow seems sometimes to involve personal emotional issues. Tim Hartnett writes, "raising objections to a proposal is an easy way to become the focus of group attention...their agreement may be courted with both attention and other forms of appeasement."

One Green Meadow member wrote the following account: *It seems that the most innovative, creative, forward-moving members have left the community because a few folks, mostly older women with a lot of time on their hands, need attention and tend to get it by blocking proposals.*

It's certainly true that older women get overlooked in the larger culture. And all of us need healing. Yet this group in our community seems to abuse the power that consensus gives them.

Many baby boomer communitarians still seem devoted—perhaps compulsively attached—to consensus-with-unanimity.

They like a slow and emotional process. How I tend to hear it is, "Either slow down and pay attention to us or you won't get your proposal passed." Other folks (often younger, but not always) have felt stopped by this energy to the point of extreme frustration and withdrawal. Many of the most passionate and service-oriented folks have actually left the community. The ones who are left don't seem to have the courage or confidence to actually create anything innovative. So we get the worst of both worlds—overly controlling older members and apathetic and discouraged younger folks.

A well-known professional consensus facilitator came to help us, only to give these women even more attention. The theory was, the more attention we give them, the more their tension will loosen. But in my opinion the facilitator brought more of the same problem we already had. And sure enough, even with the facilitator's group process, they were still not satisfied.

Baby Boomers and Consensus

Despite these problems, and even the oft-expressed support among consensus trainers for having criteria for legitimate blocks and other forms of recourse, many baby boomer communitarians still seem devoted—perhaps compulsively attached—to consensus-with-unanimity. They seem to hold the belief that the promised harmony, cohesiveness, and trust will manifest in community if only its members would just spend enough time exploring everyone's emotions and the nuances of people's differing opinions.

However, advocating more emotional processing in meetings to deal with the kinds of dilemmas Green Meadow is experiencing can *itself* create conflict. In most communities, many members, especially younger ones, can't bear such meetings. They may believe that therapy is fine but should be voluntary, and conducted on one's own time. Or they may not want to witness the emotional upsets of people twice and three times their age. They'd rather these folks behaved as wise elders—not people their parents' or grandparents' age who are expressing emotional upset about what seems like the current proposal but in fact may be long-held personal issues they haven't healed yet.

Younger community members may also not participate in these meetings because they can't afford the *time*. They don't have retirement income or trust funds. On the contrary, they usually work full-time. In rural communities they may make ends meet with several different part-time jobs—not to mention raising children too. In contrast, baby boomers can often afford the time because they may be living on retirement incomes or trust funds.

Baby Boomers and Trauma

I've got a theory about this. I think a relatively high percentage of people born in the baby boomer generation, like me (born between 1946-1964), experienced more trauma at birth and in childhood than subsequent generations. I've read that early trauma, unless healed by effective therapy later, shows up in an adult as a relatively high amount of emotional distress and reactivity, a relatively high need for attention, and a relatively high tendency to try to control the immediate environment in order to meet a probably unconscious and highly charged unmet need from childhood for safety and security.

Hospital birth and infant care practices in the 1940s and subsequent decades were exceptionally traumatic for mothers and babies. They included huge levels of muscle-deadening drugs (natural birth practices were not yet widely known), forceps, Cesareans, cutting of the umbilical cord prematurely and slapping the infants to suddenly force lung breathing, and removing infants from mothers at birth and isolating them in another room. Breastfeeding after birth was not even an option; infants received neither colostrum nor human connection, but were bottle-fed with manufactured infant formula by nurses on a rigid hospital schedule. Mothers held their infants for only a few minutes a day. All natural sources of safety, security, connection, trust, and empowerment were removed as soon as a baby was born. Psychologists theorize that these infants probably felt terrified, desperate, and powerless. (And I speculate that, in terms of encouraging healthy emotional development, this is a another Type One Error.)

Flash forward 50 or 60 years. If someone born in these circumstances has not gotten effective psychotherapy or other healing, they may have exceptionally high needs for safety and security. They may have (subconsciously) adopted a strategy of trying to control their immediate environment in order to (subconsciously) feel safe enough to get through the day. And consensus-with-unanimity allows—no, invites—people to control their immediate environment through the power to block. I think people sometimes block inappropriately simply because they can.

As Caroline Estes notes, "consensus...allows each person complete power over the group." What? We give people who are likely to have a more than usual amount of unresolved trauma—and who may not have healed it yet and are possibly compensating with strong control tendencies—"complete power over the group"? Living in a community that practices consensus-with-unanimity may be the first time any of these folks ever had social permission to place limits; to stop people; to say the "No!" they couldn't say as a terrorized infant.

So what should we do, kick out all the baby boomers? (Even though, of course, they founded most of our communities?) I think we should respect and appreciate our boomers, *and change our governance system instead.* Adopt a decision-making and governance process that *doesn't allow* anyone to stop proposals because of conscious or unconscious personal preferences or personal values, no matter if they give us protect-the-community reasons. Instead, let's shift to a governance process that doesn't just encourage collaboration and cooperation, but *requires* it. Which is exactly what Sociocracy, Holacracy, and the N Street Consensus Method do, and why I now recommend them. *(See "Resources," below.)*

A Shift at Green Meadow?

Fortunately, increasing numbers of Green Meadow members are now questioning whether consensus-with-unanimity actually serves them. A combination of demoralization, low meeting attendance, and people packing their bags and leaving—along with recent presentations about alternative decision-making methods—is apparently having an effect.

Here's what the 2012 president of Green Meadow declared to his small advisory group a few months ago: "Listen, let's face it. Consensus-with-unanimity is all but dead at Green Meadow. It'll be replaced by a something else by the end of the year."

Last I heard, they're considering Sociocracy. ❧

Diana Leafe Christian, author of the books Creating a Life Together *and* Finding Community, *is publisher of* Ecovillages, *a free online newsletter about ecovillages worldwide (EcovillageNews.org), and a columnist for Global Ecovillage Network (GEN) (gen.ecovillage.org). She is a trainer in GEN's Ecovillage Design Education (EDE) program, and speaks at conferences, offers consultations, and leads workshops internationally. See www.DianaLeafeChristian.org.*

Future articles in the series will describe the "N Street Consensus Method" in more detail, the "Four Decision Options/Choose Your Committee Members" method of Ecovillage Sieben Linden, Systemic Consensus, Tim Hartnett's "Consensus-Oriented Decision-Making" method, Sociocracy, and Holacracy (and why they work especially well in intentional communities), and politically incorrect tips for adopting a method that may work better than consensus-with-unanimity, even if older members are devoted to it.

Resources

Consensus:

- *On Conflict and Consensus,* C.T. Butler, available for free download on his website: www.consensus.net
- *Consensus-Oriented Decision-Making,* Tim Hartnett (New Society Publishers, 2011): consensusbook.com

N Street Consensus Method:

- "Is Consensus Right for Your Group? Part I," in *Ecovillages* newsletter: www.ecovillagenewsletter.org (click "Articles Alphabetically" to find it)

Sociocracy:

- *We the People: Consenting to a Deeper Democracy, A Guide to Sociocratic Principles and Methods,* by John Buck and Sharon Villines (2007): www.sociocracy.info
- SocioNet online discussion: www.socionet.us
- Governance Alive, author and consultant John Buck: www.governancealive.com

Holacracy:

- *Holacracy One:* www.holacracy.org

A Few Basic Process Points for Happy Community Life

Response to "Busting the Myth, Part II"

By Tree Bressen

Many of the points raised in "Busting the Myth, Part II" were already addressed in responses from me and others to Part I of Diana's article. I prefer not to belabor them, and at the same time i understand that some readers find this discussion useful. So here are a few thoughts to bear in mind.

1. Meetings should be fulfilling, with a good spirit. Regardless of whether your group uses leadership by elders, majority vote, or consensus, if your discussions have poor energy it's important to address that and change it. How can you reconnect with your love for one another? What will nourish your sense of unity, in a way that welcomes the individual while honoring the long-term well-being of the community?

2. In my experience, every successful consensus system—and there are a variety, including Sociocracy, Quakers, N Street, Formal Consensus, and more—restricts blocking power in order to guard against tyranny of the minority.

3. Regardless of decision process or rule, if you let someone in your group bully you, you will be unhappy. If there is a problem with bullying and you want it to stop, the group must stand up to it. If that doesn't happen, the group is enabling and co-creating the problem.

4. If the same person blocks repeatedly, that's a danger sign. While consensus allows space for legitimate different interpretations of existing group values and mission, if one or two people continually hold to an interpretation at odds with others' in a way that causes high impact, i'd be carefully and thoughtfully asking whether their membership is a good match. At a minimum such a group may need to take a step back from the particular issue and engage in some deep conversations about common values.

5. No decision-making system is perfect, nor does any decision-making system give you your way all the time. Compromise is a necessary part of collective life, part of the price we pay for the rewards of shared living. While consensus when practiced well has the potential to arrive at creative, emergent solutions, there are plenty of times when the standard of "Can you live with it?" is appropriately good enough.

The understandable desire for an outcome that brings everyone active joy needs to be weighed against the considerable investment in time and energy it may take to get there, and the costs of inaction on the topic at hand in the meantime.

• • •

All that said, here are responses to a few other specific points raised by Diana's article.

I agree that mission and values, while an important base, are naturally broader and more complex in an intentional community setting compared to a nonprofit or activist group. Having clear principles doesn't solve all your problems or make everything easy in any group, and this is even more true in the community setting. However, compared to *not* having clear principles, having them does help, including when tough decisions come up. Diana rightly emphasizes the importance of this in her book *Creating a Life Together*, which contains excellent exercises for groups to clarify their vision.

Second, in my observation while facilitating people of all ages for nearly two decades from elementary school students to seniors in their 90s, i've failed to see baby boomers having any corner on the market of poor behavior at meetings.

Finally, Diana decries tactics such as bringing in outside consultants, getting more training, improving agenda planning, creating more effective proposals, and "introduc[ing] 'process time' in meetings to deal with emotional upsets" as attempted work-arounds for addressing a Type One design error. While she may not have experienced these responses as effective, i have, many times over. Note that i'm not advocating against a structural requirement that blockers get involved in helping craft solutions (in fact i advocate for that too); i'm just saying that, depending on the situation, any of these may be helpful, and it often takes a combination of medicines to yield the best cure.

Tree Bressen is a group process consultant based in Eugene, Oregon, who works with intentional communities and a wide variety of other organizations. Her gifts include elegant process design, holding space for tough conversations, and using good process to achieve excellent product. She founded the collective that produced the Group Works deck, available at www.groupworks-deck.org, and her website, www.treegroup.info, offers extensive free resources on consensus, facilitation, and more. (Tree uses a lower-case "i" in her writing as an expression of egalitarian values.)

"Busting the Myth, Part II": More Thoughts

By Laird Schaub

Like Tree, I have many thoughts related to Diana's article, yet don't want to repeat responses already given to Part I. Here are additional points that seem worth bringing out:

❖ I am uncomfortable with Diana's term "consensus-with-unanimity," as it implies that when groups use consensus to make decisions it requires unanimity to reach agreement. Unanimity implies that everyone feels the same way about a proposal; consensus is far more nuanced than that. It's about reaching a place where everyone agrees that the proposal is the best that can be done to balance the application of group values to the issue at hand, and clarity that there are no principled objections to proceeding.

❖ In the opening example, it's my sense that Green Meadow has not worked through the right sequence. If there are known to be principled concerns (in this case, how to view right relationship to the land as a manifestation of a core ecological value) then I'd have worked through that *long* before it came to advancing specific land use plans.

The dynamic described (a pattern of repeated blocks about proposals on the topic of ag policy) suggests one of two things (or possibly both):

—There is a large (and possibly fatal) rift in how people are interpreting a core value. I'd be making *that* the focus of attention, rather than running proposal after proposal up the flagpole. If the group is unable to find a bridge that will hold the range of views, the group should reconfigure. While I fully appreciate that this will be a challenging and difficult conversation, putting it off will not help.

Working with the example given, I'd want to hear the blockers' thinking about how to balance their commitment to earth stewardship (which apparently translates into preserving the forest) and the core commitment to growing the community's food.

—The group may also (or instead) be suffering from an inability to create a resilient enough container to fully hear strongly held views and then enter into a sufficiently pliable and creative place to explore balancing. They may be trapped in an atmosphere of advocacy and divisiveness.

❖ I certainly agree with Diana that deadlocks, desperation, and dyspepsia are not good signs. And I agree with her unease with attempting to use consensus without defining what constitute legitimate grounds for blocking, the process by which a proposed block may be validated (or denied), or a defined process for laboring to resolve a block. Fortunately I don't know of many groups who don't understand the need for these things. While most groups could probably benefit from tightening up their understanding around this, virtually all groups recognize that having no agreement is a poor strategy, and I know of no groups who consider no agreement about blocking to be a sacred cow.

If the group is unable to find a bridge that will hold the range of views, the group should reconfigure.

Diana observes that a number of groups get into a stalemate because of the obstinacy of a minority—even a single individual—to considering actions that don't match with their sense of what's right for the group. Instead of looking more closely at how they can work through differences, Diana advocates that groups handle this procedurally by adopting a decision rule that allows such minorities to be outvoted.

I'm not excited about this mainly because I see what we're attempting in community (resolving non-trivial differences in a fundamentally different way than happens in the mainstream) to be one of the crucial things that intentional communities have to offer the wider society. Diana is right to point out that this work is hard (changing deep conditioning is *never* easy). Yet the stakes are high and I am not persuaded that outvoting someone is much different from what happens in the mainstream now. I worry that groups are drawn to this option as a substitute for being careful about membership selection or learning how to work differences constructively and creatively.

❖ When Diana talks about the demoralization that flows from permitting members to repeatedly block proposals because they lack "personal maturity or responsibility to handle power wisely" I'm wondering why groups allow individuals to assert rights while ducking responsibilities. I wouldn't.

After lamenting the problems at communities that have no clarity about a) the legitimate grounds for a block; b) the process by which blocks will be tested for legitimacy; or c) the responsibility of all parties to engage in a good faith effort to attempt to resolve the block (all of which I agree are lamentable), Diana moves on *without example* to suggest that having answers to those missing components merely provides band-aids and will work no better. I demur. I've found that where groups have these three elements in place—and the will to employ them—they are potent and effective tools in working with blocks.

❖ While I concur with Diana that the common values of most groups allow for a relatively wide range of interpretation, I do not believe that means they're worthless. Even vague statements can ground a conversation usefully. As a process consultant who has worked professionally with more than 75 groups, I've used this too many times with success to buy Diana's argument.

❖ Of the three reasons Diana enumerates for inappropriate blocks, I don't encounter people blocking purely for personal reasons (Diana's second reason) very often. While blockers are frequently accused of that, they almost always have an argument about why their position is tied to a group value and we're really talking about the first reason—a clash of paradigms—that I agree happens a lot. The challenge here is establishing a container of legitimacy, authenticity, and compassion in which to labor with one another. To be sure, almost all groups struggle with this—I just don't think that voting people off the island (or outmaneuvering them with supermajorities) is a good answer, or even begins to move us in the cultural direction we urgently need in this polarized world.

The third reason Diana offers—an inappropriate desire to seek attention (with the idea that negative attention is better than none)—is probably an element, yet difficult to discern. (How much is grandstanding and how much is simply distress leaking into the conversation, either because they don't expect the conversation to go well or because passionate expression comes naturally to that person?) The more fundamental issue is whether the group understands the need to be able to work emotionally. Most groups don't even have a conversation about this, and most groups don't handle it well.

❖ When I talk about being able to work emotionally, I am not talking about therapy. I am talking about understanding an individual's emotional connection to the issue at hand (therapy would be interested in the roots of that response and the potential for personal growth imbedded in that information). The point of working emotionally is that if you don't do it (and strong feelings are present), hearing is poor and the dynamic is brittle which doesn't lead to good problem solving. With that in mind I advocate listening to pertinent strong feelings for the purpose of unclogging ears and being in a superior position to solve problems. When I labor with an individual to make sure they're heard, that's coupled with the clear expectation that they then listen to and work constructively with what others have to say on the subject. Bridging is not appeasement. Being heard is no guarantee that you'll be agreed with.

Outmaneuvering people with supermajorities doesn't move us in the cultural direction we urgently need in this polarized world.

❖ I am very nervous about encouraging groups to disenfranchise and marginalize members after labeling them emotionally immature. I've found it far better to assume that people are coming from a good place until you can't find it. While I have reached the conclusion that some people are too much work for too little benefit and don't belong, I never start there, and I worry grievously about Diana's advocacy of adopting policies and decision-making processes that encourage this.

❖ Diana advances an interesting psychological theory about why baby boomers may typically have a different, more needy emotional make-up than other generations. While I am not a psychologist (and I note that neither is Diana), I work regularly with groups who struggle with particular members and I have not observed that "problem people" are concentrated in any gender or age range. ❧

Laird Schaub is Executive Secretary of the Fellowship for Intentional Community (FIC), publisher of this magazine, and cofounder of Sandhill Farm, a consensus-run egalitarian community in Missouri, where he lives. He is also a facilitation trainer and process consultant, and he authors a blog that can be read at communityandconsensus.blogspot.com.

CREATING COOPERATIVE CULTURE REVIEW BY CHRIS ROTH

Group Works: A Pattern Language for Bringing Life to Meetings and Other Gatherings

Created by the Group Pattern Language Project

2011; 91 cards plus booklet; available from www.groupworksdeck.org (also as free pdf download)

This card deck marks a milestone in group-process resources.

Inspired by *A Pattern Language: Towns, Buildings, Construction* by Christopher Alexander and co-authors (1977), which explored 253 design principles that help "create built spaces that nourish people's souls," a group of volunteers met and collaborated for three years to generate an equivalent "language" for working successfully in groups. The resulting card deck explores how to create meetings and gatherings that also nourish people's souls, this time through 91 principles or patterns, divided into nine pattern categories.

Instead of trying to replicate the many books offering specific models and techniques for running good meetings, the Group Works cards aim to "express shared wisdom underlying successful approaches...more specific than general values and less specific than tools and techniques." Each card features a pattern title, pattern image, pattern "heart" (text expressing the core of the pattern), category icon, and list of related patterns—distilling the "What" and the "Why" of a particular principle of effective gatherings and its relationship to others in the deck. Card users can explore the "How" through the many resources available on the Group Works website, and by utilizing established techniques or creating new ones.

Pattern categories include Intention, Context, Relationship, Flow, Creativity, Perspective, Modelling (readers will notice that the cards use Canadian spellings), Inquiry & Synthesis, and Faith. If those words alone (or the pattern titles) were sufficient to convey the contents, there'd be no need for the cards, but deeper exploration is what will make these pattern categories come alive. For example, "Perspective" is about "Noticing and helping the group more openly and thoughtfully explore different ways of seeing an issue. Watching, understanding, and appreciating divergent viewpoints, ideas, values and opinions. The key is in how you look at something." In this category (which includes 10 patterns), the "Value the Margins" card reads: "Edges of ecosystems are fertile ground for adaptation. Similarly in group dynamics, growth often comes from generative disturbances at the margins, perhaps from participants less invested in the status quo. Welcome and embrace people and ideas that may at first seem alien."

These cards have many potential applications, including group learning of facilitation skills, preparing for an event, debriefing after a gathering, self-assessment and self-directed learning for facilitators and participants, getting a group "unstuck" in the middle of a meeting, and even consulting as an oracle, a "Tarot card of group process." I have heard a number of positive reports about their use by individuals and groups—including a cohousing group which used them to get past major difficulties to hold a very productive, constructive meeting.

This set has reminded me of how rich group process can be if its full potential is acknowledged and nurtured. Some methodologies unfortunately seem to cram group process into a "paint by numbers" approach—or worse. The Group Works deck makes it clear that group work is an art, with endless nuance and potential for creativity—and that no simple formula will do it justice. Facilitators and participants in meetings and gatherings have an almost unlimited toolbox of methods and techniques at their disposal, if they choose to use them.

In my experience, the best consensus trainers and facilitators know how to make full use of this toolbox, and the keys to their success—the design patterns and the tools—can be learned by anyone who's caught a glimpse of the beauty of good group process. For those feeling trapped in a formulaic, limiting approach to group discussion and decision making (even if, in the words of one facilitation trainer, it's touted as the "best thing since sliced bread"), or who have lost sight of the magic of what truly participatory, effective group work can be, these cards may offer a breath of fresh air.

The core beliefs of the Group Works team are also a breath of fresh air: "We choose to assume the best of people. We believe people flourish when entrusted with the opportunity to authentically self-manage, collaborate, and make decisions collectively, as true respected equals.... We believe in sharing power, that we are wiser when we work together....Good process builds strong communities."

Whether it's used as a window into the vast world of community-building and group work, or as an aid along the way for those engaged in that work, I expect this deck will be of enduring value to anyone who chooses to explore and use it.

Chris Roth edits Communities *and is a member of Meadowsong Ecovillage outside Dexter, Oregon.*

November, 1963. In the middle of the Pentagon's grey corridors, the inner courtyard is a green haven for civilians and military on their lunch break. On a crisp fall day, an attractive young matron waves to her navel lieutenant husband. It is 12:15 pm, and Kay has nothing on her mind except the small picnic basket she has brought. Along with the rest of the United States, she is oblivious to preparations in a Dallas office building, perhaps on a nearby grassy knoll, which at this moment remain suspended in time, subject to intervention and choice, if we only knew.

If we only knew then what we know now...

Plunked down in the middle of the 20th century, reverted to his childhood body, but his memory intact, Joshua Leyden takes a run at revising his own life, and changing a future that needs some tinkering.

"Held me every step of the way. A great read, challenging ideas, fascinating and seductive." – David Kahn, Harvard Faculty.

Consider two trains heading in opposite directions, but stopped in a station. While the trains wait, it is possible to change between them. Transferring passengers would then head down their own timelines, reviewing past images incrementally. So it is with memories. So it is with dreams.

"Wonderful, touching characters, reworking our fate." – Hazel Henderson, Economist.

...and the most outrageous, yet logical path for time travel ever.

Each night, the sun went down, Nora to bed, and Josh prowled around her soul, searching for a key to unlock their mystery. While Nora slept beyond a narrow wall, Josh fought the need to break on through to the other side – replaying every mistake he'd ever made in either life. Rising, hitting the brandy, writing in a notebook lest the typewriter wake the girl. He couldn't even feel sorry for himself when he knew Nora had it far worse.

It's about time: A love story, both provocative and playful...

Paul Freundlich, Founder of Green America and Dance New England; for a decade an Editor of "Communities"; filmmaker, essayist and activist has created a journey that transcends time and reworks reality. **Available from Amazon.com [search: Paul Freundlich]**

Thinking Flexibly About Consensus

By Tim Hartnett, Ph.D.

I am very pleased to see Diana Leafe Christian's articles open up a new dialogue about the use of consensus in intentional communities. It takes courage to be willing to question the assumptions and doctrines we communitarians have lived by for many years. But this willingness to reflect and reconsider is essential if we seek to offer our communities as viable alternatives in an ever-changing world.

Since my book, *Consensus-Oriented Decision-Making,* is often referenced in Diana's articles, I feel called to join the discussion. I'd like to highlight two key points that I have found helpful in freeing our thinking about consensus and how to make it work in different types of groups.

The first key concept is an understanding of the difference between a decision-making process (like formal consensus, CODM, or Robert's Rules of Order) and the decision rule applied at the end of the process (like unanimity, majority rule, or supermajority). Unfortunately, the term "consensus" is used for both the process and the decision rule. This muddies our ability to think clearly about the difference. By using the term "consensus" to denote a collaborative, agreement-seeking process, and "unanimity" or "full consent" to denote the decision rule that requires full agreement to pass a proposal, we gain clarity and the capacity to consider these two components independently.

This distinction paves the way to see that a consensus process can be used with different types of decision rules. This means that you can have a very collaborative, cooperative, agreement-building discussion even if you do not require unanimity. This distinction also clarifies that just because a group requires unanimity does not mean that they are using a consensus process.

You can have a very collaborative, cooperative, agreement-building discussion even if you do not require unanimity.

The opposite of a consensus process is not majority rule (as is commonly claimed). Such a claim compares an apple (process) to an orange (decision rule). The true opposite of a consensus process is adversarial debate. The way that a group discusses its decisions is what determines whether it is using a consensus or an adversarial process.

Most of us communitarians are clear that we prefer a consensus process to adversarial debate (as in Robert's Rules of Order). We value consensus process because it embodies the values of inclusiveness, cooperation, collaboration, maximizing agreement, relationship building, and respect for all viewpoints. These are the outcomes we hope using consensus will provide us.

Decision rules, on the other hand, delineate the level of agreement needed to pass a proposal. But no decision rule insures that people will actually agree. When full agreement is not reached, some groups default to "status quo rules." Other groups default to "majority rule" or "supermajority rules." In either case, a decision that not everyone agrees with is made. (To not pass a proposal is as much a decision as passing one is.)

Some groups can require unanimity and use a consensus process to successfully achieve it. This is more likely in groups that are small, homogenous, mature, and well trained. When successful, a unanimous decision generally embodies the goals and values we associate with consensus.

Unfortunately, when groups require unanimity, but cannot reach it, the goals and values of consensus are not well met. In fact, the widespread disagreement that prevails when a proposal is blocked by a small number of people can be very toxic to group morale and effective group functioning.

The widespread disagreement that prevails when a proposal is blocked can be very toxic to group morale.

This problem is more likely as group size increases, as groups become more diverse, and as the maturity level of participants varies. A group of six to 10 dedicated and mature community mates may be able to require unanimity without difficulties. But a diverse, 60 member cohousing community would likely self-destruct if it were unable to make decisions unless everyone agreed.

The good news is that groups too large, or too diverse, or groups who are otherwise unable to successfully reach unanimity, can still use a consensus process paired with a more flexible decision rule. In so doing they retain the values and goals associated with consensus, but shed the agonizing problems that occur when you simply can't get everyone to agree. The Occupy Movement seems to understand this clearly. Occupy groups typically use a consensus-type process to deliberate issues, but generally require only a supermajority to pass proposals.

The second key point I'd like to make is that the consensus process model that intentional communities have been using for the last 40 years needs a major update. While the fields of conflict resolution, mediation, group facilitation, and Nonviolent Communication have all made huge advances in the past couple of decades, many consensus trainers still champion a 30-year-old text, *Building United Judgment*, or a similarly outdated manual, *On Conflict and Consensus*. It is beyond the scope of this article to articulate how the models described in these books fail to insure high levels of collaboration and agreement. Suffice it to say that using these texts is like designing your new photovoltaic system from a book written 30 years ago.

With an open mind, we can avail ourselves of new principles and methods in conflict resolution and collaborative dialogue. But first we must be willing to question our own dogma. To many professional facilitators, the "formal consensus" model intentional communities have championed as a harbinger of a new society is actually considered an anachronism. Too often communitarians struggle with formal consensus and blame themselves (or each other) without ever questioning the model they are using. There are better ways. But to see them you have to be willing to think flexibly. ❧

Tim Hartnett, Ph.D., is author of Consensus-Oriented Decision-Making *(New Society Publisher, 2011); see www.timhartnett.com and www.consensusbook.com. Tim lives in a community outside of Santa Cruz, California. He works as a mediator, facilitation trainer, and family therapist.*

How the "N Street Consensus Method" Helps N Street Cohousing Thrive

By Diana Leafe Christian

In recent issues of this magazine I've criticized what I call "consensus-with-unanimity." The "consensus" part is the *process*—the intention to hear from everyone in the circle, asking clarifying questions, expressing concerns, and modifying and improving the proposal.

The "unanimity" part is sometimes called the "decision rule"—the *percentage of agreement* needed to pass a proposal. In many communities it is 100 percent or "unanimity" or "full consent." Except for anyone standing aside, everyone in the meeting must agree to a proposal—unanimity or full consent—before the proposal can pass. (This distinction was first pointed out by Sam Kaner, et. al. in *Facilitator's Guide to Participatory Decision-Making*, New Society Publishers, 1996.)

In practice, consensus-with-unanimity means essentially that anyone can block a proposal for any reason, and there's no recourse—such as, for example, having criteria for a legitimate block, or requiring anyone blocking to collaborate with others to co-create a new proposal. In my experience, consensus-with-unanimity is what most communitarians mean when they say "consensus."

As I described in "Busting the Myth that Consensus-With-Unanimity is Good for Community," Parts I and II (*issues #155 and #156*), I don't think consensus-with-unanimity works well for most intentional communities. In fact, as noted in the articles, I think using it can cause harm. When one or more people block proposals a lot, a community can suffer from frustration, discouragement, dwindling meeting attendance, and low morale.

However, consensus-with-unanimity is only *one* possible way to decide things after the consensus process. N Street Cohousing in Davis, California, has been successfully using a different consensus method for almost 25 years.

How N Street Cohousing Uses Consensus

N Street Cohousing has a simple, straightforward way of using consensus. Here's what they do.

When the facilitator calls for consensus on a proposal and no one blocks, the proposal passes.

Up to Six Meetings: If one or more people block a proposal, however, the person(s) blocking are obligated to meet with small groups of other members in a series of solution-oriented, consensus-building meetings. Their job is to think through the issues and mutually agree on a new proposal that addresses the same problem as the blocked proposal. They present the new proposal at the next business meeting.

The small groups are required to meet up to six times and in no more than three months after the proposal was blocked. They're not *required* to take six meetings or three months! In fact, in 25 years it's never taken them more than two meetings to do this step.

The people who supported the proposal can send representatives to these meetings, but they don't have to attend all of the meetings.

The person(s) blocking are responsible for organizing the meetings, and the meetings must take place.

A New Proposal: If a new, mutually agreed-upon proposal is created in one of the meetings, it goes back to the whole group and is taken up as a new proposal.

Seventy-Five Percent Supermajority Agreement: If the person(s) blocking and the other members cannot come up with a mutually agreed-on new proposal during the series of meetings—or if the meetings don't take place for some reason—the original proposal goes back to the next Council to be reconsidered. But at this meeting, it can be passed by a 75 percent supermajority agreement of the members present.

(If more than just a few people block a proposal, depending on the size of the group, of course the proposal doesn't pass because it clearly doesn't have enough support, and the group does not invoke this process.)

Why the N Street Consensus Method Works Well

This consensus method makes anyone who wants to block take more responsibility for the effect of their block on the group. "If you've blocked," says Kevin Wolf, cofounder of N Street Cohousing and originator of this method, "you've got to be part of the solution. Anyone who wants to block has to ask themselves, 'Do I oppose this proposal enough to go through all this?'"

Satisfaction. When I visited N Street Cohousing several years ago, I asked various community members how they liked their decision-making method. "We like it," I heard over and over. "Our meetings run smoothly." An unusual aspect of N Street Cohousing is that 75 percent of their members are renters (60 percent of the homes are rentals), and having both renters and owners in the community decision-making process sometimes triggers conflict. But not in this community.

Deterrence. While this method could seem like a lot of work and bureaucracy, N Street members believe it's effective not only because it works well but also because it exists. It's a deterrent to the kind of frivolous, personal blocking one can see in many intentional communities.

"Someone blocked a proposal in one of our meetings recently," N Street member Pamela Walker told me when I saw her there. "We'd forgotten to tell this person how we work with blocks here. So when we told them, they said, "Well, if I'd known I had to do all this I wouldn't have blocked!" (Pamela told me the person then rescinded their block.)

In the nearly 25 years since N Street was founded, Kevin Wolf estimates there have probably been about 12 blocked issues total. Of these, only two or three have invoked this process. Each time the blocking people and proposal advocates reached only a second small-group meeting before they mutually crafted a new proposal. Thus they've held only about six small-group meetings in nearly 25 years to deal with blocks!

(The other 10 blocked proposals were resolved informally outside the meetings, by coming up with let's-try-it new solutions that worked, or often because assumptions just needed more time to be clarified.)

Respect for Community Members. This method is effective, in my opinion, because it respects both the person blocking and those who support the proposal.

• It respects the person(s) blocking because it offers up to three months of informal opportunities—and up to six formal opportunities—to share his or her views with others in a more intimate setting, mutually create a new proposal, or persuade at least 26 percent of the people that the proposal should not be passed.

• It respects the people supporting the proposal because, if the small groups cannot build enough consensus to reach agreement, the later 75 percent supermajority agreement will ensure that the most number of people will get the most of what they most want. "Tyranny of the minority" isn't possible.

The method is a deterrent to the kind of frivolous, personal blocking one can see in many intentional communities.

Balancing Power with Responsibility. Community-based consensus trainer Tree Bressen highly values inclusivity in community and is passionate about consensus. She considers N Street's Consensus Method to be inclusive and fair to everyone. "It seems like consensus to me," she says. "And I like how it balances power with responsibility."

Alternatives to Consensus-with-Unanimity

Over the last year I've studied Sociocracy, a governance and decision-making method developed in The Netherlands in the 1970s and used by an increasing number of intentional communities instead of consensus. I've also studied Holacracy, a governance and decision-making method developed in the US in the early 2000s, and with which at least one community, ZEGG in Germany, replaced their consensus method. I believe these methods result in more effective, productive, and satisfying community business meetings and committee meetings than when a group uses consensus-with-unanimity.

And I believe the N Street Consensus Method works very well too, and is easier for a group using consensus-with-unanimity to implement, because they don't need to learn anything new. What do you think? Want to try it? ❧

Diana Leafe Christian, author of the books Creating a Life Together *and* Finding Community, *is publisher of* Ecovillages, *a free online newsletter about ecovillages worldwide (EcovillageNews.org), and a columnist for Global Ecovillage Network (GEN) (gen.ecovillage.org). She is a trainer in GEN's Ecovillage Design Education (EDE) program, and speaks at conferences, offers consultations, and leads workshops internationally. See www.DianaLeafeChristian.org.*

Future articles in the series will describe the "Four Decision Options/Choose Your Committee Members" method of Ecovillage Sieben Linden, Systemic Consensus, Tim Hartnett's "Consensus-Oriented Decision-Making" method, Sociocracy, and Holacracy (and why they work especially well in intentional communities), as well as politically incorrect tips for adopting a method that may work better than consensus-with-unanimity, even if your older members are devoted to it.

Resources

- Tree Bressen: www.treegroup.info
- *We the People: Consenting to a Deeper Democracy, A Guide to Sociocratic Principles and Methods,* by John Buck and Sharon Villines (2007): www.sociocracy.info
- SocioNet online discussion: www.socionet.us
- Governance Alive, author and consultant John Buck: www.governancealive.com
- *Holacracy One*: www.holacracy.org

Consensus and the Burden of Added Process: Are There Easier Ways to Make Decisions?

Busting the Myth That Consensus-with-Unanimity Is Good for Communities, Part III

By Diana Leafe Christian

"I need to say something," the consensus trainer interjected. She and other visiting consensus advocates were facilitating a meeting in a real community I'll call Green Meadow. "I can see that one of your biggest problems is trust. You're talking about all these different things you don't agree on, but you really need to work on trusting each other better."

"Get on the stack!" roared one community member, annoyed by the interruption. A few others glared as well. They believed not trusting each other was a *consequence* of their problems, not a cause—one of the unfortunate results of their members' different interpretations of their community purpose. Some members consistently blocked proposals most others wanted in order to protect what they saw as the community's mission. Widespread distrust also resulted from what was seen as disruptive behaviors in meetings by a few people, some of whom were also the consistent blockers.

The annoyed meeting participants wanted to spend *less* meeting time with the blockers, not more. They'd already done too much emotional processing over the years with no visible results. They were "processed out." They wanted instead to use a decision-making method that didn't allow a few members so much power over the group. They believed trust could return only if people could feel hope for the community again.

Others in the meeting, however, agreed completely with the visiting trainer and appreciated her insights. Clearly there was massive distrust at Green Meadow. Clearly the group needed to spend even more emotional process time than they already had. They needed to really *hear* each other—to deeply understand each others' choices, values, and emotional wounds. This, they hoped, would rebuild trust.

Sharp differences had also surfaced when the community first considered the outside facilitators' offer of low-cost facilitation for whatever problems the community wanted to work on. "I'm *not* going to those meetings," snorted one farmer. "Me neither," growled another. Discouraged by the community's three consistent blockers (who had already blocked or tried to block most agricultural proposals), and no longer having the patience to do more processing, which had so far yielded neither mutual understanding nor resolution, few of the farmers or entrepreneurs planned to attend. *(See "Busting the Myth," Part II, Communities #156, Fall 2012.)*

Green Meadow chose its agricultural conflicts as the challenge requiring the most help, and asked two members to communicate this to the visiting facilitators. "Please, no more emotional processing," begged the representatives. They instead wanted the facilitators to ask Green Meadow's most frequent blocker to make a proposal for an agricultural policy she *did* want, so the visiting facilitators could facilitate a community discussion about it.

However, the facilitators didn't do this. Instead, they hosted three special meetings over the weekend devoted to...more emotional processing. Their purpose, they said, was to explore the beliefs, values, and emotional distress of anyone who felt upset about the community's agricultural dilemma. Only half the community, mostly older members, ended up participating in these process meetings. Most farmers, entrepreneurs, and younger members stayed away.

Afterwards the community rift seemed worse. And the frequently blocking member—for whose sole benefit the meetings seemed designed—sat through each one grim-faced and silent, reporting later that she'd been miserable the whole time.

Two Versions of Community Reality?

This tale illustrates what I suspect are at least two different assumptions about the amount of process time people are willing to put into community. And these two assumptions, I suspect, are themselves based on deeper, possibly unconscious, assumptions about why people join community in the first place.

Assumption A: We're willing to put in a lot of emotional process time because the main reason most of us live in community is for a deeper connection with others. Processing emotions in a group is one way to feel connected.

Assumption B: We don't want much process time. Most of us live in community for neighborliness, sustainability/ecological values, and/or changing the wider culture. *Some* of us may want more emotional closeness with others (and are fine with a lot of process time) but most of us don't.

Green Meadow's rift reflects two different assumptions about why people join community in the first place.

Here are some examples of this latter view, first from Oz Ragland, former Executive Director of Cohousing Association of the US:

While theoretically I'd enjoy a deeper connection with all other community members, in actual practice and given the limits of time, I only seek deeper connections with some—my closer friends. Besides, process time in meetings seems a poor way to grow closer compared to working together, sharing meals, and generally having fun together.

Regardless of the advice from consensus trainers to do as much emotional processing as is needed when we get stuck, I don't personally want to live in a therapeutic environment requiring long hours of meeting process. I want to choose when I do processing rather than having it forced on us because we use consensus.

Before Songaia Cohousing was built we spent many hours processing decisions in meetings. However, for some years now, we've used a decision-board rather than taking all proposals to consensus meetings, and it's working well. We're currently exploring ways to apply ideas from Sociocracy and the N Street model as we improve our process.

Lois Arkin, founder, Los Angeles Eco-Village:

I believe that what seems to me like "endless processing" with people you simply want to be congenial neighbors with, lowers the quality of community life, at least for me. Living in community with people who share some of your values does not guarantee close friends. I want to know my neighbors can be depended to help and cooperate in case of emergency, wave and give a friendly smile in passing, loan ingredients for a recipe, or just hang out with in the garden—people I enjoy working with. Mostly though, given time constraints, this is enough for those of us committed to deep and rapid change on the planet.

Steve Torma, President, Earthaven Ecovillage, North Carolina:

When you're creating all the physical and social infrastructure an ecovillage requires, especially when you have people with as widely diverse viewpoints as we do, consensus-with-unanimity doesn't make sense. We're not small and close-knit enough, and we don't have a large enough budget of time, money, and energy for the kind of group processing that consensus requires.

The community members boycotting the meetings believed that a high level of emotional processing was not only unnecessary, but onerous.

I believe the facilitators visiting Green Meadow and the community members who attended their process meetings held Assumption A about community—"We live in community for relationship and connection"—and therefore also believed that a fairly high amount of emotional processing was necessary and desirable for a well-functioning community.

And I think the community members who boycotted the meetings held Assumption B—they joined community for other reasons, including mostly (in their case) to create a sustainable village. And they therefore also believed that a fairly high level of emotional processing was not only unnecessary, but onerous.

"Added Process Overhead"—Unrealistic for Most Communities?

If I'm correct about these two assumptions, it may explain why communitarians who hold Assumption A believe consensus decision-making, which often requires huge amounts of process time, helps communities—and why those who hold Assumption B, like me, believe that using consensus often harms communities.

As you may know, many community-based consensus trainers advocate consensus because they believe it creates more harmony, trust, and connection than majority-rule voting or top-down leadership.

I now believe consensus—as practiced in most intentional communities—*may* create more harmony, trust, and connection than if they used majority-rule voting (because of "tyranny of the majority") or than if they used one-leader-decides (because of such concentrated power), but using consensus can *also* lead to disharmony, distrust, lower morale, and dwindling meeting attendance (because of "tyranny of the minority").

In contrast, three newer methods—Sociocracy, Holacracy, and the N Street Consensus Method—*do* seem to foster more community harmony and well-being.

In this article series I've criticized what I call "consensus-with-unanimity"—when everyone but those standing-aside must support the proposal for it to pass, with no recourse if someone blocks. In contrast, community-based consensus trainers who've responded to these articles *do* advocate recourse for blocking, such as (1) having criteria for a valid block (and a way to test it), or (2) requiring meetings between blockers and proposal advocates to create a new version of the blocked proposal.

However, in this article I'm using the term "consensus" to include when it's used with *or* without recourse if someone blocks, because I'm questioning whether the rather strict and specific requirements for a group to even use consensus in the first place—including its "added process overhead"—are realistic for most groups.

Pre-1980s Communities and the Hunger for More Relationship

For me, the light bulb went on when I read the following observations by community-based consensus trainer Laird Schaub in his responses to this article series *(italics are mine)*:

• "the hunger for more relationship in one's life *is one of the key reasons most people are drawn to community living."*

• "the fundamental challenge of cooperative groups...(is) to disagree about non-trivial matters *and have the experience bring the group closer."*

• "I see what we're attempting in community (resolving non-trivial differences in a fundamentally different way than happens in the mainstream) *to be one of the crucial things that intentional communities have to offer the wider society."*

• [using a decision-making method other than consensus may be] *"learning to settle for members being less involved in one another's lives."*

• "I am saddened by the choice *to accept less when you'd rather have more."*

• "I find it far more inspiring to offer hope for getting...better relationships than advising folks to *downsize their dreams."*

Laird's comments helped me realize there may be different underlying assumptions about community, relative to the quest for more relationship, because I and many other communitarians I know have a different view.

I agree that some people do join communities mostly to experience deeper relationships and are willing to put in the time required. But I don't think most people join for this reason. Most cohousers and ecovillagers I know seem to have other reasons for living in community. *(See sidebar, "So Why* Do *Cohousers and Ecovillagers Live in Community."*

Some people join communities mostly to experience deeper relationships, but I don't think most people join for this reason.

In fact, I suspect that people who might have what I'm calling Assumption A joined intentional communities formed in the 1980s and earlier. And I suspect Assumption B folks mostly live in communities founded after the 1980s, and this includes cohousers and most ecovillagers.

Please note that the two assumptions are not opposite or widely divergent, but just different points on a continuum. Each places different degrees of emphasis on the importance of wanting more relationship, more connection, and more "community" in one's life. And thus each represents different degrees of willingness to spend many hours processing emotions in meetings. And each assumption has implications, I believe, for whether slogging through consensus decision-making and its associated process time is worth it, or whether trying less time-consuming but equally fair methods—such as Sociocracy, Holacracy, or the N Street Consensus Method—may appeal more.

New Hope at Green Meadow

After nearly 18 years of conflict, heartbreak, and demoralization (*see "Busting the Myth," Parts I and II,* Communities *#155 and #156, Summer and Fall 2012)*—and with increasing numbers of members clamoring for a new decision-making method—in the fall of 2012 Green Meadow modified its consensus process.

To choose incoming new members they retained their previous method: consensus-with-unanimity with no recourse if someone blocked.

For all other proposals except annual election of officers (*see below)* they added criteria for a valid block and a way to test blocks against that criteria (i.e., a block is declared invalid if 85 percent of members in the meeting say it's invalid).

For any remaining blocks that have been declared valid, they use an adaptation of the N Street Consensus Method. *(See "The N Street Consensus Method,"* COMMUNITIES *#157, Winter 2012.)* To deal with these blocks they organize up to three solution-oriented meetings in which blockers and one or two proposal advocates are asked to co-create a new proposal to address the same issues as the first one. If they cannot do this, the original proposal comes back to the next meeting. While the group originally sought an 85 percent supermajority vote to approve any original proposals that came back, their most-frequent blocker only agreed not to block the whole proposal (as everyone feared she might) only *if* this part was changed to consensus-minus-one, so they did.

To choose officers in their annual meeting, Green Meadow adapted a technique from Sociocracy: a transparent and collaborative series of "go-rounds" to nominate and choose people for these roles. In their annual meeting in December 2012, community members cautiously tried this out. Many were nervous; in previous years these elections were characterized by hostility, contempt, and outright character assassination. However, the meeting went well. Each person around the circle described how the skills, experience, and relevant qualities of the person they nominated qualified that person for the officer role. In subsequent go-rounds people asked questions of the candidates, with potential solutions for various people's concerns built into the questions. Hearing all these solutions and getting a sense of what the most number of people most wanted to do seemed to generate a sense of confidence and good will. The officers were elected with people feeling good about it, and feeling good about each other. And, maybe, feeling some trust again.

Diana Leafe Christian, author of the books Creating a Life Together *and* Finding Community, *is publisher of* Ecovillages, *a free online newsletter about ecovillages worldwide (EcovillageNews.org). She is a trainer in GEN's Ecovillage Design Education (EDE) program, and speaks at conferences, offers consultations, and leads workshops internationally. See www.DianaLeafeChristian.org.*

So Why *Do* Cohousers and Ecovillagers Join Community?

Here's why I think cohousers and ecovillagers choose community, based on conversations with many of these folks over the years:

• Friendly relationships with neighbors—the old-fashioned neighborliness and helpfulness of former generations—instead of the more isolated, anonymous experience of mainstream culture. Feeling good about spending more time listening to each other's differing views, helping make sure people feel heard, and devoting process time to resolving differences amicably than people do in mainstream culture. But not valuing this so much that they're willing to spend the amount of process time in meetings that Laird and other consensus trainers often recommend.

• More safety for raising children and in elder years; having the assurance, comfort, and ease of finding help nearby when needed.

• The satisfaction of working with friends and neighbors on community projects and achieving shared community goals.

• *(For ecovillagers and many cohousers)* Living sustainability values in daily life; creating a smaller ecological footprint than is usually possible in mainstream life.

• *(For ecovillagers)* Learning and living ecological, social, and economic sustainability, and then inspiring and teaching others through onsite workshops and tours.

—D.L.C.

Resources

Consensus:

- *On Conflict and Consensus*, C.T. Butler, available for free download on his website: www.consensus.net
- *Consensus-Oriented Decision-Making*, Tim Hartnett (New Society Publishers, 2011): consensusbook.com
- "Laird's Commentary on Community and Consensus": communityandconsensus.blogspot.com

N Street Consensus Method:

- "How the 'N Street Consensus Method' Helps N Street Cohousing Thrive," COMMUNITIES #157, Winter 2012

Sociocracy:

- *We the People: Consenting to a Deeper Democracy, A Guide to Sociocratic Principles and Methods*, by John Buck and Sharon Villines (2007): www.sociocracy.info
- Sociocracy Consulting Group: sociocracyconsulting.com
- Video, "A Tale of Sociocracy," by members of Lost Valley community, Oregon: sociocracyconsulting.com—click "Resources," then "Videos," scroll down to the fourth video.

Holacracy:

- *Holacracy One*: www.holacracy.org

With Arms Spread Wide with Love

By Arjuna da Silva

When Earthaven was in its infancy, we were eager to learn encouraging songs and aphorisms to help us on our way to achieving our community dreams. One in particular I remember goes like this: "Sometimes I just spread my arms, wide like wings, breathe deep, and sing for my life, sing for the Earth, sing, sing, sing!" Singing for our lives and our Earth, we'd spread our arms wide and feel the love.

Some years later, a cofounder who no longer participates in community activities sent me a greeting card I actually framed. It's a Robert Andreas design, with two odd, colorful characters, hands and hearts connected, and a text that reads: "In those days, we finally chose to walk like giants and hold the world in arms grown strong with love...and there may be many things we forget in the days to come, but this will not be one of them." It's the purpose of this article to nudge those arms (mine and yours) just a little wider, maybe open them again after a sad while, and rekindle the excitement the intentional, consensus community vision is all about.

When Consensus Is a Wall You Can't Get Through

My community, like so many others in the industrialized world, has been working on how to cope with its vision of collaborative, inclusive consensus decision-making and its members' habits of debate-oriented, competitive individualism.

Only recently, after more than two years of seemingly fruitless discussion and argument, we agreed to approve a new policy for working with "blocks" (a term we might be wiser to call "unmet needs," now that we understand ourselves a little better). Sometimes, of course, a block keeps us from rushing over a cliff, or later turns out to have led to a better and not even oppositional outcome, but sometimes blocks (and blockers) just feel like a painful load of mental and emotional work.

From the point of view of folks who see no problem with their own intentions and proposals, someone "standing in the way" of approving their proposal needs to be talked down or out of their opposition. I mean, really, how often can folks say their intentions include listening deeply and with caring to the concerns of others about what *they* want to do? And when we can't please a blocker with our compromises, isn't it all too easy to fall into the trap of pegging them as someone who just has a bug up their butt?

From the point of view of someone whose block or unmet need (say, for clarity or caution) is up against others' hopelessness or just plain resistance to working through those concerns—and, if necessary, giving up some ground—that resistance is just more of the same old politics we thought we'd come to community to get away from. We have lived through this kind of tension and stalemate in my community more than once, and we don't yet know if our laborious journey coming up with a new plan for working things out will bring enough satisfaction. Nonetheless, we've decided to follow up blocks with a carefully monitored series of "solution oriented meetings" followed by an in-depth evaluation of the process, giving us a chance to learn how to be more reasonable, to help us work things out as consensus *builders*, not just consensus seekers.

That we decided to come to this outcome, even though it includes a last-ditch option of consensus-minus-one (or "soft consensus," as we called it initially), if we aren't able to find the solutions in all those meetings, means we overcame our habit of taking sides on issues and focused, *despite* our original preferences, on the essential question: what will work for this group of people?

Unity and the Yearning for Autonomy

In the years since we first started struggling with our different styles and opinions, we've taken on a whole battery of methodologies to help us through the fog and storm. We've learned Nonviolent Communication practices, we've dabbled with Worldwork, some of us explored the DISC Communication Style Profile, we're working with Restorative Circles, we've got a Peace Team, a group of "Firetenders" to help us cope with community hot spots—and now we've agreed that if we can't come to consensus after a series of solution oriented meetings, we'll accept consensus-minus-one, if it comes to that. I feel surprised and a bit proud that the current core group of members who manage our Council and Committee work for us have chosen to turn a new page.

All this effort to hold to the original vision that "Yes, we *can* be extremely inclusive with each other" clearly demonstrates that most of us still want to learn how to *build* consensus. Perhaps we'll soon decide (as Tim Hartnett suggests in his "Thinking Flexibly" article, COMMUNITIES #157) that we'll come closest to our vision if we use consensus-based processes to work things through and then a formal, less-than-perfect consensus-minus-something for decision making in the pinch. Or maybe it's not "less than perfect"; maybe even unity needs a shadow of a doubt. Perhaps our community's transition from youthfulness to maturity is when we discover that indeed (Hartnett again) if a prevailing widespread disagreement over a block festers and becomes "toxic to morale," we need stop-gaps and other ways and levels at which to work on our ability to unify.

Maybe "consensus-minus-something" is not "less than perfect"; maybe even unity needs a shadow of a doubt.

As we go through the coming years as Earthaven Council members, drawing aspects of Sociocracy into our process so the yearning some members feel for greater autonomy might also be satisfied, we will need to do much more to evaluate how each piece of the puzzle is working out, to stay on top of the "atmosphere" of our meetings, and to continue to learn and use methods for improving relationships. So far the blessings of this place, these friends and neighbors, and this opportunity to try life another way, have kept inspiring those of us who stay toward our original twin goals: to live this way, out of the box, and, yes, to be able to offer inspiration, experiential advice, and honest evaluations to other groups and families who set themselves similar challenging goals.

The Quest for Transformation

Thinking about transcending my original understanding of consensus makes me think of the bigger picture—transformation on all levels: cultural (collective) and individual (personal). Among students of spiritual enlightenment, attainment to the state of sublime inner peace (a.k.a. *nirvana*) modeled by our mentors may seem so out of reach as to be pure myth. Long-suffering practices, survival-threatening pilgrimages, tolerance of great violence—some ordeal beyond the imagined capacities of ordinary people seems required for this kind of personal transformation.

Similarly, in the realm of intentional communities, *collective transformation*—for example, the ideal of consensus decision-making—may become so elusive as to appear illusory, so that we want to leave its fruition to folks with more gumption, or to the next generation. Instead we make great efforts to change the way we decide because, basically, we don't want to spend that kind of time working things out with each other. We don't seem to have the magic, the medicine, or the miracle-workers who can show us the way out of this mind-boggling labyrinth. And working through painful discoveries about ourselves "in public" is not what we had in mind when we joined. We came for healing, not distress, but it's distress we encounter when we come face to face with how disagreeable people can be who have decisive things to say about our common resources and risks!

If this is a growing challenge for our communities, perhaps we have come to the next chapter for ICs. It seems a number of us have worked long and hard to achieve a satisfying consensus process, and may be at our wits' ends to bring its demands under control. If people don't become overtly uncooperative, they may simply withdraw their energy. Either way, community wellness falters.

Really, it's awful living in an intentional community and being stuck. Just like half-hearted monks in a monastery, doing our best to follow our agreements, we relegate the Shangri-La of our collective dreams to legend and the archetypal fairy tales that keep us dreaming. Where is the magic solution to our troubles in the annals of the movement's history? Attaining successful, satisfying results ("enlightenment" or "unity") becomes an unattainable ideal. For a growing number of cynical consensus practitioners, consensus itself becomes an unsustainable way for people from diverse spiritual and cultural backgrounds and points of view to get along.

In this case, getting along means calling forth an optimistic spirit so that collaboration can be creative and inspire more of itself. It means studying the deeper layers of meaning of ideas like mutual cooperation and enthusiastic compromise, and how those ideas have been defiled in industrial culture.

Consensing on the Right Side of the Brain

I remember, in the founding days of Earthaven, carrying out our intention to find consensus by approaching certain challenging topics from the right rather than the left sides of our brains. We used prayer, divination, ritual, or prolonged periods of meditation to seek guidance from beyond the limitations of our discursive minds. We did this several times, and each time this more receptive approach worked out well. On top of the time we saved going straight for answers without deliberating or debating them, we'd have a great time! Of course, in those days, we must have been less diverse, for we didn't have any vocal naysayers regarding this kind of woo-woo way of reasoning.

One example of this was working out the Permaculture Site Plan for the hundreds of acres we'd gained stewardship of. While considering the zones and sectors of our regenerating forest, the conversation came to ridge top development. With several ridges within our boundaries, it was inevitable some folks would start dreaming of perching on one in order to access one of the rare distant views in our narrow valley. At the time, though, we were still basking in the glow of "founders' joy," and once we saw the tug-of-war that might ensue on this issue, we decided to take a spirit journey together to see what we could see. ("Founders' joy" manifested for us as the shared, even giddy sense that a lucky star had brought us together with a noble project headed for success, and that this star would protect us from mischief and malcontent.)

Drums and toning and guided relaxation followed by an invitation to shape-shift on an inner journey must have taken a good 20 or 30 minutes of our meeting time. When we reported back, one woman told us of seeing through the eyes of a big bird, flying over its mountain home. She could feel this *native* being beseeching us to stay off the ridges, upon which its winged cousins look as they tour the local skies. Through their eyes, it was easy to imagine the scarring even permaculture-style development could cause if we agreed to go up that far. I remember the room becoming completely silent as we all saw with that bird's vision, and felt deeply the consensus that we would not build on ridge tops, which we have neither done nor ever regretted not doing.

One big problem with "founders' joy," however, is that it can obscure the need to prepare for the challenges of diversity, generational disjuncts, relational upsets, disagreements about the meanings of things—the true grit of community experience, because morale hangs in the bargain. It would be easy, now, with 20/20 retrospective vision, to give sound advice to folks starting out about what not to postpone. Once in the midst of difficulties, though, even more so than in marriage, the thing is to keep going toward the possibility of reconfirmation of commitment, with the potential for a second honeymoon down the road (they do happen, you know!).

You'll have to check in with this magazine again, probably about a year from now, to find out how we've done with some of our new policies. (Of course, you can also get in touch and ask!) Having recently begun choosing officers of our corporation (we call them Weavers) with a method we adapted from Sociocracy, already many are saying they've had a surprisingly positive experience dealing with our diverse needs for good leadership. Small signs of hopefulness are everywhere!

If we don't give up on consensus either—if we keep our eyes on its essentials, namely working through trust issues, communicating empathetically, taking the time to hear each other's true stories—we might be able to solve the dilemmas of our diversity with much needed patience, humor, and some good old-fashioned inner work. It takes a lot of time and attention to build community from the ground up, and discouragement hits us all from time to time. We want to give up, but we've already come this far! We don't want to face our own ego limitations, but if we don't, we cause suffering to ourselves and others.

If we let our troubles lead us to a deeper understanding of human nature, I'll bet we can find out how to be the builders we started out to be of a transformed, significantly inclusive culture. ❧

Arjuna da Silva is an inveterate optimist, certified alchemical hypnotherapist, group facilitator, and visionary. She lives in a beautiful, mostly hand-built home at Earthaven Ecovillage (www.earthaven.org), and offers classes locally in the mystical system called The Enneagram of Conscious Being. She can be reached at arjuna@earthaven.org.

Saying Goodbye to Consensus-with-Unanimity in European Communities

Busting the Myth that Consensus-with-Unanimity Is Good for Communities, Part IV

By Diana Leafe Christian

"Holacracy works so much better for Schoenwasser Ecovillage than consensus."
—Ronald Wytek, Schoenwasser Ecovillage, Austria

As those who've read previous installments in this articles series may know, I no longer believe that consensus, as practiced by most intentional communities, is an optimal governance or decision-making method, or that it actually fosters greater harmony, trust, and connection, as promised by consensus trainers. Instead, I believe most communities that use consensus are hobbled by this choice and experience more conflict as a result. (For why I think this is true, see "Busting the Myth" Parts I, II, and III in COMMUNITIES #155, #156, and #158.)

In the last few years several European communities created modified versions of consensus. The modified methods still embody inclusion, equivalence, and transparency, and now seem more effective and efficient as well. And these communities report liking their modified methods a lot more. I'll describe three such communities below.

Other European communities have switched to other methods of governance and decision-making method entirely, with similarly good results, as also noted below.

Modifying Consensus for More Harmony, Trust, and Connection

L'Arche de Saint Antoine, France. Housed in a 900-year-old former Catholic seminary, this spiritual community is located in the small medieval village of L'Abbaye de Saint Antoine near Valance. It's one of the network of income-sharing L'Arche ("ark") communities in France established by 20th-century Christian mystic and Gandhi scholar, Lanzo del Vasto. L'Arche de Saint Antoine's 21 adult members run a successful 90-bed conference center business, hosting over 80 groups and 3,000 visitors a year. I visited this unique "medieval" community in June 2012.

Early in its history L'Arche members modified their consensus process to use a smaller decision rule than unanimity for some of their decisions, and unanimity or 100 percent for more significant decisions. Here are their decision-rule percentages:

- Proposals in committee meetings: 66 percent supermajority vote
- Proposals in monthly business meetings: 75 percent
- Approving provisional members: 100 percent/unanimity
- Approving new full members: 100 percent/unanimity
- Electing their Director: 100 percent/unanimity
- Changing their bylaws: 100 percent/unanimity

Kommune Niederkaufungen, Germany. Kommune Niederkaufungen is a large, successful secular income-sharing community I had the pleasure to visit in August 2011. Founded in 1986 in the small village of Niederkaufungen, the community has 60 members, who live and work in seven large adjacent timberframed houses. Their community-owned businesses include a seminar center, catering service, woodworking business, car-repair business, welding shop, daycare facility for elders, a private holistic kindergarten, and several other businesses. When I was there some people had concerns about their consensus decision-making process, which they'd used for the last 24-plus years. I did a short presentation about N Street Cohousing community's modified consensus method, and am delighted they incorporated some aspects of this method into their new consensus process. Here is an excerpt from their report on their new method:

"When we couldn't reach consensus on a proposal, whatever policy was currently in place remained in place, reflecting the conservative principle of consensus. One person, through the right to veto a proposal, could stop the community from changing something everyone wanted to change. Thus that person had power over the whole group. As a result, some community members withdrew from the decision-making process altogether."

In June 2012, the community agreed to test a new modification of their consensus method. At the end of the two-year trial period they'll decide if they want to continue using it.

Here's how it works:

First, they added the option of standing aside to their previous two options of approving or blocking a proposal. As an attempt to create a better balance between those who wanted change and those who wanted things to stay the same, they strengthened the position of those who wanted change, and now a block doesn't stop a proposal. Rather they use consensus-minus-three (meaning it takes four blocks to stop a proposal).

The following five steps of their new method apply to all proposals except to approving new incoming members, which still requires *everyone's* approval.

Step One—Proposal Presented, Opinions Sampled: Written proposals are posted on the community notice board in the dining room two weeks before the plenary meeting where it will be decided. A week later, the proposal is read out loud during the plenary meeting as being up for decision for the following week.

Step Two—Expressing Concerns, Objections: If in this first meeting someone raises an existential objection to the proposal, they are asked to explain their objection. (By "existential objection" they mean a basic, foundational objection to the proposal that is more significant than simply how to implement the proposal.) Others express their opinions about the proposal too. If, during this first plenary meeting, people have pressing questions or concerns about the proposal, the proposal's advocates will attempt to clarify or modify the proposal during the following week.

Step Three—Testing for Consensus: In the following week's plenary meeting the facilitator tests for consensus by asking if there are any stand-asides or blocks.

If there are any blocks, the next two cycles of their normal small work groups/discussion groups are set aside for continued conversations about the proposal in order to create a proposal acceptable to everyone. If this doesn't bring agreement, someone in the small work group can call for the fourth step.

Step Four—Solution-Oriented Meetings: Those expressing criticism or vetoing the proposal choose two or three other members to participate in up to six solution-oriented meetings in up to two months' time in order to discuss the issue further and arrive at a decision which can be accepted by all. "We consider it a moral duty to the commune to participate in these meetings if one is asked to," they write. Any support which might help, such as another member facilitating the meetings, or using representatives in discussion, is offered on behalf of the community as a whole.

Step Five—Supermajority Vote: If no agreement can be reached after six small-group meetings in a two-month period, a decision of all members is called for on the original proposal. This is announced two weeks in advance and a written survey of opinion is posted on the notice board. The decision is called for in the following plenary meeting. The proposal is adopted if there are no more than three blocks (that is, four or more blocks are needed to reject the proposal). If there are four or more blocks the proposal is not adopted and the group continues the existing agreement or policy.

"We hope that we will now have better-quality decisions and more satisfaction with them, and we can reach agreement more often than in the past," they write. "At the same time, we hope to develop solutions that come as close to consensus as possible in situations in which we are not likely to reach full agreement."

After they use their new decision-making method for a year and a half, they'll evaluate it and decide whether they want to continue using it, modify it, or return to the more conventional consensus method they used before.

Sieben Linden, Germany. Sieben Linden is a large, successful, independent-income ecovillage on 203 acres of farmland outside the small town of Poppau in the former East Germany. One of the leading communities in GEN-Europe, it has 140 residents, who earn incomes through various private businesses and social enterprises. Some run a book printing and distributing company, publishing *Eurotopia*, the European version of the *Communities Directory*, among other books. Others teach strawbale construction or Gaia Education's Ecovillage Design Education (EDE) course. Others work as employees in the community-owned conference center business. I was delighted to finally see this famous ecovillage in August 2011.

Changing their decision-rule. Before they revised their consensus method, Sieben Linden often had what they called "lukewarm" decisions, when rather large percentages of members had strongly held views and feelings about different sides of an issue (for example, vegans' and omnivores' differing views about the issue of whether to farm with livestock). So, since everyone knew that controversial proposals would certainly be blocked, the only proposals that could pass were those which solved a problem in ways that no one really wanted much but nobody would block either.

Of course this meant they originally had far too much blocking. One evening during an informal talk I gave about governance and decision-making, I asked if they'd ever had too much blocking. People shook their heads. "No," several said. Yet one of their longtime members said she had been so demoralized by all the blocking they formerly had that she would have left the community—but stayed because her kids loved living there.

So in the early 2000s Sieben Linden modified their consensus process to specifically address these issues.

Like L'Arche de Saint Antoine and Kommune Niederkaufungen, they still use the consensus *process* itself, but they changed their decision rule to four decision options and a supermajority vote.

Their decision options are: (1) Support the proposal. (2) Stand aside. (3) Do not support the proposal. (If a person hasn't read it, doesn't know enough about it, can't decide, or has no opinion, but doesn't want to stop it either.) (4) Block.

They ask for a show of hands for each of the four options: supporting the proposal, standing aside, not supporting the proposal, and blocking, and require a 75 percent supermajority vote to pass a proposal. Thus a proposal passes only under two conditions: (1) more than 75 percent support it, and (2) there are no vetoes (blocks).

If, for example, enough people had no opinion or didn't like the proposal much or stood aside, there'd be less than 75 percent supporting it. It would be a so-so proposal and it wouldn't pass—too "lukewarm." But when 75 percent actively want a proposal, it passes.

Unless there's a block.

Blocks at Sieben Linden. If there is just one block, the person who blocked must meet with the person who brought the proposal and other, more neutral people—maybe six to eight people total—in solution-oriented meetings, like at N Street Cohousing and Kommune Niederkaufungen. The purpose of the meetings are to co-create a new proposal to bring to the next monthly meeting.

If this doesn't happen, the original proposal comes back and can be passed if 75 percent support the proposal. Thus the block is overruled and the proposal passes.

If there are two or more blocks, they use the same process. However, if no new proposal is created in the solution-oriented meetings, they just continue meeting for awhile. But if the small group cannot create a new proposal, the block stands and the proposal does not pass.

Choosing Committee Members. Sieben Linden members were getting tired of the time-consuming process of monitoring committee decisions in the monthly meetings too. Too many people were monitoring and/or deciding too many things—it was wearing them out. "Is there a way we could just trust our committees to just do their job and then leave them alone do it?" Here's how they also revised their committee system.

They reserve the monthly whole-community meetings for big-picture policy decisions only, delegate all other items to their five committees, and (through a ballot nomination process) *choose* each member of each of their five big committees—and then wholly trust the committee members to do a good job of carrying out each committee's duties and spending its allocated budget money without oversight.

This means that unlike most communities, they no longer allow any community member to volunteer to join a committee. Rather, they specifically *elect* the community members they most trust for each specific committee. Then it's easy to trust each committee and just let them do their jobs. It's like a community's new-member selection process carried out at the committee level.

Their ballot nomination process is based on each Sieben Linden member's opinion of each other member's level of maturity, skill, and experience relative to the required responsibilities and tasks of each committee. (When I first heard this my jaw dropped. It's so *radical*—communities don't *do* things like this. But I now think it's an excellent idea, and advocate this process in my workshops.)

When it's time to elect committee members, everyone gets a ballot which lists all Sieben Linden members with blank nomination boxes for each of the five committees after each name.

	Settlement Cooperative *(land co-op legal entity)* Property and infrastructure co-ownership	**Land Use and Building Policy** Neighborhood development, new buildings, etc.	**Social** Process, communication, group dynamics (including sub-committee on membership)	**Food** *(non-exempt nonprofit)* Food: purchase, storage, preparation	**Circle of Friends** *(tax-deductible nonprofit)* Sieben Linden Educational Center workshops and courses; newsletter
Member A			X		X
Member B					
Member C					X
Member D	X				
Member E					
Member F					
Member G			X		
Member H					
etc., for all 100 adult members					

Each Sieben Linden member gets to nominate five people for each committee, putting a check mark in the box next to each of the five people they believe will be the best to serve on that particular committee. The members who get the most nominations for any given committee are asked to serve on that committee.

People can let others know ahead of time that they'd like to serve on a particular committee. They can also decline to serve on a committee if they're chosen. And not everyone who wants to serve on a particular committee necessarily gets enough nominations to do so. Two Sieben Linden members told me they wanted to be on certain committees but didn't get on because they didn't get enough nominations.

(Of Sieben Linden's five committees, three are their own legal entities—one co-op and two nonprofits. All Sieben Linden members are members of these three legal entities, yet only those who are elected serve on the committee in an official capacity.)

I'm impressed with this method because it empowers committees—and thus the whole community—and reverses what happens when different people distrust a committee or certain people on it. When this happens there can be *retroactive* blocking of committee decisions after publication of committee minutes. This can result in committee members getting burned out, demoralized, ceasing to meet for awhile, and/or committee members quitting in disgust. Then the community loses valuable experience, expertise, and labor for needed tasks. And/or the tasks just don't get done at all. This happened several times at the community I've called "Green Meadow" in this article series. Ouch! (See previous articles in Summer 2012, Fall 2012, and Spring 2013 issues.)

Changing to Newer Governance and Decision-Making Methods

Some European communities stopped using consensus altogether and switched to newer methods.

Sociocracy, developed in the Netherlands in the 1970s, and Holacracy, developed in the US in the early 2000s, are each whole-systems governance methods which include a decision-making process. (Governance is how a group organizes its flow of work, money, and information, and is more comprehensive than simply a way to make decisions.) In both Sociocracy and Holacracy everyone has a voice in modifying and approving proposals and everyone's consent is required to pass a proposal. However, unlike in consensus, decisions can be changed easily, which means there is far less pressure to make a "perfect" decision. Decisions need only be "good enough for now" and can easily be changed again with experience or new information. This seems to liberate energy, optimism, creativity, and freedom to try new things. Both methods have a collaborative, win/win decision-making process which doesn't allow the kinds of power-over dynamics that can occur with consensus-with-unanimity and no recourse if someone blocks. Both methods, when used correctly, tend to generate a sense of connection, trust, and well-being in the group.

ZEGG is a 35-year-old community in Belzig, Germany, and founders of the ZEGG Forum process, which, like L'Arche and Sieben Linden, run a conference and seminar business. ZEGG switched from consensus to Holacracy in 2010.

Schoenwasser Ecodorf, a forming ecovillage in Zurndorf, Austria, switched to Holacracy in 2010. They also use Systemic Consensus, a new mathematics-based decision-making method developed by two systems analysts at the University of Graz.

In Systemic Consensus the group develops and discusses proposals just as in the consensus process; however, when it's time to make the decision, each group member expresses their amount of resistance to the proposal through a point scale of 0 to 10. Its founders, Professors Erich Visotschnig and Siegfried Schrotta, say that using this point scale to indicate the felt-sense of resistance to a proposal allows people to express a gradient of support for a proposal, which more closely matches how people really feel about proposals instead of only being able to choose between supporting, not supporting, or standing aside from a proposal. For more about Systemic Consensus, see the online article, "Systemic Consensus: Fast, Visual, and Hard to Argue With."

Other European communities that switched to Sociocracy or used it from the beginning include Bridgeport Cohousing, England; Centraalwonen Cohousing, De Doortzetters Cohousing, and Bergen Ecovillage in The Netherlands; Les Choux Lents Cohousing in France; and Ecovila KanAwen in Spain. Two communities in Australia, Blue Mountain Cohousing and Narara Ecovillage, chose Sociocracy from the beginning.

In the US, Lost Valley Educational Center/Meadowsong Ecovillage in Oregon switched from consensus to Sociocracy in 2010. (See "Sociocracy: A Permaculture Approach to Community Evolution," Winter 2011 issue, #153.) Katywil Cohousing in Massachusetts, Green Haven Cohousing in Connecticut, and Ecovillage at Loudon County in Virginia all used Sociocracy from the beginning. And Dancing Rabbit Ecovillage in Missouri is now considering the Town Meeting method, in which eight elected representatives will make decisions previously made by consensus in whole-community meetings.

In the Fall 2013 issue we'll look at how the Sociocracy governance and decision-making system works, which North American communities now use it, and how it's working for them.

Diana Leafe Christian, author of the books Creating a Life Together *and* Finding Community, *is publisher of* Ecovillages, *a free online newsletter about ecovillages worldwide (EcovillageNews.org). She is a trainer in GEN's Ecovillage Design Education (EDE) program, and speaks at conferences, offers consultations, and leads workshops internationally. See www.DianaLeafeChristian.org.*

Resources

- *Consensus-Oriented Decision-Making,* Tim Hartnett (New Society Publishers, 2011): consensusbook.com
- N Street Consensus Method: "How the 'N Street Consensus Method' Helps N Street Cohousing Thrive" (Communities Winter 2012 issue, #157—or Google the online article, "Is Consensus Right for Your Group? Part I")
- "Sociocracy: A Permaculture Approach to Community Evolution," Melanie Rios (Communities Winter 2011 issue)
- *We the People: Consenting to a Deeper Democracy, A Guide to Sociocratic Principles and Methods,* John Buck and Sharon Villines (2007): www.sociocracy.info
- SocioNet online discussion: www.socionet.us
- The Sociocracy Consulting Group: www.sociocracy-consulting.com
- Videos, "Pioneer Valley Governance," Parts 1 through 4, YouTube.com *(Author Diana Leafe Christian giving a presentation about consensus and Sociocracy at Pioneer Valley Cohousing in February.)*
- *Holacracy One*: www.holacracy.org
- Systemic Consensus: Google online article, "Systemic Consensus: Fast, Visual, and Hard to Argue With"

Community Websites:

- L'Arche de Saint Antoine, France: www.arche-de-st-antoine.com *(French)*
- Kommune Niederkaufungen, Germany: www.kommune-niederkaufungen.de/english-informations *(English)*
- Sieben Linden, Germany: www.siebenlinden.de *(click British flag for English version)*
- ZEGG, Germany: www.zegg.de/english *(English)*
- Schoenwasser Ecodorf, Austria: www.keimblatt.at *(German)*
- Les Choux Lents, France: leschouxlents.potager.org *(French)*
- KanAwen, Spain: www.valldebiert.org *(click "In English")*
- Ecodorp Bergen, The Netherlands: www.ecodorpbergen.nl *(Dutch)*
- Lost Valley Educational Center/Meadowsong Ecovillage, US: lostvalley.org
- Dancing Rabbit Ecovillage, US: www.dancingrabbit.org

Transparency, Equivalence, and Effectiveness

How Sociocracy Can Help Communities, Part I

By Diana Leafe Christian

At first the question stumped me.

I was giving an informal presentation on Sociocracy one morning in a grass-roof-covered building at Findhorn in Scotland. Sociocracy (which means "governance by peers," also called "Dynamic Governance" in the US) is a whole-system self-governance process and a decision-making method. (See *"Sociocracy: A Permaculture Approach to Community Evolution" by Melanie Rios, Winter 2011 issue.*)

The presentation was for the New Findhorn Association (NFA), a network of local friends, neighbors, businesses, nonprofits, and projects influenced by and/or affiliated one way or another with the Findhorn Foundation. Begun in 1962 in a caravan (trailer) park on the coast of northern Scotland, Findhorn was famous originally for its founders' spiritual guidance about working with Nature in its gardens. The Findhorn Foundation, a nonprofit organization founded in 1972 to offer spiritual and ecological education for residents and guests, was the first member of the New Findhorn Association, and integral to the Association's creation in 1999. Together, the Foundation, the New Findhorn Association, and the wider network of Findhorn-affiliated neighbors and friends who live and work nearby are often referred to locally as "the Findhorn Foundation Community," but usually known internationally as simply "Findhorn."

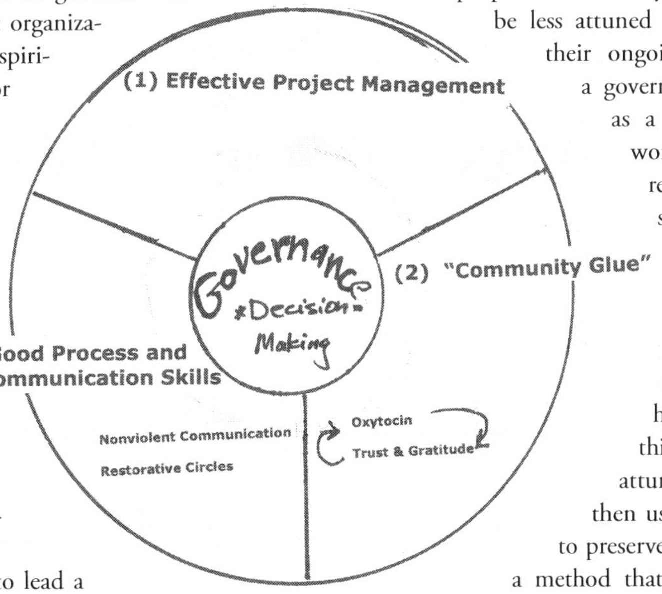

I was asked by the Association to lead a morning workshop introducing Sociocracy to a small group of Council (board) Members. John Buck, the man who introduced Sociocracy to the English-speaking world, had given two Association-sponsored Sociocracy workshops at Findhorn in the last two years, and the group had recently begun using two Sociocracy methods in their meetings. I was invited to give a presentation because, while some Council Members wanted Sociocracy, others felt uncertain about it and newer Council Members hadn't been exposed to it.

The question I wasn't sure how to respond to came from a Council Member who asked if the Association's use of Sociocracy might not diminish the group's spiritual function and impact. Sociocracy, she said, doesn't seem to acknowledge or support the spiritual principles upon which Findhorn was based.

To better understand, I asked if she was concerned that the Association using simply a secular governance and decision-making method like Sociocracy might pull them away from the deeply important spiritual reasons they were there in the first place? Yes, she said, that was her concern.

Suddenly inspired, I said that when people do gardening at Findhorn, besides tuning in to the spirits of the plants, they also use trowels and spade forks—secular tools that nevertheless help them accomplish their spiritual purpose while gardening. And that Sociocracy is similar: it's a tool that can help a group, no matter its purpose, to more easily and harmoniously achieve that purpose. And for any times when a group might be less attuned to each other for awhile, their ongoing use of Sociocracy as a governance method could serve as a safety net to help them work effectively until they returned to a more attuned state again. Smiling again, the Council Member said that's what she wanted.

Another Council Member was skeptical, he said, as he favored the way Findhorn traditionally decides things: taking time to silently attune with each other first and then using consensus. He wanted to preserve democracy and not adopt a method that might reduce fairness or equality. But by the end of the morning he was smiling too, as hearing about the basics of Sociocracy had alleviated his concerns. In fact all the participants were smiling, and me too.

Three Aspects of a Healthy, Thriving Community

This article is about what I see as the benefits of using Sociocracy in communities, especially when compared with using consensus. (See article series, *"Busting the Myth that Consensus-with-Unanimity is Good For Communities," Summer 2012-Summer 2013 issues.*) Part II, in the Winter 2013 issue, will focus specifically on how Sociocracy works.

I recommend Sociocracy for communities and similar organizations because I think that, when practiced correctly, it tends to result in more harmony and good will than using consensus decision-making often does. I see a group's governance process, including its decision-making method, as powerfully influencing and helping manifest what I believe are three crucial and mutually reinforcing aspects of a healthy, thriving community.

One aspect I call ***Community Glue***—taking time to do shared enjoyable activities that tend to generate feelings of gratitude and trust, and which also tend to create the "pleasure hormone" oxytocin. Research shows that oxytocin in the bloodstream generates feelings of trust and gratitude towards the people one is with, although it may be experienced simply as "feeling good." This oxytocin in the bloodstream keeps the "feeling good" going throughout the enjoyable shared activity.

Thus, community meals, shared work tasks, singing, dancing, drumming, playing music, playing games or sports, group meditation, storytelling evenings, describing emotionally meaningful aspects of one's life to friends and colleagues, making decisions together smoothly and effectively, accomplishing community goals—all tend to produce these feelings in the group. And this—the good will, the sense of "us" or "community spirit"—is like having good credit or a "community immune system" of trust and good will. The more trust and good will a community has, the more effectively its members can respond to and resolve conflict when it comes up. When a community draws on abundant community glue, it may be easier to just talk to each other simply and figure out how to resolve things.

A second aspect of a healthy, thriving community, in my opinion, is ***Good Process and Communication Skills***. While this is obvious to most experienced communitarians, the need for these skills becomes obvious sooner or later in newer communities too. By "communication skills," I mean the ways people talk with each other, both in groups and meetings and one on one. By "process skills," I mean the ways members gather together specifically to get to know each other better, consider ideas, understand each others' emotions or upsets, or discuss and resolve conflicts.

Nowadays I recommend what I believe are the two most effective communication and process methods for communities: Nonviolent Communication, a way in which people speak with others that tends to create a sense of connection between people and reduce conflict, and Restorative Circles, a conflict-resolution method similar in some ways to Nonviolent Communication.

The third aspect, ***Effective Project Management***, is obvious to founders of successful communities and cohousing professionals but often less obvious (or even invisible) to more idealistic or countercultural folks. It's comprised of the ways a community creates and maintains its legal entity(s); the ways it finances, purchases, and physically develops its property (including, for example, hiring any outside professional for design or construction work, bookkeeping, website design, or other work); organizes and tracks its internal community finances and member labor requirements; attracts, processes, and orients new members; and maintains the community's documents, policies, and decisions. These are all actions that well-organized businesses or nonprofits use too. Sooner or later members of new communities learn that clear, thorough, well-organized management is necessary not only to found their new community but also to successfully maintain it.

I believe these three aspects of community mutually reinforce each other. If a group has abundant community glue, for example, people will tend to feel connected enough and harmonious enough so that most of the time they'll get along well and not need to speak so carefully, and will probably need less conflict resolution as well. But if a group's reserve of community glue is low—perhaps because they don't yet realize how important it is or don't have enough time to schedule enjoyable group activities often enough—they may have to choose their words more carefully, and may need to resolve conflicts more formally and more frequently.

Similarly, if a group has effective project management, the sense of accomplishment they'll feel when people experience the community moving towards its goals can create more community glue—increasing their feelings of trust and gratitude and thus reducing their need for super-careful ways of speaking and more frequent conflict resolution sessions. But if a community is managed poorly—for example, if they miss important opportunities; experience unexpected or un-prepared-for legal

The Universal Hall at the Findhorn Community, Scotland.

Photo courtesy of Findhorn Foundation

Eian Smith

Council Members of the New Findhorn Association, a network comprising the Findhorn Foundation and affiliated businesses, nonprofits, neighbors, and friends.

problems, bookkeeping snafus, or financial shortfalls; lose documents or records of meeting decisions—this can create anger, resentment, blame, shame, and demoralization, which of course erodes the group's sense of trust and connection. A group in this situation will, once again, need to speak to one another more carefully and will probably need to resolve conflicts more often too.

(I advise groups to go for all three, of course.)

How Effective Governance Helps a Community Thrive

Community governance, in my opinion, is at the center of all three aspects of healthy community—and effective governance benefits and enhances all three. (See figure 1, p. 59.)

By "governance" I mean how the group organizes its time and work tasks, manages its money, and shares its information—along with its decision-making method for deciding these things.

When I ask groups what their method of governance is and they reply "consensus," I assume they're confusing "how" they make decisions with "what" they make them about. Solely decision-making methods such as consensus-with-unanimity, the N Street Consensus Method, majority-rule voting, supermajority voting, etc. don't specify how the group might organize and manage itself or which decisions they might make about this.

A community accomplishes its project management *through* its governance process. Its governance is the *way* it effectively organizes its legalities, finances, building and construction, membership process, work-contribution policy, how it collects and manages its documents, policies, and decisions, and so on. In my opinion, effective governance is at the heart of a healthy community.

This is why I believe using a governance method like Sociocracy* absolutely contributes to the three aspects of a healthy, successful community. Using Sociocracy for community can, in my opinion, not only eliminate some of the unintended consequences of using consensus (as it's practiced in most intentional communities), but also can help a community thrive.

Transparency, Equivalence, and Effectiveness...and the "Three Parents of Sociocracy"

Sociocracy in its modern-day version was created by Dutch electrical engineer, inventor, and cybernetics expert Gerard Endenburg in The Netherlands in the 1970s. As a boy he attended the famous Quaker Community School in The Netherlands, led by the renowned Dutch pacifist Kees Boeke, in which school decisions were made by teachers and students using Quaker-style consensus. After graduating from college Endenburg worked for the Netherlands branch of Philips Electronics, where he invented the flat speaker used in car doors and cell phones.

As mentioned, Endenburg focused on cybernetics, the science of communications and control. Communications and control happens naturally when you ride a bicycle—constantly adjusting to the requirements of whatever's happening, moment by moment. You continuously adjust your body weight over the bicycle frame, adjust the direction of the handlebars, pedal faster or slower, shift gears or apply brakes as you continuously get information about the bike's position in space through your proprioceptive sense and by what you see and hear. Your "feedback loops" are the continuous adjustments you make to keep the bike upright and going towards your destination.

Endenburg also read widely in science, mathematics, and philosophy. He was especially influenced by learning about self-organizing systems, and how everything in nature tends to self-organize...including people. He designed

* I recommend Holacracy as a governance method also, but it tends to be more expensive than Sociocracy to learn. It was designed for businesses and is marketed to them and priced accordingly.

Sociocracy for his company, Endenburg Elektrotechniek, to be a more harmonious organization, based on the values of transparency, equivalence of voice, and effectiveness.

So I like to say Sociocracy has three "parents": Quaker-style consensus (which shows up especially in Sociocracy's "Consent Decision-Making" method; engineering, cybernetics, and feedback loops (used in proposals); and Nature, especially self-organizing systems (reflected in its "circles and double-links" governance method). (*Part II of this article will cover governance using Circles and Double-Links and the Consent Decision-Making method.*)

"Plan-Implement-Evaluate" Feedback Loops

Just as we constantly use feedback loops when riding a bike, any engineer will tell us that measuring, evaluating, and learning how a product actually performs in real life, by field-testing it many times, helps ensure it does what it's designed to do and works well. An engineer first plans (designs) the product, then implements the design, measures and evaluates the product once it's made, and modifies it as needed. Thus the developing product responds and adjusts to conditions in reality—which may be quite different than what was anticipated in the planning stage. So, too, for an intentional community. A plan begins as a proposal in a meeting. After approving the proposal or a modified version of it, the group implements the proposal, putting it into effect.

Measuring and Evaluating Proposals

However, when using Sociocracy, there's a third step—measuring and evaluating the implemented proposal, and modifying it if needed. Thus a proposal, when possible, includes the criteria with which it will later be evaluated (including numeric measurement if possible and desirable) and the upcoming dates when the group will do this. *The criteria and future measurement/evaluation dates are included in the text of the proposal itself.* When possible, implemented proposals are considered as modifiable or temporary—an experiment, if you will—as the group can later decide to change it or even dismantle it and go back to what they had before or try something else. (Changing an implemented proposal later is much easier with Sociocracy's "Consent Decision-Making" method than when using consensus, as described in Part II, in the Winter 2013 issue.)

Let's say, for example, a committee wanted to create a library in the community building. So they present a proposal for a set of shelves in a particular location in the community building, and note who will build the shelves, what it will cost and where the money will come from, and who will organize and maintain the library. The proposal might have the following criteria for later evaluating and measuring the project: Do people donate books to the library? Do they check out books? Can they find the kinds of books they want? Do they return books on time and in good condition? Are library volunteers keeping the shelves clean and orderly every week?

At each of the pre-scheduled future meeting dates for evaluating the implemented proposal, the new library project would be evaluated and measured by the members according to these criteria, as well as to any other criteria the group may think of at the time. New criteria can be added to the list for future evaluations. If some aspects of the library aren't working well, such as, say, people aren't returning books on time, the meeting participants doing the evaluation can revise the library policy, perhaps by creating a new way to remind people to return books.

When using Sociocracy, people already know they might modify any future implemented proposal to adjust how it operates in day-to-day reality. Like creative engineers with a project on a drawing board, they know they have to try it under real-life conditions to see how it actually functions before they know it will work.

People can also change the dates of future evaluation times, moving them up, increasing the number of evaluations, decreasing them, stopping them altogether, or adding new evaluation times later, depending on what they find out as they respond to how real circumstances impact their implemented proposal.

"Good enough for now," "Safe enough to try"

Thus, because most proposals can later be modified or removed, community members don't need to "support" or feel they must "approve" the proposal—but simply be willing to try it. A proposal need not be perfect, but merely "good enough for now," "safe enough to try." (While true of most proposals, it's not true of one-time yes/no issues, such as fixing the sudden roof leak or not fixing it. In cases like these the group tries to do the best that can be done to address the immediate need, with the knowledge and resources available. And future evaluations, in this case, of the new roof, can inform future similar decisions.)

The plan-implement-evaluate model and proposals needing to only be "good enough for now" confers three benefits. First, the group can adjust and modify an implemented proposal to stay current with real-life circumstances, like a bicyclist adjusting his or her body over the frame and adjusting the handlebars and pedaling speed to meet existing conditions. Thus an implemented proposal can improve over time, so the various projects and processes of a community can become ever-more effective.

Second, this freedom and flexibility allows a community to try things that they might not normally risk for most proposals, because they can always change it or discard it later.

Third, knowing they can easily change a decision in the future has a beneficial effect on the mood and energy of a meeting, especially when a proposal is complex or controversial, as the group can *relax and feel confident as they consider it.* This is in sharp contrast to the consensus decision-making process, especially when there is a controversial or complex proposal.

"Evaluate and Respond" vs. "Predict and Control"

Any consensus trainer will confirm that consensus is an inherently conservative process because by the very nature of how consensus works it favors whatever agreements the group has already made. While there's no reason that criteria for evaluating/measuring a proposal later and the dates for doing so couldn't be included in a consensus proposal, it's not likely the proposal could be changed easily. Let's say a group using consensus has a complex or controversial proposal to do something new or change something. They may modify the proposal—perhaps multiple times over several meetings—to suit various concerns before everyone (except stand asides) agrees to approve it. However, it may have been so time-consuming and arduous and taken so much negotiation and compromise to finally approve it, that it's difficult for the group to imagine going through all that again in order to change it a few weeks or a few months later. This is why, when considering a proposal in consensus, there's a lot of pressure in the group to "get it right." The pressure is so much worse when a proposal is complex or controversial because it feels like so much is at stake—they'd better get it damn-near perfect right now.

This creates the energy and vibes of "predict and control"—meaning the group has to try to predict how the implemented proposal will play out in real life, and control all the anticipated factors that could come into play ahead of time. When using Sociocracy, however, unlike in consensus, the group need not clairvoyantly predict the future of the implemented proposal and the range of factors that will affect it then. Rather, they only need wait and see what happens and then adjust the decision if need be. Rather than put themselves through the stressful mode of "predict and control" they can relax into the considerably simpler and easier mode of simply waiting to see what happens, evaluate and measure what they find, and then respond appropriately. Thus they need only "evaluate and respond" instead of "predict and control." "Evaluate and respond" rather than "predict and control" removes pressure on the group to make the proposal damn-near perfect.

This, the ability to relax, feel confident, and feel free to try new things and experiment is one of the best reasons for a community to use Sociocracy, in my opinion.

• • •

All this is why I advocate Sociocracy as an effective governance method to help a community thrive.

As noted earlier, Part II, in the Winter 2013 issue, will focus on how Sociocracy works: how communities using Sociocracy organize themselves in circles and double-links, the "consent decision-making" method, how objections are not blocks but gifts to a circle, and why "tyranny of the minority" can't really happen in Sociocracy. It will touch on five meeting processes, from forming new proposals to selecting people for roles, that all use consent decision-making. It will consider the challenges of using Sociocracy incorrectly, what works well and doesn't work for communities in learning and implementing Sociocracy, how consent decision-making is similar to and different from consensus, the facilitation skills and methods common to both, and the similarities and differences between Sociocracy and Holacracy.

Meanwhile, I hear that the New Findhorn Association is continuing to implement Sociocracy in their meetings, and John Buck will teach another Sociocracy workshop there in October. I'm so glad! ❧

Diana Leafe Christian, author of Creating a Life Together *and* Finding Community *and publisher of* Ecovillages *(EcovillageNews.org), speaks at conferences, offers consultations, and leads workshops internationally. A former consensus trainer and now Sociocracy trainer, Diana specializes in teaching Sociocracy to communities, and has taught in the US, UK, Sweden, France, and Quebec. See www.DianaLeafeChristian.org.*

Some Intentional Communities Using Sociocracy

North America: Lost Valley Educational Center, Oregon; Pioneer Valley Cohousing, and Katywil Cohousing, Massachusetts; Green Haven Cohousing, Connecticut; Ecovillage of Loudon County, Virginia; Cohabitat Québec, Quebec City, Quebec.

Europe: Kan Awen Ecovillage, Spain; Les Choux Lents Cohousing, France; Centraal Wonan Cohousing, and Bergen Ecovillage, The Netherlands; Bridport Cohousing, England.

Sociocracy Resources

• Video: "Lost Valley: A Tale of Sociocracy." Youtube.com

• Article: "Sociocracy: A Permaculture Approach to Community Evolution," Melanie Rios, Communities, issue #153, Winter 2011

• Sociocracy.Info: www.sociocracy.info

• The Sociocracy Consulting Group: sociocracyconsulting.com

• Governance Alive: www.governancealive.com

• Sociocracy UK: sociocracyuk.ning.com

• Sociocracy Center in the Netherlands: www.sociocratie.nl

Sociocracy Trainers Who Teach Intentional Communities:

North America: John Schinnerer: john.schinnerer@sociocracyconsulting.com
Jerry Koch-Gonzalez: jerry.koch-gonzalez@sociocracyconsulting.com
Diana Leafe Christian: diana@ic.org

UK: James Priest: jamespriest@thriveincommunity.co.uk

Australia: Gina Price: ginaprice@optusnet.com.au

Self-Governance with Circles and Double Links:

How Sociocracy Can Help Communities, Part II

By Diana Leafe Christian

"This is one way we could re-organize the community," Malin said as she and Maria taped up a large sheet of easel paper with circles and arrows for everyone to see. Malin and Maria are members of Ängsbacka Ecovillage in Sweden, a five-year-old rural retreat and conference center community famous in that country for workshops and large festivals on spiritual/personal growth and ecological sustainability. I was presenting a two-day workshop on Sociocracy (also called "Dynamic Governance" in the US) there in June 2013.

Sociocracy is a whole-system self-governance method with a built-in decision-making process called "Consent Decision-Making" (*covered in* COMMUNITIES *#160, Fall 2013*). Sociocracy is also a method for measuring, evaluating, and, if needed, modifying an implemented proposal to adjust to how the implemented proposal works over time in real circumstances, or to account for changing circumstances, inside or outside of the community.

"The Sociocracy Circle Method" (Sociocracy means "governance by peers") was created by engineer and businessman Gerard Endenburg in the Netherlands in the 1970s. Its purpose is to create harmonious organizations, based on the values of equivalence, transparency, and effectiveness. Endenburg was influenced by Quaker-based consensus; engineering, cybernetics, and feedback loops; and chaos theory and self-organizing systems. Now, 40 years later, many businesses, nonprofits, and schools worldwide—and some intentional communities—use Sociocracy.

At this point in the second day of the Ängsbacka workshop people were applying what they'd learned. A group of participants drew a map of how Ängsbacka could use Sociocracy's circles and double links to become more equivalent, transparent, and effective.

It was clear from how they drew the map—and from people's questions and suggested improvements—that these folks really understood the basics of Sociocracy, and that many were quite enthusiastic about it. As their Sociocracy trainer, I was delighted.

Part I of this article *(Fall 2013)* covered the benefits to a community of using Sociocracy for self-governance—specifically how it can enhance three aspects of a healthy, thriving community: "community glue," process and communication skills, and effective project management. The article also described why including Sociocracy's Plan–Implement–Measure & Evaluate feedback loops in every proposal reduces the need to "predict and control" how the proposal might turn out later. This reduces pressure on community members to try to anticipate all future circumstances that might affect the decision and to keep discussing and negotiating until the proposal becomes "perfect" enough so they can approve it (as is often the case when using consensus). Rather, since decisions in Sociocracy will be examined and possibly changed later, proposals only need to be "good enough for now," or "safe enough to try." Using Sociocracy frees up energy for curiosity, learning by doing, and innovation.

The operative phrase for Sociocracy might well be, "OK...let's find out."

Community Governance vs. Community Decision-Making

Generally speaking, governance—as compared to a decision-making method—determines how a community organizes, coordinates, and tracks its work tasks, available money, and information. *Sociocratic* self-governance is more structured—and, in my opinion, more effective—than the various well-organized, loosely organized, or non-organized decision-making processes used by most intentional communities. Governance is *not* the community's decision-making method. Its governance process focuses

Two participants in the workshop for Ängsbaka Ecovillage in Sweden demonstrating how they would reorganize their community using circles and double links, June 2013.

Diana Leafe Christian

on *which* topics it will consider and decide; its decision-making method is simply *how* it makes these decisions. (As noted above, Sociocratic governance includes a decision-making method—Consent Decision-Making.)

When Sociocracy is used in businesses and nonprofits it offers considerably more equivalence among management and staff than is usually found in these organizations. They not only become more effective, but become considerably more fair, inclusive, and transparent too. And...Sociocracy can help intentional communities—which are usually fairly equivalent and transparent to begin with—to become a great deal more effective and efficient in how they manage their community and achieve their goals.

Sociocracy Circles

The organizational structure of Sociocracy consists of a group of "circles." Circles are semi-autonomous, self-organized groups of people with a specific area of authority and responsibility, whose members are tasked to accomplish a specific "aim" relative to their area of authority and responsibility. Circles are similar to what in intentional communities are called committees or teams, and in businesses are called departments.

Members of a circle make policy decisions for their circle; measure, evaluate, and perhaps modify their already-implemented decisions; keep records of their decisions and other circle business; and plan their own ongoing learning and development related to their area of responsibility.

Sociocracy workshop participants at L'Arche du Saint-Antoine community in France learning about circles and double links by forming them physically with their bodies, April 2013.

Workshop participants at the workshop in France forming circles and double links with small circles and arrows to show Operational Leaders and Representatives.

Typically there is a "General Circle" with several smaller circles linked to it. Members of the General Circle discuss and decide more abstract, longer-term community issues: strategic plans, the annual budget, and large or far-reaching opportunities or challenges. The General Circle also creates each smaller circle and gives each one its specific area of authority and responsibility (called a "domain" in Sociocracy), and allocates money for its budget. General Circles are similar in focus and scope to whole-group plenary meetings in communities. However, they are not large groups comprised of all community members, as we'll see below.

Smaller circles focus on more concrete, specific, and shorter-term issues for the organization. A community's General Circle might create, for example, a Finance Circle, Promotions and Marketing Circle, Membership Circle, Land Use/Site Planning Circle, Repair and Maintenance Circle. *(See illustration #1, p. 63.)*

"Larger and Smaller," "Higher and Lower" Circles

In Sociocratic literature the terms "higher" and "lower" circles are used to describe what I'm calling larger and smaller circles. "Higher" and "lower" do not mean "superior to" and "inferior to." Rather these terms indicate the level of abstraction the circle is responsible for—larger, longer-term issues or more concrete, shorter-term issues. But saying "more abstract, big-picture, longer-term circles" and "more concrete, specific, shorter-term circles" would be long and awkward. In order to prevent awkward phrases or connotations of "better" and "worse" I use the terms "larger" and "smaller." (But these terms are misleading too, since a "smaller" circle can have more members and thus be larger in population than the community's General Circle.)

A community's General Circle not only gives each smaller circle its area of authority and responsibility (domain) and its budget, but also its aim.

The Aim of a Circle

The aim of a circle is the specific physical and nonphysical things (i.e., "services") the circle provides the people it serves—the community as a whole, as well as any visitors it may have, or participants in any community-sponsored classes and workshops. (In businesses a circle's aim is the specific products and/or services it provides the company's customers, or, gives the company itself, such as bookkeeping services.)

The aim of a community's Membership Circle, for example, might be:

Physical things:

- New members—people—and money from any Joining Fees the community may charge.
- Member handbooks.
- Proposals to the General Circle about membership issues that may require more abstract, longer-term thinking.

Nonphysical things (services):

• Perform the tasks necessary to help new people learn about the community and meet its membership requirements (website text, handbooks, orientations, trainings), oversee how they meet the requirements (work hours, fees, community agreements), and manage meetings, interviews, references, and paperwork involved in these processes.

• Help community members meet and learn about the new people.

• Propose new membership categories if or when needed.

The aim of a circle is specific: it prevents the group from working at cross-purposes. It is described in terms of the *result* of the circle's activities, and is tangible; it can be delivered and received. It is the yardstick for measuring the circle's success. The aim is the basis on which circle members evaluate their reasons for being for or against a proposal.

A circle's aim can later be expanded or modified by either the General Circle or the circle itself, based on the circle's experience over time.

(Each circle, and the whole organization, also has a vision and mission. The vision is the better world imagined for in the future—the "why" of the circle or organization. The mission is the big-picture version of the activities to help bring about that future world—the "what" of the circle or organization.)

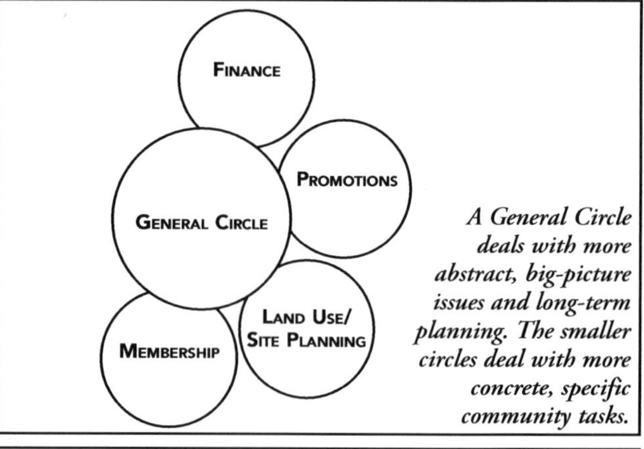

A General Circle deals with more abstract, big-picture issues and long-term planning. The smaller circles deal with more concrete, specific community tasks.

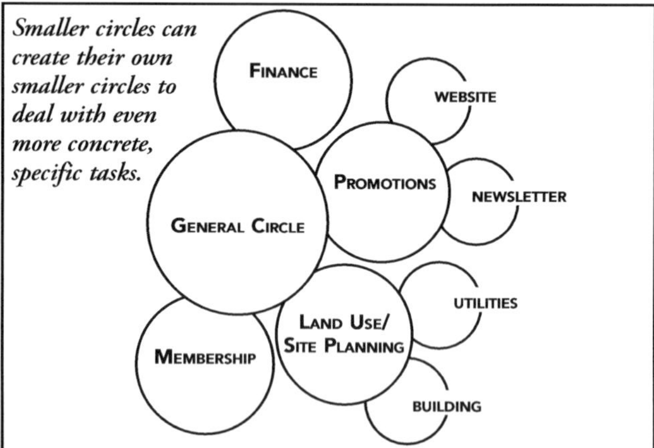

Smaller circles can create their own smaller circles to deal with even more concrete, specific tasks.

Creating Smaller Circles as Needed

A smaller circle can create one or more even smaller circles which have an even more specific focus and handle even more specific kinds of tasks. A Promotions Circle, for example, might create two smaller circles, a Website and Newsletter Circle, with the aim to write and produce these communication services, and a Visitor Circle, with the aim to welcome visitors and conduct community tours.

A Site Planning/Land Use Circle might create a smaller Buildings Circle, with the aim to build and manage community-owned buildings. It might create a Utilities Circle, with the aim to install and manage any community-owned off-grid power systems, water systems, graywater recycling systems, or composting toilets.

(See illustration #2, this page. Note that the circles on the left are more abstract and long-term, and circles on the right are increasingly concrete and shorter-term.)

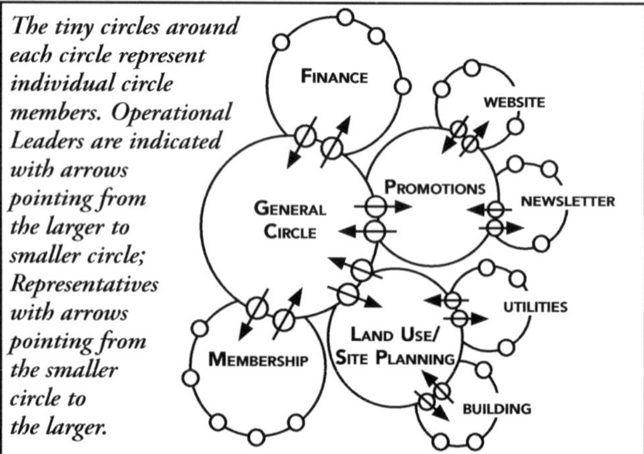

The tiny circles around each circle represent individual circle members. Operational Leaders are indicated with arrows pointing from the larger to smaller circle; Representatives with arrows pointing from the smaller circle to the larger.

Four Roles in a Circle

Each circle has four roles: a Facilitator, a Meeting Manager, an Operational Leader, and a Representative. The Facilitator is selected by the circle members to facilitate meetings, move the agenda forward, and keep everyone focused on the aim of the meeting and the aim of the circle. The Facilitator must understand Sociocracy well in order to remind any occasionally disruptive or misinformed circle members how Sociocracy meetings function properly, using any disruptions as opportunities to educate circle members in Sociocracy's principles and practice.

The Meeting Manager, also selected by circle members, either personally handles or oversees the process of creating meeting agendas, taking minutes in meetings, and keeping the records (in a physical circle logbook and/or online). (In classic Sociocracy

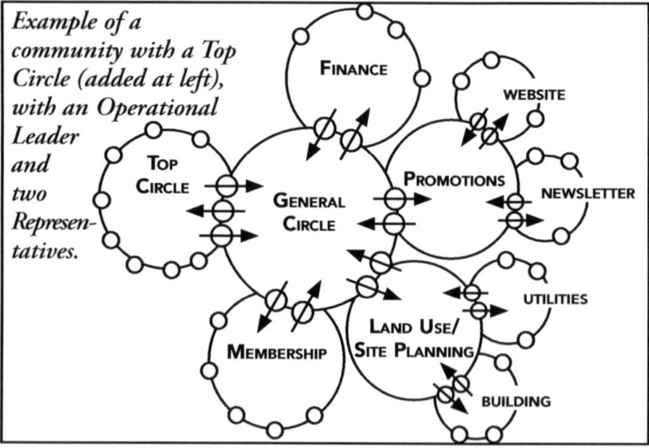

Example of a community with a Top Circle (added at left), with an Operational Leader and two Representatives.

terminology the Meeting Manager is called the "secretary.")

Circles are linked by two people, called the Operational Leader and the Representative, who participate in two adjacent circles and transmit information between the two circles.

Double Links

The Operational Leader. A larger circle not only creates a smaller circle and sets its domain and aim, but selects someone to serve as its Operational Leader. For example, a community's General Circle selects an Operational Leader for the Promotions Circle, the Finance Circle, the Repair and Maintenance Circle, and so on.

The Operational Leader's task is to convey news, ideas, suggestions, needs, requests, and proposals from the larger circle they are a member of to members of the smaller circle they are also a member of. For example a community's General Circle would select someone to be the Operational Leader of the smaller Promotions Circle. The Operational Leader would then carry the General Circle's information to other members of the Promotions Circle. The Operational Leader of the Promotions Circle is expected to help other Promotions Circle members understand the larger picture of how Promotions issues fit into the whole larger community governance process—in terms of strategic planning, finances, legalities, and other longer-term, big-picture issues. Thanks to the Promotions Circle's Operational Leader, every circle member understands their circle's role in the whole scheme of community governance.

The Operational Leader is a full member with decision-making rights in *both* circles: in this example, in the General Circle and in the Promotions Circle.

The Representative. In the same way, a smaller circle selects one of its circle members to serve as its Representative to the higher circle. The Promotions Circle, for example, would choose one of its members to serve as its Representative to the General Circle. The Representative participates fully in the governance of each circle, just as the Operational Leader does, but has the specific task to convey news, ideas, suggestions, needs, requests, or proposals from the Promotions Circle to the General Circle. The Promotions Circle's Representative helps other General Circle members understand and have updated information on the specific projects and tasks of the Promotions Circle: for example its brochures, website, blog, newsletter, community tours and tour guides.

The Representative participates in the selection of the Operational Leader for their circle too, except when the circle is first being formed (since there are no circle members yet to select a Representative).

A smaller circle can select more than one Representative to participate in a larger circle.

The two-way flow of information. The Operational Leader and Representative form the "double link" between a larger and smaller circle. The General Circle and all the community's smaller circles are double-linked like this to create a smooth, easy, and transparent flow of information, suggestions, and requests from every part of the community to every other part.

The Operational Leader of a circle *also* conveys the news from other smaller circles to their own smaller circle, because they hear the reports from Representatives of other smaller circles in General Circle meetings. While presumably most people in the community read the posted minutes of each circle, having people in these double-linked roles also helps everyone know everything. Double-linking helps create more transparency in the organization. *(See illustration #3, p. 63.)*

When a smaller circle creates one or more of its own smaller circles, it also creates its domain and aim, and it selects the Operational Leader for its lower circle. For example, if the Promotions Circle created a Visitors Circle with the aim to organize and coordinate community tours, it would select someone to be the Operational Leader for the Visitors Circle (whose members might be the community's tour guides). Similarly, the Community Tours Circle would choose one of its own members to be the Representative to the Promotions Circle. This way every circle is directly or indirectly double-linked to every other circle.

Why not just one link? Gerard Endenburg, the originator of this method, and the employees of his company, Endenburg Elektrotechniek, measured and evaluated each modification of every aspect of Sociocractic governance back in the early 1970s when they first tried it. Endenburg and his employees found that using two people to double link worked a lot better than having one person do both roles. Having the circles double-linked rather than single-linked was "field-tested" by all these people in the organization where Sociocracy was invented and first applied.

It can be difficult for one person to do two different kinds of tasks effectively. In this case, one task refers to the smaller circle's need for the General Circle to understand exactly what it wants and needs. The other task is the General Circle's need for the smaller circle to understand the whole community's big-picture plans and goals. When one person tries to do both roles it can be challenging to do either role effectively. Endenburg cites cybernetics—the science of communication and control—and engineering feedback loops, to say that these two roles must operate separately and simultaneously. Authors John Buck and Sharon Villines point out in *We the People* it must be two roles for the same reason that electric power can't flow in two directions at the same time in one wire.

I like to use the analogy of arteries carrying oxygenated blood from the heart out to the capillaries, and veins carrying un-oxygenated blood back to the lungs to get more oxygen. The oxygenated blood goes out one set of "pipes"—arteries—and the returning un-oxygenated blood comes back in a second set of pipes—veins. Both kinds of blood can't simultaneously flow in both directions in the same set of pipes!

Sometimes communities using Sociocracy don't understand the double-linking principle well. They may not know Endenburg and his employees tried it both ways 40 years ago and concluded that a double link works well but a single link doesn't. When a community creates only one link between their circles, it tends to cause them trouble later. (So please remember electric wires and veins and arteries!)

The Top Circle

A "Top Circle" offers an outside perspective and information from the wider world. It considers issues such as the economy or trends in legalities, zoning, and other factors that could affect the community long-term, including potential challenges, or potential opportunities—forming alliances with helpful, influential organizations in the wider community, for example.

A Top Circle is comprised of both community members—one or more Representative(s) and an Operational Leader (if the group desires)—and non-community members who understand and support the community, wish to serve it, and can provide information and feedback not available inside the community. These could include former members, neighbors, lawyers, accountants, bankers, as well as experts in fields especially helpful to communities, such as governance and decision-making, Nonviolent Communication, Restorative Circles, local zoning issues, state water quality issues, sustainable agriculture, and so on.

The Top Circle is double-linked to the General Circle through its community Representative(s) and the Operational Leader for the General Circle (if there is one). They are members of both circles and have full decision-making rights in each circle. *(See illustration #4, p. 63.)*

The Top Circle serves as stewards and custodians of the community's vision, mission, and aim—ensuring its legality and solvency and overseeing and supporting the executive functions of its General Circle. The Top Circle exercises an influence on governance and policy, such as creating five-year plans, 20-year plans, and so on. Top Circle members could enroll the community in carbon-offset programs and other more "big picture" ways to practice ecological sustainability, for example. Anticipating the group will need new buildings as its population increases, a Top Circle could set up a building fund and encourage the needed discipline for members to contribute to it every year. A Top Circle could plan and organize physical infrastructure and specific services for community members as they age. A Top Circle can prevent an organization from becoming a stagnant "closed system," but keep it an "open system," serving as a beneficial outside energy source.

Depending on how the community organizes its Top Circle (which it does through its General Circle), some decisions may need consent of the Top Circle before being implemented. Some decisions may be entirely delegated to the Top Circle—depending on how it's set up.

Top Circle members discuss internal community issues only when asked to; for example if there's a disagreement the General Circle or smaller circles can't resolve.

Even though the Top Circle is called "top," it doesn't have authority over the community. In Sociocracy all authority is consented to and no one person or circle has power over any other person or circle. Rather, through the circles and double-links process everyone participates in the community's authority.

While a Top Circle *could* be granted exceptional freedoms to decide things—the ability to set the community's annual budget, for example, or to reorient the group's vision, mission, and aim—this could only occur in the absence of any objection from the Representatives and Operational Leader. So please keep in mind a Top Circle serves the community and can't make it do anything it doesn't want to do.

Some intentional communities using Sociocracy have Top Circles; others don't.

General Circles Don't Include the Whole Community

A General Circle is comprised only of Operational Leaders and Representatives from its smaller circles (and if the community has one, from its Top Circle). Thus if a community had a General Circle and five smaller circles linked to it, its General Circle would have 10 members, and a few more if it had a Top Circle. This can surprise community members learning about Sociocracy, as they often expect a General Circle to be like whole-group plenary meetings.

Making decisions in many double-linked circles is more effective and efficient than making decisions in one big, whole-community circle. This is because members of each circle are focused on the circle's specific area of responsibility and authority (its domain), and on its specific aim. And...members of these circles can't just do anything they want or keep information secret in their circle—nor can individual circle members stop what all other circle members want—because of the checks and balances built into the process and the Consent Decision-Making method.

Making decisions in many double-linked circles is more effective and efficient than making decisions in one big, whole-community circle.

A community using Sociocracy doesn't have to give up whole-group meetings, however, since people can certainly schedule whole-group plenary meetings whenever they like. Some communities using Sociocracy schedule whole-group meetings several times a year to discuss larger issues, discuss and consent to their annual budget, and/or create proposals about such issues through Sociocracy's unique proposal-forming process.

Some communities create "fishbowl-style" General Circle meetings, with the Operational Leaders and Representatives sitting in a small circle to conduct their business, and all the other community members sitting in a larger circle around them, observing and possibly participating in some aspects of the Consent Decision-Making process.

Consent Decision-Making and Sociocracy's Five Meeting Processes

In Sociocracy decisions are made by "Consent Decision-Making," so-called because everyone in a particular Circle must give his/her consent to pass a proposal for that Circle. It is both similar to and different from the consensus decision-making that most communitarians are familiar with, and is derived in part from traditional Quaker-style consensus. The relationships between Sociocracy's double-linked circles and Consent Decision-Making are mutually reinforcing. These two aspects of Sociocracy are similar to the classic Taoist yin-yang symbol: one needs to understand both parts in order to understand the whole. For example, one needs to understand that objections in Consent Decision-Making must be based on the circle's aim, and for that, one must first know about circles and aims. And to understand how members of a circle can't be bossed around by the next larger ("higher") circle or by any individual circle members, one needs to understand how Consent Decision-Making works. More specifically, one needs to understand Consent Decision-Making in order to see why no individual circle member can prevent the circle from fulfilling its aim through personal, frivolous, or too-frequent objections to proposals. No circle member can bamboozle the circle with super-powerful charisma, aggressive words and energies, "you're attacking me" or "you're victimizing me" ploys, or other kinds of meeting behaviors many of us have experienced in community. The structure of circles and double links and Consent Decision-Making, working together, prevents these kinds of energy-draining behaviors.

Consent Decision-Making is the basis of each of the five meeting processes in circle meetings. These include (1) the proposal-forming process, (2) discussing and consenting to a proposal (or not consenting to it, as the case may be), (3) evaluating an already-implemented decision and deciding whether, and how, to modify it based on how it's working out in real circumstances, (4) selecting people for roles in the circle, and (5) providing role-improvement feedback to people in these roles.

We'll take up Consent Decision-Making—the second half of the yin-yang circle—in the next issue. ❧

The next article in the series, in the Spring 2014 issue, will describe Consent Decision-Making and the five meeting processes based on it. The last article, Summer 2014, will explore how communities learn and implement Sociocracy—what works well and what doesn't. Special thanks to Sociocrcy trainers Jerry Koch-Gonzalez, Sharon Villines, John Schinerer, James Priest, and John Buck for their help with this article.

Diana Leafe Christian, author of Creating a Life Together *and* Finding Community *and publisher of* Ecovillages *(EcovillageNews.org), speaks at conferences, offers consultations, and leads workshops internationally. Diana specializes in teaching Sociocracy to communities, and has taught in the US, UK, Sweden, France, and Canada. See www.DianaLeafeChristian.org.*

Why the Term "Operational Leader"?

In business and nonprofits, "Operational" means the actual work of creating the organization's products or services. Businesses and nonprofits typically conduct weekly or perhaps even daily brief "Operational Meetings" (sometimes called "staff meetings") of supervisors and employees to organize, coordinate, and track this work. And managers and bosses decide the organization's policies and strategies.

In businesses and nonprofits using Sociocracy, however, everyone in the company is part of a circle. Each circle conducts occasional "Circle Meetings" (Policy Meetings) to decide its policies and strategies, select people for roles, consider proposals, and evaluate already-implemented decisions. Each circle also conducts more frequent brief "Operational Meetings" to coordinate and track its daily work tasks. While a circle's Operational Leader is just one member of a Circle/Policy Meeting in terms of decision-making authority, he or she is the boss of the Operational Meetings—answering questions about the work, assigning and coordinating tasks, and resolving problems. Thus the terms "Operational" and "leader."

In income-sharing intentional communities the group may own one or more businesses in which community members work every day. If the community uses Sociocracy each circle may also conduct frequent Operational Meetings to organize, coordinate, and track their daily work tasks. And the circle's Operational Leader might indeed serve as the boss of these Operational Meetings (or not, as the circle decides).

In contrast, independent-income communities usually have no community-owned businesses and most people work at their own jobs or are retired. Work tasks done for the community are voluntary and take place when each member can get to it. Clerical or administrative tasks are often done on one's own at home or perhaps in a community office set up for this purpose. Physical work might take place in a group in monthly community work days.

Monthly or twice-a-month committee meetings usually combine policy-type issues and coordinating work tasks; there aren't usually separate committee meetings to only consider policies and/or Operational committee meetings to only coordinate and organize work. If the community uses Sociocracy, I recommend keeping the two functions separate, either considering Operational issues—organizing, coordinating, and tracking work tasks—in the first part of the circle meeting, and in the second part considering policy issues, or vice-versa.

—D.L.C.

Sociocracy Resources

- *Video:* "Lost Valley: A Tale of Sociocracy." Youtube.com
- *Article:* "Sociocracy: A Permaculture Approach to Community Evolution," Melanie Rios, Communities, issue #153, Winter 2011
- *Sociocracy.Info:* www.sociocracy.info
- *The Sociocracy Consulting Group:* sociocracyconsulting.com
- *Governance Alive:* www.governancealive.com
- *Sociocracy UK:* sociocracyuk.ning.com
- *Sociocracy Center in the Netherlands:* www.sociocratie.nl

Sociocracy Trainers Who Teach Intentional Communities:

North America: John Schinnerer: john.schinnerer@sociocracyconsulting.com
Jerry Koch-Gonzalez: jerry.koch-gonzalez@sociocracyconsulting.com
Diana Leafe Christian: diana@ic.org
UK: James Priest: jamespriest@thriveincommunity.co.uk
Australia: Gina Price: ginaprice@optusnet.com.au

Consent Decision-Making and Community Vision, Mission, and Aim

How Sociocracy Can Help Communities, Part III

By Diana Leafe Christian

"No objection," said the member of Park Carpool Co-op—a group of people in the Findhorn community in Scotland who share ownership of eight fuel-efficient cars. They use Sociocracy as their governance method. That evening they were considering a proposal to change their co-op's name.

Sociocracy—also called "Dynamic Governance" in the US—is a self-governance method based on the principles of equivalence, transparency, and effectiveness. *(See Part I, "Transparency, Equivalence, and Effectiveness," in* COMMUNITIES *#160, Fall 2013, and Part II, "Self-Governance with Circles and Double Links," in* COMMUNITIES *#161, Winter 2013.)* Sociocracy uses "Consent Decision-Making" as its decision-making method.

"No objection," said each person in turn around the circle. Car co-op members had offered various objections to the proposal in previous rounds, and—as happens in Consent Decision-Making—each objection was used to help modify and improve the proposal. However, in this latest round there were no more objections to the proposed name, "Eco Carshare." That meant the latest amended proposal was consented to—passed—and the car co-op had a new name.

The guest facilitator that evening was John Buck, the Sociocracy advocate who brought this method to the English-speaking world. He translated Sociocracy texts from the Dutch and wrote the book *We the People* with co-author Sharon Villines. John and I were visiting the Findhorn community in October 2013 to teach Sociocracy workshops. The co-op had asked John to facilitate that night in order to help demonstrate the six steps of Sociocracy's Consent Decision-Making process.

(Another aspect of Sociocracy is feedback loops, in which most implemented decisions are later measured, evaluated, and, if needed, modified to adjust to any real-life circumstances. At their next meeting, car co-op members evaluated their new name and realized it should include the name of their county, "Moray," and so at that meeting changed their name to "Moray Carshare.")

Moray Carshare, a car co-op affiliated with the Findhorn Community in northern Scotland, uses Sociocracy and Consent Decision-Making.

Vision, Mission, and Aim

Consent Decision-Making is based on two mutually reinforcing aspects of Sociocracy: the governance structure of circles and double-links *(described in Part I, #160)*, and the specific Aim of each circle. *(See figure 1, p. 60.)* Every organization using Sociocracy has a Vision, Mission, and Aim, and each "circle" in the organization (committee, team) has its own Aim as well.

In Sociocracy the ***Vision*** is an imagined ultimate future that provides the inspiration—the "why" of the organization, the reason it exists. Moray Carshare's Vision is "A world in which everyone has access to affordable and environmentally friendly travel options that build community and trust."

The ***Mission***—the "big-picture" intention for what the organization will do to manifest its Vision—is the "what." Moray Carshare's Mission is "To be an effective, ethical association, responsive to the needs of existing and potential members in the Moray area, providing a variety of environmentally friendly vehicles, and creating community through sharing resources with care and respect."

The ***Aim*** is what the organization produces or provides the people it serves. "Produces" can mean physical things—"products." "Provides" can mean non-physical things—"services." The Aim of Moray Carshare is "To provide well-maintained, clean, affordable fuel-efficient cars to our members; reduce greenhouse gases and air pollution in our local community; raise local awareness of the financial and environmental costs of using cars; and build a stronger sense of community."

Vision, Mission, and Aim in Intentional Community

In Sociocracy the Vision—the *why* of the organization—is external, global, and in the future. An intentional community using Sociocracy might have the Vision: "A world in which everyone can choose to live in a healthy, thriving, successful, ecologically sustainable human settlement."

In Sociocracy the Mission—the bigger-picture *what*—is internal, local, and in the present, not the future. For example: "To create an ecologically, economically, and socially sustainable ecovillage model in our area, provide a good home for our ecovillage members, and offer public workshops on sustainability."

An Aim is also internal, local, and in the present but is a more specific and detailed *what*. It specifies what the community produces or provides the people it serves. A community's Aim might be, in part: "To provide and manage all aspects of building and maintaining the social, physical, and economic aspects of the community for our members, including roads, the community building, land-use management, financial management, and membership services."

As noted in previous articles in this series, Sociocratic organizations are governed by an interconnected set of teams, called "circles." A "higher" (or "larger") circle—the community's "General Circle"—has a more abstract, longer-term Aim. A "lower" (or "smaller" or "functional") circle has a more concrete, specific, and shorter-term Aim; e.g., Finance, Membership, and Land-Use Circles. A community's General Circle sets up each smaller circle and determines its area of responsibility and its Aim. (One Danish community calls these "mother" and "daughter" circles, since the larger, more abstract circle "gives birth" to the smaller, more specific circles.) The Aim of a community's Land-Use Circle might be to develop and manage the physical aspects of the community. The Aim of a Finance Circle might be to manage the community's finances.

Policy Meetings, Operations Meetings

Circle members use Consent Decision-Making to make decisions in "Policy Meetings" or "Policy-Making Meetings." In Policy Meetings they propose and give consent to policies and procedures about work tasks and accomplishing their Aim. Think of these as "governance meetings." A second kind of meeting is an "Operations Meeting," in which circle members organize and coordinate work tasks and sometimes do the work itself, whether the tasks are physical labor or clerical/administrative work. A building and maintenance circle, for example, could have a brief work-coordination Operations Meeting before the start of a work party.

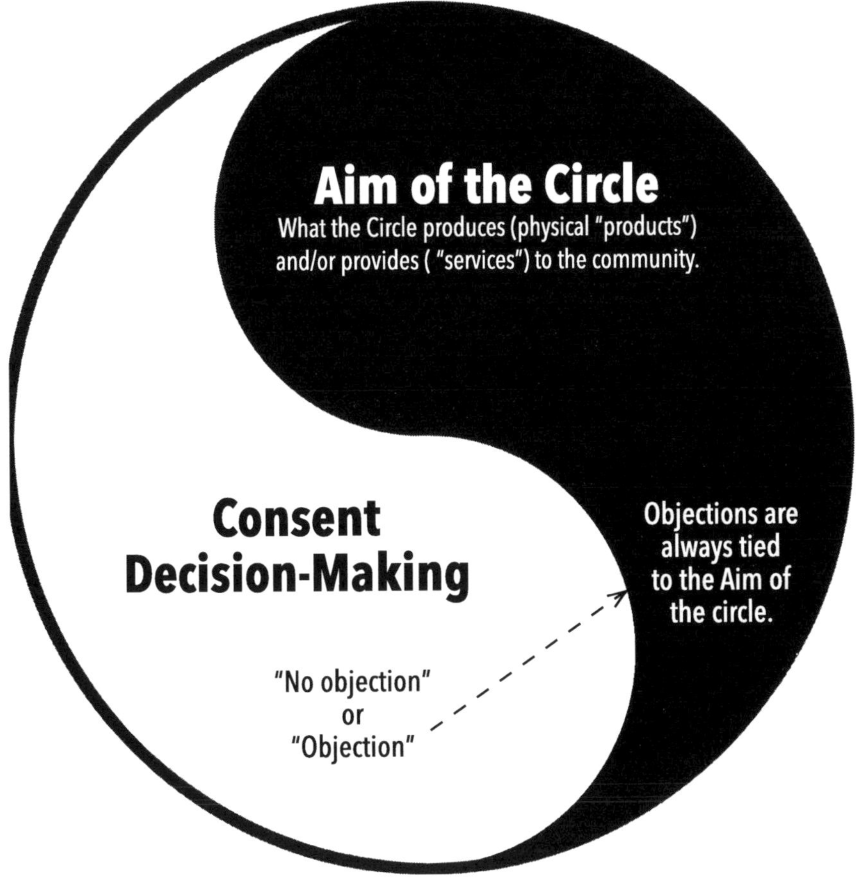

Sociocracy trainer John Schinnerer describes the two kinds of meetings as (1) "Policy-Making Meetings" in which policies about work tasks ("operations") are decided by consent among people with equivalence, and (2) Operations Meetings, in which the previously consented-to decisions are implemented.

Consent Decision-Making is used in Policy Meetings. In Operations Meetings in businesses and nonprofits decisions are often made unilaterally (that is, autocratically) by the Operations Leader—hence the term Operations "Leader." This is highly recommended for efficiency and effectiveness. John Schinnerer points out that it's easy enough to have the Operations Leader decide policy implementation unilaterally in Operations Meetings, since the policy itself was already consented to in an equivalent way by all circle members in a Policy Meeting. Think of the Operations Leader as a "straw boss" to effectively implement the circle's policies.

However, in Operations Meetings circle members can actually make decisions any way they like. This can include the Operations Leader calling the shots, but it also can include Consent Decision-Making, consensus, majority-rule voting, super-majority voting, or everyone just talking about things without any particular method.

The bottom line: in Policy Meetings decisions are made only by Consent Decision-Making; in Operations Meetings circle members choose the method they like.

The Six Steps of Consent Decision-Making

Every circle member must give his or her consent to pass a proposal for their circle. Proposals are offered in order to find better ways to help the group achieve their circle's Aim. Therefore each member gives their consent depending *on how the proposal serves or doesn't serve their circle's Aim.* That is, each circle member consents to the proposal if it would *not* conflict with their circle's Aim or with their own ability to productively carry out their specific tasks for the circle, relative to its Aim. In Consent Decision-Making, every "No objection" or "Objection" in a circle is directly related to its Aim.

In circles like the car co-op meeting, each person in the circle speaks in turn, rather than the facilitator calling on people who raise their hands. These are called "rounds."

Consent Decision-Making has six steps. When someone objects to a proposal, the *Consent Round* (4th step) and *Resolve Objections Round* (5th step) are alternated until there are no more objections. This means every circle member has given his or her consent to the now-modified proposal.

Step One—Present the Proposal: A circle member presents the proposal.

Step Two—Clarifying Questions: Each person around the circle in turn, the facilitator included, says if they have any questions about the proposal. This round is designed to find out only whether each circle member *understands* the proposal, not whether they like it. A person can ask the presenter, "Does the proposal mean X?"

Sometimes, though, people try to express a reaction in this step. They may start out with a question that becomes a reaction or comment disguised as a question. (The facilitator reminds them they'll have a chance to express their reactions in the next step.)

Because the facilitator is a circle member too, he or she participates in this and all subsequent steps.

Step Three—Quick Reaction Round: The facilitator asks if there are any quick reactions to the proposal, and each person responds. The purpose of this step is for people to express a quick general response—"I like it," "I don't like it," "I think it might be OK if we change some things," etc. The Quick Reaction Round is also designed to screen the proposal before the next Consent Round in order to make any obvious adjustments; it saves time when a proposal has significant problems that should be addressed before continuing. For example, circle members might see that the proposal doesn't include what a project will cost or an estimate of how long it will take, that the proposal is not fleshed out enough yet and thus not ready for a decision. Such comments are valuable feedback for the presenter, who might modify the proposal accordingly and bring it back to the next meeting. Or the circle could modify the proposal on the spot. The Quick Reaction Round also reveals when the proposal is fine as is.

Step Four—Consent Round: The facilitator asks each person around the circle whether he or she has a "reasoned objection" to the proposal. This is literally a call for a decision. It occurs early in the process because it's possible the proposal may pass *right then* if there are no objections.

Reasoned objections. "Reasoned" means a clear, understandable argument for why the proposal should not be passed, based on the circle's Aim. Here, "argument" means a reasoned statement of fact and the conclusions drawn from those facts, stated in a way that can be understood by other circle members. This is similar to the usage of "argument" in mathematics (e.g., a "mathematical argument").

A reasoned argument means everyone can understand the objection, even if they don't agree with it. "This is a big 'aha!' for some people," John Schinnerer says. "People are glad to realize 'Oh, I can still disagree?!'" Understanding an objection does not equal—or require—agreement!

Objection, No objection. In the Consent Round each person says either "No objection" or "Objection."

"No objection" essentially means, ***"The proposal seems 'good enough for now'—I consent to try it."***

"Objection" essentially means, ***"Hold on, I've thought of one or more arguments against the proposal as it is currently worded. I'm not ready to consent to it yet."***

The term "No objection" is used so people assess the proposal for a reason *not* try it. This is so circle members will ask themselves whether the proposal is "good enough for now" or "safe enough to try," and *won't* ask themselves whether they "support" or "approve" it enough. If the question is "Any objections?" then the answer must be "No" or "Yes." But if the question were "Do you consent?," it wouldn't be objections that were being asked for, and in Consent Decision-Making we're looking for objections, not consent. Consent is the absence of objections.

(However, some people do say "Consent" instead of "No objection," or use either phrase.)

"Arguments" for the objection. When someone objects, the facilitator thanks that

A group of members of Windsong Cohousing in Langley, BC discuss their community's Aim.

Photos courtesy of Diana Leafe Christian

person and continues on around the circle. After hearing from everyone the facilitator returns to each circle member who objected and asks what their objection is. Each objector in turn gives the clear and reasoned arguments for their objection.

Vague feelings of discomfort. As noted earlier, these arguments must be easily understood by others, rather than expressed in unclear or confusing ways. However, some objections may start out as a vague discomfort or an uneasy feeling which has not yet become a clear and reasoned argument. The facilitator and other circle members then ask questions and suggest possible reasons, in order to draw out whatever reasoned arguments may underlie the person's feelings of discomfort.

Sometimes the circle cannot uncover what the reasoned arguments are in the amount of agenda time they have for that proposal. The facilitator could propose they adjust the agenda to permit more time to discuss the matter.

If circle members simply cannot understand the person's objection, the facilitator might ask another circle member to work with that person outside the meeting to get at the argument that supports their objection, and then speak on behalf of that person to make the argument(s) for their objection more obvious to other circle members.

If there is time, the facilitator might propose an ad hoc committee (called a "Helping Circle") to explore the objection and bring a modified proposal to the next meeting.

If a decision must be made in the same meeting when it's introduced, however, or if none of the above methods help, the circle may not be able to spend more time trying to uncover the actual arguments for the person's discomfort, and may need to declare the partially formed objection invalid and move on.

Objections are not blocks. Objections are gifts to the circle. They help improve the proposal by identifying aspects that may need modification. Objections also stimulate creative thinking as circle members attempt to resolve apparently contradictory ideas. Objections are not vetoes or blocks and do not stop the proposal (unless they cannot ultimately be resolved in the nine ways suggested below). Offering clear, reasoned, arguments to support one's objection is essentially a positive, good-will action designed to improve the circle's effectiveness relative to its Aim.

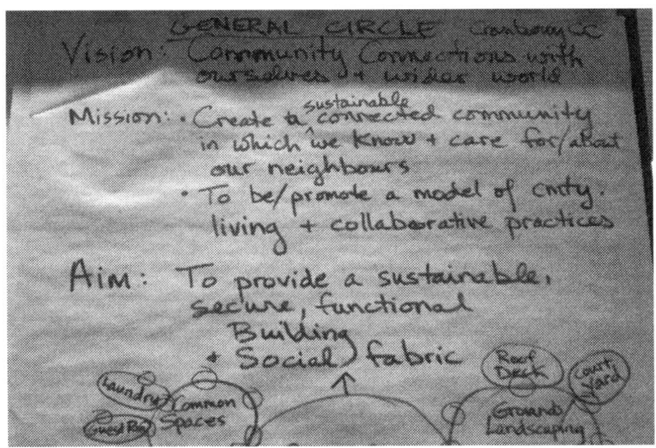

A draft Mission and Aim some members of Cranberry Commons Cohousing in Burnaby, BC came up with for their community.

Six legitimate reasons to object to a proposal:

(1) Aspects of the proposal conflict with your circle's Aim.

(2) You see one or more obvious flaws in the proposal or important aspects that were left out, relative to your circle's Aim.

(3) You see potential unintended consequences of implementing the proposal, relative to your circle's Aim.

(4) One or more aspects of the proposal may not be well-thought out or may be expressed in a confusing way.

(5) The proposal doesn't have criteria for measuring and/or evaluating the proposal after it has been implemented, or future meeting dates at which to do this.

(6) One or more aspects of the proposal would not allow you personally to carry out your assigned tasks relative to your circle's Aim.

No personal objections unrelated to the circle's Aim. When Sociocracy is practiced correctly, circle members don't allow purely personal objections. This means objections must be related to the circle's Aim or occur because a circle member could no longer effectively perform his or her tasks in the circle if the proposal passed. If someone tried to object for a personal reason, the facilitator might say, "I'm sorry, that's not related to our Aim," and the objection would not be valid. The facilitator might then read the circle's Aim out loud to remind everyone again what it is.

But what if the Aim needs adjusting? On the other hand, sometimes objections may reveal flaws in the Aim itself, or how it is stated. Like everything else in Sociocracy, a circle's Aim is subject to review and potential revision too. Some circle members' objections may indicate that they are are no longer in alignment with the Aim (good to find out!). Maybe they are in the wrong circle. Or maybe the Aim itself needs to shift.

Step Five—Resolving Objections: Circle members listen in turn to the arguments each objecting member gives for his or her objection in the Consent Round. If the group is new to Consent Decision-Making, someone could briefly note each argument on a flip chart or whiteboard visible to everyone. Having the arguments written and visible can help people still learning Sociocracy to more easily create an amended proposal.

The circle then modifies the proposal, based on these arguments, and considers the modified proposal in the next Consent Round. They can modify the proposal in a number of ways, combining the concerns revealed by the arguments with the original purpose of the proposal.

Nine ways to resolve an objection:

(1) The person(s) objecting could propose changes in the proposal to resolve their objection.

(2) The facilitator could suggest an amendment to the proposal.

(3) The originator of the proposal, one or more others in the circle, or everyone in the circle could suggest amendments to it.

(4) Circle members could add specific concerns raised in the arguments to the criteria for measuring and evaluating the proposal after it is later implemented. They could also move up the date for measuring and evaluating the implemented proposal so this will occur sooner.

(5) The facilitator could go around the circle and ask each

Consent Decision-Making

1. Present Proposal

2. Clarifying Questions

"Do you understand the proposal?"
"No questions." Or, "Yes. What about. . ?"
(In a round or popcorn-style)

3. Quick Reaction Round

"What do you think of it?" (Brief!)

4. Consent Round

"Do you have any reasoned objections to this proposal?" "No objection."
Or, "Objection." "What is your objection?"

Five Reasons to Object:

1. One or more aspects of proposal conflict with circle's aim.
2. One or more obvious flaws, or important aspects left out, relative to circle's aim.
3. Potential unintended consequences of implementing proposal, re circle's aim.
4. One or more aspects are not well thought out, or are expressed in a confusing way.
5. One or more aspects would not allow you to carry out your tasks in circle, re its aim.

5. Resolving Objections:

1. Add concern as new criterion for evaluation, and/or make first evaluation date sooner.
2. Facilitator amends it.
3. Proposal originator amends it.
4. Person(s) objecting, one or more others, or everyone in circle could amend it.
5. Round: "How would you resolve this?"
6. "Fishbowl" of two-three people in middle.
7. Refer to Research Team.
8. Refer to Resolution Team.
9. Refer to higher or lower circle.

6. Announce Decison and Celebrate

You've made a "good enough for now" decision.

person, "How would you resolve the proposal, given these argument(s)?" After two or three rounds, a way to revise the proposal might become obvious, based on people's suggestions. The facilitator and/or others could then modify it.

(6) If the arguments for an objection are not clear, the facilitator could ask two or three circle members to sit in the middle of the circle, "fishbowl-style," to talk about their feelings and arguments. Becoming more clear first about feelings and arguments for an objection may help people suggest helpful amendments.

(7) The facilitator could ask several circle members to become a "Resolution Team" to create a modified proposal, either before the next meeting or during a break in that meeting.

(8) If an objection shows that more information is needed for the proposal, the facilitator could ask several circle members to become a "Research Team" to compile additional information with which to amend the proposal, perhaps before the next meeting or during a break in that meeting.

(9) If the objection(s) indicate the proposal addresses a larger or more abstract issue than the circle's more specific and concrete area of responsibility and Aim—or that it will be controversial or is actually a community-wide issue—the circle could refer it to a "higher" (or "larger") circle such as the General Circle. Or if the arguments indicate the proposal addresses a more specific and concrete issue than the circle's area of responsibility and Aim, it could be referred to the more appropriate "lower" (or "smaller") circle.

"Resolving objections can be playful and satisfying," says John Buck, "like the group solving a jigsaw puzzle together."

Repeating and alternating the Consent Round and Resolving Objections Round. If the proposal is modified in any of the above ways, the facilitator conducts another Consent Round with the modified proposal.

If there are objections to the now-modified proposal, the circle repeats the Resolving Objections round.

Alternating these two steps, the *Consent Round* and the *Resolving Objections Round*, occurs until the proposal has been modified well enough that no circle member has a further objection.

A proposal passes when there are no more objections to it.

Step Six—Announcing the Decision and Celebrating: This step acknowledges that the circle has just accomplished one of its agenda items and can move to the next item. It may not celebrate the decision they just consented to. Rather they may celebrate that they just used the Consent Decision-Making process successfully (or more successfully than the previous time).

There is no "standing aside" in Consent Decision-Making—if someone has a concern they must express it as an objection.

Group Discussion

The relatively rigorous structure of Consent Decision-Making—drawing ideas and feelings through the filter of "Objection" or "No objection"—may seem strange at first when one is used to free-form discussion in which the discussion takes awhile and meanders because people want to be heard for the sake of being heard. Consent Decision-Making is not about being heard for the sake of being heard, however. It's about sharing clear, helpful reasons why a proposal is not fine to approve as is and pointing out how to modify it.

The issues raised in a group discussion usually emerge anyway through the "No objection" or "Objection" structure, but more efficiently. This focused, concentrated process—with people asking themselves why they can't just consent to the proposal as is—brings to light the same kinds of observations, insights, questions, or concerns

Members of Baja BioSana Ecovillage in Baja California, Mexico consider a proposal to use Sociocracy in their community, February 2014.

Using a wall poster like this, shown here in the community meeting pavilion of Baja BioSana Ecovillage, can help a group remember the six steps of Consent Decision-Making.

that might normally emerge in a group discussion. The structure hones any random insights or chatty observations into more rigorous and immediately useful information. It's like pushing unorganized, amorphous material through a fine filter so it emerges in more clear, discrete, and usable ways. When circle members learn how to do this, decision-making can becomes faster, more efficient, and more satisfying than seeking the same information through prolonged discussion.

Another purpose for doing rounds instead of discussion is to build equivalence in the group. "What we are used to as discussion is often 'dominator discussion,'" observes John Schinnerer. "The dominators argue with each other while no one else gives input, or they're given token representation when someone remembers to ask them what they think." John notes that after a group completes its first reasonably smooth process of consenting to a proposal—with self-correction on crosstalk, reactions-disguised-as-questions, random observations, etc.—he invites them to notice that they've just had a "discussion" in a different form. Then he asks them how they liked it. "Once a group has the pleasure of a Sociocracy 'discussion' like this," John says, "and they experience how quickly they get things done, they tend to save discussions for social occasions."

A discussion step can be added, however. Sociocracy is such a flexible method that any circle member can propose an open discussion, which will happen if the circle gives consent. A circle can also build discussion time into their Consent Decision-Making process for a given time period (to be assessed and evaluated later), again by making and consenting to a proposal to do this.

Communities using Sociocracy certainly still share feelings and ideas in free-form discussions with plenty of time and space to hear one another deeply. But they usually do this in other kinds of meetings outside of the official Sociocracy process, such as Check-Ins, Talking Stick meetings, Wisdom Circles, Sharing Circles, and so on.

Facilitating Sociocracy

Facilitating Consent Decision-Making requires modest facilitation skills and an understanding of how Consent Decision-Making works. The facilitator's primary job is to keep the process moving, even though all circle members hold responsibility for the quality of facilitation. Also, please keep in mind that the facilitator has no power beyond that granted to this role by other circle members.

When people are first learning Consent Decision-Making, it helps to display a large poster on the wall showing the six steps, to help both the facilitator and all circle members. The facilitator needs to keep the group to the agenda times, and needs to sense if anyone in the circle is upset at any point, find out why (is it related to an objection?), and get the circle back on track. If anyone goes off on a tangent, says "Objection" or "No objection" before the Consent Round occurs, or makes helpful suggestions when they're not in the Resolve Objections Round, the facilitator gently reminds circle members which step they're currently on, perhaps using the wall poster. Ideally the facilitator uses these times as educable moments, helping circle members recall how Consent Decision-Making works, learning as they go.

I personally have found Consent Decision-Making easier to facilitate than the consensus process, and I suspect new facilitators would find it easier too. This is probably because the structured, step-by-step process of Consent Decision-Making doesn't require the facilitator to remember so many things at once or be responsible for myriad small process decisions.

Rounds—Leveling the Playing Field, Creating Group Energy

In steps two through five each person in the circle speaks in turn, rather than the facilitator calling on only those who raise their hands. Using rounds levels the playing field. It allows quieter circle members to share their views naturally when it's their turn—they're not forced to suddenly become more assertive just to be heard. And it reins in the more outspoken or verbose circle members, who may speak too much already.

Moreover, going around the circle repeatedly tends to create a kind of spiraling group energy—it feels good! *We the People* co-author Sharon Villines observes, "Rounds are about listening. They should be transformative, not just about information-collecting." And Quebec Sociocracy trainer Gilles Charest says, "Rounds form a group!"

Must Every Proposal Be Approved?

A proposal doesn't have to be approved just because circle members are expected to modify it to meet objections. People can certainly postpone a proposal until a future meeting or reject it altogether if the arguments for objections don't seem easily or immediately resolvable or if there does not seem to be enough support for it.

If some circle members strongly support a proposal that other circle members equally reject, this may indicate the circle's Aim is so vague it can be interpreted in several different ways, or that some of them don't correctly understand it. If so, the circle may need clarification of their Aim from the next higher circle.

Consent Decision-Making as the Basis of Sociocracy's Four Meeting Processes

Consent Decision-Making is the basis of three other meeting processes, which we'll examine in future issues of this article series.

(1) *The Proposal-Forming Process*, in which people identify the elements necessary to create a proposal, and then create a proposal that addresses all of the elements they identified.

(2) *Selecting People for Roles* (also called "Sociocracy Elections").

(3) *Role-Improvement Feedback.* People serving in circle roles choose a small team of friends and colleagues to give them, in a courteous and good-will way, feedback about what they're doing well in their role and what may need improvement.

• • •

In the Fall 2014 issue we'll see how there can be no "tyranny of the minority" in Sociocracy when it is practiced correctly, and how people can remove someone from their circle if the person's behavior disrupts the circle or if that circle member objects repeatedly, and/or consistently cannot support any suggested modified proposals. We'll also look at the Proposal-Forming Process.

In the following issue we'll describe Selecting People for Roles and Role-Improvement Feedback.

In the next article we'll examine how specific intentional communities use Sociocracy, the benefits they've gained from using it, any challenges they've faced, and how they resolved those challenges.

In the last article we'll look at three ways communities can implement Sociocracy if they're now using a different governance method and consensus decision-making. ❧

Diana Leafe Christian, author of Creating a Life Together *and* Finding Community, *speaks at conferences, offers consultations, and leads workshops internationally. She teaches Sociocracy to communities in North America, Europe, and Latin America. See www.DianaLeafeChristian.org.*

"Consent Decision-Making," "Consent Round," "Consent"

"Consent Decision-Making" is the name of the decision-making method used in Sociocracy. *(I've capitalized these terms in this article to highlight them, although in Sociocracy literature they are not capitalized.)*

A "Consent Round" is a step in the Consent Decision-Making process.

"Consent" is what circle members give a proposal when they pass it. "Consenting" to a proposal offers a different emphasis than "approving," "supporting," "passing," or "consensing" to a proposal.

—D.L.C.

Consent Decision-Making and Consensus—Similarities and Differences

Both methods are based on the intention to include everyone's input in the decision-making process and exclude no one. In both, people modify a proposal well enough so everyone can approve it (consensus) or consent to it (Consent Decision-Making). Both methods use an agenda, proposals, a facilitator, and a minute-taker. In both there are times for clarifying questions and for deciding whether to approve the proposal. In Consent Decision-Making usually there is no discussion, although discussion time can be added if circle members want to add discussion.

The skills of facilitating and minute-taking are the same in both, although I believe it's easier to facilitate Consent Decision-Making. In the latter the facilitator includes himself or herself in each step; in consensus the facilitator doesn't participate in the decision-making process.

Consensus provides the option to block a proposal. In contrast, Consent Decision-Making has no blocking; an objection is not a block and does not stop a proposal *unless* the objection cannot be resolved (see "Nine ways to resolve an objection," p. 62-63).

When consensus is correctly practiced, proposals are modified based on people's stated concerns, and the group modifies the proposal before testing for consensus. However, when consensus is *incorrectly* practiced—as unfortunately can occur in intentional communities—there is often a polarized "go/no-go" energy: either a proposal is modified and passed or stopped altogether.

As with correctly practiced consensus, Consent Decision-Making is based on solution-oriented collaboration to create a modified proposal.

—D.L.C.

Sociocracy Resources

- Video: "Lost Valley: A Tale of Sociocracy." Youtube.com
- Article: "Sociocracy: A Permaculture Approach to Community Evolution," Melanie Rios, Communities, issue #153, Winter 2011
- Sociocracy.Info: www.sociocracy.info
- The Sociocracy Consulting Group: sociocracyconsulting.com
- Governance Alive: www.governancealive.com
- Sociocracy UK: sociocracyuk.ning.com
- Sociocracy Center in the Netherlands: www.sociocratie.nl

Sociocracy Trainers Who Teach Intentional Communities

North America: John Schinnerer: john.schinnerer@sociocracyconsulting.com
Jerry Koch-Gonzalez: jerry.koch-gonzalez@sociocracyconsulting.com
Diana Leafe Christian: diana@ic.org
UK: James Priest: jamespriest@thriveincommunity.co.uk
Australia: Gina Price: ginaprice@optusnet.com.au

—D.L.C.

Radical Governance Changes in Two North American Ecovillages

By Diana Leafe Christian

Two North American ecovillages—Earthaven in North Carolina and Dancing Rabbit in Missouri (www.earthaven.org; www.dancingrabbit.org)—have recently implemented new governance and decision-making methods. As an admitted community governance nerd, I'm fascinated by how communities govern themselves and make decisions, and how they innovate new methods when things don't seem to be working well. I'd like to tell you what these two ecovillages did, because they exemplify a growing trend among communities internationally to innovate new governance methods or try alternative ones.

Governance and decision-making are actually two different things. Governance is *what* the group makes decisions about, how they organize their different decision-making bodies (i.e., whole-group meetings and committees), and the responsibilities and decision-making authorities they assign to each. Decision-making is *how* they make these decisions, and is *part* of governance. Consensus, majority-rule voting, and supermajority voting, for example, are decision-making methods. Sociocracy and Holacracy are whole governance structures that include decision-making methods.

Decision-Making at Earthaven

In June 2014, Earthaven Ecovillage, where I live, changed its decision-making process radically. Many community members were so fed up with too-frequent blocking and "blocking energy" (threatening to block) that we threw out blocking altogether. We kept the consensus *process* of discussing and modifying proposals—but replaced approving, standing aside, or blocking with a way to acknowledge those who don't support the proposal, followed by a supermajority vote.

Here's how our new method works.

After much discussion and likely modifications of a proposal over at least two whole-community business meetings, when it's time to decide, the facilitator asks if anyone remains unfavorable to the proposal. If no one says they feel unfavorable to it, it passes right then and there.

However, if one or more members present don't support the proposal, each is asked, one at a time, why they believe the proposal either violates Earthaven's mission and purpose, or why passing it would be more harmful or dangerous for the community than choosing an alternative proposal or doing nothing.

Their comments are recorded in the minutes. This is followed by a minute of silence. The facilitator asks the question again, so anyone else who may now realize they don't support the proposal for either of these reasons can say why. Their comments are recorded in the minutes. This minute of silence and the request for any more non-support comments is repeated a third time.

This part of our new process is not about making a decision. It's about offering those who don't support the proposal three more

Earthaven members in front of the 13-sided Council Hall where they hold community meetings.

Albert Bates

opportunities to influence others about the proposal before the vote is taken, and to give them a chance to be heard and acknowledged.

The facilitator then calls for a vote and counts the numbers of Yeses and Nos. There are three possible outcomes:

(1) If 85 percent or more say Yes to the proposal, it passes. That's it—bang, done—passed.

(2) If less than 50 percent say Yes, the proposal does not pass. (Though its advocates can rewrite the proposal and try again in the future if they like.)

(3) But if the number of Yeses falls somewhere between 50 percent and 85 percent, the proposal does not pass—as there's not enough support for it—but it's not laid aside either. Rather, a few of the members who said No and a few who said Yes are required to participate in a series of solution-oriented meetings to create a new proposal to address the same issues. These meetings are arranged by the community's four officers, and a facilitator is appointed.

If a new proposal is created in the series of meetings it is presented at the next business meeting and we start anew.

But if the advocates for and those against the first proposal do not create a new proposal, the first proposal comes back to the next business meeting for another vote. This time it passes if 66 percent or more say Yes.

What Motivated Earthaven's Changes

The purpose of this proposal, according to its creators, was "to clarify and simplify our governance process so that it is more sustainable, fair, and effective." They wanted to give non-supporters of a proposal a chance to co-create a new one they could live with, while preventing what they described as "the gridlock and entrenched 'stopping' positions sometimes expressed by a few members."

In my opinion this new "85 percent passes" method is the inevitable outcome of the "fed up" factor at Earthaven—a factor which motivated two previous changes in our community decision-making processes, and without which this proposal would probably have gone nowhere.

For years Earthaven used what I call "consensus-with-unanimity"—meaning it takes 100 percent of people in a meeting (except stand-asides) to pass a proposal, and there is no recourse if someone blocks. In other words, in consensus-with-unanimity, anyone can block a proposal for any reason and no one can do anything about it.

At the same time we had several members who consistently blocked proposals most others wanted. One member's "blocking energy" in response to specific proposals in meetings (and even to various ideas mentioned in informal conversations) had the effect of preventing many people from creating a proposal—or even talking with others about a new idea—they knew this member would block. Thus, even though they didn't intend it, a few members held a power-over position in the community because they could, and did, stop some things almost everyone else wanted. Sometimes this is called "tyranny of the minority."

Our first two first decision-making changes were like small levers, incrementally prying us loose from feeling intimidated by consistent blockers.

Our many attempts to engage with these members—whole-group "Heartshares," mediations, pleas by individuals or small groups to please stop blocking or expressing "blocking energy"/threatening to block, didn't change anything—the blocking and threats to block continued. Our consistent blockers saw themselves as protecting the community and protecting the Earth from our community members. And while most of us know that people who block frequently may not be living in the right community (as renowned consensus trainer Caroline Estes points out), no one could bring themselves to suggest that these folks leave Earthaven and find another community more aligned with their values.

The result was discouragement, demoralization, and dwindling

The North American BioRegional Congress was held at Earthaven in 2005.

John McBride

Members celebrate Earthaven's 10th anniversary in 2004.

Susan Patrice

Before they changed their decision-rule, Earthaven used consensus decision-making since 1994.

John McBride

meeting attendance. We especially missed the participation of our young people. When younger members first joined Earthaven they'd be eager to participate in meetings, offering high energy and new ideas. But soon they'd become so turned off that they stopped attending meetings. And so in the last few years Earthaven became a *de facto* geriocracy—with most decisions made by folks over 50.

Earthaven's First Big Decision-Making Change

In my opinion, our new "85 percent passes" method passed *only* because of the two previous changes we'd made in our decision-making process.

The first change, originating in 2007 and proposed in 2012, was to create criteria for a legitimate block and a way to test it. We said that for a block to be valid at least 85 percent or more members present should believe the proposal violated Earthaven's mission and purpose or be harmful or dangerous to the community if passed. However, if less than 85 percent believed this, the block would be declared *in*valid and the proposal *would* pass.

If we had one to three valid blocks, the next step would be to convene a series of solution-oriented meetings between proposal advocates and those who blocked, in order to create a new proposal. But if they didn't produce a new proposal, the original proposal would come back for a decision rule of consensus-minus-one. This meant that if only two people blocked the returned proposal, it would not pass.

Consensus-minus-one was not what most community members wanted—the original proposal had a 75 percent supermajority fallback, not consensus-minus-one. However, our most frequent blocker, who had blocked 10 times over a five-year period, said she would not approve the proposal unless we replace the 75 percent fallback with consensus-minus-one. So the community agreed. Why? It had taken the ad hoc governance committee two years to even come up with this proposal, as it required shifting out of the paradigm that 100 percent consensus is beneficial, and it took awhile for the committee to understand this. And, fearing the effects and repercussions of shock and outrage by the consistent blockers, the ad hoc governance committee disbanded without even making this proposal. But one of the committee members, dismayed by the continued difficulty in meetings, proposed it himself two years later. Then came another year of high emotions in meetings when discussing it, and many proposal revisions, before the community approved even this truncated version.

The original proposal advocates and most community members figured that passing the consensus-minus-one version was better than nothing.

(Over the next year Earthaven used this new method twice, each time declaring a block invalid because only a few members present thought the block was valid. However, with no validated blocks during this period we never had the opportunity to convene any solution-oriented meetings either.)

Earthaven's Second Big Decision-Making Change

A year and a half later, in January 2014, we passed a second change—to keep this consensus method, with criteria for a valid block, but replace the consensus-minus-one fallback with a supermajority vote of 61.8 percent (*Phi* in mathematics). This fallback vote would be used rarely, only *after* a series of solution-oriented meetings in which proposal advocates and blockers failed to create a new proposal.

I believe the exceptionally low number of 61.8 percent for a supermajority vote—the lowest I've ever seen in the communities movement—was motivated by backlash against our history of blocking.

(And as noted above, our third and latest decision-making change in June 2014 raised the voting fallback number from 61.8 percent to 66 percent if after solution-oriented meetings no new proposal is created.)

In my opinion, our first two first decision-making changes were like small levers, incrementally prying our community loose from feeling discouraged and intimidated by our consistent blockers.

Our first decision-making change in 2012, while arduous and hard won, allowed us to even *imagine* we could pass proposals most of us wanted, and gave us the ability, in literal decision-making power, to do so. And our second decision-making change in 2014 gave us even more power to do this.

I imagine Communities readers who believe 100 percent consen-

Ecovillage members Ben Brownlow and Kassandra Brown at Dancing Rabbit's gate.

Photos courtesy of Dancing Rabbit

sus creates (or should create) more harmony and trust in a group, and/or who have experienced 100 percent consensus working well, may be appalled at our choice to replace calling for consensus with voting. Yet, as we've incrementally changed our method over the last two years, we have reversed the percentages of people who feel hopeful and those who feel discouraged and demoralized. For years now, many of us felt disheartened about our decision-making process, while a few believed it was fine. But after this series of changes, this has reversed: just a few members feel awful—certain Earthaven has gone to hell in a handbasket—but many more are beginning to feel hopeful again.

Why Dancing Rabbit Changed its Governance

In the summer of 2013 Dancing Rabbit Ecovillage in Missouri made their own dramatic change in governance—shifting from whole-community business meetings to a representational system (using consensus) with seven elected members. Their reasons for change had nothing to do with using consensus, which worked fine for them.

Dancing Rabbit began thinking about change in 2009, when they realized how their growth in membership had altered their social structure. In earlier years everyone ate together in the same place at the same time, giving them frequent daily opportunities to connect and talk informally about community issues. But as their members increased and they created several kitchens and eating co-ops, their social scene offered far less connection. They were no longer the same kind of cohesive group that could informally discuss community issues on a daily basis. As a result, their governance system didn't work as well: meeting attendance was down, people formerly involved in governance were getting burned out, the smaller number of folks who still attended meetings had more say than anyone else, and some decisions took longer than they once would have. This was partly due to the community's increasing size, and partly due to simply not knowing each other as well as they once had.

The Village Council System

Dancing Rabbit's new Village Council consists of seven community members elected by the members for staggered terms of two years each. These seven representatives now make the decisions formerly made by whole-community meetings:

- Creating and dissolving committees and approving committee members
- Approving and modifying job descriptions for specific community roles and paid staff
- Approving the group's annual goals and priorities; approving the budgets for Dancing Rabbit's two legal entities (an educational nonprofit, and a land trust through which daily community life is organized)
- Making committee-level decisions when requested by a committee
- Making membership decisions, including revoking membership, when these decisions can't be resolved by the regular membership process
- Revising group process methods; clarifying or weighing values on various topics, including covenant changes
- And any other responsibilities not already covered by a committee that Council members or Dancing Rabbit's Agenda Planners think are worthy of Village Council attention.

"It's refreshing to work with a smaller group that's been picked to be good decision-makers, and to be able to move forward despite concerns from people not on the Village Council," says Dancing Rabbit cofounder Tony Sirna. "The community seems to be adapting well to this process, with people accepting that they won't always get what they want (just like in full-group consensus but without as much time spent on the process)."

Empowering Committees with "Power Levels"

Dancing Rabbit has many committees, all of which essentially report to the Village Council. A committee called the Oversight Team provides the executive function of staffing committees and making sure they do their jobs. Committees have the power to propose policies in their area of responsibility, and implement policies.

The power to make decisions, however, depends on which of four "power levels" a committee has. The "propose" level is the power to make a proposal, and every committee and individual member or resident has "propose" power.

Some committees also have "review" power, which means they can send a proposal to the whole community by email. This starts a two-week comment period, during which concerns can be expressed, changes can be made, and everyone has a chance to suggest changes to or buy in to the decision. At the end of two weeks, if there are no unresolved concerns, the committee's proposal automatically passes.

Other committees have "recall" power. This is almost identical to "review" power, but the committee doesn't need to wait until the end of the two-week period and can implement a proposal immediately. However, if concerns are expressed in the two-week period, the committee may need to modify the proposal.

"Final decision" power means making and approving a proposal immediately, without a review period. The Village Council has this power for most decisions, as do meetings of the whole community, if such a meeting were to be called. At first it was rare for a committee to have "final decision" power (the Contagious Disease Response Team uses this power to declare a quarantine, for example), but the power to make decisions has become more common as the community delegates more authority to committees.

A committee can also have multiple power levels for different types of decisions. For example, a committee could use "review" power to propose a budget, and after receiving approval could use "final decision" power to approve minor changes in it.

After creating the Village Council, Dancing Rabbit added two more power levels. Committees or individual members may be given a "Village Council review" level, in which they send a proposal to the Village Council and the whole community. Everyone is free to comment on it during a two-week period, but the final decision rests with the Village Council.

Similarly, in the "Village Council recall" level a proposal is given a two-week comment period but the Village Council can implement it immediately.

"It's refreshing to work with a smaller group that's been picked to be good decision-makers, and to be able to move forward despite some concerns."

Selecting Village Council Members

While the process for selecting Village Council members doesn't involve consensus *per se*, it seems infused with the spirit of Dancing Rabbit's consensus culture.

Here's how it works. The names of every community member and resident (who has lived there at least three months) are listed alphabetically on a ballot form given to everyone. (Exceptions are the community's Selection Shepherds, who serve a one-year term to manage Village Council elections.) Each person fills out the ballot form, evaluating each person in terms of how they might serve as a Village Council member.

Evaluation choices are:

+2 "I think this person would be good in this role."
+1 "I feel OK about this person in this role."
0 "I have no opinion about this person re this role."
-1 "I don't think this person would be good in this role."

The Selection Shepherds tally the points and the 20 people with the highest number of points are eligible to be nominated for the Village Council on a seven-member slate. A slate includes returning Council Members and the three or four new ones.

A whole-community meeting is held in which people present and discuss various possible slates of seven eligible members each, and choose from one to five of what seem like the best slates of nominees. The nominees are considered according to the following criteria: the person knows how to consider what's best for the community as a whole; understands the community's mission, sustainability guidelines, and ecological covenants; has the time; is willing to participate in conflict resolution if needed; is a member in good standing (paid up on dues and fees and up-to-date with labor requirements); and preferably has the use of a computer and has had consensus training. And at least some nominees for a slate need good verbal, written, and/or financial skills.

In this meeting, ideas about people for these slates are discussed, combined, and whittled down, and the group ends up with up to

Hundreds of people visit Dancing Rabbit each year, like these folks taking a tour.

Dancing Rabbit members eat in various dining co-ops. Here's the kitchen and dining room building of Ironweed Co-op.

five different slates, chosen either by consensus or, if agreement can't be reached for one slate by consensus, by a dot-voting system.

At that point all members vote on the slate of nominees they want, using a computer-based instant runoff system. The slate with the most number of votes becomes the new Village Council.

Consensus at Dancing Rabbit

Village Council members use consensus to make decisions, as do the smaller committees. As in many other intentional communities, the basis of Dancing Rabbit's consensus culture is the belief that people should always have a chance to share their opinions and concerns, and decisions aren't made until everyone who speaks up is taken into account. And...they expect community members to take responsibility for how their own consciousness may affect community decision-making. "Consensus requires us to make decisions that are best for the group as a whole, and being able to distinguish between our personal wants, fears, and agendas and the group's good—which is essential to making a positive contribution," they write in their Process Manual.

As advised by most consensus trainers, Dancing Rabbit members believe that blocking should be a rare occurrence if the community is functioning well and its members are in alignment with its values and process. Thus they have a clear blocking policy and a way to test for the legitimacy of a block. For example, someone objecting to a proposal is expected to stand aside, not block, if their objection is based on personal values rather than on shared common values. And conversely, it is expected any block will be based on one or more shared community values, or by the belief that passing the proposal would damage the community.

Dancing Rabbit used consensus in its whole-community meetings, and a block was considered valid if it was based in one of the stated community values and at least three other members could understand (but did not necessarily agree with) why the person felt this way. If someone were to block frequently, the Conflict Resolution Team would help the person and the whole group talk about it, with the possibility of setting up an ad hoc committee to work through the issues.

Now, in their seven-member Village Council, a block is considered valid if one other Village Council member can understand (but not necessarily agree with) the blocking person's position in relation to shared community values. It is also expected that any Village Council member who blocks has made a reasonable effort to participate in the group's discussion. It is also expected that other Council Members have been reasonable too, giving the person adequate time to consider and comment on the proposal. (Village Council decisions can also be recalled by 25 percent of Dancing Rabbit members.)

I'm impressed by how Dancing Rabbit innovated a whole new governance method in response to the social effects of their increased membership. This took foresight and pluck! While I've called the new methods of Earthaven and Dancing Rabbit "radical," Tony Sirna points out that their new method isn't actually radical (except for using consensus instead of majority-rule voting) because they intend to grow to the size of a town of 500 to 1000, and small towns typically use representative governance with elected Councils.

I hope you've found these innovative new methods stimulating food for thought. Working to shift a whole community's paradigm about governance and decision-making takes courage, energy, and time. And...it can be really worth it! ❧

This article was adapted from a piece that first appeared in the online GEN Newsletter: gen.ecovillage.org/en/news.

Diana Leafe Christian, author of Creating a Life Together *and* Finding Community, *speaks at conferences, offers consultations, and leads workshops internationally. She specializes in teaching Sociocracy to communities, and has taught Sociocracy in North America, Europe, and Latin America. See www.DianaLeafeChristian.org.*

Many Dancing Rabbit members have built strawbale cabins with white plaster, like this one.

Why No Tyranny of the Minority in Sociocracy: How Sociocracy Can Help Communities, Part IV

By Diana Leafe Christian

In Sociocracy, a "circle" is a committee or team. *(See "Self-Governance with Circles and Double Links," COMMUNITIES #161, Winter 2013.)* Every circle has an "Aim"—a statement of the things the circle produces and/or provides and delivers to the people it serves, stated as an overview. For most communities "the people it serves" are the community members themselves. So a community's Finance Circle, for example, provides financial services—collecting funds, paying bills, and so on. If the community also has an educational mission, "the people it serves" include the visitors who take the community's tours, classes, and workshops. In this case, the community's Education Circle, for example, provides workshop trainers and services and logistics for the workshops and classes for the public.

As described in the last article in this series, "Consent Decision-Making and Community Vision, Mission, and Aim" (COMMUNITIES *#163, Summer 2014)*, all of a community's circles are guided by Sociocracy's three values: equivalence, transparency, and effectiveness.

The six steps of Consent Decision-Making are: (1) Presenting the Proposal, (2) Clarifying Questions Round, (3) Quick Reactions Round, (4) Consent Rounds alternating with, (5) Resolve Objections Rounds, and (6) Celebrating the Decision.

Step Four, the Consent Round, and Step Five, the Resolve Objections Round, are repeated until there are no more objections and the proposal is "good enough for now" and "safe enough to try." There are at least six legitimate reasons to object to a proposal *(see box, p. 63)* and at least nine ways to resolve an objection *(see box, p. 63)*.

Objections must be reasoned and "argued." This means the objection is based on observable facts and the reasonable conclusions the person draws from those facts, and other circle members can understand these conclusions. Usually objections don't stop a proposal, but flag the need to modify the proposal to improve it in needed ways. [Some Sociocracy resources say that reasoned, argued objections must be "paramount," meaning significant, not trivial objections. However, several Sociocracy trainers suggest not using that potentially confusing word.]

Not every proposal must be consented to, since responses in the Quick Reaction Round can show that there's little to no support for the proposal, or it has substantial deficiencies and needs more work, or is written unclearly, and it's dropped. But usually the circle members themselves create the proposal (in Sociocracy's Proposal-Forming process), and they don't spend time making proposals about issues they're not interested in.

Practicing Consent Decision-Making at an IPOEMA Permaculture teaching center in Brazil, April 2014.

Some communities use what I call "consensus-with-unanimity" as their decision-making method. This is when everyone in the meeting except those standing aside must approve a proposal for it to pass, and there's no recourse if someone blocks. When communities use consensus-with-unanimity, sometimes the same few community members can consistently block some, or many, proposals. These members thus control the community by virtue of what they won't let it do—the so-called "tyranny of the minority." However, when a community uses Sociocracy and practices Consent Decision-Making correctly, tyranny of the minority doesn't happen.

Jack's Many Objections

Let's say a member of a circle, Jack, objects to a proposal. And let's say it seems to one or more circle members as if the objection may really be Jack's personal preference about how we carry out the Aim and not a reasoned "argued" objection. Or his objection may not necessarily be tied to the circle's Aim at all, or to the aim of the proposal. The facilitator or any other circle members could point this out, and could ask Jack a series of questions designed to help him understand the process better and clarify his thinking.

Only the person who is objecting can withdraw their objection. This usually happens in the Resolve Objections Round, or when they say "No objection" in the next Consent Round. (I was mistaken in the third article in this series, in COMMUNITIES #163, when I wrote that the facilitator can declare an objection invalid.) If Jack objects to the proposal but can't seem to show how his objection is related to the Aim, there are several things the circle can do:

The facilitator and/or other circle members can ask Jack, "Can you show how your objection is related to our Aim?" Hopefully he can, and his reasoning is clearly understood by the other circle members. If not, the facilitator or someone else might ask Jack this question again, gently and courteously, perhaps changing the wording of the question.

Someone might ask, "Is this your personal preference—something you'd personally really like to see happen? And if so, how does it also relate to our Aim?" Or, "How does this proposal directly affect you?"—a question which might bring out new information. Or, "Can we resolve your objection in another way—for example, in a future proposal?"—helping Jack understand that this proposal is confined to a certain scope, and another, future proposal can address the issues he's concerned about.

Maybe Jack cannot show how his objection relates to the circle's Aim. Or maybe he believes it relates to the Aim but other circle members don't see how it does, and Jack is not willing to remove his objection.

As noted in earlier articles in this series, every proposal includes criteria for later evaluating and measuring the proposal after it's implemented. So someone could ask, "If we added the criteria 'X' to the proposal, we can evaluate it later to see whether the problem you're concerned about might be starting to happen—if so, we could change things then. If we added this criteria, do you think the proposal would be safe enough to try?"

If these questions help remind Jack that he has recourse for his concerns—that new criteria for later measuring and evaluating the proposal can be added—he might agree that it's safe enough to try, and withdraw his objection.

Consent Decision-Making

1. Present Proposal

2. Clarifying Questions

"Do you understand the proposal?"
"No questions." Or, "Yes. What about. . ?"*(In a round or popcorn-style)*

3. Quick Reaction Round

"What do you think of it?" *(Brief!)*

4. Consent Round

"Do you have any reasoned objections to this proposal?"
"No objection." Or, "Objection." "What is your objection?"

Six Reasons to Object:

1. One or more aspects of proposal conflict with circle's aim.
2. One or more obvious flaws, or important aspects left out, re circle's aim.
3. There are no criteria or dates for later evaluating implemented proposal.
4. Potential unintended consequences of implementing proposal, re circle's aim.
5. One or more aspects are not well thought out, or expressed in confusing way.
6. One or more aspects would not allow you to carry out your tasks, re circle's aim.

5. Resolving Objections:

1. Add concern as new criterion for evaluation, and/or make first evaluation date sooner.
2. Facilitator amends it.
3. Proposal originator amends it.
4. Person(s) objecting, one or more others, or everyone in circle amends it.
5. Round: "How would you resolve this?"
6. "Fishbowl" of two-three people in middle.
7. Refer to Research Team.
8. Refer to Resolution Team.
9. Refer to higher or lower circle.

6. Announce Decision and Celebrate.

An Experienced Facilitator Responds to Repeated Objections

Earlier this year Sociocracy trainer Gina Price from Australia and I led a workshop in Brazil. Gina asked these kinds of questions as she played the role of facilitator in an exercise on Consent Decision-Making. A workshop participant objected to the proposal in the exercise but it wasn't clear how his objection related to the circle's Aim. Gina gently asked if his objection was based on a personal preference or whether it might be specifically tied to the circle's Aim. His response didn't convince the others that his objection was in fact related to the Aim.

So Gina, still playing the role of facilitator said, "What if we added a criteria to the proposal that specifically addresses your concern? So that when we evaluate the proposal after it's implemented, we can find out whether your concern is happening. And if it is, we can change things. If we added this criteria, would you find the proposal safe enough to try?"

The man still didn't believe the proposal would be safe enough to try by adding this new criteria. Gina repeated this question, gently and courteously, a second time.

He still didn't believe the proposal would be

Participants at the IPOEMA workshop in Brazil in a discussion of the Resolve Objections Round.

Photos by Diana Leafe Christian

safe enough. Gina then asked, "If we added this criteria to the proposal and we *also* moved the first evaluation date up sooner, do you think it would be safe enough to try?"

At this point the participant believed the proposal *would* be OK to consent to with these changes. He was convinced by Gina's suggested proposal modifications: (1) adding his concern about a potential negative consequence to the proposal's criteria for later evaluating it, and (2) moving the evaluation date up, so the evaluation would happen sooner. Finally he understood how it was possible to resolve his objection in a way that seemed reasonable and safe, and he withdrew his objection.

As you can see, the facilitator and other circle members do everything they can to help the person find ways to resolve their objection so the proposal seems "good enough for now" and "safe enough to try."

Time-Sensitive Proposals

If all of these methods for modifying the proposal did not result in Jack's withdrawing his objection, and if the proposal is not time-sensitive, it could be saved until the next meeting. In the meantime a few circle members in a smaller "helping circle," or Resolution Team, could meet with Jack before the next policy meeting to help him find a reasonable resolution to his objection. Sometimes all a person needs is a little time and some psychic space away from the issue; time to "sleep on it," so to speak.

However, when a member like Jack repeatedly objects to a time-sensitive proposal in a community and is not willing to withdraw his objection after circle members offer multiple ways to modify it to resolve his objections, I recommend that someone propose that the objection is invalid. And if everyone except Jack consents to this, they regretfully and courteously declare his objection invalid and move on.

As Sociocracy trainer and *We the People* co-author John Buck points out, this procedure is like temporarily removing Jack from the circle, but only for the duration of this specific proposal. While many Sociocracy trainers may not recommend declaring an objection invalid and moving on for time-sensitive proposals, I recommend it because I've seen what often happens when any one community member has complete decision-making power over everyone else: they can delay or even stop the group from making a crucial decision. This is one more protection against "tyranny of the minority."

Consistent, Repeated Objections by a Circle Member

Why would Jack object to proposals often, and no proposal modifications seem adequate enough for him to withdraw his objection or help come up with a modification that will work for him? I see at least three possibilities:

(1) Jack may not understand that Sociocracy and Consent Decision-Making work quite differently than consensus. And he may be, consciously or unconsciously, trying to stop the proposal—using an objection as a "block," rather than seeing the proposal as an experiment, something that can be tried and perhaps later modified further or thrown out altogether.

A remedy for this is for circle members to arrange to get Jack additional training. If he is not willing to get more training, or he believes he understands Sociocracy well enough, or he argues about it, the circle could also ask for advice from their Sociocracy trainer to help Jack understand better. (If this doesn't help, however, there is a recourse. See "The Remedy of Last Resort—Asking Someone to Leave the Circle," below.)

Members of Baja BioSana Ecovillage in Mexico learning Sociocracy in their open-air pavilion, February 2014.

(2) Jack may have a different interpretation of the circle's Aim than other circle members do. A remedy for this is for circle members to discuss the issue—through free-form discussion, a "fishbowl" process, or any format they like—in order for everyone to understand the circle's Aim better. And they could perhaps revise the description of their Aim so it's more easily understood, or change the Aim itself. They would do this with the consent of the next "higher" circle, such as the General Circle, since the General Circle sets the Aim of each functional circle, at least in classical Sociocracy.

(3) Jack may have an unconscious emotional pattern that compels him to stop or disagree with what other circle members want. Doing this, consciously or unconsciously, may meet a need he may have to feel seen and heard, or a desire, conscious or unconscious, to rebel against perceived authority figures and "not be pushed around."

A remedy is for circle members to talk openly and compassionately about this possibility. Jack may feel quite uncomfortable, since the group is talking about the possibility of his having psychological issues compelling him to object for personal reasons, rather than for one of the six reasons to object. *(See box, p. 63.)*

When using Consent Decision-Making a circle must face and deal with the issue of someone repeatedly objecting to proposals no matter how the proposal may be modified to meet their objections, or how diligently others try to help the person understand Consent Decision-Making. The circle must deal with the issue directly, because of its mandate—its Aim—to deliver certain physical things and/or services to the community it serves. And one circle member's personal issues can't be allowed to stop them. So what can a circle do?

The Remedy of Last Resort—Asking Someone to Leave the Circle

What if nothing seems to help a circle member understand the process better, or differentiate between personal preferences or unconscious motives and objections based on the circle's Aim? After trying everything else first, another option is for the circle to ask the person to leave the circle, either for a specific period of time, or indefinitely.

Any circle member can propose that Jack leave the circle for a specific period of time, or indefinitely. And if everyone except Jack consents to this proposal, he must leave the circle. Jack wouldn't have consent rights in this proposal because it's about him. Please note, this process does not ask Jack to leave the community, just the circle. And it doesn't mean he cannot apply to join another circle.

If not everyone in the circle consents to the proposal, though, then Jack stays in the circle, and the group keeps dealing with the issues. Jack may change, in which case the problem is resolved. Or, if he doesn't, sometime later someone can propose this again. And by that time, enough other circle members may believe it's best if Jack *does* leave their circle so they can move forward to accomplish their Aim.

In my experience leading workshops and as a consultant to communities, I've seen, over and over, that most community members are loathe to take actions like this to improve a difficult situation if it means another community member might feel discomfort, no matter the amount of discomfort that member may have triggered in others—and even if that member did and said things that caused other people to feel so much discouragement and demoralization they quit their committees. Many community members would rather suffer in silence than believe they had caused someone to feel hurt.

And Jack probably *would* feel hurt if he were asked to leave the circle. When he understands that other committee members find his behavior too difficult to continue working with, he may react with hurt feelings, shame, anger, or blaming. Yet being asked to leave a circle is feedback—and getting this feedback may be crucial in Jack's own conscious or unconscious quest for self-awareness and knowing how to live a better, more satisfying life. It's a wake-up call, a "request from the Universe" that he do some course-correction.

Ideally, Jack would learn from this, and benefit. But let's say he doesn't, and continues to feel hurt, and withdraws from the community for awhile, or for good. Even so, I believe it's better to be real and authentic with him—with kindness, compassion, and empathy, if possible—than for the circle to continue to limp along in a stuck, dysfunctional manner. Doing so could even be considered as creating a codependent relationship with Jack, unintentionally preventing him from learning from the natural consequences of his own actions.

If the circle asked Jack to leave, temporarily or indefinitely, other circle members would feel bad for Jack too, and they might be tempted to believe they *caused* his feelings. However, most likely they would soon feel relieved as well, if not uplifted and energized as they experience themselves moving forward toward their circle's goals without disruption, conflict, or being repeatedly slowed down.

While I certainly have compassion for a community member like Jack, I also have compassion for the community as a whole, and for its potential to become healthy and thriving. I want community members to feel the satisfaction of moving forward towards their community's goals, and their committee's goals. This can feel wonderful—and this is why I recommend Sociocracy to communities. While I realize some communities may not want to use the option of asking to someone to leave a circle, I want to let people know this option is built into Sociocracy governance, and can be used if needed.

The next article in the series will cover giving consent to circle members, and the Proposal-Forming process. ❧

Diana Leafe Christian, author of Creating a Life Together *and* Finding Community, *speaks at conferences, offers consultations, and leads workshops internationally. She specializes in teaching Sociocracy to communities, and has taught Sociocracy in North America, Europe, and Latin America. This article series will be part of her forthcoming booklet on using Sociocracy in Intentional Communities. See www.DianaLeafeChristian.org.*

Six Legitimate Reasons to Object to a Proposal

(1) One or more aspects of the proposal conflict with the circle's Aim.

(2) The proposal has one or more obvious flaws, or important aspects are left out, re. the circle's Aim.

(3) There are no criteria or dates for later evaluating the implemented proposal.

(4) There are potential unintended consequences of implementing the proposal, re. the circle's Aim.

(5) One or more aspects of the proposal are not well thought out, or are expressed in a confusing way.

(6) One or more aspects of the proposal would not allow a circle member to carry out their tasks, re. the circle's Aim.

Nine Ways to Resolve Objections

(1) Add the person's concerns as a new criterion for evaluation, and/or move the first evaluation date earlier so it happens sooner.

(2) The facilitator amends the proposal.

(3) The originator of the proposal amends it.

(4) The person or persons objecting or everyone in circle amends it.

(5) Do a round: "How would you resolve this?"

(6) Organize a "fishbowl"—two or three people sit in the middle of the circle and discuss how to resolve the objection while the other circle members observe.

(7) The proposal is referred to a Research Team—several circle members who will get needed information for modifying the proposal.

(8) The proposal is referred to a Resolution Team—several circle members who will work with the person objecting and modify the proposal in order to resolve it.

(9) The proposal is referred to a "higher" (more abstract) circle or a "lower" (more focused and specific) circle.

The Proposal-Forming Process

Sociocracy has four major meeting processes: (1) Consent Decision-Making, (2) the Proposal-Forming process, (3) Selecting People for Roles (Sociocracy elections), and (4) Role-Improvement Feedback. Consent Decision-Making forms the basis of the other three meeting processes.

Proposals are created with the Proposal-Forming process and then considered using Consent Decision-Making. Most Sociocracy trainers teach the two together as one long process, from the first step of the Proposal-Forming process to the last step of Consent Decision-Making. This is called the "long format." Practicing Consent Decision-Making only, after a proposal was created earlier, is called the "short format."

I teach these two processes separately, however, because I've found it makes each one easier to learn. A circle can first create a proposal and then consider it immediately with Consent Decision-Making, or make a proposal and consider it in another meeting. Or someone could propose that their Representative take the proposal to a higher circle, and if they all consent, it goes to a higher circle.

—D.L.C.

THE TOP 10
Most Common Mistakes in Consensus Process and What to Do Instead

By Tree Bressen

Editor's Note: For decades consensus has been the decision-making method of choice for many baby boomer communitarians and activists, as well as for younger generations of cooperators inspired by them. In this document crafted originally for the Occupy movement, long-time group-process trainer and consultant Tree Bressen shares tips on common mistakes in consensus and how to help the process work more smoothly.

1. Inappropriate Blocks

Blocking because you disagree, object, don't like the proposal, it doesn't match your personal needs or values, it goes against tradition, you'd have to leave the group if it passed, etc. Also includes premature blocks, where someone threatens to block if a group explores a particular direction.

• Consensus works only when the power to block is restricted to concerns that are demonstrably based in the core principles of the group. Consensus means giving a fair and heartfelt hearing to substantive points—it does not mean you always get your way.

• Remember the Stand Aside option exists for people with passionately held concerns and objections.

• Establish a clear procedure regarding how the validity of potential blocks is assessed and what happens when one arises. Create a robust response to inappropriate blocks.

• Blocking does not have to mean end of discussion. Some of the most effective consensus groups require the blocker to help work out a solution.

2. Enabling Bad Behavior

If disrespectful statements or behavior from one member toward another or the group are tolerated (yelling, sarcasm, put-downs, jokes at someone's expense, etc.), this degrades the meeting environment for everyone, impacting the whole group's safety and well-being.

• Set a constructive tone and insist on following it, kindly but clearly putting a stop to any meanness, attacks, undercutting, oppressive "isms," etc. We are fully capable of disagreeing fervently with respect.

3. Poorly Planned Agendas

People's time and life energy are precious; when this is not respected, they stop showing up. Prioritize clearly and be realistic. Reserve the bulk of time for the things that appropriately call for widespread active involvement.

• Put advance time into creating the best possible agenda—and then be willing to shift it if the group as a whole needs something different.

• Put the most important items early so they don't get squeezed by less important items.

• Avoid lengthy reports (just get the highlights, or put it over email) or announcements (use a big sheet by the door instead, so people see it when they come in and when they leave).

• Provide breaks at least every 90 minutes (and don't pretend you can have a five-minute break).

4. Having the Same Person Facilitate and Present Topics

When the facilitator is also the person offering information and context on an issue, it lessens safety for those who may disagree with the general thrust, putting them immediately on the defensive.

• Presenters supply information and context and should be free to advocate.

• Facilitators need to be neutral so that everyone in the group feels supported by them.

• Mixing roles can work OK in small, committee-like groups (seven people or less?); the larger the group, the more need for facilitator neutrality and formal roles.

5. Starting from a Proposal instead of an Issue

In situations where people want to feel fully empowered and included, any overly developed proposal on anything important will inevitably evoke resistance. At that point, the recipients of the proposal feel scared that they'll be steamrolled, while the developers of the proposal feel unappreciated, and no one is happy.

• For smaller proposals that don't require many people's energy for successful implementation, starting from a proposal can be fine.

• For more complex or controversial situations that touch many people, start by describing the situation and exploring ideas together in the larger group. A committee can be useful in helping frame the topic, as long as they don't go too far down the road. Later, once a basic direction is established, a committee might work out details. Or if the larger group doesn't easily come to resolution, they may request a task group of people with diverse viewpoints to work together on it.

6. Too Many Details

There's nothing like a tedious, overly detailed conversation among a few involved people to put the rest of the meeting to sleep while everyone checks out.

• See #3 above.

• Delegate! Send the rest to committee.

7. Rushing the Process

Leads to inappropriate blocks, situations where legitimate concerns were not dealt with in an integrated way and so the only option left to the person raising it is to block the whole process, which feels rough on everyone involved.

• Allow plenty of time for discussion. Take the space to really listen to people's diverse viewpoints and concerns. Trust the wisdom of the whole.

• If you have time and if it's important, discuss the matter, then let it sit and settle, then return to it.

• Wait to make the official call for consensus until a sense of unity emerges.

8. Spending All Your Meeting Time in Open Discussion

In general discussion, only the boldest get their voices heard—many others never even raise their hands.

• Change formats (planned in advance or on the spot): break into pairs or small groups (three to five people), line up to show the spectrum of opinion, use dot voting, fishbowls, roleplays, write stuff on sheets around the room, etc. See treegroup.info/topics/handout-formats.pdf for a bunch more ideas.

9. Attaching Proposals to People

Once something is out on the floor, it belongs to the group, not an individual member. Thus it's better to refer to an idea as "the proposal to do X" than as "Jenny's proposal." For this same reason, avoid the taint of "friendly amendments," a holdover from Robert's Rules and voting process where you ask the proposer's permission to modify. You wouldn't ask one person "Can i add this bed to the garden?" unless it was their garden; since it's the group's common plot, it's up to everyone whether and how the proposal gets modified.

• Expect every proposal to get modified a lot before adoption.

10. Fuzzy Minutes

Failing to accurately record the sense of the meeting can mean hours of lost group work. Don't record verbatim who said what, because it's too long for others to read later and it ties issues too closely to personalities.

• Make sure the decision and reasons for it are written clearly for the records. Record any stand asides (names and reasons), and tasks for implementation (who will do what, by when). ❧

Tree Bressen lived in intentional communities and shared households her whole adult life until she discovered in 2011 to her surprise and dismay that she enjoyed living alone. She is the founder of Group Pattern Language Project, authors of the deck Group Works: A Pattern Language for Bringing Life to Meetings and Other Gatherings, *available for free download at www.groupworksdeck.org. She is based in Eugene, Oregon, where she consults with a wide variety of organizations on how to make meetings better.*

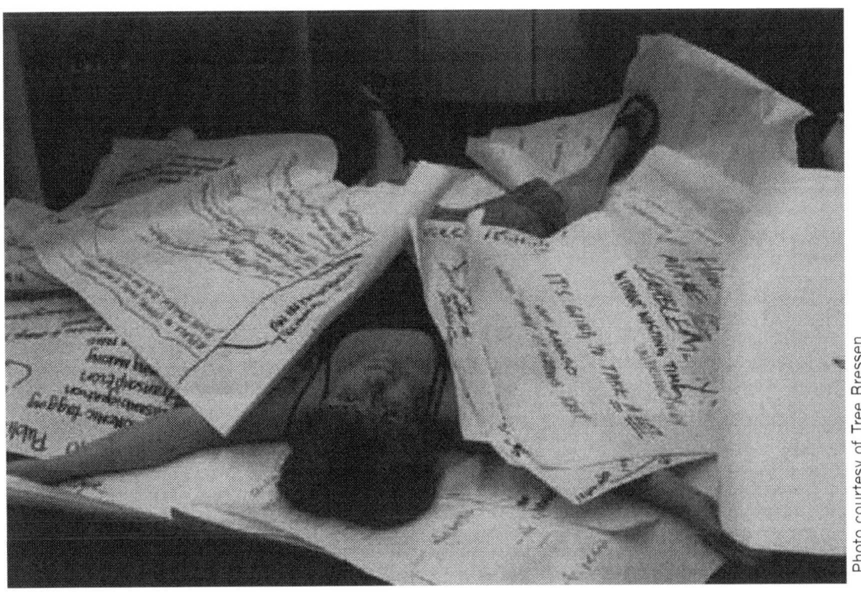

Photo courtesy of Tree Bressen

Misconceptions about Sociocracy

Diana Leafe Christian

Participants in the author's ecovillage workshop in St. Petersburg, Russia, discussing governance issues in community.

Laird Schaub, Executive Secretary of the Fellowship for Intentional Community (publisher of this magazine), expressed eight concerns about Sociocracy in the Winter 2014 issue (#165, pages 80, 77-79).

Some of Laird's concerns involve Sociocracy; others address an inaccurate perception of Sociocracy—as if Sociocracy were an alternate but less effective form of consensus. However, in my experience it's quite different from consensus.

1. Sociocracy "Does Not Address Emotional Input"

Laird wrote that understanding and addressing emotions that arise in meetings is an essential component of group dynamics. He believes Sociocracy does not do this, which is a serious flaw. Fortunately this isn't true.

(1) Circle members have several ways to address emotions when considering a proposal, including open discussion, fishbowls, and other processes. They can do this if someone proposes one of these formats and the circle consents to it.

(2) Emotional distress is less likely than when using consensus in considering a proposal because there is far less pressure to "get it right," since proposals are measured and evaluated several times after they're implemented and can be modified to suit real conditions in real time. Taking this pressure off people in meetings tends to foster more peaceful, relaxed meetings.

(3) Communities using Sociocracy can create a Process Circle to specifically help resolve conflicts between members and assist with the emotional issues and challenges of individual members.

(4) Sociocracy is designed for a different set of assumptions and expectations about meetings and self-governance than consensus. More specifically in relation to Laird's concern about handling emotional content in meetings, Sociocracy is designed for groups in which a circle fulfilling its aims, performing its tasks for the community, and moving forward towards its goals is more important than the emotional upsets of any individual members during those instances *when the group cannot or is not willing to take the time to deal with both.* Methods for doing this are described in previous articles in this series ("Consent Decision-Making," Fall 2014; "Why No Tyranny of the Minority in Sociocracy," Winter 2014).

People well-trained in Sociocracy know that their personal prefer-

(continued on p. 79)

MISCONCEPTIONS ABOUT SOCIOCRACY

(continued from p. 80)

ences are not valid reasons to object to a proposal or to advocate for what they want instead if their preferences conflict with the aims of their circle. Also, people don't volunteer for a circle but apply to join it. Each member of a circle must be consented to by every other member, so the circle will consist of people who can work well together to help it fulfill its aims for the community. And in Sociocracy decision-making bodies are relatively small—perhaps four to six people in functional circles and maybe eight or 10 people in a General Circle.

In my opinion Sociocracy exists in a different paradigm than the one I believe Laird advocates—that most people join communities in order to have deep, personally satisfying relationships with other community members, and so it logically follows that consensus is the best choice for decision-making. And while for many people living in community personal relationships may be very important—especially with friends and neighbors one feels drawn to—a more important reason for their living in community may be to create a great neighborhood, as in cohousing, or to create a settlement where people learn and teach others about living in more ecologically sustainable ways, as in ecovillages. In my experience many members of communities founded since the early 1990s, like most cohousing and ecovillage projects, may prefer a governance and decision-making method like Sociocracy which favors moving forward toward community goals over emotional processing in meetings.

So while Laird sees addressing emotions that arise in meetings as essential, I see it as essential for some communities but not for others.

On another note, while Laird reports that a Sociocracy trainer assured him that all certified trainers are experienced in working with emotions in meetings, I don't believe this is true—in my experience Sociocracy trainers, certified or not, are no better and no worse than anyone else in working with emotions in meetings...and they don't need to be.

2. Double Linking of Circles

Laird's concern is that there may not be enough people to fill both the operations leader and representative roles in every circle. But when this is true people join more than one circle. And when a community is new or has few members, they can combine this role until they have enough members for both roles.

3. Sociocracy Elections Allow Criticizing Candidates on the Spot

The elections process doesn't do this. Before anyone is nominated, proposed, or consented to for a role in a circle, the group selects the term length and the tasks the person will do in the role, the requirements the person will need to carry out those tasks, and some desired characteristics for the role. These can include characteristics like "gets along well with others in meetings," "has good communication skills," and "has high skills in cooperation and collaboration." Circle members base their nominations, and any objections and resolutions of objections, on these factors, but not on any personality characteristics of the proposed candidate.

4. Objections, and Consent vs. Consensus

Laird writes that, if the concepts of consensus and Sociocracy's consent process are substantively different, then this difference makes sense only if using Sociocracy allows people to consent to a proposal sooner than people using consensus would approve a proposal.

Yes, people using Sociocracy would most likely consent to a proposal sooner. However, "to approve a proposal" in consensus and " to give consent" in Sociocracy are like apples and oranges, since objections in Sociocracy are not blocks (three are no blocks); they are more like concerns, but far more specific. And objections to a proposal and resolutions of objections are tied to the circle's very specific aims, rather than to the values or lifestyle choices of any individual circle member.

5. "Rounds Are Not Always the Best Format"

As noted above, other formats are used when proposed and consented to. Laird also said he believes rounds are slow and repetitive. Actually rounds in Sociocracy are quick and tend to give the circle energy; for example, clarifying question, quick reaction, and consent rounds usually just involve a few words, although people say more when describing an objection, and in rounds to resolve objections. In my experience, the quickness of rounds and their "include-everyone" energy feels really good. Sociocracy trainer Gilles Charest in Quebec says, "Rounds build the group."

6. Starting with Proposals

Laird wrote that people start with an already-created proposal, but actually proposals are created through the multi-step proposal-creating process, and are almost always created by the same people who decide them, either a few minutes earlier in the same meeting or in a previous meeting.

7. Governance System or Decision-Making Structure?

Sociocracy is a governance structure with several parts, including consent decision-making.

8. "A Structural Response to an Energetic Challenge"

Laird wrote that some groups may want an alternative to consensus because they're frustrated by it, but they may not realize that using consensus requires a commitment to culture change for it to work well. He says Sociocracy appears to offer a structural approach, but the most important issues in meetings are energy issues, not structure.

In contrast, Sociocracy does not require a commitment to culture change nor must people aspire to a higher level of consciousness or behave more nobly than they usually do or possess exceptionally good communication skills. Sociocracy doesn't require a gifted facilitator or a high level of trust in the group. It only requires that the group understands and practices Sociocracy correctly, rather than trying to combine parts of it with consensus, which tends to create an awkward hybrid that doesn't solve old problems and generates new ones.

Diana Leafe Christian, author of Creating a Life Together *and* Finding Community, *speaks at conferences, offers consultations, and leads workshops internationally. She specializes in teaching Sociocracy to communities, and has taught Sociocracy in North America, Europe, and Latin America. This article series is part of her forthcoming booklet on using Sociocracy in intentional communities.*

Sociocracy, Feelings, and Emotions

By Jock Millenson

A few weeks ago I found myself returning to my seasonal eco-community in Greece for the 13th year, about to dig and plant one of our vegetable beds which had lain covered and dormant all winter.

After uncovering the straw and cardboard mulch laid down last autumn to keep the weeds from overwhelming the bed during our seven-month absence, and before starting to work, I took a few moments to sit next to this 25 x 6-foot bed to "attune" to it. I let the warm May sun, the smell of last year's compost mixed with that of newly cut grass, and the fragrance of wild mountain herbs mingle with the sight of the rich brown clods of fertile Greek soil and the songs of the birds. As I sat there on a stump, my wellies in contact with the soil, I invited thoughts about what might grow best in this bed and reminded myself of what we had planted there in previous years and how the bed had fared last summer.

After a few contemplative moments, I got up and selected my trusty Smith and Hawken four-tined stainless steel fork and began digging. Although this bed has been "improved" every year since we first dug it in 2012, I still found a few large rocks to remove and many clods of earth that needed breaking up with the fork so that any seeds sown directly would not be prevented from germinating and reaching the light.

Eventually I was satisfied that the bed was nearly ready, set down the fork, and fetched a rake to smooth over the bed and ready it for the corn seeds and cucumber seedlings that I had decided to plant.

Now as I write this it is early July and the corn stalks are up about a foot and the cucumbers already have started twisting around them and I can see a few immature cukes already on the vines. If all goes well, in a few weeks we will be eating cucumbers and corn cobs.

• • •

You might be wondering why I've started this piece on Sociocracy and feelings by writing about gardening. It is because I see a close analogy. In Laird Schaub's article "Further Reflections on Sociocracy" (Communities #165), he expresses his concern that Sociocracy fails to deal with the emotional and feeling aspects of community process. In this article I will not be considering all of Laird's points, only the two that I have the most personal experience with: #4, the difference between formal consensus (C.T. Butler and Amy Rothstein, 1987) and consent, and #1, how to deal with feelings in decision-making situations.

For the past 13 years I have lived nearly every summer in an intentional community in Pelion, Greece consisting of some six to 10 ever-changing members and coworkers whose stated mission is to demonstrate the value of authentic community as a vehicle for teaching and researching holistic education through a living-learning environment.

Ever since we at this community, called Kalikalos, were introduced to Sociocracy by the late Emile van Dantzig in 2010, we have used some of the principles of Dynamic Governance in our decision making. However, because we are a small group of never more than a dozen people, we do not make use of the full suite of Sociocratic tools. For instance, although we do have some small sub-committees—the six managers of our three campuses, the boards of directors of the two nonprofit companies that run our three campuses, and various ad hoc committees (e.g., the two people currently looking into the construction of a solar shower at Kissos Centre and the three people who are doing social media)—we have never seen a need for double-linked circles.

Similarly, we do not use the Sociocratic guidelines for selecting managerial (focalising) roles for people. These seem to emerge organically out of our everyday interactions and the degree of commitment and leadership people are willing to take on. Nor do we use the formal rounds in evaluating proposals. Because our circles are quite small (six to 11 people typically) we accomplish the same ends by free-form discussions with our daily morning meetings always held (facilitated) by one person whose job it is to keep us on track and to remind us of time constraints. As we are a working community servicing workshops, we cannot spend the entire morning in a meeting; our guests are expecting lunch, the fruit and vegetable seller arrives at noon, the plumber or electrician may also be waiting for us at 11 am, and callers expect to find the office functioning in the morning.

• • •

We use Sociocracy primarily to guide our decision making. Without going through the formal process of picture forming, making a proposal, inviting a reaction

Staff circle.

round, adjusting the proposal for objections, etc., we mix it all up together. Most of the time this is a free-for-all. If the facilitator decides that the discussion is getting out of hand and straying from the issue, or sees that one or two people are dominating the discussion and others are not speaking, she (and we are about 70 percent women) brings out the talking stick and turns the discussion into controlled rounds.

Little by little the issue either becomes clarified and the proposal sculpted so that the facilitator invites the group for a consent round; or the group has such wide views on the issue that it's clear no proposal at this stage is likely to receive general support. It is then referred back to a small subgroup of two or three members, self-selected from the most disparate opposing viewpoints, to come back to the next meeting hopefully with a synthesis.

Alternatively, if a coherent proposal has emerged that appears to have the general support of most of the group, the facilitator calls for a consent round. This is very simple: either the facilitator or the original proposer reads out or says the proposal as precisely as possible. Those of us who have no paramount objection to it put our right thumb up, those who aren't sure or need more information put their thumb horizontal, and anyone who has a paramount objection puts their thumb down.

Those who require more information are asked what isn't clear and the proposer or any other member endeavors to provide sufficient additional information to allow the person to either go thumb up or thumb down. Frequently the very process of providing more information results in a modification or refinement to the proposal. We may then try another consent round which may or may not result in all thumbs up and if so the proposal is immediately written down in our agreements book, the wording checked with everyone, and an agreed time for re-evaluation is noted in the agreements book.

Suppose one or more persons still voice paramount objections. Such an objection means either: (1) the member believes that the proposal violates the mission of the community; (2) that it is likely to have consequences that will violate the community's mission, or which will be undesirable for the group; or (3) that the dissenting member thinks there is a better way to achieve the same end.

Whenever there remain people with thumbs down, the facilitator reminds the group that they are not being asked if they agree with the proposal. They are being asked if they can "live with it," or if it is "good enough to try"; it will always have a time limit as to when it must be brought back to the circle to be re-evaluated.

This simple reminder constitutes the core difference between formal consensus and Sociocratic consent and why we prefer the latter. We do not require agreement from everyone in the circle, we merely require that they can live with the proposal and allow us to try it out. This subtle but crucial difference between formal consensus and Sociocratic consent is what prevents our group from being held hostage by one or two members who cannot agree with it. Many equalitarian communities have found that attempting to achieve consensus agreements can create such lengthy processes that people lose energy and may eventually drop out altogether.

Although Sociocratic consent differs subtly from formal consensus, I agree with Laird that consent is a variation of consensus. In our Articles of Incorporation we hold consensus to be a fundamental spiritual principle, a core value of our community, and the basis for all our decisions.

What does a group do if there is one person consistently objecting to nearly every proposal put forth, arguing that in their view of the mission all these proposals violate it, hence their paramount objections are fully valid and must be respected? I cannot agree with Diana Leafe Christian (Communities #165, page 62) that the group is then empowered to bypass the objection and pass the proposal anyway. This undermines the very principle of consensus which we at Kalikalos hold to be a central core value of our community.

First of all, let's affirm that the lone consistent dissenter might be right! (Remember the film "12 Angry Men.") The objections must be considered. However, very often such consistent blocking of proposals is a reflection of a quarrel with the leadership—either a personal one, or a clash of values. If the latter, the group can endeavor to clarify its mission and vision, to make it more clear to itself and to its members. (This exercise is one we at Kalikalos have been carrying out this summer, so that we all know to what we are subscribing and potential new members know what they are joining. We've arrived at this: "Exploring the value of authentic community as a vehicle for teaching and researching holistic education within a living-learning environment.")

On the other hand, if the blocker is engaged in a personal struggle with the leadership

Morning attunement.

(the core group in our case) then a process of last resort is a proposal to remove that member from the group. This is the only proposal in which the member has no power to block. Asking a member to leave is a drastic step, one which is at odds with our aim to be as inclusive as possible, but we have over the 13 year history of the project invoked it three or four times. Whenever there is a clash of our own paramount values (say, inclusivity vs. the ability to function and carry out the mission) one is obliged to prioritize. Power struggles do occur in communities and even with the best communication tools they can be very unpleasant. Their resolution can frequently be acrimonious, leaving in its wake damaged egos and hurt feelings which only time can heal. In the final analysis we are obliged to refer to the common good.

• • •

Now let me turn to Laird's first concern, that Sociocracy offers no place for processing feelings and emotions. I agree, it does not. However, we do not rely on Sociocracy to help us with emotional issues. This is where my garden analogy is useful.

I do not use a rake to dig the soil, I use a fork. The rake will be useful only after I've dug the soil and gotten out the rocks and broken up the clods. So too with meetings. We would not dream of starting a morning circle with decision making. First we take a few minutes of silent attunement (meditation) to bring us into presence—the place where we are all one. (This is the social equivalent of what I did by sitting quietly by my vegetable bed before getting up to dig it.) After that, we use the talking stick to go 'round (usually more than once) to hear how each member of the community is feeling now. Issues may arise, there may be conflicts between members, there could be held resentments; these all have to come out, be heard, and the co-intelligence of the group is needed so that everyone can see the big picture. Many conflicts and resentments have their roots in poor or inadequate communication. Whenever one party sees a situation in one way and another person sees it totally differently, these disparate viewpoints must come to the surface and be made transparent for the whole group so that the protagonists can see each other's viewpoints and hear what other group members who are not involved think. We would not dream of going on to the decision-making portion of our daily meeting until we had thoroughly processed the feelings and emotions that are in the group.

It is only when these have been thoroughly processed that we are ready to talk ideas and make decisions. In the emotional sharing portion of our meetings (which can take anywhere from 10 minutes to two hours) the process is controlled by the talking stick with strict guidelines: the talking stick confers the power of speech; speak deep, brief, and from the heart in "I" statements; talk about people who are present in the circle; don't talk about "we"; don't give a philosophical lecture; don't formulate proposals; don't use "you" in speaking to a person in the circle, instead use their name and speak to the group at large or to the centre of the circle, which has a lighted candle and usually a bowl of fresh flowers.

Just as we would not begin to rake our garden bed until we had dug it fully, we do not not turn our tripartite morning meeting to "business" (decision making; both evaluating previous decisions and making new ones) until we have fully dug up and processed all the emotional clods and feeling rocks that exist.

Notice that I said "processed." I did not say "resolved." Emotional issues sometimes arise from personality clashes that can recur time and time again in a group with a common vision. I have lived on and off for many years in the Findhorn ecovillage in Scotland and one of the things I had to learn early there was how to live and work with people who shared my values and vision of a new world of peace and partnership, but with whom I would not in the natural course of life become friends. This is a learning; it requires flexibility and tolerance. Even in a small community of a dozen members one may not like everyone, but we are joined together to help build a new world. To do so we have to learn to work with others with personalities very different from our own.

• • •

In conclusion, elements of Sociocracy seem to us at Kalikalos to be extremely helpful in making community decisions both easier and quicker. At the same time, as Laird emphasizes, other tools (ZEGG Forum, psychodrama, fishbowls, Scott Peck community building, creative writing, meditation, and more) are available to work through feelings and emotions. At every Kalikalos meeting we make a place for both decision making and processing feelings, but we try not to do them both simultaneously. This is not to say that strong feelings may not come up in the decision-making portion of a meeting, and conversely people will get ideas during the emotional sharing rounds. Human interactions are messy; they cannot be boxed in so neatly. Nonetheless, establishing one time and place where emotional issues take priority and the group's intention is on them, and another time and place where decision making has the priority and intention, has proved a valuable method of giving both these key aspects of community living the respect they deserve.

Jock Millenson is an associate member at large of the Findhorn ecovillage in northern Scotland, a cofounder of the Kalikalos Holistic Network in Pelion, Greece, and the author of Liberating Love *(1995), the first book in English about the ZEGG Forum process.*

RESOURCE:
C. T. Butler and Amy Rothstein, *On Conflict and Consensus: A Handbook on Formal Consensus Decisionmaking* (Portland, Maine: Food Not Bombs Publishing, 1987).

The Six Steps of Proposal-Forming in Sociocracy

By Diana Leafe Christian

Editor's Note: *The following is an abridged version of a longer article on Sociocracy's Proposal-Forming process, forming part VI in the author's "How Sociocracy Can Help Communities" series. For specifics of each step and tips on how to implement it in your group, email the author at diana@ic.org.*

The six steps of proposal-forming in Sociocracy (a.k.a. Dynamic Governance) can be used independently by a community even if it doesn't use the rest of Sociocracy. Proposals can be either considered immediately or saved for another meeting to decide. They can be also proposed to other circles or subgroups within the community to decide.

Here are the steps:

One: Present the Problem.

A circle makes a proposal to solve a problem or benefit from an opportunity, relative to its specific aims or objectives.

Let's say a Community Life circle, with the aims to provide enjoyable community-building events and services, takes on the problem that their community doesn't have a library. Someone presents the problem: "No community library," and writes "Library" in large letters at the top of a flip chart.

Two: Identify Aspects of the Problem ("Picture Forming").

The facilitator asks circle members to suggest various aspects—facets, characteristics, attributes—of the problem.

These are not specific proposal ideas, which come later in Step Four, but large, overarching categories that describe the problem. Identifying aspects of the problem first—"picture forming"—will help circle members create a more thorough proposal.

For example, if a circle is considering the lack of a library, various aspects of the problem could include "LOCATION," "LIBRARY MATERIALS TO LOAN OUT," and "SHELVING MATERIALS."

As in classic brainstorming, people don't criticize, praise, or otherwise comment on other people's suggestions. They can suggest more than one aspect of the proposal at a time. They can also pass, as they'll have other opportunities to offer suggestions as the facilitator keeps going around the circle.

Step Two is complete when no one has any more aspects of the problem to suggest.

Three: Consent to Completeness of the List.

Next is a consent round in which circle members are asked to consent to whether the listed "Aspects of the Problem" seem thorough and complete.

This step basically asks, "Have we thought of everything we'll need to thoroughly address the problem and not omit anything important?" Consenting to the completeness of the list is simply a consent round like those in the Consent Decision-Making process, but people say "Complete" or "Incomplete" instead of "No objection" or "Objection."

Saying "Incomplete" means the person has thought of another aspect of the problem, and then they state the aspect they've just thought of.

This step is finished when after several rounds no one says "Incomplete" anymore and there are no more suggested aspects of the problem.

Step Four: List Specific Proposal Ideas.

The purpose of this step is to collect one or more specific proposal ideas to address each of the already-generated aspects of the problem. These are not whole proposals but small, discrete parts of a proposal.

(4a) Generate proposal ideas in rounds. Circle members post the flip chart pages listing aspects of the problem on a wall where everyone can see them.

Some proposal ideas will be criteria for measuring and evaluating how well the library is functioning after it's built and dates of specific upcoming meetings in which these evaluations will take place—the "feedback loop" part of Sociocracy.

Different proposal ideas can also contradict each other, which is fine.

(4b) Include at least one specific proposal idea for each aspect of the problem. One way to do this is by comparing the listed "Aspects of the Problem" to the listed "Specific Proposal Ideas," and checking off each aspect of the problem for each proposal idea that addresses it. For example, next to the aspect, "LIBRARY MATERIALS TO LOAN OUT," the scribe could make three check marks,

Participants at a Sociocracy workshop in Montreal play in a skit to learn Proposal-Forming, 2014.

one each for "Books," "CDs and audiotapes," and "DVDs."

Once every aspect of the problem has been checked off and no more ideas are suggested, the circle does a consent round to make sure each aspect of the problem is addressed by one or more proposal ideas.

Circle members will have at least three additional opportunities to add proposal ideas or otherwise modify the proposal: (1) next, in Step Five of the proposal-forming process, (2) in Consent Decision-Making when they're deciding the proposal, and (3) each time the circle evaluates the proposal after it's been implemented.

Five: Organize Specific Proposal Ideas.

(5a) Select "tuners." These are circle members who write the first draft of the proposal. Tuners can be the whole circle, two or three circle members, or just the facilitator, depending on how complex the problem is and how the circle wants to do it.

If it's two or three circle members, they can be selected informally in a variety of ways, including "volunteering with consent." For example, if someone says, "I'd like to do this and I'd like Fred to work with me," this is a proposal. So the facilitator does a round to check for consent.

John Buck, coauthor of the Sociocracy book *We the People*, suggests that one of the best uses of a whole-community meeting is to use the proposal-forming process for controversial or complex topics, like a pet policy. If this is the case he recommends selecting tuners through Sociocracy's "Selecting People for Roles" (elections) process *(described in next article in the series)* because with controversial proposals some members may feel suspicious of whoever might be in the role of tuners unless they can consent to those who will fill this role.

(5b) Tuners shape proposal ideas into one or more draft proposals. Using the lists generated earlier, the tuners organize the specific proposal ideas into a draft proposal. If the issue is complex this could be several related draft proposals.

For a relatively simple proposal they might do this during a break in the meeting. For a more complex proposal or set of proposals they could do it in a later and bring their draft proposal(s) to the next meeting.

As noted earlier, proposal ideas can contradict each other, such as suggestions for different locations of the library (including when half the community might prefer one location and half the other).

John Buck recommends two different ways for handling contradictory proposal ideas:

(1) Just pick one of the contradictory proposal ideas, or

(2) Include both or all of them.

In either case, any part of the proposal, including contradictory parts, can be addressed later by objecting during a consent round when the proposal is being decided, and ideally by also participating in finding a way to resolve the objection.

(5c) Tuners share the draft proposal(s) with other circle members. The tuners share the draft proposal(s) with the circle.

Six: Consent Round—Does the draft proposal (or set of related proposals) address all identified aspects of the problem?

Next is a consent round to make sure the draft proposal includes at least one and ideally several proposal ideas that address each aspect of the problem. The facilitator might ask, "Any objections to the proposal as complete enough to address all aspects the problem?"

People *don't* say "Objection" if they personally would not consent to the proposal as it is currently written, or if they want to add an idea they especially liked that the tuners didn't include. Rather, they would simply object in a consent round later.

Similarly, they don't say "Objection" if they suddenly want to add a whole new proposal idea, *unless* it seems as if the proposal would not serve their circle's aims unless the new proposal idea were added. In that case the circle would then propose the new idea and do a consent round. If they consented, they would add it.

When after several rounds everyone says "No Objection" and no one says "Objection," this means the draft proposal has been consented to. It is no longer a draft; it is now a finished proposal.

Circle members have not consented to the proposal itself. They've simply finished the sixth and last step in the Proposal-Forming process. Now they're ready to either decide the proposal or save it for a future meeting.

Diana Leafe Christian, author of Creating a Life Together *and* Finding Community, *speaks at conferences, offers consultations, and leads workshops internationally. She specializes in teaching Sociocracy to communities and has taught in North America, Europe, and Latin America. She is currently teaching for the Global Ecovillage Network (GEN) in an online course. (Each weekly session is posted on youtube.) This article series is part of Diana's forthcoming booklet on using Sociocracy in intentional communities.*

Participants at a Sociocracy workshop at Aldeafeliz Ecovillage in Colombia practice Proposal-Forming, 2014.

Diana Leafe Christian

SELECTING PEOPLE FOR ROLES (SOCIOCRACY ELECTIONS): How Sociocracy Can Help Communities, Part VII

By Diana Leafe Christian

Selecting people for roles (elections) is one of the four meeting processes in Sociocracy, and like the other meeting processes, is based on Consent Decision-Making. In an intentional community, for example, this process can be used to select people who will lead special projects, its annually elected officers (depending on the group's legal entity), and the four roles in a circle.

Selecting People for Roles has six steps.

Step One: Review Role

The most important aspect of the Selecting People for Roles process is to first agree on the following four criteria before nominating anyone for the role. Nominations are based on these four things:

1. *Length of term.*
2. *Responsibilities of the role.*
3. *Qualifications of the role (in order to fulfill its responsibilities).*
4. *Desired (though not required) characteristics of the person filling the role.*

Can the person do these responsibilities? Does the person meet the qualifications? Does the person have some of the desired characteristics? *(See "Role Description: Community President," page 63, for these criteria in one community.)*

Author Diana Leafe Christian facilitating the Selecting People for Roles process at the Jewish Intentional Communities Conference, Baltimore, 2016.

The reasons people would nominate someone for a role, the facilitator would then propose someone for the role, and circle members would either consent to or object to the proposed person are based solely on the responsibilities, qualifications, and desired characteristics of the role.

Step Two: Submit Nomination Forms

The facilitator hands out small pieces of paper that serve as nomination forms. Each circle member, including the facilitator, writes their own name at the top of the paper, perhaps also writes "nominates," and writes the name of the person they nominate for the role. They hand their papers to the facilitator. People aren't nominated for personal reasons, such as liking or being friends with someone, but only because the person meets the qualifications to perform the responsibilities of the role and may have one or more of the desired characteristics.

Step Three: Share-Reasons Round

The facilitator reads the first nomination, and says something like, "Jill, you nominated Jack. Would you tell us why?" Jill then tells the circle why she suggests Jack, saying why she believes Jack fits the qualifications for the role, and has demonstrated one or more of the desired characteristics noted for it. The facilitator does the same with each nomination form. (The facilitator might write on each paper the reasons that person nominated someone, which is easier than trying to remember what everyone said later.)

The facilitator reads each nomination paper (including their own), until each one has been read and everyone has heard the reasons for everyone's nomination. Hearing everyone's reasons for their nomination is important, and leads to the next step.

Step Four: Invite-Changes Round

The facilitator asks each person if they would like to change their nomination or keep it the same, based on the reasons they've heard other people say for why they nominated their candidate for the role. People may say things like, "Keep my nomination," or "No change." Others may change their nomination to another circle member who was nominated, because they were convinced by the reasons for their nomination when they heard them stated by others. The person says *why* they are changing their nomination. Reasons for changing a nomination, again, are not based on personal preferences.

NOTE: Changing one's nomination from one person to another is not designed to be insulting to the first person and is not taken that way in Sociocracy. Rather, Sociocracy trainers emphasize and well-trained circle members assume that the person changed their nomination because of the strength of the reasons given for nominating the other person.

Optional Step Five: Open Discussion or Questions

Circle members can choose to have an open discussion or ask each nominated person more questions at this point if they like. However, two Sociocracy trainers in the US discourage a discussion, and Gerard Endenburg did not design it into the process. John Buck, Sociocracy trainer and coauthor of the Sociocracy book *We the People*, notes that the elections process was designed to proceed seamlessly through each step without the need for discussion. This is because the process of objecting and resolving objections tends to bring out the points that would arise in a free-form discussion anyway, but takes less time. This step is not usually needed, he says, and he recommends it only in one specific situation *(see below)*. Sociocracy trainer John Schinnerer, who's quite familiar with typical intentional community meetings, finds that the elections process is more effective without a discussion, because not using it promotes more understanding of Sociocracy and helps change former meeting behaviors "once people get used to really listening to reasons for nominations without reacting and focusing on the responsibilities and qualifications rather than personalities and popularity." If people want to try a discussion for some reason, John cautions people to watch out for the discussion becoming typical election behavior in our culture. "These include 'campaigning' for a candidate (and the resulting loss of equivalence), domination by a few, arguing, negative comments about a nominee, 'attacking questions' (comments disguised as questions), and so on."

In any case, if circle members want a discussion, as in Consent Decision-Making, they would propose a discussion with a specific time limit, such as five or 10 minutes, and then either end the discussion when the time was up or propose more time.

Step Six: Consent Round

The facilitator chooses someone who was nominated and proposes that person for the role. The facilitator might say something like, "I propose Jack for the role of ________, based on the reasons you stated in your nominations and changed nominations," and then states those reasons.

The facilitator doesn't propose the person with the highest number of nominations, but the person for whom the most convincing arguments have been given for fulfilling the role. Here "argument" means a reasonable, convincing reason. The facilitator proposes the person for whom the reasons—arguments—given by circle members seemed the most convincing in relation to the responsibilities, qualifications, and desired characteristics of the role, rather than the number of nominations. However, the relative number of nominations the person received can be one of the factors that the facilitator considers.

The facilitator then conducts a consent round, with people saying "No objection" or "Objection." Saying "No objection" means they consent; saying "Objection" means they don't consent yet. People cannot object because they want a different person for the role instead. Just as in the Consent Decision-Making process, the same principle applies of "Good enough for now," "Safe enough to try," and "OK—let's find out." The proposed person doesn't have to be perfect for the role, just good enough and safe enough to perform the responsibilities of the role.

Objections. People might object to the proposed person for several reasons—for example, because they could not fill the role for the stated term length, as when the term is for a year and the person will be away traveling for several months that year. Or someone might object because the person doesn't have one of the skills required for the role, and thus doesn't meet its qualifications; e.g., the role is Bookkeeper and requires skill in using Quickbooks software specifically, but the person is unfamiliar with that software. Again, disliking someone is not a valid reason to object.

People write their name and the person they nominate on a nomination form..

Resolving objections. Objections are resolved just as in Consent Decision-Making, with the person objecting, or any others in the circle, including the facilitator, suggesting ways to resolve the objection. In the first instance, above, circle members might modify the proposal to shorten the term length to accommodate the person's schedule, or have another nominated person fill the role after the first person leaves. The proposal could be modified so that two people share the role, with the second person taking over after the first one leaves, or it could propose a different person fill the role instead.

In the second example above, circle members might suggest the proposal be modified so that the current bookkeeper would train the proposed person in Quickbooks before they took over the role. Or, that a different nominated person who did know Quickbooks was proposed for the role.

Just as in Consent Decision-Making, the circle returns to a consent round after suggesting ways to resolve an objection. And as in Consent Decision-Making, consent rounds and resolving objections may alternate several times as objections are raised and circle members resolve these objections. The process is complete when there are no longer any objections and someone is selected.

I once observed a community using this process to select a Land Use Manager for the next year, and one of the responsibilities was to facilitate meetings. After reviewing the term length, responsibilities, qualifications, and desired characteristics for the role, and after the nominations, the facilitator proposed Carol. Two people objected, explaining rather diplomatically (since Carol was right there) that she was ideal for the role in terms of land use skills and experience; however, she didn't like to facilitate meetings and didn't have as much skill in it as Tom (also sitting right there) who also had the same skills, though was not as experienced as Carol. One person objecting said she thought meetings might be awkward and people might feel put off, given that, "Excuse me, Carol, but sometimes you seem kind of grumpy when facilitating a meeting, since you don't much like it." "I sure don't!" Carol affirmed. "Would you potentially be available to facilitate the meetings?" the Facilitator asked Tom. He said he would.

The circle then modified the proposal to something like, "Carol as the Land Use Manager for the next year, but she won't facilitate meetings; Tom will facilitate them instead." Everyone consented to this modified proposal, and Carol was elected for the role for the next year.

NOTE: The facilitator does not *choose* the person for the role, but only proposes someone who has previously been nominated. As you can see, the actual choice is made by the circle members through the principle of consent.

When Two Nominees Seem Equally Qualified

John Buck suggests that the optional Step Five, Discussion, can be used when there are equally strong arguments for two different people. In a discussion, and before proposing one person for the role, the facilitator could ask about the potential availability of each person during the term length, in case one was less available, and whether each might be willing to fill the role or if one were less interested in it.

However, John Schinnerer suggests a different solution and recommends *not* having a discussion. "What value would an open discussion add?" he asks. "I suggest it would be a waste of time; like going for the 'perfect' candidate instead of knowing that either one was already more than adequate." He suggests the facilitator simply proposes one of the nominees, and then checks for consent. "If there are purely practical reasons why one person cannot serve (and then that person would then object), then simply propose the other, similarly well-qualified person."

The facilitator might say something like, "Well, it seems either Jack and Jill could do a great job in the role. But since we need to select someone today, I propose Jill."

In my experience, it works well for the facilitator to acknowledge to circle members that two nominees seem equally qualified. This helps people understand that the facilitator is not proposing one of them without realizing the other would be equally good. The facilitator might say something like, "Well, it seems either Jack and Jill could do a great job in the role. But since we need to select someone today, I propose Jill."

Don't Volunteer for the Role—Nominate Yourself!

The Sociocratic value of equivalence is reduced when someone volunteers ahead of time or volunteers at the beginning of the elections process. Let's say Marcia volunteers for the role and several of us planned to nominate Peter. We might hesitate to nominate Peter or not nominate him at all, because we fear that nominating someone else other than Marcia might offend her. Maybe we will all nominate Marcia so she won't feel slighted, even though she's not who we really want. As Sociocracy is designed, Marcia would not volunteer, but would simply write her name on the nomination form. When asked why in the second step, she would say she wants to do the role and why she qualifies. This is perfectly legitimate in Sociocracy.

Do's and Don'ts—Selecting People for Roles

• *Don't do this process without already having a clear, already agreed-upon term length, responsibilities of the role, qualifications, and desired characteristics for the role.* I suggest writing these criteria in big letters where everyone can see them. Seeing this information visually helps people focus on why they might nominate someone for that specific role, or why they might consent to or object to that person for the role.

• *Don't ask who is interested in the role and who's not.* This has the same unintended consequence as volunteering for a role. Encourage those who are interested to nominate themselves.

• *Don't select someone for an unlimited term.* It's much easier to suggest someone if you know it's for a specific period of time, not indefinitely, and if you know you will later do the Role-Improvement Feedback process *(described in next article in the series).*

• *Ask for the candidate's consent last.* This helps the proposed person enjoy the impact of other circle members consenting to them in the role. Also, if the person didn't want the role and planned to object, they might change their mind and consent to it after they hear all the other circle members consenting to it.

• *Don't have a dialog* during *a round.* If a brief discussion is proposed and consented to, do it in-between steps rather than in the middle of a step, as that can disrupt the process.

• *If you're nominated and don't want the role, just object when it's your turn in the consent round.* When asked why, let the circle know you don't want to do the role, and why.

• *Don't seek the perfect candidate.* Each candidate will have specific strengths and weaknesses, and you're going for "good enough for now" and "safe enough to try," not perfection.

• *Use Sociocracy's Role-Improvement Feedback process* to help the person get even better in their role's responsibilities.

Remember, the number of nominations a person receives is far less important than the strength of the reasons for nominations, relative to the responsibilities, qualifications, and desired characteristics.

Why Do Facilitators Have So Much Power?

They don't! The facilitator proposes the person based solely on what other circle members have said about their reasons for nominating that person—not according to the facilitator's personal preference. If people don't want the person the facilitator has proposed they simply object during the consent round and say why, based on the role's responsibilities, etc. as described above.

"I find that people constantly project power on facilitators that they do not formally have in Sociocracy," John Schinnerer says, "especially in elections." In terms of resolving objections, he reminds us that the facilitator is not more important in suggesting the actual resolution itself, which should be the work of the circle as a whole. Any one or several members may suggest ways to resolve objections, and one of those may be the facilitator, but only in equivalence with other members, John says.

Also, the facilitator is originally chosen through this very same elections process, and fills the role for only a specific term length. Further, if circle members don't like how the facilitator does the job, they can convey this and suggest solutions in the Role-Improvement Feedback process. If that doesn't work well they can also propose to replace the

Role Description: Community President

Here is a description of the role of President in one intentional community.

Term Length: One Year

Responsibilities:

1. Maintain overall community vision for the community with the other officers.
2. Oversee and provide support for the Care Circle, Safety Circle, Ritual and Celebration Circle, and Peace Team Circle.
3. Provide direction in handling community conflict.
4. Sign official documents and perform official duties of the President as outlined in Bylaws.

Qualifications for the Role:

5. Willingness and ability to perform the responsibilities of the President.
6. Ability to see, draw out, and weave together all perspectives of an issue—being "multi-partial."
7. Ability to perform or delegate the facilitation group processes, such as meetings and conflict resolution.
8. Demonstrated ability to collaborate, cooperate, and work well in teams.

Desired Characteristics:

9. The wisdom to discern when to act quickly and when to wait in a crisis; keeping a balance between action and patience.
10. Remaining impartial and hearing all sides of a conflict; not causing dissension.
11. Confidence in processing conflicts.

—DLC

When Someone with a Reputation for Conflict Volunteers for a Role ahead of Time —John Buck's Advice

Someone "running for office" by publicly volunteering ahead of time can generate the same unfortunate consequences for the community as volunteering during a meeting instead of nominating oneself. Volunteering ahead of time violates the Sociocratic principle of equivalence, because it puts people in the awkward position, described above, of having to decide whether to nominate someone one truly wants for the role, or nominate the person who volunteered in order not to potentially trigger their hurt feelings by nominating someone else.

This awkwardness is especially poignant—and challenging for the group—when the person who publicly volunteers ahead of time has a history of triggering conflict but appears not to realize this.

John Buck advises that if this situation occurs, various people should take this member aside and describe what could and maybe would be said about their past behaviors if they publicly seek the role, and ask the person to publicly withdraw their nomination ahead of time if they don't want to experience this possible outcome.

—DLC

facilitator before their term length is up. If everyone consents, the facilitator stops doing that role and they choose someone else.

Objecting to Someone With a Reputation For Conflict

To help reduce the likelihood of triggering someone feeling hurt, please consider including a phrase like "Has a reputation for getting along well with others" or "Demonstrated ability to collaborate, collaborate, and work well in teams" *(see #8 in "Role Description: Community President," page 63)* as one of the desired characteristics or even one of the qualifications for the role. This can reduce the triggering of hurt feelings later, in the unlikely scenario that the facilitator proposes a disruptive or uncooperative person for a role they are otherwise qualified for. If the group does not include a requirement like this, they risk the possibility someone might nominate such a person (or that the person might nominate themselves). However, requiring that a candidate must be personable and cooperative as one of the desired characteristics or qualifications for a role will reduce the likelihood that circle members will nominate a disruptive or uncooperative person, or that the facilitator would propose them.

If, however, someone *does* nominate such a person, whom I'll call "Reginald," and for some reason the facilitator proposes him, the group has two hard choices. One is to consent, watch how Reginald does in the role, and give him appropriate feedback and request any desired changes in one or more Role-Improvement Feedback processes while he's filling the role.

The other choice is to object, and when asked why, to say you believe he currently doesn't meet the specific desired characteristic or qualification: "Has a reputation for getting along well with others." (One could add a conciliatory phrase like, "although this could always change in the future.")

This option takes courage, and one certainly does run the risk of triggering hurt feelings in Reginald and discomfort in other circle members too, although some might also feel relieved. So consider choosing the option of objecting to Reginald only if his actually doing the role would be worse for the circle than the painful feelings and discomfort for everyone if he were denied the role.

If most people in the circle know his reputation for conflict, others might object also. And please keep in mind community consultant Tree Bressen's advice, "There's no substitute for personal courage when living in community!"

Overview: Selecting People For Roles

1. Review Role
- Term Length, Responsibilities of Role, Qualifications to Perform the Responsibilities, Desired Characteristics for the Role

2. Submit Nomination Forms
- "I _______ nominate _______."

3. Share-Reasons Round
- "I'd like _______ in this role because _______."

4. Invite-Changes Round
- "I change my nomination to _______ because _______."

5. (Optional) Open Discussion or Questions

6. Consent Round

Facilitator proposes candidate with strongest arguments re. responsibilities, qualifications, and desired characteristics.
- Numeric majority is less important than the strength of the reasons.
- Ask for candidate's consent last.
- Re. objections, use "Resolving Objections" in Consent Decision-Making: i.e., modify the proposal and repeat Consent Round.

DO NOT!
- Elect someone for an unlimited term.
- Ask for a volunteer.
- Ask who is interested in the role and who's not.
- Have a dialog during a consent round or any other round.
- Seek the perfect candidate. Each has strengths and weaknesses, so the proposed candidate needs only be "good enough for now."

—DLC

Reducing the Likelihood of this Challenge Ahead of Time

Sociocracy is a whole system, and if a community uses all of Sociocracy, this kind of awkward situation would most likely not occur. Why? Because circle members would have previously had the opportunity to consent to each person in the circle, and with a reputation like this, Reginald would most likely not have been chosen as a member of the circle in the first place. ("Consenting to Circle Members" will be described in a future article.) So while some communities use the Selecting People for Roles process alone, without using the other parts of Sociocracy, I don't recommend it because of the potential for this kind of unique challenge in an intentional community.

The next article will describe Sociocracy's fourth meeting process, Role-Improvement Feedback.

Diana Leafe Christian, author of Creating a Life Together *and* Finding Community, *speaks at conferences, offers consultations, and leads workshops internationally. Specializing in teaching Sociocracy to communities, she has taught in North America, Europe, and Latin America. She is currently teaching an online course for the Global Ecovillage Network (GEN). This article series is part of Diana's forthcoming booklet on using Sociocracy in intentional communities.*

The Seven Steps of Sociocracy —Putting it All Together

By Diana Leafe Christian

Sociocracy workshop participant in Sweden summarizing Role-Improvement Feedback for the group.

Diana Leafe Christian

Participants in Sociocracy workshop at Huehuecoytl Ecovillage in Mexico finishing skit on Role-Improvement Feedback.

Jan Svante

In every community there's plenty of work to do, from typing reports and sending emails to physical labor like weeding gardens and chopping firewood. Even though many people may mostly imagine community as lovely social gatherings with shared meals, kids, dogs, and volleyball—and not as a lot of "work"—work it certainly is, and it never stops.

Every community needs governance and decision-making. What may not be obvious is that governance is about management, and management has to do with planning, accomplishing, and monitoring the flow of work. Community governance is mostly about effectively managing the community's projects and work tasks and the funds needed to accomplish them. Since Sociocracy was designed specifically to plan, accomplish, and monitor the flow of work in an organization, it has been adopted in the last few years by various intentional communities. How does it help communities? They have faster meetings and get more done!

"We've made more decisions in the past two months than we have in the past two years!" *—Davis Hawkowl, Pioneer Valley Cohousing, Massachusetts*

"The biggest thing is that we get things done. We don't have a backlog of things that people are afraid to bring up." *—Mike April, Pioneer Valley Cohousing, Massachusetts*

So far in this Sociocracy series we've examined the governance structure of circles and double links; specific Aims for each circle; feedback loops—including ways to measure and evaluate a proposal built into the proposal itself; and three meeting processes: Proposal-Forming, Consent-Decision-Making, and Selecting People for Roles. This article describes how a community uses all of these parts together. It also includes brief descriptions of the last two meeting processes, Role-Improvement Feedback and Consenting to Circle Members.

A Circle's Work—"Operations"

"Operations" is a term used in business management to mean "work."

A circle, for example a community's Finance Circle, has Aims—what it produces or provides for community; in this case, ongoing management of the community's finances.

The Aims of a functional circle are ongoing, and can change only if the General Circle changes them, but the details or specific goals or tasks that express these Aims can change or stop, depending on circumstances. (For example specific tasks or goals derived from the Aims of the Finance Circle could include proposing annual budgets, paying bills, sending invoices, collecting money, doing bookkeeping, managing bank accounts, and providing reports about the group's assets and cash flow to the General Circle and/or to whole-group meetings.)

When circle members perform their individually assigned tasks for the circle, they're doing its work —its "operations."

In most intentional communities people propose and decide policies for how to accomplish needed tasks, and the same proposal might also include details about those tasks. In Sociocracy, however, there are two kinds of meetings: "Operations Meetings," which are relatively frequent, informal, shorter meetings for organizing and coordinating work details; and "Policy Meetings," more formal and infrequent meetings to create policies for the circle's work. In Sociocracy the larger and more abstract issues of creating policies to guide the work, and the more focused, concrete issues of coordinating the details of the work, occur at different times and in different meetings, which helps organizations function more effectively (and get more done).

Policy Meetings

In a Policy Meeting circle members use one or more of Sociocracy's various meeting processes—creating new proposals through the Proposal-Forming process (including creating feedback loops in each proposal), making decisions through the Consent Decision-Making process, choosing people in the Selecting People for Roles process, and/or two more: Role-Improvement Feedback (p. 65), and Consenting to Circle Members (p. 66, this issue). Circle members can also discuss and decide ways to measure and evaluate

Four Parts of a Policy Meeting

1. Opening Round:
- Check-In, transition into meeting

2. Administrative Matters:
- Requests for changing agenda items
- Announcements, if any
- Consent to minutes of previous meeting
- Confirm next meeting (date, time, etc.)

3. Matters of Content (any or more of the following):
- Proposal-forming
- Consider proposals with consent decision-making
- Evaluate implemented proposals
- Select people for roles (elections)
- Role-improvement feedback for circle members in roles
- Consent to proposed new circle members (Consent to removing a circle member)
- Accept reports from lower circles

4. Closing Round:
- Evaluate facilitation, group effectiveness: "What went well? What can we improve?"

—DLC

A Circle's Logbook or Log Website

For a more thorough description of Logbooks and Log Websites, ask the author for her "Logbook" handout at diana@ic.org.

Logbook sections about the whole community that are the same for every circle:

1. The community's Vision, Mission, and Aims.
2. Diagram of the Community's circles and double-links structure, showing the General Circle, Top Circle, each functional circle, and any attached smaller or "lower" circles, and the Domains and Aims of each circle.
3. Community Bylaws.
4. Community agreements about how they do things that apply to all members and to all circles.

Logbook sections for the the circle itself:

5. The circle's Domain and Aim.
6. Each circle member's name and their general and specific responsibilities and tasks for the circle's specific work for community.
7. The term length, responsibilities of, qualifications for, and desired characteristics of each role in the circle, including (but not limited to) Representative, Operations Leader, Facilitator, and Meeting Administrator.
8. Minutes of each Policy Meeting of the circle.
9. The circle's Development Plan. This includes any training, experience, teaching, and research that circle members may need for their circle to function effectively.
10. Individual work plan. A description of the responsibilities and tasks of each circle member for which they are solely responsible in the circle, including each person's own development plan or "plan for improvement" from each Role-Improvement Feedback session.

—DLC

and possibly change a proposal they've previously implemented. They also hear reports and approve meeting minutes. (See, "Four Parts of a Policy Meeting," this page.)

Policy Meetings are facilitated by the circle's Facilitator. Every circle also has a Representative and an Operations Leader. In a Policy Meeting of the Finance Circle, for example, one circle member would function in the role of Representative to the General Circle; another would function in the role of Operations Leader from the General Circle.

A fourth role in Policy Meetings is the Meeting Administrator.

The Meeting Administrator

Before each Policy Meeting the circle's Meeting Administrator (called "Secretary" and "Circle Administrator" in Sociocracy literature) gathers items for the agenda and helps prepare the agenda for the next meeting, along with the circle's Facilitator, and, in most businesses that use Sociocracy, with the Operations Leader as well.

The Meeting Administrator is also responsible for seeing that someone takes the minutes at each Policy Meeting, and can either take the minutes themselves or arrange for another circle member to do so.

The Meeting Administrator also maintains the circle's Logbook and/or Log Website. This is a three-ring binder or a website or both, with documents that contain the history of the circle and its relationship to the whole community. For Logbook/Log Website documents, see "A Circle's Logbook (or Log Website)," this page.

Operations Meetings

In Operations Meetings circle members organize and coordinate the details of their specific work tasks. (These could also simply be called "Work Meetings.") A Building and Grounds Circle, for example, could have a brief work-coordination Operations Meeting before the start of a work party.

The specific details of how policies or projects are implemented and which circle member does which specific tasks and coordinating these tasks and arranging the logistics for them are decided in Operations Meetings. If the circle wants to coordinate work or decide the details of how it gets done, it's an Operations Meeting.

Difference between Operations and Policy Meetings

Sociocracy trainer John Schinnerer describes the difference between the two kinds of meetings like this:

"In Policy Meetings policies about work tasks are decided by consent among people with equivalence.

"In Operations Meetings, previously consented-to decisions are implemented."

In businesses, Policy Meetings take longer and might occur once a month. Operations Meetings are quicker and might occur more frequently or whenever needed. They are separate meetings, and separating the concepts of operations/work and policy-making is an important part of Sociocracy.

In businesses and nonprofit organizations, each member of a circle usually works five days a week, and at the same time and in the same place. Thus it's easy to have quick, stand-up Operations Meetings several times a week to discuss and coordinate details of everyone's work.

But in an intentional community, each circle member is a volunteer who doesn't work five days a week like in a business. Each circle member of the Finance Circle, for example, might perform their different tasks at different times and in different places, probably in their own homes. The circle members would still do all the work of their circle, but not at the same time or in the same location.

(However, there are exceptions. Members of a community's Grounds and Landscaping Circle, for example, might perform their landscaping tasks all at the same time in a work party, in which case they would be working at the same time and in the same places).

But even though members of most circles in intentional communities don't work together every day in the same location, they still need periodic Operations Meetings. So it can work to schedule an Operations Meeting at the end of a Policy Meeting, with a break in-between the two kinds of meetings, to clearly indicate they have completely different functions.

Decision-Making in Operations Meetings—the Circle's Choice

In Operations Meetings circle members can make decisions any way they like. They need only propose a decision-making method for Operations Meetings and consent to it (which they would do in a Policy Meeting).

The Operations Leader could decide everything unilaterally, and this is how it is done in most businesses and nonprofit organizations using Sociocracy. The Operations Leader decides the details of how policies are implemented in terms of discrete tasks, which circle member will do which tasks, and how these tasks are coordinated. This is why this role is called Operations "Leader." If the circle discovers they don't have a policy for something that comes up, the Operations Leader decides in the moment how to handle it, and the circle creates a policy for it at their next Policy Meeting.

But since circle members can decide how they'll make decisions in Operations Meetings, if they didn't want the Operations Leader to decide they could use consent decision-making, classic consensus or one of its modifications, or majority-rule or super-majority voting. Or circle members could just talk about how they'll orga-

Eight Steps of Role-Improvement Feedback

For a more thorough explanation of and details about this Sociocracy meeting process, request the author's comprehensive article on Role-Improvement Feedback at diana@ic.org.

1. Feedback Team meets, comprised of:
- Person in the role who will receive feedback
- One to two people in his/her circle
- One to two people from smaller circle who work with the person
- Another person as Facilitator

2. Facilitator goes over:
- Term length, duties, requirements for, desired qualities for the role

3. Person states:
- Positive aspects of their work in role so far

4. Team members state:
- Positive aspects of person's work so far

5. Person states:
- Any improvements he or she could make

6. Team members add:
- Their views of any improvements if needed

7. Person summarizes things going well and needed improvements. Proposes plan for improvements.
- Plan can include actions other circle members take too

8. Consent Round for person's circle to consent to plan

—DLC

Huehuecoytl workshop participants getting a sense of Policy Meetings.

Jan Svante

Five Steps to Consent to a Circle Member

For a more thorough explanation of and details about this Sociocracy meeting process, request the author's workshop handout on Consenting to Circle Members (and when needed, asking people to leave a circle) at diana@ic.org.

1. (Optional) Applicant's questions/comments
- Person can ask circle members questions or makes comments.
- Person could ask more questions in addition to those asked during earlier interview process.

2. Circle's questions/comments round
- Circle members ask person questions or make comments about their potential inclusion in the circle.

3. Circle's consent round
- Assuming nothing alarming or difficult comes up, facilitator proposes the person be invited to join the circle.
- If there is a concern, proposal can have conditions; for example, a Garden Circle can ask applicant to not bring their dog to garden work because he loves to dig holes, and the person agrees.
- Consent round involves all circle members except the person (since the proposal is about them), but the person is still present.

4. Applicant's consent
- Facilitator asks applicant, "Do you consent to be part of the circle?" (And names the condition to return, if there is one.)

5. Celebrate decision
- Applicant consents; circle celebrates the decision.

Four Steps to Remove a Circle Member

A circle might ask someone to leave for a specific period for further Sociocracy training or to improve communication skills, or to leave indefinitely. Person can be present and offer reasoned arguments but does not participate in consent round. (Or they may choose to not be present.)

1. (Optional) Person's questions/comments
- Person can ask circle members questions or makes comments.

2. Circle's questions/comments round
- Circle members ask person questions or make comments about their potentially being asked to leave.

3. Circle's consent round
- Assuming nothing changes, facilitator proposes that person leave the circle, temporarily or indefinitely.
- If temporary, proposal can have conditions for their return.
- Consent round involves everyone except the person but they are still present (unless they choose not to attend the meeting).

4. Acknowledge decision
- Assuming there is consent to remove the person, facilitator offers everyone present the opportunity to say how they feel (sad, frustrated, relieved, and so on). If person is not present, circle determines who will tell the person about the decision.

—DLC

nize their work without any particular decision-making method.

Bottom Line: In Policy Meetings decisions are made solely by Consent Decision-Making. In Operations Meetings circle members choose whichever method they want.

By the way, if the Operations Leader makes the decisions in Operations Meetings, that role is the only role that is really "active" in these meetings. The roles of Facilitator, Meeting Administrator, and Representative are inactive when performing the circle's work tasks and in Operations Meetings. These three roles only apply to Policy Meetings.

Why is the "Operations Leader decides" the default method? Because if the Operations Leader decides these details it's easier and faster for the circle. It can be a relief to know that every small work decision doesn't have to be made by consent decision-making, which is rather unwieldy for such simple, straightforward issues. John Schinnerer suggests that it's easy enough for an Operations Leader to make unilateral decisions about implementing the circle's policies and coordinating work activities, since each person in the circle already proposed and consented to these policies in the first place. This is a "circular hierarchy," since an Operations Leader can't carry out any policy the circle members didn't already decide themselves.

Remember, some of the main reasons a community uses Sociocracy in the first place are to help projects and work tasks go more smoothly and effectively, to save meeting time, and to get more things done more quickly with more enjoyment.

"People are happier and more satisfied and getting more things done." *—Laurie Nelson, Pioneer Valley Cohousing, Massachusetts*

"A visitor said she'd never seen a community meeting be so effective, efficient, and fun!" *—Hope Horton, Hart's Mill Ecovillage, North Carolina*

The next article, the last in our series, will examine the specific benefits experienced by various communities that have used Sociocracy for several years, and what can go wrong when well-meaning community members use only some parts of it and use it incorrectly.

Diana Leafe Christian, author of Creating a Life Together *and* Finding Community, *speaks at conferences, offers consultations, and leads workshops internationally. She has taught Sociocracy to intentional communities in North America, Europe, and Latin America, and recently offered an online course for the Global Ecovillage Network (GEN). This article series is part of Diana's forthcoming booklet on using Sociocracy in intentional communities.*

Huehuecoytl workshop participants discussing the differences between Policy and Operations Meetings.

Jan Svante

Facilitating Diverse Groups

By Starhawk

Edges or ecotones, where two different systems meet, are places of enormous diversity and dynamism in nature. Where the ocean meets the shore, the varying conditions of waves and tides create hundreds of niches where different forms of life can thrive.

But edges can also be places of enormous conflict and destructive change. In an old-growth forest, the trees that grow on the edge develop extra strength in their fibers and a spiral twist that helps them resist the wind. Cut them down, and the next storm may take out the forest.

When we open our groups up to more diversity, we create social edges. They can be places of immense learning and enrichment, but they can also become places of intense conflict and pain. We live in an historical moment where sensitivity is extremely high and society is deeply polarized around issues of race, of gender, of sexual orientation and class division and all the other factors that may be subject to discrimination. While we've made great strides in some areas—legalizing gay marriage, for example, and electing a black president—in other ways we are bombarded with the rhetoric of hate and the relentless tide of murders of people of color by police. On the edges of diversity, we often feel on edge—wary of receiving or inflicting pain.

Skilled facilitation can help us assure that diversity brings growth and resilience to our groups. Below, I would like to share some of the insights and lessons I have learned in half a century of wrestling with this issue. I have been fortunate in having many wonderful teachers and co-conspirators, including Pandora Thomas, Rushelle Frazier, and Charles Williams who work with me in Earth Activist Training, the permaculture training organization I direct. We offer Diversity Scholarships for people of color and differently-abled people, and making these resources available has significantly changed the demographics of our trainings—from mostly white to sometimes more than 40 percent people of color. Providing enough resources for groups instead of just one or two recipients also shifts the overriding culture of the group, and raises many challenges for the facilitators.

Creating a Welcoming Environment

A facilitator's first task is to create a truly welcoming environment, where everyone can feel seen and valued. When people come to a new group, they are often a bit nervous. There's a bit of the child in each of us, wondering "Will the other kids like me?" For those in a target group for discrimination, that question broadens out. "Will people see beyond my race/gender/class/age/sexual orientation/physical ability and really see me?" How do we create an atmosphere that encourages people to do so?

First, beware of formulae that promise to do the work for us. Each group is different, and each constellation of needs and gifts may require its own response.

For example, it is customary now in progressive circles to ask people to state their preferred gender pronoun when they first introduce themselves. The idea is to make gender-fluid or non-binary people more comfortable and safe, so that they don't have to be the only ones to explain how they identify and whether we should use "he," "she," "they," or something else. And in many situations, this process can be a welcoming way of showing awareness and support.

But what if you have a group that includes some gender-fluid folks and many others from different cultures and backgrounds that have never encountered these ideas before and may find them disturbing or challenging? Sometimes stating gender pronouns might function more as an in-group ritual, a marker that displays our political savvy. It can leave the uninitiated feeling clueless and wrong.

How do we resolve these conflicting needs in a way that can further growth? Especially at the very beginning, when we have not yet established any group norms or support?

I began thinking about the complexities of identity after hearing Gregg Castro, speaking on a panel at a Pagan conference on indigenous experiences. "For a California Indian," he said, "your identity is your place."

Now, I often introduce groups by talking about the many and varied ways we each experience and construct our identities. Is it our place, our tribe, our clan, our gender, our work, our religion, our political affiliation, or whether we're a Mac or a PC person? I am a Jewish-American Pagan aging woman Wiccan author, activist, permaculture designer, teacher, change-maker, and many other things. Who are you?

I often start groups by breaking people into small groups or pairs to discuss the nuances of how they identify themselves, and then introduce each other.

Often, someone in the group will ask if we can each state our gender pronoun. Because the request comes from the group, and is not just something imposed by the facilitators, people feel more free to ask, "What is that about?" And the question then can lead to a truly meaningful discussion about gender and how we experience it.

Of course, that leaves us as facilitators vulnerable to being seen as clueless and unsophisticated, or worse, as unsympathetic to the needs of gender-nonconforming folks. So I might make special efforts to give off other signals that I am, indeed, aware of those issues and supportive. I might explicitly mention non-binary gender or say something like "women, men, and those who are gender-fluid or transcend the categories" in conversation.

There are other, simple things facilitators can do to create a feeling of welcome. Introduce yourself to new people, or introduce them to one another. When I think back on groups where I've been an outsider and yet felt very welcome—a neighbor's Filipino wedding, a music festival where everyone else was 20 or 30 years younger—it was because people came up and introduced themselves. Even if you're a shy person—I am!—push past it and extend yourself. And build into the group many chances for people to interact in pairs or small groups, so they get a chance to connect more intimately with a broader group of people.

Seek people out socially, outside of the classroom—sit with different people at meals, for example, not just your friends. A good facilitator is a bit like a good host at a party, introducing people, starting conversations, making sure shy people don't get left out.

Say "racism." Say the word, talk about it, early on. You don't need to go into a political diatribe, but make racism present in the discussion, for that sends a message to the people of color in the room, "This aspect of my life is seen and acknowledged here."

And acknowledge your teachers and influences. People who have been devalued need to know their contributions will be seen and valued, and honoring your influences can help set that tone. This article does not just reflect my own thinking and experience—it also comes from what I have learned over many years from working and struggling with many people. Here are some of my teachers and learning partners around these issues: Pandora Thomas, Charles Williams, Rushelle Frazier, Isis Coble, Luisah Teish, Ynestre King, Rachel Bagby, Margot Adair, Bill Aal, Shea Howell, Lisa Fithian, Juniper Ross, George Lakey, Fran Peavy, Johanna Macy, and many more.

The Issue of Safety

If we truly welcome people into a group, how do we make sure the group is a safe place to be? We can make rules against using racial slurs or threats, but how do we protect against the micro-aggressions, those little digs that come from ignorance or unconscious bias?

There is no protocol or set of agreements we can make that will guarantee that no one will ever make a thoughtless remark, or say something insensitive. In our attempts to provide that safety, we may actually create the opposite. If we start out by saying, "This is a space in which we have zero-tolerance for racist, sexist remarks or name-calling or harassment," the subtext is "This is a space full of people who are likely to use the N word or tell sexist jokes if not explicitly told not to!" Because otherwise, why would we need the rule?

I prefer to frame agreements as positives: "Can we agree that we want to treat everyone with respect, and use language that is respectful?" Or, more fully, I might say: "We've worked really hard to make this a diverse group, in many ways. Some of them are visible—like skin color, or the gender we present with. Many, many more aspects of diversity are invisible—our character, temperament, achievements, many aspects of our history, background, and culture. There's a lot we don't know about one another. We come out of a dominant culture where racism, sexism, heterosexism, and all the other 'isms are endemic, built into the structure. But can we agree that in this space, we want to value everyone here for the fullness of who they are? That we will strive to look beyond stereotypes and wrestle with our own prejudices, to see one another in our wholeness?"

I also want to establish an atmosphere that lets us all be less than perfect and encourages us to open up and learn rather than close down and defend. So I might say: "We all make mistakes. We all say things, at times, that are less than sensitive or that hurt someone else's feelings, intentionally or not. Can we agree to be

Photos by Brooke Porter

open to feedback? That we'll do our best to learn from it, and take it as valuable information?

"And if we need help in that process, if we need someone to vent to or to run something by and give us perspective, or if we need support in confronting someone openly or bringing an issue to the group or the teaching team, who here is willing to offer that kind of support?"

Generally, almost everyone raises their hands, and now we've established the group as a pool of supporters rather than a bank of critical judges.

But what happens when somebody does make an insensitive or hostile remark? Then, as facilitators, it is our duty to intervene. But how do we do that in a way that educates, rather than simply polarizes?

There are two concepts that are helpful in understanding how our words or actions may have hurt somebody. The first is to recognize the difference between intent and impact. Maybe Joe's intent when he wolf-whistles at Betty is only to express his admiration at how good she looks—but the impact may be to reinforce a lifetime's worth of experiences of men's entitlement to judge women's bodies.

Discussions of race, gender, etc. can be painful. But working through that pain is how we grow and make change.

The second concept is the difference between text and subtext. Text is the words I say; subtext refers to all the underlying meanings we intuitively understand, from tone, body language, and subtleties of language itself.

When a flamboyantly gay man says to an African-American roommate "Thank you for not being like all those other black men," the subtext is "Black men are homophobic." When an enthusiastic group member welcomes a new Latina participant by saying, "It's so good to have someone of your kind here," the subtext is "People like you don't really belong here—you're out of place."

Discussing these concepts in a group before incidents happen can give people a framework for understanding why a remark that seems innocent on the surface might actually be hurtful. Facilitators can encourage participants to let go of defending intentions, and instead open to feedback, take responsibility for the impact of their words and actions, and increase awareness and understanding.

When Pain and Conflict Erupt

We are all wounded by a dominant culture that does not value our inherent worth as human beings. Some get stabbed to the heart by being continually devalued because of something extraneous to our true worth: skin color, gender, physical ability or looks, age, sexual orientation, etc. Others suffer more subtle wounds by being overvalued for one of those same extraneous features. When we name the wounds, they often bleed afresh. So discussions of race, gender, etc. can be painful. But working through that pain can be immensely valuable, for that is how we grow and make change.

Racism and other forms of structural oppression are endemic, a constant, low-level or acute pain. I think of it like tinnitus. I have a hearing loss and a constant, irritating buzzing and hissing in one ear, that never goes away and interferes with every conversation. Tinnitus has been called "audible pain." Most of the time, I simply ignore it and focus on other things, because if I didn't, I'd go out of my mind. Discrimination is like that—always present, a static that comes into every relationship, a chronic, low-level pain that sometimes erupts into acute agony. And chronic pain can be exhausting and debilitating.

Most often in groups, the weariness comes from the micro-aggressions, the little digs, the jokes that go awry, the unconscious assumptions and insensitive remarks that the aggressors may not consciously intend to be a slight or even be aware of. It's the suggestion that isn't acknowledged, the smile that's not returned, the norms we unconsciously expect others to follow.

When we open up the topics of racism, sexism, or other forms of oppression, we inevitably must confront the question of privilege—unearned social power and advantages accorded to us because of our skin color, gender, presentation, etc. People of privilege often go through a fairly predictable set of responses, similar to the stages Elizabeth Kubler-Ross identified people go through when confronted with death: Denial—"I'm not racist!" Anger—"You're just playing the race card!" Bargaining—"If I call someone else out on their language, I can be the Good White Guy." Fear—"What will happen if we let these people take over?" Grief, guilt, and sometimes excruciating discomfort—I feel so bad about my privilege and your pain that I can only see you as a walking wound, not a person.

Why should acknowledging privilege feel like a kind of death? It's the death of a comfortable sense of self, the belief that whatever precarious sense of value you've achieved in your life is suddenly in question and rests on the broken backs of others.

The facilitators' task is to patiently shepherd people through this process, toward acceptance—"I am a person of value. I hold value that I have earned, and I also benefit from unearned privilege that I cannot escape, but can turn to the service of making a world of justice."

But people from targeted groups are often dealing with another kind of death—the kind where a cop shoots you when you are stopped for a traffic violation, or a homophobic attacker breaks your neck, or a rapist stabs you. Understandably, they may feel impatient with those responding to a purely symbolic death, and exhausted from being the objects of projections. So facilitators also need to make space for people from targeted groups to voice their pain and be recognized for their strength and contributions.

Facilitating can feel a bit like brokering a peace between warring nations, or attempting to reconcile a feuding couple. Good facilitators remain neutral, yet successfully establish an alliance with all sides. Skill, compassion, and training are all required, as well as a goodly dosage of pure dumb luck! We can also do the following:

1. Do your own work. Read, counsel, take workshops, ask for help from friends to move through your own deep feelings to a place where you feel comfortable with yourself.

2. Whenever possible, have a co-facilitator that represents diversity. If you're white, work with a person of color. If you are a person of color, a white co-facilitator can be a great asset in facilitating a mixed group. If you're a man, work with a woman.

3. Set a strong container. Pain will surface in these discussions. Make sure the space is safe, protected from interruptions or disturbances. Choose a time when discussion will not need to be cut off. Afternoons might be better than late-night sessions, so people don't go to bed in distress.

Who or what is going to contain the pain when it surfaces? Is that you—and are you ready for it? Or is it a process that you use, for example, a talking stick or Way of Council process specifically designed to let people share deep feelings without others responding or commenting? But be prepared to break the form if someone is saying or doing something deeply hurtful.

4. The group may need to separate at times. People of target groups may need a space where they can relax, share honestly what's going on with them without the fear of offending or the need to caretake. People of privilege may need an opportunity to vent and emote without the burden of further triggering those from the target groups.

5. Rebuild group cohesion. Bring people back together again, to reconnect and share learning. This can take many forms—for example, a fishbowl where people of color talk and white people listen, or a sharing in pairs, where a man is paired with a woman or person of fluid gender. Group cohesion can also be rebuilt through collective work—moving a giant tree trunk together, or building a cob bench—or celebration. That wild dance party late at night may be just what everybody needs.

Working and learning together with a diverse group of people is one of the greatest opportunities we can have to grow. We can build true relationships and heart connections with amazing people and form strong friendships that have stood the test of conflict. Groups that embody the diversity of our world become richer, more colorful, more intelligent, resilient, vibrant, and fun—edges of creativity and positive change.

Teachers and leaders in the broad permaculture world are now understanding the need to strengthen the social aspect of regenerative design.

The ability of individuals and groups to collaborate successfully is one of the largest constraining factors in all forms of organizing, and as we succeed in creating more functional groups, all our work in every area of life will be strengthened. ❧

Websites:
Starhawk: *starhawk.org*
Earth Activist Training: *earthactivisttraining.org*
Black Permaculture Network: *blackpermaculturenetwork.org*
Pandora Thomas: *www.pandorathomas.com*

Starhawk is the author or coauthor of 13 books on earth-based spirituality and activism, including the classics The Spiral Dance, The Empowerment Manual: A Guide for Collaborative Groups, *her visionary novel* The Fifth Sacred Thing, *and its long-awaited sequel,* City of Refuge. *Starhawk directs Earth Activist Trainings, teaching permaculture design grounded in spirit and with a focus on organizing and activism (www.earthactivisttraining.org, starhawk.org). She travels internationally, lecturing and teaching on earth-based spirituality, the tools of ritual, and the skills of activism.*

Saying "No" to Prospective Members

By Laird Schaub

One of the trickiest issues that intentional communities face is screening prospective members.

Some groups find this so odious (judging whether others are good enough) that they don't even try. Instead, they rely on prospectives to sort themselves out based on what the community has said about itself (on its website, in brochures, in listings, or in informal conversations with members), and how the new person relates to the community when they visit.

Another factor when it comes to screening is that communities in the US are subject to Federal and their state's Fair Housing Laws. Federal Fair Housing Law prohibits the discrimination (in housing sales, rentals, advertising housing, loaning for housing, etc.) against people on the basis of race, color, religion, national origin, sex, disability, or familial status. State Fair Housing Laws may mirror the Federal law, or they may add additional characteristics such as age, military status, sexual preference, etc. to the Federal list. Some groups mistakenly translate this into a proscription against using *any* discernment about who joins the group (or buys a house) but that's not true. It's perfectly legal to insist that people be financially solvent, not have been convicted of felonies, or agree to abide by common values and existing agreements. In fact, it's legal to choose against a candidate for any reason *other* than the Federally and state protected characteristics in your state.

What's more, there are any number of people who are attracted to community for the right reasons but are not a good fit, and it's better all around if the community plays an active role in screening for decent matches. In many cases (unless the would-be member is a community veteran) the new person is still wrestling with the question of whether *any* intentional community is a good choice for them, much less *your* community. There will be many new and strange things that people have to make sense of during their initial visit, and in the process they can easily miss clues as to whether the visit is going well or not as seen through the host's eyes.

Finally, when you take into account how important it is to have your membership aligned about what you're trying to create, it becomes clear why it's not a good plan to rely mainly on the new person figuring it out on their own. Yes, this may mean that someone washes out sooner, but isn't that better for them as well—rather than getting a false impression about how things are going and discovering the mismatch six months after moving in? Delayed disclosure may relieve the community of having a difficult conversation up front, but at what cost?

OK, let's suppose I've convinced you that communities should get actively involved in membership selection. In broad strokes, there are four possibilities about how a prospective visit may go:

a) Both the community and the prospective realize it's not a good fit. While there's the possibility of some hurt feelings if the prospective feels that what they found did not match what the community promised, mostly this ends amicably and there's no problem.

b) You both like each other and the prospect converts to becoming a new member. Hooray! That's what you had in mind and you're off to a good start. Of course, the honeymoon will end and not everything that starts out well stays that way. While there's no guarantee of long-term happiness, you did your best and now you take your chances.

c) The prospective doesn't feel there's a good fit, though the community likes what they see and wants to encourage the prospective to hang in there. Most of the time when this occurs it's because the prospective comes across as a "good catch" and will likely be attractive to a number of communities. In short, they have options. In this situation also, there's unlikely to be hard feelings. The community may be sad at losing a good prospect, but dating doesn't always lead to marriage and you knew that all along.

d) The hardest combination—and the one I want to focus on in the remainder of this essay—is when the prospective likes the community but it's not reciprocated. Now what?

In general, this is because of one or more of the following factors:

• Poor social skills

There's a high value placed on good communication skills in community and it can be a serious problem if the prospective is not good at:

—Articulating what they're thinking
—Articulating what they're feeling
—Hearing accurately what others are saying
—Expressing themselves in ways that are not provocative
—Taking in feedback about how others are reacting to their behavior
—Being sensitive to how their statements and actions are landing with others

The issue is not so much whether the prospective fits right in, as whether the members feel they can work things out with the prospective when there are differences—because there will always be differences (eventually).

• Weak finances

Sometimes it's a question of whether the prospective has sufficient assets or income to meet the financial obligations of membership. Not everyone who is drawn to community has their life together economically.

• Too needy

Occasionally prospectives come to the community to be taken care of, and there appears to be a frank imbalance between what the person can give relative to the level of support they're needing. For the most part communities are looking for a positive or break-even balance from prospectives and will tend to shy away from those with mental health issues, emotional instability, addictions, or extreme physical limitations—unless there is a plan offered whereby those needs will be taken care of in a way that works for all parties.

Note that there are some excellent examples of communities that have built their identity around serving disadvantaged populations:

—Gould Farm (Monterey MA) focuses on mental health
—Innisfree Village (Crozet VA) focuses on intellectual disabilities
—Camphill Village (the first in the US was located in Copake NY and now there are 10 others) focuses on developmental disabilities
—L'Arche Communities (the first in the US was located in Erie PA and now there are 17 others) focus on intellectual disabilities

• Failure to keep commitments

It's hard on communities when members make agreements and then don't abide by them; when they make commitments and then fail to keep them. Sure, everyone has a bad week, but with some people it's a pattern and communities are leery of folks who aren't good at keeping their word.

To be sure, it can be difficult to discern a pattern during a visitor period, yet it's one of the reasons groups like to ask prospectives to lend a hand in group work parties—so they can assess follow-through and work ethic. People who come across as allergic to group work don't tend to be viewed as good members.

• Too different

This factor is something of a nebulous catchall. It can be an unusual personality, a quirky communication style, strange tastes or habits… Perhaps this traces to a different cultural background, but regardless of the origin it can be hard when there are no others like this person already in the group. Members may feel awkward in this person's presence and questions arise about whether they can make relationship with this person.

Even where there is a group commitment to diversity, that doesn't mean that *everyone* can find a happy home there.

• • •

One of the measures of a group's maturity is its ability to have authentic and compassionate conversations about hard things. And discussing the sense that a particular prospective is pushing the group's edge around the limits of what it can handle is an excellent example of a difficult conversation.

Saying "no" is not fun, and it can be very hard to hear it if you're the one being voted off the island. Yet sometimes groups have to do it, and putting it off doesn't make it easier later. The best you can do is anticipate that this is coming and discuss ahead of time what qualities you want in new members, so that you've already established the criteria you'll use before you start applying them.

Saying "no" is not fun, and it can be very hard to hear it if you're the one being voted off the island. Yet sometimes groups have to do it.

There will still be challenges, such as the dynamic where one member wants to stretch to take a chance on a prospective that another member is convinced is a poor risk, but at least you'll have established a basis for the conversation—in this case: what is the perceived risk, and how much is too much?

While living in community can be a wonderful experience, it isn't always easy.

Laird Schaub used to be the Executive Secretary of the Fellowship for Intentional Community (FIC), publisher of this magazine, and was a cofounder of Sandhill Farm, an egalitarian community in Missouri. He now lives with his partner, Susan Anderson, in Duluth, Minnesota, where their community is an old-fashioned neighborhood, complete with book clubs and backyard barbecues. He is also a facilitation trainer and process consultant, and authors a blog that can be read at communityandconsensus.blogspot.com. This article is adapted from his blog entry of October 13, 2014.

AVOIDING "SOCIOCRACY WARS": How Communities Learn Sociocracy and Use It Effectively...Or Not

By Diana Leafe Christian

Members of Hart's Mill Ecovillage near Chapel Hill, North Carolina, meet the three requirements for learning Sociocracy well and using it effectively.

"We've made more decisions in the last two months than in the previous two years!" observed Pioneer Valley Cohousing member Davis Hawkowl a couple months after Pioneer Valley Cohousing in Amherst, Massachusetts agreed to try Sociocracy for an 18-month period. Sociocracy, sometimes called Dynamic Governance, is a governance and decision-making method created for businesses in the 1970s. In recent years it has been adopted by some intentional communities too. But groups don't usually just replace their current governance and decision-making method with Sociocracy. Rather, they decide to try Sociocracy for a specific period of time, usually two years or 18 months, and then take a member survey to learn if they like it, how it may have benefited them, and if they want to keep it or return to the method they used before.

So after 17 months of using Sociocracy, in July 2014, Pioneer Valley conducted a member survey to see if and how many community residents liked using it. Before, the same relatively few members had done almost all the administrative work. After implementing Sociocracy, their survey showed that far more members became involved in community governance. The survey also showed that more people took on leadership roles, including newer members who had not participated in community governance before. And an overwhelming majority reported they were "highly satisfied" with Sociocracy.

Pioneer Valley and other communities using Sociocracy have generally experienced four distinct kinds of benefits. These include more enjoyable and effective meetings, a greater sense of accomplishment, becoming better organized, and a feeling of more connection among members. However, certain conditions are required for effective implementation of this method, and not meeting these conditions can be a recipe for failure—as I'll describe below.

Three Requirements for Learning Sociocracy and Using It Effectively

After teaching Sociocracy for intentional communities since 2012, I learned—from observing communities where it wasn't working well—there seem to be three requirements for using Sociocracy in order to truly benefit from it. And not meeting these requirements tends to result in ineffective meetings and conflict. The requirements are:

1. Everyone learns Sociocracy. They learn the basic principles, governance structure, and meeting processes, and this includes organizing periodic trainings for new people. This way no one is likely to misunderstand a facilitator's role. Or characterize the facilitator as a "dictator" when the facilitator leads the circle through the steps of a meeting process, seeks everyone's consent first before agreeing to a request for a (time-limited) open discussion, or calls on people in rounds rather than responding to random raised hands.

If not everyone can learn Sociocracy relatively soon after the group decides to use it, I recommend that these members sign an agreement saying they will learn it as soon as they can, and specifically that they won't try to stop the facilitator from doing their job, or try to induce the group to use a process more like the one they're used to, which is usually consensus.

2. They use all seven parts. (See "Seven Parts of Sociocracy," p. 61.) Sociocracy of course has more than seven parts, but in my experience there are seven main parts groups need for it to work well. This is because each part reinforces and mutually benefits the other parts. Consent decision-making, for example, can tend to trigger conflict unless the group uses three other parts of Sociocracy: a governance structure of circles and double-links, a clear, well-understood domain and aims for their circle, and feedback loops built into each proposal. With these other parts in place consent decision-making tends to work beautifully.

3. They use it as it was designed. The group doesn't try to change Sociocracy into a hybrid method with what they're used to. When some community members want to stay with consensus, they may try to induce the group to try a kind of hybrid Sociocracy-consensus so they can feel good, and they can threaten to block the proposal to try it unless they change Sociocracy this way. Unfortunately a pseudo-Sociocracy/consensus hybrid usually triggers more frustration and conflict than either method alone. In my opinion Sociocracy is in a different paradigm altogether from consensus (and making it more consensus-like dilutes its effectiveness).

For the most part, Pioneer Valley does all three things. Everyone has learned it, they use it correctly, and most circles use all the parts. While some circles haven't used Role-Improvement Feedback yet, and not all circles have built feedback loops into all of their proposals, increasing numbers of Pioneer Valley members are becoming aware of and including these parts of Sociocracy.

When These Requirements Aren't Met–"Sociocracy Wars"

Unfortunately the following two communities didn't do these things. Learning about their painful experiences is what convinced me how important these three requirements are.

The first is a community I'll call Cypress Commons. Their founders began using Sociocracy early in their history, in their property development and financing phases. At first it went well; several founders told friends how much they loved using Sociocracy. But unfortunately, the group didn't periodically train the new people who joined, believing they'd "just pick it up" by being in meetings. By the time construction was finally finished and people moved to the land three years later, as is common in communities like this, approximately 80 percent of the members had not taken the original workshop or had training in Sociocracy.

The four remaining founders had done the best they could to convey Sociocracy to people during meetings, and over the years they served as meeting facilitators. However, their ability to help others understand and use Sociocracy correctly was countered by almost 30 newer residents who'd joined over the years—people who were familiar only with consensus or else top-down management.

The community fell into what I call "governance drift." With approximately 30 out of 34 people barely understanding Sociocracy—and often projecting onto it the top-down management or classic consensus governance methods they already knew—the original Sociocracy principles and meeting processes gradually shifted into something else. Increasingly in meetings people insisted on speaking whenever they wanted to regardless of the steps of a process the facilitator was attempting to lead them through, and the facilitator, wanting to be accommodating, just let them speak. Most didn't understand the need for double links between circles, and because increasingly fewer people participated in governance, the group gradually began filling the operations leader and representative roles with one person.

Furthermore, feedback loops were not built into proposals, so objections were not resolved by adjusting the ways people might later measure and evaluate the proposal. Instead of benefiting from this easy and collaborative way to resolve objections, people argued for and against objections and treated them like blocks. Meanwhile, many people also insisted on attending meetings of the General Circle and functional circles even though they weren't members of those circles, and worse, insisted on having full decision-making rights in creating or consenting to proposals. Clearly, most Cypress Grove members didn't understand the basic Sociocracy principle of consent.

People also argued about *how* they were supposed to organize circles and make decisions. Some members really did seem to understand how Sociocracy works, but others had different ideas. The arguments about this, in meetings and on email, were fierce. At one point I did a Sociocracy review workshop, hoping to help Cypress Grove. (One of the founders paid for it, as the community as a whole didn't think they needed and wouldn't pay for a review workshop.) Unfortunately the workshop didn't help much. My attempt to present the basic principles of Sociocracy and the simple steps of its meeting processes only intensified the conflict. "You're taking their side!" one member blurted out.

Cypress Grove had recently elected a newer member as Operations Leader for the General Circle, who had not learned about Sociocracy. He was involved in the issue of conflicting statements in the Sociocracy book *We the People*, which described making decisions in Operations Meetings two different ways on two different pages. I forwarded my email from co-author John Buck to this new Operations Leader and other members. John explained that these were not contradictory but two optional ways people could make decisions in Operations Meetings; the circle could choose. But the new Operations Leader was convinced that since the page saying the Operations Leader makes decisions unilaterally appeared later in the book, that was the actual truth, and so he'd make all decisions in Operations Meetings. He also believed that any issues in circle other than actual proposals must be operations, and so he'd unilaterally decide those issues too. This is not true, of course. So I offered the new Operations Leader a series of one-on-one Sociocracy training sessions on Skype at no charge. But he declined, saying he was too busy, and it was unnecessary anyway since he already understood Sociocracy.

These difficult experiences, and those of several other communities I visited, didn't seem to result from anyone's quality of character or harmful intentions, as everyone seemed motivated by a genuine desire to help the community. The problems occurred because, in my opinion, not everyone in the group had learned Sociocracy, they didn't use all the parts, and they used most parts incorrectly!

When These Requirements Aren't Met–Sociocracy Gets a Black Eye

A few years later I did a Sociocracy workshop with participants from three nearby intentional communities in a rural area I'll call Orca Bay, including homeowners in several small adjacent private housing devel-

Hart's Mill members build a fence during a work party. This community uses all seven parts of Sociocracy.

opments, which I'll call the Orca Bay Homeowners' Group. Many had taken two previous workshops by a Sociocracy trainer colleague, and he told me the Homeowners' Group was now using Sociocracy.

I later met the president and meeting facilitator of the Homeowners' Group, whom I'll call Sam. He told me about a series of difficult meetings they had since they began using Sociocracy. A building with a kitchen and dining room on an adjacent property, which the group leased for weekly common meals, had become overrun with mice. So they created and consented to a proposal to have two cats live in the building to take care of the mice, and they'd look at the issue again in six months. Six months later they reviewed the now-implemented proposal, looking at the effect of the cats living in the building. The mice were gone and most Homeowners' Group members had grown fond of the cats and wanted to keep them, but two members intensely disliked cats and a third was highly allergic them. As the meeting facilitator Sam had tried to conduct an evaluation discussion but the meeting was so contentious nothing was resolved. Those who wanted to keep the cats used what Sam called "bullying and shaming tactics" to try to silence those who had problems with the cats. This didn't sound much like Sociocracy!

In the process of asking more questions I learned that only Sam and a few other members of the Homeowners' Group had actually taken my trainer colleague's Sociocracy workshops. The rest knew relatively little about it, and they weren't interested in learning more. In addition, Sam and the members who did know about Sociocracy didn't seem to understand much about the process of building feedback loops into proposals. In their first meeting, for example, they had not included a clear list of ways they would measure and evaluate the proposal later. They didn't appear to understand that based on what they might learn by measuring and evaluating specific impacts of the cats on the building and on the people, they'd have the choice to keep the cats, change how they lived in the building, or remove the cats. Instead they worded the proposal to say they'd keep the proposal after the six-month period "if we can live with it." This is not how feedback loops are used in Sociocracy. This wording was more like a kind of "sundown clause" used in consensus, in that the implemented proposal would have to be disbanded unless it met the vague criteria, "we can live with it," and this criteria was not defined either. No wonder they were stuck.

Even more significantly, the Homeowners' Group didn't actually have the basic structures that an intentional community needs in order to decide something all members must comply with, like their governance and decision-making method. In this group, anyone immediately became a full member of the Homeowners' Group and had full decision-making rights as soon as they bought a house from a departing homeowner. They had no membership process, which would include first getting to know and then choosing new members based partly on their willingness to learn and use the group's chosen governance and decision-making method. Furthermore, homeowners who attended meetings included the small group that always attended and those who only came when there were agenda items they cared about. Thus the relatively few people who participated in the meeting where it was proposed the group adopt Sociocracy agreed to a process only a few had learned about and most were unwilling to learn, and which couldn't be enforced in any case.

This was the group that Sam as facilitator bravely tried to lead through the various steps of proposal-forming and consent decision-making—with the controversial issue of what to do about the cats as the topic!

At first I thought Orca Bay's problem was their misunderstanding about including feedback loops in proposals. So I suggested that, if the group consented, to try again with another trial period for the cats, this time with clear and specific ways they'd later measure and evaluate their impact on the mice, the building, and the people, and clear and specific ways to mitigate the effect of the cats on the several members who'd been adversely affected. And to make sure knew that their options about the cats after the trial period would be to keep them, change how they lived there, or remove them.

But this turned out to be bad advice. Sam later emailed to say the group tried to do this but endured another whole year of conflict. They finally agreed to remove the cats, which pleased three people but was a painful loss for almost everyone else. And their additional year of conflict, Sam told me, was the direct result of my advice to try again. Not only that, he said, but most people in all the Orca Bay communities now had a poor opinion of Sociocracy and were no longer interested in using it.

Ouch! I was appalled to think I contributed to this. But my actual mistake, I now think, was in not advising them, given their situation, to *not use Sociocracy at all.* They didn't meet the basic criteria to use it! No group can use a governance method without having a way to make sure everyone learns it and uses it. For example usually Sociocracy is taught to businesses and nonprofits: if the bosses of a company or nonprofit agree to try Sociocracy, all the employees will do so. In teaching Sociocracy to intentional communities I now know this only works if the group passes a proposal to try Sociocracy for a period of time with the agreement that everyone will learn it and use it. (And members who don't learn it will of course still be welcome in meetings but wouldn't be able to participate adequately.)

Learning the painful experiences of the Orca Bay Homeowners' Group, on top of the previous painful experiences of Cypress Grove, absolutely convinced me that these three requirements are needed in order to benefit from Sociocracy.

Hart's Mill members celebrate a work party on their 112 acres. All members learn Sociocracy.

Workshop participants at Huehuecoyotl Ecovilage in Mexico discuss the three requirements for Socicoracy.

Jan Svante

Meeting the Requirements–"Our Meetings Rock"

It doesn't have to be like this. Hart's Mill Ecovillage, a forming community near Chapel Hill, North Carolina, meets the three criteria. Everyone learns Sociocracy, and they regularly offer in-house trainings for new members. They use all seven parts. This includes building feedback loops into proposals and later measuring and evaluating the effects of their proposals after trying them for awhile. They choose Operations Leaders and Representatives for each circle. They use all four meeting processes, including Role-Improvement Feedback. And they use them correctly.

"Our meetings just rock," observes cofounder Hope Horton. "Recently we had a huge amount of business to conduct in one large-group meeting that lasted for three hours. We moved through it easily, spending no more than about 10 minutes on each issue. It took a lot of preparation and training to accomplish this, but there's a group coherence around this process now, and people tend to have more energy after a meeting than before. When new people learn the steps of the process, and learn how to do rounds, they feel amazed at how much we can get done. They feel confident that when they come to a meeting it will be productive, so people don't mind coming to them—lots of them!"

Rocky Corner Cohousing, a forming community near New Haven, Connecticut, also meets the three requirements. They regularly offer in-house Sociocracy workshops for new members. Most circles use most of the seven parts and some circles use all of them. They use Sociocracy correctly and have easy, enjoyable, effective meetings. "I personally place so much value on Sociocracy that I have become critical of every other organization in my life," wrote Rocky Corner member Marie Pulito in the Spring 2016 issue of COMMUNITIES. "The redundancy of tasks where I work is horrendous. My church meetings make me cringe. The annual meetings of my small New England town fall far short. Where is the equivalence of voice, the power of many minds coming together to find a solution to a problem? I now want every organization in the world to use Sociocracy!"

Diana Leafe Christian, author of Creating a Life Together *and* Finding Community, *speaks at conferences, offers consultations, and leads workshops internationally. She specializes in teaching Sociocracy to communities, and has a reputation for a teaching style that is so clear that communities can start using Sociocracy right away after a three-day workshop, with additional consultation help on Skype, if needed. Diana has taught Sociocracy in North America, Europe, and Latin America, and is currently helping train the Board of Directors of the Global Ecovillage Network (GEN). This article series is part of her forthcoming book on Sociocracy in intentional communities. See www.DianaLeafeChristian.org.*

The Seven Parts of Sociocracy

Sociocracy has more than seven parts of course, but these are the main parts I believe are minimal for a group to learn Sociocracy well and use it effectively. In the same way the seven main parts of a bicycle mutually benefit and reinforce each other (frame, front wheel, back wheel, handlebars, pedals and gears, brakes, and seat), so too the seven parts of Sociocracy mutually benefit and reinforce each other.

1. Circles and Double Links.
2. A clear domain and clear aims for each circle.
3. Feedback loops built into every proposal.

And four (really five) meeting processes:

4. Proposal-Forming.
5. Consent Decision-Making.
6. Selecting People for Roles (Elections) [and Consenting to Circle Members].
7. Role-Improvement Feedback.

—DLC

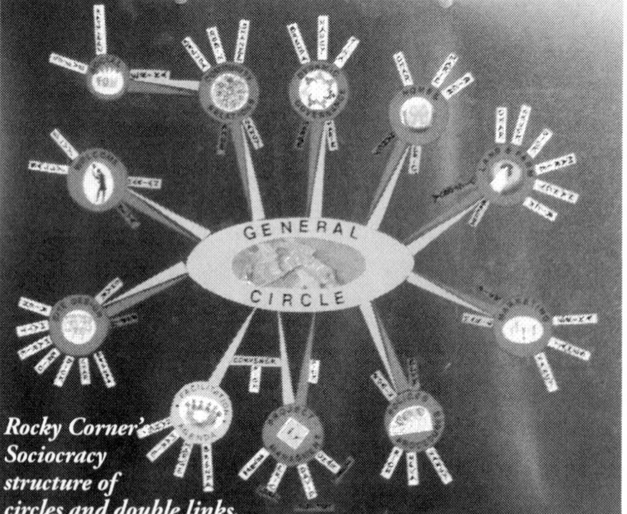

Rocky Corner's Sociocracy structure of circles and double links.

Rich Wilbur

Members of Rocky Corner Cohousing in Bethany, Connecticut celebrating Winter Solstice on their land. They also meet the three requirements.

Rocky Corner Cohousing Winter Solstice celebration.

Photos courtesy of Diana Leafe Christian

III

POWER, GENDER, CLASS, AND RACE

COOPERATIVE GROUP SOLUTIONS Advice About How to Handle Challenging Dynamics

The Bully Question

Q: *How can we deal with a member who frequently gets their own way by force, skating close to the edge of what's acceptable behavior, and yet does nothing bad enough in itself to warrant expulsion?*

From time to time we find ourselves living with someone we might label a bully. Usually a white male, older than 40. This person has developed a pattern of non-cooperation, ignoring agreements, ignoring established policy, ignoring decisions made by those with the responsibility to make them.

We're a large decentralized community (no guru). We delegate responsibility and authority for different areas to managers. We don't make decisions in whole community meetings. Bullies here manage to separate us and ignore decisions.

We have policies that spell out our decision-making methods and who is responsible for what. We have a list of expellable offenses and a process for calling for expulsion, and that of course is a last resort. We don't have any agreement or requirement for people to engage in mediation or feedback even when these are offered or requested. Most of us do agree to hear feedback, and to have a mediated discussion, if someone asks, but one of the difficulties of dealing with these difficult people is that they refuse.

These uncooperative people get their own way by force, by being so unpleasant that no one wants to deal with them. They disrespect other people (especially women), belittle them and call them names. They succeed by "picking us off one at a time," targeting one person, even baiting her, pouring scorn and nastiness. Each of us treated this way gives up the fight at some point and avoids contact with this person.

By now you might wonder how these people ever got accepted as members, or why there hasn't been a unified uprising against them. Not every facet of everyone's personality comes to light during provisional membership. Every human has some good characteristics, and these troublesome people may be appreciated for their hard work, technical skills, or artistic nature. Not every member is affected by the person's nastiness. Publicly, the person may seem mild-mannered, only to turn into Mr. Hyde when disputing land use with another member in the back 40.

Some people wish we did require people to participate in conflict resolution, but given that we don't, and we like to base a lot on trust of each other rather than policing, what can we do to spot such people and select against them joining? What can we do to deal with them once they have slipped in? How can we become more courageous as individuals and how can we better unite and support each other in tackling the problems such people introduce? How do we recognize when someone is making too many infringements on our accepted ways of treating each other? What do we do then?

Tree Bressen responds:

You raise fascinating questions here. I think there are a variety of paths open to you and your group on this, some of which you already pointed to in what you wrote.

Your community is not alone in including some members who refuse to talk over conflicts or listen respectfully to feedback. Because i don't think there is any surefire method for screening such people out, i'm going to focus here on how to respond once the person is a member.

From what i have seen in situations of this nature, it is going to take concerted group action for anything to change. However, lest you despair, that concerted group does not necessarily have to include every person in the community. The key is to expand beyond stories from a few members who've been burned to the typically "silent majority" middle. When more people who are not known for raising issues and are reasonably well-liked (and whose skills are seen as just as valuable as the bully's) join the chorus, my experience says that's when change happens. It is truly unfortunate that a bunch of people usually get hurt (and the community often loses one or more good members) before a sufficient number of people are willing to set an appropriate boundary.

People perennially push on boundaries in groups. If you want your decisions taken seriously, that means finding a way to push back. Something needs to happen when someone doesn't follow an existing decision: a conversation between a committee and the offender, a discussion in community meeting about the incident, a fine or penalty, etc. Agreements only become real when members are committed enough to stand up for them.

Whether or not your community has an agreement about feedback, feedback happens. And with sufficient feedback, offending members almost always change or leave. In the really bad cases, no one believes they will leave until it actually happens, but i've seen it over and over again. Most members do not leave as a result of formal expulsion process deciding against them; just having such a process start is often sufficient. Outside of any formal process, if a dozen members go to that person and say, "I really think it would be better if you moved out," they probably will. If you can help the person find a face-saving way to do this, all the better.

The people who have the most leverage with the bully are their friends. So it's especially powerful when their friends (or political allies) are willing to say to them in some form, "Hey, i love you dude, but what you are doing is not cool."

Regardless of who raises the topic, the bully will usually get defensive, counter-accuse, come up with all kinds of rationales for their behavior. Don't let them change the subject, or focus on how other members are hypocritical because "look at what they did," or engage in other avoidance tactics: acknowledge what they are saying, then bring the talk back to the subject of their own behavior. Express sincerely how their behavior impacts you and others you care about—be willing to be a bit vulnerable about this.

Some groups have found it useful to document incidents over time, so that when a public confrontation happens (with or without the bully present), there will be a record demonstrating the pattern, that this is not just about a few "over-sensitive" people.

Once members who are concerned gather enough momentum to attempt a group discussion, the bully or their allies will typically try to prevent that. They'll have some reason why the discussion should be delayed, threaten to boycott, or turn and accuse others of being a lynch mob. This is bullshit, and you should not stand for it. Perhaps my experience is not the norm, but i've seen the "scapegoating" charge used tactically to prevent dealing with problem behaviors more than i've ever seen real scapegoating happen. (More often the opposite is the problem—everyone bends over backwards to be nice and avoid scapegoating, and thus they allow the bullying to continue.) Community culture naturally favors direct communication, but the problem person doesn't need to be present to make progress on the situation. You are allowed to have a meeting on whatever you want, with or without all parties there.

Recipients of mistreatment typically feel helpless. You need to get back in touch with your power. Listing what your options are, even if you choose not to act on any of them, can feel very liberating. Those options may include revenge scenarios, public satire, formal shunning, and a wide variety of other behavior previously considered off-limits even in the privacy of your own mind. Remember, i'm not saying you should necessarily act on these ideas. But allowing yourself to list all the possibilities can open up space for creative options no one has considered before. And most important, it allows you to take personal responsibility for the choices you are making. Instead of "John did this to me," your self-talk becomes, "In this circumstance, i chose to do X."

I recently worked with a group facing a long-term bully situation. In that meeting (which the bully chose not to attend), we first provided an opportunity for members to express their emotions about their experiences, choosing a movement-based, time-limited format for this so that the energy would keep moving and would not feel too heavy, while allowing intense expression. Then people took turns doing sentence completions: "I give my power away when I..." and "I can choose to reclaim my power by..." in order to help them reclaim personal responsibility for what was happening. Finally, we did a series of roleplays, some about that specific situation and some more general, closing with one that looked into a future where the situation had been satisfactorily resolved years earlier and the community had learned how to prevent such dynamics from arising again.

Throughout the planning process, we were sensitive to the

In order to yell back i had to get past my self-identity as a professional facilitator.

possibility that people might attend in defense of the bully, and we wanted space for the legitimacy of that viewpoint as well. Therefore our formats were deliberately neutral: someone could just as well stand up and say, "I am angry at the community for how they have treated this poor person," as say, "I am angry at how this person has treated me and our community."

Drawing from my personal past, i used to live with a community member who regularly yelled at me inappropriately. My typical response to this was the same as when i was a kid: run to my room and cry. After a while i was able to stay in the room and cry: no real improvement. Eventually i got fed up and recruited an outside friend to coach me on offering a different response. After a bunch of rehearsal, i was finally prepared. *At that point i'd already essentially "won," because the power dynamic had shifted.* If the bully did not yell at me, i won, because i did not want to be yelled at. If he did yell at me, i was ready to practice my new behavior. One evening it happened: he yelled at me, in the living room, and i shouted right back! We went back and forth at high volume for several minutes, until another member intervened (at which point i went out on the front porch to celebrate). In order to yell back i had to get past my conditioning as a womyn, and my self-identity as a professional facilitator that says polite conversation is the way to go—to this day i believe that in this case, yelling back was a good response, one that successfully reset the boundary between us. The icing on the cake? A week or two later, the yeller gave notice that he was leaving the community—surely not a coincidence.

If other members are reluctant to get involved, invite them to reflect on how one toxic personality can bring down a whole group, and ask yourselves whether that's the kind of community you want. Y'all are working hard on the tasks of community every day; do you really want your efforts undercut by one or a few people's bad behavior? How do these behaviors reflect on the community's core values (fairness, equality, democracy, peacemaking, feminism, etc.)? Allowing hurtful behavior to go unchallenged hurts everyone, not just the immediate target.

Never let a community member hold the group hostage. No one's skills are irreplaceable, and no one's contributions are worth the sacrifice of your self-respect.

Tree Bressen is a group process consultant based in Eugene, Oregon, who works with intentional communities and other organizations on how to have meetings that are lively, productive, and connecting. Her website, www.treegroup.info, offers extensive free resources on consensus, facilitation, and more. (Tree uses a lowercase "i" in her writing as an expression of egalitarian values.)

Laird Schaub responds:

This is a good topic, because, at root, it's about how cooperative groups can responsibly and effectively respond to a form of violence without being violent. What could be more important?

There's a lot going on here. First let's explore the behavior and how tricky it can be to define what's acceptable. The bully label implies intimidating behavior (which may or may not be intentional—sometimes it's just style or even class differences). Where some people cultivate directness, others experience the same behavior as confrontation. Sarcasm and cutting humor are disrespectful and mean to many; yet can be normal jocular discourse to others. A lot depends on what was normal behavior around the dinner table for each player when they were growing up.

For example, anger is a class issue. It tends to be a middle class taboo and a working class staple. Thus, a member who comes out of a blue collar (or even pink collar) upbringing will typically incorporate the expression of anger into everyday speech, and are at immediate risk of being labeled a bully for that behavior in a middle class culture that tends to feel intimidated in the presence of openly expressed anger.

But let's suppose you've sorted out "appropriate" from "inappropriate," and you're satisfied that the protagonist fully understands that their actions are intimidating—yet they continue acting in a patterned way to push their own agenda. Now what?

While I question the assumption that it is solely up to the "bully" to make adjustments (you could just as reasonably ask others to work on how they react to bullying behavior), it can't be good for the group that members are allowed to refuse to make a good faith effort to hear and work constructively with critical feedback from other members about their behavior as a member of the group. This can be so destructive of group morale and functionality that I advocate explicitly adding it to the list of member responsibilities—even to the point of making it grounds for an involuntary loss of rights if a member consistently refuses to talk. To be clear, I am not saying that the person needs to agree with the critical assessment that they've done something wrong, or that need to accede to the request—or demand—that they change; I'm only saying they need to sit down and talk about it (without smirking, crossing their arms, or rolling their eyeballs) and try to work it out.

To turn this around, the group is going to have to find the will to deal with it. If a person crosses the line of acceptable behavior, then you have to have the spunk to hold them accountable. Part of the dynamic that makes this difficult is the style and class issue mentioned above. One of the reasons bullies do what they do is because they've learned that it works. That is, people tend to back off and give in because it's too unpleasant to object, and bullies tend to have a higher tolerance for tension (and even rawness) than others. If the bully can succeed in making objectors feel like confrontation is their only active choice, then they may succeed in creating paralysis—as people will be reluctant to engage in the very behavior they are objecting to.

Fortunately, there is a way out of this paradox. It's possible to be a "gentle, angry person" who stands firmly for their values without being an asshole. If the bully rants, you don't have to rant back. Yet neither do you have to give in. You can be caring about their concerns and yet still stand strong for your boundaries around acceptable behavior. (**Hint:** this kind of conversation will often go better if you can start by demonstrating a clear understanding of the bully's concerns, *before* you state your objection to the way they are being expressed.) Consider it a form of tough love. Often this goes better in a group, where people can support each other—both in being firm and in being compassionate.

The idea here is to pair rights and responsibilities, and the bully's right to raise objections or otherwise speak their mind about group issues can legitimately be curtailed if they are not fulfilling their concomitant responsibility to behave acceptably and work cooperatively with the concerns and interests of others on the same topics. Of course, this isn't going to work well if you haven't spelled out what constitutes acceptable behavior. Make sure your footing here is solid before going toe to toe with the bully.

If you have a clear sense that the bully has broken group agreements, it will help if you have in place a pathway for working constructively with this dynamic. I suggest adopting something like the following graduated sequence, at the end of which a member could suffer an involuntary loss of rights. By spelling this out ahead of time, you will have options short of expulsion, which is a very heavy step and hard to take. Note that each step below involves more effort and group resources than the previous one. You can stop whenever the matter is resolved to the satisfaction of all parties.

Step 1. Can you let it go?

Step 2. Speak directly with the person.

Step 3. Get informal help to speak with the person.

Step 4. Get help from the team or committee that has responsibility for the area that the agreement covers and/or from the Reconciliation Team group (if you have a subgroup or committee whose job it is to help resolve interpersonal tensions in the group—and if you don't have such a team, I recommend that you create one) to talk with the person.

Step 5. Go to the whole group, in plenary.

Step 6. Recognize formally that the problem persists and all reasonable attempts to resolve the problem have been tried.

Step 7. Discuss in plenary the possibility of imposing sanctions.

One of the key concepts in this sequence is that it's important for the group to feel that you have exhausted all reasonable attempts to resolve an issue short of sanctions before applying them. Note: not all steps make sense in all situations and it is permissible to skip ones that offer no apparent prospect of relief. The overriding principle here is getting the problem solved as unobtrusively and expeditiously as possible. While you want to be compassionate, in the end you must be resolute in holding the bully's feet to the fire.

Unfortunately, it can be even worse. On occasion, I've encountered bullies who were not that bothered by social ostracism. In the extreme, I've seen people who could tolerate a degree of social isolation that others couldn't even imagine, generally because they've had very little social connection in their life and have no real prospects of it being better somewhere else. At the end of the day, if social sanctions are ineffective, your group may have to grapple with the possibility of simply doing the best you can to be non-reactive to the bully and going on with your lives with this dysfunctional person remaining in your midst (because they don't care to leave and they haven't done anything clearly expellable).

Last, let's look at how to screen prospectives to keep bullies out—on the theory that it's easier than dealing with them once they're members. If your group is experiencing a patterned behavior problem—whether bullying or anything else—learn from it! That means discussing and identifying which behaviors are unacceptable and then screening prospective members to see that they fall on the acceptable side of the line. While no one wants to start a courtship by discussing divorce, you may be well served by a frank conversation with prospectives where you make it clear if they become members and run afoul of the boundaries of acceptable behavior—which you have carefully laid out—they can expect to be the subject of group scrutiny, and it won't be fun for anyone.

Laird Schaub, a member of Sandhill Farm community in Missouri, has been doing consulting work on group process since 1987. A longtime activist in community networking, he has lived in community since 1974 and been involved with the Fellowship for Intentional Community (FIC) since 1986; he is currently its Executive Secretary. laird@ic.org; 660-883-5545. Laird authors a blog which can be read at communityandconsensus.blogspot.com.

Beatrice Briggs responds:

To fully understand the situation it would help to know a few more details, such as: How long has the community been in existence? Is this problem new or has it always been present? How many people are in the group? What is the ratio of men to women? Is there only one bully or several? Does the bullying

> ***As a group, consider ways you could vary your habitual response to the bully. Call 911? Smile sweetly and walk away?***

usually center around one issue (you mention land use) or does it vary?

Lacking more complete contextual information, here are some generic thoughts, focused on your question: How can we become more courageous as individuals and how can we better unite and support each other in tackling the problems such people introduce?

Form a support group. Convene those that have complained about being victims or witnesses to bullying behavior. Do not make a big public announcement—just get a few people together at first. Make it clear that the intention is not to indulge in whining and complaining, but to support one another in a learning process. Assume that there are important lessons for each of you, whether the bullies change or not. Spend time establishing trust within the group. Confidentiality (at least at the beginning) may be important. Other possible agreements: commitment to attend the first three sessions (or whatever number you agree on); no new participants until members of the first group begin to feel stronger.

The following exercises might be helpful for the group's learning process. Ideally, a skilled facilitator would guide you. Look in the community or beyond to find a resource person.

• **Uncover the ghosts.** In pairs, talk and listen (perhaps three-five minutes each for the first round) to each other about the ways in which the individual bullies remind you of people from your past. (Here is a place where the commitment to confidentiality is important.) Describe the similarities in behaviors and the response they provoke in you. Cry and tremble as needed. The listener does not interrupt, only provides complete attention. Switch roles. Repeat a few times. End by affirming something like "That was then and this is now."

• **Discover your inner bully.** Working in groups of three, assign these roles: the bully, the listener, and the observer. The person taking the role of the bully conjures up a clear image of how the community (or other) bully behaves (physical posture, tone of voice, gestures, etc.) and begins to act in that manner. The listener's job is to *understand* (not agree with) what the bully is saying, using the skills of paraphrasing and questioning to see if he/she has grasped the essence of what is being transmitted. The listener also tries to discern what emotions and values underlie the bully's behavior—again verifying that his/her perceptions are correct. The listener should NOT try to change the bully's opinion, show him the error of his ways, prove how wrong he/she is, etc. Just listen and seek to understand. Continue for several minutes or until there is evidence that the "bully" feels understood. Then stop. Let the "bully" de-role. Ways to do this include shaking the body to disperse the energy, answering questions such as "What is your name?" "Where are you?" "Which way is north?" Once the person playing the bully is back into the present, the observer comments on what he/she saw. How successful was the listener at capturing the bully's opinions, feelings, and values? Was there a turning point in the conversation? What helped or hindered the communication?

After everyone has had a turn in all three roles, gather the whole group together to debrief the experience. What was it like to be the bully? Listener? Observer? What did you learn about your self?

• **Change your personal rules.** Reflecting individually, answer these questions. Be specific. Write down your responses.

1. What rule of *mine* (not necessarily the community rules) is the bully breaking?
2. Where did I learn this rule? Who taught it to me? (It may feel like a "universal" rule, but clearly not everyone is guided by it—e.g., the bully.)
3. What might I gain/lose by abandoning or modifying this rule? What inner power could I tap? What new options might I have?

Share your answers with one other person (or the whole group if it is small) and than demonstrate how you might break your old rule. Act it out! The idea is not to turn yourself into a bully, but to tap into strengths that your own rules have prevented you from accessing. Note: this is hard for some people. It feels risky, perhaps impossible. Encourage them to make a one-to-two percent change in the rule and test out how that feels.

• **Brainstorm and practice alternative responses.** As a group, consider ways that you could vary your habitual response to the bully. Call 911? Smile sweetly and walk away? Practice active listening as described in the "discover your inner bully" exercise? The key idea is that you cannot change the bully, you can only change how you react—and that can produce magical results. ❋

Beatrice Briggs is the founding director of the International Institute for Facilitation and Change (IIFAC), a Mexico-based consulting group that specializes in participatory processes. The author of the manual Introduction to Consensus *and many articles about group dynamics, Beatrice travels around the world, giving workshops and providing facilitation services in both English and Spanish. Home is Ecovillage Huehuecoyotl, near Tepoztlán, Mexico, where she has lived since 1998. bbriggs@iifac.org; www.iifac.org.*

Do you have a question for our Cooperative Group Solutions panelists? Please send it to editor@ic.org.

Balancing Powers: Leadership and Followship in Community

By Elizabeth Barrette

Power in community can work differently than in the mainstream. We acknowledge more types of power and value a wider set of skills. We move more fluidly through roles so that instead of "leaders" and "followers" we often have the same people playing both those roles in different contexts.

Leadership

On a spring afternoon, the turnspit assembly team finally admits defeat: no spit-roasting today. The whole lamb carcass won't fit in the oven. People stare dolefully at each other. "Okay, we need to cut this nice lamb into pieces," I say. "I know some anatomy and I've helped butcher chickens. Raise your hand if you've ever done home butchering, or field-dressed game, or have any other relevant experience." Several people volunteer. With much tugging and laughing and sharing of ideas, we divide the meat into small pieces.

In considering leadership, look at what a leader needs to be and do. Most concisely, a leader provides guidance and direction. Community leaders direct a particular settlement; task supervisors see that jobs get done; workshop facilitators teach numerous people new skills. So "leader" covers all the people who make things happen in intentional communities and lend their vision to get us where we're going. Overall, people want leaders to create a sense of community, organize activities, provide services, and help in times of need. Leadership expectations break down into practical and personal roles, among others.

The practical sphere encompasses most group functions. *Founders* define a vision and create new communities. *Event organizers* dream up festivals and workshops, then make sure the activities run smoothly. *Entertainers* include our musicians, dancers, theatre troupes, and so forth. They add spice to the work we do—but they also transmit our culture. *Networkers* connect the dots into a vast web of human resources spanning the world. They make it possible to pull together people needed for a community, a publication, or a special project.

The personal sphere encompasses things that usually happen behind the scenes, but can intrude into group space. *Greeters* welcome new people and help them mesh. They make communities grow. *Crash crew* leaders are the people you turn to when disaster strikes. They clean up after messy divorces, personality meltdowns, and storm damage. *Cheerleaders* urge people to grow and try, providing encouragement after failures and applause for successes.

Qualities of a Good Leader

Each leader has a unique combination of leadership qualities. Skills may come from education or experience—ideally both, but don't overlook someone who can do the job just because they only have one or the other. Different roles also call for different traits and skills. However, some things are essential for most or all leaders in community.

Determination—A leader provides the energy and focus to get people moving and keep them on track.

Competence—This includes not just the ability to do things correctly but the self-confidence to do so smoothly, in a way that reassures other people they're in good hands.

Patience—Effective leaders allow for calm handling of delays and difficulties, as well as teaching people.

Honor—People can look up to a leader who is worthy of their respect and who behaves with integrity.

Vision—A leader illuminates a path from where we are to where we want to be, and inspires people to follow it even through the rough spots.

A sense of humor—This eases tensions, fosters connection, and discourages harmful forms of pride.

Communication—Necessary for most community functions, this is a fundamental ability to gather information, guide meetings, talk people into doing things, and mend misunderstandings.

Problem-solving—A good leader can recognize signs of trouble, identify the source, and take steps to fix it.

Resource management—This entails fundraising, gathering tools and supplies, finding volunteers, and using them efficiently to meet established goals.

A well-calibrated bullshit detector—A leader must be alert when people are trying to deceive her...or themselves.

Leadership Techniques

Leadership is not one skill but many. People sometimes learn the obvious ones but overlook more subtle aspects. Here are some useful techniques for community leadership:

• Learn what your neighbors do well. When assembling a team for a project, connect each task with a person who has relevant expertise.

• Find the work that needs to be done and take care of it. You know how people are always saying, "Somebody should do something about that"? Be "Somebody."

• Always pad your budget and your timeframe. Things *will* go wrong; it's your job to make sure the problems get buffered, so they don't make matters worse.

• Watch for members whose skills are growing. Cheer for their progress. Offer them more responsibility.

• Watch for burnout. Be prepared to reduce or change someone's tasks (including yours) to avoid this.

• Observe body language. If folks are leaning forward and nodding, you're on the right track. If they're fidgeting, it may be time to stop talking and switch to something else, like physical activities.

The intentional community movement offers numerous models of leadership. Some communities have one leader, or a small group of leaders. Some try to avoid the temptation of putting anyone in charge, instead sharing responsibility equally. How does your community assign (or withdraw) authority? Who organizes things, and why? What do members expect of the person(s) in charge? What do the leaders get, and what do they give? How well does your system work for you? Discussing these and related topics can help a community fine-tune their leadership structure so that it works for everyone.

Followship

Several friends gather to disassemble a fallen tree. A chainsaw growls in the background as we work on breaking up the smaller twigs and branches for kindling. Sometimes I help hold the bigger branches to be cut by handsaw or chainsaw. Upon request I fetch and carry gloves, earplugs, and water bottles. Later, I retire early to the house and start supper for the team.

People often discuss leadership without ever touching on followship. Followers are as essential as leaders, because leaders can't lead if nobody follows. Similarly, if the leaders outnumber the followers, nothing gets done because of too many arguments over who's in charge. Ideally, people have both leadership and followship skills so that they can switch roles.

Good followers enable leaders to accomplish great things. The leader supplies the direction, and the followers provide the motile power. Bad followers don't provide enough power, or pull in different directions, or support wretched ideas as well as good ideas. So a leader really depends on having good followers. Many communities teach and reward that kind of teamwork, which helps expand our skills.

Qualities of a Good Follower

Leaders and followers share some of the same virtues, while others differ. A follower's qualities should complement those of a leader. Not all followers necessarily show all of these qualities, and there are other qualities, but these can help identify people with followship potential.

Humility—A humble follower helps leaders relax, because they don't have to worry about that person trying to take over their position. The modern mainstream culture pushes success to excess, often pressuring people to "get ahead" and "be a star" even if they hate being the center of attention or being in charge. Humility means deriving contentment from who you are and what you do without feeling compelled to reach for the pinnacle. Not everyone is, can be, or should be a leader. If people's personality, skills, and desires suit them to be followers, they should take satisfaction in that. Explore until they find a level and area of responsibility that feels comfortable.

Loyalty—Loyal followers support a chosen cause or leader through good times and bad times. They stick around when others leave, and won't switch sides as long as the cause is just or the leader honorable. This helps minimize turnover, which can strain communities.

Honesty—The best followers display excellent communication skills. They speak the truth gently if possible, firmly if necessary. They give an honest opinion of ideas and people.

Integrity—Good followers can be trusted to carry large sums of money or use equipment responsibly. They will keep an embarrassing secret, but not one that could harm innocents. They carry out honorable instructions in honorable ways; they won't lie, steal, or cheat to accomplish goals.

Disagree constructively. Don't let a bad plan or improper request pass unremarked. In problem-solving sessions, open, vigorous discussion promotes effective solutions.

Reliability—This means getting things done right, on time. Be organized. Only promise what can be delivered, and always deliver it. If necessary, find a substitute to cover responsibilities.

Utility—The most useful followers are competent, confident, and good at diverse skills. They avoid false modesty and their community knows what they do well.

Flexibility—An effective follower finds ways to make things work. Be willing to implement whatever is assigned. Be prepared; expect the unexpected. Adapt to changing circumstances.

Synergy—This precious ability enables a follower to combine the available people and resources to best effect, creating a whole that is more than the sum of its parts. The synergist may be an expert teambuilder or ceremony coordinator, unifying what the leader provides.

Followship Techniques

Like leadership, followship spans a variety of skills and methods. By learning and teaching these, we can expand the pool of good followers in community. Here are some things you can do as a follower.

• Support your leader's ideas. Voice agreement; also use body language by nodding or leaning forward. Speak well of your leader to others.

• Accept direction from your leader. When asked to do something reasonable, do it without hesitation. This helps avoid the awkward scenario caused by everyone waiting for someone else to move first.

• When volunteers are requested and your skills match, step forward. Volunteering strengthens community bonds.

• Ask the right questions. If you don't understand what is needed, seek to clarify the needs and processes. If a proposal is under discussion, ask questions to reveal its strengths and weaknesses.

• Disagree constructively. Don't let a bad plan or improper request pass unremarked. In problem-solving sessions, open, vigorous discussion promotes effective solutions—even if people argue a lot before reaching conclusions. Otherwise, it's usually best to deliver criticism in private, and praise in public. Avoid saying things publicly that could discredit your leader or their plans, unless the situation poses a danger. Save face as much as practical without allowing real harm, because when people feel threatened they tend to switch from problem-solving to defensiveness.

• Build consensus. Bolster teamwork. Seek suitable people and encourage them to get involved.

• When following instructions, pay attention to the *spirit* as well as the *letter* of

What gets in the way of learning, community, productivity, or just plain fun? How can you avoid making the same mistakes that you've seen other people make?

the instructions. Deliver what your leader wants and needs, not just what they said.

• Pay attention to everything around you. Be observant. Report interesting details, task progress, potential problems, and possible solutions.

• Listen actively. Serve as a sounding board or a shoulder to cry on. Good listeners are valuable.

• Take care of your leader. Many leaders are "big picture" people who easily forget small details while focused on wider issues. If necessary, pick up cell phones, ensure notes are in order, or remind your leader to eat and sleep regularly. Divert unnecessary distractions; encourage people to handle things within their own responsibility.

• Remember that your leader is only human. Allow for some mistakes and flaws; accept apologies with grace. Do what you can to compensate for weaknesses and encourage improvement. Be patient with growth processes.

As you did with leadership, now think about followship in your community. Who are the followers? How are they chosen? Are the followers good at what they do? Are they always the same people? Do they want more responsibility, or do they prefer following to leading? What does your community do to thank people who take this role? By discussing these and similar topics, you can help make sure that people feel satisfied with their role in community and that they have opportunities to shift around so they don't get bored.

Developing Skills

The drums make pleasant thunder as we strive to stay in rhythm, one eye on our neighbors, one eye on the workshop leader. He guides us only by hand signals, not words—we respond by intuition, speeding or slowing. Afterward he explains how this type of drum workshop builds teamwork skills.

Intentional communities depend on the membership having a good balance of leadership and followship skills. Because our values may differ from those of the mainstream, people haven't always had a chance to learn the interpersonal and organizational skills needed in community. In order to meet our needs, we need to teach those skills so that residents and guests can get along and accomplish their goals. Conferences, festivals, and workshops provide formal opportunities to learn both leadership and followship skills. However, a lot of education in community happens on a casual, everyday basis.

Understand that there are better and poorer ways of teaching, and that not all methods work equally well for all teachers, students, or topics. One mistake is to let people volunteer to lead a project without providing any guidance, which can lead to fumbling and failure. A better approach is to pair a new volunteer with an experienced member who can teach what they wish to learn. As people gain experience, they may take on new responsibilities so that they remain challenged and invested in their work. Also remember that leaders may get tired and want to let someone else take charge for a while. That's a good time for them to focus on a followship skill they want to improve.

For best results, learn from both good and bad examples. Which classes or workshops have you enjoyed the most? Which ones did you hate? What techniques do you find most effective? What gets in the way of learning, community, productivity, or just plain fun? How can you avoid making the same mistakes that you've seen other people make? How can you make skill development enjoyable and effective? Do your members know how to lead and how to follow? Do they know how to get things done in an egalitarian group? When planning educational activities or pairing teachers and students in your community, discuss these points together.

As a general rule, treat other people with respect, whether they serve as leaders or followers or both. Consider how they wish to be treated; for instance, some people like attention while others don't. Also think about how you prefer to be treated; it may not always be the same as other people's preferences, but it's a good starting point. Avoid doing things to others that annoy you when someone does them to you.

Look for ways to strengthen community ties. If you admire an experienced person, ask them to teach you something. If you're organizing a project, invite skilled people to help with it. Get together and discuss your community's skill set. What's missing? Where could your members gain those skills? Reach out to your friends in other communities—whatever it is, somebody knows how to do it! ❧

Elizabeth Barrette writes nonfiction, fiction, and poetry in the fields of gender studies, speculative fiction, and alternative spirituality. Her article "Householding" appeared in Communities *#144. She supports the growth of community in diverse forms and is active in local organizations. Her favorite activities include gardening for wildlife and public speaking at Pagan events and science fiction conventions. Visit her blog at ysabetwordsmith.livejournal.com.*

More Perspectives on Leadership and Followship

A Response to Elizabeth Barrette

By Ma'ikwe Schaub Ludwig

I love it when someone takes the time to break a complicated topic down into component parts that are easier to understand, and I like a lot of what Elizabeth has offered in her lists of leadership and followship traits. I teach about leadership, and so have spent a lot of time thinking about that side of the equation. Elizabeth's done an excellent job of getting me to think about both sides, and I'm grateful. If I could sit down at my kitchen table with her, here are some things I'd love to chat about.

Leadership Qualities

I found myself wanting to add some aspects to the leadership list. Mostly, it seemed odd to me that there was more focus on communication, integrity, and honesty for the followers than for the leaders. Being a teacher-type and a life-long seeker of great role models, I wondered from whom the "followers" would be learning all these great skills (as our mainstream culture is hardly great at them)? So here are my additions:

Self-honesty and the ability to recognize alignment. Effective leaders are ones whose passion matches the passion of the group. People turn into martyrs when their personal life's work doesn't match the group's life work. "Know thyself" is a credo for everyone; for leaders, it is also an imperative.

Ability to hold to the group purpose and set aside one's own agendas when needed. This is two-fold: being able to keep one's self on track and not introduce extraneous agendas to the group's work; and being able to hold the group to their focus, gently reminding people when they are starting to get too complicated or when they are adding aspects into the project that aren't the group's work.

The ability to nurture others. The best leaders are on the lookout for the next generation of leaders, and actively nurture the spark of enthusiasm and self-development in others. I've spent hours with interns and students over the last couple years talking about their lives and what inspires them, acting as elder and mentor. I'm starting to see this as a more matured version of my own leadership.

A willingness to model humility and the fine art of apology. When it comes down to it, some of the most important skills we can model are those that involve humanizing ourselves in the eyes of others (which makes leadership look accessible) and being able to admit when we've been (or done) wrong. Both of these are rooted in a philosophy that says that we are all human and we are also all capable of some form of leadership, despite our flaws and shortcomings. (Paired with Elizabeth's *sense of humor* element, this is the cornerstone of authentic leadership.)

A strong sense of fairness. Sometimes leaders have to arbitrate tough moments where the people in their group seem to have contradictory needs. Leaders need to be even-handed in their rewards, chastisements, and division of resources. If you aren't fair, you (rightfully) lose the trust of the group as a whole, and create an environment where your perceived "favorites" have to struggle to be seen as part of the gang. Responsible leaders don't set up their group for the fissure lines caused by favoritism.

The ability to think ahead several steps. While I don't buy into the "idle hands are the devil's workshop" philosophy, I do think that when folks show up enthusiastic to work on a project and there is nothing to do, this experience can be pretty frustrating. A good leader has to serve the function of thinking things through in terms of timing, order of steps, and having materials and personnel available so that the work can continue and flow well.

Responsible Followship

While I like a lot of the advice that is offered in this article, I want to note a pitfall of adopting this whole package. The way Elizabeth talks about followship makes me nervous: while I don't think this was her intention, the way she has things framed could be read as too much passive and potentially blind support of leaders for my tastes (particularly without a strong focus on integrity in leaders). On the other hand, groups sometimes want to switch in midstream, handing over power and then attacking their own leaders for wielding it.

Here's my bottom line: if a group has abdicated power to a leader, then you damn well better back the person up. It is deeply unfair to hand over responsibility to one person and then hang them out to dry when you disagree with what they do or say. However, I prefer the model where you don't abdicate and you therefore have the right and responsibility to call your leaders on bad behavior. While I don't think this article is entirely one-sided in this area, I prefer to lean more on the active end of engagement between leaders and followers.

In fact, when it comes right down to it, I found myself wondering as I was reading this why the list of traits of leaders and followers didn't overlap more. Strongly defined categories of "leader and follower" feel a little too dichotomous for my tastes—not what I'd like to see in an alternative culture. I'd like to see us all working on developing flexibility as a bottom line: be able to lead when it is needed and follow when it is needed, and do both with grace and a cooperative attitude. I like the philosophy that says that there aren't "leaders" and "followers" but rather that these are roles that everyone plays at one time or another. "Leaders" are really the servants of the moment and role models for how to be a good human. Presumably, they once learned those skills from others and are now passing them along.

One of the places where I see us strongly agreeing is in this idea that leaders are human: they mess up, don't think clearly all the time, and sometimes forget who and what they are serving and have to be reminded. Fear of messing up (and either feeling humiliated or being punished for it) is a huge factor in people being unwilling to step up to the plate and lead. Creating a kinder, gentler culture where power and leadership are shared, and where giving and receiving feedback are regular (and non-traumatic) events, can go a long way to making leadership accessible to everyone. Ideally, leaders are people you can look up to because they are genuine about their struggles and flaws as well as their passions, and unapologetic about caring and wielding power in service to your shared goals. Leaders are best when vulnerable; this is possible when the culture makes that safe. Everyone in the group has responsibility for creating that culture.

Power in Cooperative Groups

Finally, I'd like to touch (briefly) on a largely missing topic, which is power in cooperative groups. Traditionally, power is seen as residing in leadership. While this is certainly true, it

(continued on p. 75)

Photo courtesy of Ma'ikwe Schaub Ludwig

Students in Laird and Ma'ikwe's Integrative Facilitation training learn about facilitation, cooperative leadership, and themselves. (2009)

MORE PERSPECTIVES ON LEADERSHIP AND FOLLOWSHIP

(continued from p. 35)

Ma'ikwe works with students in the Integrative Facilitation course preparing for an even-handed, participatory meeting. (2009)

isn't the whole truth. My theory is that there are many different types of power, some blatant (like who is leading the project, who has a lot of social capital because of past good deeds, and who has expertise) and most more subtle. This subtle list includes a lot of territory: Who neglects to read the notes ahead of time, and then gets the whole group to tell them everything they should already know, wasting 15 minutes of everyone's time and getting a lot of attention? Who is really good at getting folks to pick up their slack? Who is really good at honesty? Who isn't? Who is really good at fun? Who is internally strong and has power because they don't need to be coddled? Who does need to be coddled, and takes energy from the group to get their personal needs met? Who rarely speaks, saving up their input for times when it is likely to be more influential?

Instead of asking, "Who has power?" I'm more interested in the question of how each person within the group gets and wields their power. The list of things above that are examples of types of power are (mostly) things that can be used for either good or ill in a group. Power itself is necessary to get things done, and neither good nor bad. And I believe that everyone has some power in a cooperative group (and that claims to complete powerlessness are themselves a form of wielding power, because no cooperative group wants to be accused of that depth of power imbalance and will generally bend over backwards to not have that impression persist).

Here's the kicker, though, and the one addition I'll make to Elizabeth's basically sound list of follower traits. Because leaders generally can't effectively lead a discussion about their own power in the group, good followers will occasionally bring this topic up. (This could just be an addition to the list of other important topics Elizabeth suggests groups grapple with.) The purpose of this conversation is not to drag down the leaders, but to encourage an even-handed consideration of how the group wants to relate to power in general, and how well everyone is doing with taking on their share of both power and responsibility. If a "follower" can successfully serve the group in this way, they'll be well on their way to blurring the lines between leadership and followship, and that is all to the good. ❧

Ma'ikwe Schaub Ludwig has lived in intentional community for 14 years, and is currently a member of Dancing Rabbit Ecovillage. She is the author of Passion as Big as a Planet, *which looks at the relationship between self-awareness and effective earth activism. Ma'ikwe teaches facilitation and consensus with her husband, Laird Schaub, and offers workshops on starting communities, leadership, and spiritual activism.*

Power and Powerlessness in Community

By Markus Euler

In university I was already keenly interested in issues of power and authority, but my studies of these topics have become much more real since I started living in community. Now, rather than focusing on academic questions such as how power comes into existence and what legitimizes authority, I care more about coming to terms with power differences in specific structures and clarifying existing problems on this basis.

Strangely, sometimes I feel just as powerless in my community as in normal society. At these moments, I think I am just a lonely voice crying in the desert with no power to change anything. Since the population in my community is much smaller than in the society as a whole, my voice should have more weight here.

And probably it does. One out of 60 (in ZEGG) is certainly more than one out of 80 million (in Germany). But that does not mean that I actually feel this way. What I say to myself is important in relation to how powerful I feel.

I noticed this when we had a small kitchen crisis in our community. We are organized so that every community member belongs to a cooking group which is in charge of the kitchen once a week. Each group has about 10 people who distribute among themselves whatever tasks have to be done. When new members arrive, or old members leave the community, we always try to ensure that the number of people in cooking groups remains the same. However, because of a big fluctuation, once only five members remained in one of the cooking groups and could therefore no longer handle the workload efficiently. They were still somehow able to keep things running through heroic self-sacrifice, but it was pretty unfair since people in well-staffed cooking groups had to work significantly less.

Though it was obvious to all that this group needed more people, attempts to lure members from other groups failed. This happened partly because people did not want to leave their familiar group and partly because the other groups feared that they would become too small. It became clear to us that we could come to a solution only with the entire community. Thus, we called for a Plenum in order to try to resolve this problem. In our community, a Plenum is a meeting to which

It was actually by* not *expressing my needs that I had inhibited the problem-solving process.

Markus Euler

all community members are invited and where all those who attend are entitled to make a decision.

Not everybody was present at the Plenum. This happens often in our community, since our members are usually very busy. We decided to set up our cooking groups in the room. Thus, all those who belonged to a cooking group stood together and the names of the missing people were written on slips of paper and placed at the appropriate groups. It became immediately obvious that one group was much smaller than the others. The attempts to shift people back and forth so that all groups could have the same number of members failed once more, for the same reasons as before.

I kept myself out of the whole process. I thought I could not contribute anything to the solution. My cooking group was still big enough. Although I was not really happy in this group, there was nothing that particularly bothered me. Above all, I did not want to move to a smaller group. When the situation started looking really hopeless, I felt powerless to do anything. At some point, however, following a spontaneous impulse, I said: "I would really like to cook with people I like." The statement was well received, but still no one had any idea how it could bring us closer to a solution. The whole process had come to a standstill.

We were all aware of the problem, but there was no one who had the power to solve it by decree—for example, by compelling some members to change groups. Since it was clear that nothing had helped, and also that things could not continue as they were, we decided to start considering crazy solutions as well.

Then a community member said: "I think Markus' idea is really interesting." I was intrigued that she described my statement as an idea, as I myself would have never perceived it as such. I had simply expressed my own needs, but did not wish to stand in the way of the overall process. But all at once it occurred to me that it was actually by *not* expressing my needs and by *not* going fully for what I wanted that I had stood in the way and inhibited the problem-solving process.

I would call this an example of empowerment at the right time, and what happened next showed that she was right to support me as she did.

I looked around the room. Unfortunately, none of the people that I would have liked to have in my group were present. However, their names were written on slips of paper. So I plucked up all my courage, authority, and power and I simply took the papers I wanted and put them around me. Immediately, a new cooking group was formed and I was inevitably its manager. The remaining people, including the papers with names that were left over, quickly found their way to other cooking groups without any major difficulties.

For me, this experience proved several truisms that one hears again and again in communities.

First: If everyone takes care of oneself, then everyone is taken care of.

Second: Everybody has something to contribute to a solution, even if she or he does not think so.

Third: Sometimes it takes a nudge from the outside, so that you do what you wanted to do anyway.

The process I just described took place about two years ago and our cooking groups still work perfectly. For me, this process symbolizes that when someone in our community wants something and the time is ripe for it, then things can change completely.

We are open and free enough to implement even crazy solutions. ❧

Markus Euler lives in the ZEGG Community near Berlin (www.zegg.de). He works there as an accountant and a workshop leader. As a writer he publishes articles about several issues, including community, money systems, love, and relationship.

Dancing with Discomfort: Thoughts on Empowerment from a Reluctantly Powerful Person

By Kristina Jansen

In an essay I read recently about advocacy and citizen participation in Zimbabwe, I came across this statement about the difficulty of empowering women in Africa:

> *Institutional change is often easier than at the personal level... most people resist changes to their personal space even when it involves extending their horizons. It is not easy for people to reach critical consciousness in their personal lives due to an intrinsic need to belong.*
>
> —Hope Chigudu, Chair, Global Fund for Women, personal correspondence, 2001

What struck me about this quote was how much I identified with it, and it resonated with what I was writing about for this issue of Communities. I was trying to describe how I felt as a child growing up in the midst of a vibrant intentional community in southern California, which I call Orinda in my writings. The basic tenets at Orinda were all about self-discovery, psychological empowerment, and personal integrity, but when I was a child growing up here, I experienced it differently.

My parents were among the early members of Orinda, moving here in the mid 1970s, and I was brought along. I was five or six years old when we moved into a cooperatively owned apartment building and I stopped living under their direct care. They weren't particularly good at being parents, and even before we moved, our family was rapidly falling apart. Needless to say, I was a deeply insecure child. Somehow I got it in my head that I had to be a "right" sort of person to be cared about, and this made me feel constantly on edge. While there were many ways that living in Orinda allowed me to develop and flourish as a person, I always felt oppressed by this need to be good, to say the "right" thing, to think and feel in a way I believed was in line with how the majority of everyone else was thinking, feeling, acting. Living with this belief meant there wasn't much room for me to figure out what I actually thought or felt, and I was not happy—which was a problem, since I thought "happy" was what I was really supposed to be. The pressure I felt is perhaps not so different from what a small-town girl with aspirations to go to the big city for college might experience, and even the guilt I felt at having different opinions and different wants was perhaps not unusual. It's part of that impulse in many of us to go out into the world and find our place in it, to leave our parents behind and make our own life. But at the time I didn't know this was a part of human nature. I thought I was a freak.

When I was 19, I left Orinda to go to college and live independently. Since there was no precedent for a young person in the community to go off to college (before me most of the younger people involved had dropped out of mainstream education, and were focused on working in one or another of the community's business enterprises), I did not know how to do this and keep close to my family, which was how I thought

about the community by now. Because I had never trusted my community friends and family enough to really talk about what I wanted and why I felt I needed to move away, many were surprised and felt hurt when I left for school. They assumed I would be estranged and antagonistic to Orinda. Other people who had left in the past were quite sour by the time they said goodbye, and bitterly rejected their whole experience here. I did not feel this way, and in fact I deeply believed in the goodness of living more communally. I believe humans are social animals, and our social experiment felt right to me. I loved the adults who had acted as parents, role models, mentors, guides, and I cherished those relationships even as I planned to leave. I loved my age-mates like siblings, and there were many people of all ages in the community that I considered dear friends. Leaving was not an easy choice on many levels, but it was something I felt I needed to do if I was going to find my own path.

At 28, I found myself back home for a spell. The intervening years had changed me, and being back I found myself in a different relationship to my former "parents." Life in Orinda turned out not to be as oppressive as I had once thought. Over the years I had lived on my own, I had gotten to know that I have an innate tendency to look for definition outside of myself. I learned that I could not blame the community for my own reluctance to have and express a dissenting opinion. I discovered I have an almost neurotic desire to blend in, while always holding myself slightly apart as an observer. In graduate school I studied anthropology, putting my natural tendencies for "participant observation" to professional use. Living in India during this time made me know that no matter how exotic the society was within which I found myself, I would find ways to disappear into the woodwork. If I was the only fair-headed woman in the village, I'd be sure to cover my hair, duck my face, and keep my mouth shut as long as possible—without creating waves, that is. So, when my time in India came to a natural end, and other life issues brought me home, I had the chance to revisit some of my old ideas about the society I grew up in with a fresh perspective.

I found that I was more than welcomed back into the community as an adult. Instead of being regarded with suspicion over my prodigal adventures, I was treated with respect, especially because I had a different point of view. I had been expecting to be shouted down, or otherwise silenced if I voiced an offbeat preference, like for yoga over tennis for example. I loved yoga, but when I came back only two or three others were quiet practitioners. When I started to go to classes in town, and then chose to practice regularly in the open, these few others joined me. Then more people got interested. Then more. Now even the most die-hard anti-yogis among my friends take the occasional class.

It was not easy for me to live as boldly or with the equality my friends and family members at Orinda were eager to allow. I've been home again now for more than a decade, but it is still hard for me to say what I think, to act as I see fit, or to express dissenting opinions. I fell into a job within the community's central office, and turned out to be good at communicating with people and organizing things around here. And in fact, I now find myself being called on to make decisions that affect lots of others with surprising regularity. Usually I make sure to take a reading from a handful of other people, and then communicate the results to the masses. In a funny way, I think my reluctant style might actually be more effective than if I was a more overtly controlling sort of person. Many of my friends now come to me for advice or to be a sounding board for some community event. I still get the occasional "Who are you to tell me what to do?" thrown back at me, to which I usually just reply, "Hey, I'm not telling you what to do, I'm just letting you know you are welcome to participate if you like." Since I personally don't have a stake in anyone actually listening to me, even the most defensive reaction can just slide off my back.

As I've gotten older here and more established as a person others turn to, I have had to face that I'm intrinsically uncomfortable with being in charge of anything.

As I've gotten older here and more established as a person others turn to, I have had to face that I'm intrinsically uncomfortable with being in charge of anything. Hell, half the time I don't really want to be in charge of myself. And here is the secret problem with living in a large and vibrant community: there are always a number of people who are not fully able or willing to take care of themselves on a practical level. Instead of someone or some small group of people trying to run everything, seeking power wherever they can, it seems there are a lot of people here who'd be perfectly happy just being told what to do. A lot of times, I am one of those people. On the other hand, there are always decisions that need to be made, and in the end someone needs to take action. Sometimes now, I am one of those people.

What is power at Orinda? It's not money, though being generous financially does get respect, and being self-supporting means a person has the security of financial independence. It's not force, though being able to express one's anger or opinions forcefully and effectively does get respect. It is not manipulation, though there are times when a person's weakness seems to have the whole community focused on him or her; it's just not usually a positive focus. I guess the people who have the most power here are those that have the most respect, and the way you get respect at Orinda is to live a generous, open, forthright life, in accordance with your individual nature, while being responsible for yourself and respectful to others. Being a powerful person here requires saying what you think, feel, and believe, without trying to ram it down anyone else's throat. It requires asking for what you want, knowing full well you may not get it. It requires showing up and sharing life. It's pretty simple, but surprisingly difficult.

But the main path to power here at Orinda is the willingness to give back, and to be of service. This past weekend marked the start of the summer season, when a large contingent of our friends and family members are off traveling until September. This is always a challenging transition for those of us left behind, who need to work and keep things at home going. My friend Alice called me on Friday to ask what was happening over the weekend. I made it up. "We should get together for dinner Saturday and maybe talk after." She was happy with this idea. I sent a message to everyone still in town that I was putting a meal together: "Show up if you like, I'll be home around 5 to start cooking, and would love your help if you have time. We'll serve around 6:30, talk after. I would love to see everyone." Donny offered to shop, so I sent him the grocery list. Alice wanted to take care of dessert, so I suggested she bring pies. "What kind? How many?" she asked. "Apple, cherry, and one more," I told her. Miguel said he'd help, so I asked him to make the main course. Lonnie sent me a note that she had already harvested lettuce that morning. It was washed and ready in the main fridge. At 5, when I got home to start preparing the meal, Annika, Dee, and Dennis arrived and wanted to help. It felt like a stone soup sort of meal, and in the end, my efforts were mostly directorial. Twenty-five friends showed up, helped cook our meal, clean up, and then we sat down to talk about our week, and share where each of us was at. As I looked around at the many friendly faces, I realized I had made this happen just by saying let's do it. I felt amazed by what a little initiative and a willingness to stick my neck out could create. It might not have been the most comfortable position for me to be in, but that night I certainly felt like I was creating my own life, and there was not an ounce of inequality in the room. ❧

Kristina Jansen grew up in the community she writes about here, and has dubbed "Orinda" for publication purposes. She left for a while to explore the wider world, and then returned as an adult to have her own children and live among close friends. She works in the community's central office—managing projects, people, and activities, or doing whatever needs to be done. She gardens, raises kids, writes essays, travels the globe, and spends as much time as she can with her friends.

Illustrations by Ethan Hughes

Power and Disempowerment on the Ecobus

By Chris Roth

I arrived for my first day on the Conservation Society Ecobus (not its actual name) wearing my Conservation Society t-shirt. I was happy and proud to finally be part of a tribe—to join something larger than myself that I could actually believe in. To me, the t-shirt symbolized this new beginning in my life, and the larger movement to which I was now dedicating myself.

Imagine my surprise when I was told to turn my t-shirt inside out.

The guides explained that by wearing t-shirts with writing on them, I and other students were serving as advertising placards, presenting images to other people in an effort to create impressions-by-association, rather than presenting our true, unbranded selves. T-shirts with writing showed inner insecurity, and furthermore, they were offensive and tiresome to look at during hikes. By turning our t-shirts inside out, we would be reclaiming our power and our integrity, instead of giving them away to societal forces by buying into something that wasn't really us.

Not everyone agreed. While many of us had never considered this issue before, some had already sworn off corporate t-shirts but felt good about wearing environmental ones. A few people said they liked to wear t-shirts representing groups and causes they cared about, because it helped promote those causes and also was an excellent conversation-starter with others who had similar interests. But the guides and second-year students immediately became more emphatic, and the dissenting voices soon piped down. We apparently needed to agree on this. No one wanted to get off on the wrong foot. We all agreed to reverse our t-shirts, or wear plain ones.

Thus began a two-year journey during which I simultaneously gave away power and empowered myself with an expanded perspective on the world—lost my voice and aspects of my self while also discovering both. I've heard similar tales from others who've joined intensely focused, insular groups (what some label "cults," though that is not a term that the Fellowship for Intentional Community considers useful or fair, as it's an oversimplified, judgmental term in every case).

The questions that arise are similar among many of us, whether our experiences were in separatist Christian communities, ideologically-driven social experiments, radical environmentalist enclaves, groups guided by charismatic leaders (a category that can overlap with others), or any similarly focused community endeavors:

Were we being controlled, or had we found a new freedom in our adopted tribe? Had we lost our individuality, or gained a new sense of self? Were we simply conforming to new standards, or were we gaining the courage to resist conformity to the larger society's norms? Were these the best times of our lives, or the worst?

The answer was often: both. But I'm getting ahead of myself. So far, I'd only flipped my t-shirt inside out.

* * *

At 20, feeling isolated, alienated, and out of harmony with the world around me, I had left my traditional liberal arts college and set off on an entirely different course. The Ecobus' parent organization, the Conservation Society, had been a cornerstone of American environmentalism for decades, and had taken this traveling, consensus-run experiential education school, and its nine-month-long experiments in community living and outdoor learning, under its wing.

The Ecobus aimed to help its guides and students rediscover the awareness and practices needed to live in balance with ourselves, each other, and the natural world—to restore healthy individual, social, and ecological relationships. I stepped onto the bus brimming with idealism and enthusiasm (as well as some understandable fear at the newness of it all), and met the 22 people who'd be my fellow students and community-mates for most of the next year. The first lesson, about t-shirts, while unexpected, felt strangely liberating. The nuances of the issue seemed less important than the opportunity to be "in this together." Something about the black-and-white framing of it, the radical shake-up of the default mode of being in the modern world (in which advertising was so pervasive that few questioned putting it on their bodies), comforted, even exhilarated me. The t-shirt decision solidified us as a tribe. Many more such decisions followed.

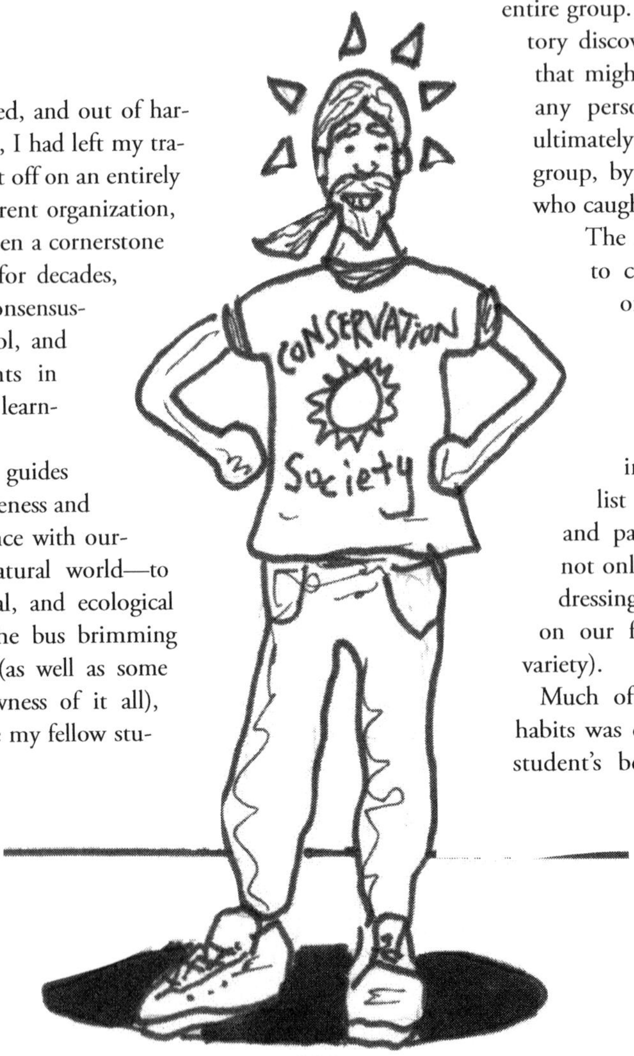

When applying to join the bus program, all of us had already consented to certain norms. We'd agreed to eat whatever was served, rather than following different diets. (Catering to individual dietary needs, we were told, would be too complicated and would also divide the group.) Dedicated meat-eaters, the guides made it clear that meat would be a regular element in the group diet. Although I'd been vegetarian for three years, I had agreed to this change in diet because I'd felt desperate for an actual group experience that would bring me back into harmony with the world and myself. There would be no alcohol, drugs, or tobacco, restrictions which were fine by me. Quite significant for many students, we had also agreed to refrain from "exclusive relationships" while on the bus—meaning not only sexual relationships, but "best friend" and confidant-type relationships. Our primary relationship was to be to the group as a whole—nothing could be said to any individual that was not OK to share with the entire group. (As those who tested this territory discovered, anything said to anyone that might raise any "issues" or indicate any personal or interpersonal tension ultimately would be aired in the whole group, by that person or by the person who caught wind of it.)

The men on the bus had also agreed to cut their hair so that the tops of the ears were visible, and to remove facial hair, because we didn't want to offend some of the "resource people" we'd meet on our travels by appearing to be hippies. We'd received a list of suggested clothing to bring, and partly as a result, we ended up not only cutting our hair similarly, but dressing similarly (though the patterns on our flannel shirts showed a bit of variety).

Much of the uniformity in our living habits was dictated by our situation. Each student's belongings needed to fit in a small cubby on the bus and a backpack on the roof. Living outdoors and camping, essential parts of the educational experience, were the only options

available to us. Some of us tended to sleep in tents, others under tarps, others under the stars, but we all slept outside except in the direst weather emergencies (which occurred on perhaps two nights during my two years with the program).

* * *

I found the new experience of sleeping outside deeply satisfying. I'd grown up in a suburb of New York City, and had been camping only a few times in my life. The Ecobus took us to beautiful natural places all over the country, exposed us to environments more varied and awe-inspiring than I could ever have imagined, and put us in direct, tactile contact with the earth every night. Not every camping experience occurred in the wilderness—in fact, wilderness hikes comprised just a fraction of our time together—but whether camping in a town, on a Native American reservation, in a developed state park, at a KOA campground, or in the backcountry, we were opening ourselves up to the outdoors, becoming comfortable with the earth (rather than a building) as our home. Given the previous trajectory of my life, I probably never would have done this on my own.

Camping felt quite empowering. Not only was I less dependent on "civilization," and able to take care of my own (minimal) shelter needs (with a little help from modern tent and tarp materials), but I shared my bedroom with the natural world, which I realized held more beauty and endurance than anything we humans can construct.

Sleeping outside together in a group of 23 people every night also offered a unique experience of community. Even when we spread out (as we often did), I felt a sense of solidarity with others that I have rarely felt in my life. For years afterward I would periodically miss that feeling—especially when I was continuing to sleep outside, as all good Ecobus students did, but no one around me was. Where were my Ecobus mates? At those times, I would miss the tribal togetherness that had us all sleeping out together, whether the weather was balmy or extreme (as it sometimes was).

Dedicating ourselves to this practice, especially when it wasn't easy, challenged us and brought us together. If any of us had slept inside (in those rare situations where that might have been possible), it would have felt like a betrayal. In fact, sleeping outside was not only a practical matter—it was a moral statement and essential sign of our alignment. It embodied our commitment and loyalty to the group and to the earth. It was a nonnegotiable part of being an Ecobus participant. It was part of the same reassuring, black-and-white package of lifestyle choices that had us flipping our t-shirts inside out, eating whatever the group as a whole ate, refraining from couple relationships, and grooming and dressing ourselves nearly identically. It unified us as Ecobus students. It brought power to the group.

* * *

And at least once, it brought unexpected discord. On a night fairly early during my first year on the bus, we had set up camp in a state park, and many of us had chosen to sleep without tent or tarp, under the clear, star-filled sky. Part way through the night, an unanticipated rainstorm wakened us. Those without weather protection faced a choice: take their tent or tarp down from the roof of the bus and set it up in the pouring rain, or crawl under the large, roofed picnic shelter that was next to our campground. Most of the unprotected campers chose the latter course, and woke up in the morning relatively dry, grateful for the fortuitous location of that shelter.

But not everyone was so happy at this good fortune. At our

morning meeting (we met, always as a whole group, for several hours on most days), one of the guides uttered the "magic words" (words that were repeated, by various people, quite frequently—and that almost always resulted in a stoppage of all other activity and a devotion of the entire group's attention to the issue, for as long as it took to deal with it): "I have something to bring up."

He described what had happened the previous night, and asked if the people who'd chosen to sleep under the pre-constructed shelter had anything to say for themselves: What had they been thinking? How did their choice reflect our desire to be self-reliant, to set up our own shelters? Hadn't it been an example of taking the easy way out? Didn't it contradict what we stood for as a group? Wasn't this the first step on a slippery slope that would have us sleeping inside shelters built by others elsewhere as well? Had they honestly believed that this was the best choice to make? How serious were they about this program, anyway?

The students offered some explanations and apologies, but by this time most people knew that genuine debate was not wanted, that acquiescence was the only safe route, the course of least damage. They promised never to do it again. Had someone felt empowered enough to challenge the guide's assertions, they might have said:

That park shelter was built much more sustainably, using more local and durable materials, than our nylon tents and tarps made in China. The more we set up and take down those tarps and tents, especially in inclement conditions, the sooner they will wear out. The environmentally responsible choice is to make use of an existing resource rather than, for arbitrary ideological reasons, using an alternative with larger negative impacts.

The guide might well have responded that sometimes the best choices *do* exact environmental costs, and that in this case the purity of our camping experience, our direct contact with the earth, held more importance than the negligible wear and tear on our equipment. But that conversation never happened, and none of us actually got to make that choice. Or rather we *did* make it—we ran by "consensus," after all (in unfacilitated meetings dominated by the loudest voices and without any training or formal consensus process)—but we made it under great duress. We had already given our power of choice away to those who ran the Ecobus. We already understood that we were there not to learn by making choices and seeing the results of those choices—we were there to learn by following the leaders' choices and adopting their worldview, or at least trying to.

* * *

In the first week or two, actual multi-sided conversations, exchanges of ideas held independently by individuals on the bus, had still attempted to occur. But the pattern established by our initial t-shirt discussion asserted itself quickly: if given a chance, people might start to share their own perspectives, but the guides and second-year students quickly moved in with the "Ecobus" interpretation of whatever we were discussing. Most problems were the result of "Prejudice Against Nature." "White-smockers" (soulless reductionist scientists, obsessed with measurements and logical arguments and cut off from the living, breathing earth) shared the blame for the plight of the planet with greedy corporations and clueless consumers. Most educational institutions (except the Ecobus) deliberately separated us from the earth in order to mold us into cogs in the machine of western civilization, which was destroying the planet and the native peoples who once lived in harmony with it. Our feelings were the voice of nature speaking through us, and they connected us with the rest of the living earth. By returning to actual, experiential connections with "Culture, Nature, and Self"—by recreating our understandings of and relationships to those, as we formed a subculture more attuned to them—we could help heal the damage the dominant culture had done.

The worldview was compelling in many ways, and I still believe that much of it has validity. I also now see other aspects of it as oversimplified, black-and-white interpretations of a nuanced, "gray" world. But during the Reagan years, that world seemed to have gone mad, as ecological concerns had been pushed to the margins (and often off the edge) of the national discourse. Corporations had seized power in Washington. The agencies responsible for our parks and wildlands had been deprived of enforcement power and taken over by corporate lackeys, and even most environmental groups had been forced to compromise until there was nothing left to give away. Our Secretary of Interior believed that the end of the world was near, and that if humans failed to use up all additional natural "resources" by that time, we would have sinned by failing to utilize the gifts that God had given us. He gleefully urged mining, drilling, and resource extraction everywhere—the more the better. In this atmosphere, the radical, often antagonistic response exemplified by the Ecobus seemed not only understandable, but justified.

Conversations would not end until all seemed to have "agreed" or at least acquiesced to the guides' point of view—until all dissenting voices were silent. The processes of forming consensus in our day-to-day decisions and of figuring out the meanings and reasons behind the issues we discussed relied on attrition, on wearing down the will of those who may have seen things a bit differently but got tired of arguing. Ultimately, resistance to the dominant view seemed futile—an ironic twist, in that our group prided itself on resisting the worldview of the dominant culture. Perhaps, in holding strong to that resistance, we needed an unusual degree of unity—one that, if it didn't come naturally, had to be forced or constructed.

By a month into the program each year, most students wouldn't even bother stating an obviously alternative viewpoint—in fact, they seemed in competition with one another to articulate the "Ecobus" viewpoint first. How did we feel about the stripmine? As student after student reiterated (reinforced by the guides' approval), it was a rape of the earth. I had also noticed how colorful and awe-inspiring the rock exposed by the mining was—I had actually enjoyed seeing it—but I didn't dare say so. I kept quiet.

* * *

I noticed that I kept quiet a lot. Long discussions would go by and I wouldn't say a word. Some other students wouldn't either. Near the end of each discussion, a guide or one of the more voluble students, usually a second-year, would say, "I wonder why so-and-so [often 'Chris' during the first year, until I learned to prevent it by saying at least *something* before being called out] hasn't said anything? What is s/he thinking? Where is s/he at with this?"

In a group that discouraged alternative or more complex viewpoints, that pressured its participants into ideological conformity, it seems little wonder that some of us clammed up rather than giving our power away by saying things we didn't wholeheartedly believe, or that didn't express the full picture as we saw it. Instead, we chose to give our power away by *not* talking. I remember a period when I had difficulty articulating anything, even in normal conversation. I felt almost as if I'd lost my voice entirely; when I did manage to squeeze something out of my voicebox, it seemed to me strained, feeble, full of tension. People often asked me to repeat it, to speak up so they could hear me. I would, but I didn't really feel like talking. In retrospect, I'm sure my physical voice faded away because I didn't feel safe speaking about what was really going on inside, of which I was often in denial.

And yet, in a sense, I did also find my voice during those two years. I had been trained to be polite, socialized to not "rock the boat." I had often censored myself rather than raising difficult questions or offering potentially critical perspectives. The Ecobus turned this formula on its head. The guides encour-

aged us to criticize ourselves and each other, to "bring things up" whenever we saw a hypocrisy or inconsistency, to hold each other accountable to our group covenants and ecological principles. Experienced Ecobusers made it a habit of *not* saying "good morning" or "hi" or even, it seemed, smiling—those would distract, apparently, from the weighty business of focusing on how we each were failing to live up to our ideals. Displays of affection, casual touch, and hugging were absent from our culture, and actively discouraged by the guides; in fact, predictably, one of them blocked a proposed group hug at the beginning of my second year on the bus (such a thing had never even been proposed the first year), ensuring that the suggestion would never be repeated. A community we certainly were—but one committed to mutual challenge and confrontation rather than mutual support. The guides saw this as excellent training for challenging and confronting the people in agencies and companies who were ruining the planet—and we even got some practice with that, as we visited government offices and power plants and asked questions that made our hosts squirm.

Interestingly, the higher-ups seemed relatively immune to confrontation and challenge. Having figured out the "Ecobus way," they were responsible for embodying and articulating it. When our bus got together with the two sister buses in the program, I noticed that the guides and students on those buses seemed to act in the same ways, have the same discussions, hold the same worldviews and opinions as our bus. In fact, all the guides seemed to hold the same philosophy and even use the same jargon as the original founder of the Ecobus program, who guided one of the buses. It turns out that all five of the non-founder guides had been proteges of the founder on the original Ecobus, and were now doing their best to spread his understandings, which had become their own.

And during the course of those two years, many of those understandings became my own as well. I found that a lot of them did make sense to me; they helped me understand and interpret the world in ways I hadn't before. Especially in my second year, I became more outspoken on the bus. I felt that I agreed with most of the philosophy but didn't always agree with how we were attempting to embody it.

Increasingly, I felt able to "rock the boat" when I thought it needed rocking. I challenged the meat-eating dictum on environmental grounds, and almost succeeded in converting my bus to vegetarianism on a trial basis (stopped only by a couple holdouts who were unwilling to even attempt it). I remember questioning how much time we spent driving around instead of staying in one place. I found myself able to express my perceptions of other people and their personal challenges (as well as my own), and I rediscovered my ability to write. I was no scientist, just a beginning student of ecology, and a very poor naturalist at that point in my life, but in the areas of "psychology" and "English" I got high marks from fellow Ecobusers (both figuratively, and literally, in our very awkward mutual-grading ritual at the end of each semester). I also discovered a passion for Native American culture, which led me, upon graduation, to move to a reservation I'd first visited with the Ecobus. For the next four years, I continued to follow the "Ecobus code" by sleeping outside in all but the very most inclement weather, including all through the winter. And to this day, I have continued to be influenced by the ecological and cultural perspectives I gained on the bus, although I see that they were infected by varying degrees of fundamentalism, intolerance, decidedly *un*compassionate communication, pseudo-consensus, dysfunctional power dynamics, self-righteousness, hypocrisy, and naivete.

* * *

When I tell people about my times on the bus, they have one of two reactions: "That sounds *amazing*!" "That sounds *awful*!" Often the same person says both things during the course of the conversation; the order of the statements depends only on which parts of the story I happen to tell first.

Our group had experiences in natural ecosystems, on Native American reservations, in other land-based subcultures (from communities of Mennonite farmers to Appalachian mountain dwellers to remote Sierra Nevada homesteaders) that affected many of us profoundly, and permanently expanded our ideas about the world and its possibilities. We also witnessed power plants, mines, chicken factories, and environmental devastation; we spent time with policy makers and wild food foragers, folklorists and archaeologists, activists and conservationists. We all picked up musical instruments, sang together (learning songs particular to each region of the country we visited), and held our own contra-dances. We eschewed consumerism, mass media, and electronic entertainment of all sorts (although laptop computers and cell phones didn't yet exist, we would likely have boycotted those too). In their absence, we created, however awkwardly, our own culture and lives together during those years.

We talked and formed community. Were we always speaking our full truth, and was it a community of equals? No, and no. We each gained some inner power, and lost some inner power, by joining this tribe. Fortunately, most of us still had many decades ahead of us to continue to figure out how best to speak about our feelings (which we'd been told were the most important things, nature's way of expressing itself through us); how to relate most effectively with others (by being more compassionate, and less judgmental, than we'd been on the bus); how to connect most fully with the earth (for me, it wasn't riding around in a bus and camping, but rather gardening and immersing myself in local ecosystems in place-based intentional communities); how to distinguish between choices that were truly ours and choices that we made under pressure; and how to integrate everything we'd experienced on the bus in ways that empowered rather than disempowered us.

* * *

An intense, 24-hour-a-day, seven-day-a-week world unto itself, the Ecobus asked for total commitment from its participants. Was it a "cult"? In the sense that most people mean it, maybe it was. But the ease with which that label can apply to many aspects of it proves to me the uselessness of that label. I learned and grew through my time on the Ecobus in ways that I value to this day. My experience on the bus made unique contributions to my life, both through its "positive" and "negative" lessons, influencing everything I've done since. And it left me with many memories (most more comical than troubling in retrospect, and many of them beautiful) that continue to inspire me, or at least provide good fodder for conversation. You haven't heard the half of them.

The Ecobus asked for total commitment from its participants. Was it a "cult"? In the sense that most people mean it, maybe it was. But the ease with which that label can apply to many aspects of it proves to me the uselessness of that label.

But here are a few more: there was the night we were drenched by the municipal sprinklers set on "automatic" in the town park; the frigid winter evenings sitting in a circle around a non-campfire talking about how cold we were, but how the act of enduring extreme low temperatures was more aligned with nature than building a fire; the hike along Baxter State Park's narrow Knife Edge, during which several of us had uncontrollable bowel ailments...and the welcome we felt at southwestern pueblo dances; the quiet of a backcountry canoe trip; the transcendent beauty of the song of the canyon wren; the glimpses we offered each other into our own complex, tender inner worlds, in which the answers were seldom quite as easy as those offered by any single worldview, no matter how comprehensive. And there were the many times when we got past the words and I felt, on a much deeper, more tactile level, that we were indeed part of the earth, living in community with one another in ways that were *not* forced, finding our power from sources more fundamental and enduring than the relatively insignificant human power dynamics of the day.

About the t-shirts: I now wear them right-side out...except when I choose not to. ❧

Postscript: In the decades following my two years on the Ecobus, the program evolved considerably. A new generation of leaders replaced the original guides, introducing new ideas, a much greater emphasis on diversity (in everything from thought to diet), increased bioregional focus, and more compassionate communication. Yet there were also tradeoffs; latter-year students, who could enroll on a single bus for only a semester at a time (a shortened and more-expensive one at that), by most reports experienced less intensity, less unity, less commitment, fewer contra-dances danced, and fewer folk songs learned. Regrettably, financial and organizational challenges eventually forced the cessation of the Ecobus program. It is sorely missed and still mourned by many of its alumni, from every era.

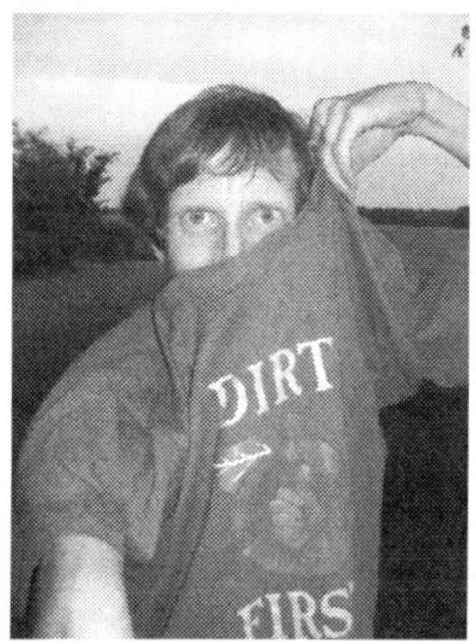

Chris Roth edits Communities *and currently calls Rutledge, Missouri's tri-communities area home.*

Communities Editorial Policy

Communities is a forum for exploring intentional communities, cooperative living, and ways our readers can bring a sense of community into their daily lives. Contributors include people who live or have lived in community, and anyone with insights relevant to cooperative living or shared projects.

Through fact, fiction, and opinion, we offer fresh ideas about how to live and work cooperatively, how to solve problems peacefully, and how individual lives can be enhanced by living purposefully with others. We seek contributions that profile community living and why people choose it, descriptions of what's difficult and what works well, news about existing and forming communities, or articles that illuminate community experiences—past and present—offering insights into mainstream cultural issues. We also seek articles about cooperative ventures of all sorts—in workplaces, in neighborhoods, among people sharing common interests—and about "creating community where you are."

We do not intend to promote one kind of group over another, and take no official position on a community's economic structure, political agenda, spiritual beliefs, environmental issues, or decision-making style. As long as submitted articles are related thematically to community living and/or cooperation, we will consider them for publication. However, we do not publish articles that 1) advocate violent practices, or 2) advocate that a community interfere with its members' right to leave.

Our aim is to be as balanced in our reporting as possible, and whenever we print an article critical of a particular community, we invite that community to respond with its own perspective.

Submissions Policy

To submit an article, please first request Writers' Guidelines: Communities, RR 1 Box 156, Rutledge MO 63563-9720; 660-883-5545; editor@ic.org. To obtain Photo Guidelines, email: layout@ic.org. Both are also available online at ic.org/communities-magazine.

Advertising Policy

We accept paid advertising in Communities because our mission is to provide our readers with helpful and inspiring information—and because advertising revenues help pay the bills.

We handpick our advertisers, selecting only those whose products and services we believe will be helpful to our readers. That said, we are not in a position to verify the accuracy or fairness of statements made in advertisements—unless they are FIC ads—nor in REACH listings, and publication of ads should not be considered an FIC endorsement.

If you experience a problem with an advertisement or listing, we invite you to call this to our attention and we'll look into it. Our first priority in such instances is to make a good-faith attempt to resolve any differences by working directly with the advertiser/lister and complainant. If, as someone raising a concern, you are not willing to attempt this, we cannot promise that any action will be taken.

Please check ic.org/communities-magazine or email ads@ic.org for advertising information.

What is an "Intentional Community"?

An "intentional community" is a group of people who have chosen to live or work together in pursuit of a common ideal or vision. Most, though not all, share land or housing. Intentional communities come in all shapes and sizes, and display amazing diversity in their common values, which may be social, economic, spiritual, political, and/or ecological. Some are rural; some urban. Some live all in a single residence; some in separate households. Some raise children; some don't. Some are secular, some are spiritually based; others are both. For all their variety, though, the communities featured in our magazine hold a common commitment to living cooperatively, to solving problems nonviolently, and to sharing their experiences with others.

PUBLISHER'S NOTE BY LAIRD SCHAUB

Gender Dynamics in Cooperative Groups

I've recently been in a dialog with a thoughtful friend who has lived half his life in a consensus-based community and shared this reflection about gender dynamics (which I have lightly edited to preserve anonymity):

As I see it, there is a distinct difference between the genders that has persisted for decades, well beyond the behaviors or personalities of particular men or women. When our group experiences open conflict in arriving at consensus it almost always becomes positional/territorial "lines" between one or two men, not women. I have recently seen the group get close to agreement only to have the consensus founder because one or two males believe they have a better understanding of: a) how consensus works; or b) what the real problem is that the rest are missing. It happens repeatedly...and heatedly.

Recently, I was standing in a circle of members when I expressed a concern that a committee had sent out a written message to a departing member that had not been cleared in plenary. When anger erupted in response to that revelation all *the women took a physical step back, while the males exchanged heated words. Though we worked through the anger over the next days, it has made me look more closely at male-female dynamics during our plenary conversations—to read the body language, to observe if females are speaking out or not, and to see who is helping us move collectively and who is holding onto some "sacred" place that cannot be touched.*

Lately, I've been finding a wonderful amount of courage and inner clarity to challenge these positions, yet I admit to almost wishing to be part of a community where the women's views were weighted a bit more than the men's (I know that's a big generalization, but there are threads of truth for me), because women can sense much of what is being felt in the group and what is being lost that the males often miss while proving themselves "right."

I replied:

I can certainly resonate with your observation as someone who gets to peek behind the curtain of many groups (people don't hire me to confirm that everything is going well).

The way I've made sense of the gender phenomenon you described above is that women in our culture are conditioned to be more relational than men; and men are held up to the standard of John Wayne, the archetypal rugged individualist. (To be sure, I know plenty of women who are every bit as roosterish as those men whose behavior you have highlighted in your community, but in general I think your observation is sound.) For relationally oriented people it's not so difficult to set aside personal preferences for the good of the group. For those taught to trust their inner truth above all else, it can be the very devil distinguishing between personal preference and divine inspiration. In that context, asking them to think of the whole is an insult because they believe that their inner truth is always about that. They just have trouble accepting that other people's inner truth might be different, and just as divinely inspired.

On the whole, it's been my observation that strong women tend to run intentional communities. Not because they are naturally better leaders, but because it's essential for leaders to have developed fairly sophisticated social skills to be effective in community, and girls tend to be steered in that direction more than boys. While you want leaders to be good at both relational skills and systems thinking, it's my sense that it's easier for a woman to learn systems than it is for a man to learn to see an issue from another person's perspective.

What do I mean by relational skills? It's the ability to:

- Articulate clearly what you think.
- Articulate clearly what you feel.
- Hear accurately what others say (and be able to communicate that to the speaker such that they feel heard).
- Hear critical feedback without walling up or getting defensive.
- Function reasonably well in the presence of non-trivial distress in others.
- Shift perspectives to see an issue through another person's lens.
- See potential bridges between two people who are at odds with each other.
- See the good intent underneath strident statements.
- Distinguish clearly between a person's behavior being out of line and that person being "bad."
- Own your own shit.
- Reach out to others before you have been reached out to yourself.
- Be sensitive to the ways in which you are privileged.

Intentional communities (at least the ones that don't espouse traditional gender roles, which is most, but by no means all) tend to be especially attractive to strong women for two reasons. First, communities tend to be progressive politically and are therefore likely to be committed to breaking down stereotypical gender roles. Thus, women are far less likely to encounter glass ceiling dynamics in community. That means openings for *everyone* without reference to their plumbing. Hallelujah!

Second, communities are committed to creating cooperative culture, and that means *how* things are done tends to matter as much as *what* gets done. This is in striking contrast with the mainstream culture and its fixation on results. In consequence, those social skills (that women have been conditioned to excel at) stand out as a big plus.

Going the other way, community can be a challenging environment for strong men because their behavior may trigger knee-jerk suspicion about whether their strength is rooted in a desire for personal aggrandizement (the mainstream tendency) instead of service to the whole. It is not enough that the strong man *thinks* he's clean (by which I mean not ego-driven and working on behalf of everyone); it matters more how he comes across to others, and this is all about social skills, not facility with rhetoric or branding.

It's even more nuanced than that. Given the historic privilege that men have enjoyed in the wider culture, the determination to create a more feminist culture in community (by which I mean egalitarian—not woman-centered) translates into encouraging women to step up and men to step back. In practice this can result in women being celebrated for being assertive (in the interest of encouraging their stepping up) while men *taking the same action* are criticized for being too aggressive (in an effort to encourage their stepping back).

While this may be demonstrably unfair, a more subtle question is whether it's an appropriate strategy for closing the gap in societal prejudice that favors men. While there's no doubt that this strategy won't work long term (because it would just reverse the inequity), it's an open question whether this exercise in affirmative action is justified in an effort to accelerate getting to the promised land of equal opportunity—and if so, for how long it should be supported.

All in all, intentional community is an incredibly potent laboratory for experimenting with gender dynamics in pursuit of the holy grail: a better life for all.

• • •

After I shared the above thoughts in a blog post, I received several comments, including this one, from a reader named Abe:

I have had a lot of experience visiting communities and hearing this bigoted viewpoint about men being one way and women being another way. I mean, I hear it outside communities as well, but I would have imagined more critique, in communities, of the concept of the gender binary or the idea of gender being anything more than a concept in our heads. I have heard quite a bit of critique of these ideas of "men are this" and "women are that" in the circle of Acorn, Twin Oaks, and Living Energy Farm. Still, there is a womyn's gathering and a womyn's collective at Twin Oaks.

I remember, at an early Gaia U board meeting, a proposal to divide the board by gender (just women and men, no one else). It was decided there be two heads of the board, because, you know, "you have to balance the feminine and masculine energies" and "men and women have a different way of looking at things."

What does this idea that men and women think and do things differently serve? Let's say it's not being said from a biological perspective of sex, rather than gender, and you're only talking about the cultural norms and how people were raised. Even then, what can this thought even serve? First, it is said from a cisgender perspective, speaking only of women and men and no one else. It excludes intersex people. It excludes transgender people. Beyond that, what do you do with an idea like that? You apply it to the people around you and make judgments on individual people based on what your belief is about people of their gender. The problem with prejudice like that is that there is no way to take a whole classification of people and accurately apply it to any one individual within the classification.

I wrote the original piece because I believe there are important differences in the way that boys and girls are conditioned in the mainstream culture. It was not my aim to encourage stereotyping or to promote the assumption that all feminine-presenting people act one way and all masculine-presenting people act another; it was to describe a gulf that I see played out repeatedly in cooperative group dynamics and which I believe we must learn to recognize and develop the capacity to bridge between.

The most important part for me is the ways in which cooperative culture differs from competitive culture with respect to how it solves problems. In the wider culture, we venerate rational problem solvers and systems thinking. In cooperative culture those qualities are still an asset, yet so is the ability to work relationally and empathetically.

What was intriguing for me about my friend's observation (which was the inspiration for my original blog entry) was: a) that both styles persisted in his well-established community; and b) that the clash between the styles was *the* major impediment to peaceable resolution of conflict. I was not so interested in the analysis that women were never strident, or consistently did a better job of setting aside their egos to think of the whole, yet I *was* interested in how gendered cultural conditioning could explain what my friend observed.

That's exciting because it means that there is every reason to believe that if *all* children were trained to be skilled at human relations, then we could all be better cooperative problem solvers. ❧

Laird Schaub is Executive Secretary of the Fellowship for Intentional Community (FIC), publisher of this magazine, and cofounder of Sandhill Farm, an egalitarian community in Missouri. He is also a facilitation trainer and process consultant, and he authors a blog that can be read at communityandconsensus.blogspot.com. This article is adapted from his blog entries of November 30 and December 3, 2013.

NOTES FROM THE EDITOR BY CHRIS ROTH

Chris Roth

Gender: Is There a "There" There?

As best I can remember, my first diary contained scant or no evidence of any kind of emotional depth, social intelligence, or even sensitivity of any kind. In it I ecorded my exploits, batting average, and other baseball statisics as a member of Edgewood School's fourth-grade boys' "B" eam. It was hardly a stepping stone to the Major Leagues, but evertheless my lone grand slam (the result of a couple fielder rrors, to be honest) was apparently the highlight of my year, liciting the largest capital-letter writing in the entire diary. In his journal, at least, I was all "boy," sports-obsessed, competiive, and almost charmingly unaware of the relative insignifiance of my achievements.

Fast forward 15 years, though, and I'd embarked on decades f working in fields in which three quarters or more of my colagues were women. I could care less about sports, and most of ıy close friendships turned out to be with women, with whom could relate so much more easily than I could in stereotypial male culture. I went out drinking with buddies exactly zero ımes; eventually, I would spend hours at a stretch conversing bout personal and interpersonal matters with women friends, ot as any kind of male conquest (I was mostly celibate) but ecause it was where I felt most at home. In relationship, I ound myself attracted to women with a strong mix of "mascune" and "feminine" characteristics, and I often seemed to be e one dwelling in the emotional realm more of the time. If d once hewn closely to my culture's gender expectations, I had xperienced at the very least some slippage.

My first draft of this editorial started by listing six statements that could be interpreted as sexist and oppressive of the feminine, all of which I'd heard from fellow intentional community members over the last 30 years. Four out of the six, however, had been uttered not by a man, but by a woman. In the interests of not reliving or perpetuating those sentiments, or the disharmony and imbalance I associate with them, I've removed them from this piece of writing. (I'd like this magazine to embody what we want to manifest more of, rather than get too mired in places we don't want to be—or at least to offer a representative balance—and my experiences in intentional community have been overwhelmingly positive in terms of overcoming sexism.)

But my point remains: both men and women seem capable of embodying a large spectrum of characteristics, of varying degrees of suitability to cooperative culture—from qualities we think of as extremely masculine to those we think of as quintessentially feminine. What emerges in each of us may have as much to do with social circumstances and pressures as it does with our inherent natures...at least until we become aware of the full range of being and expression of which we are capable.

Once we start making our own choices about who we allow ourselves to be, we may find ourselves throwing cultural gender expectations to the wind, as many of this issue's authors do—and also discovering that our identities and relationships are much more nuanced and rich than traditional gender definitions would have them be.

In the final stages of assembling this issue, we received text for a sidebar to Oblio Stroyman's "Evolving Gender Consciousness in New Culture Camps" (p. 28). In a passage we didn't have room for, Michael Rios wrote:

"Though I present as white/male/heterosexual, my reality is anything but. I grew up in a multicultural environment where men (and women) cried with each other, kissed on the lips, and touch was a near constant. Men were considered to be the emotional gender, and the women, if anything, were expected to keep the level head in the family. So my experience of being physically male left me with virtually nothing in common with what US males in a men's group talk about. ...

"Realizing how different my experience was from others here in the US, I had spent years in both neurobiological and sociological research, trying to determine what the core reality of gender must be. The more I explored, the less I found that could be considered essential gender—and the more I concluded that 'when you got there, there wasn't any "there" there.'"

Is there any "there" there, when it comes to gender? For me, the jury is still out—I have many more questions than answers within myself about gender and how it correlates with biology and sexual identity. At the very least, gender is a continuum, not a strict duality. Perhaps, if there's truly no "there" there behind our current theme, we have nothing to talk about in this issue...

Yet judging from the bulging contents, apparently we do.

Rather than making gender, sexual identity, and gender relationships seem irrelevant in a sea of "we're all the same," the intensity of community living can bring these issues to the fore as nothing else does. In this issue we hear from a multitude of contributors, with diverse gender and sexual identifications, about the issues they've encountered in community. The Table of Contents provides just a hint of the breadth and depth you'll find inside. We hope you find this exploration as fascinating as we have. As always, we'd love to hear your feedback and additional contributions to this discussion. Please let us hear from you!

Speaking of fascinating subjects, we're excited to announce that you can delve into a wide range of them in new materials now available from the FIC. Our "Best of Communities" article compilations distill the most incisive and enduring stories we've published this millennium in Communities (with a few holdovers from the 1990s). Fifteen collections, each with a different theme, are now available for purchase and digital download at ic.org/products/communities-magazine.

They're a perfect complement to an ongoing Communities subscription—which also, for the first time, now includes a digital subscription. (Another first: international subscriptions, when digital-only, are now available for the same price as US subscriptions.)

We've also prepared complete digital files of all Communities back issues, from the first one (in 1972) to present, also available at our online store.

Please support the magazine and enhance your own library by taking advantage of some of these new offerings! (For more information, see the ads on pages 1, 9, and 76.)

And thanks again for joining us!

Chris Roth edits Communities.

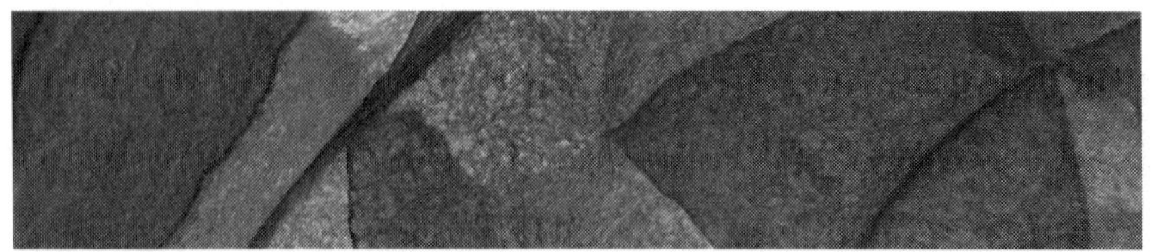

CREATING COHOUSING
Building Sustainable Communities
CHARLES DURRETT & KATHRYN McCAMANT
$32.95

... a must read for anybody who wants or needs to know about cohousing.
–Craig Ragland, Cohousing Association of the United States

FINDING COMMUNITY
How to Join an Ecovillage or Intentional Community
DIANA LEAFE CHRISTIAN
$24.95

This charming and commonsensical guide...should be read by every serious community-seeker.
–Ernest Callenbach, author, *Ecotopia*

These books and more available on line at **www.newsociety.com** and from fine print and ebook sellers.

On This Episode of "Girls with Tools"...

By Cole Wardell

A Midden is an intriguing or marvelous rubbish heap, much like our house. Located in the middle of urban Columbus, Ohio, our income-sharing community (The Midden) finds that its greatest resources are the artifacts (groceries, furniture, shoes) thrown away or overlooked by mainstream society. We use all this stuff to build more whole, egalitarian systems for ourselves.

But thriving off mainstream trash still means we're immersed in mainstream society every day, including the forces and behaviors that make the status quo so painful: sexism and street harassment, bosses and jobs, poverty and evictions. The primary way that our community members struggle with the dominant paradigm is outside the house: negotiating a sexist boss, organizing a campaign against fracking, or protecting a neighborhood from encroaching development.

With so many projects it can be easy to forget that the status quo lives inside our community, too. If we fail to take time and energy to undo learned behaviors, heal ourselves, and reflect on our relationships, we risk making our community no different from any other group of activist roommates—except with more trash. That's why we've made space this past year for deliberate conversation (and sometimes conflict) to work through the ways that patriarchy and gender inform our community and our relationships with each other.

Caring to Work—and Working to Care

This all started with a conversation about working together, which we decided to have after a major house project came to a standstill—and remained stuck—as we failed to resolve major conflict.

After some time, we decided that the broadest and safest way to talk about these concerns was to discuss working together in general. As our conversation continued, it became clear that "working together" was a topic that highlighted ongoing tensions around gender in our house. Sure, it also had to do with personalities, communication styles, and other factors—but the tension we encountered had to do with the *patterns* of our shared work, for which gender is a driving force.

Patriarchy divides skill sets along gender lines: When young girls are given dolls to learn caregiving while boys are given legos to learn how to build things, the result is a gendered divide in adult skills that *all* people need—especially when living in community.

This was (and is) the clearest example of gender informing our collective activities: our women members have less experience with construction and manual labor than our male members. However, our increasing difficulty in working together occurred for more complex reasons. For one, we failed to acknowledge all of the associated cultural knowledge that goes along with manual labor, such as technical terminology, muscle memory, and confidence in working alone or in leadership. In other words, you can't just teach someone where the on/off button is. In order for a project to have truly shared investment and participation, we have to work extra hard to teach, demonstrate, and practice skills with each other. We have to care for our comrades as

much as the end product.

One of my housemates describes the self-conscious voice that plays in her head when working on construction projects as a TV show called *Girls with Tools*. (*GWT* is a reality show documenting women struggling with power tools. We're trying to copyright it.) Our community's challenge was that women were alienated from these projects, even when participating in them. I spent more than one construction job primarily fetching and handing over tools after my ongoing questions received unsatisfactory answers, and I fell quiet out of frustration.

Women members in our house have responded to this in a variety of ways. One housemate decided to avoid the stress of group construction projects altogether and contribute in other ways. Another more recent member chose to take the time and emotional energy to work through the frequently painstaking conversations necessary for preparing, learning, and fully participating in manual labor projects. I've chosen to be selective in my participation, or to work on these projects alone, until I can build more trust in our process and communication.

When the experience of working on manual labor with men alienates women from this type of work, male members avoid (temporarily) the challenge of confronting how male privilege informs our shared work—not to mention how it informs our relationships in general. And when women do want to contribute to construction projects, we risk making ourselves vulnerable to criticism, dismissal, and low self-esteem.

In talking, we also observed ways this problem played out in our shared labor system by rewarding certain behaviors and ignoring others. We eventually decided to try an experiment in which we pro-rate "skill share" hours and leave gender out of the equation entirely. By incentivizing mutual aid instead of "gendered" labor we avoid a host of complications, not the least of which is that "gender" itself is a socially-constructed category that creates falsely-restrictive divisions between individuals. Gender builds walls, and we want our community to break walls down.

What Community Gives Us

If we truly want a new (ab)normal—and we do—we should desire that in our lives as much as in our activism. This means recognizing and confronting systems of oppression in our intimate relationships, even when it feels more risky or painful than with strangers. (In general, we're quite good at yelling back at street harassment.) It also means that desiring freedom isn't enough: transforming our daily, sometimes trivial behaviors requires a lot of effort.

Living in community isn't an answer to the problems of larger systemic oppression, but it can serve as an intentional space to minimize or resist their authority. By living in an egalitarian, income-sharing community, we've freed ourselves to a degree from landlords and financial precarity, and created more opportunities for horizontal cooperation and community activism. But despite all the things community offers, it's still up to us to experiment and hopefully shape our interpersonal relationships to be a little more free. ❧

A resident of The Midden (themidden.wordpress.com), Cole Wardell is a writer and artist with a background in feminist/queer and environmental organizing. Her current efforts include growing deeper roots in Ohio. Her work and blog can be found at colewardell.com.

1. For the purposes of this article, I'm defining patriarchy as a system of oppression that organizes our practices and culture along gendered lines. In a patriarchal culture, masculine qualities are valued over feminine ones, power is held primarily by men, and women—as a category—are economically, emotionally, and physically oppressed.
2. Since our community's values are oriented around radical anti-authoritarian politics, we like use Peter Kropotkin's idea of mutual aid to describe the way we voluntarily cooperate with each other, rather than acting out of obligation or guilt.

Particulate Matter

By Molly Shea

Editor's Note: By the author's request, we are alerting readers that references to sexual assault occur in this article (paragraphs six and seven).

Holding each other accountable to the vision we share isn't simple. Living in community involves challenging each other to become better, stronger, more full people. It gives us the opportunity to learn from each other, and share our experiences. We're able to gain understanding and analysis about the world and the ways in which we interact together. Using our interactions and experiences to evaluate gender and oppression can get really, really complicated.

It can be unbearably challenging to pinpoint and dig into "gender issues" in our community (The Midden—see "On This Episode of 'Girls with Tools'...," page 12). The way it forms my interactions with strangers, coworkers, family, friends, and fellow community members is pervasive. Gender issues are often small and nuanced. They're not always dramatic or clear cut. It's the thoughts that go unsaid, but become visible through body language and heard between the lines. In our community, we can't look to one person, one conversation, or one trend to identify the ways gender impacts our lives. It's seeing the ongoing patterns and build up of all the little interactions that allows us to grasp the depth and breadth of the situation.

All the Little Interactions

Often when we host visitors, women in our community feel a deep sense of obligation and desire to make them feel welcome and comfortable. I clearly recall a quiet visitor who stayed with us for a short time last year. Despite earnest attempts on my part, I failed to deeply connect with him and as he left to continue his travels, neither of us reached out to say our goodbyes. I felt blamed for his lackluster experience, and can clearly see the ways in which my gender made it feel unacceptable I did not wish him well. I felt guilty for not being able to graciously host him during his visit.

Women in our community tend to have easier intimate connections between each other than with men. Late night conversations allow us to process our emotions, ask each other questions, and simply lend an ear to create a lot of trust and empathy between us. On the other side of the story, men around here often process their emotions on their own, by writing or daydreaming. This often creates a gendered division between ways of emotionally connecting to each other, and leads men and women to different relationships.

Our rage is not unjustified, but a lack of empathetic communication between men and women can build the fire instead of allowing it to simmer down.

This undercurrent became present recently when I found myself feeling frustrated that a male housemate had asked another male housemate to work a paid landscaping job together for the day, while none of the women (some of whom have landscaping experience and are looking for employment) were asked or included. Standing in the kitchen, I found myself sharing my frustration with the women who were there with me—but it took several weeks before I shared that with my male housemate. Ultimately, both of the conversations were useful and productive, but frequently tensions like these stay between women until bubbling over as rage. Our rage is not unjustified, but a lack of empathetic communication between men and women can build the fire instead of allowing it to usefully simmer down.

Women also tend to experience and carry a lot of trauma in our lives. That's true of men too, but it's less pervasive and systematic. Sexual assault against women is a prime example of the ways trauma enters women's lives—a stunning one-third of women report being sexually assaulted. While systematic control of women through sexual violence is not small or nuanced, the ways experiences of assault can impact our daily lives can be quite hard to see and identify. Trauma can be triggered at almost any moment and sometimes by things we wouldn't expect.

The impacts of trauma came up less than a month ago when a long-term guest described someone she knew as having "rape face." While it was meant in a light-hearted and funny way, it immediately flooded my head with memories of being assaulted, and what, exactly, their faces looked like. Instead of letting her know what was happening, I froze up and had to slip away as quickly as I could, spending a long night alone trying to change the image inside my head. In some ways, this example is too obvious or straightforward. Smells, particular words, tones in someone's voice, songs, food, conversation dynamics...you name it—these also can trigger experiences of trauma. For me, trauma can be flipped on more easily than turned off, which means women are pretty likely to carry these experiences and emotions forward into interactions, decisions, and generally our lives. It can prevent me from being present with those around me, can make "small problems" feel like huge ones, and a loss of agency over my life can unjustly become applied to all aspects of it, including creating a shared life with my community.

Gender normativity is the particulate matter that swirls around in the air and slowly fills our lungs until we simply can't breathe.

They Are Everywhere

It is these small, sometimes unnoticed, interactions that perpetuate gender inequality and force us into limited ways of being. There are large and incredibly present normative systems that hold us down. They show up as massive inequalities like the wage gap, where as of 2010 women earned only 77 cents on the dollar compared to men for equivalent work. Examples like this are worth noting, talking about, and changing, but these systems are not the thing that really gets under my skin. The gender norms that shape my life and prevent my freedom are more ubiquitous than that; they are everywhere. Gender normativity is the particulate matter that swirls around in the air and slowly fills our lungs until we simply can't breathe.

Our community is finding itself immersed in gendered norms, and ways we choose to resist them, as we build a microcosm of what we do want. Not all males who have been a part of The Midden fall into these examples. Not all women do, either. When we perpetuate oppressive norms, as our society has trained us to do, it hurts. It can feel easy and acceptable to ignore patriarchy at our jobs, at the bar or coffee shops, and on the streets, because we simply expect it there. We keep our defenses up and are ready to brush it off. But in our community, we want so much more. We hold each other to higher levels of accountability for tearing apart the systems that oppress us. We aren't prepared for a surprise attack of patriarchal behavior, and the ways we feel it cut us when it pops up and penetrates our lives so deeply.

We continue to struggle to find balance between critical analysis and allowing ourselves forgiveness. Talking through the big and small ways we find ourselves engulfed in gender norms allows us to start to transform our relationships with ourselves and each other. That is, if we can stomach the conversation and begin to clear our lungs of all the dust that's settled inside of us for so long. ❧

Molly Shea is a member at the egalitarian community The Midden in Columbus, Ohio (themidden.wordpress.com). Born in rural central Ohio, she's lived in a variety of collective and communal environments and uses her energies as a change maker doing social and environmental justice work.

Sexism at Dancing Rabbit

By Sam Makita

Dancing Rabbit is a growing community outside Rutledge, Missouri, made up of about 70 individuals with different backgrounds and experiences. We're an ecovillage, founded in feminism but not focused on it and without a unifying idea of exactly what feminism looks like. I'm offering my perspective, which is certainly not universal, on how sexism affects us here. What you're about to read is my opinion, and not the official stance of Dancing Rabbit by any means.

Sexism

I'm a woman. I am genetically and physiologically female. I have some masculine traits but I don't think I'm mannish. I'm pretty tall for a woman, but not at all tall compared to all humans. I have pretty strong arms for a woman, but they're probably less strong than the average adult's. I'm extremely messy compared to the women I know, but only sort of messy when compared to my friends and neighbors who are men.

Dancing Rabbit has much looser gender expectations than most of the wider culture, as demonstrated by member Coz Walker.

Josi Nielson

Let me be clear: I absolutely do not think that we can make a conclusive statement about the relative heights, strengths, or messinesses of two people based on their gender. I *do* think we can draw some bell curves based on observations, and make statistical predictions based on what we see. Maybe the curves will change with time and culture shifts, or maybe they won't. I might be able to pass as a tenor, but how many women are there who can pull off a baritone or bass part as well as an average man? That's not to say that a woman couldn't be a very good bass singer, only that those people are more rare and it's reasonable that their representation in their field should reflect that.

Noticing, speaking, or accepting that different genders have different tendencies is not what I would call sexist. Some folks might, and I think that's their way of helping others avoid making assumptions and decisions based *solely* on gender. We're sensitive to the fact that the assumption that a person of a certain gender is necessarily incapable of a given task has led to many missed opportunities for people to rise to their full potential and created much injustice in the world. That sensitivity helps us to be aware of what sexist mistakes have been made and to avoid them.

Discrimination is what happens inside a person when they lack the information, the energy, or the motivation to make decisions based on what they see, rather than assumptions based on culture, habit, or previously observed trends. At Dancing Rabbit we're pretty good at making many choices based on actually taking the time to look at people's characteristics rather than just lumping them according to gender. For example, this past spring a woman announced at the WIP (our weekly meeting) that she needed "some strong people" to help with moving her propane tank. By identifying the trait she was hoping to maximize she got what she actually needed.

What if I were looking for a wet nurse? I could advertise for a "person who is lactating" instead of "a nursing mother" so I don't exclude anyone based on their gender alone, even though I'm pretty sure the best person for the job will be a woman. In short, sexism is making decisions or having reactions based on gender instead of some more relevant characteristic.

Avoiding sexism is not as easy as I just made it sound. People are generally pretty bad at knowing why they make the choices they do and even worse at accurately communicating those motivations to others, which makes it really hard to know whether sexism is at play in a given individual action. Plus, we make so many decisions throughout our days and years, and so many of them are sub- or barely-conscious, that some amount of lumping into groups seems necessary for getting though the day.

In order for people of all genders to have the same opportunities and rights, we need to put in the extra effort necessary to consider the possibility that people might surprise us, to be open and aware enough that we can see things even when we don't expect them. The surprise could come from a person being an outlier for their gender or from the assumptions of previous generations being wrong, or both. Such a moment could cause confusion, fearfulness, and insecurity, or curiosity, wonder, and humility. Openness to people being their very best selves, whatever their gender—that's the antidote to sexism.

Counter-Discrimination Tactics

Folks at Dancing Rabbit are generally good at being open to the possibility that a woman might be the best choice for a job that has historically been done mostly by men, or vice versa. I've seen folks get really excited about it. In fact, I've seen us consider as a group whether we should choose a woman for a traditionally male role even if there's a more qualified male available. During that discussion I heard from my fellow community members that the aim of this calculated sexism would be to give an advantage to women in historically male fields to help correct for disadvantage they've experienced otherwise. I think there's merit in that. I also think we have to acknowledge that it is a kind of sexism, because it includes or excludes people based on gender. On the whole, I think Dancing Rabbit is in favor of this kind of corrective discrimination.

I personally have concerns that giving preferential consideration to one gender over others, especially for paid work, could have the opposite effect that folks are hoping for.

In addition to the offensiveness of the implication that a woman in a man's world must need our help to succeed, I have concern about how giving such advantages affects the resulting workplace. Imagine, for example, that you're hiring a work crew of six carpenters and want to have 50/50 gender balance. If you get applications from qualified candidates in a ratio proportional to the ratio of carpenters in the US as a whole, which according to the Bureau of Labor Statistics was 1.4 percent women in 2010, you have to turn down about 194 qualified men even if you hire all of the female applicants. If the three men you hire are the best three for the job, then those men are almost certainly going to be better at the job than the women, not because men are necessarily better carpenters than women overall, but because you had to hire the best, middle, and worst woman candidates available, but only the top 3 percent of the men. On the worksite, then, those guys, *and those gals*, are certainly going to see more evidence to back up the very stereotype we were trying to counteract.

It's hard to be patient, but I think that's what we need to do to effectively correct the erroneous perceptions that are harming women's ability to earn a living, participate meaningfully in fields that excite them, and live up to their full potential. Pushing men out of the way isn't the way to do it. My suggestion to folks at Dancing Rabbit who wish to help women who have interest and talent in very male-dominated fields is that they should run educational workshops in those fields and welcome women to join, and show them as much respect and encouragement as the men in the group.

Pushing men out of the way isn't the way to correct misperceptions about women's abilities.

There have been a few workshops at Dancing Rabbit open only to women. This is another example of sexism aimed at counteracting the historical trend. I appreciate that some women might not feel comfortable exploring a new skill while there are men around, and they should have a chance to learn. At the same time, though, it's that very argument that feels degrading to me, which bothers me even more than the simple, overt sexism of excluding men and other genders out of hand. It feels degrading because it implies that women are not emotionally strong enough to do something we want in the face of discomfort or fear—that we need to be protected from our own feelings of embarrassment and inadequacy in order to succeed. To me that feels patronizing. It also seems counterproductive to building a global culture in which we are equally open to accepting the particular gifts of everyone, and in which we feel able to confidently offer those gifts, regardless of gender.

While I am thankful for folks' efforts and good intentions in offering skill-building opportunities to a segment of the population less likely to have gotten those opportunities elsewhere, I question the overall wisdom of using sexism to fight sexism.

The Boys' and Girls' Clubs

One of the behaviors that comes up the most for me when I think about sexism at Dancing Rabbit is the gathering of people together for emotional support, divided by gender. Men's Group and Women's Circle are not official Dancing Rabbit events or organizations, just gatherings of people who want to get together for a shared activity, open to anyone to participate in, with one catch: Women's Circle is for people who identify as women, and Men's Group is for people who identify as men. There is not yet a group of or for people who don't identify as either of those genders.

Were a group of people to decide, after getting to know one another, that they feel safe together and want to get together to talk about some tender things, without the whole village looking on or bringing unwelcome energy, and they all happen to be of the same gender, I would not call that sexist. Choosing all woman friends does not make a person sexist, it simply belies a preference. On the other hand, being explicitly open to any woman-identifying person and closed to any non-woman-identifying person is overt sexism. Ditto with men. I don't go because I'm not sure the kind of sexism embodied by the existence of gender-specific groups is healthy for the kind of culture I hope we're growing here. Many people think it is healthy, the groups are well attended, and the reports I get from Men's Group, at least, are that those who attend are better people for it.

But I can't help wondering what the reaction would be if Dancing Rabbit had a richer racial diversity than we do and there existed something like "Whites' Night" which anyone who identified as white could attend. They'd participate in deep sharing and mutual support in their whiteness, and everyone else was explicitly excluded, though free to form their own group if they so desired. The reason for that racism might be given as some white people not feeling safe sharing some parts of themselves in the company of other races, perhaps because in the past they've been hurt by a non-white person. That's kind of how Women's Circle looks to me.

I can't help wondering what the reaction would be if Dancing Rabbit had a "Whites' Night."

It's hard for me to lodge a complaint with something that my fellow communitarians find so rewarding, and it's not totally clear to me whether the net effect will be toward an end I'm hoping for or not, but, if you ask whether the gendered support groups are sexist, the answer is clearly yes. Genderist? I'd say so. Will I participate? No thank you. Will I think less of those who attend? No. I wish we had a culture in which people could be more thoughtful about including and excluding people based on criteria more relevant than their gender, but it takes so much energy to do so, maybe that's better spent on other things.

Gender Balance

Another clearly sexist occurrence at Dancing Rabbit is the pretty frequent talk of seeking or needing "gender balance" on a given committee. We are likely, as a group, to give preference to people who round out the gender diversity on a committee, over those who might be more interested or more proficient in the task at hand. Honestly, I haven't seen it happen very often, but it is talked about an awful lot.

Warren Siting is the committee responsible for helping people figure out where and how to build their homes and other structures in order to be harmonious with the existing village and with the plan for growth. I heard a concern that with all men on the committee there was no one that a woman might feel comfortable talking with about the sensitive topic of where and how to build her house, that she would feel intimidated. That's both sexist in the assumption that a man cannot be easy to talk to and disempowering in the implication that women shouldn't be expected to communicate with a man without a woman-savvy liaison. On the other hand, it could be that it's another kind of discrimination to not accommodate the needs of everyone, and maybe help communicating with men after a lifetime of oppression by them is a need some people have.

It's hard to know how much unequal representation of genders in certain fields reflects inherent gender differences instead of cultural influence.

Our mission at Dancing Rabbit is partly to be an example for others to follow, so I can see the merit in creating a tableau of what we hope the future will naturally look like. It's hard to know how much of the unequal representation of genders in certain fields is related to inherent differences among genders, and how much is due to cultural influence stemming from some long-standing and arbitrary or outdated bias. Maybe in a perfectly un-sexist world those committees would still end up mostly made up of one gender. We won't know that until we live in an un-sexist world.

Are We Sexist?

Yes, there's sexism at Dancing Rabbit. Of course. We're a community made up of individuals who came from the wider US culture and tens of thousands of years of human history before that. Some of our sexism stems from noble intentions, some from confusion or lack of energy to examine our motives and our goals closely. At the organization level, our membership agreement contains a pledge of non-discrimination based on sex, among other things. It seems to me that we're letting some things slide as far as overt discrimination, but at least our paperwork is in the right place.

Men wear skirts, women wear pants, and we have at least a stated norm that wherever a woman must wear a shirt, so must a man, though that last one's not always remembered and observed. Long hair, short, whatever. Armpit and leg hair is totally acceptable, regardless of gender.

We're also doing well insofar as sharing chores across established gender lines. Most people here take a cook shift, most people clean public and private spaces, all parents (and many others) participate in childrearing. There're men and women in leadership roles here, and on physically, technically, and socially strenuous tasks. More importantly, there's not the expectation or requirement that people of a certain gender are the ones who perform a certain task. We're free to choose how to contribute based on our interests and talent—one reason I am proud to be a part of this community.

We're far beyond most of the country in terms of accepting people for who they are and the contributions they bring, regardless of their gender. Part of that's thanks to Dancing Rabbit's foundation in feminism, for which I'm grateful. I think there's room for us to be more open-minded and objective around gender, and I look forward to watching that unfold at Dancing Rabbit and beyond. ❧

Sam Makita moved to Dancing Rabbit Ecovillage (www.dancingrabbit.org) in late 2009 from suburban New Jersey. Among other things, Sam writes for the weekly newsletter and runs the village dry goods store.

Gender-Bending on the Commune

By Valerie Renwick

As a self-identified feminist ecovillage, Twin Oaks (Louisa, Virginia) definitely has gender as a social construction on its radar. Many aspects of our culture reflect this, from the work we've done eliminating gender bias from our labor, to the way our egalitarian values blend seamlessly with a feminist approach to life, and also including the experiences that the community has had with transgendered people and the experiences that they've had with us.

For people who want to delve more deeply, a lot of information about gender at Twin Oaks is available on our webpage, specifically in our online newsletter from Spring 2013 (www.twinoaks.org/leaves-of-twinoaks/leaves-pdf-archive.html). Meanwhile, here is a glimpse into several aspects of gender on the commune.

• **Our Gender-Neutral Pronoun "Co":** This is used when the gender of a person is irrelevant or unknown, as in, "Each week, every member should turn in co's labour sheet so that the Labour Assigner can get all the jobs covered." It's much less unwieldy than her/his or even s/he. Also handy for thickening the plot in conversations like, "I hung out with a special someone last night, and co wants to spend more time with me" (effectively doubling the number of people that this might mysteriously be referring to). We use this word in policies and also to some extent in daily life, sometimes somewhat facetiously and at other times genuinely. The grammarians among us get antsy when people start using phrases like "Each co should..." (using a pronoun as a noun) and often a lively grammar-geek conversation ensues.

• **"Addressing the Dress":** This is a policy we adopted for our Saturday Tour guides. Each weekend we offer a tour for the public who want to learn more about the community, and sometimes male members of the community who are giving the tour happen to be wearing a dress or skirt. (At Twin Oaks, men as well as women wear dresses and skirts for comfort and fashion during warm weather.) For us this is normal, but we are aware that for many of the people who come for a tour, it is not. And so if a Twin Oaks man is giving the tour and is thusly attired, he must "address the dress," and consciously explain to the tour group that at Twin Oaks, our culture does not limit this style choice to female-bodied members, and that we'd prefer all members be able to be comfortably attired instead of having to adhere to an arbitrarily-imposed fashion norm.

• **Our Shirtlessness Norms:** Virginia gets very hot in the summertime, and some people would like to take off their shirt to be cooler. In the mainstream, it is socially acceptable for men to do this but not women. We would prefer not to incorporate this gender bias and male privilege into our lives, and so our Nudity Policy (yes, we have one) states that at the times and places where it is acceptable for members to be shirtless, this applies equally to women and men. However, we don't want our mail carrier or UPS delivery person to be uncomfortable and so in the generally public areas of the community, both men and women need to wear shirts, and in the more sheltered areas, both genders are free to be shirtless.

• **The Collective Menstrual Calendar:** In our main dining hall, on the wall of the bathroom, each year a member creates a beautifully artistic menstrual calendar. In addition to the wonderful artwork on it, it is large enough for a square for each day of the year, and every menstruating woman can write her name on the day that her menstrual cycle starts each month. This is one way that gender intersects with our alternative culture—in the mainstream, this information would not be considered suitable for public sharing. For us, it is both a convenient way for women to track their cycle, and a fun art installation as well, without stigma around its subject matter. Although it is true that when it was first proposed, we had one member who was in general quite vehemently opposed to gender-segregated activities of any type, and who made an alternate suggestion that we post a "masturbation calendar," which both genders would be equally able to participate in. While many members appreciated the humor in this (mostly-facetious) suggestion, nothing ever came of it.

• **Homemade Edits of Kids' Books:** This is a familiar scenario to progressive and radical caregivers everywhere—you're reading a book to a child, and as the story unfolds, you realize the gender biases that are woven into the plotline, and find yourself starting to change pronouns to model a more eclectic reality. A group of Twin Oakers wanted to take a more direct approach, and so, wielding a bottle of white correction fluid and a pen, they methodically went through our children's books, and altered the gender and features of some of the characters with relation to who was the farmer and who was the nurse, changed select "Mrs." and "Mr."'s to "Friend" (we do not use honorifics at Twin Oaks), and generally enjoyed re-imagining the storylines created by various authors.

Coda: I was just about finished writing this article when my four-year-old god-daughter came by my desk, and saw the current COMMUNITIES magazine (Youth in Community, Fall 2013), the cover of which features a child with blue eyes and shoulder-length reddish hair. She commented on it, asking, "Is that boy eating popcorn?" My partner and I exchanged glances, silently remarking on the fact that upon seeing a child with medium-length hair, her baseline assumption was that the child was male. Perhaps the perfect final commentary on the subject...

Valerie Renwick has been helping to raise gender awareness at Twin Oaks (www.twinoaks.org) for 22 years. She was an organizer with the Feminist Ecovillage Project (www.ic.org/eco) and her work at Twin Oaks includes Outreach, Forestry, and teaching Yoga.

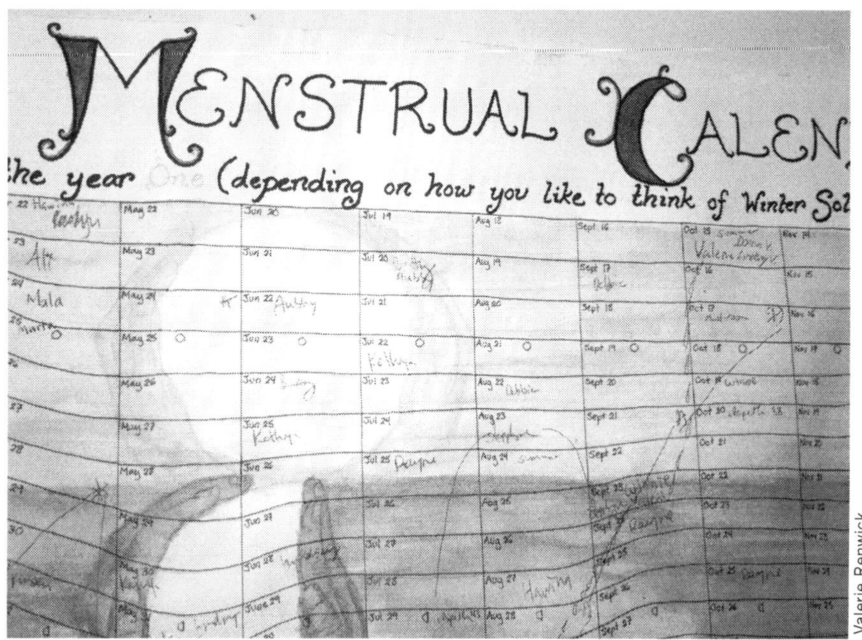

Valerie Renwick

Evolving Gender Consciousness in New Culture Camps

By Oblio Stroyman

*[Editor's Note: For more information about Network for a New Culture (NFNC), the focus of the following article, see www.nfnc.org and also the articles "New Culture Perspectives for Everyday Life" (*Communities *#159) and "Network for a New Culture Camps" (*Communities *#142).]*

It's the year 2000 and I am 24 years old, sitting wide-eyed and wide-open in a slightly musty and incredibly magical "women's tent." It is "gender circle" time at my first Network for a New Culture's (NFNC) Summer Camp West and we have finished our "check-ins."

"Now we're going to play the dating game," the sparkly-eyed facilitator instructs. "The women will write on slips of paper to request dates with the men and change things up!"

There is chatter and excitement in the tent, and a woman quietly speaks up, asking "what if" she wants to request a date with another woman. The energy in the tent tangibly shifts; the air feels a bit heavier, a bit mustier. I never hear her request addressed directly. While I am pretty sure she is not told no, being told "you are at choice" does not feel like the same support the majority of the women are getting around asking the men out. I never will find out if she asks for a date with another woman. I'll never feel comfortable.

I spent my first two years with NFNC as a camper, boldly going where no Oblio had gone before. I wholeheartedly threw myself into the NFNC experience, choosing to live with 100ish relative strangers for 14 days at a time deep in the woods, without cell phone signal, without wi-fi, doing personal growth and community-building work. I found a home in NFNC. For the first time I was surrounded by people who shared and furthered my understanding of polyamory, sex positivity, nonviolence, eco-consciousness, and transparent, authentic, respectful nonviolent communication.

It was through this experience that I recognized the power in community, in collective intention and accountability, in shared resources, vision, and values. I felt healthier in this community than I had ever felt in the nuclear style living situation I was enculturated into. With my head in the clouds, the niggling pain I felt over experiences like the one in the women's tent seemed transient—more like the nagging of a thorn stuck in the bottom of my foot, a foot that was too involved in its joyous dance to stop and take stock.

Over time, the smallest of thorns unaddressed work their way into debilitating agony. In 2000 and 2001, I didn't have the skills to take the thorn out myself, nor the language to ask my community for help, I just knew I didn't feel good. After a nine-year break, a B.S. in Sociology and Women and Gender Studies and M.Ed. in Couples and Family Therapy, I developed an understanding, a language, and sense of embodiment to wrap around what did not fit for me in this New Culture space: the community's old culture relationship to gender norms and sexuality.

Since this realization, I have run the gamut of emotions regarding the ways the community as a whole reinforces, challenges, rewards, and punishes adhesion to gender and sexual norms. I have seen this in a number of areas including heterocentrism, gendered space allocation, gender identity, and LGBTQ inclusivity, to name a few.

So why do I return? Every time I feel decimated and torn down by gender/sexual ignorance in NFNC, I find myself rebuilt by the community's capacity for compassion and willingness to expand its consciousness. I understand we are all working together to create New Culture, of which my pain, process, and showing up is an integral part. Isn't this what community-building truly is?

This story started in 2000 in the women's tent, a "sacred space" for women to gather and discuss what was present for them in a "safe container." This was a protected space, set up for the duration of camp to be used by women at will, a container blessed with altars and decorations. I noticed right away that there was no space dedicated for the men except when a common space was off limits at the designated gender circle times. When I shared that I did not feel that the community demonstrated that it valued men's space, I was told that "it is up to the men to make that happen." At the time I did not challenge that answer, though now I would say it is up to the community, not male-identified people alone, to show that it values "men's space" equally.

A decade later this dilemma still exists at Summer Camp West. While there is no longer a women's tent, it was not until 2013 that the men at this camp were offered a comfortable, private meeting place during gender circle time, and this was because *I* chose where the gender circles took place. The women were asked to meet in "the lounge" where the men had met previously, an outside living room in "downtown" summer camp, between the kitchen and showers. The feedback was that it was "too loud, too public, too hard to make a container, too hard to focus." This was a step up from where the men had met the previous year, in the beautiful-but-damp, dark, and chair-less garden. Often times we have to experience some discomfort to recognize the extent of our privilege; this year it was the women's turn.

The gender circles taught me a lot about the relationships women were in, but not so much about them as individuals.

In the 2000 and 2001 women's gender circles, I was struck by the way the bulk of the conversation focused on romantic relationships with men and/or negotiating how to feel comfortable sharing "their" men. I left those years feeling that the gender circles taught me a lot about the relationships women were in, but not so much about who the women were as individuals. As a female-bodied person I was not invited to sit in the men's circle, though a male lover of mine shared that he felt disappointed by his experience that the men kept a physical distance from one another, did not share the space in a way that felt like everyone was heard, and did not have a designated space that stayed sacred to the men during camp. He shared that he did not feel closer to the men at camp after these gender circles and was uncertain what to do, so he didn't attend any more. He never returned to camp and I never returned to the women's circle.

Since then I have heard from women who continue to attend the West Coast women's circles that the conversation has not changed much. From the men I have heard that their circles have changed for the better year after year, increasing physical and emotional intimacy and improving communication skills to include everyone in the circle.

In 2010 when I returned to NFNC Summer Camp West, I was delighted to see that in addition to men's and women's gender circles, a third "gender fluid" group had been established the year before. The existence of the group and the potential awareness it represented was an oasis and an invitation for me at camp. I ended up co-facilitating the group with the person who had started it, and the three-hour discussion time was abundantly filled with only six attendees. It became strikingly apparent that there were OTHER people who did not feel at home in the gender normative environment that had always existed, and in this I found my calling at NFNC. I joined the NFNC Summer Camp West organizing team (SCAMP) for the following year to become an unrelenting voice for the change I wanted to see.

I could feel my heart rate increasing before it was my turn to speak. The only thing I was certain of stepping into the 2010 debrief of summer camp was that it was a "make it or break it" moment for me and NFNC. As the only genderqueer/queer-identified person on the Summer Camp West organizing team, I felt very passionate and a little nervous to state my feedback and make my proposal, imagining that many would not understand the gravity of what I was sharing. I took a deep breath in, and I came out. I shared that I felt that gender was at the foundation of *all* the healing work we were doing, that in order to truly do the work on a core level we needed to address gender and sexuality directly, and I proposed that gender be one of the early and primary camp workshops.

I could feel my heart rate increasing. It was a "make it or break it" moment for me and NFNC.

Deep breath back in and holding. The response was not only yes, but an enthusiastic, rapid-fire cascade of support! Deeply moved, I recognized that a powerful aspect of NFNC is that though it is also wrought with the challenges and limitations of the "default" world, it is different in that it is a community open to owning and examining growth edges.

Running with the momentum into 2011, I excitedly invited my dear friend, the Dean of Students and Director of LGBTQ Services from the University of Oregon, Chicora Martin Ph.D., to open the gender discussion at the West Coast camp. She and I worked together to shape a presentation that would challenge and support the community. We raised consciousness regarding sex, gender identity, sexual identity, and LGBTQ identities. We offered experiential exercises to demonstrate the concept of gender norms as a social construction, encouraging the community to think meaningfully about how they may want to create NFNC tenets around gender.

I expected some people to be inspired, some people to be challenged, and some people to be completely clueless as to why this topic mattered. Many people met my expectations, though I was particularly intrigued by the reactions I did not anticipate. When it came time to move into gender circles, after the presentation, many campers were frustrated and confused about which one to attend. They began questioning: "Are these biological sex circles or gender circles?" They began processing what it would mean to choose to participate in any one of these segregated circles. Chaos ensued.

"All of the people with penises are invited to attend the men's circle," the leader of the men's circle stepped up and asserted. "Do you mean attached penises?" I inquired before the community. "Are trans men who have not had bottom surgery welcome?"

The men's facilitator did not seem enthusiastic to have that discussion on the spot, and he was even less prepared than I to figure it all out in the five minutes before lunch. The participants were again invited to self-select and continue to dialogue about the challenges with others, as we were to break for lunch. As if on cue, a beloved community leader entered the circle, enthusiastically announcing that the next day would be "Sadie Hawkins Day, where the women (female-bodied people?) instigated connection with the men (male-bodied people?), who were to await to be approached.

My heart and mind imploded. A couple of my trusted confidants just held me while I sobbed in anger and frustration. I spoke in an unfiltered stream of consciousness: "Can this community change? Are they willing to? Are they even listening? Am I in the wrong place?" I could see that so much work in this area was needed, and I was uncertain if I was the one to hold it for them when I could be so personally affected.

I have since come to believe that it is because I am so personally affected that I am the perfect one to hold space for the community. To witness me, a beloved community member, hurt by the ideas and behaviors takes the topic from conceptual to personal, semantic to humanistic. The next morning the man who had made the announcement asked to sit with me at breakfast, sharing that he realized that he had perpetuated the very thing we were working so hard to deconstruct. He spoke in the morning circle, humbly shifting his invitation to ask the extroverts to step back that day, encouraging the introverts to take a risk and instigate connection with others. He apologized publicly and the experiment was a success. In 2011 the Summer Camp West "gender fluid" circle was twice as big as the year before.

Between 2011 and 2012, I received a number of personal correspondences regarding the way that people were affected by the gender presentation, "coming out" about the alternative unexpressed gender and sexual identities of individuals in the community or in those they loved. This included a personal story from a set of parents who shared with the community the triumphs and challenges in supporting a gender-non-conforming child. Their pain and triumph became the pain and triumph of the community. Again I felt profoundly moved and resolved to continue to spearhead the topic of gender and sexuality in NFNC. Through fully showing up and being out and open, an environment was starting to take shape where others were able to come out. Very Harvey Milk.

In 2012, I continued to have the full support of the West Coast SCAMPS, and I worked with behavioral specialist and educator Shanya Luthier from Portland, Oregon to shape a presentation that took the work to the next level while still including new campers. We raised the consciousness of the community regarding the rewards and punishments for "passing" and adhering to gender/sexual norms. Through experimental exercises Shanya offered the community the opportunity to assess the ways unconscious biases affect views of self, views of others, and all interpersonal interactions. This "gender fluid" circle once again grew in size, though the discussion that year helped me realize that I was selling myself, and other members of the community, short. I realized it was time to invite the group to step into the next level of consciousness.

We raised community consciousness of rewards and punishments for "passing" and adhering to gender/sexual norms.

I do not identify as "gender fluid," shifting from one gender to the other as inspired, but rather as "genderqueer," something entirely different and non-binary. Once I was able to identify this, develop a language, and assert this, other campers came out to me as feeling similarly. Before the 2013 camp, I attended Gender Odyssey, a Seattle conference for trans and gender non-conforming people. For the first time I was immersed in a New Culture specific to gender and sexuality. Not only did I not have to advocate and educate people regarding my identity, I was clearly perceived and desired for who I am. Sometimes I do not realize how tense my muscles are until I release, and as I was able to release for even a moment into the Gender Odyssey community, I was gifted with clarity about how to hold NFNC in 2013.

"Hello, my name is Oblio and this is Shadow, and we will be your hosts through the topics of gender and sexuality today. Let's start with assumptions, and let's start with us. The most dangerous assumptions are the ones unspoken, so what do you think you know about Shadow and me regarding our gender and sexuality?" I began.

"Check Your Junk at the Door: Exploring and Expanding Concepts of Sex and Gender Identity" was my playful, personal, and heartfelt offering to Summer Camp West in 2013. I walked into this workshop feeling more supported by the community than ever as they had requested that I be the primary presenter, showing me that that they appreciated the challenges I posed to their paradigms. The presenters for the other workshops jumped on board and took the initiative to coordinate with me before camp to incorporate the topic of gender and sexual diversity as threads that ran through their presentations. At the very least they were using same-sex and non-gendered examples in their work, and in that they watered the seeds of change.

"Do you have assumptions about my sex? My gender? Do you assume I was always the sex you perceive me as? Do you have assumptions about how we would interact sexually? Do you have assumptions about my sexuality? Do you have questions about yours in relation to me?" I inquired.

I relaxed into my trust of myself first and foremost, and trust of the community's willingness to be kind while pushing their edges. It became clear that the best way to present *to* them was to be present *with* them. I shared my knowledge and personal experience from the heart, opened non-shaming and inviting dialogue with the community, and took them through experiential exercises in which we all looked one another in the eye and "came out" about our assumptions, the way these affect our abilities to connect, working on letting them go. In this space we all became more deeply transparent with one another. This year I introduced the "trans*" group in place of the "gender fluid" group. It was open to trans-identified and gender-non-conforming people by self-identification, including gender fluid and questioning people. It was the largest of the three gender circles.

"Do you have assumptions about my sex? My gender? Do you assume I was always the sex you perceive me as?"

"They are lovely and worth it, they are just very gender normative and hetero-centric. It is not intentional, they just don't know what they don't know. We all have our blinders, and they are patient with mine." It is 2011 and I am talking with one of my partners, a gay man who is considering Summer Camp West for 2012.

"It is hard to be in the Summer Camp environment as a queer person for many reasons, and I still believe it is really important. I am already seeing change," I continue.

He chooses to attend in 2012 and 2013 for his own reasons, and is affected by the community's biases in ways he did and did not expect. As a gay man he is certainly accustomed to the dangers, prejudices, judgments, and triumphs involved in being who he is daily. What is different about NFNC is that he lives in the woods for 10 days immersed in a group primarily comprised of people still ignorant about how their unconscious gender/sexual privilege affects him personally, developing bittersweet heartfelt connections and doing deep personal work.

"I am not gay but let's have lunch. I am not gay but I feel attracted to you. I am not gay but let's be sensual...I am not gay but...I am not gay but..." His experience of being able to freely relate from a heartfelt space, especially with male-bodied campers, is deeply affected by these ideas and attitudes. In 2013 he comes back as a SCAMP, and what seems clear to us both is that as long as the pros outweigh the cons we will continue to stay engaged as leaders in the community.

"Are there showers with a curtain?" my transgendered partner asks me concerned. "Have there been other transgendered people who have attended, and how were they treated? Will they let me in the men's circle? Will they be open to me if they do?"

I wish I could allay his fears, but the best I can do is share that I believe Summer Camp West will hear and help with his concerns, though he will have to advocate for them. He is already sharing heartfelt connections with many NFNC community members and the road is less bumpy than 10 years ago. I imagine his journey, and NFNC's journey, will be wrought with its own unique triumphs and challenges that we cannot anticipate. I believe that all will be furthered through growing pains.

In NFNC currently, we are having the discussions about the changing role of gender circles, and ways we can create an inclusive environment that draws in people across the gender and sexuality spectrum. No longer do I hear the ignorant hands-off remark, "We are open, they just aren't attending."

With all of the growth still needed regarding gender/sexuality in the NFNC community, I continue to be soulfully grateful that I, my partner, and other gender/sexual-non-conforming folks are able to see through what is painful in the community to the beauty that also exists. I am grateful for our individual decisions to expend the energy and emotional fortitude it requires organize, teach, model, mentor, and be students in the community. With all of the growth still happening within my partners, myself, other LGBTQ and gender-non-conforming folks, I continue to be soulfully grateful to NFNC's commitment and willingness to welcome us as teachers, students, and cherished community members. I believe we are all owning that as a community we are still at the beginning of an ever expanding gender/sexual consciousness and are actively choosing to walk willingly hand in hand into this social experiment. ❧

Oblio Z. Stroyman is a queer-identified former relational therapist turned Ecstatic Dance DJ who lives in Oregon's Eugene/Springfield community. She is the steward of "The Point" studio, an intimate venue that supports community by hosting events and skill share opportunities. She has always been passionate about community and social trends, focusing her undergraduate and graduate studies on family, gender, and sexuality. She has been connected to the Network for a New Culture community (www.nfnc.org) since 2000, participating as an organizer since 2010, helping to bring gender to the forefront of New Culture dialogs. She also offers regular trainings that focus on raising awareness in professional organizations regarding polyamory, gender, LGBTQI concerns, and community. Oblio strives to weave together strengths from her communities into group processes that cultivate increased intimacy, depth, learning, and social change.

Gender at Summer Camp East

I first attended Network for a New Culture Summer Camp in 1999 in Oregon, and encountered many of the same gender dynamics Oblio describes in her article. Over the next few years, as a far-from-gender-normative camper, I worked to create change—specifically, to "queer things up" within the men's group. Then in 2004, in addition to attending the Oregon camp, my nesting partner and I started New Culture Summer Camp East in the Mid-Atlantic area. Beginning fresh, we were able to eliminate some of the most oppressive gender structures, but we were still learning ourselves, and many of the people who came to camp had not explored the issue at all.

The first year of Summer Camp East, we had several exercises to raise awareness around gender. One of the first stereotypes we encountered were men who were resistant to touching other men, claiming among other things that they could tell the difference between a man's touch and a woman's. We created an exercise where half the people were blindfolded, and the other half would give them non-sexual touch, on the cheek, the arm, or the back, and had the blindfolded people guess whether it was a man or woman touching them. The men who had been most adamant about there being an important difference found that their guesses were no better than random chance—they got it wrong half the time!

Over the next several years, the organizers and experienced campers were able to create more and more of a culture that saw gender as malleable and diffuse, rather than binary and fixed. Grappling with the concept itself, trying to identify *anything* that could tie gender to biology, we came to the realization that there was far more difference between some men and other men, and some women and other women, than there was between the average or normative man compared with the average or normative woman. Other than basic reproductive functions, there was nothing that was true for the vast majority of men that was not also true for large numbers of women, and vice versa. For virtually any characteristic we examined, we saw two bell curves that overlapped, with far more overlap than separation. Coupled with a deeper understanding of how societies shape and control behaviors that tend to exaggerate whatever natural differences might exist, we came to the realization that gender, for all practical purposes, is an arbitrary construct.

From the beginning, the mix of participants at Summer Camp East included a range of gender expressions and sexual orientations, starting with bisexual women and men, and expanding to include gay, lesbian, transgendered, non-gendered, and intersex people. Perhaps because of the culture of radical acceptance that we were creating, there was never much attention focused on these variations, nor did people express difficulties with the issue. Where queerness at the West Coast camp seemed controversial or political, at the East Coast camp it just seemed "normal." People were who they were, they did what they did, and no one seemed to be particularly concerned about it.

Over the years, most returning campers have come to see gender as an arbitrary choice, with few if any assumptions associated with any individual's choice. Rather than focus on identifying gender differences of any kind, we prefer to see each individual as being who they are, and making choices to present however they wish. Each year, we continue to have discussions and workshops on gender issues, and we keep discovering new dimensions that need to be explored, tested, and included in our shared perspectives.

—Michael Rios

Gender Identity and Sexual Orientation
Sharing a Heartfelt Conversation

By Niánn Emerson Chase

I realize that gender identity and sexual orientation for any individual are very complex issues, with not only biological factors but also environmental, social, and cultural elements to consider. In our modern society, with its fast pace and digital device onslaught, we all need to slow down and take time to have honest and thoughtful conversations about this sensitive and important aspect of today's culture.

I lived most of my childhood on an Apache reservation in Arizona. I grew up in a home where my mother and father had strongly-identified female and male roles. Both parents were comfortable with their identities within our family arrangement as woman, mother, homemaker and man, father, provider, protector. My three siblings and I benefited greatly from our parents' mutual commitment to their shared spiritual ideals and to their family, as well as their ease and harmony with their gender identities.

We children also benefited from the wide range of friends and associates of our family who were of different cultures, religions, politics, and social leanings. None of us felt pressure from our parents to be exactly like them but rather to become what God designed us to be—the smartest, most compassionate, and ethical women and men that we could become, always doing what was right in the eyes of the Creator. I still have that basic theological foundation and hopefully have passed it on to my children, grandchildren, and all of those in the spiritually-based intentional community that I co-founded.

Living on the reservation, I had friends who experienced the various dynamics and circumstances that plague families living in dire poverty and racial discrimination. So even though I came from a harmonious and well-ordered home with much love and support, many of my friends did not have that stable foundation of physical, emotional, social, and economic security. Regardless of our different racial, cultural, and economic circumstances, my friends and I still shared the struggles of living in the larger dominant culture, which I grew to consider greedy, materialistic, and run by imbalanced white males. These men determined the politics and social standards of our nation, that in turn perpetrated the environmental and social ills that we all still suffer from today in various ways.

As children and youth, we females wrestled with our own perceptions of our self-worth because of the societal messages we accepted from our peers in school, from most human institutions, and from the media of the larger society—messages that indicated females were not as worthy

Ellanora DesManae DellErba, Global Change Multi-Media

A beautiful circle of sharing and appreciation in honor of one of our community's beloved sisters.

Amadon DellErba, Global Change Multi-Media

The most important thing for any soul is to grow into a sense of personhood, being "at home" within her or his personality, and having self-esteem.

as males. Many of my friends received those kinds of messages from their own grandfathers, fathers, and brothers, some even suffering physical and psychological abuse as females, which enraged me.

An especially strong message for us females in our young years was that if we girls were not pretty and sexy, we were not cool, and most females have carried this "programming" into their womanhood, which still deeply affects how they see themselves as human beings. But many males suffer too from this type of programming and do not meet their potential as whole human beings who are able to be in truly loving, complementary relationships. I eventually came to the realization that any type of societal programming that promotes misunderstanding and any kind of prejudice, bullying, and social injustice harms both the victims and the victimizers.

In my grade-school years I handled any male bully or sexist by simply beating the hell out of him, so any male friends I did have (and I had quite a few) appreciated my "tom-boy" ways, and I became their "equal," even though I was a girl. In my teen years I had outgrown my angry reactions to male bullies and withdrew from all male and female peers who pressured me to become something I was not and did not want to become. I became an excellent student and studied independently, feeding my ever-expanding curiosity about reality on this world.

In college I became more radical in my views of social and political issues and proactively took part in the civil rights, feminist, and anti-war movements that were all going on simultaneously in the 1960s and into the early '70s. I had an active social life with a large group of friends who shared some of my passions, but my closest friends were those who shared my love of spirituality, which was applied in every aspect of our lives.

Though I have always been consistent in my own gender identity as female and in my heterosexuality, I have had friends—from childhood on—who were not so clear in their own identity or sexual orientation and some who changed their sexual orientations in mid-life. I grew up with two males who always seemed uncomfortable in their "maleness," and eventually both, as adults, identified themselves as females and now dress and act within that identity.

One of my closest female friends, whose friendship has lasted from third grade into the present, displayed much confusion and distress over her mother's tremendous pressure to be a "fluffy" girl and do all of the girly things expected of her. After a stressful marriage with a man that involved having a child and experiencing a deep sense of betrayal when he had an affair with one of her "best" friends, she divorced him and spent many years in and out of lesbian relationships that never panned out. Finally, she found a woman with whom she has been in a committed relationship for many years, though she still seems to be tortured about her gender identity.

As souls ascending, we humans are born into physical mechanisms (bodies) that in most cases are either female or male. I believe that within divine pattern the God-gifted personality circuitry of each individual fits the body of that person, thus being either female or male in gender identity. But due to many reasons, not every person identifies with the gender body with which she or he was born.

Interestingly, within the Apache culture is a beautiful tradition that promotes self-esteem for both genders—the Sunrise Ceremony for a girl at the threshold of womanhood, in her puberty years. This takes at least one year of planning and preparation, involving the whole extended family and friends of the designated girl, and culminates in a three-day, coming-of-age ceremony for the entire tribe/community. Throughout the process, the men have well-defined roles and the women have theirs, and they work closely together to create this spiritually-based, socially-uplifting ceremony.

The year (or more) planning process provides the opportunity for communion and cooperation among family and friends, with love and support extended to each other in the careful, methodical training and preparation that is given to a girl-becoming-a-woman. Ideally all persons involved can experience a sense of self and place within a loving family and community that gives the message that all individuals, female and male, are highly valued and needed.

In the decades that I have attended these ceremonies, I continue to observe and personally experience the tremendous sense of healthy pride and respect that the people have for each other during those three days. Even those individuals who are handicapped in some manner, or "different" from most, are treated with love and included in some function that makes them an integral part of the event. If only this sense of personal and social "wellness" could be extended for the rest of the year, but unfortunately those three days have not yet been integrated into the whole of the culture of the reservation for the rest of the year. Nor has the overcontrolling dominant culture changed enough to provide the opportunities needed for each individual, family, and society to unfold into the divine pattern of wholeness, wellness, and personality integration.

Here in the culture of the EcoVillage at Avalon Gardens, we have implemented our own form of coming-of-age ceremonies for our girls and boys respectively, which include a series of activities over a two-year period for children of pre-puberty and puberty ages. The entire community is involved at some level, with a team of parents, school instructors, and mentors being part of the planning. For the children, the two-year process includes individual vision-questing, artistic creations, rugged and gentler outdoor activities, study and contemplation, interaction with older mentors, service projects, and so on.

The purpose of these various activities is to assist each girl and boy to identify with her or his unique individuality as a person, a soul ascending. The most important thing for any soul is to grow into a sense of personhood, being "at home" within her or his personality, and having self-esteem. When an individual experiences a sense of personality integration, she or he then can become more compassionate and respectful of other persons and more regardful of our natural and social environments.

What our community realizes is that ecosystems, social systems, and person systems are interrelated and cannot be separated when trying to solve the many problems and ills within ourselves, as well as in our world, which include inequality of opportunities, spiritual and economic poverty, physical and psychological violence, the unraveling of most ecosystems, and so on.

When an individual is confused and imbalanced within her or his personhood, then she or he is not encircuited with her or his true Creator-given personality and thus experiences a sense of lostness and not knowing oneself. That lack of personality integration can result in various mental and social disorders that are acted out in many ways, one of them being difficulty in relating to those of the opposite gender or anyone who is considered "different." So, as with the coming-of-age activities for children, we adults need coming-of-age experiences throughout our lives to assist us in the unfoldment into our personality integration and ability to relate to others more lovingly and respectfully.

When an individual experiences a sense of personal integration, she or he then can become more compassionate and respectful of other persons and more regardful of our natural and social environments.

Ellanora DesManae DellErba, Global Change Multi-Media

Intentional community living can provide opportunities daily for individuals to feel loved, supported, and assisted in their own healing and growth. The culture of congruency that is more possible in an intentional community can provide a paradigm for living with compassion and respect for others as ascending souls, children of God. The entire community culture can be designed to help individuals outgrow various unhealthy attitudes and behaviors that are disrespectful and at times even hateful to others.

And community offers something else wonderful: the gift of a genuinely "safe" environment, where ideally the sexual pressures and "images" of men

(continued on p. 75)

GENDER IDENTITY AND SEXUAL ORIENTATION SHARING A HEARTFELT CONVERSATION

(continued from p. 53)

and women are basically nonexistent, thus allowing each adult a healing opportunity and emotional support to test out new waters, so to speak, and discover their beautiful, true, and higher selves within their male or female circuitry design without fear of ridicule or peer pressure.

We have found that most individuals who have a difficult time relating respectfully and compassionately to others, including those who may even use the intimidation tactics of a bully (whether with a lover or with just about anyone), suffer from a lack of true self-esteem within her or his Creator-gifted personality circuitry. If the "bullies" or "bigots" or misogamists or "whatever" are willing to become proactive in their own healing and growth processes, they can be transformed as they find themselves within their unique personhood and thus no longer need fear or hate other persons or individuals.

A culture of congruency provides opportunities for people to think about and discuss with each other how mindsets, certain ideologies, and behaviors are counterproductive in building a society of wholeness and wellness. And such a culture encourages people to "take off the mask(s)" they hide behind to seek refuge within the facades of "image" they've built in order to protect themselves from further emotional pain.

At Avalon Organic Gardens & EcoVillage we have group and individual counseling and sharing sessions where people can attempt to respectfully and regardfully work out their differences, which include counsel for couples who are having difficulty in relating to each other. We have found that couples often conclude that they need to put some space between each other in order to attend to their individual healing processes, with the hopes of reuniting again.

Regardless of someone's racial, national, religious, cultural, or gender identity, I believe we all need to consider ourselves and each other as beloved children of the Creator and planetary citizens—true "brothers and sisters"—who have a responsibility to personally find ourselves within our own unique personalities and support one another in that process. Thus we can become more whole, healed, and compassionate beings who contribute to the genuine progress of human civilization by helping create cultures of congruency within divine pattern. I invite everyone to begin having more conversations in this vein, with open hearts and minds, for the restoration of our world and all its majesty, including its peoples.

Niánn Emerson Chase grew up on four different Native American reservations in the southwestern United States. After earning her Bachelor's Degree in Literature/English and Education, she returned to the San Carlos Apache Reservation in Arizona where she lived and taught for 15 years. In 1989, she co-founded Global Community Communications Alliance—currently a 100+ member intentional community and working ecovillage (at Avalon Organic Gardens & EcoVillage) located in southern Arizona in the historic southwest towns of Tubac and Tumacácori. Within the community, she serves as the Director of the Global Community Communications Schools for Adults, Teens, and Children, as well as serving on the Board of Elders and as a pastor.

Communities Editorial Policy

Communities is a forum for exploring intentional communities, cooperative living, and ways our readers can bring a sense of community into their daily lives. Contributors include people who live or have lived in community, and anyone with insights relevant to cooperative living or shared projects.

Through fact, fiction, and opinion, we offer fresh ideas about how to live and work cooperatively, how to solve problems peacefully, and how individual lives can be enhanced by living purposefully with others. We seek contributions that profile community living and why people choose it, descriptions of what's difficult and what works well, news about existing and forming communities, or articles that illuminate community experiences–past and present–offering insights into mainstream cultural issues. We also seek articles about cooperative ventures of all sorts–in workplaces, in neighborhoods, among people sharing common interests–and about "creating community where you are."

We do not intend to promote one kind of group over another, and take no official position on a community's economic structure, political agenda, spiritual beliefs, environmental issues, or decision-making style. As long as submitted articles are related thematically to community living and/or cooperation, we will consider them for publication. However, we do not publish articles that 1) advocate violent practices, or 2) advocate that a community interfere with its members' right to leave.

Our aim is to be as balanced in our reporting as possible, and whenever we print an article critical of a particular community, we invite that community to respond with its own perspective.

Submissions Policy

To submit an article, please first request Writers' Guidelines: Communities, 23 Dancing Rabbit Ln, Rutledge MO 63563-9720; 800-462-8240; editor@ic.org. To obtain Photo Guidelines, email: layout@ic.org. Both are also available online at ic.org/communities-magazine.

Advertising Policy

We accept paid advertising in Communities because our mission is to provide our readers with helpful and inspiring information–and because advertising revenues help pay the bills.

We handpick our advertisers, selecting only those whose products and services we believe will be helpful to our readers. That said, we are not in a position to verify the accuracy or fairness of statements made in advertisements–unless they are FIC ads–nor in REACH listings, and publication of ads should not be considered an FIC endorsement.

If you experience a problem with an advertisement or listing, we invite you to call this to our attention and we'll look into it. Our first priority in such instances is to make a good-faith attempt to resolve any differences by working directly with the advertiser/lister and complainant. If, as someone raising a concern, you are not willing to attempt this, we cannot promise that any action will be taken.

Please check ic.org/communities-magazine or email ads@ic.org for advertising information.

What is an "Intentional Community"?

An "intentional community" is a group of people who have chosen to live or work together in pursuit of a common ideal or vision. Most, though not all, share land or housing. Intentional communities come in all shapes and sizes, and display amazing diversity in their common values, which may be social, economic, spiritual, political, and/or ecological. Some are rural; some urban. Some live all in a single residence; some in separate households. Some raise children; some don't. Some are secular, some are spiritually based; others are both. For all their variety, though, the communities featured in our magazine hold a common commitment to living cooperatively, to solving problems nonviolently, and to sharing their experiences with others.

Notes from the Editor BY CHRIS ROTH

Undressing and Addressing the Elephant in the Room

Chris Roth

With this issue, Communities faces head-on a theme that has seemed increasingly timely in recent years—particularly over the last six months during which we've been assembling these articles. Especially in the context of broader discussions happening in society, Class, Race, and Privilege often seem like the "elephant in the room" in the intentional communities world. This issue makes an attempt to undress and address the issues that elephant raises.

The questions of Class, Race, and Privilege in intentional community are not simple or clear-cut. I see two simultaneous impulses—one in which intentional communities expose people to greater diversity in their social and working circles; broaden people's empathy and ability to understand and embrace those different from them (coming from different class or racial backgrounds or amounts of inherited privilege); level out social inequities; and serve as models for the coming-together that can help us understand how related we all are, that we're all in this together, that socially constructed differences of power and privilege are arbitrary and deserve to be jettisoned and rectified. Intentional communities can become places where the trappings of prejudice, power-over, and separation on superficial grounds are transcended, and replaced by new ways of relating that show what is possible.

The other impulse, often hidden or overlooked in communities' own understandings about themselves, is in the opposite direction: intentional communities can become refuges for people to escape to in an effort to be with a closer "tribe," which unfortunately often turns out to have the same racial and class backgrounds and amounts of inherited privilege. Even when this is not a conscious intention, and even when there is a clear, stated desire for greater diversity, less class and racial diversity can become the default mode, and power imbalances can persist in communities, for a host of reasons examined in this issue: economic barriers, cultural barriers, unacknowledged or invisible racism, fear.

In my own life in community, I've witnessed both impulses at work. Along with the idealized (and usually inaccurate) notion that communities bring together a rainbow of people in an alitarian utopian lifestyle, I've also heard the generalization that North nerican intentional communities are populated almost exclusively by hite, middle class people. While we don't have comprehensive statistics ailable across the broad spectrum of the communities movement, the tter generalization may be true in many (but not all) cases, at least as r as the "white" goes—and often in the area of class as well, especially more expensive communities, though as always there are exceptions.

My own journey into community is a bit more complicated than ei-er of these scenarios (the inspiring or the dismal) in relation to social stice. I grew up in a setting that was ethnically and even racially some-hat diverse but fairly homogeneous economically and socially; my wn's inhabitants ranged from middle class through upper-middle class upper class, and my friends were almost all in the first two categories. he working class people I had exposure to were the blue-collar workers om adjacent towns with the technical skills and willingness to get their nds dirty that kept most residents of my town comfortably detached om too much (or in some cases any) physical work.

It took moving to an intentional community for me to start learning al-life skills in areas that, in my hometown, were below the pay scale or gnity or social class—while being well above the practical aptitude lev—of most residents. It also took moving to an intentional community start mingling with people from significantly different backgrounds, cluding working class as well as the middle class from which I came, d including (because of the communities I was attracted to) people ith international backgrounds, including from less developed coun-ies. By becoming downwardly mobile, I (and many like me) became ore adept at the skills of self-reliance and resilience, while learning om others who had already been acquiring those skills while we had en marooned in suburbia and/or academia. In these settings, the work community became the great equalizer among people from disparate ass backgrounds.

Two groups were notably absent from these places: the very rich, and e very poor. But in other ways, I found that community living greatly oadened my class horizons, removed class barriers in ways that stay-g in my hometown and in the circles within which I grew up would ot have. This mixing of classes has presented some challenges: cultural fferences, varied attitudes toward such things as diet, tobacco, com-unication styles, etc.—but ultimately I have always been thankful to ve entered into a world where people of different class backgrounds nd common ground and can share their lives together, much more an I experienced in the social world from which I came.

The same cannot be said for race. The communities I've lived in have cluded fewer people of color than the town I grew up in or than the wns in which my parents and my brother now live. This is partly be-use both Oregon—where I've spent the great majority of my time in mmunity—and rural northeast Missouri—where I've spent most of y few adult years away from Oregon—are predominantly white, and rthermore have a history of racism whose legacy lives on in the racial akeup of the states (see "Oregon History and Politics" in Kara Hun-rmoon's "Why Diversity Is Good for Intentional Community," page 3). It's also partly because of the various factors explored in articles roughout this issue.

In my early 20s, I had the experience of being a racial minority—in ct, the only white person I dependably saw every day—for a year-and-half, and since then I've gravitated toward communities with missions education and creating cross-cultural bridges, sharing what we've en fortunate to gain access to with others who may not have had ac-ss to it otherwise. At the same time, the relative racial homogeneity has been among the most disappointing aspects of most of my formal intentional community experiences. And while the IC world has greatly broadened my experience of class diversity, it's also true that for many in the communities world, their home intentional communities are, if anything, less diverse than the settings they came from, more of a class-restricted, unintentionally racially homogeneous enclave.

In short, intentional communities have a lot of potential for address-ing questions of class, race, and privilege. And, as we see in this issue, they also have a LOT of work to do in all of these areas to create the conditions where reality can catch up to ideals. In many ways they are no further along in addressing these issues than the wider society is—and in some ways, they are often less far along in practical terms, even if they're further along in "intention."

We hope that this issue will help communitarians to discuss this el-ephant in the room without shame, denial, rationalization, "fragility," or any of the other reactions that impede real progress. This kind of progress (in our own understanding and awareness, and in our exter-nal actions) can and must be made in order for the world many of us envision—in which the wounds created by conscious or unconscious classism, racism, and privilege are healed, and are replaced by a culture in which all have equal access to fulfilling, cooperative, resilient ways of life—to become the world we are living in.

We encourage your Letters (sent to editor@ic.org) in response to the articles in this issue, for publication in issues #179 or later. This is a conversation we hope will be an active, ongoing one within the communities movement until there is no longer a reason for it—a day which is unlikely to come until a lot more reflection, discussion, and work are done, until broad efforts are made to act upon some of the insights and suggestions shared in this issue, and upon others yet to emerge.

• • •

In concert with publication of this issue, we are undertaking an initia-tive intended to make it—and hopefully future issues as well—acces-sible to anyone, anywhere with an internet connection. As detailed in Kim Scheidt's Accountant's Note on page 5, in order to facilitate wider distribution and readership of this issue, **we are offering digital copies of issue #178 for free download from ic.org/communities**. Because of software upgrades, these include formats fully compatible with every variation of electronic device. The FIC is soliciting donations to support this offering, but not as a condition of digital issue download. If this model brings in enough support, we hope to make this arrangement permanent, greatly increasing our digital readership while still bringing in enough income to pay our bills from those who are willing and able (thank you!) to contribute monetarily to this effort. Also:

We are asking for your help in spreading word about this offering. Who do you know who would appreciate reading this issue? Please send them to ic.org/communities for their free digital copy. Please share news about this issue and this offering on blogs where you think they would be appreciated, in social media, in any other venue through which you reach people who might benefit from reading Communities. We are excited to share this issue with the world in hopes that it can make a difference, both in the world of intentional communities and in the larger culture.

Thank you again for joining us in this issue!

Chris Roth edits Communities.

Moving Beyond White Fragility: Lessons from Standing Rock

By Murphy Robinson

Last winter I spent six weeks living with the indigenous water protectors at Oceti Sakowin Camp, supporting their efforts to turn back the oil pipeline being built under the Missouri River next to the Standing Rock Reservation, part of the homeland of the Lakota people. As a white person from New England, this was the longest period of my life that I'd spent in a space where I was the racial minority. The thing I missed most deeply when I left the camp in late January was the vibrant and continual negotiation of racial and colonial privilege.

Oceti Sakowin Camp was not a safe space physically: police violence was endemic on the front lines, the camp was under constant threat of being raided or razed by militarized forces, and despite the no-alcohol policy in the camp, illicit alcohol use and unhealthy interactions were recurring problems within the Water Protector community. The camps were the most visible manifestation in recent times of the colonial war of genocide and land theft that has been going on in North America since the first European settlers arrived, and it did feel like a war zone. As one indigenous water protector observed, "This is the exact same war we've been fighting for 500 years...except now they are shooting us with rubber bullets, and we have iPhones to record it with."

Non-indigenous allies were welcomed in to join the resistance against the pipeline, while the movement remained under indigenous leadership, with a clear call for peaceful prayer as our sole tactic. I was one of the white people who came to support the work. My first few days in camp were a crash course in what NOT to do, mostly learning by making mistakes. After attending the newcomer orientation I understood how to avoid causing the most common offenses, but it immediately became very clear that I was unconsciously embodying a lot of colonial culture, and needed to shut up and listen so that I could relearn some very basic ways of being in community. One of the most impactful concepts taught in the orientation was this: When an indigenous person corrects you, the proper response is gratitude. Rather than being offended or defensive, recognize that it is a huge gift and act of trust for someone to take the time to tell you how to do something properly in our culture. When you react with resistance and protest, you dishonor and reject that gift. Just say thank you and change your behavior, that is all that is required.

In late December I found a home in Two Spirit Camp, which was a community for queer, transgender, and two spirit water protectors and white allies. The camp was led by a Lakota two spirit woman with an intact lineage of spiritual tradition, and out of the 16 or so residents, just over half were indigenous. Most of the camps or *oyates* (smaller sub-camps within the larger water protector camp area) were for either specific tribal groups (such as the Oglala Lakota Camp or Michigan Camp where most of the Anishinaabe water protectors lived, which were usually wholly indigenous) or specific task forces (such as the Medic Oyate, which was predominantly white). Two Spirit Camp was one of the few camps where indigenous and non-indigenous people lived together and supported each other as a family group.

Everyone in Two Spirit Camp had a keen awareness of colonialism and white culture, and the ways those systems of privilege pervade all our lives. While Oceti Sakowin Camp was in a war zone, the Two Spirit Camp commu-

nity felt like one of the safest places I've ever been when it comes to racial tensions. Unlike what I've seen in groups working on racism in the outside world, we were able to move beyond the White Fragility and White Guilt that completely bog down many attempts to communicate about privilege and oppression. Our community was built on a common mission (stopping the pipeline), and all of us had given up a great deal to come and live in the subzero temperatures of a North Dakota winter to defend the waters. We depended on each other for daily survival tasks like chopping firewood, cooking meals, and keeping a fire going in each tipi or tent. We had good reason to trust that everyone's intentions were good, and that gave us the safety to speak honestly about white privilege when it manifested in our camp.

Nearly daily, I would receive feedback about my unconscious acts of racism: using a phrase with derogatory roots, displaying impatience that betrayed my sense of entitlement to any space I was in, making a joke about Spirit Animals that made light of the sacred traditions of Lakota culture. Because everyone at camp understood that we had all come to earnestly fight against colonial oppression, we could correct each other with an attitude of "Let me help you correct something you don't realize is offensive" rather than an attitude of "You are such a bad person!" I did genuinely feel grateful every time I was corrected, because I knew it was a key way of helping each other unlearn patterns of oppression that are unconscious. We all felt an emotional freedom to speak our needs and reactions in a community bonded by love. We laughed constantly in that camp, letting the joy of community give us strength against the massive forces we were facing. When one of the jokes struck a sour note, someone would speak a correction, the jokester would apologize briefly, and then we'd keep on laughing.

The freedom to talk about these acts of unconscious racism without the fear of offending someone was something I deeply mourned when I returned to Vermont. Here, making a simple observation about colonial and capitalist patterns I see us enacting in our communities has lost me long-standing friendships very quickly. We don't have a culture of "correction as a gift" and instead see correction as criticism. When I make observations about the white supremacist culture that is endemic even in our politically correct liberal communities, people get very defensive. I get these reactions as a white person talking to other white people, so I can't imagine how much worse it would be to try to speak these things as a person of color in this environment. I've come to see our collective White Fragility as one of the key roadblocks that is holding us back from creating a more inclusive culture.

I wish I knew a magic formula for moving past White Fragility. So far what I have seen work at Standing Rock was a combination of five things:

1. Bring people together over a common cause that is greater than themselves.
2. Create a community where white people are in the minority.
3. Create a standard of People of Color being in leadership.
4. Give everyone a basic orientation to how privilege works and why we are trying to dismantle it.
5. Create a norm of prayer, ceremony, offerings, and gratitude.

Under these five conditions, White Fragility seemed to evaporate. I'm not sure if the same thing can be achieved in a predominantly white space like rural Vermont. Creating a norm of prayer and ceremony could certainly be done very poorly in a white space, since the tendency is to use culturally appropriative practices from other cultures.

The one space in Vermont where I've been able to consistently have the conversations I want to be having about colonialism and racism is a local decolonization solidarity group that has spent a year and a half educating themselves about colonization and received a lot of mentorship from a local indigenous elder. We are an entirely white group, but we can toss around ideas and analyses freely because we all trust that everyone is there to unlearn their unconscious habits that are harmful. We receive correction from each other gently and gratefully. Sometimes our conversations start to seem circular, as if we are only preaching to the choir, and we struggle with finding ways to bring these ideas to the wider community where we live.

Intentional communities tend to have strong shared value systems, and I think they would make wonderful environments in which to do this work of transmuting White Fragility into White Humility. Another thing we can do as white people is to get off our butts and put our time, money, and physical bodies into the struggles for an end to racial violence in this country. For me the pilgrimage of putting myself in service to an indigenous-led movement taught me things that have forever changed how I see the world. Both at home and on the front lines, we all need to be doing this work. ❧

Murphy Robinson lives on unceded Abenaki territory, sometimes known as Vermont. She runs Mountainsong Expeditions, where she teaches archery, ethical hunting, and wilderness skills in a feminist, anti-racist environment. She is grateful that Mountainsong Expeditions recently acquired land through a beautiful community fundraising effort, and is also deeply uncomfortable with the colonial system of land ownership. She welcomes students and interns on this mountainside property for those who want to deepen their sense of nature connection and grapple with privilege together while building community. You can contact her through her website at www.mountainsongexpeditions.com.

Growing Inclusivity in Cohousing: Stories and Strategies

By Rosemary Linares

For me, it is impossible to separate my professional training and personal identities from my experience living in my Midwest cohousing community. As a queer, Latina, cisgender[1] woman, I easily pass as a straight, white female. I have been married to a cisgender Mexican male for the past seven years. We have two children who were both assigned male at birth and who will determine their respective gender identities and sexual orientations over time. My eldest is technically my step-son, but our bond is beyond biology. He is half-white and half-Mexican. Our youngest is half-Mexican, a quarter-Cuban, and a quarter-white. My white mother lives two doors down from our house in the same cohousing community.

My family lives in a relatively wealthy, highly educated town, but we would not have been able to purchase our home in this cohousing community had it not been for the post-recession drop in housing prices. We purchased our home from a bank after an eight month waiting period for a "short" sale. We learned about the short sale opportunity through my mother, who has lived here since 2002.

I share all of this very personal information to locate my intersecting identities of privilege and marginalization, as they inform my viewpoint. These identities also guide my personal and professional work for self determination and liberation. My background and social identities influence how I experience the world and how others view and make assumptions about me. As a result, I have dedicated my academic and career trajectories to focusing on social justice, diversity, equity, and inclusion. I launched a consulting company in 2010 to support nonprofits and universities in strengthening these areas.

Yet, when I moved with my family to this predominately white, progressive cohousing community, I was initially stunned by the implicit bias, microaggressions, overt acts of racism, stereotyping, and other racist and homophobic experiences we have had to overcome in order to continue living here. While these struggles have been, and continue to be taxing, I know that we would face similar issues in other neighborhoods that were not also trying to build intentional community. We stay here because there are also many bright and positive advantages to living in this community. For us, the biggest draws are twofold: my mother lives two doors down (our kids have two refrigerators to raid!) and our children delight in having a solid group of supportive friends of different ages, always ready to play zombie tag at any given moment. What a double blessing!

While we have enjoyed these advantages, our initiation to living in cohousing was quite jarring. Three months after moving into our new home, a serious conflict erupted regarding a display for Día de Los Muertos in the Common House, and we were the catalysts. Our idea was to assemble a temporary, traditional altar for Day of the Dead in a well trafficked area of the Common House where neighbors could leave photos of loved ones who had passed. The display would last for two weeks and culminate in an evening celebration with neighbors, drinking atole, eating pan de muertos, and sharing stories. Typically in Mexico and Central America, beginning in October, families create ofrendas to celebrate loved ones who have passed, and leave them on display for weeks. My husband shared with me that where he is from, families first present sugar skulls, sweets, toys, and other food to honor deceased children (angelitos) to help their spirits return to earth on November 1st. This annual tradition culminates in the afternoon of November 2nd when families head to the cemeteries to clean and decorate the tombs where deceased members of their family are buried. Families spend all night through the morning of November 3rd in the cemetery with candles and food, sharing stories to remember their ancestors.

I was initially stunned by the implicit bias, microaggressions, overt acts of racism, stereotyping, and other racist and homophobic experiences we have had to overcome in order to continue living here.

In our community, we came upon an unwritten rule that prohibited religious or seasonal displays in the Common House, such as Christmas decorations, lasting over a period of multiple days. This rule came about, in part, because a neighbor whose Jewish ancestors were brutalized during Christmas was very triggered by such displays. It was not a formal policy. Being new to the community, I did not know about this unwritten understanding. After collaborating with other neighbors to sponsor this event, we were surprised when several community members were very displeased with our community-wide invitation to set up this Day of the Dead display. My neighbors' general disagreement emphasized that "it was inappropriate" for there to be Christian iconography on display in our common spaces over the period of two weeks. While my husband and I shared that this ceremony was rooted in pre-colonial indigenous spirituality that was syncretized with Catholicism due to European colonization and imperialism, this historical context did not change our neighbors' objections.

A painful conflict ensued. I set up the display in spite of the dissension from several community members and I take responsibility for my contribution to the escalation of the conflict. In the end, the display was beautiful (please see the photo) and the event was well attended by many adults and children. However, we have not had another Día de los Muertos, done in its original cultural context, in the Common House since.

Determined to prevent future pain like the hurt my family experienced, I launched an ad hoc committee called the Cultural Expression Committee. Returning to my community organizing roots felt productive, and I convened this group over the span of one year. Organically the work of the group shifted. Rather than dissolve the committee, several members continued to work together to support a transformative process to change the community decision-making rule from "consensus decision making" to "consensus-oriented decision making."

One year after the Day of the Dead conflict, Tim Hartnett, author of *Consensus-Oriented Decision-Making: The CODM Model for Facilitating Groups to Widespread Agreement,* presented a dynamic training in our community. Stemming from this training, the community changed key policies in our Book of Agreements. Five years later, we have seen the paradigm shift with regard to our decision-making processes. In some ways, I think CODM allows us to make certain decisions at a faster pace, and for other decisions, the process feels more tedious. All in all, our ability to include and honor multiple perspectives during the process of making a decision is laudable. I am grateful for the evolution of our decision-making rules resulting from the adoption of CODM.

My initial orientation to cohousing made an indelible impact on me. I realize now that I naively made certain assumptions about my neighbors and expected them to all be friendly with me. I quickly learned that this was not the case, and that is ok. Exactly six years later, I would like to say that I turned this experience into an opportunity for learning and practicing setting boundaries with others. Now I share intimate information with only a few close neighbors who have become friends. As I reflect on other times of conflict in the community, I recognize that we all bring into community our respective social identities of privilege and marginalization, relationships, histories of childhood trauma, and present-day struggles. All of these factors influence how we interact and show up in conflict.

Because oppression permeates and manifests itself in cohousing, as in all facets of society, I encourage those of us living in or studying cohousing to apply a racial equity lens to this experience of intentionally building community. A starting place is with the examination of disparities in the membership of people of color in cohousing communities. According to a 2011 study conducted by Angela Sanguinetti and highlighted in the article, "Cohousing's Diversity Problem" by Amanda Abrams, 95 percent of cohousers are white, 82 percent identify as Democrats, 66 percent hold a graduate degree, and the majority are relatively affluent.[2] However, Angela Sanguinetti's research has highlighted the importance of differentiating between new-build cohousing communities and retrofit cohousing communities, as the latter tend to be more diverse by race and socioeconomic status.[3]

This overrepresentation of white people in new-build cohousing communities is similar to the demographics of the leadership of the nonprofit, corporate, and public sectors. In her article "No I Won't Stop Saying 'White Supremacy'" critical race author and scholar Robin DiAngelo points out that the leaders of this country's institutions are primarily white. For example, for the period of 2016 to 2017, "congress is 90% white; governors are 96% white; top military advisers are 100% white; the [current] president and vice president are 100% white; the current POTUS cabinet members are 91% white; teachers are 83% white; full time college professors are 84% white; people who decide which TV shows we see are 93% white; people who decide which books we read are 90% white; people who decide which news is covered are 85% white; and people who decide which music is produced are 95% white."[4] Fortune 500 CEOs are 96 percent white, according to the Center for American Progress.[5] For the last 20 years, BoardSource has tracked the racial and ethnic demographic data of board members of nonprofit organizations. Over that period of time participation of

Photos courtesy of Rosemary Linares

people of color on boards has never reached more than 18 percent.[6]

NPR highlights that as of July 1, 2015, 50.2 percent of babies born that year were babies of color in the United States.[7] This statistic includes my preschooler. The US Census predicts that by 2044 the racial and ethnic demographics of our country will have shifted so that there will be more people of color than non-Hispanic white people. Given this future shift, at what point will these sectors, including intentional communities, also shift to reflect the demographics of our country? How can we accelerate this change so that cohousing communities actively engage and reflect the demographics of the general population? What are the barriers to making this shift happen? This is an area of focus I tackle on a daily basis in my professional role. But at home, I recognize that my cohousing community and the intentional communities movement are at the beginning of collectively designing strategies to effectively move the needle.

To start moving the needle, those of us in the cohousing movement need to overcome the barriers that prevent inclusion and promote racial and ethnic homogeneity. From my personal experience and observation, the following is a list of barriers to inclusion in cohousing. While not exhaustive, this list may help spark important conversations, leading to action:

1) As noted in the data above regarding the demographics of intentional communities, the majority of members reflect privileged identities. Those with privileged identities include people who are white, male, heterosexual, middle-to upper class, able-bodied, and/or Christian adults. I do not highlight these identities here to attack, blame, or shame anyone with any combination of these privileges. Encouraging guilt leads to inaction. Rather, I advocate that people with privileged identities leverage their privilege to learn and make change. This momentum forward starts with explicitly naming and recognizing one's identities that hold privilege. In my experience, the homogeneity reflected in cohousing communities lends itself to a severe lack of collective awareness and action regarding issues of power, privilege, and oppression. Most of my white neighbors have not actively evaluated their implicit bias, white privilege, white fragility, white savior complex, bias toward colorblindness, or complicity with white supremacy. It's hard stuff, and I've certainly made mistakes along my path to understand and accept my racial identity. But this remains a primary barrier to cultivating inclusive and diverse cohousing communities in terms of race, ethnicity, socioeconomic status, gender identity, sexual orientation, ability, age, and other markers of difference.

By 2044 there will be more people of color in the US than non-Hispanic white people. At what point will intentional communities shift to reflect the demographics of our country?

2) Social networks tend to be comprised of people with the same racial and ethnic backgrounds as one another. One of the most powerful recruitment strategies for new cohousing community members is through current members' individual spheres of influence. This is how my family moved to the same community where my mother lives. So when 75 percent of white people have only white friends, they are not likely to actively recruit new neighbors of color who fall outside of their social network.[8] Also, people of color want to avoid being tokenized and marginalized by their neighbors. For some, joining a homogeneous neighborhood of the powerful racial group feels like a threatening proposition, regardless of any positive intent from the current residents.

3) Diversity in background and styles of communication and behavior will lead to explosive conflict when unconscious bias is also present. People have different communication, behavior, and conflict styles, which show up in daily interactions as well as moments of division. This is actually an asset, but it can serve as a barrier when we unconsciously, collectively ignore this fact. A study mentioned in a September 2016 *Harvard Business Review* article demonstrated that "homogenous teams feel better—but easy is bad for performance."[9] For example, if a community is comprised of primarily introverted white baby boomers, then an extraverted millennial family of color with a child moves in, the community is primed for conflict. Why? Because if some members hold an unspoken assumption, or unconscious bias, that this new family should conform to the cultural norms of the more seasoned residents, it is only a matter of time before conflict will erupt. This was basically my experience. Howard Ross says, "We do not think the way we think we think," which means that we do not consciously recognize if we are taking part in unconscious bias.[10] This is why it is important to be aware of intent *and* impact. My neighbors were positive in their intent to inform me of the unspoken rule regarding the presence of Christian imagery in the common house, but the impact of their communication and behavior resulted in painful conflict.

4) Conflict aversion will result in ostracizing and marginalizing individual members and their families. In general, those within white culture do not have to consciously realize that their cultural norms are upheld as the standard. It is possible that individuals involved in a conflict within community are already marginalized in the broader society based on their oppressed social identities. When a conflict arises, these power dynamics are present. Often the voices of those with privilege are elevated and those with marginalized identities are further marginalized. While this may not always be the case, we cannot separate systemic and structural oppression from any interpersonal interaction.

In the spirit of systems change, to overcome these barriers, I suggest the following recommendations for individuals living within intentional communities to shift the paradigm, in order to cultivate inclusion and diversity:

1) Create and commit to an action plan. An action plan can help a community strategically increase racially diverse households, tying together goals with activities, outcomes, a timeline, and resources. Action planning starts with establishing strong, shared mission, vision, and values statements that all members embrace. Refer to these statements and action plan at every community meeting.

2) Volunteer community leaders need to address conflict immediately. Managing conflict is not easy, but it is critically important. As soon as a conflict arises that impacts three or more members of a community, leaders within the community need to draw from existing norms, processes, and policies to engage the broader community in the conversation. If these norms do not exist, they must be created in order for the community to function effectively. Anyone aware of the conflict will have an opinion on the situation, and those impacted will desire to communicate their perspectives. There are structures to facilitate difficult conversations, such as restorative or listening circles and other participatory facilitation techniques. Make sure to intervene using these participatory methods immediately to not allow the conflict to quietly fester, because the community will reach a boiling point. Once the conflict explodes, community members' energy must shift to damage control. Heading off an explosion is generally a more pleasant course of action.

3) Hire an outside facilitator, trainer, or mediator. Someone who

does not live in the community may best assist with leading community change processes. Because we all come with our implicit biases, relationships, and histories, no current cohousing member will be seen as impartial or neutral on contentious topics or areas of serious conflict. Plus, each member should be able to participate in the change process and it is very difficult to be both facilitator and participant because of the inherent power dynamics involved.

4) Acknowledge your community's contribution to perpetuating systems of inequity. Recognize the indigenous community's land on which your community is built. Acknowledge and reconcile if your community is actively contributing to the gentrification of the area where you are located. Pool a donation to support a local community-based organization that promotes economic justice and/or fair housing.

5) Recognize this is a lifelong journey and evolution for each of us as individuals and as a collective community.

6) Collectively organize and engage in opportunities for individual and interpersonal learning and growth:

a. Set guidelines and group norms: ALWAYS collectively agree on a set of guidelines or group norms to help structure any community conversation or dialogue focusing on issues of conflict, race, all forms of oppression and –isms, and other difficult topics. Examples could include:

- Practice active listening; seek first to understand
- Use "I" statements[11]
- Share the air time[12]
- Create space for silence
- Be aware of intent *and* impact[13]
- Practice "both/and" thinking[14]
- Challenge oppressive remarks and behaviors without blaming or shaming
- Expect/accept discomfort and unfinished business[15]

b. Trainings: Host annual trainings that examine systems of power, privilege, oppression, implicit bias, microaggressions, childhood sexual abuse and trauma, homophobia, transmisogyny, white fragility, white savior complex, and/or white supremacy.

c. Dialogue: Hire trained facilitators to co-facilitate a series of at least eight intergroup dialogues on race.[16]

d. Activities and events: These can be related to themes of race, racism, anti-racism, racial justice, and racial equity, targeting residents or opening up to members of the broader community, town, or city to attend.

e. Workshops on personality, conflict, and/or communication styles: Individuals can complete the Myers-Briggs Type Indicator, TKI Thomas-Kilmann Conflict Mode Instrument, or the Intercultural Development Inventory about intercultural communication to begin a meaningful conversation at the individual level and then explore a community's unique landscape of different styles.

f. Avoid using the word "safe space": Interracial, mixed gender spaces to talk about race are historically unsafe for people of color, women, trans, and non-binary individuals. In my role as a facilitator, I have heard participants with marginalized identities say this because these individuals experienced that the "safe place" was not meant for them, but for the participants with privileged identities. Frame the space as a "brave" space instead.

7) Begin collecting data on the racial and ethnic demographic composition of community members. Any respondents should self-identify, and no one should assume anything about another's identities. Track other demographic markers of difference as well, including gender identity, sexual orientation, age, ability, socioeconomic status, religion, etc. In order to illuminate the demographics of those who comprise the intentional communities movement in this country and track any changes over time, we need these data. Likewise, we need to provide opportunities for those who have done this work in the broader community to share it with others in the cohousing community.

8) If you are a white person, listen to people of color. Engage current and prospective members who are people of color in conversation. Listen to them when they speak at meetings. Do not interrupt. Notice if you start feeling defensive. Do not make the conversation about you. Just listen. Hear what they have to say and thank them for sharing their opinions. Do not expect them to teach you things; that is not their job.

9) Read *The Four Agreements* by Don Miguel Ruiz. It is a quick read and valuable resource for life, as well as living intentionally in community.

Unfortunately my cohousing community has not updated its vision, mission, or values since 2003. One of our values still reads, "Deal with diversity of thought." That is not language that is likely to inspire and intrigue potential members of color to move here. In fact, our ongoing efforts to update our internal vision and values have started, stopped, and sputtered over multiple years. While I am hopeful that we will be able to revise and update this critical, unifying component to building our intentional community, I do not know when it will happen. But I do know that for as long as I continue living in this cohousing community, I will approach each experience as an opportunity for learning and growth. My mother's late friend said, "Cohousing is the most expensive self-improvement project you can find!" I wholeheartedly agree. The cost is not just monetary, but also emotional. For me, this cost is worth it because I continue to learn so much about myself and others in an environment filled with people who are also intentionally growing alongside me.

A mother, entrepreneur, and social justice activist, Rosemary Linares is devoted to promoting social change through capacity-building work in the nonprofit sector. Connect with her via her website at www.cmsjconsulting.com.

---

1. Cisgender means identifying with the gender assigned to me at birth and not identifying as transgender, non-binary, or gender nonconforming.
2. Diversifying Cohousing: The Retrofit Model by Angela Sanguinetti, March 2015: www.researchgate.net/publication/282050459_Diversifying_cohousing_The_retrofit_model
3. Ibid.
4. www.yesmagazine.org/people-power/no-i-wont-stop-saying-white-supremacy-20170630
5. www.americanprogress.org/issues/economy/reports/2012/07/12/11938/the-state-of-diversity-in-todays-workforce
6. leadingwithintent.org/wp-content/uploads/2017/09/LWI2017.pdf
7. www.npr.org/sections/ed/2016/07/01/484325664/babies-of-color-are-now-the-majority-census-says
8. www.washingtonpost.com/news/wonk/wp/2014/08/25/three-quarters-of-whites-dont-have-any-non-white-friends/?utm_term=.1993a60e9ca5
9. hbr.org/2016/09/diverse-teams-feel-less-comfortable-and-thats-why-they-perform-better
10. www.theplainsman.com/article/2017/09/critical-conversations-speaker-confronts-unconscious-biases
11. By avoiding generalizations about groups of people and speaking from our own personal experiences, feelings, or beliefs, we demonstrate the act of holding ourselves accountable and avoid attributing these feelings, beliefs, or judgments to the listener.
12. Make certain that all participants are explicitly given an opportunity to speak. Invite participants who tend to remain quiet to "step up," and if they tend to dominate conversations to "step back."
13. Although I may have positive intent in saying or doing something, if the effect of my statements or actions is negative, I need to hold myself accountable for the impact I made, in addition to the intent I brought forward.
14. "Both/and" thinking is a discipline that can replace thinking in terms of "either/or." For example, "race and ethnicity" can be both a social construct with no real basis in science and it can have very real historical and present-day implications.
15. This work is challenging and ongoing. We may never come to any conclusions in our lifetimes, but we can commit to the learning journey and evolution, accepting nonclosure. We also need to lean into the discomfort in order to stretch and grow.
16. There are multiple models to hold dialogues on race; for resources please visit www.racialequityresourceguide.org/guides/guides-and-workshops

Bridging Social and Cultural Divides in Cohousing

By Alan O'Hashi

What's been on my mind lately is how intentional communities can help bridge socioeconomic divides.

I live in a cohousing community, consisting of privately owned homes and shared common spaces. Everyone lives independently, but shares in some of the chores of maintaining the community. After living here eight years and volunteering for the National Cohousing Association, I'm convinced that intentional communities—including cohousing—are one way to help bridge cultural and socioeconomic divides, one community at a time.

Confronting Privilege and Prejudice

The aura around social and economic "privilege" is subtle—I've experienced it from varying angles most of my life. Being a Japanese-American Baby Boomer, I grew up under the post-World War II anti-Asian sentiment. While I may speak English with an American accent and am a third-generation Yankees fan, I continue to find myself as the brunt of privilege, which is a separate story.

My partner in crime Diana and I moved here from a nearby two-story condo after the cohousing community had opened. A home became available when the owner died. It was ground floor, with no stairs, and wheelchair accessible, which turned out to be important when I was in rehab recovering from a debilitating illness.

Complicating the social culture here is the combination of market-rate- and affordable-housing-owners. The city housing authority provided free/cheap land to developers in exchange for 40 percent affordable homes. We were able to qualify for the local government affordable housing program. Affordable homeowners are restricted by a set of rules in exchange for the low purchase prices. For example, appreciation values are limited, as are sales prices.

Being part of an affordable housing program, coupled with stereotypes about people who reside in affordable housing, exposes us to oppressive language—"charity cases," "think different," "lower class," "no pride," "don't fit in," etc. Those long-engrained attitudes are difficult to reverse even for the most progressive and socially aware.

The current political climate doesn't help things. Whether liberal or conservative, the national mood amplifies how individuals deal with their perceptions about differences among people. Unmasking prejudice is more common now, meaning that others are faced with learning how to be allies.

Instilling Cultural Competency

Unless communities are intentional about unpacking their self-perceptions of privilege, "on-the-job" training can cause hard feelings. In my experience over the years, oppressors don't like to be called on their sh*t by the oppressed. Cultural competency is a long, ongoing process and it takes some stumbling and falling, losing friends and making new ones.

I've been presenting at a lot of different meetings lately. Diversity issues seem to be of great interest. I get approached by attendees who agree they intellectually understand the importance of inclusivity, but don't know how to change themselves and their organizations. They are eager to learn.

The simple answer is to infuse cultural competency into the day-to-day operations of the community. This involves fostering awareness and change at multiple levels: organizational, interpersonal, and personal.

Cohousing vision statements generally mention "valuing diversity." When I talk with forming communities, I ask them to have honest discussions about what influenced their views about diversity and some ways the vision can be implemented based on changed attitudes. Governance based on shared responsibility, rotated leadership, and norms about accountability are big departures from majority rule and top-down decision making, and can help with this transformation.

Living in a community facilitates neighborly support if a ride is needed to the store, or help needed to move furniture, or caregiving needed by sick neighbors. Friendships form, BBQs happen spontaneously, and formal community events are planned around holidays. In the process, intentional communities enable conversation among divergent opinions. But individual effort must be put into understanding the perspectives of others and changing personal courses of action.

Increasing Diversity

Cohousers may intellectually "value diversity," but diversity doesn't always play out, considering that the typical cohouser is white, educated, high income and high perceived social class, and, about 70 percent of the time, a woman.[1] So forming community members should discuss what they would be willing to give up—attitudinally and/or financially—to include diverse members.

The need for personal introspection doesn't end once the houses are constructed and residents unpack their boxes. Over time, the community evolves and residents need to keep unpacking their personal histories and values as families move, people pass away, and new neighbors arrive.

Professional and lay cohousing developers can choose to make personal transformations. There are markets other than those of the "typical" cohouser, particularly in gentrifying and abandoned neighborhoods. More culturally competent developers can expand their markets by finding easier outreach paths into diverse communities. As a cultural broker myself, I know that this approach gets results and opens doors without the appearance of "tokenism."

Some Next Steps

- Step out of your comfort zones to start.
- Who do you sit next to in church? Sit next to a stranger.
- Do you stand up as an ally? Take a risk when you hear an offensive comment in the grocery store checkout line.
- Social justice marches and political elections may be personally transformative events that bring people together.

It's when individuals collaborate and alter their behaviors that bridges are built to close social and cultural divides—one community at a time.

Alan O'Hashi is a Board member of the Cohousing Association of the US. For more of his writings, please visit alanohashi.wordpress.com. A version of this article first appeared as a blog post in FIC's 30th Anniversary series.

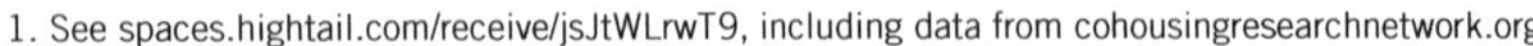

1. See spaces.hightail.com/receive/jsJtWLrwT9, including data from cohousingresearchnetwork.org.

Reflections on Class from a Newbie at Rocky Hill Cohousing

By Jennifer Ladd

I moved into Rocky Hill Cohousing in Florence, western Massachusetts at the end of August 2017 and I am very glad to be here. I love that people will send out emails asking for all kinds of things, from bananas to send to school with their child's lunch to cloaks for Halloween. People in this 28-unit community ask for help moving things, getting a ride, and babysitting in an emergency. I enjoy the community meals, monthly meetings, workdays, and the ease with which I can walk across to my neighbor and share food, watch a movie, participate in a book group, or strategize how we will plow the roads together.

All of this I thoroughly enjoy. And, I seem to have chosen to live in a predominately white, mostly middle and upper middle class, formally educated neighborhood in a predominately white town. Not everybody shares these characteristics but many do.

Though race, class, and gender are braided together and very difficult to separate, for the purposes of this article I am going to limit my comments primarily to class because of my history with Rocky Hill. One of the reasons I moved here is that I know people in the community who are actively involved in climate organizing, peace movement, and anti-racism work. I also know that the community worked purposefully on class issues at the beginning: I had been a co-facilitator of that exploration in April of 2005 with my cofounder of Class Action, www.classism.org, Felice Yeskel. We had worked with Rocky Hill members on class and money issues just as they were breaking ground.

The goals of that work were:

1. To create safety to begin a dialogue around money and class.
2. To better understand and respect each other's feelings and values about money.
3. To share some of their histories around class and money that may be relevant to their current feelings.
4. To begin to discuss openly their feelings about the money and class differences in the community; including: having vs. not having,

spending vs. not spending, giving vs. receiving.

This proved to be very useful as it helped members know themselves better and to better understand the history behind opinions strongly held by other members.

Some of the exercises we did together included answering these two questions:

1. In what ways do you think people in the community judge and/or make assumptions about you around money and class?

2. In what ways do you judge and/or make assumptions about others in the community about money and class?

We asked people to line up according to their self-defined class background when they were 12 years old. This exercise stayed with people: people on both ends of the class spectrum had the courage to step forward and risk feeling exposed. People shared the strengths they gained from their class backgrounds and the limitations—especially as they pertained to living in community.

At the end of our time together people identified next steps:

• Continue to discuss cost-sharing.

• Talk about inequality and power.

• Explore different values and ideas about money; why do we have them and what are the implications?

• Look at personal interests versus community interests.

• Think about the contingency budget—how do we negotiate our different values?

• Name and explore different kinds of power, not just focusing on financial power.

• Talk about shame that we carry in relation to money and class.

• Talk about unconditional acceptance.

So as I have entered into the community, I am curious about how those conversations have manifested today.

Rocky Hill is located in a predominately white town, Northampton, where the median home value is $269,800; most of the houses at Rocky Hill are valued above that. Low-income families, even some middle class families cannot easily afford to move in. The real estate market in the Northampton area seems to be going up every year and it is more expensive to live here than in the surrounding towns. At Rocky Hill we live in a dilemma: we want to be open to anybody who is in alignment with the mission and values of cohousing, but we can't escape the relatively expensive real estate market that does affect the availability of homes here.

Some of the members I have talked to say, "Access was at the center in the beginning—and it was hard to do." However, there are a number of things that the community has already done and is working on to reduce the costs of being here and to therefore be more welcoming to people with fewer financial assets.

• **Offer homes with a range of size and cost.** There are three basic designs for houses ranging from one to four bedrooms, which are charged by the square foot. If one has less money for housing one could purchase a smaller house; more money, a bigger house.

• **Charge for improved square footage.** Another way of adding to the community coffers is that people who decide to add on to their condo—building a deck, finishing the basement, adding a screen porch—are charged an initial amount per square foot (that they would have had to pay if the house had been designed with the proposed addition, at the beginning). This acknowledges that the family is privatizing what was previously community space. And people's condo fees are increased to reflect the additional square footage they now have. Different kinds of additions are charged different amounts.

• **Buy building materials in bulk.** Again, at the beginning the originating group made the decision to order materials in bulk or wholesale to reduce the cost. However, a few members now say, in retrospect, that this may have also caused people to design bigger houses with more than they needed for fear that if they decided they wanted something later on it would be more expensive because they would have to pay the retail cost.

• **Sell no higher than the appraised value.** There are no enforceable rules about selling one's house but people are encouraged to sell at the appraised value of the home rather than going to the highest bidder. This is challenging when housing is expensive and people want to take their proceeds and buy somewhere else which may be even more expensive than here in Northampton.

Photos courtesy of Jennifer Ladd

• **Have some rental spaces.** A few people have built small apartments in their houses that are rented out, again making it possible for individuals or small families to live in cohousing without buying a full condominium. These members participate actively in the community. Others are renting out rooms to people who are more transitory and not active members of community. We hope to find more ways to engage them.

• **Plan for big expenses.** The community is striving to be considerate of people on limited incomes by raising condo fees at a predictable rate for the purpose of building up the reserve fund. The Reserve Fund is specifically for doing large capital projects like replacing roofing, siding, painting, and redoing the asphalt road. The community brought in a professional to help estimate how much money needs to be put aside so when there is a very costly repair community members don't have to pay an assessment—a large lump sum per household all at once—to cover the cost of the expensive project.

• **Reduce community costs.** We do our own plowing, cleaning, leaf raking, and landscaping in general, which keeps condo fees lower.

• **Create and now possibly expand an Affordability Fund.** In the beginning the community and a few wealthier families pooled approximately $25,000 into an Affordability Fund, the purpose of which is to help people with down payments for a house. At least three families took advantage of this. The community is now considering other uses for this fund (which is now half its former size) such as temporarily assisting people struggling to pay condo fees or assisting someone to create long-term rental space. This has yet to be worked out.

• **Develop close, mutually rewarding relationships with low-income families.** It just so happens that this community is part of a Circle of Care supporting a refugee family from the Congo. And though this is not primarily a financial form of support—it's mostly the moral and day-to-day support of helping with jobs, transportation, healthcare, setting up a home—all contribute to this newly arrived family's capacity to live in Northampton while having a close warm tie with this community even though they live outside of the community.

• **Continue to ask the question:** How can we be more affordable to those who are currently here and to potential newcomers? We have some members who keep up with what other cohousing communities are doing and people in different committees keep these questions alive as well.

All of these ideas are very specific. Just as the devil is in the details, the "class issues are in the budget"—and it demonstrates some of the ways that values can be integrated into the system of cohousing operations rather than just being discussed as a good idea.

But questions remain. One person I talked to wondered out loud about what is going to happen when people get older, with less income and more needs? Will they need to move or will the community find ways to help people financially so that they can stay? He said, "I have my ideals and values of inclusion, and we are connected—yet, I have to admit that I like my comforts. I am not sure how much I am willing to give up to enable others to stay; I'm just being honest about my ambivalence."

Though class and classism can be addressed in the budget, there is more to the picture than that. The community culture can absolutely reflect class and racial (gender, ethnic, religious, etc.) predominance and marginalization, comfort and discomfort, inclusion and exclusion.

Just as the devil is in the details, the "class issues are in the budget." Values can be integrated into cohousing operations rather than just being discussed as a good idea.

Every workplace, community, group has a culture—a set of norms that may be very close to the dominant culture's norms or may be very different. Culture includes ways of decision making, showing respect, dealing with conflict, food choices, norms about noise, sound, child rearing, humor, manners—on and on. The more we can name and know our class culture the more we are apt to see misunderstandings as cultural and possibly take them less personally.

I think it is worthwhile for every group to acknowledge that it has a culture with underlying or hidden rules and then to articulate what those rules are so they are not so hidden to those within the sea they swim or to others who enter the community. We as a community have yet to tackle this!

Next steps from my newbie point of view:

1. Be clear about the community culture—what are our norms and practices, spoken and hidden. Clarify who we aren't.
2. Continue to get to know about each other, including our class backgrounds and childhood attitudes towards money that are playing out today in our decision making.
3. Engage in white awareness work as a community.
4. Find ways for those who are renting temporarily to feel as included as possible.
5. Create policy that makes emergency/backup funds available to community members who really need it.
6. Have frank conversations about aging and sickness—how does the community want to be with those who can no longer afford to pay condo fees and live here?
7. Alert community members about city, state, and federal initiatives that enable low-income people to have decent housing so we continue to ground our solutions in the larger town, state, and national context.
8. Get comfortable with being uncomfortable as we explore class, money, and for that matter, race, gender—any of the deeply ingrained dominant patterns in our society. Liberation often requires going through the metaphorical fire of openness and conflict to get to the other side.

Every day I have some concrete reason for enjoying being here, much of it having to do with people sharing who they are and what they have with one another. I also know that good intentions to be welcoming across race and class are very, very difficult to really achieve. The weight and momentum of historic/systemic patterns is very heavy. These pockets of experimentation are essential. May we keep on learning, reflecting, and taking action.

Jennifer Ladd, Ed.D. is a philanthropic advisor, fundraising coach, and anti-racism/classism trainer. She cofounded Class Action (www.classism.org) with Felice Yeskel. In her consulting work she is dedicated to creating resilient community by helping resources move where they are most needed in a way that serves all involved.

CONVERSATIONS ON CLASS AT DANCING RABBIT ECOVILLAGE

By Sasha Adkins

When I was living at Dancing Rabbit (Rutledge, Missouri), I participated in a "Train the Trainer" weekend with ClassAction (classism.org), and came back eager to try out some tools that were new to me. The Rabbits gave me space to experiment. It turns out that more Rabbits were "diggers" than "pavers," and our conversations were rich and thought-provoking.[1]

We incorporated the "Power Walk" exercise into our annual retreat. Participants began by standing in a straight line facing in the same direction, as if we were all looking towards a common goal, and then we repositioned ourselves in response to 20 statements such as: "If there were more than 10 books in your house growing up, take one step forward" and "If you ever went to bed hungry because there wasn't enough food, take a step backwards." After the statements were read, folks were invited to add their own. We discussed what surprised us looking around at where each other was standing, and some of us noticed how closely the configuration of who was out in front mirrored who had the most influential voices in our governance. Some of us asked who was present in our community and who was not.

We also held a forum which we called, "*Are Ecovillages Inherently Elitist?*" In one brainstorm, we imagined that we were going to create the most elitist ecovillage possible and listed all the written and unwritten rules it would have. (Sometimes dysptopia is initially easier to describe than utopia.) After that, we reflected on our own. Here are some of the thoughts and questions that came out of this exercise.

• How can the "visitor" phase be made more accessible for new residents? Taking two or three weeks away from job and family responsibilities to try out life in an intentional community may not be possible for someone who has no paid vacation, for example, or no back-up for elder care. At the same time, an extended visit is an essential part of discerning whether the community and the potential resident are a good match. Beyond that, our visitors were asked to either pay for overnight accommodations in the Mercantile or to bring a tent and a sleeping bag. For those who don't own one and whose friends don't spend their leisure time exploring the wilderness, this might add another layer of potentially insurmountable financial burden.

• Do our expectations for comportment follow white middle-class norms? This may show up in procedures for conducting meetings and structures for resolving disputes, to name just a few examples. Are residents from other class backgrounds and other cultures pressured to learn and conform to these norms, or is there room for new residents to help shape a different way of doing things?

• Some folks in community spend a great deal of time unpacking their emotions, and often in a compartmentalized way ("inner sustainability" sessions or co-counseling or check-in). At other times and in other spaces, open—particularly loud—expressions of anger, grief, or even joy may not be encouraged. (Of course, this depends on who you hang out with!) Emotional restraint may be experienced by some as cold and unwelcoming.

• For those who have experienced food insecurity, evictions, and having their belongings sold or pawned to pay bills, minimalism as a voluntary "lifestyle" may not feel safe or appealing. In particular, Dancing Rabbit's rule that members may not own a car represents a different level of risk (and freedom?) for some than it does for others.

• Dancing Rabbit is rural, and the surrounding towns are largely white, and heavily Old Order Mennonite. One African American visitor shared that she felt trapped and isolated and that the thought of needing to interact with local police or hospital staff (who were all white) was more than unnerving. Some members take extended trips abroad or to other parts of the country when claustrophobia sets in, but this may not be an option for folks who are from poor or working class backgrounds.

• Folks who rely on WIC or SNAP (the program that used to be called food stamps) need to purchase groceries from local supermarkets where their benefit cards are accepted, to supplement whatever food they grow or raise. Though in some areas, farmers' markets accept EBT cards, many do not. Members supported by trust funds and others with access to wealth are able to source (and take more risks in growing) a more organic, sustainable diet. Do ethical judgments about the folks who "support" conventional agriculture and confined animal feedlot operations crop up? Do folks on government assistance feel that they are perceived as not contributing as fully to the community's mission and values?

• Because the cost of living at Dancing Rabbit is lower than that in many other areas of the US, DR may attract some members who are primarily seeking affordable living/survival, while other members who have a wider range of choices are drawn to the ecovillage because they are excited to be part of an experiment in sustainability. All members contribute to the work of building Dancing Rabbit. How can we be sure we aren't, even unconsciously, privileging one motivation over another?

I don't pretend to have answers. I offer my recollections of our conversations simply as an invitation to others to help me think through it more deeply, and as conversation starters for other communities. I appreciate that so many folks at DR were willing to have these conversations, and to listen to each other's experiences with compassion and an open mind. I have been inspired by the depth of honesty and trust that I saw modeled there and hope to carry that spirit into the wider culture.

Sasha Adkins was raised a nomad, traveling on a sailboat in the Atlantic with family. Sasha has yet to settle down and stopped keeping track after the first 50 addresses, but spending six months at Dancing Rabbit in 2012-2013 was definitely a highlight. Sasha has also lived in community at the Beacon Hill Friends House (Boston) and the Discipleship Year House (Washington, DC). Sasha, a fellow with GreenFaith, teaches environmental health, with a focus on plastic marine debris as a symptom of the toxicity of disposable culture.

---

1. "Diggers" want to surface the root causes of conflicts, while "pavers" value harmony and would rather smooth over differences to preserve cordial relationships.

Potluck Circle at Dancing Rabbit Ecovillage.

Cecelia Watkins

CLASS, RACE, AND PRIVILEGE in Intentional Community

By Kara Huntermoon

Community members watch solar eclipse in the North Field.

In my first year as a co-owner of Heart-Culture Farm Community's land, I was shocked to learn that new residents, particularly raised-poor and people of color, felt I had pressured or forced them to vote yes on particular people moving in. I thought I was expressing an opinion, in the context of everyone having an equal right to their opinion. Certainly those who felt "forced" hadn't said anything during the consensus process about not liking the new people. Nobody ever accused me of "forcing" them to vote a certain way during the seven years when I was only a renter!

The problem was one of privilege—not necessarily the "privilege" of being more officially responsible for helping our intentional community function well, which is what ownership actually means at Heart-Culture. The privileged status of my class and race backgrounds, combined with the experiences of our residents of living in the wider oppressive culture, made it hard for them to accept that they had a right to participate with an equal voice. In our resident consensus process, a block is a block, regardless of owner or renter status. How could I make that clear?

I learned to withhold my opinion and listen first, even calling on people who tend to remain silent, ensuring their voices are heard before mine. My position as a white middle-class educated person holds meaning in my relationships, especially when one knows that I am a community co-owner and 10-year resident. I'm also the rental manager, a job I got because nobody else was willing to sign eviction notices (even when all agreed one was needed).

Initially in my liberation work, I tended to focus on my hurts, on the ways I have been oppressed. As a woman who became a single mother at 23, sexism and male domination hit me especially hard. I now had a very important job to do, and one for which I would be frequently judged by complete strangers if I failed in even the tiniest detail—like the day a woman screamed at me on the street because my toddler was not wearing shoes. However, my important high-stakes job came with zero income. In fact, it increased my expenses. Though raised middle-class and educated at an excellent high school, I had not finished college. I joined the ranks of the extremely poor when I chose to parent full-time. My daughter and I spent two homeless years living on the grace of friends, and then found an intentional community that charged $85 per month to live in an eight-foot-diameter cardboard and scrap-wood dome and share facilities in a support house. I advertised at the local Organic markets until I found a job nannying for $80 per week (eight hours), and suddenly I had stable housing and extra income! Wow! Intentional community can totally rock for single mamas!

As I explored the ins and outs of sexism and male domination, and the effects of sexual assault, domestic violence, and the institutionalized exploitation of female labor on my own life, it slowly dawned on me that my own personal constellation included many aspects of privilege. A 40-hour volunteer training at our local domestic violence shelter included an exercise called "The Shape of Privilege." To do this exercise, draw a circle, then intersect it with four lines to make eight spokes. Label each spoke with an oppression—for example, sexism, racism, able-ism, age-ism, classism, gender oppression, immigrant oppression, religious oppression. There are others; choose the eight that make most sense in your life. Then imagine that the center of the circle, where all the lines intersect, is the point of zero privilege, or most oppressed. The place where the lines intersect with the outside of the circle is the point of maximum privilege, or least oppressed. Now mark a point along each line to represent where you feel you personally fall along the continuum of oppression. Connect the points, and color in the resulting shape. This is the shape of your privilege.

When I did this exercise, I was shocked. While my point along the continuum of "sexism" snuggled up in the center (most oppressed), most of my other points ranged near the outer edge of the circle. I have a lot of privilege! Most inspiring, the facilitator of this exercise claimed that the position of privilege is the power position in terms of making lasting change. It's easy for white people to ignore or dismiss people of color complaining about racism, but when white people stand up against racism, their voices are more likely to be heard. This argument hooked me. I resolved to use my privilege to make change towards ending oppression of all people.

I came to understand that the systems of oppression for all other constituencies function in much the same way as sexism and male domination: in order to exploit the labor and value of a large number of people (let's say people of color) to benefit a few power-holding elites, a continuum of behaviors is needed. A minority of individuals in the privileged group do extreme violence (like routine police shootings of black people), and a majority of individuals in the privileged group perform microaggressions and fail to reform the institutions of oppression. The majority of white people can then deny being racist, without actually doing anything to end racism or recognizing the way racism personally benefits them.

As this light went on, I started a life-long learning. I will never be done with this personal work, but I have a few insights to share. The question: How can I use my personal life and my position as a leader in intentional community to break down the barriers between people caused by oppression? How can my intentional community be a microcosm of a society free from systems of oppression based on the visible markers used by our wider society, such as class, race, sex, or age? Here are some initial answers:

Lead from behind, listen first, listen longer, and keep my opinions "last and light." This helps counteract the tendency for my voice to carry more weight because I am white, articulate, middle-class-educated, and in a leadership role in the community.

Relationship is more important than being right or being smart. Respect other people's thinking, even if I totally disagree. Keep my opinions to myself if that might help the person who is talking feel more accepted. Really try to understand where they are coming from. As an example, I have eaten only Organic food for years, but instead of judging others in our community, I try to understand why they might make different choices around food. I have learned a lot about food access inequality, both from listening and from researching on my own (try Googling "Food Desert"). I have also had a positive impact on others. One of our residents (a person of color) told me he is trying to buy Organic food more, because he thinks it will be healthier for himself and his daughter. When he moved in several years ago he believed Organic food was impossible for his family; he felt separate from "judgmental hippies" and their "weird food rules." I believe my consistent focus on caring about him and listening to him has given him room to make changes in this area.

How can I use my position as a leader in intentional community to break down barriers caused by oppression?

Invite feedback and thank people for it. Make it safe for people to tell me how they are affected by me, even if they are in an oppressed group (for example, people of color) in relation to my privileged group (white). Don't defend myself—just listen.

Proudly join the working class: the only class with a future (to paraphrase Harvey Jackins). Do the dirty work. If I don't do it, some other person will have to do it. Do what needs to be done and don't complain. Pick up the trash, put away the tools left out in the rain, and don't bother to ask who left it that way. (It could easily have been me.)

Make sure every voice is heard. Notice if someone has not spoken about a topic of discussion, and call on them to do so. Someone who attends meeting after meeting in silence does have a valuable perspective and important things to say, and needs to know that their voice is welcome. In the history of our community, those who won't offer to speak in meetings have been immigrants, women of color, and people who were raised poor (particularly those who spent several years living on the streets during their teens). If they are not willing to speak up in the group, even when called upon, it is helpful to delay any decision on the topic until someone can ask the person privately to explore their thoughts and feelings. This extra effort to make safe space pays off in the long run in greater retention of diverse residents.

Create financial structures that level the playing field. Every community needs capital to start, and continuing inputs of money to continue functioning. At Heart-Culture Farm Community, our mortgage payment alone is $2,600 per month, and utilities, taxes, and maintenance add another several thousand dollars. That's before we add any "progress projects," like installing water catchment systems, planting orchards, or building new housing. Creating a level financial playing field is tricky when the money needs to come from somewhere, quick.

This is a place where those who already have privilege (in this case, money) can leverage that

Jumping on the trampoline at sunset.

Three community children, from three different families.

Photos by Myriad Huntermoon

privilege to make necessary change. Communities do better with "financial angels" who are willing and able to take on responsibility for funding projects until the community can support itself. These people are "angels" because they play a specific role, and use their specific gifts to seed the community, but they remain humble in their relationships with people; they don't use power-over control tactics to micromanage the residents. Personality and ethics are really important in a financial angel. Other people in the community can help by making a commitment to see the angel as a valued and important human being, one who is approachable and wants connection and closeness as much as any other person.

Residents with lower incomes have a valuable role to play in community. We charge rents between $250 and $800 per month, including utilities and community fees, depending on the size of the space. This amount is low in our area of the country, but it covers our community's needs, and allows our residents to do more than chase the dollar. One of our owners, for example, works three days per week in a near-minimum-wage job, and spends the other four days working on community projects and building relationships with residents. He isn't going to bankroll any large projects with his monthly buy-in payments, but the attention he gives to community well-being during his days off is invaluable to the community's good functioning.

Encourage sharing. Good relationships lead to innovative ways to help each other. When we can borrow a tool, there is no need to buy it. On a larger scale, we can help each other through stressful life transitions. Several times our community has taken up collections to pay for a resident's rent for a month, when an injured resident temporarily couldn't work, or when a new parent wanted to bond with a baby but didn't have paid parenting leave. Because many of our residents live month-to-month, sharing brings a resiliency to our lives that wouldn't otherwise exist.

Make ownership accessible. Anyone who can afford to live at Heart-Culture can afford to buy in to the ownership structure. This system was created for my family, and has since been extended to two other owners and codified into our policies. In writing, it says that anyone who lives here for at least three years and attends owners' meetings for at least one year can buy in to the ownership of the land, provided they can obtain consensus from current owners to accept them as a new owner. The new owner can, if needed, receive a loan from the current owners' group, which allows them to buy in to the ownership by paying the same monthly amount they paid for rent. Anyone who can afford to live here can afford to buy in.

In practice, the current owners look for certain qualities in a prospective new owner, and the three-year time lag exists to give us time to identify those qualities. We want people who will resolve conflicts that come up while living together, and who are guided by values we hold in common. They need to be able to form trusting relationships with the current owners, and participate well in consensus during both resident and owner meetings. We want them to think beyond themselves and their families, to consider how to help the functioning of the entire community go well. Ownership means more responsibility, to both the financial and social well-being of the group. Owners rely on each other to help solve problems and hold a strong container for the community culture. This container is especially important at Heart-Culture, because we do accept residents who are very diverse, including those who have no experience with social sustainability structures (like consensus and mediation) or physical sustainability structures (like composting toilets and greywater systems).

Learn about race, class, oppression, and privilege. Study the history of different groups of people. Why are race relations the way they are today? What were they like 100, 200, or 400 years ago? Learn the life histories of community residents; how do they relate to the histories of groups? For example, how does my life history relate to the history of white people in the United States? How does my Latina community-mate's life history relate to the history of Spanish colonization of the indigenous peoples of Latin America? Don't be "color blind" or "class blind." Blindness isn't a way to end oppression; it's another way to avoid admitting to our own privilege. Unless we look squarely at the problems that face us, we will not be able to dismantle institutions of oppression and create a society where people are truly equal.

In the last six months I have seen signs that my efforts are paying off. One of our raised-poor long-term residents recently started speaking up in nearly every meeting, after years of cursory answers to invitations to contribute. An immigrant resident gave an unusually long speech in reaction to an emotional topic in a recent meeting. People are telling me they disagree with me—and I think that's a good sign. I can tell we like each other, and I'm glad they feel safe arguing with me. I'm looking forward to seeing how our relationships evolve into the future! ❧

Kara Huntermoon is one of seven co-owners of Heart-Culture Farm Community, near Eugene, Oregon. She spends most of her time in unpaid labor in service of community: child-raising, garden-growing, and emotion/relationship management among the community residents. She also teaches Liberation Listening, a form of co-counseling that focuses on ending oppression.

Serifina, three years old, was born at home on the farm.

Riverside mandala.

WHY DIVERSITY IS GOOD for Intentional Community

By Kara Huntermoon

Eight Heart-Culture Farm Community children, ranging in age from two to 13.

Why is diversity good for intentional communities? Challenging systems of oppression takes place on all levels, from the micro to the macro. Understanding the macro dynamics, the patterns of the wider society, lends significance to interactions on the personal level. The work of linking the macro to the micro can help us make personal choices that affect our bigger society. In my life, as a white woman in an intentional community in Oregon, I can tie these levels together through three vignettes from different levels of reality: macro (Oregon history and politics), micro (personal feelings and relationships), and community-scale (interpersonal decision-making).

Macro Level: Oregon History and Politics

Segregation practices over 500-plus years have succeeded in making close interracial relationships harder. For example, 12 percent of Oregon's population is non-white, so one out of every nine people I meet on the street ought to be a person of color. But I do not meet that many people of color, and I notice when I see one because it seems so rare. We have to reach out specifically across segregation lines to make relationships. Our separation from people of color is one sign of white privilege.

Why do I have to seek out people of color in order to find them? Oregon's history is strongly racist, including active recruiting of KKK residents with advertisements describing Oregon as a "white haven." The entire state was a sundown town, with an 1859 Constitution that banned blacks from living or working in Oregon, owning property, or voting.[1] Black people who failed to leave the state could be physically beaten until they complied. While these laws have been repealed, and today Oregon is known as a liberal state, we are still living in strongly segregated communities. White liberal people have little opportunity to learn, through relationships with people of color, about their own privilege and racism. This leads to a kind of white denial, where we are genuinely liberal and anti-racist, but unaware of our own privilege, so we perpetuate the institutions of racism without even knowing it.

Intentional communities in Oregon are generally white dominated and attract mostly white middle class people. If we want to change this (and I do!) we have to reach across color lines to create diverse communities. For communities to succeed in retaining residents long-term, we have to develop an awareness of the larger societal dynamics that affect our personal relationships. History, sociology, anthropology, liberation theory, and co-counseling are my favorite resources. If we don't seek out education about race, class, and privilege, we will remain well-intentioned but ineffectual—perhaps claiming to be "color blind," but actually incognizant of colorism, classism, and their remedies. Our communities will suffer as a result, usually by unawarely repeating the social dynamics of the oppressive society.

Micro Level: Personal Feelings and Relationships

It is very healing to have close relationships with people who are different. For example, two of my close friends are heterosexual men, and both relationships help highlight the fact that not all men will rape and attack me if I don't give them sex. I occasionally have to educate one of them about microaggressions they've aimed at me or at another woman, but since they respond positively I experience this as an empowerment exercise. I *can* stand up against oppression in my personal relationships and move those relationships forward, even if I am shaking with fear.

On the other side of the oppression spectrum, I have several friends who are Latinx, black, or Asian-heritage. As a white woman I tend to be hesitant to express myself around people of color, but my close friends encourage me to be big and make mistakes. When they tell me I have erred in my treatment of them, I thank them. I am genuinely glad they feel safe enough to tell me some version of "Shut up, white girl, you have no clue." Both my self-education on racism, and the corrections I receive from my friends, serve to sink me into a deeper sense of security. I *can* have close relationships with all kinds of people, without fear of acting oppressively towards them. Since the last thing I want is to hurt others, it's reassuring to have evidence that my relationships can recover from my mistakes.

Community Level: Interpersonal Decision-Making

The oppressive society hurts groups of people in patterned ways, and those hurts shut down some aspects of emotional and mental functioning. For example, boys and men repeatedly hear admonitions like "Boys don't cry"; "Buck up! Be a man!"; and "You're a sissy!" As a result, most men find it difficult to access tears as a healing process. Girls and women generally are allowed to retain more access to their emotions.

A diverse group of people includes individuals who have been subjected to different patterns of oppression. The areas of functioning impaired by these hurts are different for members of different identity groups. That means the areas of functioning retained or developed are also different. Each person has a piece of the truth, and together we can make a whole story; we can make more functional accurate responses to challenges that arise in our communities.

For example, our community once agreed to help a pregnant homeless couple be housed long enough to birth and recover from it. The family was not eligible for residency at Heart-Culture because of several details, including drug use, communication style, and the number of residents who felt triggered or unable to relax around them. About half of our residents gave impassioned pleas to accept them temporarily, as we didn't like to see a hugely pregnant woman on the streets. "The difference between this pregnant homeless woman, and all the other pregnant homeless women, is this one is asking us for help," explained one resident.

The deciding argument came from several raised-poor residents, including some people of color. They explained that they had spent some time interviewing the homeless couple, and assessed that though they weren't a good fit, they also weren't dangerous. "They're not going to steal from us, hurt us, or make life hard on us," explained one young man. Those of us with "safer" more sheltered, more privileged backgrounds trusted their judgment, because they *knew*. They had lived through conditions where these kinds of assessments had to be made over and over, and empirical evidence collected from the outcomes. We trusted our community mates. We may not have trusted the homeless couple, but we trusted each other.

Several white middle class residents insisted that we not allow the homeless couple to birth on the property. Even though the community had several born-at-home babies, they felt it was too much to risk when we didn't know the parents. As it turned out, the mother needed the hospital to save her life during a true birth emergency, a rare complication that would have killed her before she could reach help if she had tried to birth unassisted on our land. Because we insisted they not birth here, they chose the hospital, and both mama and baby turned out fine.

Our community mates were right: the couple was safe for us, and we shouldn't allow them to birth here. Two positions, from diverse voices combined to create a good outcome. We housed the couple for two months, they birthed safely, the dad found a job, and they moved on. Although several residents felt relieved when they left, all agreed it was a good experience.

Conclusion

Most intentional communities are motivated by a goal to be different from the mainstream: more ecological, more egalitarian, or more supportive of personal and spiritual growth. Social justice consciousness and intentional diversity are one possible response to the problems of racism and classism in the wider society. Taking on the challenge of creating diverse communities can lead to personal and interpersonal growth for residents. Successful relationships with all kinds of people strengthen our communities, adding to our long-term resiliency. ❧

Kara Huntermoon is one of seven owners of the community land at Heart-Culture Farm Community, where the ownership structure encourages low-income residents to buy in. She has lived at Heart-Culture for 10 years with her husband and two daughters. Kara teaches Liberation Listening, a form of co-counseling that focuses on understanding and ending systems of oppression.

---

1. "Oregon's Racial History, Diversity Explored." Mail Tribune, www.mailtribune.com/article/20131020/News/310200330.

Photos by Myriad Huntermoon

Sunset over the North Pasture.

August 2014 action led by the Organization of Black Struggle, attempting to ask Gov. Nixon to de-escalate police tactics in Ferguson and not bring in the National Guard.

Jenny Truax

The October 2014 "Requiem for Mike Brown" action included a banner drop and added an important song to the St. Louis Symphony program that night: "Which side are you on, friend? Justice for Mike Brown is justice for us all!"

Jenny Truax

Demonstration following Stockley acquittal.

Richard Reilly

Combating Racism, One Community at a Time

By Jenny Truax

"Where are all the people of color?" This question has come up frequently at gatherings during my 20 years with the Catholic Worker (CW) movement, a network of faith-based intentional communities that focus on direct service (often hospitality to the homeless) and justice work. Our current movement seems to attract largely white, middle class folks (myself included), and while our lack of racial diversity has been noted, we haven't made a lot of progress in becoming more inclusive. In the past few years, CW communities in St. Louis and throughout the Midwest have been doing some exciting (and scary!) work examining ourselves, changing communal structures, and reaching out to become more anti-racist communities.

For white folks, dismantling white supremacy first requires an honest reckoning with ourselves as both individuals and communities. This work can be vulnerable, messy, and painful and needs to be an ongoing process. Secondly, it requires white-dominated communities to build relationships and concretely support organizations led by people of color, using the resources at our disposal—property, finances, a broad network of support, newsletters, and other means of communication—to uplift the work these groups are doing. These are two essential "feet" of anti-racism solidarity, and cannot be done well in isolation from each other. If we try to engage in action without first examining the damage our own whiteness and racism has done to us as individuals and communities, our efforts will be surface-level at best, and can do real damage at worst. Alternately, if white people remain in the realm of navel-gazing without taking action, we can end up becoming paralyzed in our own self-righteous anxiety. I'll recount some concrete examples of both of these strategies.

Looking Inward

After the murder of Mike Brown and uprising in Ferguson, our communal energy in St. Louis expanded to join and support the Black Lives Matter movement while we continued to do hospitality. A shift occurred for us during this time; we gained a new urgency to directly confront the racism present in our own community and in our larger movement. Looking inward, we began revisiting our founding principles through a specifically anti-classist, anti-racist lens. This process helped us understand more deeply why our movement is largely one of white, middle class, able-bodied people. It has been important (and painful) to acknowledge that something about our mission and the way we practice it makes us appealing to a very narrow (and socially privileged) group of folks, despite our own sense of being a radical movement. In re-reading our foundational documents and mission, we asked the questions, "Who would this speak to? Who does it explicitly welcome and unintentionally exclude? How have these ideas been interpreted by our friends who are not white or middle class?"

We were very nervous to talk about simplicity and voluntary poverty, because they are central tenets of our movement. As we talked about both the ideal, and the current practice of it in our own community, we asked: Does our practice of simplicity presume that members begin with some level of material wealth? In what ways does "downward mobility" appeal only to those who have experienced a life of financial stability? How do poor and working class people interpret this value? Does our practice of this value acknowledge the differences between voluntary downward mobility for middle class folks, and achieving economic stability for poor and working class folks?

We also looked at our writings on nonviolence, a central principle of the Catholic Worker since its inception. In the midst of the Ferguson uprising here, and the Black Lives Matter movement nationally, our community has heard the feedback that people of color are fatigued and angered at white people trying to dictate how they should respond to racist oppression. We've also noticed the ways that the term "nonviolence" has been used to silence the voices of people of color to actually promote the status quo. We also see that the behavior that white folks label as "violent" is very often a reflection of a culturally-white practice of politeness and compliance with police and

The 2014 #FergusonOctober national march in St. Louis.

Jenny Truax

The 2017 Women's March in St. Louis.

state power. Speaking for myself, adding these nuances has been vital to my growth as someone who seeks to exist in the Catholic Worker movement and also be an accomplice/ally to our local Black Lives Matter movement.

It's often difficult for white people to recognize how racism may be playing out in our communities. All communities have a specific culture: expectations, assumptions, shared values, beliefs, and symbols that are generally accepted without too much thought. We create culture out of our own socialization, experiences, and identities that we bring to community. Culture is powerful precisely because it affects everything from an underlying level, like the air we breathe. Our community has used the following list of ways that white supremacy shows up in the group culture to help us unveil how racism is operating in our community. This tool is from the Catalyst Project and Criss Crass, with summaries created by the St. Louis Anti-Racism Collective. As a mostly white community, we have come to understand that external tools like this are essential to help us become more self-aware in examining our practices and underlying assumptions.

Universalizing White Experience

This phenomenon happens when "white" is considered standard and normal, and we assume that most people have had similar experiences. In intentional communities, white folks can view their way of doing things—organizing styles, meeting culture, style of communicating, and living practices—as normal and average, just "the way things are." In this

2017 Highway shutdown following the acquittal of police officer Jason Stockley for the killing of Anthony Lamar Smith.

The 2014 #FergusonOctober national march in St. Louis.

dynamic, white folks may react poorly to suggestions, challenges, or different ways of doing things from people of color. Some questions to ask about your community:

• Is it an expectation that people joining our community will learn about the culture and history of the folks we serve and the history of the land on which we are working?

• In what ways does our community prioritize efficiency over relationship-building?

• Does our community recognize that a white-led community has specific cultural ways of communicating and of running meetings, campaigns, and programs, which can inadvertently marginalize people of color?

• In talking about protest and direct action, does our community recognize that there are different risks for black, brown, and undocumented activists?

The idea of "recruiting" people of color into "the" movement ignores historical and contemporary reality.

De-racialization

De-racialization involves removing an issue from the larger context of racism and failing to challenge the impact of racism on that issue. De-racialization restricts the self-determination of the people who are most impacted by that issue to define their own struggle. This term was developed by Critical Resistance, a prison abolition organization. Some questions to ask about your community:

• When our community addresses issues like homelessness, war, or climate change, do we name and challenge the intersection of racism with these issues?

• How have we treated injustices like climate change and war as if they affect all people equally?

• In what ways are white people in our community encouraged to speak in newsletters, to volunteers, and publicly as experts on subjects that disproportionately affect people of color (while groups and people of color are often ignored or not believed)?

Contradictory Resistance

In the dynamic of contradictory resistance, white folks work to end oppression but simultaneously fight to maintain the privileges they have. This can look like fighting to maintain positions of power in an organization. It can look like white activists sacrificing the goals of activists of color in order to win short-term gains for their own agenda. One example of this is when white leaders ignore the asks of organizers of color and prioritize their group's perceived reputation by "playing it safe" or avoiding the appearance of being "too radical." Some questions to ask about your community:

• If our community addresses an issue that disproportionately affects people of color, are they in leadership on our projects and campaigns—or even at the table?

• Does worry about the perceptions of our (mostly white) members and donors prevent us from taking strong stands against racism?

• Are the white folks in our community willing to share power, and have less control?

Centered on the White

This is a dynamic of white activists ignoring or misunderstanding the resistance coming from communities of color. Five-hundred-plus years of liberation struggles on this continent have been led by people of color, from colonization through today. The idea of "recruiting" people of color into "the" movement (defined as white radical struggle) ignores this historical and contemporary reality. Some questions to ask about your community:

• Do we get stuck on the questions, "How can we get more POC to join our group?" or "Why don't more people of color realize how important this issue is?" without doing any deeper digging?

• Has our community prioritized building relationships in our neighborhood, and with

Karen House, a Catholic Worker house in North St. Louis.

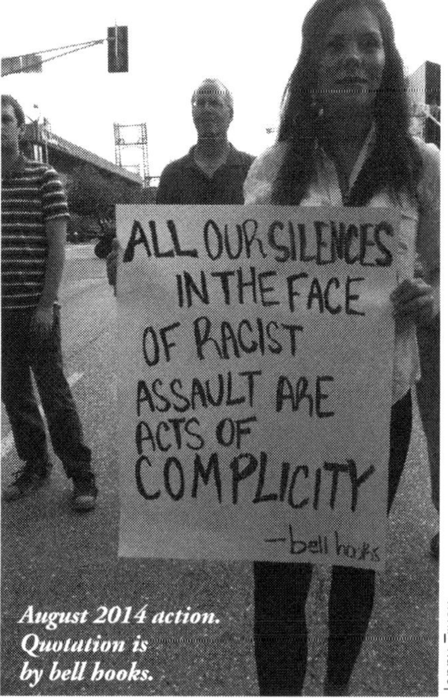

August 2014 action. Quotation is by bell hooks.

Jenny Truax

Act of civil disobedience at the downtown courthouse on the one-year anniversary of Michael Brown's killing.

Jenny Truax

2017 Demonstration at St. Louis police headquarters following the Stockley acquittal.

Kristen Trudo (@radicallytender)

the local groups led by people of color?

• Has our predominantly white organization ever used black and brown icons (like Dr. Martin Luther King, Jr., Gandhi, etc.) to further our mission without challenging present-day racism?

• Is our community supporting local or regional efforts led by people of color?

Taking Action

As we move from introspection to action, knowing that the two are both ongoing, constant, and self-feeding processes, I'll give some examples of recent actions taken by Midwest Catholic Worker communities. These communities, most of which are majority-white, are doing work to address their own racism, change their structures, and support local groups led by people of color.

• Appreciating that dismantling white supremacy cannot be done within a white bubble, many Midwest communities have begun to deliberately partner with groups and organizers of color. Instead of trying to get people of color to join *them,* these communities are supporting organizations where people of color *already* feel safe and welcome—even if they do not philosophically align 100 percent of the time.

• Understanding that racism makes it much easier for white communities to raise money, the Minneapolis CW has committed to tithing a portion of its fundraising efforts to organizations led by people of color.

• Many Midwest communities are doing both internal and external education on decolonization, racism, and white supremacy. Communities have led book discussion groups on *Witnessing Whiteness* and *Waking Up White.* Other have brought local anti-racist speakers to lead discussions.

• Noticing that material support is a concrete way to support groups led by people of color, many communities are sharing their space, volunteers, and resources. The St. Louis CW

In response to the uprising, many white Ferguson businesses and citizens erected "I love Ferguson" yard signs. One creative action repurposed the message. Art by Kristina Kvidovic and the St. Louis Artivists.

Jenny Truax

This dystopian scene played out nightly during the winter of 2014: police armed with tanks, tear gas, and military equipment advancing towards demonstrators, just under the Ferguson sign "Seasons Greetings."

Jenny Truax

organized, and directly offered hospitality to out-of-town activists during the national #FergusonOctober demonstration. The Minneapolis CW has cooked food for events that they themselves were not leading. In Chicago, the Su Casa community repurposed a portion of their building to provide low-rent office space to the #LetUsBreathe collective. The Milwaukee CW redirected a large bequest that they had received to help cover some of those costs to make the necessary repairs. #LetUsBreathe plans to convert even more of their space to welcome organizations typically excluded from access to affordable and private meeting space in Chicago.

• Remembering that each intentional community has specific strengths, the Minneapolis CW recognized that the Catholic Worker movement has a large number of people steeped in the tradition of civil disobedience. In 2016, they organized a large group of Catholic Workers to do a series of direct actions, taking direction from their local Black Lives Matter group. (Historically, these direct actions have been conceived, led, and executed by white Catholic Workers, who are often not directly affected by the injustice they protest. Needing to lead actions, rather than trusting in the leadership of people of color, is a symptom of white supremacy.)

Our radicalness, good work, and good intentions do not make us immune from racism. Geographical proximity to communities of color does not automatically grant us the badge of "anti-racist community."

• Recognizing that structural changes are necessary to combat white supremacy, the St. Louis CW has adjusted many policies and practices. We wrote down and published our process for accepting new guests and new community members in order to be more transparent. (A particular way that racism shows up in communities is when we base membership on "who you know" and therefore also subject it to the implicit bias of current members.) We are more intentional in how we welcome volunteer groups, trying to balance the (sometimes opposite) needs of volunteer groups seeking "face-to-face" interactions with the privacy of our guests who consider Karen House their home. Our weekly meeting features questions that presence our efforts to combat white supremacy: "How have you brought people of color closer into your own life and the life of the house? What are you doing, especially with self care, to combat the sense of urgency and scarcity?" In our newsletter and website, we seek to amplify the voices of those impacted by violence and oppression, rather than speaking on them as (white) experts.

White folks (myself included) in majority white intentional communities must reckon with the ways that racism has isolated us and limited our communities. Our radicalness, good work, and good intentions do not make us immune from racism. Geographical proximity to communities of color does not automatically grant us the badge of "anti-racist community." Our sense of being countercultural should not morph into an arrogant delusion that we are not influenced by white supremacy. This engagement requires vigilance, vulnerability, and bravery. And our liberation as white people absolutely depends on it.

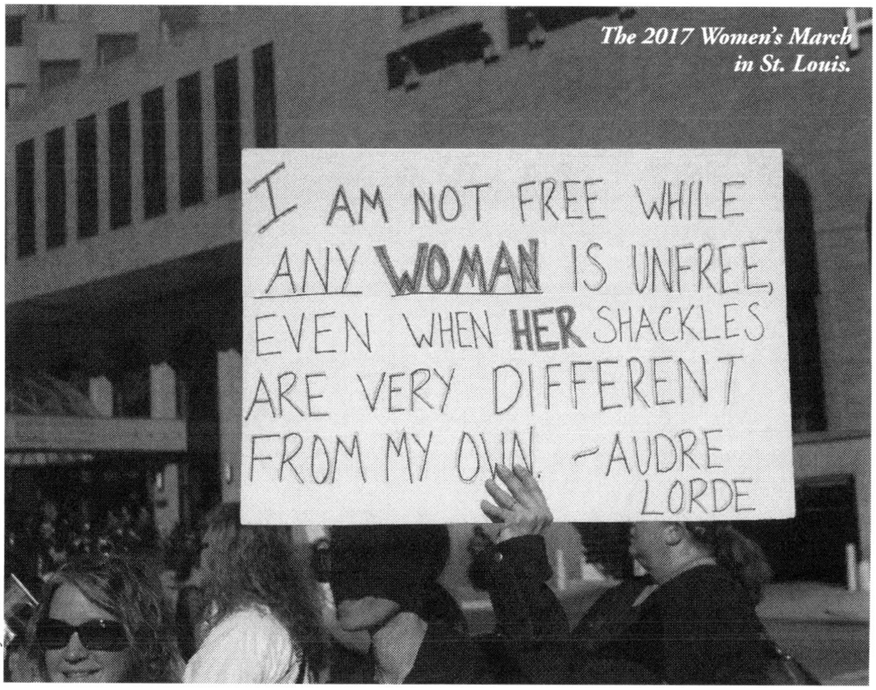

The 2017 Women's March in St. Louis.

Jenny Truax

Author acknowledgments: I'm grateful to Brenna Cussen Anglada, the current and past members of the St. Louis CW community, the St. Louis Anti-Racism Collective, and Annjie Schiefelbein, all of whom contributed ideas, editing, and content for this article.

Jenny Truax has been a member of the St. Louis Catholic Worker since 1998. She does anti-racism education and action with several St. Louis groups and has a deep love of all things related to Star Wars, pit bulls, and tennis. She also maintains the website of the St. Louis Catholic Worker, which has a vast repository of anti-racism resources: www.karenhousecw.org.

Sources and Further Readings

Links to all of these resources can be found at the St. Louis Catholic Worker website at newsite.karenhousecw.org/ic

Catalyzing Liberation Toolkit by Catalyst Project and Chris Crass

"White Supremacy Culture" by Tema Okun

"On Showing Up, Staying in our Lane, and Doing the Work that is Ours: 8 Guideposts for White People Supporting Black Lives Matter" by the St. Louis Anti Racist Collective

"Racism in our Communal Structures: A Community Assessment Tool" by the Western States Center

Dismantling Racism: A Resource Book for Social Change Groups by the Western States Center

"Decolonizing Together: Moving beyond a politics of solidarity toward a practice of decolonization" by Harsha Walia

www.exemplars.world - a resource for communication

Forty years ago, in "Diet For A Small Planet," Francis Moore Lappe proposed that simply by adjusting our carnivorous feeding habits, the human population of Earth could achieve a harmonious balance with resources. Half a century ago, Buckminster Fuller was promoting his vision of a Dimaxian world where technology served the greater good, and we should be "thinking global and acting local." Books, articles, films, video and photography offer a treasure trove of creative material to strengthen the case for sustainability and community. As the technology has made information radically more accessible and affordable, smart phones, cable, Zoom and on-line services join word processing programs and miniaturized cameras to expand communications into the virtual. Even so, environments like the Impact Hubs continue to demonstrate that much of the best jams continue to take place where humans gather.

Exemplars.world is a portal to help us understand and organize; a searchable, on-line library of the possible. There is a narrative that ties it all together, and for each organization or community, there is a brief description and a link to their web page. To add Exemplars, or comment, contact pfreundlich@comast.net

example: Impact Hubs

Starting Point: Isolation of urban workers, decline of structured office space. **Organizing Strategy:** Collaborative workplaces foster social entrepreneurship, tech savvy, warm hosting, hip presentation. **Tools:** Downtown, public transport accessible locations; cool, comfy furniture, state of the art communications. **Outcomes:** Depth (the experience of being a local HUB member) and reach (awareness of being part of a widely spread, international network) is provocative. **Primary Resource:** http://www.impacthub.net/where-are-impact-hubs/. Impact Hubs are a global network of people, places, and programs that inspire, connect and catalyze impact. Impact Hubs are where change goes to work. On five continents, the HUBs mix socia and environmental concerns by breaking down the traditional barriers between for-profit and non-profi

IV

RELATIONSHIPS AND INTIMACY

Nudging at Boundaries

By Julie Boerst

The sun brushes the treetops and I hear Buster crowing. I go to the chickens, open up the coop, clean it up like it's a big kitty litter box, and listen to the soft clucking as the birds begin their foray into the acreage that surrounds our homes. I take the eggs left behind and put them in Steve and Laura's fridge. Why am I taking care of these chickens not my own? Because it comes to me to do it. Because the chickens eat the bugs out of my yard. Because I'm fond of watching them pecking in the clover and love to throw some corn in their direction.

This is how family is taking shape here at White Hawk Ecovillage—a sort of soft, friendly give and take that nudges at the boundaries that exist in traditional neighborhoods. If you're going to nudge at boundaries, you've got to be sensitive—to the stiffness in a posture, the downcast eye, when someone's tone leaps into nervousness or agitation, when my own tone does that. You need to know when to come and when to go if you're living in a community where you're in and out of each other's houses, yards, and chicken coops.

Food that I did not make shows up at my house—popcorn, spring rolls, muffins, pie. Food shows up at my neighbors' houses—cookies, cakes, squash. Some of my family's food is cached in Greg's root cellar, which he has opened to all of us. We are getting the hang of effortless sharing. It's interesting to see how a *quick! quick! reciprocate!* alarm went off inside me when I first received, obscuring the gift someone offered. Now I know to just do my job—to give when it occurs to me and to receive when it comes to me, to say no when that comes to me, too.

Sometimes what occurs to me is funny. Bring nettle tea to Greg! Bring nettle tea to Greg! Why? He's probably busy working. I don't want to interrupt. Bring nettle tea to Greg! So I give in and just do it. There. It's not so hard.

There are fun little uproars. Someone has taken all the shovels! Where have they gone? I need a shovel! I should have a shovel! We learn to rub the rough edges off each other, communicate honestly and directly, hear when that querulous and utterly nonproductive note creeps into our voices. We are seeing the little stories about ourselves that emerge, settling down into more plain and simple fact. It's exactly the same as learning how to get along with a partner, a daughter, a mother.

Kids are allowed to be who they are. No one remarks about my child in his extended hermit phase, preferring to spend the bulk of his time inside with trains rather than roaming our 120 acres. Children may play naked or half-naked.

White Hawk Ecovillage

The author lives at White Hawk Ecovillage, a growing intentional community on 120 acres near Ithaca, New York, with 30 home sites and three households in residence. Members value the kind of sustainable living, interaction, and sharing that emerges spontaneously in community.

Parents don't have to worry about the stigma of having kids outside without coats in cold weather. All of us know when and how to indicate a need for more warmth, for more or less of anything, and we are all free to do that.

As people come and go, come and go from our home, I am fortunate that I am unable to maintain a standard of cleanliness that would say something nice and orderly about me. I am grateful for that. I drop another layer of identity and obligation and just let myself clean the house exactly when I do. I notice I don't apologize anymore for the way my house looks. It seems preposterous to me now, almost like telling the clerk at the grocery store, "I'm so sorry I'm probably not pretty enough to please you!" Entirely unnecessary.

The day I sweep Laura's floor, I have a breakthrough. Her girls have been playing with salt and her hands are full. It occurs to me to grab a broom, simultaneously terrified that I may be saying something about the house or her ability to handle things. But really, I'm just sweeping the floor—the floor gritty underfoot, the floor she's sighing over. She comes to my house and helps herself to juice. Good! So this is how it is—boundaries easing, no need to play hostess or capable mother. It feels nice.

I'm writing this article before dawn with all my shades up, exposing me entirely. We installed shades before we got here because we value our privacy and love having the option of enclosing ourselves. I notice that I don't care as much about being enclosed, though. Before, I put the shades down to smother an uncomfortable sense of being on display, on stage. Now that occurs to me less, maybe because I act a little less like I'm on display in my day-to-day life. Being in community brings me face-to-face with the image that I make of myself more often, and it invites me to let the image crumble. At the same time, hooray for shades. I love them.

I like to drink Coke. I used to prefer to do so with the shades down. How could I let them see my terrible weakness? Terrible weakness or not, I do it with shades up or down now, with a still-perceptible degree of self-consciousness. So is this the definition of family? The people who are allowed to see you drink Coke? The people who are allowed to see you greedy, sheepish, ashamed, and happy about it?

Photos courtesy of Julie Boerst

I notice I don't apologize anymore for the way my house looks.

My day-to-day experience is family, as the stay-at-home mother to a one-year-old and four-year-old. Two-year-old twins live two houses down. No, they're not all best buddies. No, they don't spend all their time together. There's no need to create a cheery and idealistic picture of that. They come and go when they do, sometimes sharing smiles and moments. Laura (the twins' mother) and I bounce back and forth between our homes, adding variety to our days. My daughter is currently fascinated by her daughters, staring at them in awe, reaching up to stroke their hair. Sometimes two whole days go by and I think how odd that I haven't seen them. Sometimes I'm over there five times a day. Today it was three times by 7 a.m.—once to tiptoe in and put eggs in the fridge, once to add one more, once to put a plate of cookies on the table.

I wonder what it will be like when there are more homes, more bouncing, more exchange. I wonder if a certain stiffness will arise, an image of community to uphold, an identity grasped with white knuckles or a sense of self-importance. I realize that's up to me. What will I uphold in any particular moment? What will I allow to unfold?

Opposite page top: Arvelle, Laura, and Sylvanna Woinoski visit Julie. Middle: White Hawk Lane. Bottom: Buster the rooster. This page top: Community playground construction: Steve Woinoski and Greg Nelson working with visiting family helping out. Above: Danby Fun Day Parade (Alana Peterson; Beauty Peterson; Joe Italiano; Sylvanna, Laura, and Arvelle Woinoski; Dmitri Italiano).

A couple from Long Island is coming to visit today, and I have forgotten entirely. I am pleased that I have done this, that I have not spent the entire preceding day attempting to make my home appear like a suitable image of White Hawk, one that will entice and convince. Today this home will be what it is. Maybe it will invite new members into our extended family. ❉

Julie Boerst lives at White Hawk Ecovillage with her husband and two children. She enjoys baking, reading, and walking (www.whitehawk.org).

Morehouse—Choosing Your Family

By Judy St. John, Ilana Firestone, and Marilyn Moohr
with Arlene Goens and Ben Oliver

Lafayette Morehouse is a community that has been living as an extended family in San Francisco East Bay for over 40 years, while actively researching pleasurable group living. In addition to unrelated community members, the group includes brothers and sisters, mothers and fathers, aunts and uncles, grandparents and grandchildren, in all the traditional meanings of those terms. Lafayette Morehouse supports its ongoing research on pleasurable group living by presenting its findings in courses for the public. Members of the Lafayette Morehouse community tell their experience of family within the group.

Judy St. John, 52
Finding my extended family

I have often heard it said that you can pick your friends but you can't pick your family. That never sat right with me. From a young age I knew I could feel a sense of family with a lot of people under the right circumstances.

I discovered this at summer camp. Raised in New York City with working parents, each summer starting at age five my sister and I were sent off to the same camp in the Catskills. Since I saw the same people each year, the other campers felt like siblings to me. The counselors and adults running the place were like parents, aunts, and uncles. In my experience, all those people became my extended family, at least for the summer. I didn't know it then, but basically what I was experiencing each year was communal living. The variety of personalities to bounce off of allowed me to express all the sides of myself. It was a rich, full, joyful existence that was what I thought family was meant to be: all these people behind my goals, interested in my life as I was in theirs. Returning home at the end of the summer to our nuclear family unit, as wonderful as my parents were, my sister and I felt like we were going back to a kind of fabricated social construct. We would wait patiently until summer came around again.

Later in life I looked for a way to recreate that environment. Living at college had some of the elements but it was transient. After graduating and getting a job and my own place, I longed for that feeling of being surrounded by people I care about and who care about me. But how was I going to create it? I considered the Peace Corps, the Navy, working on a fishing boat—something that would entail living closely with other people—but I didn't want to go to a foreign country and, being a poor swimmer, was deathly afraid of floating around in water.

It looked like I could possibly find a reason to live with people if I would just subscribe to a philosophy or religion or take up some kind of a cause, like organic farming. Unfortunately I didn't have any of those callings. What I did have was the desire to have a big family and I didn't want to have to give birth to most of the members.

In fact, even marriage was not something I aspired to, which set me apart from my girlfriends growing up. I knew that, even if I were to find the guy of my dreams and fall in love, going off into the sunset and setting up a home with just him would likely turn into a nightmare. It just seemed unreasonable to expect one person to fulfill all of my interests and yearning for social interaction. From my experience of summer camp, it was clear to me that it would take a composite of several different people to keep me fully entertained.

Arlene Goens.

Photos courtesy of Ilana Firestone

Ben, Marilyn, and Sylvia.

Arlene Goens, 79
Moving into community as a senior

I was 67 when I moved into Lafayette Morehouse. I'm 79 now. My daughter Diana had lived there for over 35 years, and my granddaughter Sugar, 9 at the time, had been born there. My original goal in moving from Indiana where I owned my own home was to find a low-cost apartment and live near the children. Because low-cost housing is basically non-existent in the area, as a last resort I asked if I could join the Morehouse community. I had visited my daughter here for short periods over the years, but no one really knew me, nor I them.

The life I left behind in Indiana could not have been more different. I was a leader in a close-knit ultraconservative Christian church where I was involved in all activities and I had close relationships with many people as friend and counselor. I was often asked for advice in church and interpersonal relationships. I had lived alone in my own house for over 20 years.

I was shocked to observe what by my standards was parenting that was beyond permissive. What Sugar wanted, Sugar got. No argument, no exceptions. Example: Sugar's grandfather came to visit, and the four of us went out to eat. After Sugar (then 10) decided that none of the five places we chose were where she wanted to go, we ended up going home and she and Diana fixed their own meal. I was sure she would grow up to become the most selfish, self-centered person ever. I eventually was able to come to terms with the fact that this method was Diana's choice.

Diana and Sugar enjoyed (and still do) an extraordinarily close relationship of which I was not a part. My initial response was to feel sorry for myself while at the same time acknowledging that realistically this was bound to be so for whatever period of time.

Gradually, Diana and Sugar and I began to communicate some of our feelings. I expressed my sense of isolation, and we began to do more things together.

Today, Sugar, now 21, has become a thoughtful, caring, charming young lady, responsible and willing to take responsibility in every way. She has chosen this way of life as an adult and plans to stay in the group for now. The three of us (affectionately dubbed "the Goens Girls" by the community) have fun going out together or sharing whatever we choose to do, enjoying a mutually loving, caring, delightful relationship. For the first time in my life, I am truly happy.

Arlene Goens has lived at Lafayette Morehouse for the past 12 years.

So there I was, a group dweller in search of a group, knowing I would not be satisfied with the conventional model of a marriage and family. I wanted to be part of a pack where I could carve out my own lifestyle and live as I wanted in the middle of a bunch of people.

Fortunately my sister was looking for this too. Thanks to her, I found Morehouse. She had been living there for six months and knew I would love it too, just like we both had loved summer camp. I visited and liked what I saw. The central goal of the group was to live closely and overtly study the dynamics of pleasurable group living. Through deliberate living, could everyone have everything they wanted while getting along? This was clearly an active exploration that included a lot of communicating and examining of goals and interactions and discussing all proposed actions before they happened.

I also liked the diversity of the group and their acceptance of people with all different lifestyles. There were single people with and without romantic partners, married monogamous couples, couples with outside romances, divorced people who still lived together in the community but kept their friendships and raised their kids. It seemed like you could create the life and relationships you wanted as long as it didn't make anyone else's life uncomfortable. It was the Burger King of communal living. I could have it my way.

So at the age of 23, as a relatively shy, single person, I moved into Morehouse. I delved into the group social experiment investigating what it takes to have my life and the lives of those around me be pleasurable. I quickly befriended a nice guy in the group who was also single at the time. He did not seem like the man of my dreams so I felt free to enjoy myself around him and felt no pressure to have our friendship be anything other than it was. As the months passed he became the best friend I had ever had and a wonderful roommate. Because I had made friends with the other people living so closely with me, there was no pressure for him to be my dance partner, my tennis partner, my shopping buddy, or even like to eat the food I liked, read the books I liked, or watch all the shows I liked. I had the rest of the group from which to pick people to share my various interests.

Community members enjoy food and fun.

I was happy. I had found my lifetime summer camp and a relationship that was thriving largely due to the interest and support of the other people in the group. After living here for a year it dawned on me that I could be married without making my husband be my sole companion. We got married and became parents.

Twenty-seven years later we are still together. Our son was born and raised in the community and had the kind of childhood I had dreamt of. I have an unconventional relationship within a large unconventional extended family and it suits me perfectly. Of course having this large, extended family brings with it exponential problems. There are more people to disagree with, be betrayed by, leave messes behind, and to see through difficult times. It doesn't get easier with more people in your "family," but it's never dull and there's always someone to relate to over something crucial. One thing I am certain about is that my relationship with my husband would not have started and certainly not have endured or increased in intimacy over all these years without the group around us for support, an extended family beyond what blood relationships could provide.

Ilana Firestone, 56
Keeping a marriage together

Like many Boomers, I grew up with women's lib. I had seen how my mom, a spirited free thinker, nevertheless became a housewife whose freedom turned out to be doing everything at home and also working a full-time job. I was certain I was never going to get married, have kids, and get into that trap, and I thought I had the new freedom to help me along.

But after fending off my cute husband-to-be for a couple of years, he prevailed in his insistence on giving me everything I wanted, even those things I protested about. He convinced me

Marilyn Moohr
Living with elderly family

Sylvia is my 93-year-old mother. She and I have always been close, even though we lived thousands of miles apart ever since I graduated from college. My mother and father came from very traditional backgrounds and they and my older brothers were initially somewhat challenged by my decision to live in a group. However, over the years they all visited our community many times and fell in love with the people. My undeniable happiness and the way my son was thriving thoroughly won them over.

When my dad died eight years ago, after being married to my mom for 65 years, she was bereft. She still had a wide circle of friends, yet I knew she faced spending most of her days alone in her apartment. With the support of my community, I encouraged her to come live with us. It took quite a bit of reassurance before she said yes. It was a brave move for her. Many of us have invited our parents to live with us but over the years only a few have accepted.

We, as a group, had to make some adjustments to accommodate having Sylvia here. Drawing on our experience of having had a few elderly people live with us and knowing how devastating isolation and boredom can be for old folks, we gave her a room in the center of our busiest house, making contact easily available. We refurbished her bathroom to include safety rails and also added rails to the hallways she uses. As time has gone on and Sylvia has transitioned from cane to walker, we have had to alter access to the house she lives in so she can more comfortably move about. The old-age-friendly changes we have made and continue to make will be needed by us eventually (we hope to be 93 someday too), so it's been great to have a reason to begin them now.

Sylvia's life here at Morehouse is rich, filled with relating with people of all ages and interests. Each morning, she and I begin our day together having coffee in the group dining room with the "girls," catching up on all the gossip, planning the day's activities, and greeting other friends as they arrive or pass by. The excitement and social drama inherent in close group living sometimes reduces Sylvia to shaking her head, mystified, saying, "This place is not to be believed!"—but she loves being where things are happening. If there is a meeting, party, or event, Sylvia is usually the first one there. Some days she can be found at the hairdresser and out to lunch with other women from the community or attending the Greek Orthodox cathedral in Oakland. Her daily exercise includes doing laps around the large dining room and long hallways, laughing and chatting with people along the way. On a typical day at least a dozen community members stop by her room to say hi, show off a new outfit, bring her a treat, or to confide in her and ask her advice. We tease her about being a party animal. She often says with a laugh, "I'm spoiled—and I love it!"

For me, having my mother's life be so rich and full is an indescribable blessing. My brothers, who live on the East Coast, are grateful for the good time my mom is having living with us and they enjoy visiting us as often as they can. While I am my mother's primary caregiver, I am not burdened by that responsibility in the way that I would inevitably be if we didn't live in this group. Since we are on a 24-hour clock around here, there is always somebody up in case Sylvia needs anything. Within the community various people help with her physical care and her daily needs. It's enjoyable and rewarding for them and fun for Sylvia. With so many others actively involved in my mother's life, I am free to spend time with her in ways that pleasure us both. I get to cherish her with love, rather than obligation. My Morehouse "family" has helped me take the best care I could possibly imagine of my mother and provide her with an enviable, vibrant, and rewarding old age.

Ben Oliver, 35
When your parents divorce

The only way for me to talk about being raised by divorced parents is to start by saying, "Really? I didn't notice." I couldn't say how old I was when my parents divorced, because as a child, it was never anything I had to think about. Either I was very naïve and/or my parents did an outstanding job of making sure that I never knew what it could feel like being raised in a "broken" home. Not a day goes by that I don't appreciate my parents and the way they raised me; however, I know things would have gone a much different direction if it wasn't for Morehouse.

Growing up in Morehouse, whether you were a child of a "single parent," from a "broken home," or any other variation from the societal norm, everyone looked after you, loved you, and treated you like their own. I saw my parents when I wanted to see them and they saw me when they wanted to see me. My dad might make me breakfast or take me to school, while someone else might pick me up and make me dinner. My mom might help me with English class or help me clean my room while my "other" parents might help me with math or tuck me in at night. The reality is, I always had a community of people looking after me and making sure I was taken care of.

What is divorce? What our society has come to define it as is not the same as when you live in Morehouse. Compared to a societal norm, I don't consider my parents divorced. Fighting? Lawyers? Custody? Abuse? Distrust? Separation? These words do not reflect the childhood I experienced—it was quite the opposite.

I consider my upbringing as extremely blessed. I had the best of everything and never considered life would be better under a traditional roof. My parents were happy. Did they sleep in the same bed with one another? No, but what did I care? I was a kid. Did my parents ever fight or show signs of what a traditional divorce might look like? Surprisingly, no. To this day I have no memory of them ever fighting or showing dislike towards one another. As a child, I would selfishly only consider how something would affect me, and I have only positive memories. My family loved me and I was happy.

To me, Morehouse has always been more about the extended family than the traditional family. As an only child with divorced parents, I had brothers and sisters and dozens of parents. I never had to go without, choose one parent over the next, witness fighting parents, or feel like my happy home was being torn apart.

As an adult looking back on my life and thinking about my childhood, the truth is, I couldn't have asked for better. My parents are still in each other's life and love one another. I can come home and see both of them at the same time, all the while knowing there isn't animosity in the room. Yes, my parents are divorced, but they are happy and that is all I could ever ask for. While society would define my childhood as one from a "broken" home, thanks to Morehouse, mine was "fixed" and I never knew there was anything wrong.

Today, I'm married with a family of my own. My wife and I are more in love and happier than ever. We live in a traditional family environment and I get great gratification from the life I've provided for my wife and children. I learned so much living at Morehouse that I use today in my family, my group. Life is good.

Ben Oliver, son of Marilyn Moohr and Bill Oliver, grew up in Lafayette Morehouse.

Before I could say "I will never be June Cleaver," some friends introduced us to Morehouse.

that I could be married and be my own person.

Still, two-in-a-box was not going to be for us.

Communal living seemed to be my destiny. Even though my parents immigrated to the US, I was raised to eventually go live on a kibbutz, my mother's unfulfilled legacy.

I went off and lived on a kibbutz for a few years after college and found a lot of good ideas there—you were friends with your neighbors, worked for a common goal, there were parties and holidays at home with the extended family, and the kids lived in their own house with nannies 24/7. You could be with them as much or as little as you wanted to be.

But when all was said and done it was hard to shake the freedom and multi-cultured society available in America. I found the mores and values of kibbutz life to be just too restrictive. I came back to the US but the communal living paradigm stuck with me. In fact, my husband and I lived in an apartment alone together only for the first few months of our relationship. We quickly moved people in with us including my sister, Judy *(see article)*, who was also looking for that group feeling.

But he wanted kids; we were getting close to buying a house, having a mortgage, and growing our business. I was headed for being a vegetarian, Californian version of my mother...and without her tremendous patience!

Before I could say "I will never be June Cleaver," some friends introduced us to Morehouse, which was everything I had been looking for! It was structured in many ways like a kibbutz, including having a house where the kids are raised together. But Morehouse had much more, including an emphasis on pleasurable group living, an interesting and dynamic philosophy of the perfection of life, members of varying backgrounds, and the idea that fun is the goal, love is the way.

The best part was that shortly after we made the move, my sister came too—she and I fulfilled our childhood dream of being able to live together our whole lives while having our own families and careers.

Of course, like everyone, we hit relationship snags along the way. I remember first moving in, a fairly starry-eyed newlywed, mesmerized by all these fun people with whom I was now living, all of whom seemed to have so much more experience in ways to enjoy life. I wondered if I had made the right choice (in having picked my husband) and considered perhaps jumping ship and starting a relationship with someone else. It was Marilyn *(see article)* who talked to me, so many years ago. Seeing my husband through her eyes reminded me what I loved about him and why he was then and still is the right one for me.

In this milieu, knowing that I had the backing of my blood

More fun at Lafayette Morehouse.

relations and of the whole group, I decided to have kids—yes, two, much to my own surprise. I was fortunate enough that at the time there were many other kids being born and the whole "herd" of them lived in their own house, where they could enjoy each other's company, color on the walls, and do what kids like to do, with constant adult supervision by people who loved them just about as much as we did.

A couple of other times Jack and I got very close to splitting up. We even separated once for a few weeks. But the good part was that we still lived in the same community, just a building apart on common grounds, and were able to share our friends, spend time with our kids, and be together when we wanted to. Our friends were a close enough part of our lives that they could help us sort out our differences and eventually to reconcile. With the support of the group, my relationship with my husband has flourished, rather than diminished as it often does with couples left to their own devices.

I attribute the great relationship we have had with our sons as they grew up, and continue to have with them now as adults, to having raised them in this group. Throughout their childhood we spent exactly as much time together as we wanted to and my husband and I did not have to sacrifice our relationship or private time together. As far as I can tell, happy parents make for happy children.

Marilyn Moohr, 65
A Morehouse divorce

Bill and I met in Morehouse, fell in love, got married, and had a son. We had a lot of very happy times, but we had rough ones too. With the help of our friends we navigated the shoals pretty well whenever things got rocky between us, but after 10 years, we realized that being married to each other really didn't suit us. When people in our community realized that our relationship was in trouble, they came to our support. For example, one couple whom we loved and respected met with us for an hour or two every day for about six weeks to help facilitate our communication. Their goal was not to persuade us to either divorce or to stick together, but rather to make sure we made decisions about our future not out of anger but rather with love and compassion for ourselves and each other. We had seen other couples in our community divorce and continue to care for one another, and that really helped us to see that we could end our union yet still keep all the parts of our relationship that we enjoyed and valued. Bill and I both felt strongly that we wanted to remain friends, continue to live in the community, and raise our son in a loving environment. Together we looked to how to make this situation as good as possible for us and for our young son, Ben.

With this level of support we got from our friends, Bill and I were able to end the marriage without bitterness and acrimony, but rather with keeping the best parts of our friendship. There were adjustments we had to make and they weren't always easy or comfortable, but neither of us had to leave "home" to have things be the way we wanted. Our friends were able to go on being friends with us both, and didn't have to join my camp or Bill's camp. There were no camps to join! There was no custody battle, no attempt to make Ben choose between us. He was able to grow up with total access to both of us without ever having to doubt our love of him or each other. We talked with Ben about how we were sad about divorcing, but that the fundamental relationship between the three of us had been and would continue always to be love. Bill and I continued our partnership parenting together. Now, almost 30 years later, Bill and I both continue to live in the community with other partners that we are deeply committed to. Ben is grown and has a family of his own and Bill and I both get to freely enjoy our grandchildren together and separately. So although Bill and I divorced many years ago, our "family" flourishes. ❉

Judy St. John, Ilana Firestone, and Marilyn Moohr are long-time members and on the faculty of Lafayette Morehouse. For more information, visit www.lafayettemorehouse.com.

Second Family

By Arizona Nashoba

The dreaded day in every mother's life finally arrived for me. All my children were out on their own, scattered around the world. It quickly became apparent that living in the family home, quietly waiting for the kids to have time to come visit me, was not a lifestyle I could adjust to. So, I sold my house and started moving around the country trying to find a place that would feel like home. Inevitably, everywhere I went included four empty walls that were devoid of the laughter, conversations, and shared work that I had become accustomed to while raising my children. Working, cleaning, and cooking for myself alone was just not worth the effort. I was stuck and I was going crazy. Empty-nest syndrome left me feeling lonely and without a purpose.

Photo courtesy of Arizona Nashoba

Author's housemates and second family, "The Nashobites." From left to right: Mr. Tom, Shakaya, Steve, Gwyn (a regular primary child of Madge), Madge, Jayel, Eve, Diane, Arizona, Marione, and Piper.

Four years later, in total desperation, I took my search to the internet looking for unique community living experiences. I thought that I could find a neighborhood that shared occasional potluck meals and truly interacted with each other. What I found instead was the Federation of Egalitarian Communities. The more I read about these intentional communities, the more excited I became. Could I have found my answer?

After days of carefully reading about each community, I decided to write a request to visit Twin Oaks. That single decision has led to a series of life-changing events.

The three-week visitor period provided me with ample opportunity to see how the community functioned. I worked alongside community members, ate with them, socialized with them, and quickly fell in love with the community lifestyle. My decision was made. I was applying for membership. The 10-day wait for 100 people to decide the fate of my choice was one of the longest periods in my life, but finally the wait was over—I had been accepted for provisional membership.

The move and subsequent adjustments to life at Twin Oaks were not quite as easy as my visitor's period had led me to think they would be. The labor scene was difficult to balance. Most days ended with me feeling totally exhausted and just wanting to climb into my bed and escape into dreamland. The social scene was also not as I had anticipated after my visitor's period. Now that I was a member and not a visitor, it was up to me to make the effort to reach out to other community members. They had their lives and routines and I had to attempt to become a part of that.

The days passed by quickly and each day I wondered if I had made the right decision. Perhaps I had made the choice too quickly. I wondered if lack of former community experience meant that I was not going to adjust or be accepted. And still I plodded through each day, reaching out to people when I had the opportunity, fulfilling my responsibilities, and trying to grow.

Around my three-month mark, halfway through my provisional period, I was walking to the writing group that I co-facilitate. One of the topics I had chosen for the group to write on—"Home"—was leading me to serious contemplation about my life here at Twin Oaks. It certainly isn't a perfect utopia.

Personal and community dramas are on display for everyone

(continued on p. 77)

SECOND FAMILY

(continued from p. 40)

to see and comment on. Everyone has their own beliefs about how the community should operate, which many times cause lively discussions about community intentions, finances, and businesses. Members have different viewpoints on just about every part of life, from work ethics to what should be served at dinner. Living here has provided me with daily challenges regarding personal interactions.

I continued walking and contemplating the lifestyle I have here at Twin Oaks. Tonight I have the writers' group, tomorrow is art therapy, and Wednesday night is cards with my housemates. On other evenings I may go to a dance party or make a walking date with another Twin Oaker. Sunday mornings bring a pancake breakfast with my housemates, at which we share Steve's delicious pancakes heavily seasoned with lots of good conversation and laughter. My work scene has begun to balance out; I know every day what tasks I am going to perform. Somehow or other, I too have quietly fallen into the nice comfortable routine filled with the laughter, conversations, and shared work that I was looking for. I have a new family, friends, and a purpose for this second part of my life.

As I walked along the forest path enjoying the acceptance of my new lifestyle, I heard the voice of one of the community's children call out. "Arizona! Arizona, I love you." I took a deep breath and smiled. I was home. ❋

Before joining Twin Oaks, Arizona worked as a software engineer. The fall of WorldCom/MCI soured her perspective on the modern corporate world and led her to work completely for herself while researching the problems with businesses in today's world and our impacts on that world. Her findings left her searching for a better way of life.

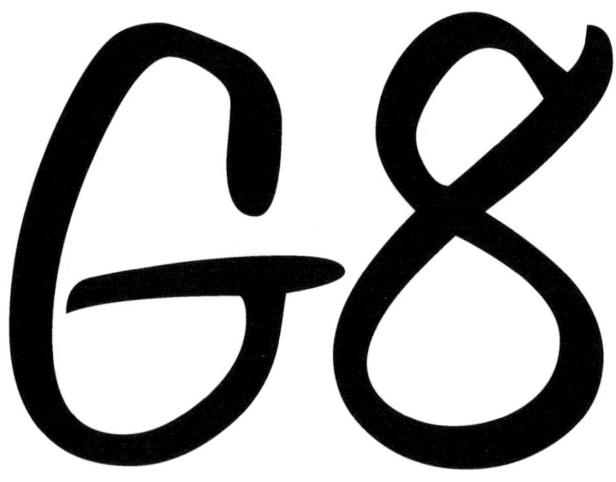

By Lawrence Siskind

Two and half years ago, P and M, a couple close to me, put out a call to a few friends. They asked if we would be willing to meet regularly, one night a week, to support them in their partnership by helping them communicate and process thoughts and feelings with which they had been struggling. Six of the invited responded, and we quickly decided to make the Thursday evening gatherings about all of us, rather than just the one couple who had inspired us to meet. The rest is history, at least for eight of us, plus D, who joined us earlier this year. We continue to meet every Thursday night, and our connections to each other, already deep and growing at the beginning of the experimental meetings, have grown to such a degree that we unabashedly use the f-word, "family," to describe what we are doing.

It certainly is difficult to use any other word since each of the nine of us would describe differently what we might be up to. Though we are all, to varying degrees, polyamorous and intimate with each other, we have no particular intention when we meet other than to honestly connect and to support each other in whatever ways to which we are moved. We gather in one of our living rooms—we live, three couples and three individuals, spread out over six houses, in compact Eugene, Oregon—and we usually begin with short check-ins during which each of us shares (holding our red, polished heart-shaped stone) what's been going on for us that day or that week. After we hear from each person, we decide who wants more time and attention, or occasionally, we decide to experiment with some process or activity that one of us wants to offer, a meditation or an energy work modality. For example, recently, we went around the circle telling stories from our lives that the others were not likely to know with the intention of revealing more about ourselves, and another week we expressed gratitude for each other in a completely darkened living room. At the end of two hours, or thereabouts, we indulge in desert (homemade cobbler and ice cream are our favorites), and often repair to the hot tub. Though several of us are lovers, in varying degrees of intimacy, sex is not a part of Thursday nights (except there was this one time...).

Although Thursday nights made us the family we are, we are much more than some "poly" folks who meet on Thursday nights to process their relationship baggage. We suffer the weight of many other varieties of baggage which can often make for some heavy lifting. We struggle with how honest we want to be with each other, how much we want to share, how much we want to receive, and whether expanding the size of the group to others in our lives will raise our collective energy or dilute our intimacy. Since we have no particular goals for our meetings, no personal growth agenda, we have to face whether we really want to consistently show up and be with each other, because each other is all we can agree to. Early on, we floated the idea of learning Nonviolent Communication (NVC) together, but a few of us were less than enthused. Nothing, other than being present with each other to the best of our abilities, has inspired us to get serious

> ***We are much more than some "poly" folks who meet to process their relationship baggage. We struggle with how honest we want to be with each other, how much we want to share and receive.***

about something, and I doubt anything will. We simply love each other as a family. But in this family, we strive to uncover our secrets, to expose our deep behavioral patterns in order to prevent the building up of petty resentments that undermines connection.

Although we socialize in many ways other days of the week, and with a wider circle of people, we have trouble doing much together as a group, other than meet on Thursday nights. Seven of us went to Burning Man together a couple years ago, and it was a strain to do much, other than the arduous set-up of our camp. Four of us, my partner S and I and another couple, L and M, spent some time together in New York during the holidays, and we had trouble getting along. For example, S and I like to walk a lot, even in the cold, but L and M wanted to jump on a bus, subway, or in a cab whenever possible. We like abstract expressionistic paintings, L and M, figurative works, so even museum visits led to separation rather than connection. Because we are a group of people with such varied interests and needs, it is particularly important and challenging to communicate clearly.

Courtesy of Lawrence Siskind

The G8...or is it G9...or 10?

I do think it's unlikely that we all will live together any time soon. We're far too eccentric and set in our ways, and we're a bit old to start building residential community; I'm the youngest at 45. I imagine us, in our old age, living more closely and sharing more resources. At the present moment, we remain very independent souls. We came together in an attempt to try to help a single couple stay together. (They're still together, despite ups and downs, both economic and emotional, and we're still working at it.) That said, I truly believe that our group is stronger than the individuals and couples it contains.

At the Network for a New Culture Summer Camp, at which we all met (at different camps over the years), we're an exciting item to other Campers. Questions are asked: What are you G8 folks up to? Can we join you? How can we create a group like yours? And isn't it all about sex? The answers to the questions, I believe, are actually quite simple: We connect in whatever way is true in the moment. To join us, you would have to fall in love with each of us, then we would demand (actually we're too lazy to demand, but we would be unable to resist) your presence. You can create a group like ours by assembling those individuals who you think love you, and seeing who keeps showing up. And no, it isn't much about sex... but we can still dream. ❁

Lawrence Siskind, despite having lived his entire adult life on the West Coast, considers himself a New Yorker in exile. He currently lives in Eugene, Oregon, where there is more opportunity for loving connection than there is for teaching high school English. He and his partner are involved in a "committed," "open," "codependent" "experiment" that they call a "relationship." They reside at the Du•má community, where he loves to empty the dish rack and hone his backgammon skills. He spends much of his time and energy processing and funning with the G8, and participating in the planning of the Network for a New Culture Summer Camp.

Smoker and Mirrors?

"Well, I could probably see it the way you do if I were an a••hole!" P remarked to me. I had been curious as to why P was so much more attached, felt so much more betrayed, by his partner M's admission that she'd been secretly smoking cigarettes away from home for months. P read in my objective-sounding curiosity a lack of concern for his partner M's health, and he was angry because I wasn't more understanding about his disappointment in the dishonesty of her behavior. My reaction to getting called "an a••hole," when my intention had been to try to help shed light on the emotions we all were feeling about M's coming clean, was to shut down emotionally. When the discussion about P's feelings continued on with others in a pretty heated manner for our group of lovey-dovey "family," I requested that we simply stop trying to talk further at this time about the issues. For me, the heated emotions were too painful to witness. I was that upset, and I am the one of us who almost always wants to push and push in the group, to get us to share more deeply. The intensity of the emotions showed us all how difficult it can be, among partners, lovers, and deep friends, to even try to disentangle loving concern from emotional codependency. Do we care so much about our loved ones' behaviors because we are concerned for them, or because we believe their behaviors are a part of ours? If M risks her health by smoking and fails to be honest about it, is my health at risk? If I were her partner, would I be able to remain civil while others wondered why I was so upset? These complex issues of intimacy are the kind with which our group is dealing on Thursday nights, and beyond.

—Lawrence Siskind

Exploring Family

By Chris Roth

Questions from the Hopi

"Where's your family?" This was the most common question I was asked as a white person living and working on a pueblo reservation in northern Arizona, 2,250 miles from the New York suburb where I'd grown up. The Hopi have occupied their traditional villages for nearly a millennium, with familial and inter-familial ties spanning generations. Each Hopi family is known and connected in some way to every other Hopi family; each clan has a memory going back as far as memory will reach, explaining each individual's place in the intricately woven fabric of the family, clan, village, and tribe. The question might as well have been "Where is your community?," because, for Hopis, family, extended family, and community are so intertwined as to be virtually inseparable.

My nuclear family of birth—meaning my father, mother, and brother—lived back in New York at the time, although my brother spent much of the year at college in Ohio (where my parents were to move years later, although by that time my brother was back in our home town, later to move into the city). My only surviving grandparent lived in upstate New York. My uncles, aunts, and cousins lived in various locations up and down the East Coast and Midwest (later to extend to the West Coast). Except for those still living with their parents, I believe no two siblings within this family (at least what I knew of it) lived in the same state, let alone the same town.

I actually experienced more rootedness and family in my life than many of my peers did. I had grown up in the same home town until I left for college. Our family spent lots of time together as a unit, including on every school vacation. My parents usually worked within a half-mile of our house (my father even bicycled home daily for lunch, weather permitting), and were present every day for their two children. My maternal grandmother lived in the same town until my teenage years; she was our most frequent babysitter and a major presence in all of our lives. We stayed in touch with immediate relatives (including far-flung ones) and were part of a relatively close-knit church community as well. Although some of my friends left my home town part way through my childhood (their parents' careers taking them elsewhere), others stayed until high school graduation (almost all then dispersed). Unlike many of my peers' parents, mine stayed married (for 50 years as of 2009, and counting).

And yet here I was, more than 2000 miles from where I'd grown up—something that would have been unthinkable to

any Hopi—seeking a new way of life and new "community" for myself—which would have been unnecessary for any Hopi. For a person from my background, however, the *un*usual thing would have been to stay with my family, even if I could find more than one or two of them in a single location. Coming from a dominant culture based not on inherited traditions and principles of ecological and social sustainability, but instead on a process of nearly constant change, progress, and reinvention, I was naturally seeking to figure out how to reinvent my own life as made best sense to me—how to choose among the seemingly endless choices of how to be. (In my case, "progress" meant moving back closer to the earth rather than into ever-more-advanced technological civilization.)

That this path led me there might have been somewhat comical and counterintuitive to the Hopi, as many of them had learned to aspire to elements of the life I'd left behind. However, despite encroaching modernization and western culture, family and community still held central places in their lives, and were not fading away any time soon. As examples of people who have found ways to live together and "stay together" in place, the Hopis have few rivals.

I was not looking for a Hopi bride, or any bride. A "relationship" would be a distraction. My "family" was everyone.

"Do you think you might meet some nice Hopi girl?," I was also asked occasionally. (I was not only the sole white person in my workplace, but one of the few male employees there, and an eligible bacheler in my early 20s.) Inevitably, I was embarrassed and didn't answer. I was not looking for a Hopi bride, or any bride (although, in retrospect, I sometimes have to ask myself, *"What was I thinking?,"* before I remember). I wanted to find harmony within myself, with the earth, and with people who knew how to live on the earth. A "relationship" would be a distraction. My "family" was everyone.

But why wasn't I married?

On Marriage and John Keats

I've never been married. I've never even really been close to it, nor to starting a family. In my approach to and history of romantic relationships, I seem to have much more in common with Romantic poet John Keats (moviegoers, see "Bright Star") than with Casanova or others who, for better or worse, seem to have had no problem living in the moment sexually with whoever was in front of them.

However, I'm also different from Keats: I failed to die of tuberculosis at the age of 25, and therefore have had the opportunity to be inspired by several muses (not just one) over my lifetime, virtually all of them (like Keats') solely platonic friendships, never "consummated" in the conventional sense. As a result of my greater comfort with platonic rather than sexual relationships, and the generally deeper, more long-lasting connections I've felt in friendship in general, uncomplicated by sex, I have never been part of a biological family except my family of birth—and may never be.

To be fair, Keats was planning to marry Fanny Brawne when he was inconveniently written out of life's script—and they might well have started a family (albeit probably a tubercular one). Furthermore, I've deliberately steered my romantic impulses away from the kind of sexual tension that made Keats' unconsummated relationship so cinema-worthy—and, after a brief, frustrating, imagined career as a tormented writer, I also stopped attempting to write poetry that is "half in love with easeful Death." I know through experience that I am fully capable of feeling tortured by longing for a person who embodies life's beauty and mystery for me (and simultaneously thwarted by—well, I'm not sure what), but I've generally tried to redirect my energies in ways that eluded or were simply not available to Keats—who also left no offspring, although he left some terrific poetry.

In my closest brush with a Keatsian relationship, near the end of high school, I finally overcame my shyness enough to establish a real friendship with the person in question (or allow it to be established by not running the other way). (The previous time I'd fallen hopelessly in love, in first grade, had caused me to become mute in the presence of the object of my devotion for the next eight years, so our imagined engagement and wedding never happened.) But this time, for one poetry-filled summer, and for much of the next year, I felt that someone else could perhaps supply everything that was missing from my life, a feeling that had some basis in my own experience.

But although the "myth of romantic love" (as a substitute for everything else) dies hard, it almost inevitably dies, and it did for me. My soulmate ended up in and out of mental institutions, and I myself barely escaped what I realize in retrospect was a loony bin itself, my college, after what I self-diagnosed as a very quiet mental breakdown. Although I was better at recognizing my mental patterns in the "illnesses" section of a psychology textbook than I was at identifying my actual feelings, I see now that underneath it all, I was feeling depressed, adrift, and unconnected to others or to my life source. This was not the stuff of which happily-ever-after dreams—nor families—are made.

Nor, in truth, is tuberculosis. Keats was obviously not one to emulate too closely.

...good times, hard times, dreams, disappointments, "tempests in teapots," transformative moments, and everything in between...

Missing: Family

I wanted a way back into the feeling of connection I'd had as a child. Although I'd grown up in a tight nuclear family, and with some sense of extended family (both related and unrelated to me biologically), I seemed to have grown apart from them through my process of education. Seen from one perspective, my high school had taken in a human being and spit out an over-intellectualized super-student with a gnawing feeling of emptiness and almost no time (or even skills) to cultivate relationships with others. (High school also taught me to edit, so depending on your opinion of this magazine it may not have been a total disaster.) I'd grown apart from most of my peers, who tended to be into all the teenage things that I was not. Henry David Thoreau spoke my mind more than anyone I knew personally or witnessed in popular culture. While others drove, drank, and dated and dumped one another, I got my fulfillment through long-distance running, bicycling, taking a very full course load, and holing myself up with books and a typewriter. This seemed to work at least tolerably well as long as I was surrounded by family and the larger community in which I'd grown up (even if I was ignoring them, preoccupied with schoolwork and running).

But gaining and then "losing" a soulmate, being separated for the first time from my family and home town, and having

my self-story crumble midway through college, left me seeking the connection to others that was now so obviously missing. This process helped launch my involvement in community (described in more detail in "How Ecology Led Me to Community," issue #143—I won't repeat the entire story here).

Nuclear family did not seem like the answer to me, and was not what I aspired to. For better or worse, owing to reasons I understand and reasons I don't (including my previous experiences, my sense of broader connection, my upbringing by parents who modeled concern for others over self-interest, and my particular mix of personal strengths and insecurities), my interpersonal energy usually goes towards a number of people—both close and casual friends—rather than just one, and toward the non-human world too, not strictly the human.

Family in Community

I've lived in community for most of my adult life—when not in a formal intentional community, then on a farm or at an educational center in which people live and work together. My sense of family has broadened to encompass many hundreds of people by now—people with whom I've lived and worked closely, shared meals, good times, hard times, honest conversations, music-making, gardening, dreams, disappointments, joys, traumatic events, humor, "tempests in teapots," transformative moments, and everything in between. I can't imagine not having these things in my life, nor people to share them with.

That sense of extended family endures even with people who are no longer my community-mates. In fact, most people who feel like family to me fit into that category now, owing to high rates of residential, membership, and staff turnover in the places I've resided. In my most recent community, I've stayed about twice as long (a dozen years) as anyone else who lives here now, and the second-longest of anyone who's ever lived here. After all that time, and all the change that's occurred during it, I'm recognizing that my need for family is still just as strong as it was early in my life, and that I want to explore some other ways of meeting it. By the time you read this, I will have started that exploration.

One advantage of finding "family" in community is the ability to be part of many families. I've spent more than a decade in a usually child-friendly community in which I've been able to enjoy the presence of children, be one of many adults in their

lives, provide whatever guidance, modeling, cultural enrichment, or at least child-friendly verbal banter I feel capable of, play catch, read books, and make sure they don't fall off stone walls.

At the same time, none of these children were mine, and all of them (except the most recent arrivals) have left. A disadvantage of finding extended family in a high-turnover community is that the people in your life can be here one day, gone the next—gone forever, because busy lives mean you may not stay in touch. That doesn't happen with biological family—even with physical separation, that kind of family seems (at least to me) as if it's for life. I expect to stay in touch with some of my ex-community-mates for life as well, but probably not with many of the children (for whom we were once surrogate aunts and uncles), especially if they were very young when in community. I know that blood ties would add a different dimension to our ongoing commitments and connection.

I wonder: Who *is* family for each of us?

Leaving

I am walking away from a place I love—from people, animals, land, and weather I love. I am leaving home. The first time this happened was the most difficult moment of my life. I was leaving behind family to join people unknown to me (who, that first time, never ended up seeming like family). The second time was easier. Eventually I came to see that even when I stay in one place—as I have for more than a decade—people, animals, weather, landscapes change. My adopted, extended family changes, leaves, lives in flux—sometimes almost as much as if I myself were the one who'd left and arrived somewhere new.

When I move on, I am no longer just leaving family—I am going towards family. I am reuniting with family from whom I've been separated by distance, and I am discovering new family. I am sorry to leave behind all the non-human family, especially plants and birds, who, in many ways, have been more steady companions than the ever-changing human population here. They are as big a part of my ongoing daily experience, and in some ways as connected to my heart and my being, as all but the closest human friends. But I know that wherever I go, I will find their relatives. And while my sense of tribe is quite different from that of the Hopis, less rooted in bloodline and tradition, I do experience it, and it is not limited geographically. My contribution to it seems not necessarily to be as one who's adding to the gene pool or helping the population rise—but I do feel I have a role to play.

What motivated John Keats moves me as well: No matter how many well-reasoned lists I might make balancing pros and cons of various life choices, ultimately it is my heart that draws anywhere. It is a sense of connection and strange familiarity, even when this family I've discovered is new to me. It is the beauty and mystery of life reasserting themselves, pushing aside distractions and fears. When I am in touch with these truths, separation from "family" no longer provokes anxiety, and the world becomes again a place of wonder, existing in the moment, ever-new yet more familiar than my own experience of time would seem to account for. Whether involving individuals, groups, or places, these feelings of family never fail to remind me of the value of gratitude and the cyclical, ancient-feeling newness of every day...as if I had discovered an unknown, long-lost sister; a bunch of siblings, elders, nieces, and nephews that inadvertently got erased from my family tree; a piece of ground I know from a dream; a sacred spot on the earth. Few statements are indisputable, but I think this one may be: we are all more related than we can comprehend. ❁

Chris Roth edits Communities *and spends much more of his time in practical action (especially growing organic food and combing through articles for typos) than the above reveries might indicate.*

REVIEWS BY CHRIS ROTH

Together and Apart
A Memoir of the Religious Life

By Ellen Stephen, OSH

Morehouse Publishing, Harrisburg, New York, 2008
Paperback, 148 pages

If you're a secular communitarian, you may assume that a book about living in a convent will have little or nothing to do with you. *Together and Apart* will almost certainly cause you to uncloister your thought habits in this area.

Ellen Stephen writes with more wisdom, insight, and candor about residential intentional community than most authors I've read. This is partly because she herself has spent more than four decades immersed in it; she is also a gifted writer and seasoned observer of herself and of human nature. While I have never been a member of a religious community (monastery, convent, ashram, etc.), many of her stories about her life in the Order of Saint Helena (in several different convents) resonated with what I've experienced and witnessed in secular communities. In her memoir, the life of a monastic and the life of a secular communitarian—including the issues that confront each—do not emerge appearing so different after all. In fact, they are in some respects almost identical.

While a popular conception is that religious communities tend to be hierarchical and dogmatic—and therefore perhaps different from more egalitarian secular communities—these do not appear to be the dominant themes in Ellen's life in an Episcopalian community. In Ellen's group (once nominally answerable to a monastery, but now independent of any male authority), sisters rotate through roles, share power, and actively question both theology and day-to-day guidelines they set for themselves. She describes her order's "bad old days" when she first took her vows, during which fear and subservience to the superior ruled too often, and its subsequent evolution over the decades into a far more egalitarian, mutually supportive, mutually empowering paradigm emphasizing connection. "A call to the religious life is first and foremost an invitation to be *together*," she writes. "There is always a consciousness of the importance of human relationship, of love."

The sisters are committed not only to each other but to a path that respects the earth. Although Ellen's community is not explicitly ecological in its focus, its commitment to "poverty" (understood as simplicity and sharing) and social justice mean that it may actually be more ecological and sustainable in its practices than the majority of secular communities. The sisters wear mostly used clothing, not only because they need to operate within a very low budget but because "using what others no longer need seems like a kind of recycling, and recycling in all its forms is an important aspect of poverty today, as well as a witness against consumerism and waste." The amenities in their daily lives are simple and shared, as the sisters seek alternatives to the excess, exploitation, and economic disparity that they see in a society of individualistic materialism and ownership.

This approach is not always easy. "Sharing a kitchen or any other space with other people," she remarks wryly, "can be a real challenge to serenity and sisterly or brotherly love." In fact, even deciding on décor in a convent can pose difficulties, now that the traditionally austere guidelines have loosened up a bit: "'Homey' to one sister may mean frilly white curtains and flowered throw pillows. That doesn't signify home to me."

But perhaps the biggest challenges come from simply learning to live together as individuals with differing personalities, priorities, needs, and personal issues. Ellen repeatedly disabuses readers of any rose-colored glasses through which they may wish to look at community living, while also explaining why she has found the challenges worth confronting. Her descriptions and perspectives are, if anything, on the "dark" side, but they are meant to counteract false images. If she doesn't speak for you in these passages, she likely speaks for someone with whom you have lived:

"[Sometimes] the hardest thing for me in community is respecting another sister who does not seem to me to be choosing the 'road less traveled,'" she writes. "It has taken slow-growing knowledge and acceptance of my own failings to begin to see beyond the faults of my sisters to the true self within that is to be accepted and loved." At another point, she observes pithily, "We human beings are complex creatures, and complexity is hard to live with."

The solution, she has found, is not to bottle up the difficulties, but instead to say what needs to be said to community mates, if it truly needs to be said (or to process it internally, if reflection shows that to be the best course). "Repressed feelings are like toothpaste in a tube—under enough stress a capped tube will crack open and the paste will ooze out at an inappropriate point. On the other hand, freely choosing to bear a

(continued on p. 78)

REVIEWS

(continued from p. 80)

difficult thing may be a gift of love."

She gives her perspective on the supposed "holiness" of religious communities with characteristic candor: "Someone once said of the cloister that it does not automatically ensure holiness: a wall may enclose a lovely secret garden, or a stinking rubbish heap." Elsewhere, she writes, "When our order was in the early stages of self-study and renewal, our superior said in jest that she was going to write a book about the life called *The Grunge and the Glory*. Living a life that is both culturally apart and intensely together is exacting. There is a lot of grunge."

This book contains many more gems: thoughtful observations on the balance of work, relationships, and one's own inner life in community (and how different individuals' approach to that balance can itself create tensions); the importance of having well-designed, protracted processes for incorporating new members, as well as graceful, deliberate ways to deal with a member's separation or exit from the community; reflections on the challenges faced by founders and elders witnessing change within their own communities; and some simple, sage one-liners: "Some of the stress that arises in community life comes from insecurity trying to clothe itself as power." "Even the most desired outcome is much better chosen than imposed."

While describing "fair and efficient leadership, whether designated or undesignated" as the "'oil' that keeps the 'machinery' of relationships and daily life moving along smoothly," Ellen sees the ideal form of that leadership as "almost invisible"—not ostentatious or concentrated, but flowing through different people in different circumstances. Ellen's houses function with no one sister in charge, but with delegated responsibilities, and with whole-group decisions made in weekly house meetings, by consensus when possible. These meetings start with a few moments of silence, then the setting of an intention, then personal "check-ins." (Does this sound familiar to anyone in community?)

A few final notes: if you don't resonate well with the word "God" as a descriptor of ultimate reality and the source of one's guidance, you may want to substitute "Gaia," "the Universe," "our essential being," or some other term throughout this book. If you are averse to the idea that we are part of something larger than ourselves—"family members" with responsibilities as well as opportunities—or believe that everything is meaningless, disordered chaos, or think that monastics and "seekers" of every kind take things *way* too seriously, you may not like this book (or, on the other hand, you might take perverse pleasure in it). Otherwise, I can almost guarantee that this very personal story of hearing and answering the call to community living has much to teach even the most secular communitarian.

Communities Editorial Policy

Communities is a forum for exploring intentional communities, cooperative living, and ways our readers can bring a sense of community into their daily lives. Contributors include people who live or have lived in community, and anyone with insights relevant to cooperative living or shared projects.

Through fact, fiction, and opinion, we offer fresh ideas about how to live and work cooperatively, how to solve problems peacefully, and how individual lives can be enhanced by living purposefully with others. We seek contributions that profile community living and why people choose it, descriptions of what's difficult and what works well, news about existing and forming communities, or articles that illuminate community experiences—past and present—offering insights into mainstream cultural issues. We also seek articles about cooperative ventures of all sorts—in workplaces, in neighborhoods, among people sharing common interests—and about "creating community where you are."

We do not intend to promote one kind of group over another, and take no official position on a community's economic structure, political agenda, spiritual beliefs, environmental issues, or decision-making style. As long as submitted articles are related thematically to community living and/or cooperation, we will consider them for publication. However, we do not publish articles that 1) advocate violent practices, or 2) advocate that a community interfere with its members' right to leave.

Our aim is to be as balanced in our reporting as possible, and whenever we print an article critical of a particular community, we invite that community to respond with its own perspective.

Submissions Policy

To submit an article, please first request Writers' Guidelines: Communities, RR 1 Box 156, Rutledge MO 63563-9720; 660-883-5545; editor@ic.org. To obtain Photo Guidelines, email: layout@ic.org. Both are also available online at communities.ic.org.

Advertising Policy

We accept paid advertising in Communities because our mission is to provide our readers with helpful and inspiring information—and because advertising revenues help pay the bills.

We handpick our advertisers, selecting only those whose products and services we believe will be helpful to our readers. That said, we are not in a position to verify the accuracy or fairness of statements made in advertisements—unless they are FIC ads—nor in REACH listings, and publication of ads should not be considered an FIC endorsement.

If you experience a problem with an advertisement or listing, we invite you to call this to our attention and we'll look into it. Our first priority in such instances is to make a good-faith attempt to resolve any differences by working directly with the advertiser/lister and complainant. If, as someone raising a concern, you are not willing to attempt this, we cannot promise that any action will be taken.

Tanya Carwyn, Advertising Manager, 7 Hut Terrace, Black Mountain NC 28711; 828-669-0997; ads@ic.org.

What is an "Intentional Community"?

An "intentional community" is a group of people who have chosen to live or work together in pursuit of a common ideal or vision. Most, though not all, share land or housing. Intentional communities come in all shapes and sizes, and display amazing diversity in their common values, which may be social, economic, spiritual, political, and/or ecological. Some are rural; some urban. Some live all in a single residence; some in separate households. Some raise children; some don't. Some are secular, some are spiritually based; others are both. For all their variety, though, the communities featured in our magazine hold a common commitment to living cooperatively, to solving problems nonviolently, and to sharing their experiences with others.

PUBLISHER'S NOTE BY LAIRD SCHAUB

Being Vigilant about Vigilante Dynamics

One of the most telling aspects of groups is how they handle controversy. When you're driving down the road and suddenly hit a pothole, is your dominant response compassion, despair, or assignment of fault?

While cooperative groups never start out intending to struggle, all eventually do. To be sure, the frequency and severity of encounters with road hazards can vary widely: some just get into the soft mud long enough to spray the fenders, requiring only a quick trip to the car wash to get cleaned up; others come to a full stop buried past the axles, and it takes a tow truck to get back on the road. Nonetheless, *all* groups stray off course now and then.

When bad things happen, does your group tend to: 1) blame the driver; 2) blame the road; or 3) see if anyone is hurt, dust yourselves off, and get the car back into service?

Before exploring these options, I want to hit the pause button long enough to explain my motivation for this essay. The theme for this issue of Communities is Mental Health, and I am writing to describe a disturbing tendency that I want to place into the context of everyday wear and tear on group function. As a process professional I've seen groups misuse "mental health" as a pejorative label when they're unhappy with the behavior of a challenging member. While this doesn't happen often (thank goodness), it's common enough to warrant a description of how it can surface as part of the blame-the-driver syndrome.

OK, now let's walk through the choices, paying particular attention to Door #1.

Blame the Driver

If somebody was perceived to be behind the wheel when you hit the bump (I say it that way because there are plenty of accidents where it doesn't appear that *anyone* was in the front seat), it's relatively common for there to surface a knee-jerk upset with the driver, expecting them to take the full hit for what happened to the car. Could the driver have gone more slowly? Sure. Yet that doesn't necessarily mean they were being reckless (or that they wouldn't have been chided for proceeding too cautiously if there *hadn't* been an accident).

The interesting case is when there's clear evidence of imprudent driving (going too fast, not keeping one's eyes on the road, having a couple drinks before firing up the old engine) and the person(s) in charge undoubtedly does have some degree of responsibility for what occurred. If the group is habituated to looking for a fall guy, then the driver is the obvious candidate.

The key here is understanding that having *some* culpability is not the same as having *sole* responsibility. When a member is difficult, or has some patterned behaviors that the group struggles with, it's easy to slide into groupthink that labels that person

PUBLISHER'S NOTE BY LAIRD SCHAUB

as *the* problem. There are a lot of ways to get there. Maybe the person comes from a different class background; maybe they have an unusual style of communicating or unfamiliar ways of processing information; maybe they have a strong accent; perhaps they have an abrasive or confrontational personality. Maybe they suffer from ADD (attention deficit disorder) and rely on emotional intensity as a coping mechanism; perhaps they have Tourette Syndrome and express themselves using unprovoked swearing; possibly they have Asperger Syndrome and don't recognize normal social cues. Once multiple people start labeling the "odd" person as "other," it's only a few easy steps to seeing them as "the problem."

While it may be true that a person has difficult behaviors, that doesn't necessarily mean they don't have valuable viewpoints or can't be worked with constructively. There is, to be sure, delicacy around how much diversity a group can handle and whether the group has the resources and resilience to make it work with every member. (Regardless of how good the value alignment is, not all combinations of people can effectively communicate with one another or successfully manifest healthy internal dynamics. Some configurations are just not meant to be.) It has been my experience though, that rather than addressing the difficult dynamics directly, some groups have a nasty tendency to vilify and ostracize the odd person, isolating them in the group. The odd person gets pigeonholed as a troublemaker, the group stops seriously considering that person's input, and the group gets lazy about looking at the ways *it* has inadvertently contributed to creating and maintaining the dysfunctional dynamic. It can get ugly.

> ***While there's no doubt that the mental health of members impacts community living, it can be chilling to observe groups engaging in pack behavior to stigmatize a challenging member.***

One of the more insidious ways this plays out is when groups label the odd person as having a mental health problem, and indulge in amateur diagnosis to make an assessment that is not recognized by the individual or corroborated by professional observation. Mental health is a serious and not well-defined field. While there's no doubt that the mental health of members impacts community living—sometimes profoundly—it can be chilling to observe groups engaging in pack behavior to stigmatize a challenging member, all the while washing their hands of responsibility for such labeling.

Among other things, the tendency to blame the driver leads to *all* members being reluctant to drive (take responsibility) and cautious about disclosing fender benders. (After witnessing how the odd person has gotten crucified, who wants that to happen to *them*?) Worse, this response reinforces the habit to both assign blame and to make sure that it falls on others. It leads to a culture of finger pointing instead of problem solving, and debilitates the group's energy.

Blame the Road

Why wasn't that pothole fixed? Why don't "they" maintain the road better? Why aren't the brakes on cars more responsive? Why are we so unlucky? This is essentially a disempowered response. The group is at the mercy of outside forces over which it has no control. Buffeted around by the winds of Fate, you just try to hang in there and escape the attention of capricious gods. Life is dangerous and it's best to do what you can to minimize risk and stay below the radar. Yuck!

Shit Happens

In this response, the focus first is on whether anyone was hurt, and then shifts to fixing the problem. This includes making any necessary repairs to the vehicle and it may also call for a review of what the driver could have done differently, and what might be done to repair the pothole.

This doesn't pretend that people aren't damaged or upset, yet it prioritizes problem solving over punishment.

It's crucial, in my view, that the upset be attended to first. Pretending that upset doesn't exist never works, yet groups are often reluctant to go there because of fears that the strong energy associated with distress will get out of control and cause even greater damage to relationships than the accident did. The key here is welcoming the expression of the feelings (hurt, anger, fear, disappointment) while objecting to blaming and attacking.

Once you get the air cleared, you're well poised to get practical about auto repairs, driver training, and highway maintenance. The thing you *don't* want to do is sit around the bar with your upset friends and rail about bad drivers. The world already has plenty of road rage; what we need is more road grace (and fewer vigilantes). ❧

Laird Schaub is Executive Secretary of the Fellowship for Intentional Community (FIC), publisher of this magazine, and cofounder of Sandhill Farm, an FEC community in Missouri, where he lives. He is also a facilitation trainer and process consultant, and he authors a blog that can be read at communityandconsensus.blogspot.com.

NOTE FROM THE EDITOR BY CHRIS ROTH

Crazy About Community

The articles in this issue are among the most candid and personal we've ever published. Rich with lessons learned (sometimes painfully) through experience, and with insights about healing and wholeness, they say almost everything this editor's note could have said, and much more. They also got me thinking about my own relationship to the theme. At the risk of getting myself committed (or at least judged), here's some of what I thought about:

I used to take mental health for granted, both in myself and in those around me. Mental illness was what the crazy mother of those two girls at church had—there was something "off" about her. The rest of us were normal.

The veil gradually fell away as I noticed that more adults didn't exactly fit the model of mental wellness. How else to explain the paranoia and incessant negativity of one of my father's employers or, later, the suicide of a family friend? Certainly by the time one of my high school classmates took his own life, I'd started to realize that all was not well in Normalville.

Love is sometimes described as a form of insanity. Certainly, my most serious adolescent encounter with it brought on feelings and insights that made much of my previous "status quo" and routines seem comparatively meaningless, emotionally and spiritually. And when the object of my head-over-heelness encountered her own mental health challenges (eventually landing in a psychiatric ward, then becoming a permanent part of the mental health system), I had to face the fact that the way I, too, saw the world was "different," and the people I related most closely to were different, from what was deemed normal in our society. Self-styled seekers of what was "real" and "true" in ourselves and on the earth, we felt maladapted to a frenetic consumer culture (and its associated work world) that provided many superficial distractions but no deep answers. I came to see us as islands of sanity in a world gone mad, but I also knew that revealing one's thought-dreams in the wrong circumstance could easily get one classified as "mad" oneself, and in need of treatment.

I did go through a period of feeling as if something major must be wrong with me mentally (beyond the personality challenges that we all encounter in ourselves). I've also had a few brief recurrences of feeling "crazy" (or at least genuinely depressed/anxious), almost always at moments of significant change in my life. At those times, not only has modern civilization seemed off-kilter (not a stretch, to anyone paying attention), but I myself have felt equally off-kilter. Looking at the circumstances that have precipitated this feeling can help me understand some of the vital ingredients of mental health.

My most profound sense of emotional/psychological dis-ease has come when I've uprooted myself from a place with which I'm very familiar, and put myself in a place that has not yet become "home." Even when many other ingredients for wellness are present, this loss of an intimate connection to a piece of land or bioregion has deeply unsettled me. And because close connection to the land is not built into the dominant society, I have needed to discover myself how best to achieve that in each new place. So I've learned to ask now: "Am I actually crazy, or has my larger ecological self, my self in relation to the land, just not established itself here yet?"

Other elements playing major roles in generating distress: separation from family; separation from friends; disruption or shift in my work life; loss of roles or projects that were meaningful to me; loss of a community or a sense of community. Even in community, an absence of loving relationships among those around me can profoundly impact my own sense of well-being.

By contrast, these ingredients always seem to boost mental health: genuine affection among community mates; the presence of children; elders; music-making; meaningful group work; people committed to inner and outer exploration and communication; a mission of service to the larger world; creative homegrown culture; abundant opportunities to be outdoors; and the sharing of food grown and prepared consciously.

But being in a favorable environment is not enough; wellness also requires our own initiative. Only I can tap into my own creativity, ability to relate to others and the earth, and desire for community and connection. If life is not a spectator sport, mental health isn't either. Nor is it a solo sport: mutual support, encouragement, and recommended-ingredient-sharing are essential.

If life is not a spectator sport, mental health isn't either. Nor is it a solo sport: mutual support and recommended-ingredient-sharing are essential.

Intentional community, however, is not a one-size-fits-all recipe for happiness and sanity. I've seen various mental health issues play themselves out, without full resolution, in community, just as they do in the wider world. Sometimes, instead of soothing the distresses of isolation and cultural alienation, community can seem to make life even crazier. Obsession, fear, paranoia, and/or hostility (whether inner- or outer-directed) can take root and spread, and members may forget to balance the wisdom they can gain only on their own with the wisdom to be found in the group.

At these times, rather than being an obvious model of something saner than a "world gone mad," community instead becomes a powerful learning laboratory and mirror that, through adversity, may lead us to both understand that ill-at-ease world and get clues as to how it could become better.

Likewise, we hope this issue provides both models that inspire and lessons that teach. Please enjoy! ❧

Chris Roth (editor@ic.org) lives at Dancing Rabbit Ecovillage, Rutledge, Missouri.

Photos by Chris Roth

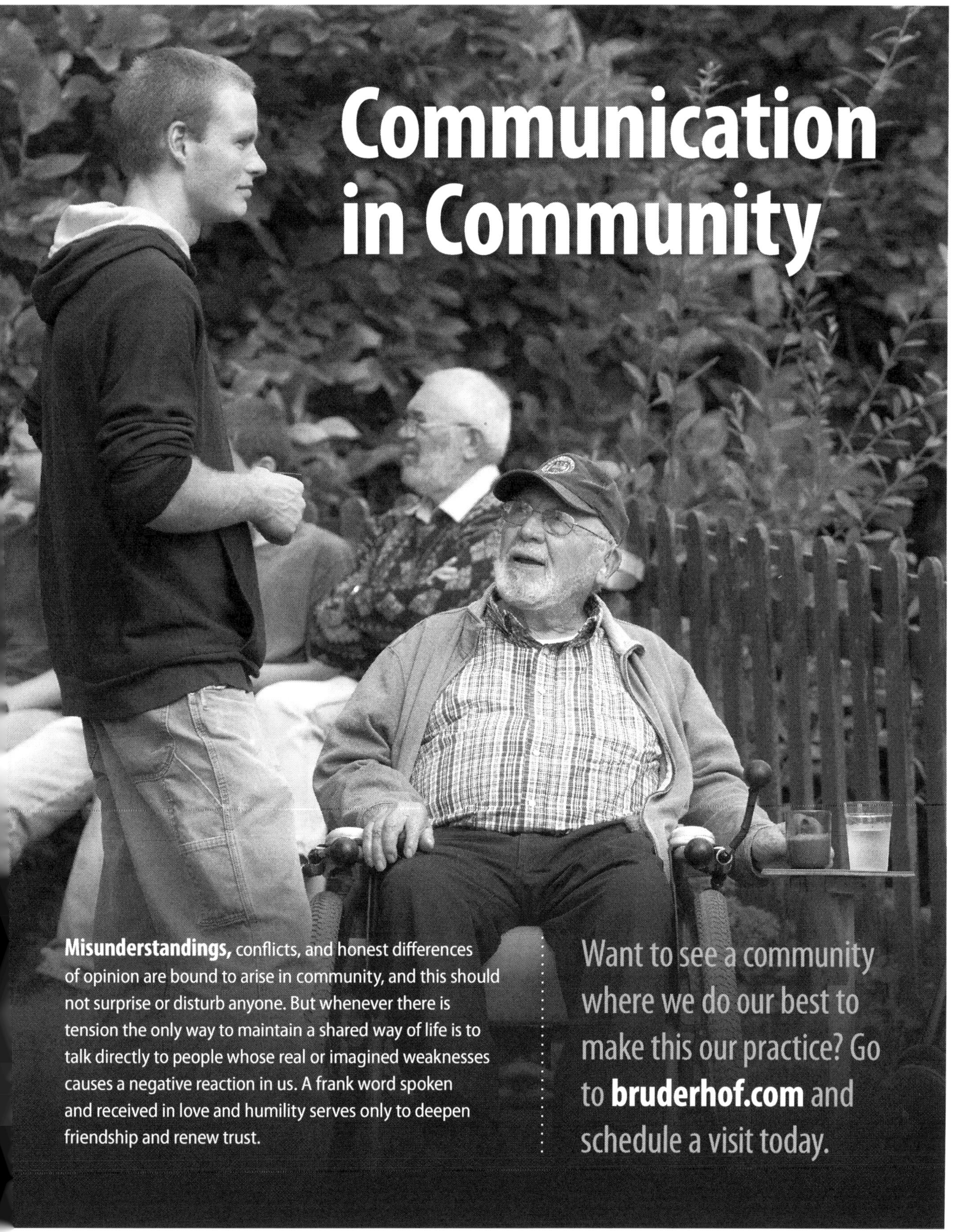
Communication in Community
Misunderstandings, conflicts, and honest differences of opinion are bound to arise in community, and this should not surprise or disturb anyone. But whenever there is tension the only way to maintain a shared way of life is to talk directly to people whose real or imagined weaknesses causes a negative reaction in us. A frank word spoken and received in love and humility serves only to deepen friendship and renew trust.
Want to see a community where we do our best to make this our practice? Go to **bruderhof.com** and schedule a visit today.

Gifted, Mad, and Out of Control

By Alexis Zeigler

"I have a heart, remember to tell them that."
—Delancey, the evening she took her life, July 1993

What if there were a serious disease affecting millions of Americans, sometimes with deadly consequences? What if it had no clear cause or cure, but some treatments existed that had been scientifically and systematically shown to be the most effective? What if these treatments were so effectively ignored and disregarded by doctors that they had become all but completely unknown inside and outside of the medical establishment?

All of these things are true, and I am not talking about some half-baked "cure" for cancer. All of these things are true about serious mental illness. It impacts millions of Americans, though we are forced to hide it because it bears such strong social stigma. We have spent incomprehensible sums of money to build hospitals, research drugs, and develop all manner of invasive techniques with horrifying side-effects. And repeated studies in third world villages where people live in very meager circumstances show that they, with no "technology" at all, have a higher rate of recovery from serious mental illness. Yet you will never hear that most extraordinary fact from a psychiatrist. (Warner, Richard, *Recovery from Schizophrenia: Psychiatry and Political Economy*, New York, Harper and Row, 1985)

Modern intentional communities fall somewhere in between mainstream America and a traditional village. Intentional communities generally lack the intensive kinship systems that make up the basic social fabric of villages. But modern communities do reclaim some of the intensive social support of traditional villages. It is perhaps because of this increased support and a sense of safety that one sees mental illness more openly in community. And while I would not want to make disparaging comments about my fellow communitarians, I think it is also true that misfits are attracted to community. That is nothing to be ashamed of.

Activist groups are likewise full of crazy people. Most of history's famous people, especially those who took upon themselves to be agents of change, were misfits who by today's standards would have been called mentally ill. Sigmund Freud, the granddaddy mind-doctor of them all, had "disorders" and addictions that would have been labeled obsessive-compulsive in modern

times. Abraham Lincoln and Winston Churchill both suffered bouts of deep depression. Isaac Newton, Beethoven, Vincent Van Gogh, and a long list of other famous and highly accomplished individuals suffered from what would now be called "bipolar disorder." If each of them had been hospitalized at a young age, stigmatized with that most horrific of labels of being "mentally ill," how many of them might have failed to continue with their life's work? One can only wonder.

The difficulty in community is that we can take the lid off of the can, but we don't have a clue what do do next. Mental illness can be terrifying and extremely fatiguing. I live in a small community that has been referred to as "the Asylum" because we did support work for mentally ill people for a number of years. I have spent many sleepless nights, and I have dug too many graves. Sometimes the demons play for keeps. The terrified family and friends often run to the psychiatrists. I try to explain to them that the doctors may help or harm in the short term, but the support that community can offer is far more important. After a year or two of brutal disappointment, they see what I mean.

In the early days of the Asylum, one of my friends whom I will call James came to live with us. He experienced extreme states of unrelenting anxiety, racing thoughts, sleeplessness, sometimes also struggling with sudden visual and auditory hallucinations. Had we taken him to the hospital, he probably would have been labeled, medicated, and shamed. Instead, we kept people with him as much as we could. Someone often slept in the same room with him, as he found that comforting. Aside from any grandstanding about the superiority of community support over drugs for treating mental illness, it's clear enough why the medical establishment can't offer that kind of treatment. It is a lot of work. It can be extremely fatiguing, physically and emotionally. With James we traded off between friends. It took about seven months, but he got better. For years now he has run a state-wide and now nationally recognized social service agency that offers support for self-help organizations comprised of mentally ill people.

If I take all the crazy people I have known and draw a circle around the ones who are alive, some amazingly productive and happy to boot, they are the ones who maintained their social networks. In spite of periods of extreme pain or stress, broken hearts, broken promises, and damaged goods, they put their energy into maintaining their relationships. If I draw a circle around the crazy people I have known who are now dead, they failed to maintain their social networks. The lesson is clear enough.

One learns from the losses as well. When I lived at Twin Oaks, I befriended and fell very much in love with Delancey, a young woman who had come there from a troubled past. We were never sexually or romantically involved. That for me is the meaning of community, to fall deeply in love with people, many people, whether or not they are romantic partners. She told me things that were so shocking as to be incomprehensible. That was the first lesson—believe the unbelievable.

Without wanting to divide the world into petty dichotomies, I see people having different coping mechanisms for their pain. Some people dig into their memories and express their emotions with great vigor. Some people develop a strong discipline to keep a lid on their bad memories and are more stoic. At the Asylum, our shorthand for this dichotomy was "diggers and pavers." One of the greatest problems with helping crazy people is that diggers and pavers often do not get along. Each

Crazy people test our boundaries and force the dirt and filth of bitterness right out into the light of day. Craziness can be an opening, a healing for all of the community, but it's not easy.

feels deeply threatened by the other. The pavers have the greater social sanction of mainstream America, which is a paver-oriented culture to a rather extreme degree. (One hears a constant refrain from anthropologists about how much more expressive are people in non-western cultures.) Abuse survivors can be infinitely compassionate with other abuse survivors, or seemingly cruel, depending on the adaptive techniques each person is using and the chemistry between them.

I have found, quite consistently and much to my chagrin, that when I try to help someone in crisis, almost all of the work goes into dealing with and helping the people around the person in crisis who are triggered and agitated by the person in crisis. Crazy people test our boundaries and force the dirt and filth of bitterness in community right out into the light of day. I have a belief that many traditional cultures understood this painful and necessary process, and made use of it. Crazy people often held a revered place. (That assertion is based on ethnographic information, not romanticized visions. Richard Katz's *Boiling Energy* is one amazing book on the subject.) We struggle to understand. Craziness can be an opening, a healing for all of the community, but it's not easy.

Taking care of crazy people is often very hard work. In our hyper-individualistic world, we try to shove that burden onto the medical institutions, or onto anyone we can find. In the end, you get what you pay for. Crazy people test our compassion, and can re-enforce or destroy it.

Delancey was a digger to the extreme. She was deeply compassionate and poured herself into trying to help others. Her digger tendencies were too much for some. Some people were overwhelmed by her. A surprising number of people were jealous and resentful for all the attention she got, in spite of the fact that she was in extreme pain, in a most precarious situation. Her death was nothing short of a bomb in her community. We open the lid, and then we do not know what to do with what jumps out. We can try to put the lid back on, which is what America says is right. It's not right for me.

I believe we are all crazy. As soon as you get over that, it starts to get a little easier. You can't run from it, whether it is manifest in yourself or your loved ones. You can bury it or deal with it; there aren't any other options. The impact of crazy people in community is different because the social fabric is different. We all feel it when someone is having a hard time.

Crazy people are not a rare species. In the mainstream, people hide it. In community, you see it up close. A lot of people suffer manic and psychotic episodes if they are subject to extreme stress. Beware the labels. The term "schizophrenic" is simply a trash bin into which the doctors sweep everything that they do not understand. The manner in which labels are assigned by psychiatry is cursory and often extremely damaging. Most people, when they are dealing with bad memories or other highly stressful circumstances, will display symptoms that could be labeled mental illness. Some crazy people want to be labeled because it makes them feel a little safer that they have a specific illness with a specific treatment. I have heard the refrain from the docs too many times, "treatable condition." To them, "treatable condition" equals "profitabl pills." There is a real treatment, and it' called community.

In the meantime, if you are young anc have one episode of mental disruptio caused by extreme stress, you may b told, based on a three-minute intervie with a psychiatrist, that you have a serious lifelong mental illness and told yo will need to take powerful, expensiv psychoactive "medication" for the res of your life. The carelessness with whic such drugs are prescribed, sometimes i contradiction to the instructions provided by the manufacturer, is stunnin to people not familiar with the system.

An activist friend of mine had a classi manic-psychotic break a few years ag She is young, and fits well into the cat gory of people who are most likely to g better with support. She was hospitalize told she had a "treatable condition," an medicated. She was taking the drug s was given for about a year before som one in the family bothered to look on the manufacturer's website and discovered that the drug was intended only for very short-term use. (This particular drug has also since been the subject of thousands of lawsuits.) Based on one three-minute interview with a psychiatrist, she was given the drug and forgotten. Her health improved considerably once she stopped taking that drug, or "medication." (In the end, poor people sell "drugs," rich people sell "medication." Such is the nature of things.)

The heart of the issue is that doctors can't sell love. They can't sell a social network. So they have constructed a fairy-tale land where madness is all biology and they sell pills. A friend of mine who worked on the "psych ward" for years made the comment that the psychiatrists have become nothing more than sales reps for the pharmaceutical industry. Be careful. They can kill your friends. The stigma of being labeled "mentally ill" hits people when they are most vulnerable. Some of them never get over it.

The psychiatric establishment created a myth that most crazy people do not get better. This is a lie with potentially deadly consequences. Most crazy people get better. Particularly for young people who are not habituated to psychoactive "medications," chances are that they will get through a mental crisis and return to full function, though changed by the experience. Your job to help them will mean, in the beginning, dealing with their freaked-out friends and family. You do not need to figure out what is broken, try to fix it, or doubt your credentials. Your job is to try, as best you can, to provide a safe and supportive shell. You, or someone in the support group, will have to provide limits as well as support. Consistently, those closest to a crazy person think they need support and those further away will say they need limits. In the end, they need both. But the bottom line is that they need to stay integrated, woven into the human fabric of community. That is their best hope.

Beware psychoactive substances, legal and illegal. Many people under extreme stress "self medicate." Such behavior introduces powerful and unpredictable variables. I would suggest avoiding drugs of all kinds if possible. There are a small group of people with biological disorders who can benefit from modern chemistry, but that group is very small. In the end each crazy person has to make their own choices.

Chemical addiction to legal or illegal drugs, whether psychoactive "medication" or cheap beer, is likely to do more harm than good. One definition of addiction is the use of chemicals to avoid pain. Crazy people, and indeed all of us, are much better off if we can find ways to manage and integrate pain, not perpetually run from it. Marijuana is not the harmless substance that some of its proponents would claim, at least not in this context. It is a powerful stimulant for people with manic tendencies. That generally does not help.

The people who came together to help Delancey called themselves "the tribe." Helen was among the tribe, and we found a kindred cause in trying to help people in crisis. Helen and I were partners for a couple of years. In time she drifted thousands of miles away. Over time, her situation deteriorated. I tried to stay in touch with her. I went and visited. I got in touch with her friends and tried to get them to stay in touch. Helen's adult identity was radical, strong, and powerfully contradictory to the paver culture in which we live. But it was at great contradiction to all the pressures of family and the society around her. In the end, her adult identity succumbed to the pressure, and nearly disappeared under an accommodationist facade. It wasn't her, and it didn't work. She isolated herself. She too took her life, a few years ago now.

For me, Helen's death was a turning point. I am not looking for new crazy friends at this point. I have no regrets. I hope I have learned some things, and I do not fear loss. I have come to cherish the victories. We brought people to the Asylum who had attempted suicide, or made other dramatic gestures looking for help. Many of them now have families, and are actively involved in social change. Coming to terms with your own pain is often a long and arduous process with no specific ending. Most people get better, often through a long and difficult process of learning what does not work.

Neither the diggers nor the pavers have the final answer. The people who can make use of the energy and insight in the deepest recesses of their minds, hold onto their true identity and bind it to a community around them, are the people we call leaders. This often comes at the price of many mistakes, many hard lessons about what not to do. For me the choices are clear enough. I will live and I will die among my people. I will not turn my back on them when the demons come to call. ❧

Alexis Zeigler has lived in intentional communities all of his adult life. He is also an activist, writer, and orchardist, currently living at Woodfolk House in central Virginia and helping start a sustainability-focused education center and community nearby called Living Energy Farm (www.livingenergyfarm.org). His website is conev.org.

Walking Wounded

By Gigi Wahba

Circle before mealtime for tri-community potluck.

First off, my personal bent: I feel that our whole society is suffering from mental stress/illness so, of course, we see it in intentional community.

How do we define mental illness or mental health? In American society it's about functionality and temperament. If you can keep your calm and do your work, you will likely be considered normal, healthy, and stable. The same is true in the communities I have lived in.

Most people coming into community have had some kind of trauma in their life that has put a part of their emotional system into disarray. They may have grown up without one parent, so that the remaining parent was often stressed emotionally and financially. They may have grown up with a parent who couldn't handle their own emotions and turned to alcohol, work-ahol or church-ahol—leaving, again, the other parent to handle the normal ups and downs of daily life. Still others suffered from verbal or physical abuse.

Even in the so-called "normal" families where all members talked and did fun things together, it is rare to find someone unscathed in their emotional responses, unchallenged in their self-esteem, unaware of some skeleton in their personal history.

And this is just childhood trauma. Most of us as adults have been in compromised, disempowering, even dangerous situations. We weren't given th tools for healthful sexual relations, conflict resolution, introspection, or eve basic nutrition.

We are all the walking wounded, i community as in the greater society The difference is that in the intimac of community a person is compelle to face how their words and behavio impact others. When the impact i understood and compassion and sup port are offered, some genuine heal ing happens. All too often, howeve isolation results. Either the distresse person self-isolates until the mood lif or shifts, or the person experiencin mental stress is avoided because he/sh feels like an energy sink to the others.

Yet even when deep healing is n available to the individual, I still belie the overall atmosphere of commun living is a great container for anyo in distress. In the communities I ha lived in, a person pretty much mak their own schedule, takes part in dignified work activities, is able to participate in communal meals, meetings, rituals, and other gatherings. So the isolation is gently challenged and a draw toward healthful pursuits is always there.

For myself, I come from a lineage of bipolar, depressed, obsessive compulsive, and schizophrenic—and their partners who typically were highly functional, highly intelligent, extremely calm and compassionate, but...conflict avoiders. So on the one hand, I feel blessed that I have drawn my sensitivity from a wide range of perspectives on what we call reality. On the other hand, couldn't we have just been a normal American family eating at McDonalds three times a week and going to church on Sunday?

No way! My parents were immigrants to this country and their extended families were scattered all over the globe. We rarely visited with cousins and there was no such thing as a family reunion. We were three kids, born on three different continents, and my parents living on a corner lot in the suburbs of New York. We weren't connected with other families in any significant way.

My mother was adoring and wacky while I was young and then her illness progressed to obsessive and verbally abusive as I got older. She was later diagnosed as bipolar and always refused care either in the form of psychotherapy (that was for crazies) or medicines (she intuitively distrusted allopathic ways). By high school I was ready to catapult out of the family home and take whatever risks I needed to find my own identity.

Needless to say I did a lot of experimenting with life, relationships, attitudes. For most of my young adult life, I didn't know if I had mental illness or if I was just suffering from a normal dose of angst, rage, and uncertainty. I had strong emotional swings in the context of being highly attuned to the needs and moods of others. Mostly I knew I wanted independence and did not want to end up at my mother's doorstep.

I emerged as a civil engineer at a time when the field was mostly men. I felt powerful if also a bit ridiculous (since I had never picked up a drill or hammer in my life). My career was short lived, since I felt I was missing the real work of life—learning about myself, my surroundings, and my calling. I stumbled into a rural community setting while living abroad and it immediately felt like a homecoming. Since then I have had a total of 20 years of intentional communal living.

Homeschooling 2004: Gigi and her daughter, Renay.

Photos courtesy of Gigi Wahba

Annual Party to celebrate fertility of land and of friendships.

So how have I seen mental health handled? My first community was a spiritual group in the Netherlands with a clearly defined leader figure. As far as the social security office was concerned, we were all crazies that together took care of each other and were minimally subsidized with the "dole." I lived there for two years before I understood this amusing dynamic, but it did explain the wide range of emotions, and especially intimacy difficulties, that were talked about in our group. I learned that several members had attempted suicide, many had been raped or otherwise abused, and a few had diagnosed psychological illnesses. Within this mix, I felt safe to share my own confusions, despair, inadequacies, and fears.

We worked very hard on our rural farm and we mostly isolated ourselves from the

Sorghum seedlings being transplanted into field with tobacco transplanter. Stan driving, Thea, Apple, Renay, Kevin riding.

observe, for example, how a mare accepted or refused a stallion. Some mares were very clear, others submissive, others unsure, some dominant over an inexperienced stallion. Which behavior looked healthiest? Which more problematic?

I wish I could say that that community still exists today, but it actually disbanded some time after I left due to power struggles between those perceived as "enlightened" and those feeling disempowered to create their own spiritual ascension.

In my current rural farming community, we generally do not display our most extreme emotions—sorrow, anger, frustration, etc. It's too scary and, when it happens anyway, there tends to be a big mess to clean up. However, we do talk about the range of how we are feeling and try to articulate the source so others can understand our behavior. We give feedback carefully but reluctantly for it is often perceived as exhausting and unsettling work. If a person can

At any moment of a day, someone's emotional needs would become the focus of either a small group or, at mealtime, the whole group of 40.

greater society. However, we were 100 percent dedicated to each other. At any moment of a day, someone's emotional needs would become the focus of either a small group or, at mealtime, the whole group of 40. Over and over we practiced how to hold each other emotionally, how to open our own hearts, how to work with the fiercest emotions that came up. Often our dinner conversations would go for three to four hours interrupted only by the animal chores we needed to accomplish.

Our work involved natural healing of horses and dogs, primarily. We cared for about 15 dogs and 100 horses at any given time. We both showed and bred the horses as a way to prove and display their full health to the conventional horse community. Observing the social behavior of the animals—their power struggles, shows of affection, orneriness, playfulness, etc.—gave us many metaphors for our own tendencies. Believing animals are generally closer to their true nature gave us a kind of pathway to our own behavioral health. One could

clearly state their needs, I feel our group will stretch to meet them. However, it is my experience of observing mental stress that this is often too much to ask of the person in distress.

There have been a few times in my history here where I have asked the group to reconsider a recent decision. Because we already have a consensus process where decisions can be belabored, this request has been met with annoyance and judgment about my process. On my behalf all I could say was that I wasn't in a good headspace to make the decision or see its consequences. Sympathy is hard earned in these circumstances. Instead, I have learned that, in my group, it is better to halt the decision process in the moment and share the momentary overwhelm. In this way, people can better trust that my intention is to make a good decision for the group rather than to push some agenda later on.

I think it is very challenging to live in close quarters with one another. I remember when the first reports of the trapped Chilean miners came out, there was news that NASA had sent experts to give tools to ward off depression and worse, aggression. We humans do not instinctively cooperate like a beehive. So too in my community, I often feel we just scratch the surface of what is being triggered, just enough so that some relief is experienced. How often do I look around and see someone moody, agitated, stressed, taciturn, or isolated?

Concerned Citizens group at Memphis, Missouri Courthouse. Petitioning to reinstate a local ordinance for the control of confined animal feed operations.

When tensions rise, we make earnest attempts to hear each other's concerns yet we have difficulty creating spaces where we can share our full vulnerability.

When tensions rise, we make earnest attempts to hear each other's concerns yet we have difficulty creating spaces where we can share our full vulnerability. Uncomfortable emotions are heavily managed. Instead, we tend to be pragmatic, conveying the edges of what we can tolerate and what we can accommodate. Energy does get blocked, sometimes for years.

I think this lack of deep inquiry and empathy inhibits shifting of unhealthy patterns and leads to emotional/mental stress. To our credit, we recognize our shortcomings in the field of emotional caretaking. We hold ourselves to the expectation that we will engage with each other when hard feelings are in the air so that we keep striving for clarity together. We also bring in outside help for new tools in this pursuit. It's wonderful to have an outside facilitator bring new energy and enthusiasm to our stuck places and help us move through some difficult conversations and interpersonal blockages.

I think as an alternative culture we are slowly recognizing the importance of this work. It is challenging to realize that just as we must regain the basic skills for self-sufficient living, we must relearn the ability to be compassionate and supportive toward one another. ❧

Sandhill Farm.

Gigi Wahba has been a member of Sandhill Farm in Rutledge, Missouri since 1994.

The Influence of Community on Mental Health

By Cindy and Friends
[Cindy Baranco, Ilana Firestone, Marilyn Moohr, and Judy St. John]

Living with a group of people you are bound to run into some mental health issues. The National Institute of Mental Health estimates that over 25 percent, one in four, of adults suffer from *diagnosable* mental health conditions in any given year. That's quite a staggering number. Our experiment in intentional communal living, with a philosophical basis of perfection (meaning, essentially, that we take the deliberate outlook that life is good), has yielded a much-reduced overall percentage and an ability to deal with many problems as they arise, within the group, often before the conditions become serious enough to require professional help.

If a condition isn't actually diagnosed, the situation is somewhat subjective—is a person a little unhappy or actually depressed? Are they trying to lose a few pounds or struggling with a full-blown eating disorder? Is it youthful rambunctiousness or Attention Deficit Disorder? Often the stigma and shame of having a mental health problem and the inevitable attempts to hide one's condition only exacerbate things.

> ***An important part of supporting someone with a mental health issue is to keep them involved in the life of the group.***

Our community, Lafayette Morehouse, has been together in the San Francisco Bay area for over 40 years, averaging 75 to 100 people, and in that time we've had only two or three incidents of psychosis serious enough to require short-term hospitalization. There have also been a handful of varying degrees of depression—in one case serious enough to undergo long-term therapy. Also some cases of alcoholism, "ADD," drug addiction, Obsessive-Compulsive Disorder, and the like.

We have chosen to live very closely together, like a big family, and consequently, distress can't be ignored for very long. When you go through all facets of life's ups and downs together—marriages, divorces, births, deaths, cancer, broken bones, the whole range of human experience—episodes of mental illness are more able to be a part of life; not a taboo, but rather just another challenge to face together. We've found that openly handling issues of any kind makes life better for all involved.

Even in a long-term, loving, committed community, people face a variety of conditions—physical and mental. At times we've gathered together to "babysit" someone whose behavior warranted it; used alternative modalities, or encouraged taking the more traditional route of seeing a psychiatrist or getting other professional help, including temporary hospitalization until the person has been able to regain their balance. In that situation, community members are at the hospital as much as the rules allow so that our friend can be assured of our ongoing love and support.

How many of the growing number of ADD diagnoses are a function of weary parents looking for some relief? Among the dozens of children we had over the years, there were at least a couple who could easily have been diagnosed and given medication. We resisted saddling these young people with a lifelong stigma and instead were able to increase the attention they received. In one of our most interesting lifestyle experiments, conducted over two generations, the kids lived together in their own house—sort of a kibbutz model bu with different goals and motivations. Even with 24-hour adul supervision, they had a big hand in raising each other. Ou system allowed parent and child to spend as much (or in som cases, as little) time as they wanted together. The kids also ha a variety of role models to emulate, providing them with mor behavioral options than in a traditional living situation. Thos kids who were on the brink of being declared ADD? They'r grown now, happy and productive, and only the stories remai of their younger days.

Whether a person is in crisis or has a chronic problem, we'v found the most effective approach is to not lose sight of th person as a full-fledged human being. Just because they hav a diagnosis or are behaving aberrantly, they are not defined b their condition. We have noticed that once a person starts ge ting treated as if they are a mentally ill patient, then they are no longer part of their group in the same way as a "normal" person and the separation intensifies their distress. An important part of supporting someone with a mental health issue is to keep them involved in the life of the group and not marginalize them by categorizing them as a victim.

In our decision-making system of "one-no-vote," *everyone* has the power to cast an irrevocable no-vote that stops any proposed action. Knowing that you have a vote puts you on equal footing with others, confirms your power, and could help obviate some of the feelings of paranoia and worthlessness which are so often part of the basis of mental illness.

One example is of a long-time member of our group who was born with water on the brain. Through the tireless efforts of her mother and the help of cutting-edge doctors in the field, she achieved a relatively high level of functionality. A cyst on the right lobe of her brain caused schizophrenia, making it difficult for her to handle stress, and also caused some minor physical disabilities. For most of her life she's been on psychotropic drugs to help her maintain an appropriate mental balance. She owns up to her illness and is grateful to be able to get help in the parts of life she's not particularly adept at or comfortable with—she'll say, "you handle my money, I'm not good at that." Friends in the community take care of her medication and make sure she takes it on schedule.

Not having to resist her condition or pretend it doesn't exist makes being taken care of not a wrong part of her but just a part of her. Her condition actually seems to contribute to the sweet person she is. It certainly hasn't stopped her from having everything she wants and being a full-fledged, contributing member of the group. She has the same communal responsibilities as everyone else. If there's a task that falls within her interest and abilities, she volunteers enthusiastically. She takes care of others as much as they take care of her.

There are also times when she becomes somewhat delusional and angry. That's a signal that it is time to have her meds adjusted. It sometimes takes weeks before her psychiatrist is able to determine the next appropriate cocktail so we have to pay special attention to ease her way through these difficult periods. When we are taking care of someone who is on medication, we've found we have to consider that it's not the person just being unpleasant or "crazy" but that the medication may be having an effect—it's time to check with their doctor. Also, usually nothing is a permanent answer—what works this time may not work next year.

In her early 20s she wanted to have a child and with the support of the group, she was able to carry a pregnancy to term, even though it proved at times quite stressful to her and those around her as her hormones, fluctuating during pregnancy, affected seriously her mental stability. Nevertheless, she made it through her pregnancy, and has a fabulous daughter who, also with the support of the community, survived growing up with a single mom who was "different," and is a lovely and talented adult today.

While most children, particularly teenagers, are often ashamed of or embarrassed by their parents, she was exceptionally challenged by having a mother who wasn't "standard issue." While she was growing up, other people in the community often "filled in" for her mom when needed or accompanied them to parent-teacher conferences and the like. There was actually more than one person in the role of "mom," who helped to provide consistency and stability for the family. That ongoing help took a lot of pressure off of the relationship, and mother and now-grown daughter have been able to access and

(continued on p. 78)

Photos courtesy of Cindy Baranco

Ilana Firestone, Marilyn Moohr, and Judy St. John

THE INFLUENCE OF COMMUNITY ON MENTAL HEALTH

(continued from p. 31)

express the love between them. Despite all odds, a woman with a fairly serious mental health issue, who easily could have been relegated to an institution or lived life as a cripple, was able to be the good and caring mother she wanted to be. With community support, an illness doesn't have to hold back you or your loved ones.

The relatively low incidence of mental illness in our group may also be because each individual has more personal freedom to carve out whatever lifestyle suits them; to pick and choose what they do and don't want to do. That tends to take a lot of stress out of life and reduces the kind of emotional breakdowns that come from trying to cover obligations and responsibilities that don't necessarily suit the individual's particular nature. The challenges and demands of day-to-day life are distributed so that not everyone has to know how to cook or garden or fix things. We help take care of each other.

Friends are at hand to help when you are having difficulty with situations or people in your life. Parents are not on their own to nurture their children; spouses are not on their own to support and care for their partners. Friends are involved and interested in your wants and your successes and victories as well as being there for your downfalls and defeats.

Chronic illness, mental or physical, can be most overwhelming to the people closest to the stressed person, and can really wear them down. If you have friends who can help you, there's less chance for upset between the parties, less inclination to take it personally or to succumb to anger. If being a couple means you are solely alone or stuck with whatever illness your partner gets, whether it is cancer or chronic depression, it's pretty frightening. Having friends to spell you, help you, and possibly be more objective, eases the burden for the caregivers and reduces the guilt of the cared for.

Living closely with many other people allows us to share in more of life's joys than just our own. It also means we share in more problems than just our own. In our group we think of ourselves as responsible hedonists, and that means if someone is acting out in an inappropriate or self-destructive way we have to get involved because they are in our lives and their unhappiness affects us. So we take each other on for the good times and the bad times. And as far as we can tell, that results in more good times. ❧

Cindy and Friends are all long-term members of Lafayette Morehouse. "In our 42 years of living together, we have found that things are more fun when done with others, including writing." For this article, this group-within-a-group consisted of Cindy Baranco, Ilana Firestone, Marilyn Moohr, and Judy St. John. For more information, visit www.lafayettemorehouse.com.

Hand in Hand, Heart to Heart: Peer Counseling in Community

By Amara Karuna

Class connecting.

What happens when we decide to get together with some friends on a lovely piece of land, and build family and community together, and after a few months or years the rosy glow of our idealism wears off and it seems to become so much more difficult than we imagined? Why do we find ourselves arguing, feeling jealous, greedy, and uncooperative? It seems that if the others would just do it our way, and stop being so unreasonable, things would work out great!

How do we communicate what we want without being controlling? How do we stay connected when our needs seem to be conflicting with others? How do we truly share power and not be co-dependently giving in to please another? What do we do when we feel like punching the other person, or we seriously consider whether there might be some way to never speak to them again? How do we handle our attraction to someone else's lover? Why do we find ourselves willing to back off and give up on what is important to us, just to avoid conflict?

I have noticed that emotional problems between people are the main reason for breaking up relationships, businesses, and communities. Part of permaculture is making a human culture which is healthy and sustainable, just like creating a healthy balanced culture with plants and animals on a farm. Because our Western culture is so emotionally repressed, most people have no models for how to handle their own emotions in a responsible and healthy way. We go through life hoping for peace and pleasure, and if we get triggered or have our "buttons pushed," we tend to blow up out of control, and then try to get out of the unpleasant emotions as fast as possible, without really understanding where they came from or why they are so intense.

Most people have trouble even keeping a healthy relationship going with one person, so the idea of living with a whole group is overwhelming. Other people are like mirrors, and sometimes they reflect parts of us we don't really want to see. If one mirror is too much, then what about five or 10? There is nowhere to hide then! Each relationship adds levels of interconnected complexity. A number of my friends look at my busy, complicated situation from their quiet, sedate lives and wonder why I am even interested in such a challenge. A community is an emotionally intensive experience. It is also a fantastic way to grow, if you are committed to your own healing and are willing to look carefully and fearlessly into your own shadows.

The shadow is any part of the psyche that is unpopular and judged as undesirable. It exists because of an accumulation of past hurtful experiences. We can see our own shadows in the places where we find ourselves doing things that we have already decided we do not want to do, such as indulging in addictions. It is also seen in chronic illnesses that we can't seem to heal—or where we feel blocked in moving forward toward the things we want to create in our lives.

Shadows live in our unconscious, so by their nature they are hard to see. It is far easier to notice something you do not like about another person, thus projecting your shadow onto them. There is also a well-known tendency for any group to pick a scapegoat, or "identified problem person," who manifests the shadow energy of the group mind. The problem with shadows is that no matter what attempts are made to control or ignore them, they keep popping their ugly little heads up in the most inopportune and embarrassing moments. This is because they want healing, and they want to be honored and acknowledged. The longer they are pushed away and repressed, the more energy they build up until they really seem like monsters lurking somewhere under the thin veneer of our "nice" conscious personalities.

When I was around 25 years old I joined a small intentional community that was egalitarian in structure and involved income sharing. They were six adults and a baby living in a large house in a small town, living communally in a very intense way. Income sharing is challenging for many people, because it involves pooling the income made by the various members, and then using it for all the group expenses and giving each member a small stipend for personal use. This required a lot of bookkeeping and a lot of emotional processing to be sure that everyone felt that the resources were being dealt with fairly. In addition, living, working, and eating in one house created an emotional pressure cooker from all the intimacy. I loved it. And I also noticed where it was not working well.

The members had various levels of emotional skillfulness and awareness. I became aware of a pattern in which someone who was emotionally upset, and not taking responsibility for their feelings, would use the group meetings to process all their emotional problems. There would be a lot of projections onto others, and a tendency to have the group attention focused on the upset person for long periods of time. This was very draining and time-consuming for the group, and eventually led the group to dissolve. This experience led me to seek ways that people could live together in harmony, and work out emotional difficulties.

The good news is that shadows and old emotional distresses can be cleared and permanently resolved, with loving help from others. I studied and practiced many different group processes and therapies, and the two I have found most useful for community are Nonviolent Communication, or NVC, and peer counseling, also known as co-counseling. We use NVC when we need to communicate something and listen well to others, and use co-counseling when we want to explore inside and deeply feel and release emotions. They complement each other well. In La'akea Permaculture Community, we train people in both skills in our internships, and use them as a basis for having common language and agreements about how we choose to relate to each other.

Listening to each other.

Photos courtesy of Amara Karuna

Emotions are natural waves of energy that arise in response to a stimulus, and if they are allowed to flow and are not repressed, they naturally resolve themselves.

Co-counseling is a worldwide network of non-professional counselors, who trade sessions for the purpose of clearing emotions, dissolving rigid patterns of behavior, and recovering our ability to be present and think clearly and rationally. It is a people's liberation movement that started in the '50s, has spread all over the world, and has many permutations and offshoots. You can check out the original organization at www.rc.org, where you will find all the basic ideas and many resources for learning the skills.

Emotions are natural waves of energy that arise in response to a stimulus, and if they are allowed to flow and are not repressed, they naturally resolve themselves. It is natural for a child to get angry if another child steals a toy, or if they are denied a food that they really want. The emotion can be validated and allowed space to be felt, and yet not be the deciding factor in how the situation is resolved. Hurtful things happen to us as a natural part of life, and our emotional responses to them are our natural way of healing the hurts. A child who is sad about not having another cookie can be

Mini session.

We make room for the shadows to come forward in a safe way, at the right time, by invitation. This prevents them from having to burst forth in dramatic desperation.

allowed to cry, and have the feeling acknowledged in a respectful way. They can be given empathy, but not another cookie, and soon the tears will wash through and the inner sun with shine again.

In our lives, in this culture, we experience many disappointments and moments of neglect, abuse, and not having our needs met. If we are not given loving empathetic attention around the emotions stirred by these hurts, they tend to get stored in our subconscious shadows. There they wait, and when anything later happens which is similar enough to the original hurts, we experience that unpleasant phenomenon known as being triggered, or having our buttons pushed. Then we find ourselves re-experiencing the old feelings, saying and doing things that don't work well, and generally being unable to stay present and think clearly in the moment.

If we can recognize that we are triggered, and ask for help from our friends, we can move through the pain into clarity by allowing space to deeply feel the emotions. We often need and deserve support from others in working with these old pains. The most useful kind of support is calm, loving presence and empathy from another person. We avoid giving them advice to solve their problems, and trust that when the emotions have washed through, they will be able to think again and work out their own best solutions. It takes training and practice and personal inner work to offer this to each other, and it is well worth the time invested.

We hold space for people to talk, cry, laugh, rage, and tremble out fears. Emotions are messy, physical things that involve lots of movement, sounds, inner chemistry, and body fluids. When releasing anger, a few moments of really beating up a pillow are often more effective than hours of verbal processing. Laughing and shaking the whole body are really useful when people feel scared and nervous. Crying helps us let go and heal from a loss. Emotional releases are deeply healing when they are welcomed, held in a safe space where no one is hurt, and allowed to finish.

How do we use this in community? Mostly it is coming to a group agreement that emotions are important, and we can feel them fully and then make our choices based on our clear thinking. We make room for the shadows to come forward in a safe way, at the right time, by invitation. This prevents them from having to burst forth in dramatic desperation just to get any attention.

Specifically, we have opportunities at our weekly Heartsharing meeting to express our deeper feelings. We ask every week at these meetings if someone has something to clear with another person, and hold space for that to happen with group support. We do morning check-ins every day where we are open to shorter sharing about anything that is coming up for people. We do group processes like the Forum, where the whole group gives attention to one person at a time as they freely move and express whatever is alive for them in the moment. We play theater and psychodrama games so that we can laugh and be creative together.

We take time to trade sessions in pairs on a regular basis, so that our needs for personal attention and emotional expression are met. We hold space for each other while we struggle through the hard places. When someone has a sudden injury or emergency, we take time to allow the feelings, scream, or yells to come through, so that the energy does not stay stuck in the body and healing can happen fast. When two people are in conflict, we can give each a time individually to blow off steam and explore what in their past is getting triggered. Then we can meet together in a mediation session and work out solutions. We help the children work through their feelings using NVC, Connection Parenting, and counseling. We have small support groups on specific topics, such as parents getting together to talk about childraising challenges, or the older women having a meeting to listen to each other.

When everyone feels safe to be truly authentic, and express whatever is real for them, no matter how ugly or uncomfortable it seems, then the hurts that have been relegated to the shadows are able to be brought into the light of awareness. They can be explored, understood, and released. We can look for the old roots of what happened in the past, and re-program the old habits into new, more healthy patterns. We can truly come into a place of closeness, trust, and safety in relationship with each other.

This is where community can be a path of both personal growth and spiritual awakening. To fearlessly face one's deepest pains, with the loving help of others, creates a situation where we can go much farther and faster together than we could go alone. We can free each other from old chains and cages, with patience and compassion. This is why I love community. As we each become free of old fears and blocks, and open into our own unique, beautiful power, we can more effectively create a new and healthier world.

"One by one, everyone comes to remember

We're healing the world one heart at a time..."

(song by Michael Stillwater) ❧

Amara taught Re-evaluation Co-counseling, a method of peer counseling, for over five years, and has been studying and practicing it since 1983. She developed her own approach to peer counseling in 1988, called Wholistic Peer Support, integrating many ideas from RC with spiritual meditation practices, psychic healing, and body-centered techniques. She is a member of La'akea Permaculture Community, near Pahoa, Hawaii. See amarakaruna.webs.com for information on trainings and services from Amara, www.karunaarts.com for her interfaith prayer flags, art, and Goddess clothing, and www.karunapublishing.com for inspirational music, books, and children's books. For more information on La'akea trainings, see www.permaculture-hawaii.com.

Shadow Sides of NVC and Co-Counseling

By Dona Willoughby

My heart is pounding out of my chest, my palms are sweaty, and my shoulders held tight. I feel like I might explode. Words come spewing out of my mouth louder and sharper than I seem to be able to control. I am throwing my feelings and needs like daggers into my friend/lover's face.

But I'm using Nonviolent Communication! Or am I? Although I am using the NVC process, I am more than angry. I am triggered, and a bit irrational. I want respect, support, love; the list goes on and on. I am intent on relieving my pain by giving some to my friend and lover. I want to show him his inadequacies. In this moment, I am not interested in connecting at the heart; I could care less about his needs. I am in too much pain myself. I would prefer he NOT come from free choice (an NVC intention). In this moment, I want to blame, change, and control.

I experienced the above incident years ago. Should I get this triggered again, I hope to: 1. Take a deep breath. 2. Ask for a specific time later to discuss the issue. 3. Promptly call one of my co-counseling partners to make a date for a session.

Both NVC and co-counseling are tools which can move us toward peace, joy, connection, and love. However, they can be ineffective or misused if our intentions and boundaries are not clear.

Shadow sides I experienced in co-counseling include:

1.THE CLIENT NOT TAKING CHARGE OF THEIR SESSION. I have been given advice and had releases interrupted during my sessions. I have had counselors recommend actions that were not helpful. I am now aware that I am in charge of my session, and it is my responsibility to make it clear what I want from my counselor.

2. NOT HAVING CLEAR BOUNDARIES. The interns at La'akea take the beginning co-counseling class. Yesterday one of the interns had a practice session with another student. He had not completed the class about boundaries. He became triggered by what the other student, now his client, said. Instead of telling his client he was not able to be present for the session, he pretended to be present, when he wanted to scream and run away. He was in need of a session after the session. I have been asked to give touch in ways that were not comfortable for me in sessions. I have learned to establish clear boundaries and let clients know when I am unable to be lovingly present.

3. NOT BELIEVING THE CLIENT HAS THE ANSWERS. The client's distress is exactly that, the client's. It is easy to confuse this and blame the triggering stimulus, or the person who functioned as the trigger. Counseling with those closely involved in the client's distress or the stimulus can be dicey and difficult to keep clear. We prefer counseling with those outside of our community. This involves coordination, time, effort, and fossil fuels since transportation is often involved.

4. NOT BEING VULNERABLE. To be completely open and vulnerable in a session I need to trust that my counselor will keep everything I say confidential. If this trust were broken pain and harm could ensue.

5. RELEASING DISTRESS BUT NOT GETTING TO THE ROOTS. We can continue to release distress until the cows come home but until we identify the roots of the issue and heal our core patterns, our time is wasted. People can get caught in rehearsing the same complaint over and over, without getting to the cause and reprogramming of the original hurts.

In closing, the benefit I gain from co-counseling that does not occur in a "shrink on a couch" counseling session is the healing I receive when I give loving presence to another person. I learn from the other's distress and healing process. I am attracted to counselors whose path to healing is in alignment with and helpful to mine.

Dona Willoughby, co-creator of La'akea community, teaches Nonviolent Communication, yoga, herbal medicine, natural farming, and permaculture.

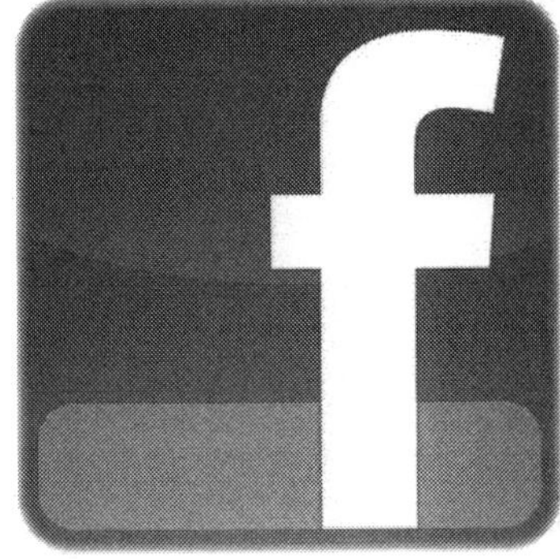

Prescription Facebook:

How can Facebook act as an agent of mental health to a community fragmented 20 years ago?

By Sandy Brown Jensen

I've heard the bad news about Facebook: it's community-busting, time-consuming, and addictive for unwary users, as well as a profitable stalking ground for predatory cyber-bandits and advertisers alike. I've got plenty of friends who have better things to do with their time than log in and waste time chit chatting with people they weren't even friends with 20 years ago when we were in community together, and they have no interest in knowing now. I understand that "evil, evil social media" mentality. Oddly enough, I just don't see it that way. I've found Facebook has been a tool for re-uniting a lost community I had long grieved had passed from my life forever.

I was an Emissary of Divine Light (EDL) from 1972-1992, and in my heart, probably still am. I lived those 20 years in EDL communities, 10 of them at the Glen Ivy Community in southern California. What can I say? That's a really long time to live in community. Those friends were soul friends, forever, as we thought then.

The World Health Organization (WHO) defines mental health as "a state of well-being in which the individual realizes his or her own abilities, can cope with the normal stresses of life, can work productively and fruitfully, and is able to make a contribution to his or her community." Within our busy center, for many of us friends, mental health bloomed. For others, a variety of challenges arose that made it difficult to cope with stress, to work fruitfully and make the contribution to "the good of the all" they may have wished. Professional counseling in the 21st century is well-known to be useful for countless interventions in the troubled lives of citizens, but, in early to mid-20th-century EDL, the roadblocks to professional mental health started at the top.

When Lloyd Arthur Meeker, known as Uranda, drafted the foundational principles for the Emissaries of Divine Light back in the 1930s, the profession—the art and science—of psychology was in its infancy. Popular access to books, tapes, and the national pop-psych lecture circle was far in the future. To Uranda, mental health meant finding your place in the whole. The tools for this included daily reading of his publications, such as *The Seven Steps to the Temple of Light*, and working with higher consciousness within your Emissary community.

I discussed this recently with his daughter, Nancy Rose Meeker. She said, "From a young age I was aware of the struggle of adults around me with their psychological dilemmas. Uranda was very interested in what he called 'spiritual psychiatry,' but resistance to him and his vision of Truth were not allowable."

Uranda also developed a healing practice called attunement that worked with the energetic patterns of the body. His son, Lloyd Meeker, Jr., is still an active attunement practitioner. He correctly resists any inference that attunements might be used as a vibrational sedative; however, one by-product of attunement is often to return a distraught person to calm and balance, so attunements often were the prescription of choice for troubled Emissaries.

In the early to mid-20th-century Emissaries of Divine Light, the roadblocks to professional mental health started at the top.

On August 4, 1954, Uranda's plane went down in San Francisco Bay, killing all on board, orphaning his children. Lloyd, Jr. told me, "Nancy Rose and I were told explicitly that there was no need to grieve Uranda and Kathy's death. They had fulfilled their purpose on Earth. That we children were thus informed that we were not part of our parents' purpose for being on Earth was devastating to me. I still believe that the lack of collectively grieving the death of our parents and attaining the resolution grief brings was a tragic watershed moment in the collective EDL story."

British–titled Lord Martin Cecil (later Exeter) assumed the leadership of EDL. His relationship with the mental health field was more personal and more influential over my generation of Emissaries. His first wife suffered from symptoms that began with postpartum depression, which was not well understood in the 1930s. Eventually, she was institutionalized and died quite young. Again, the field of effective psychiatry was light-years from where it is now. It is my own view that Martin witnessed early-day attempts to help his tragically ill wife, and he lost her. It seems to me that Martin, as Lloyd observed, did not come all the way through his own grief cycles. This is an issue of mental health, and one that spilled over to affect the entire EDL community.

While he was EDL guide and spokesman, I think Martin's knowledge about and attitudes toward the mental health field got caught in the amber of time. As more and more trained counselors became Emissaries, it became painfully obvious that Martin did not embrace their profession. This is not to say *all* Emissary leaders; some were more supportive of these inner explorations.

However, by the late 1980s, I observed that this suppression of the mental health field had grown into a subterranean point of tension within worldwide Emissarydom. There were many articulate, radical speakers who spoke truth directly to power. Some were quickly quashed by the power of silence. But in the gossip underground, there was a lot of pushback as leadership itself began to fragment along this and other fault lines contingent upon the changing psychic landscape of the late 20th century.

When Martin died in the late 1980s, chaos ensued. His son and heir apparent, Michael Cecil, said, "My own perception suggests that a lot of the unrest after Martin's passing had to do with a lack of understanding (in me and others) of how to navigate the grief cycle within the community, and that many got stuck at the anger and depression stages." Thus, as I see it, the collective failure to learn how to grieve Uranda's passing came back to haunt the Emissary collective when Martin died.

In the lower-level circles of the Emissary world where I lived, gossip became viral. Talk flew from community to community—incessant talking about leadership, about what cult was, and if we were one; some people were "de-programmed"; anxious talk swirled, flowed, boiled over. The truth probably was that a whole lot of people could have used a whole lot of grief therapy at that time to help them think through the grief of losing Martin and their own changing life choices.

In Emissary history, the late 1980s and early 1990s were marked by diaspora. Emissaries left the communities in droves, and I don't think I'm far off by saying this demonization of psychology at the highest levels by some leaders was one powerful root cause among others, which included issues around feminism, democratic or consensual decision making, and gay rights.

I would like to say I left my community for many well-thought-out reasons—lots of my friends use the term "cognitive dissonance," but I can't honestly claim that

The collective failure to learn how to grieve Uranda's passing came back to haunt the Emissary collective when Martin died.

Body Mind Connection. See the original at www.CherylRLong.com.

Watercolor by Cheryl Renée Long

I don't think I understood how important the human heart bond is to individual mental health.

phrase as my own. I felt like a slugger's batted ball. A colossal stroke sent me flying out of the ballpark—over the familiar field of my community, over the upraised faces of my fellow communitarians, out past the big lights into the distant darkness. I know I'm supposed to take responsibility for everything that happens in my life, but I couldn't have felt less in control. It felt as if mysterious forces were rushing together to shape my destiny, and all I could do was go along for the ride until I fetched up on the farthest end of the legendary Oregon Trail in Eugene, Oregon. Then all those powerful forces sort of lost interest and wandered away, leaving me to reinvent a life.

Few things rend the heart and mind like grief, and in so many ways grief and its resolution lie at the core of mental health for so many ordinary people. For 20 years, I had lived and breathed and had my being in the vibrant embrace of my community. I didn't live that long with my biological family growing up from birth to age 18! When I left home to go to college, the separation from my bio-fam was hard enough. But I had letters and visits, and summers at home. The bonds loosened slowly and naturally while our relationships became richer in more adult ways. But the bond with my community was severed like a bunch of grapes clipped off its vine.

I didn't know it then, but I had left most of my heart and pieces of my soul in my community at Glen Ivy. My heart was always full of tears in those days as I struggled to learn how to get jobs teaching and then with teaching itself. I was depressed and full of unacknowledged grief.

I tell my own story of the soul loss that came with leaving my community as one story among perhaps hundreds. So many of my friends in their 30s and 40s, who left EDL in the late '80s, found themselves alone, in grief, with no money and no education. Each of them has a story to tell, and none of the stories is easy. We all left part of ourselves with each other and struggled alone through the 1990s finding our individual paths to peace. Many marriages broke up after community-bonded couples tried to survive in the arid air "outside."

Let's take another look at the WHO definition of mental health in context of our broken community: we were no longer in a state of well-being realizing our own abilities. I for one was not coping well with the normal stresses of life, working neither productively nor fruitfully. We were all floundering to recover those states of healthy equilibrium which had been ours so easily for so long. We'd lost our emotional support system, our social network that had held us intertwined.

During these years, while hundreds of ex-Emissaries fought to reinvent their lives without our accustomed social network, virtual social networks came online. In 2004, Facebook went public, and as of July 2010, it had over 500 million active users, or about one out of every 14 people in the world. It has met criticism on a range of issues from data-mining, to censorship, to intellectual property rights.

So if I am such an aware media consumer, why am I not more wary? I was a fairly early adopter of Facebook, so I have been witness to its birthing pains, but I have also been on the welcoming committee as, one by one, my old communitarians have found their way online.

I have around 300 ex-EDL Facebook "Friends," and they are still showing up. People are posting their old EDL photos, and the rest of us flock in to tag familiar faces, to recite stories of those who have died, to discuss where a picture was taken in what year. I have fallen into Facebook conversations with a woman who lives in Auckland and whom I met only once or twice—we talk about the best way to make sauerkraut. I talk every week to an ex-Em in Amsterdam, whom I knew of "back in the day," but I have never met in person. Like others, I post short memoir pieces for others to read and comment on, and I enjoy engaging in the back and forth in the mix of memory and everyday life.

With every old friend who becomes my Facebook "Friend," I feel pieces of my soul coming back on line. And it's not that we are once again propounding the meaning of Martin's words or our origins in the sun—that was great when we were kids in the '70s. We talk about everyday things, we tease each other, we organize parties—one in New York last summer, one coming up in Canada, one in California to usher in the New Year 2011.

I don't think I understood how important the human heart bond is to individual mental health. In my connection to others, whether online or face-to-face, I experience a state of well-being in which I can realize my own abilities as a communicator. Knowing my friends are, as the saying goes, "there for me," helps me cope with the normal stresses of life. Many people may think I'm crazy, but having a Facebook widget in the lower right hand side of my computer screen streaming the background chatter of my "Friends" helps me work productively and fruitfully. Writing memoirs and posting them on Facebook makes me feel I am able to make a contribution to my many communities: EDL, bio-fam, college.

Reunited on Facebook, our friendships have become virtual, and I suppose I have to speak for myself, but I'm starting to feel whole again. The old grief of separation is finally healed, and I have found my way back home. ❧

Sandy Brown Jensen lived for 20 years in Emissary of Divine Light intentional communities, primarily at Glen Ivy Community in southern California. She blogs at sandybrownjensen.com. Her articles on community may be found in the Communal Studies Journal, Community College Moment, *and elsewhere. Sandy teaches English and is an Instructional Technology Specialist at Lane Community College in Eugene, Oregon.*

Name ______________________

Address ______________ Date ________

Rx for "Mental Illness": Caring Community

By Brian Toomey

Editor's note: a footnoted version of this article, with links to many additional sources and resources, appears online at communities.ic.org.

How We Talk About Our Struggles

In the spring of 2007, in a cafe off of Shattuk Avenue in Berkeley, California, I found myself sitting across from my close friend Alissa. "My cousin was just diagnosed by one psychiatrist as schizoaffective," she told me, "a second psychiatrist diagnosed her as bipolar, and a third with borderline personality disorder. Can you help me understand what's going on here?"

I could understand Alissa's frustration; she was seeking to understand her cousin's suffering and she wanted to be able to trust those aiming to help her. She came to me in part because I had some knowledge in the field—along with years of working with distressed homeless populations, I had recently dropped out of a Ph.D. program in clinical psychology.

I left the graduate program because I needed more community, and also because I had deep concerns about the scientific and political integrity of mental health treatment in America. I shared with my friend that as a result of my studies I was concerned about the accuracy and values that underlay modern psychiatric diagnosis.

I first developed this concern when I was working with homeless populations in Seattle, Washington. One day I asked a long term resident of the shelter why he seemed glum. "Because I am bipolar," he replied. I felt scared hearing this. I feared that if he saw "bipolar" as something he was, it would, by definition, never be something he could change. In my experience, choosing to see mental health through the lens of a static diagnosis which defines our identity, as opposed to a temporary and personally meaningful struggle, blocks our ability to shift internally and seek solid support.

I later learned that multiple scientific studies have confirmed that, in general, two psychiatrists who interview someone independently and do not confer are not significantly more likely to agree about a diagnosis than they would if they made purely random diagnoses. I also worry knowing that it was not until 1973 that homosexuality was removed from the the standard guidebook containing diagnostic categories of mental illness, the DSM. Similarly, in the 1990s the psychiatric establishment pushed to establish premenstrual distress as a mental illness. Indeed, a recent study showed that the overwhelming majority of people who served on

MD ______________________

Signature ______________________

the scientific committee tasked with defining mental illness have received direct funding from drug companies. This situation raises similar concerns for me around accuracy and bias that I feel when I look, for example, at the funding of modern US elections.

My reading of the history of psychiatric diagnosis suggests, unfortunately, that cause for such concern is not a recent phenomenon. Many of the terms we commonly employ, "schizophrenia" for instance, date back to a dark period in European and American history when doctors and other medical professionals, motivated by the the philosophy of eugenics popular at the turn of the last century, engaged in forced sterilization of people diagnosed as mentally ill. Indeed, *The New England Journal of Medicine* and *The American Journal of Psychiatry* (to this day two of the most respected journals in the field) published editorials in the 1920s that were supportive of Hitler's forced sterilization program and eugenic approaches to mental illness.

How can we talk about mental illness and distress in a way that preserves individuals' humanity and supports community? Overall the evidence suggests that human distress and madness are not comprised of distinct diseases, but rather that they are better construed and studied as clusters of individual symptoms. These symptoms can be described perfectly well in natural language, which has the potential to be much less stigmatizing. For example, I would request that my fellow communitarians consider moving away from describing themselves with static diagnostic categories like, "I am (or have) ADHD," and instead say, "I struggle with distraction and impulsivity." Likewise, instead of saying of someone, "She is clinically depressed," we can choose to say, "She is experiencing deep sadness and a desire to withdraw socially." I have found Marshall Rosenberg's writings and his model of nonviolent communication to be an excellent resource for shifting language. I believe that such language, which focuses on personal feelings and needs, is not only more scientifically accurate, it is also more empowering and more aligned with the values of the communities movement.

What Really Helps? Faked Concussions and Real Caring

When a person in distress receives care and is helped, what exactly is it that helps? Journalist Gary Greenberg offers the following story of a participant in a clinical drug trial. Janet Schonfeld had suffered from serious depression for more than two decades when she read about a trial for the antidepressant medication Effexor. She felt hopeful and excited about the possibility of a cure, and within a few weeks of enrolling in the study she *was relieved to feel fewer feelings of worthlessness and suicidal ideation*—a dramatic improvement. She also experienced nausea, one of the drug's known side effects, leading her and her nurse to assume that she was receiving the active drug.

However, at the completion of her six-month participation she was alarmed to learn that she had been taking an inert placebo and that her improvement could not be attributed to pharmacological action. If, as the drug companies would have us believe, a chemical imbalance in her brain had been corrected, that correction had happened without the assistance of any drug. Her story is not an isolated incident, as more recent studies (which include information drug companies attempted to hide and which was obtained via the Freedom of Information Act) have also shown that SSRI depression medication consistently fails to outperform placebos meaningfully. The surprising and powerful takeaway here is that even in situations where people think they are being helped by a chemical agent, it may well be those steadfast communitarian values of hope and concerned attention that are actually what is healing.

A similar tale unfolds when we look closely at Electroconvulsive Therapy, a form of treatment made famous in Ken Kesey's *One Flew Over the Cuckoo's Nest.* In ECT (commonly known as electroshock or shock therapy) a strong electrical current is passed through the brain of a patient, deliberately inducing a concussion. Patients often report large improvements after receiving treatment, but also (not surprisingly) tend to suffer additional negative neurological effects. However, as with Janet Schonfeld's story above, patients who have their heads shaved and receive anesthesia but receive no electrical shock show the same improvement.

Even when people think a chemical agent is helping, those steadfast communitarian values of hope and concerned attention may well be what is healing them.

If it is not the drugs or the electrical shock that is helping people get better, as these results strongly suggest, then what is it? I believe that the healing comes both from having the caring attention of the doctors, most of whom are compassionate people who chose their profession to help people heal, and from being able to engage in a healing ritual.

What does this mean for the communities movement? I believe it means that in most cases we can work to largely (but perhaps not entirely) replace the mainstream medical treatment of mental illness, and that we can work to build our own rituals of caring, healing, and support. (NOTE: I strongly discourage abrupt withdrawal from psychiatric medication. Please shift current treatment only under the direction of a licensed medical doctor who is sympathetic to your needs and reasons for doing so.)

By analogy, in most cases folks can lose weight with sensible eating and exercise, and it is only in rare cases (such as thyroid malfunctions or the rare condition known as Prater Williams Syndrome) that there are medical reasons that people cannot maintain a healthy weight. Similarly, in most cases we can take care of our own mental health. We can look to feelings and needs and seek to establish habits of healthy living, rather than trying to correct malfunctioning neural synapses.

One might protest that this can make sense for the average worried neurotic of the Woody Allen variety, who maintains relationships and a job, but not for the more deeply disturbed. Even in these cases, however, I think there are viable community-based solutions. For example, World Health Organization Studies show that people who experience a first episode of psychosis (e.g. serious delusions, hallucinations, or hearing voices) in the developed world are more than twice as likely to end up having those experiences chronically as their counterparts in India, Nigeria, or Columbia. These countries often have stronger webs of community and extended family support systems, and they also make room culturally for intense distress to run its natural course.

Inspired by tales of human connection with those struggling with psychosis, Loren Mosher, M.D. has created experimental healing centers known as Soteria houses to provide a low- or non-drug option for the treatment of first episode psychosis. In these homes, people in the throes of a mental health emergency receive round-the-clock empathy from compassionately attuned, nonprofessional caretakers. Randomized clinical studies tracking the outcomes of the people who undergo the Soteria project show that they do better than those receiving traditional medical care. I believe that this shows that even in the most dire of cases (the psychiatric emergency of a first psychotic episode), creative community-based solutions can perform as well as or better than traditional medical alternatives.

Who Really Helps: Professionals, Amateurs, and Amore

In the late 1970s Hans Strupp, a professor of psychology at Vanderbilt University, heard the following concern from a colleague: "How do you know that training works—that people would not get just as much help getting well talking over their problems with a kind, intelligent layperson as they would with a Ph.D. psychologist?" Strupp was intrigued by the question and designed a study to test it. College students enrolled in a program for free psychotherapy. Half of the students received therapy from Ph.D. professionals; the other half received caring attention from non-psychologists, college professors who had been identified by their peers as kind and good listeners.

What did Strupp find? People improved considerably in both groups, but there was no difference in efficacy between the professors and the professional psychologists. Feeling a bit like the emperor with no clothes, the clinical psychology establishment has replicated the study in slightly different forms more than 30 times, in an attempt to show that trained professionals are, on average, better at therapy than untrained kind paraprofessionals. The results have been surprisingly consistent—common professional training in mental health does not appear to make people more effective healers.

In a related line of research, over the course of a large number of trials, it has been shown that one type of therapy (Freudian, for instance) does not outperform another form (say, cognitive behavioral). If training and therapeutic modality do not appear to affect effective support, you might ask, what does?

Research has routinely shown that certain people are better at giving support than others, and that quality of caring attention matters. Indeed, one multi-million dollar study by the National Institute of Mental Health found that some psychiatrists are consistently more effective healers than their peers even when just prescribing inert cornstarch placebos.

What does this all mean for the communities movement? I believe findings like these have the capacity to embolden us. We do not necessarily need to rely on expensive, HMO-based, rigid therapies and drugs administered by professionals who might not share our culture or values. We can provide amateur care for one another, reclaiming the positive connotations for "amateur"—from the French *amateur*, "lover of," ultimately from the Latin verb *amare*, to love. Better to base our care for one another in love is the message I get both from my personal intuitions and from my reading of the primary research.

Principles for Community-Based Mental Health

Freud once commented that the aim of psychotherapy was to help people ascend "from hysterical misery to ordinary unhappiness." I think we in the communities movement can strive for more. To that end, and with a nod to the famous poster on how to build community, I offer the following in closing:

How to Support Community Mental Health

- Support (neuro)diversity, recognizing and honoring the huge variance in the human experience.
- Promote economic equality and opportunity.
- Seek natural health, making sure to get plenty of B vitamins, omega three fats, and vitamin D.
- Spend time outside.
- Exercise with vigor.
- Avoid toxins like heavy metals.
- Devote a great deal of time to family and friends, and nurturing and enjoying those relationships.
- Express gratitude, listen, and practice forgiveness.
- Continuously seek to be helpful in daily life.
- Connect with and care for nature.
- Eat together.
- Practice optimism when imagining the future.
- Savor life's pleasure, and try to live in the present moment.
- Commit to lifelong goals and ambitions.
- Live in connection with your values. ❧

Brian Toomey lives at Dancing Rabbit Ecovillage, and is a co-owner and editor on Sustainablog.org, an online blog covering environmental issues. He enjoys reading, vegan whole foods cooking, and meditating. He also has a fanatic love of basketball and the Boston Celtics, and shares the Buddha's desire that all beings be liberated from suffering.

Nina Rey

A Nomad Ponders Family and Community

By Molly Hollenbach

My friend Nancy goes to family reunions a thousand miles away with at least 50 people, and I marvel. I'm an only child from a small family, not married, no kids. We moved around a lot, and my parents didn't actually live together much, even when they were married. I'm not sure why. They moved to change jobs, to be near her brothers and sisters in Detroit or his in Los Angeles, or maybe to split up, to get back together. We had relatives but didn't live near them; I had friends but frequently had to say goodbye.

My mother was the only constant in my life, and we had an edgy relationship. She came of age on a Missouri farm in the Depression, I grew up in a California town in the '60s. She worked two jobs as a medical secretary to put me through high school, and I, of course, lounging around reading the Existentialists, had no appreciation for what she must have given up to raise a child alone. We blamed each other for our differences.

I have, like my mother, itchy feet, the travel bug, the nomad's belief that there really is greener grass in the next valley over. Being able to move along when things aren't going well is a very American form of freedom, and it produces a very American kind of person: a lonely one. Although I've kept up the family pattern, with variations, I've also yearned for closer relationships. This story is about my personal quest for intimacy in family, friendship, and community, and what I learned along the way.

•••

The common element of intimacy is some kind of openness. You meet each other's eyes without dissembling—it's an open-eyed, mutual regard. It could be called a loving regard; but not all intimacy is loving. There's the quiet comfort of knowing and being known, such as one feels in a family, a long marriage, or a small town. There's also the intimacy of extreme moments—in crisis or celebration—the stuff movies are made of. You're standing together on the deck of the sinking Titanic. You're in bed. You're halfway up the glacier. Or someone has a gun to your head, and you look into his eyes. You are fully, mutually present.

And there's what Romain Rolland, an early 20th century French philosopher, and then Sigmund Freud called the "oceanic feeling," *"le fait simple et direct de la sensation de l'éternel (qui peut très bien n'être pas éternel, mais simplement sans bornes perceptibles, et comme océanique)."* [literally: The simple and direct fact of the sensation of eternity (which might not be eternity, but simply without perceptible boundaries, oceanic).] Freud rephrased this as "a feeling of an indissoluble bond of being one with the external world as a whole."

I think of it as a moment of grace, an ecstatic, mystical oneness—the far end of the range of feelings of intimacy. It happens; it's not something one can consciously direct. My first experience of this sort came at a lonely moment in my life, when I was 11. My mother filed for divorce and took a secretarial job in La Jolla; my father went to work for the Los Angeles Department of Water and Power. They put me in a small boarding school for girls on a ranch in the live oak hills of Fallbrook, California. On the second day of class, the teacher in the one-room schoolhouse skipped me two grades—from fourth to seventh—and thus I became both the youngest and oddest member of this small community.

Each girl was assigned a horse to ride and take care of. Mine, a swaybacked brown pony named Prince, became my best friend. Because of the swayback he couldn't wear a saddle much, so I learned to ride him bareback. One afternoon I was out in the back pasture with Prince, stretched out on his warm, dusty back, with my toes in his mane and my head on his rump, watching the clouds. Something happened that I called afterwards "merging with the sky." The air became luminous. I had a deep sense of absolute belonging in the world. I couldn't tell whether it lasted for a moment or for a while. Since then, whenever that perception comes, it fills me with gratitude. It infuses my life with meaning. It is what I stand on, my bottom line.

•••

When I was younger I think I expected that feeling of ecstatic, mystical oneness to happen in human company, as well. I believe I've seen it in Sufi dancing or the ecstatic devotional dance of followers of Rajneesh, though I haven't experienced it that way myself. It is an extraordinary kind of intimacy in a crowd, closely related to the bliss of sex, the feeling of union with god. It is one of the elements of charisma. It is a human universal, although many people have never felt it, might not even want to feel it. This feeling can be manipulated, controlled, and directed by those who know how to use their personal power over others.

As a graduate student in cultural anthropology, I read about the wide varieties in human experience and social forms, and thought there were probably better arrangements in some societies than ours. For example, I found gypsies fascinating because they, like my family, never settled down, yet they seemed to have a closeness and emotional freedom so different from ours.

Carol Miller, a cultural anthropologist who lived among modern-day, Serbian-American gypsies in the 1960s and '70s, writes about the gypsies' love of a blissful feeling of togetherness in extended family groups. Although they moved around a lot, they maintained close ties through phone calls and parties and religious events throughout the year. Miller explains, in her book, *Lola's Luck: My Life Among the California Gypsies*, that gypsy ceremonies held on occasions such as births and deaths were intended to be more than just a good time, to create more than good feeling: the goal was euphoria, unforgettable moments, heroic moments—what I'm calling ecstatic, mystical oneness. All the elements of community were there: close relatives, food, music, dance, and formal elements invoking spiritual beliefs. But it wasn't considered a successful event if that shared good feeling didn't arise and sustain itself among everyone present. A mean-spirited remark could ruin the whole ceremony.

•••

The Be-Ins, Love-Ins, rock concerts, political demonstrations, group therapy, and communes of the '60s were experiments in intimacy—intensely shared experience, openness, honesty—in new social forms that flew in the face of the cautious, conventional '50s. Toward the end of that era, after hugging strangers at Love-Ins and standing shoulder-to-shoulder in protests, I dropped out of graduate school in anthropology and joined a commune.

At the height of the hippie Revolution, a group called The Family coalesced in Haight-Ashbury and left the city, eventually settling in northern New Mexico with high hopes of creating a new and better society. In early 1970 I met two representatives of The Family at the World Affairs Conference, a semi-academic, radical thinkers' conference at the University of Colorado in Boulder, where The Family was invited to talk about their communal way of life. They gave a demonstration of Gestalt therapy to a large audience, which I found thrilling. At the end of the week, I quit my waitress job, said goodbye to my roommate, and left for Taos. The calm self-possession of these two folks, both bright dropouts from higher education, impressed me. I

Bligh Gillies

hoped they could help me get what they had: "the self you've always wanted." And I was hoping to find a real family.

At that time, The Family had about 55 members and lived in a small adobe house about 10 miles outside of Taos. They considered themselves a group marriage and practiced their own form of group encounter and Gestalt therapy as a means of breaking down psychological barriers. They had a rule of "24-hour encounter." Every member was supposed to be emotionally available to the others at all times. If someone wanted to interact with you, you had to give the encounter your full and honest response, including showing anger or irritation if that was how you felt. All conflicts were supposed to be resolved by face-to-face confrontation, which they called "hassling"; no passive avoidance, no forming alliances to gang up on someone. Everyone had an equal voice, they said. This vision appealed to me. I hated hypocrisy

Sunrise Ranch, little chapel.

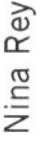

Nina Rey

Sunrise Ranch, pavilion and sculpture pond.

and believed that people are essentially good. I believed that if I could get in touch with my "real" self, I would be OK; I would know what was going on, know what to do, know how to be a good person. And I would be loved.

As it turned out, there was no politeness encountering each other, and no privacy either; even toothbrushes were shared. But more significantly, there was no psychological privacy. I was horrified to hear things I had said to a lover thrown in my face by someone else. Intimacy in The Family proved painful, as it was based on psychologically invasive techniques without corresponding safeguards. The Gestalt sessions often turned accusatory and bullying—all in the name of love. In The Family's version of Gestalt therapy (probably not recognizable to its founder, Fritz Perls), the person on the "hot seat" in the middle of the circle faced a crowd of interrogators who gave no quarter. For me, the message was: "You don't know where you're at!," "You don't know what you really feel" (the implication: We do.), "You're so fucked up." When I was on the hot seat, I usually ended up humiliated, sobbing apologies for not being whatever

I thought I was supposed to be according to the group.

Nothing in The Family's rules said anything about nonviolence or compassion. The leader was called "the strongest among us"—not the kindest or wisest, though some considered him wise, but the strongest. The rule of hassling, which was presented as a means of giving everyone an equal voice, in fact created a hierarchy in which the strongest and most aggressive members got their way and directed the life of the community.

Yet there were moments—many moments—of peaceful being together in the little adobe house on a field outside of Taos, or crowded together on the floor of the white van on the way into town, or working side by side in the kitchen, that touched some part of me seldom touched. It was like having lots of brothers and sisters—the larger family I had yearned for as a child. Though I left The Family after only a few intense months, I held onto the possibility that somewhere, somehow, there could be that open sharing of selves without the invasiveness, whether in the intimacy of one-to-one relationships, or in therapy, or in a community of a different kind.

•••

Now, in my 60s, I have finally realized that relationships deepen when you stay put. I live in a high mountain town where I've lived several years, gone away, visited, and moved back, to be with the same friends. The post office and grocery store are a short walk away, and I see faces I recognize even if I've been gone for a while. I cherish this community that others have built and take comfort from their sense of permanence. My own small circle of friends is teaching me what it means to know one another over a long time and to see one another grow and change. Simply choosing to stay in this town, in a landscape I love, with these particular friends, has taught me a lot about intimacy. I'm not looking to move—at least not for a while. Not unless I have a really good reason.

Sunrise Ranch, dome.

•••

An article in the "Elders" issue of Communities magazine by Victoria Albright moved me to think again about my own family. She is about my age and is writing about a mother-daughter relationship transformed by a group process in community. My mother died 12 years ago, before I ever found a way to let go of my anger and blame. My clumsy efforts at encounter-style honesty with her after I left The Family didn't work well for either of us. She looked back bitterly on "that terrible time when you got involved with the hippies and hated your mother."

Albright described an experience of intimacy within a group that sounded so different, and so much kinder, than what I had seen in The Family. It sounded secular; not mystical oneness but a way of building close relationships while keeping ego boundaries respectfully intact. She and her daughter had a very positive outcome from a group process that seemed intrusive to her at the beginning.

Albright had come for a visit to Lost Valley Educational Center, an intentional community near Eugene, Oregon, where her daughter was living. When she was invited to share disagreements with her daughter with a third person—a mediator—present, she almost turned around and left. But she stayed, at her daughter's urging, and found it was possible to be herself, communicate fully, and honor the generational differences. Albright visited Lost Valley many times and grew to love her role there as an elder, able to help other parents and children understand each other better.

I decided to call Albright and ask her to consider in more detail what made this potentially painful or even harmful "processing" of differences in values and worldview both positive and growth-inducing instead of widening the conflict between herself and her daughter. If my mother and I could have had something like that, I thought, it would have changed our lives. Albright said the ground rules made the group process positive—the rules for peaceful, nonjudgmental communication, and the dedication of all the members to following those rules. There were several practices that made deep sharing at Lost Valley safer than it was in The Family or in my family of origin.

The Lost Valley community's rules were based on the principles of Compassionate Listening, developed initially to help Israelis and Palestinians talk to each other in the quest for a lasting peace, and Nonviolent Communication, developed by a psychologist, Marshall Rosenberg, for similar purposes. The idea is that conflicts can be resolved if the parties agree to listen to each other with empathy and speak honestly without judgment, blame, shaming, guilt, or

Nina Rey

"Would you be willing to wait until later in the day to use the vacuum cleaner?" It wasn't about oneness; it was about allowing, differentiating, and working together.

other kinds of manipulation that increase the conflict. Nonviolent communication is a four-part process: first, making observations based on perception, e.g. "I hear you vacuuming the living room at 8 in the morning"; then a feeling statement, "I feel irritated"; then an expression of a simple human need, such as "I need to be able to sleep in after working late"; and finally a clear, concrete, feasible request, such as "Would you be willing to wait until later in the day to use the vacuum cleaner?"

Surrounding all this at Lost Valley were hours and hours of just listening and allowing each other to say what they meant. It sounded delicious to me, but it wasn't about oneness; it was about allowing, differentiating, and working together.

•••

Because, after The Family, I remain suspicious of hierarchy and distrustful of charisma, I was intrigued to hear from a former member of another communal group who considered her patriarchal leaders benevolent, even though she eventually left. I asked for more information from Taylor Goforth, a bright-faced, slender woman now in her 50s. Goforth spent nearly 20 years with the international spiritual group, Emissaries of Divine Light (EDL), living for six years at an EDL community in Oregon, and another 12 years at Sunrise Ranch, in the foothills of Rocky Mountain National Park.

The beautiful land at Sunrise played a large part in her experience of community.

"The land spoke to me so deeply," she said. She loved to climb the hill of huge granite boulders to the west and look out over the valley and north to the mountains. The 345-acre ranch provided the group a solid economic base, with a dairy herd, a five-acre organic garden, and enough land to raise alfalfa and hay. Some 125 members worked hard together, growing and processing much of their own food. They found joy in the work, Goforth said.

EDL had a hierarchical structure, but in this case there were many leaders, not just one, and according to her they were mostly benign.

"The spiritual focus was represented by the community and the leaders. We considered the hierarchical structure the design of heaven on earth; the heavenly design could be made manifest," Goforth said. "The community was a vehicle to experience oneness with God and with the creative process and the Whole [of existence].

"When we were together there was a hugely moving experience that happened, with the group resonating around ideals and high feelings of ecstasy, compassion, serenity, illumination."

In the best of times, Goforth said, "I felt like everything I did had significance; I had a purpose, a direction; I was surrounded by others with the same purpose, having the same experience. It was mind, heart, and body together. Life was suffused with meaning."

What could possibly have been missing? For Goforth, it was critical thinking and a strong connection with the big world outside the community. She felt subtly set apart as an intellectual. She saw the patriarchal leadership growing rigid and resistant to change. The teachings emphasized the positive to the extent that the negative couldn't accept-

Despite their struggles, those who left these communities took something with them, as I did from The Family—new knowledge of themselves, questions, a determination to build something more.

ably be spoken.

It's hard to sustain utopia. As Shakespeare put it in *The Taming of the Shrew:* "My tongue will tell the anger of mine heart, Or else my heart, concealing it, will break." Jealousy, aggression, a carping, bitter anxiety—there will be a stain on the white tablecloth, and eventually it will have to be washed. The Taos Family ran up huge debts, lost members, and left town in the middle of the night. The communities described by Albright and Goforth did not last, at least not in the same idyllic form. For Lost Valley, the gradual changing of the generations, as well as economic and other factors, both internal and external, brought in new goals and approaches that also changed the social dynamics (part of an evolution, perhaps a spiral one, that continues today). In the EDL community, Goforth said, "people felt their idea of or commitment to what Martin Exeter (and Uranda before him) had taught in terms of spiritual truths was being betrayed, left behind, changed. The group's trust of each other was deeply shaken." Many, including Goforth, left. (Sunrise is, however, still a working farm community, still part of EDL, and, according to Goforth, again manifesting important elements of its initial spirit.)

But despite their struggles, those who left those communities took something with them, as I did from The Family—new knowledge of themselves, and some questions, and perhaps a determination to build something more.

"After I left I felt very fragmented," Goforth said. "No one around me had anything in common. I wondered what brought people together [in mainstream society]."

•••

After my brief but often painful experience in The Family, I had no interest in living in a commune, ever again. But while I was still with The Family, I had the opportunity to visit another kind of place that also left a lasting impression, this one positive. The Family had made a film about itself and the other Taos communes of the time, and had a grand plan for distributing it and becoming rich and famous. The leader sent four of us off in a car with a copy of the film and instructions to arrange showings at university campuses throughout the west. Our first stop was the University of Arizona, and someone had arranged for us to stay at a community of artists north of Tucson called Rancho Linda Vista. Rancho Linda Vista was a cohousing community before the term was adopted. A group of artists and art professors from the University of Arizona had bought a piece of land that was formerly the home base of a working ranch; houses were scattered out among the desert landscape and there was a central building for meetings and shared meals. But there was privacy; there were separate houses; there were psychological and social boundaries and breathing spaces in which to make art.

When I visited Rancho Linda Vista in the spring of 2003, more than 30 years after its founding, it was still there, still beautiful, and they were still doing art. Some of the original members had passed on, but the community continued. I chatted with Joy Fox McGrew, one of the cofounders, sitting on her porch in a cool desert breeze. I asked if there had ever been a time when someone tried to take over and run the place their way. Joy mulled it over and said that someone once did get into writing up the rules and making them into a book and telling everybody what to do, but that effort didn't get very far. There was no way to get a leg up on that particular horse. It seemed that when conflicts arose and meetings got long, someone would likely say, "Aaahh, let's go get drunk and make art."

•••

I'm happy in my *un*intentional community with good friends, but here's what I would look for if I wanted something more consciously designed: First, a secular mission statement. I'm no longer looking for ecstatic, mystical oneness in a group. That's religion. I believe in the separation of church and state, on the micro as well as the macro level. Second, a means, whether formal or informal, part of the rules or part of the group's culture, to acknowledge and prevent the ascension of those who want power over others. Exercising limited personal authority based on character, experience, and/or skill is different from control, manipulation, coercion. Let that distinction be maintained.

I would look for a place where there are separate quarters for partners and families and others who choose to live alone. I'd look for a community with permeable boundaries and lots of involvement with the wider world. And I'd want to find people who know about Compassionate Listening and Nonviolent Communication and are committed to living by those rules of engagement, because I think such practices allow intimacy to develop where it will—like grace—like belonging in the world. ❧

Molly Hollenbach is a freelance writer. She is working on a revised edition of her book, Lost and Found, *a memoir about The Family commune in Taos, New Mexico, 1970 (University of New Mexico Press, 2004).*

Honesty and Intimacy

By Damien Friedlund

Intimacy is like a drug. If you're brave enough to take a taste, you'll get high. By intimacy, I mean honesty. To practice honesty, we expose ourselves, make ourselves vulnerable. If my friend knows that I look at internet porn, once aspired to become a billionaire, and am attracted to his partner, and he still loves me, then I have overcome one of humankind's worst fears. If he loves me more because he knows me that much better, then we have reversed a basic human dynamic much of society takes for granted: that we will tell the truth and lose love directly because we did so. When my secrets are no longer secret, and I am loved in spite of them, or even because I have shared deeply, intimately, I am free. It's my experience that the most powerful social and emotional bonds are created by this process.

When I was 30, I joined a rather extreme community (some might call it a "cult," though FIC discourages use of this ill-defined, usually pejorative label) because I could see, upon visiting them, that the 40-odd members had some kind of powerful family-like love between them. They so casually expressed affection with playful, light touch. Because of loneliness and isolation in my life, I readily gave up my unappreciated autonomy and what few worldly goods I possessed

Illustrations by Yulia Z.

to gain a chance to experience this other-worldly kind of connection. I was not disappointed, though the path towards intimacy was not a clear one. After a couple months of pleasant warm social interactions while performing simple rural labors such as harvesting potatoes and milking goats, two of my closest new companions took me aside in the hay room of the goat barn to let me know, to my horror, that I wasn't working out in the community. After years of solitary, ambitious toil in large cities, I was thoroughly enjoying my new, rich social life among 40 seeking souls in rural America. The problem they told me was that I was hiding myself behind the mask of my personality.

I had no idea what they were talking about. What did they mean that I was lying from deep within my personality? I had thought I had been so congenial, so willing to work hard, so open to what this new strange but powerful communal life had to offer. I was distraught at the prospect of my return to the mean streets of mainstream America. They told me that they could tell that I was hiding and lying, that they did not feel close to me in the way that I imagined I was close to them. The only way to stay was to come clean and honest, tell them about my real feelings about the pain they said they could feel right beneath the surface of my persona. I dug into my memory trying to excavate some childhood (their suggestion) wrong that could possibly redeem me in their, and apparently the whole community's, eyes. The best thread I could pick at from the garment of my life was pain I had experienced in high school, heavy ostracism, that led to me retreating emotionally, becoming much more guarded in the way that I expressed myself. I was 32; high school seemed so long ago. I had thought that pain was safely discarded in the past. Perhaps, I wept, the pain of those experiences, a cruel taunting that went on for several years while I was marooned at a chilly New England boarding school, was what they were looking for. I had never voluntarily told anyone about those years. Bingo! My friends yanked at the thread of my story until the whole garment of that old pain lay in a pile of thread at my feet. I had never told my family or any of my friends outside of prep school about this painful part of my life. I had just tried to bury it and forget about it.

Later that day, I related my sad tale to an audience of the entire community. Crying, expressing my emotions, in front of everyone led directly to my acceptance and success in this community. Reflecting on the experience, I know I was, consciously or unconsciously, being recruited into what some call a "cult," but the social transaction that was taking place was one of the most important events that has occurred in my life. By revisiting the painful chapter from my past, which I had long relegated to a mental dustbin, I regained a measure of my youthful enthusiasm, the innocence and naivete that had been crushed at prep school. Now I profited socially by undoing the layers of defense and protection I had built up over the years. A fundamental human dynamic of fear and truth was reversed. The truth—that I was treated as, had been, a loser in high school—did not lead to people continuing to reject me. On the contrary, the revelation led to profound empathy and my acceptance into a community and a way of life I craved.

The important lesson I learned was that revealing the truth led to love and intimacy because sharing it was a form of love and intimacy. With intimacy as the payoff, honesty, both emotional and intellectual, became my new religion. Though the community was not sustainable over the long term for myself and for almost everyone else—how could it be sustainable, when the religion of honesty came up against the practically inevitable desire for autonomy?—the lesson imparted, that honesty rather than strategy would lead to love and intimacy, has, for me, never diminished. I learned how to breathe a healthier, more powerful atmosphere, and I would continue to seek that air, choosing to live where it flourished.

But can we always be honest, and expect to receive the love and intimacy we crave? Unfortunately, no. I'm writing this article anonymously. For professional reasons, I do not want my colleagues to be able to Google my name and read about my past experiences or know details about my personal life. My professional life, for better or worse, is not the appropriate context for expressing myself honestly or seeking intimacy, except in individual doses that I control. There is some truth to the common perception that if we are truly honest we will be crushed. We cannot expect those who hardly know us, and who did not choose to work in the world with us, to respond favorably to unusual and uncommon expressions of honesty. Most people in impersonal situations just want our social interactions to go smoothly. Practicing an unusually high degree of honesty will not make one's interactions go more smoothly. Quite the contrary, it will point out the hard work that building intimacy requires, and is likely to make them very uncomfortable. The joke phrase we hear so often, "Too much information!," will assume a new air of seriousness. If, for any of the parties, the goal of the social transaction is other than intimacy, then honesty has a limited role to play.

Attraction tends to work much more mysteriously, or at least eccentrically, than matching values and lifestyles.

So, what contexts are the best for seeking intimacy? Not surprisingly, in family and community, we have the best chances for building deep intimacy. Despite the faults of the community at which I took my crash course in honesty, the degree of intimacy practiced there was exceptional. That's what attracted me in the first place. When I left, I knew I would seek that intimacy in a more sustainable context.

I researched intentional communities and I ended up living in another rural one where 30 people, in addition to gardening, building, practicing permaculture, and running a conference center, met weekly for several hours specifically to cultivate connection and build intimacy. On paper, the situation seemed the perfect place to continue my quest for communal intimacy. And I did make strong connections. Many of the members of this intentional community practiced a high level of honesty and experienced a deep intimacy with each other. But this community of intention, over time, was hardly more sustainable than the group I had left. Over the years I have seen every member I knew leave to meet some need they could not meet there. Most often members left to pursue a professional ambition or to seek and cultivate personal relationships. Although intentional communities often have built the social structures to encourage honesty and to promote intimacy, like meetings and rituals devoted specifically to this purpose, they are usually, nevertheless, challenged to hold on to members.

Most communities are not big enough to foster enough loving partnerships. People usually want to find someone with whom they can fall in love. A population of 30 people, many already partnered, is rarely enough to provide a suitable variety of potential partners. Fifty unattached people is closer to what I imagine would be the lowest possible number of members of an intentional community that would be likely to be able to hold on to members for social reasons alone. Though communal intimacy is a powerful draw, loving partnership, along with meaningful vocation, is the fuel that powers most peoples' lives. Unfortunately, most people are drawn to intentional communities because they believe in the values of the community, the mission statement, and they are attracted to the lifestyle the members live. But we don't really choose our friends, lovers, and partners by such criteria. Attraction tends to work much more mysteriously, or at least eccentrically, than matching values and lifestyles, though these factors certainly come into play. Though the process of deepening honesty and building intimacy with any willing like-minded person is thrilling, at least for extroverts, most seekers of communal intimacy long to do so with their best friends, those to whom they are most attracted. Ultimately, I believe, profound intimacy springs from "affection," not "intention." The good old-fashioned chemistry of attraction and affection is more likely to create the incentives that will galvanize individuals to overcome the inevitable challenges that come with relationship building, community building, intimacy building.

I left that community to pursue a professional goal, and eventually I ended up drawn to another communal experiment, this one smaller and urban. I moved in with a partner and her extended family consisting of an ex-husband/co-parent and

Relationships are almost like sharks: they don't have to keep moving to survive, but if they're not moving forward there is a high likelihood that they'll move backwards.

their two children and another long term member of the community. With room for 10 members, I hoped we could foster a community of affection that would provide the foundation for life in a beautiful and stable community of intention. I believe that goal may be possible, but we were not successful. My partnership was not as solid as I had hoped, and when it broke up, and when we both fell in love with new partners, though we were still friends, our new social lives did not lend themselves to building the degree of intimacy I believe is necessary to create a "community of affection." My energy flowed across town to where my new partner lived and where many of my best friends ended up living. The point of offering these details is to show to how much fluidity our lives are subject, and the difficulties this condition places on the building of a community. And we were middle-aged, slowing considerably down. Try to build a solid anything with a group of young people. It might be that a community most likely to thrive would be comprised of retirees approaching senior citizenship. You think I'm joking, but the older age demographic has the best qualifications for creating stable community.

I'm presently involved in an extended family of sorts, non-residential, but quite intimate. Our average age is 54, including those in our 40s and our 60s. We're financially stable, more geographically stable than most younger people, and we have the time to connect and do things with each other, when we want to. What, exactly, it is that we want to do with each other has emerged as our biggest challenge. When we first realized that we were a "community of affection," we didn't exactly intend it, and we were all so thrilled. At last a community, no larger than a big nuclear family, in which we all really liked each other. We shared and shared. We helped each other through all sorts of knotty personal issues with each other and within our various partnerships and friendships. But the first blush of love wears thin in a group, even a small group, just as it tends to in a partnership of two. Differences clarify.

At the beginning of this essay, I put forward a definition of intimacy based on honesty, or shared emotional experiences. But honesty is a game in which the ante is continually being raised. It's not easy, or necessarily sustainable, to put the brakes on honesty, to say, "only this honest, and not any more so." Don't all relationships, whether comprised of two or 20, tend to chafe against their limitations? I don't know whether those with whom I feel most intimate, by my own definition, those with whom I must express myself as honestly as I am able, will agree to meet me in a place in which we are both vulnerable, in which we both show each other our naked and imperfect souls. There is no guarantee that honesty will be reciprocated, that others, even those closest to me, will share my notions of intimacy. I don't need everybody I love to believe in the religion of honesty, but relationships among people who believe in different degrees of emotional sharing come under a pervasive strain. Relationships are almost like sharks: they don't have to keep moving to survive, but if they're not moving forward there is a high likelihood that they'll move backwards. And receding relationships, even if the recession turns out to be merely seasonal, are particularly awkward creatures with which to play.

Though our family of old fogies is relatively stable, we may not blaze new trails towards greater intimacy. What we already have, which I hope will continue to be extraordinary, may be as much we get. If our collective age is the key to our success as a "community of affection," it may also be our limitation. Old dogs may not be capable of learning new tricks, new ways of being with each other. It's often quite difficult to tell whether we're creating a new way of being intimate, or whether we're just holding each others' hands on the long, inevitable walk towards death. But I suppose that is a rather intimate stroll.

Over the past six months, my partner has been more honest with me about my dysfunctional behaviors, themselves manifestations of my selfishness or self-centeredness. She calls me out on things I say or ways that I act of which she says she would not have made an issue in years past. She realizes she must be honest with me or the foundation of our relationship will be corrupted. In actuality, we will have no relationship, even if we are living together and are sharing the logistics of our lives. In turn, I really must hear, must receive, what she is sharing, if I value our relationship. To resist her emotional truth would likewise nullify our relationship. Whether I can change my behaviors, heal my dysfunction, is another question, but I must, at least, deeply respect what has been bravely offered if we are to move forward, to continue to build intimacy. Each of these decisions to hear each other's truth is individual. We do not know if it will be heard, reciprocated, or if its sharing will change our dynamic.

Despite my quest for intimacy in partnership and community, I realize the most important decisions about intimacy—in my opinion, how to pursue honesty—will have to be made alone and stand alone, whether reciprocated or not. Just as the essential decisions affecting my partnership, I believe, are individual, decided by each of us, the future of our communal family will come down to individual decisions about what each of us wants and is able to express. Ultimately it is quite ironic that intimacy—honest, deep sharing between people—is expressed, both in partnerships and communities, by individual actions. ❧

Damien Friedlund writes pseudonymously.

Love Is the Answer

By Satyama Lasby

I love the topic of love. Being "in love," falling in love, finding one's true love. It depends on where you are in your life, of course, for as we know, everything changes. One year you may find yourself with a beautiful partner, and in another moment you are going through a breakup or a unique healing process that has occurred through relating with another.

It was after a breakup with my partner of four years that I made the New Year's resolution to discover unconditional love, and I have been on this journey ever since. The breakup occurred because I had slept with another man during a vacation and held this event close to myself for several months. It was not a happy or free time in my life. In fact, I lost a lot of sleep, worked too much, and lived with stress. I decided to take a group I had heard of called the enlightenment intensive, otherwise known as "Who Is In." I returned to my partner to share the truth of being with another man, which resulted in the end of the relationship on his part. Emotionally I journeyed from the bliss of the truth and emotional emptiness I had found in the group to being devastated and rejected as he ended the relationship.

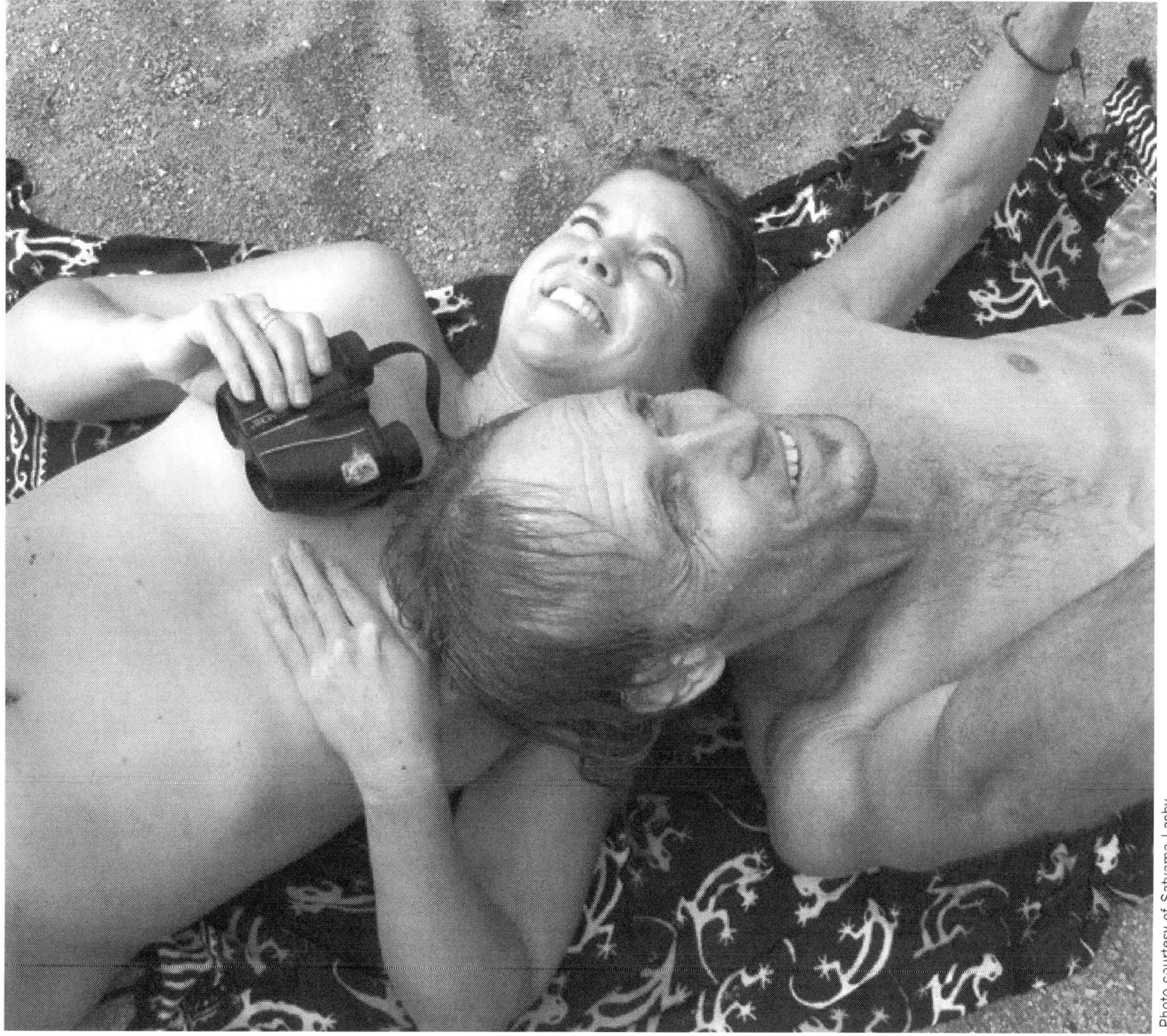

Photo courtesy of Satyama Lasby

Tantra for Greater Understanding

Here is an idea for a group of men and women inspired by Karam and Raji, the tantra teachers of Pachamama in San Juanillo, Costa Rica.

The men and women meet in separate groups to begin. In each circle, each person says something aloud on what they would like the opposite gender to know about their gender, for greater understanding, sharing, and intimacy among the sexes. Each person also shares what they appreciate about the opposite sex.

For example, I have shared:

"I would like men to know that they are free to be who they are, and that women are not trying to keep them down or get something from them."

and

"I would like men to know that we appreciate it when they communicate honestly and openly with us, and listen to us even when we are trying to explain something that may be emotionally difficult."

After the same-sex groups share amongst themselves, they come together to share what was discussed. People have the option to pass if they do not feel comfortable. Each person lets the next person know when they have completed their sharing.

I have found this exercise to be deeply intimate, beautiful, and heart-opening.

—S.L.

It was a turning point in my life, however, as I launched into the quest for truth. Living and speaking this way brought a feeling of incomparable bliss. I quit my career two years later and decided to finally live my dreams by traveling the spiritual path and living in community. I wanted to live in community, with people who felt that the truth was as important as I did. I also wanted to be among people who could share love freely, even be in relationships that were open enough to sustain and accept other lovers. It was at the Osho International Meditation Resort in India that I began a way of relating that would change and expand relationships for me.

As Osho attests, love is freedom, and freedom is truth. The meditation centre in India is a juicy and ethical place. People have multiple lovers, open relationships, exclusive partners, with little marriage or children in the Osho sanyassin world. Sanyassins are spiritual seekers and followers of the master Osho Rajneesh. I decided to take sanyass after several experiences with men that taught me two very important lessons...one being to share the truth upfront when relating, and the other being the principle of detachment.

When it came to intimate relating, I had one partner who told me he was sleeping with several people yet still invited me to join him. While at first I was taken aback by the conversation and proposal, I spent several weeks processing, doing emotional cleansing through groups, and came to a place where I decided to accept his offer. The decision was one based on my respect for the truth given outright. The next lesson that came very quickly for me after accepting his proposal was one of detachment, especially detachment from people. Many women experience this in the commune and in our lives because our ingrained and conditioned nature is to find a man to keep for raising of children in order to keep our species alive. I experienced feelings of anger, jealousy, and rejection, because of my conditioned expectation for this man to continue to want me, yet when he pulled away, or went with another woman, I was hurt, despite having the cards laid on the table for me.

I have since had several experiences like this, and in the reverse. Men come to me energetically with desire, and I do not want them because of this pull. I am always grateful for experiences in relating, as it is such a mirror for me. It is a journey of course in finding love, but as we know, love can only come when we love ourselves, which I truly do.

My spiritual journey has led me to the place of observation, letting things go, and learning the art of non-doing, as the universe works to provide us with what we need. It was after an experience of moving to a new city and meeting a fellow sanyassin in Ontario that I learned the lesson of detachment, once again. I thought this might be the "one," as it is quite rare to meet someone having Osho as their master in this part of the world. I fell for him of course, as the pattern went; I wanted him too much and he went with someone else, backed away and eventually told me he wanted only friendship. While all this was happening, along with the feelings of rejection that came with it, I was naturally becoming friends with another man, going to spirit conferences, festivals, and the Rainbow Gathering in Pennsylvania. What started with absolutely no attraction to this other man ended up in a very deep love, for I truly wanted nothing from him. I had no expectation on the relationship. I was simply having beautiful experiences with this man, as a friend and as a lover. I could be in my full power, express my full truth, and be intimate with other people if I wanted.

The Path of Love is one that runs quite deeply for us all. I feel that in the work I have done on myself, doing exactly as I want to do is key, every time. True love came when I wasn't trying to make anything happen, and it continues to work this way. My relating with my lover is open and free; I can travel the world and live in community. He is raising two children and teaching spiritual living to ESL students while I am following my dream of being in the community of Pachamama for the winter, and teaching yoga workshops and writing in Canada for the summer.

It is also possible for us to have other lovers, and be open about it. Love, intimacy, and the truth are interconnected, and all come when we are truly free and in love with ourselves.

Satyama is a freelance writer, yoga teacher, and Thai massage therapist living in both Pachamama in Costa Rica and in Guelph, Ontario. Passionate about travel, she puts on yoga and tantra workshops internationally. See www.satyama.ca or contact her through satyama@satyama.ca.

Dreaming It Up: Our 20-Year Experiment with Open Marriage in Community

By Jake and Bell

Bell: I remember when it all started. We had been married a year, together for four. And I still hadn't answered the question, "Can I really be in love if I am attracted to other people?" I had this belief that in serious relationships you put your blinders on and never look at other men. But after a while, I realized this restriction was sapping my zest for life. Then we moved into this big intentional community and, in our first week, I met Rain.

Jake: I remember that long walk we took when you said you were attracted to Rain and didn't know what to do about it. I didn't know either so I gave you a yellow light and said we should "Proceed with caution…" I think I also made some silly rule I didn't want you to touch each other where you would wear underwear. I remember the fateful night a few weeks later when I came back early from making tofu (coincidentally, with your next lover!). And there the two of you were, in our bed, and you clearly had broken my rule!

I was devastated. I felt like you had pulled the rug out from under me and I lost all trust in you. We slept apart for the first time that night and I remember having one of the most profound dreams of my life. I was driving a beautiful red car and all our photo albums were in the back seat. We stopped at an amusement park and when we came back, we found the car was broken into and all our photos were stolen. And I knew this happened because you left your door unlocked!

Suddenly it all made sense! I think the car represented our relationship, which is interesting because, like a car, we can both be "in it," but also have our own doors—our own ways of relating to the outside world. In my relationships, I always "lock my door." I can roll down my window—and relate with my head, even my heart—but I always keep my seatbelt on.

My fear was that you would be "careless" and let someone else into our car, and this person would steal that which made us special, made us unique... And that's exactly how I felt. Around that time, you would say you loved me and I would think, "So what?! You love me… You love him… You love the dog… What's special about that?"

It was a difficult time for us! You kept wanting to open up the marriage and I was angry and scared. This went on for around five months, but slowly I started asking new questions about

© Photos8.com

that dream, like "Why am I driving?" Why am I the one responsible for keeping us on straight and narrow road? And perhaps even more important, "Is there even a road out there?" Over 50 percent of marriages end in divorce. Maybe we'd do better heading off in our own direction.

I also started to recognize some of the cultural stories we were trapped in. Continuing with the car metaphor, it occurred to me that the cars we drive were designed before we were born. We don't build our own cars, we go to a lot and say things like "I'll take the red sedan with the good safety record." In a similar way, we don't create our relationships and they have rules and norms that were created millennia ago! "I'd like a heterosexual, serial monogamous relationship please. Ah, come right this way…"

So, I started to wonder, if I could really *design* our relationship, using the metaphor of a car, what would it look like? And it quickly came to me that I'd want a solar powered car! Solar energy is abundant! Today, most cars run on fossil fuels—a limited and zero-sum resource. The more one person has, the less another has. And I think many of us have a similar story that love is a finite resource we have to hoard. "I can't let you love someone else because that would be like putting a hole in our gas tank. All our love would leak out and there would be nothing left." I dreamt up a new *story* for us in which our "car" is powered by a source of energy so abundant we couldn't imagine even beginning to use it up. Love is the fabric of the universe! It's limitless!

This new story helped me feel more connected to you and also brought back a sense of specialness to our relationship. I realized what made us unique was not only the "photos" or experiences we shared, but who we are in the world together. As a couple, we take this omnipresent love and manifest it in the world in a unique way. Who "Jake and Bell" are *together* is unique. And that uniqueness is not lessened by your sharing love with someone else. In fact, in a way, it actually increases it!

I also came to realize that most of us have very different interpretations of what the word "monogamy" means and that this disparity is often what gets couples in trouble. In almost every relationship, one partner wants more intimacy, more love, outside the relationship, and this partner always "wins." They either get what they want or are seen as "noble" for sacrificing and coming back to the relationship. Meanwhile, the other partner either feels awful for restricting their partner or like a doormat if they let the other go. I realized the only way to make this work was to make it a two-way street.

Now, instead of our own struggles, it was our friends in the community that were challenging us. It was always, "Poor Jake. Bell is such a slut. Brandon is a homewrecker."

Bell: And that's what we did! We worked out a 10-rule agreement for ethical non-monogamy. 1. Alerting each other to "upcoming attractions"; 2. Getting permission before acting; 3. Getting permission from love interest's partner, if there is one; 4. Confirming that a love-interest is aligned to spiritual principles...and a slew of sexual health and safety protocols. Finally! Liberation Day! Just knowing this was possible made me fall in love with you all over again.

And others… Soon after, I also fell in love with Brandon, a builder in the community. He was the strong silent type, but spiritual too. Just what I wanted off the menu. But now, instead of our own struggles, it was our friends in the community that were challenging us. And here, *you* always came out the winner. It was always, "Poor Jake. He deserves better." or "Bell is such a slut. How dare she have her cake and eat it too!" or "Brandon is a homewrecker, breaking up their marriage!"

The irony is that, while we were trying our best to be transparent and honest with each other and those around us, there were several secret affairs that came to light around this time. The resulting chaos rocked the community and none of those rela-

What broke them up was not so much that their partners made love to someone else, but the breaking of trust between committed best friends.

tionships recovered.

The lying and dishonesty were so powerful, they could never explore anything deeper. It was all about "How could you have done this to me!" and "I was the *last* to know!" The pain of the deceit was so overwhelming, they couldn't ask "What did this mean?" or "Can you still love me and him/her at the same time?" What broke them up was not so much the fact that their partners made love to someone else, but the breaking of trust between committed best friends.

Jake: Yes. I remember deciding early on that if we were going to open our relationship we had to do it with the utmost integrity and honesty. I didn't want to repeat these old, painful stories, but rather to create something new. I found it amazing that, even in this new-age community, members were still clinging to traditional stories. It's like we were floating in this river of culture yet somehow swam to shore and could see these cultural stories for the first time.

Bell: It was quite a year! In the end, we left the community, to move closer to our families. I had dreams of the three of us living together happily ever after. But then I went to Costa Rica and blew it big time. I met another guy and got your permission to sleep with him, but totally forgot to ask Brandon. He didn't like that at all. And that was that. Later, you started having other lovers as well.

Jake: It took me a few years though. I thought I "locked my door" because I was a "sensitive new-age guy," but really, when I was honest with myself, I was just scared of rejection. Opening our relationship took away my excuse and my hiding place, which was challenging, but also wonderful! I had a number of short-term lovers and one relationship that lasted four years and recently ended when she chose to enter into a monogamous relationship with another friend. These all were incredible opportunities to share love and intimacy. They were also opportunities to "unlearn" many of our cultural stories. For example, I learned that I'm not a very jealous person. I didn't know that about myself! And I learned that love for one person doesn't preclude love for another. In fact, it often increases it! I don't remember learning that in any Disney movie!

Bell: And that brings us almost to today. My most recent relationship happened when the kids were three and eight. I was in my early 40s and having a mid-life crisis of sorts. I fell in love with someone much younger while traveling and later supported him to come and live with us. You were very generous around this, for which I will always be grateful.

And our kids were so used to "alternative" families in our progressive neighborhood (as we're writing this, they are both at play dates with friends who have two mommies) they just rolled with it. When our eldest asked about my lover, I explained that people can love more than one person and we were different in our beliefs about love and that mommy could love daddy *and* a boyfriend. That relationship ended over two years ago and I've been a bit more "quiet" about my sexuality since then.

I now look at non-monogamy in terms of its usefulness developmentally. At this stage in my life, my spiritual practice and career development require a lot of focus and these kinds of relationships absorb a lot of energy and attention. I'm also questioning if non-monogamy at this point in my spiritual development is an inhibitor given our present cultural context and understanding of how to do love. I think in 50 years, spiritual practice and non-monogamy will fit together more easily because the cultural waters are getting clearer.

So, here we are. Twenty years later! And, many thought, surely one of us would find someone else and leave the marriage. I was always clear that was (and still is) possible, but chose to take the risk because I really wanted to learn something about myself, us, love, and our world.

Jake: Ironically, I think we wouldn't be together now if we *didn't* open our relationship then. And to be clear, we have never advocated that others do as we did. We had four years of relationship, including a year of marriage under our belt, before we even considered these questions.

Bell: These are changing times and individuals need to stay true to their own hearts for guidance as we evolve into a more compassionate and awake world. ❧

"Jake" and "Bell" live in community with their children and can be contacted through editor@ic.org. While they are open to sharing on these topics, they understand these are controversial issues and thus names and locations have been changed to provide "plausible deniability."

The Relationship of Relationships to the Group

By Laird Schaub

Recently I was asked to facilitate a sharing circle for a group where there had been a shift in an intimate relationship among members. The change—an old partner out and a new partner in—naturally spurred a complex set of reactions among the other members and the group was undecided about whether to talk about it as a group, and if so, how. That's where I was asked to help.

On the one hand, the precipitating events were intimate decisions that the group clearly recognized as outside the group's purview. That is, no one was trying to make the case that the individuals needed any kind of group sanction to proceed. At the same time, it was equally clear that the shift was demonstrably affecting the group. In addition to the two people who were starting a relationship, there was a break-up of a longstanding relationship that resulted in a long-term member exiting the community. So joy and grief were commingled in a volatile emotional stew and it was anything but simple figuring out how to proceed with caring and authenticity.

To what extent is the group a stakeholder in this dynamic? To what extent is it helpful to create a forum at the group level to explore this tender territory? This is a great topic. Shifts in intimate relationships are not rare and groups often stumble over this dynamic, in part because groups seldom address how they want to handle it ahead of being in the situation that exposes the ambiguity—and it's hard to have an even-handed conversation about the *theory* of discussing the impact of relationships on the group, when everyone knows that what they're itching to talk about is how unresolved tensions in one *particular* couple regularly manifest in the form of sarcastic comments that poison the ambience of community potlucks.

In the particular situation I was working with, the pathway was further clouded by one member of the emerging couple wanting the chance to talk in the whole group, while the other partner dreaded it. The latter had never been comfortable sharing in groups, yet was willing to talk with anyone individually. Why, this person wondered, couldn't that be enough?

While much sharing might have been accomplished through one-on-one sharing, not everyone feels comfortable doing that when they're upset, and there is considerable power in everyone hearing from everyone else all at once. Not only does this cut down on speculation and gossip about what's happening and how people are responding, it gives depth to each person's knowledge of other members, and enhances the trust that you can build as a consequence of weathering a complex dynamic together.

By creating an intentional community, the group had made an explicit choice that members would be more in each other's lives than is the case in typical neighborhoods. That is, they purposefully chose to be closer with one another. That said, there was still substantial ambiguity about how close they wanted that to be, and the request to have a group conversation about how the group was impacted by intimate events begged that question. While some members definitely wanted this opportunity, others thought it was inappropriate and was inserting the community too far into members' private lives. Nonetheless, the group proceeded, and most members, to their credit, were willing to give it a try, with even some of the skeptical attending (for which I was thankful and impressed).

The sharing circle was an explicit attempt to help the new couple in their continuing relationships with others in the community—which everyone wanted to proceed in a healthy, authentic way—yet we established at the outset that no one was intending this session to encourage people to take sides between the new couple and the exiting member. In fact, one of the clearest benefits of the session was our ability to successfully establish that no one was asking anyone to choose between them, so that support extended to any of the principals should not be construed as an implied withdrawal of support for any other principal. Whew!

In this instance, the group did a terrific job of speaking from their hearts and listening closely to each other. This was all the more impressive in that a number of people had hard things to say.

Here is some of what came out:

—Anger that one member would make themselves available for a new relationship before the old one was dissolved. Some thought this violated a standard of morality, even though it was recognized that was a personal position and not something that the group took a stand on (though some groups do, this one did not).

—Lament that the group was not able to find a way to better help the struggling couple work through their issues, with the hope that either they'd come through it with their relationship intact, or that it was possible for the old couple to separate without the group losing a valued member.

—Fear in the new couple that others were holding them in judgment and that they might be shunned.

—Anger that people might have been used by the new couple to create opportunities for them to get together—that the third party was asked to hang out not because the couple wanted to spend time with them, but so that their presence could make it "safer" for the new couple to spend time together without arousing suspicion.

Note the power of the whole group hearing about all of this in one go, rather than trying to piece it together from a series of one-on-one conversations.

—Upset that people were hearing "dirty laundry" about the old couple that no one was comfortable with, or knew how to respond to.

—Confusion about whether it was appropriate to express happiness for the new couple without coming across as callous and uncaring for the person losing their partner.

—Upset that the group was intruding on private matters, and that the conversation might lead to traumatization and polarization that would preclude or at least delay healing.

—Fear among single people in the group that their spending time with married members might be misconstrued as an attempt to seduce other people's partners.

—Relief that the group cared enough about each other—and the whole—to make this attempt to discuss what was going on, without judging one another for their individual reactions.

—Thankfulness that there was finally an opportunity to say openly how difficult it had been to try to befriend all parties and have no one to share that with because of an overriding commitment to confidentiality (the underlying relationship struggles had been going on for more than a year).

One of the most powerful things that emerged in the sharing was people witnessing difficult things from their past that strongly influenced how they saw this development, which included their personal stories around intimacy and the boundaries they have developed about what is private and what is suitable to be shared with others. When revealed, it made it much easier for others to understand their perspective. In the absence of such knowledge, we tend to assume that others have similar life experiences to ours, and this can considerably muddy the waters when trying to make sense of why someone reacts as they do. Often, these things don't emerge until such tender moments occur and people are given an unexpected safe forum to share their histories.

Note the power of the whole group hearing about all of this in one go, rather than trying to piece it together from a series of one-on-one conversations. None of what I've written here is meant to criticize one-on-one sharing—I'm all for it. I'm only trying to make the case why sharing in the group offers unique benefits. Done well (which is not a slam dunk, yet is demonstrably possible), it undercuts hearsay, establishes a common basis for moving forward, enhances trust, and accelerates healing.

While no one wants people to suffer and go through deep hurt, such things inevitably occur. I'm excited when groups are willing to make the attempt to trust their ability to help each other through hard times by being real and vulnerable with one another, trusting in our basic humanity and desire to piece together our myriad and confused responses into a tapestry of authenticity and support when coping with crisis.

Relationships don't exist in a vacuum, and I think it works better when groups don't just look the other way and hope for the best. It gives me hope when communities are willing to extend themselves and recognize they can have a role in helping to create a healthy container in which relationships can manage struggle, and the individuals whose lives are affected can get support in finding their way to a constructive response. I'm proud to be a midwife of such moments.

As a group process consultant, this is as good as it gets. ❧

Laird Schaub is Executive Secretary of the Fellowship for Intentional Community (FIC), publisher of this magazine, and cofounder of Sandhill Farm, an FEC community in Missouri, where he lives. He is also a facilitation trainer and process consultant. This piece originally appeared September 30, 2010 on his blog at communityandconsensus.blogspot.com.

Three Perspectives on Intimacy in Community

Three members of Lafayette Morehouse (in the San Francisco Bay area) reflect on various forms of intimacy and how community fosters and supports it.

The Cavalry is Just Around the Corner

By Kiva Lindsey

I had a tumultuous relationship with my first husband, although we loved each other deeply. I really believe that we split because I kept the details of our relationship so private. We loved each other, but anger and resentment built up over time.

Somewhere along the way I became quiet about how I was feeling, not wanting to rock the boat or disturb the façade of "we have it all together." It was just the two of us, living on our own, and I felt more separate from him than ever. I am a "put on a happy face" kind of gal, but behind the big smile I was an unhappy woman, afraid to tell anyone what I was feeling. I was lonely and estranged from everyone, especially the one I loved the most.

I am grateful for my "starter marriage." It was a true learning experience and luckily we have stayed great friends. I learned what not to do, which for me was trying to make a marriage succeed without getting much support from other people. It is still my instinct to hide any troubles with my relationship but now, living a communal life closely with others, hiding out is no longer an option and I have found unexpected benefits in including friends, both in good times and bad.

For example, recently I had a blowup with my second husband, Michael. It had been one of those days; I could tell I was getting sick and was just annoyed by everything. I got very upset when Michael came home 20 minutes late without bothering to call. I know, I know...20 minutes seems really petty, but like I said, it'd been one of those days. So we argued and ended up sleeping in separate rooms.

The next day there was no denying that I had a massive head cold. Michael walked into the room and I immediately started barking orders at him. I was distressed about getting sick and felt it was my right that he drop everything, especially his grudge, and take care of me. "I am the one who is sick!" I screamed. (Attractive, right?)

He was still upset from the night before and frankly, I was still angry with him for coming home late. In no time our fighting escalated and was on the verge of violence. Michael stormed out of the room; I buried my head in the pillows.

He went directly to see Alec and Marilyn, friends of ours who have lived in our community for many years and have had a lot of experience successfully navigating intimate relationships. They've helped us many times before, quickly and gracefully getting us to a place where we could talk calmly about what was going on in our relationship.

It was a brave and loving move Michael made, calling in the Cavalry. I, of course, was not in the room to hear their wise words. I was home feeling sorry for myself for being sick and chasing off my best ally. But amazingly, 15 short minutes after he stormed out of the room, he was back, he was calm, he was happy, and he was offering to run me a bath and make me tea. When he walked *in* the room, feeling sane and full of love again, I immediately let my guard down and felt like I could surrender to him and the bathtub and the cold. We both knew that we were teammates again, with the common goal of getting me well.

Michael and I often say that we wouldn't have stayed together without our group. Including other people and their viewpoints has been one of the most important ingredients in the success of our intimate partnership.

I am 38 years old and I have spent the

last 16 years in two different intimate relationships. I am just starting to really understand that having true intimacy with my partner doesn't mean not arguing. Arguing can be incredibly intimate; and we all know that making up can be very sweet.

Having a good marriage is what I wanted all my life. I was blessed with the ability to pick great men, but keeping them was a different story—I had no idea how to have an intimate partnership. By the time I graduated from high school, my parents had been through three divorces. What I knew of relationships was that when the going gets rough, you walk away.

But I am sticking this one out, with some help from my friends! The best part is I am not only more intimate with my husband but with everyone I share my life with. ❧

Kiva Lindsey Goldstein, a Colorado native, took her first Morehouse course 16 years ago, and has been living in the community the past seven years. It was at Morehouse where she met and married her husband, Michael. Kiva studied at Naropa University in Boulder and was staff member of The World School of Massage in San Francisco, where she was certified in Holistic Health Education and massage therapy. She is currently training to teach Morehouse courses, which includes participating in ongoing research in sensuality and pleasurable living.

When You Feel All Alone

By Jane Hillis

The intimacy in my life was unexpectedly increased recently when my 77-year-old husband broke his elbow in three places. He was completely immobilized in a position where he could not even lift a glass of water. At first he depended on me 24 hours a day for everything.

There were many moments of extreme appreciation for each other during this time. I realized Joe would not always be there for me; he appreciated how willing I was to take care of him. The simplest acts of everyday life, like giving him a drink of water, were opportunities to love.

There were also times when I was stressed out and overwhelmed to the point of snapping angrily or crying. Couldn't I have my morning coffee before tending to him?

Our struggles were opportunities for us to get to know each other better and others also, as we talk frequently to people in the group about our lives. My husband was vulnerable, struggling with issues of mortality and physical inability to take care of himself or be productive. At 62, I was now facing taking care of a rapidly aging husband. Wasn't life supposed to get easier now? Who would take care of me?

As time went on, I realized I could not do everything myself. We reached out to the group for help and found we developed a much more intimate relationship with many people. Although people had offered to help from the beginning, it was not easy for me to accept. As for asking, what if they said no? A good friend finally said "You're so busy rejecting yourself you won't give us a chance!" So I began to ask.

People were happy to contribute different things. Some brought Joe snacks or drinks. Some spent time with him. One person was even willing to empty the bedpan!

I was now able to go out and have time to do other things. Joe and I got to experience the love people had for us. There were still stressful times during Joe's recuperation period, but the intimacy and love had increased dramatically—not just between us but with lots of people in our group with whom we wouldn't otherwise have shared so much. ❧

Jane Hillis has been a resident of Morehouse since 1992 and involved since 1974 in group living. She has a Ph.D. in Sensuality from More University and is a faculty member of the Lafayette Morehouse Sensuality Department. Jane studied psychology at UCLA and later completed her liberal arts degree at Antioch University in Venice, California. Jane and her husband Joe enjoy living communally and finding ways to have life improve as they age.

Little Intimacies

By Lynne Goodman

I grew up in a solid New England family. We had dinner together every night, the beds were always made, and clean clothes magically appeared in my closet every week. It was a good way to grow up; at the same time, it wasn't heavy on drama. Since I wasn't privy to any households that did have drama, I always wanted to know what was really going on with other people. Kind of like when people crowd around the friends of celebrities and ask, "What are they REALLY like?" I wanted to know, "What is everyone REALLY like?"

Living in a community, in my case specifically Morehouse is, for my money, the best way to know. You get to see your housemates fighting, being romantic, going through crises—all the really juicy stuff. In fact, the moment I truly wanted to live in a Morehouse was when I went to visit one. As I walked in, a resident I knew was coming down the stairs—and as he rushed out, he yelled bloody murder at another resident who was at the top of the stairs. "Wow!" I thought. "Cool! People aren't pulling punches—they're just saying what they feel. They really get into it here!" I wanted in.

Once in, I discovered that it's not just the dramatic moments that create intimacy; it's also the raft of all the little ways you get to know other people. In our communal environment, we like to take time to do things for each other and thus we find out what each other's preferences are. Like exactly how someone likes each of the seven pillows on her bed positioned. That one housemate likes his coffee the almondy color of another housemate's skin. One woman, who only ever seems to eat healthy food, always has a can of Pringles and a Lindt chocolate bar on her bedside table. When you ask Deborah to help out with something, she'll always say "No." But we're not bothered by that because we know you just have to wait a little while, ask again, and she'll likely say yes.

We've seen each other at our best and worst and funniest moments. Like the time one couple had a fight and he threw all her clothes out the window. Another couple would sometimes ask me to wake them in the morning. I discovered how they looked entwined and asleep, their skin beautiful against their dark purple sheets. Once someone slipped into the kitchen and spiced up the soup Millie was making for the house. (You should have seen when Millie found out...). When a friend's little girls would visit, one housemate painted their fingernails and showed them scary movies like *Jurassic Park*; they loved that. Once I had a boyfriend over and after we'd gone to bed a housemate came into our room with a video camera. We laughed. (No, he didn't get any footage!)

It always feels great when someone from outside the house comes to me for advice on what to do to please or impress one of my housemates. "Do you think she'd like lemon bars?" they might ask. And I can answer, "Oh, gosh, I'm afraid not, she's got a sensitivity to citrus. But you know what she does love?... " And then I feel good, like I myself am "A Celebrity's Friend," because I am the one being asked, "What is she REALLY like?" And I know. ❧

Lynne Goodman lived in the New York Morehouse for 18 years, the last seven of which she and her husband took the leadership position of being the "housemothers." They have led many Mark Groups, introductory social evenings held around the country. Last year they moved to the Bay Area to live at the Oakland Morehouse. Lynne graduated from Oberlin College with a degree in English. She is now a graphic designer.

Yulia Z.

Intimacy in the Village Setting

By Ted Sterling

Since first I met Dancing Rabbit Ecovillage cofounder Tony Sirna at the Communities Conference in Willits, California in 1998, I have understood that the "village" part of ecovillage here was meant as more than a euphemism. Dancing Rabbit was intended to be more or less like the village of popular conception—small, rural, surrounded and supported by agriculture and practical arts, and made up of villagers whose lives would doubtless be intertwined in many ways.

When I subsequently arrived at Dancing Rabbit (located on 280 acres outside Rutledge, Missouri) for an internship in July 2001, I found a small group of people (at that time, members numbered perhaps 10, and the village hosted upwards of 20 interns over the warm season) with a lot of commitment to a beautiful vision. It was not a village yet. It did feel intimate, in the ways that we all worked together and relied on each other to feed ourselves, survive in our tents, and share the very small amount of sheltered space while trying to build some of the first structures. We were pioneering. Intimacy was born out of necessity, though aided by common purpose.

I met my future partner Sara, another intern at the time, that first morning as I reconnoitered the budding village. I had been deeply missing the intimacy of a close relationship prior to my arrival, and felt deep gratitude to the world and to circumstance when I quickly found that intimacy. Within a few weeks we were sharing a tiny tent in a field of tall grass. Within a couple months, I was beginning to think seriously that I might like to spend the rest of my life with her. This July we'll celebrate 10 years together alongside our five-year-old daughter Aurelia.

In our village I sooner or later see my community mates in nearly every shade of their existence.

At the time of that 1998 conference, I had already lived five years in the student co-ops in Berkeley, California, mostly in the co-op known as Lothlorien. The intimacy of that setting was like a drug to me; we cooked beautiful vegetarian food for each other, cleaned for each other, created and took part in elaborately prepared social events, sometimes fell in love with our house mates, and even studied together occasionally. It was the parallel education to my academic pursuits, and turned out to be the more important for me. I was hooked on the intimacy with my community mates that came from living in such close proximity and sharing so many events both routine and unusual in one of the most formative moments of our collective lives.

Sadly I began to see that I was facing an end to that particular intimacy; transience is built into the BSC (Berkeley Student Co-ops) experience, since you must be a student to live in them and are allowed only one grace semester. Lothlorien (my then home) possesses amazing cultural coherence under the circumstances, but at that time I agonized over the loss of important house members every year as they graduated (or moved into private housing, the wisdom of which I thought dubious at best). The pain of it was visceral. The idea of starting my own community, based on good land that I'd never have to leave, offered salvation for my particular torment, and grew deeply rooted in my dreams.

I worked on organic farms, homesteaded for a year, traveled around the world and across the US in search of community in its many forms as my desire for a more permanent home increased. At first that five-month stay in northeast Missouri seemed just another stepping stone to me. I still pictured mountains and forest and perhaps the ocean or a big river looming not far off in the distance when I dreamed about my own community. Sara was more sanguine than I about Dancing Rabbit, but indulged my fantasies so far as to begin looking for land with me in the Appalachians.

Then one day, home alone at our temporary abode in some quiet (and lonely) woods on the Maine coast while Sara was off visiting friends and family for a few weeks (including at Dancing Rabbit), it hit me: I could spend the next 10 years trying to start my own community, hoping I had enough charisma to attract others and instill dreams of community similar to mine in them; or I could give it a go in an existing community where I knew it was possible to do all or most of what I dreamed of, and spend the next 10 years doing instead of trying. Sara already thought Dancing Rabbit was the way to go, and I realized that if I really wanted community to succeed, I ought to support existing communities instead of splintering the energy still further.

We wrote a fateful letter to Dancing Rabbit, and arrived as members in April 2003. In the intervening years I have learned a great deal of intimacy. To be sure, my understanding and experience of closeness in a partnership with one person dwells in a different realm now than it did then. Alongside Sara I have stretched and molded the rudimentary sense of fulfillment in love I began with into a glittering, jeweled orb of deepest intimacy. We have changed each other, grown individually and together, built a house, birthed a child, and much else.

Without the supporting web of context, however, I cannot imagine having traveled so far or with such meaning. Dancing Rabbit and our neighboring communities Sandhill Farm and Red Earth Farms provide that context, and I will likely spend the rest of my life trying to fully appreciate the fathomless depths of intimacy inherent in building a village in all its lurid detail from scratch with 30-1000 friends and acquaintances. Whether by upbringing or predilection, I did not begin with a deep appreciation of intimacy beyond that of family or lover. I always thought of myself as having friends, but in retrospect I hardly understood what friendship really meant.

In our village I sooner or later see my community mates in nearly every shade of their existence. I do not have to share a bed or income with most of them to see it. We are building a pedestrian-based village whose human zone is "thickly settled," to borrow a New England term. Between one dwelling and the next a frog often requires no more than a few leaps. In hot summer weather when the barriers between inside and out fade to nothing, I can hear my neighbors snoring, having sex, arguing, cooking, and just about everything else related to the act of living. It is both startling to my staid American sense of propriety and independence, and at the same time deeply humanizing.

These observations are perhaps nothing remarkable to a city dweller, but there is a certain anonymity to city life; the individual typically leaves those unintentional intimacies of home for work, play, commerce, and so on, losing his or her self in the multitude.

Here at Dancing Rabbit, I share limited space in often-cooperative facilities with my neighbors, and beyond the village are farm fields and forests. I may dine in an eating coop with them, share shower facilities, build compost piles with buckets of their mixed excrement, dive naked into the pond to cool off alongside them, grow, sell, trade, and eat produce with them, share a ride to town with a handful of them, sit through and participate in every conceivable form of meeting with them, find myself in conflict and its resolution with them, quietly lust after them, build a house with them, cry, laugh, run, scream, or die with them. I will also just watch them do many of these things. I share myself and so do they. Some more than others, but you cannot really hide from anyone here.

This is not the first time I've felt like I was re-learning and experiencing a life that was commonplace to the vast majority of my ancestors in the not-too-distant past. Yet for all that, I never experienced a tenth of it before deciding to embroil myself in the exquisitely mundane daily realities of this particular place and collection of people.

Before living in community, I found it very easy to play the mental game of comparing myself favorably to the blind, benighted masses of the world who didn't care or didn't know better about whatever it was I was concerned with (and whom I didn't know). Since rooting myself in this intimate setting, I have found that game far harder to play, because I daily observe a much broader range of human behavior and foibles than just my own or my partner's or child's examples. I can plainly see, and cannot readily ignore, that my way is only one among many, and that I have a great deal still to learn.

Each time I see and learn, gratitude grows in me for this shared humanity, the vulnerability we each show each other, the gifts of love, time, and energy we daily give and receive, the example we show to every new person that sets foot here, which subsequently seeps out to help change our collective culture.

Despite this undeniable intimacy, we still struggle sometimes with elements of it, particularly in the more intentional forms like friendship. Without the situational closeness I share with all here, I fear I would rarely grow true friendship. I would be far lonelier. But I'm not. I do have this.

My friend Thomas wrote a poem of sorts to each person in the village one year for Validation Day (our version of Valentine's Day). Most were typical, brilliant Thomas, with deep meaning likely hidden in apparent nonsense if only I was sharp enough to find it. I read mine many times, and have carried it since as encouragement to pursue as many more opportunities as I can to know him more:

two ants
wished to treat
bones here & there
with pond elixir.
welcome spirit
nurtured being
becoming bee.
friends not far?
true joy ❧

Ted Sterling lives at Dancing Rabbit Ecovillage. See also his article about Lothlorien in our "Student Housing Co-ops" issue, Communities *#110, Spring 2001.*

Photo courtesy of Dancing Rabbit Ecovillage

The Solace of Friends in Community

By Alline Anderson

It all started with Amy. She, like many of the women here at Dancing Rabbit Ecovillage, felt dissatisfied with the quality and depth of her relationships. Looking for a format that encouraged and developed closeness among women, she found the Woman Within Journey (womenincircle.org). She went for a weekend, learned about Women's Empowerment Circles (e-circles), and was profoundly moved. One by one she approached women in our community who she hoped would be interested in participating in a circle of discovery and sharing, and with whom she felt a level of comfort. I was fortunate to be among these women. Oh, how I count my lucky stars!

In the beginning there were seven of us. It was scary, uncomfortable, and often painful. We had a lot to work out. For all of the closeness of our lives here, we seemed to have developed a culture filled with emotional barriers. This makes sense if you think about it. In "normal" (non-intentional community) life one resides with a partner, or room mates. You go to work, where you interact with an entirely different set of people. After work you might get together with friends, or volunteer somewhere, or belong to a gym—all with an expansive group of individuals. I found I missed the safe anonymity found in a wide circle of friends and acquaintances. For example, if I were having a conflict with a room mate I could run it by my co-workers, or friends in my book group, who might have ideas on resolutions, or help me with perspective. But when all of these people are the same it can become problematic.

Here at Dancing Rabbit, we (members, residents, and work exchangers) eat, work, and play together. There are occasional shorter-term visitors and guests, but basically it's just us. And therein lies the difficulty. If everyone knows everything about everybody (or thinks they do), where are the boundaries? Where is the safety?

So with Amy gamely leading us into unknown territory, we began. At first, we used the Woman Within text. We were reluctant, unsure that we would reap any benefits, nervous, and not entirely trusting. Many of us, each week, said the same thing "I didn't really want to come, I don't know if I'll keep with this, two hours is a lot of time..."

After a few months we ditched the text. We took turns leading. And amazing things happened. We found many more commonalities than differences. The differences we discovered provided insight and understanding rather than being divisive. We realized that prior to e-circle we were comparing our insides (filled with flaws) with other women's (seemingly perfect) outsides—not accurate, and certainly not helpful. We found that we shared many of the same insecurities and fears. Even better, we found that we really liked and admired each other, even when we knew that each of us was less than perfect. It was eye-opening and yes, empowering. Oddly enough, as the weeks and months went on, we found that we really looked forward to going. Or that at least after our e-circle session was over, we were grateful for having attended.

Our gatherings look like this: Every other week, we get together in a place where we'll have no interruptions. After lighting a candle, we sit in a circle and have personal check-ins—each woman can take up to half an hour. Daunting at first ("Am I boring you? Oh, this sounds so stupid...") we came to revel in our sharing time. I mean really, when is the last time you had half an hour of anyone's undivided attention? We speak of what is happening in our lives, what we're feeling, what we're struggling with. There is no back and forth—this is each woman's opportunity to share without interruptions. The rest of us listen in supportive silence. If, at the end, she asks for feedback, or help, we share what we're feeling and thinking. We don't gossip, and do not talk about others in any way other than how they intersect with our lives. We work hard at being constructive. Everything is entirely confidential,

even from spouses/partners. This creates an incredible sense of trust. We are creating a force of support, a silent yet fierce network of women who believe in each other. We have created a space where we can be vulnerable safely.

When I asked the women in my group why they like e-circle, one told me, "It's not just what is happening in my life. It's bigger stuff, the growth edges. We can receive support with what we're working on, get and share empathy and compassion. We are able to expose the raw spots where we're trying to grow—no one holds back when sharing." Another replied, "E-circle has enabled me to share more openly with more people, especially women in this group. It encourages a depth in relationships and trust. I am able to expose more of myself. I am learning to be more accepting and empathetic." Another said, "I so desperately want to feel understood. In e-circle I feel I am, and I feel safe" and "best of all, the relationships carry beyond e-circle. There is not a lot of space in our community for 'what's really happening for you' conversations. But now there are five people I actually know well, who know me well, and who have my back."

We have created a space where we can be vulnerable safely.

For me, the beauty of e-circle comes from the support we receive from each other. For example, one of our members has a lot of fear and anxiety speaking in groups. So when she musters up the courage to speak in the community's Sunday meeting, we are there cheering her on. No one else knows what's going on behind the scenes, but we do, as does she. We have found that we each have a deep sense of appreciation and pride when we have a full vision of another person, in this case the members of our circle. We're on the same ride together. It's not always fun, and sometimes involves screaming, but what the heck!

In the year and a half since we started, much has changed. One of our members passed away last September, and Amy is taking a sabbatical away from Dancing Rabbit. Those of us who are left continue to meet regularly.

We now look forward to our meeting every other week, and joke about how we'd like to have a daily e-circle, if only our busy lives would allow it. We truly appreciate the gift we've inadvertently given ourselves and each other—the solace of friendship, and the balm of caring women. I feel incredibly humbled to be the recipient of the trust of these amazing women.

One of our goals is to establish a number of e-circles here at Dancing Rabbit. We hope to add more women to our circle, and empower several other circles to begin and flourish. More women supporting women, and therefore making our community stronger and healthier. What could be better? ❧

Alline Anderson wishes to thank the women of her e-circle for their continued support and anonymous quotes for use in this article. Alline has been a member of Dancing Rabbit Ecovillage since 1999. She and her husband Kurt run the Milkweed Mercantile, a strawbale, solar- and wind-powered Inn and Seminar Program. Contact her at alline@milkweedmercantile.com—she'd love to hear from you.

Fascinating Selfhood

By Kim Scheidt

I recently reread a book that I originally purchased five years ago when I was trying to "fix" my failing marriage. The book, *Fascinating Womanhood* by Helen B. Andelin, purports to teach the reader what characteristics define the ideal woman. It explains the laws which she must obey if she is to be admired, loved, and appreciated, and gives instructions on how to go about becoming more feminine.

Originally published in 1963, this book is written from a patriarchal, Christian viewpoint. Virtually every page provides material that would cause any good feminist to scream out in indignation, or perhaps go searching for a match with which to send it all up in smoke. My now-partner picked up the book from where I had left it lying on a table and when I came back to the room asked, "why in the world are you reading this crap?" So, I want to make it clear that I'm not actually suggesting that anyone go out and buy this book...

But I guess even the murkiest of literary works can sometimes provide nuggets of wisdom, and *Fascinating Womanhood* has its share. Much of the advice the author provides is specific to a married woman's relationship with her husband following traditional gender roles. However, a lot of the focus is on self-improvement of one form or another, and there are quite a few ideas that could be adopted to help any person in any number of their relationships.

Acceptance

Complete acceptance of others is one quality that is often touted but seldom followed. How many times have we heard the adage that you can't go into a relationship with the idea of changing the other person? But so many people still try, usually with frustrating results. If we cultivate the attitude of complete acceptance of others it can be very freeing. Recognize that we are all human beings who are part virtue and part fault. Honestly accept the total person, including all imperfections, and don't try to change them. Being less concerned with the other's faults allows you to concentrate on all the good qualities they exhibit. And probably the best way to help someone else's self-growth is by recognition and belief in their better side.

Admiration

Every person has qualities or characteristics that deserve appreciation, be they intellectual gifts, physical prowess, or other skills or special abilities. When you become interested in another person and listen to them talk, find traits they exhibit that deserve recognition and admiration. Then express your admiration in a way that is heartfelt and sincere, and also be specific.

The desire to be admired, which we all possess, can go hand-in-hand with a fear of humiliation. If someone has been ridiculed or belittled in the past, or treated with contempt or indifference, they will very likely suffer from injured pride. In addition to expressing admiration of others, it is best to eliminate remarks that have the effect of crushing another's ego. Be sure not to ridicule or belittle others, even in humor.

Sympathetic Understanding

There are bound to be times when people around you become discouraged, and it is a great relief to find someone to confide in. When you develop the attitude of complete acceptance, then those around you feel able to trust their precious thoughts and emotions with you. When a disheartened person comes to you, it is usually not practical help that they need. The most valuable help that you can provide is to build the person up with approval and hope. Do your best to remove self-doubt and reestablish self-esteem in the other. Picture the person as a success, even if they aren't one right now. And don't let their gloom rub off on you.

Inner Happiness/Worthy Character

It is uplifting to be around those who are genuinely happy. Deep inner happiness is something you can cultivate to carry you through the ups and downs of life with tranquility. It comes from a development of the personal spirit and is not to be confused with seeking temporary pleasure. Two essential ingredients to this happiness are the complete acceptance of yourself and the appreciation of the simple joys of life.

Inner happiness evolves from development of the entire character, and this is an ongoing process. Important qualities of a worthy character are traits such as self-mastery, unselfishness, patience, gentleness, honesty, and self-dignity. Be accepting of your weaknesses and mistakes, but continue to strive toward greater character development.

•••

I realize that these pieces of advice are not always easily followed. But I recommend trying to incorporate them into your own life, and then witness the positive reaction in yourself and those around you.

Kim Scheidt is a founding member of Red Earth Farms community in northeast Missouri. She works at the national headquarters of the Fellowship for Intentional Community. She initially intended to write an additional sidebar outlining "advice from the book that didn't make the cut"—for example, "women shouldn't wear herringbone prints, make financial decisions, or be educated for a career"—but decided against it.

What To Do When You're Angry??

The author of *Fascinating Womanhood* uses the analogy of steam gathering in a teapot to depict the inner turmoil one feels when angry. Anger is a real emotion that we all experience, and at times it can be intense. But how to properly express yourself without causing the situation to escalate? There are different techniques for dealing with anger:

Suppressing anger, like turning the flame off under the teapot, is a mistake. Suppressed emotions can be seriously damaging and can lead to a self-induced numbness, an inability to feel both pain and pleasure.

Releasing anger with harsh words or violent actions is like turning up the heat and blowing the top off the teapot. This is obviously not ideal.

Self-control, tightening the lid on the teapot, causes steam to build up pressure inside. Presenting a calm exterior while holding emotions within will lead to inner turmoil and resentment towards others.

Talking things over with the person you're angry with is an attempt to turn down the heat. However, in the author's experience, doing so will probably lead that person to feel defensive and result in an argument.

According to *Fascinating Womanhood*, none of the above methods of dealing with anger truly solve your frustrations without causing further damage to yourself or your relationship. Thus the successful way of dealing with anger is with a

Spunky display of emotions. This causes the teapot lid to gently bobble up and down, releasing steam. It is important that this fiery show of anger be mostly on the surface, that underneath you aim for an inner calm. Acquire a list of adjectives that are fitting for the occasion, and make use of exaggeration in your speech. The idea is that you give vent to your emotions in a way that is not harmful. It is a way to communicate your thoughts when you have been offended or mistreated, and a manner of preserving your self-dignity. Releasing steam in this way will allow for a tranquility of spirit to emerge. Even if the situation that provoked your anger does not change, your reaction to it can. Anger can become just another fleeting emotion that you embrace and then let go.

—K.S.

Photo by Chad Knepp

The Path of Community

By Barbara Stützel

Photos courtesy of Barbara Stützel

Many of my friends are on a spiritual path. They are Buddhists or study shamanism or the like. Sometimes they ask me: which is your path? I tell them that my spiritual path is the one of community. I dedicate myself to exploring the human being.

I've been living in a community with 100 people for 10 years. We share not only our daily life, but also a dream, and all the joys and frustrations along the way leading us towards this dream. The dream is a life in peace and love between human beings and nature. I am sure that many people share this dream. In my community we decided to dedicate our lives to finding a way to get there, and to share our experiences on this way. We have land, houses, our own water, and a conference center which guarantees us income—the fact is that our physical needs are fulfilled. Now the interesting question is: how do we create peace and love?

The dream unites us. In the first phase of living in community that is enough. We share everything; we feel united and love the collective, because it supplies us with all we want. There is always someone to embrace, somebody to share with, someone to inspire us. But soon the urge toward individuation pops up.

Our histories separate us: each person has different experiences and develops his or her values and strategies out of this life experience, wanting to repeat what caused happiness, fleeing from all that was painful in the past. Each person's experiences lead to individual capacities and likes. A living community doesn't deny these differences, but benefits from the various capacities. The more an individual discovers his or her potential and applies them in the community, the better the community functions. Whatever we do then, we do it with enthusiasm and passion.

The danger comes when we start to confuse our experience with reality and our opinion with the truth. Then we insist on our opinion, even though this is only one part of reality. In the last 10 years of collective living I have discovered more and more how different the inner realities are. We hardly ever think of the same thing when we use the same word—each individual has a world of emotions underneath, that we often don't perceive in its depth. To reach this phase of living together is very frustrating. It seems impossible to reach an agreement. Many times this is the point of separation in groups.

The next step is to recognize that everything I believe and live is relative and that other truths exist. Many people experience these moments of listening in depth on special occasions with a friend. In community we go beyond that: we open up to the possibility that there exists a collective intelligence which goes further than what each one knows, and which we discover in spite of all the individual truths. To get there each one has to leave behind his or her history. It is a way to transcend the Ego and listen to the essence of the human being.

Today when I share with my friends from other spiritual paths, I realize that I could call this essence of human being by the name God. The process of opening oneself to real listening is a state of attentive consciousness. This is why I say that my spiritual path is the one of community. ❧

Born in 1966, psychologist and culture creator Barbara Stützel has lived at ZEGG community for 10 years. She is engaged in linking people and helping them to crystallize real utopias out of their potential. To achieve this she creates cultural events, theatre pieces, and seminars. ZEGG, founded in 1991 near Berlin, Germany, currently has 100 members. See www.zegg.de. Thanks to Agnes Hannack for translation assistance.

Expressing Gratitude in Community

By Devon Bonady

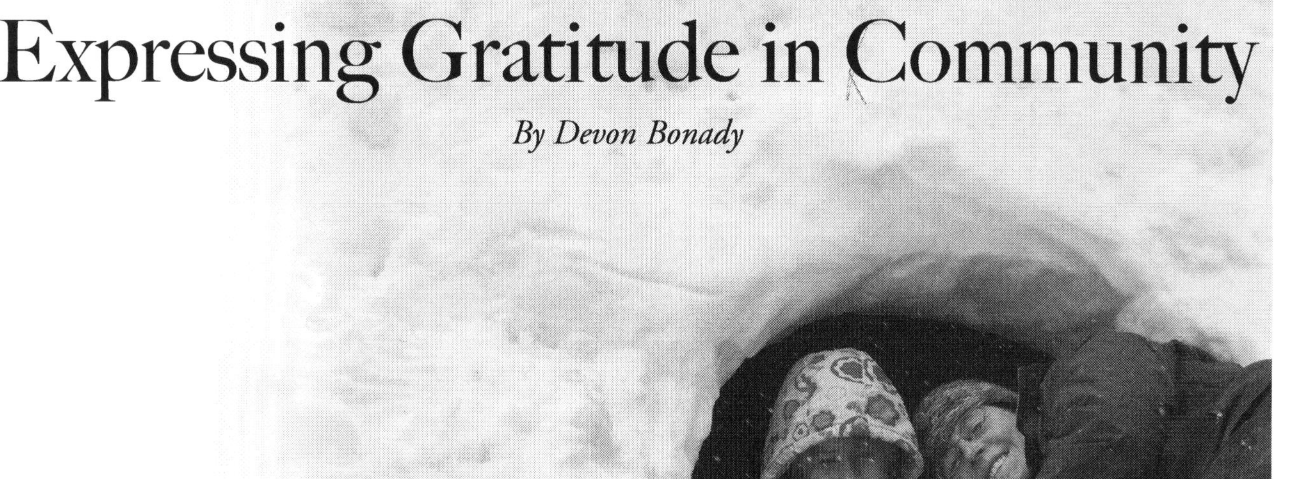

Brian Basor

It's a warm fall day on the shady pond, with a cool breeze, birds singing, and dragonflies buzzing. My dear four-year-old neighbor Ella and I sit silently in the paddle boat wandering the pond searching for water insects to catch. Leaves rustle in the breeze and a few even fall from the canopy into the water. Ella is poised at the back of the boat with her colander, directing me to a certain nook and then waiting for the perfect moment to dip the colander into the dark water. If we are lucky, a few species of water insects will appear as the water drains from the colander and she can swiftly transfer them to the temporary shelter of a plastic bucket on the back of the boat for examination and identification. Today she has already taught me the names of two species that we did not see last time we paddled together.

This is not the first afternoon I have spent this way, but it will be the last with her for quite a while. This peaceful pond exploration day, although in some ways like many others, is different because it is just a few days before she and her family move across the country to begin a new adventure. It is a painful time for me, but also an extremely precious time. One thing I learned while living in community is that I must appreciate and savor the present moments I have with special people in my life while they are with me, as they often move on. The vivid memories and strong feelings I carry with me from even simple days with special people lift me up in hard times and help me to remember the beauty and strength of connection in community. Ella's family has been contemplating and preparing to move away for over a year by this time, and as I deal with my grief, I also appreciate every moment I have to spend with them. Pond paddling, sandbox playing, coloring, or camping, I have been blessed with many opportunities to connect with this family, my neighbors, the biggest piece of my little neighborhood community.

Today, I reflect on the day, almost five years ago, when she was born. I was already a close friend and neighbor of her parents; her birth welcomed a new sense of family, closeness, and community into my life and our little neighborhood. Her birth gave me the opportunity to be of service and give back to my dear friends in a new and different way. As they met the challenge of raising a baby, I brought them meals, split firewood, and entertained the baby for a few moments to give Mom and Dad a break. Not only did I come to realize how much I love to show my gratitude by helping others, I experienced the magic of reciprocity in that, by giving to my community, I receive so much more than I could ever imagine.

From a very early age, Ella and I became friends. In the early days, I took her on long walks. For me, this opportunity was not just about getting to know a small child intimately, but also about learning what is important to me. My time with her started out as an act of service—to help her parents find a little time to get work done or a quick nap while the baby was away. I felt joy in giving, of course, and yet what I received in exchange from this budding relationship was more than I ever could have imagined. Now I have a very dear five-year-old friend and pen pal who sends me beautiful artwork by mail. Her brother, mom, and dad become dearer to me each day and provide love and support even from their new far-away home. Thanks to this family, I have tools and experience to guide me through the new and overwhelming process of becoming a new parent.

By my sharing appreciation for my neighbors through service, we all benefit greatly. My experiences in community throughout my life have shown me that serving and appreciating others while living in community is essential for personal and group connection. At this time in my life, as I begin motherhood, the lessons of appreciation, gratitude, and reciprocity that I have learned in a variety of community situations will be essential for my well-being and that of my family.

The opportunity to reflect on and learn from my experiences in a variety of communities is a gift in itself. I appreciate the wisdom that comes from others who share their stories, whether in conversations, films, Communities, or other venues. Learning from others' experiences helps me to glean more from my own experiences. It seems to be a never-ending and always enriching process. I have lived in a variety of community settings: a rural intentional community with about 25 year-round residents, a rural educational center with 10 year-long residents, a three-family farm with 10 seasonal interns, a loose-knit community of eight people living in a cluster of houses, and a rural homestead with five to seven adults and a varying level of community "intention." My current community, the latter, also consists of neighbors and friends within a five-mile radius, and friends in a town 25 miles away. All of these community configurations have offered me a multitude of lessons in gratitude. In particular, I think of two ways that I have learned to express gratitude: by appreciating others and by offering myself in service to others.

While living in community, I have learned the value of appreciating others for the work that they do. In intentional community, each resident invests a lot of time and energy into people and projects. People are busy and do not always take the time to notice the work of others, nor do they always have the opportunity to hear how their work has been received by other residents. Members want to feel that their personal gifts and the work they do benefits everyone and allows them to feel part of the group vision and goals. They want to know that their efforts are valued and worthwhile. A successful community requires people with a wide variety of skills to accomplish tasks, and sometimes members are not aware of all that each member does to keep the gears in motion. How many of us feel like others do not realize how much work it takes to do our job?

I lived in a 25-member intentional community that derived most of its income from conference center management. Members worked in diverse jobs such as facilities management, conference coordination, and growing fresh vegetables for the community and conference center meals. At that time, the main garden was a 10 minute walk from the community center. Some community members who worked in the conference center office had not even been to the garden after a year or more of living on site. Those unfamiliar with gardening, farming, and manual labor did not realize the amount of time and effort that the gardeners and interns put into growing food. The gardeners did not feel appreciated and their perspective on some community decisions was misunderstood. In an effort to boost their morale, community members initiated a community day in the garden. We had everyone out there planting potatoes, singing songs, having fun, and experiencing the work that is required to grow food.

At that time, I was a gardener, and I received helpful positive feedback after the community day. As a result, I reflected on my own perceptions and judgment of other community jobs and work styles. I am a "do-er," and I tend to focus on physical projects.

This page: Devon and Ella playing in the snow. Opposite page: Devon and Ella on a special summer day.

Matt Emrich

My job as land steward covered so many arenas that I tended towards immediate needs like keeping trees alive, and fixing fences. I did not always take the time to understand and appreciate those who were "talking" and "planning" or those who were dealing with community conflict, both of which are essential roles in the functioning of a healthy community. Over time, thanks to our community's emphasis on personal growth work, I became very grateful for the healers, planners, and elders in our community and came to see how their gifts, although very different, were way more valuable than mine (though some may argue, just as valuable). Expressing interest and curiosity in what others do to help hold it all together helps community succeed.

While living in this intentional community, I learned how to appreciate others for who they are, not just what they do. That started with myself—learning to separate my identity from my work, which was very difficult for me and came about only because of all the emotional support I received from my fellow community members. As a community, we placed a high value on direct communication and appreciation. We set aside times for members to gather and share their appreciations with each other. Using a practice of one-on-one sharing, each week when we met for our well-being meetings we took time to mingle and connect with one person at a time, first silently and then by speaking. Usually, one person would be moved to speak and share something with the other. Certain days, facilitators asked us particularly to share an appreciation for the other person who simply listens and takes in the appreciation without judgment.

This activity was very uplifting for me. By practicing with a variety of people with whom I lived and worked, I came to understand that we always have things to appreciate in each other, even during conflict and challenge. If we can focus on the gifts we have received by connecting with an individual, we will always find something to appreciate. Through practicing this activity, I also realized how much of what we appreciate in others is related to their way of being or connecting, not just the things they accomplish. This allowed me to give myself permission to put more effort into connecting with others instead of always pushing to get the physical work done and "prove myself" by what I have accomplished that others can see.

The varied work that we all do as members of a community is an expression of our appreciation for the land and physical structures in community, and for the founders and members of the community. Our work is an act of service. As I learn the history of communities in which I live, I begin to grasp the effort required, and the risks that people have taken to make it possible for me to experience community in a particular place with certain people. From purchasing and investing in land and buildings, to long hours of labor and meetings, to dealing with challenging neighbors and uncomfortable living situations, founders and sustaining members work hard and dedicate themselves to a vision from which we continue to learn and benefit. I like to think that the work I do now, whether it be helping my neighbor build a greenhouse, caring for someone's goats while they are away, or organizing a benefit to raise funds for someone's health crisis, is a service to those who came before me and laid the foundation for my community as well as those who keep it thriving today.

Ella

Now that Ella and her family as well as other friends here have moved to a new place and a new focus, it is time for me to re-envision my sense of community. It is a prime time, as I am also learning the meaning of family as community with a newborn son. Before my son was born, a friend of mine gave me a bead to wear as a reminder of the strength of community. As a neighbor and friend, with the bead she offered some wisdom for me as I learn to parent while also adjusting to a shift in my neighborhood community. She reminded me of the support that I have in this quirky and beautiful community in which we live. Together, she and I are choosing to focus on appreciating this community that we already have, and to reach outside of our comfort zones to connect with people new and old. Since her blessing and my son's birth, I have been reconnecting with a few neighbors and getting to know new ones. Through this process, I once again feel gratitude for all of my community experiences, for my friendship with Ella and her family, and for the opportunity to help them and many others. ❧

Devon Bonady lives with her family in a cabin in the treetops of the Oregon forest. She appreciates her new lifestyle as a mother, gardener, and environmental educator. She continues to learn many lessons from her constantly evolving community.

Fostering Vulnerability

By Eli Winterfeld

Vulnerability has played different roles for me in the various settings I have called home. I was born and raised in an intentional community in Georgia; from there my family moved to Kitchener-Waterloo, Ontario to live as a nuclear family. My other homes have been my university town, summer camp, and most recently, a collective house of like-minded peers.

My community experiences have shown me how essential vulnerability is. The breakdown of community that we are experiencing as a society can be attributed partly to individualism and pride in providing for oneself. People place great emphasis on independence—both material and emotional. Our society views people who "depend" on others as weak. Being open about one's needs is taboo in our society. Many people do not feel they can allow themselves to be vulnerable and receive help from others graciously. I believe it takes great humility and strength to allow others to help you with your various burdens. Deep, genuine community cannot emerge without personal vulnerability. Additionally, openness to interdependence and resource-sharing can also help us live more frugally, with a greater respect for the environment, and help meet our need for human connection.

I grew up, until the age of 16, in an intentional community. Jubilee Partners, a Christian service community in Georgia, focuses on assisting refugees who are transitioning to life in the United States. Of course many organizations could facilitate such a program, but what makes Jubilee special is the intentionality of the work and lifestyle they demonstrate. The members of the community live on the same rural property as the refugees and they share together many aspects of life: work, meals twice a day, food production, games of soccer and volleyball, parties, worship, and other communal activities.

One of the most intentional and invested aspects of life at Jubilee is its communal income sharing. Resources are pooled to provide each individual or family with everything needed for a fulfilling life—which is largely non-material, in my own experience. As a child I sometimes felt materially vulnerable in a negative way when compared to my peers at school, especially because I didn't have a TV or a trampoline. However, as I grew older, I began to appreciate the purposeful, interdependent life that comes with common resources and a focus on relationship, rather than material goods. My friends would visit and would be struck with awe as we built skateboard ramps in the communal workshop, borrowed a car simply by writing a name and a time on a blackboard, and received weekly groceries to our doorstep. I felt rich even though the income we lived on fell well below the poverty line.

This intensity of sharing time, energy, resources, and emotional fluctuations necessitates personal vulnerability. Members, volunteers, and refugees become quickly and deeply connected because of the atmosphere of openness that allows for deep vulnerability. Though I could not have articulated it at the time, as a child and youth I found this interdependence comforting and empowering. I felt surrounded by support and lived a fulfilling life, both emotionally and materially.

Another place I have found belonging is the summer camp where I have worked for the past six years. To initiate community during staff orientation, each evening we set aside time for staff members to share openly about their experiences during the previous year. With these reflections, we open ourselves up and invite others to partake in the joys and hardships of our journeys. We welcome support and embrace our own vulnerability.

This setting has allowed people to feel comfortable enough to "come out," discuss mental health issues, and share concerns about the future. As each person shares, they light a candle from a circle of candles in the centre of the room. At the end of the five days, the ring of connected lights is a beautiful symbol of our common embrace of interdependence and vulnerability. This process is nourishment for relationships and community building and creates a sense of trust and community that I have not experienced in any places that do not intentionally create space to actively foster interdependence and vulnerability.

Because the current measurements of success stress individualism and competition, we must actively seek alternatives.

My experiences at university were quite different, as they lacked the intentionality of camp and Jubilee. I want to note that there are many positive aspects of university settings in terms of networking, collaboration, knowledge development, and personal growth. However, in the realm of fostering vulnerability and interdependence, the institution seems to be moving in the opposite direction. University was one of the most individualistic, prideful cultures I have ever been a part of. In most academic settings, students and professors are pressured to be as independent and competitive as possible. Most students strive to appear more knowledgeable and articulate than their fellow classmates. The existing systems of appraisal in the university setting channel one's energy into personal achievement rather than interdependence and personal vulnerability.

Different forms of community create different atmospheres in which individuals operate and varyng attitudes toward vulnerability. Some types of community make it very easy for an individual to be vulnerable. In other community settings, not only is vulnerability not facilitated, it is discouraged and made inaccessible. These types of settings focus on individualism, pride, and personal achievement.

I currently live with a number of my peers from the camp I discussed earlier. Now, in a collective living situation yet still in a new neighborhood, we try to determine how to create space that encourages the kind of vulnerability and interdependence that can lead to deeper communal and neighborhood relationships. We hope to host gatherings and initiatives that are part of creating this space, but it also must come from a very personal level.

I learned this first-hand in November when we moved in. We did not have internet or a printer and I was leading a session for a youth conference the next day and had no way to access or print the proposed lesson plan. Being my relatively disorganized self, by the time I set off in search of a computer, the library was already closed. So, barely even knowing the subject of the lesson the next morning, I began to think of options.

I had met only one couple (in passing) on my street so far. So I mustered all my courage to be vulnerable, walked over, knocked on their door, and asked to borrow their printer. After hearing my plight my neighbor was very gracious and invited me in and set me up in her office to allow me to print a 20 page document. Before this, I had assumed, without a doubt in my mind, that my first act of community in my new neighborhood would be through giving rather than receiving. I guess I needed to practice a little vulnerability myself.

In my past experiences with various forms of community the spaces that encouraged vulnerability were already established. Now, the space must be discovered through a combination of active creation and of tapping into the existing energies of the neighborhood.

I believe our communities, neighborhoods, and institutions would benefit from creating atmospheres that facilitate vulnerability. Because the current measurements of success stress individualism and competition, we must actively seek alternatives. The importance of intentionality cannot be overstated here. I believe we need to encourage both material and emotional vulnerability, because the two work in tandem and perpetuate one another. If we create atmospheres that invite vulnerability, our relationships will be deep and genuine. ❧

Having grown up in intentional community, Eli feels a strong draw to creating community in everyday contexts. He is currently working at a nonprofit organization on a "localism and livelihood" project that helps facilitate local, relationship-based economy. Living in an urban collective house of six, Eli and his friends build community mostly through having fun: hosting dinner parties, playing board games, making music, growing food, and other projects with similar themes.

Bringing Home Lessons from Community Living

By Melanie Rios

A few months ago I landed in the "real world" after 35 years of living in intentional community. I was ready for a break from being the director of the Lost Valley/ Meadowsong Ecovillage sustainability education center, where I'd lived for two years. I moved into a house in nearby Eugene, Oregon that my sister and I had been renting out to individuals in anticipation of moving there eventually.

In my first days living in this house, I noticed a difference between the norms of this household and the norms I had become used to through living in community. No one from the household offered to help me carry in boxes, and one was reluctant to move his car that was blocking access to the door. The fridge and cupboards were divided into four separate territories, and no one ate together, or even seemed to talk to each other. The yard had been neglected such that paths had been obliterated by weeds taller than my head. When I came down with the flu, a housemate became unhappy that a friend of mine was in the kitchen making me tea for me while I was in bed. He gave notice by email rather than discussing his concern with me, and another housemate followed suit, saying he was ready to live by himself.

And so I found myself experiencing the economic uncertainty, ecological decay, and social isolation that so many folks in the "real world" are facing. How could I apply the lessons I had garnered from decades of living in intentional communities to this situation in a way that might be helpful in addressing challenges faced not just by me, but by many others?

I crafted a vision for a community and nature-based household, put it out on Craigslist, and within three minutes, received a call from Alicia. "I could have written that ad!" she said with enthusiasm, grateful to have connected with a like-minded person. And so the ALEA (Alliance of Life-Enriching Advocates) homestead was born. This article describes how we are setting up our household based on what we've learned from living in intentional communities in a way that we hope will be successful not only for us, but potentially serve as a model to be replicated in homes in cities, towns, and suburbs across the nation.

Lesson #1 from living in intentional communities: Create a safe climate for expressing concerns, including issues of power.

While serving as director of Lost Valley, I was a natural lightning rod for folks who had a distrust of authority, and other kinds of concerns also erupted from time to time, so I learned ways to diffuse resentments and conflicts. Especially helpful was the practice of "Worldwork" developed by Arnold Mindell. We'd gather in a circle to discuss a hot topic, such as "drug policy," "child-raising practices," or "power relationships within our community" as a form of theater.

The goal of Worldwork is not to change our agreements, but rather to simply

A visit from friends.

ear each other, with folks speaking to ach other from flexible perspectives. For xample, someone steps into the circle nd says "I'm speaking for my grandnother, and she says 'Children should sit quietly during the dinner hour.'" Someone else steps in and says "I'm speaking or an indigenous village elder, and he ays that we are all responsible for the ehavior of our children, not just their iological parents." All voices have a hance to be heard, even those that aren't n the room, and ideas are shared in ways hat don't lock someone into a rigid idea f who they are and what they believe.

We found that concerns that were xpressed in this venue would often esolve themselves without needing to ewrite policy. This practice of Worldvork can be helpful in other settings esides that of intentional communities, rom the individual household to the eighborhood to larger "town hall" type gatherings. When we understand each ther well, it is easier to care for, respect, nd adapt to each other.

Arny Mindell also offers us the concept hat differential rank or power isn't necesarily a problem, just lack of consciousness bout power. Valuing *earned rank*, which is onferred based on someone's knowledge r experience, can be helpful in supporting a wise, effective, and cohesive community. At the same time, it's important to talk openly about the potential dangers of *unearned rank*, which is conferred based on something such as someone's skin color, gender, or inherited wealth.

Applying this understanding to our forming household, I initiated a conversation with Alicia and her partner Robert about power differences amongst us. They acknowledged feeling concerned that they might feel like second-class citizens in the household given their relative age and non-ownership of the property. They shared their desire as responsible folks in their mid-20s to step into fully functioning adult roles. They also expressed wanting to commit long-term to being stewards of a piece of land without being worried about being asked to leave, as had happened to them recently when a house they had been renting was sold to different owners. I shared with them my desire to step back from the center of power and daily responsibilities to function more as a mentor or contributing elder. I also shared my gratitude that they saw this half acre as a place to steward, as it is a larger amount of land than I want to dedicate myself to on my own.

Fostering good power dynamics requires not just a good structure and clear initial understandings, but also ongoing maintenance.

As these intentions are mutually compatible, we thought of ways to encourage Alicia and Robert to step up into their power and for me to step back. One strategy was to give them a long-term lease so that if conflicts arise between us, we either work it out or I leave. Another strategy has been to give them prominent roles of responsibility. Alicia has become the website designer, membership recruiter, and first screener for potential new housemates, and Robert is manager for the greenhouse and gardens. To deal with the potential problems associated with a structure in which Alicia is responsible for recruiting members while I'm responsible for paying the mortgage, we have decided to ask new folks coming into the household to give us 60 days notice before they leave rather than the normal duration of 30 days. This gives Alicia 30 days to fill a room before I might feel a need to step in and do so for financial reasons.

I know from experience living in community that fostering good power dynamics requires more than a good structure and clear initial understandings—it also requires ongoing maintenance. We have instituted weekly meetings that include time for sharing appreciations and concerns about each other. In daily interactions I have made it a practice to defer back to them when they ask me a question about their areas of responsibility. "What would you do if I weren't here?" I ask. I see this as helpful as we

Melanie Rios.

Chuck and Alicia making pea trellis.

Photos courtesy of Melanie Rios

get to know each other, when our natural tendency is to fall into socially proscribed roles. I'm guessing that soon they'll be confident enough that I can offer my opinions without unduly influencing the outcome of decisions.

When creating the social and power norms within a shared household, I believe many different arrangements are fine as long as they are clear and consensual before people move in. I could have chosen to retain more power, and would have thereby attracted folks who are happy to live somewhere without major responsibilities. While equalized power is not essential to creating a successful household, I do think it is helpful if people living in close quarters have something they care about in common, whether it be a spiritual practice, a passion for a particular form of dance, or as in the case of ALEA, a shared interest in homesteading. It's also helpful if people are compatible in what they eat, how clean they like to keep the house, and their relationship with drugs and TV. The more clarity one has during the interview process the better, so that people know what they're getting into before choosing to live together.

Lesson #2: Life feels rich when we live with a diversity of ages, genders, and species.

Robert and Alicia are both eager to start their own family, but are not feeling financially ready for that step. They were hoping to get a dog as a substitute for a baby in the meantime. I had learned from living in intentional community how much children contribute a sense of connection, wonder, and exuberance to a home, and how dogs can be great sources of affection and protection. So we decided to look for a child and a dog for our newly forming household.

It wasn't hard to find just the beings we were looking for, as Alison had been turned down by many landlords before she found us because of her four-month-old baby and her dog. She says "I felt so isolated before I moved here, as the folks I lived with both worked during the day, and were busy with their own projects in the evenings. I feel so grateful now to be living with people who talk with me, are willing to stay with my dog when I go out with friends, and who are helpful in so many ways. It was great when you all helped me move in, and played with my baby while I assembled my dresser."

Soon after Alison arrived, we interviewed a man in his 50s who was potentially about to become homeless. He had recently received a Master's Degree in counseling and was setting up a private practice, but didn't yet have enough clients to pay a deposit or a full month's rent. He came with good personal references from friends of mine, so we welcomed him into a vacant bedroom on a temporary basis while he stabilizes his finances. The arrival of three generations of people and a dog has jelled for us in the ALEA household a sense of abundance and connection.

Lesson #3: Ritual and storytelling help create a sense of meaning and connection to each other and the world.

Alicia learned from living and working at the Living Earth School in Virginia how much she loves daily rituals such as singing and expressing gratitude before meals, and sharing "stories of the day." "Telling our stories helps us create meaning from our lives," she said. Sobonfu Somé, whose name means "Keeper of the Rituals" in her native African land of Burkina Faso, was asked recently what she feels is the most important thing to do for nurturing the health of a community. "Mark the comings and goings of people with ritual," she replied.

We at ALEA are creating our new family rituals drawing on resources such as the Singing Alive! repertoire of songs that express our values so beautifully, and the book *Coyote Mentoring*, which teaches the arts of questioning, storytelling, and nature awareness. We'll invite the larger community to gather for storytelling, beginning this Sunday to celebrate the Jewish holiday Purim, which honors

(continued on p. 71)

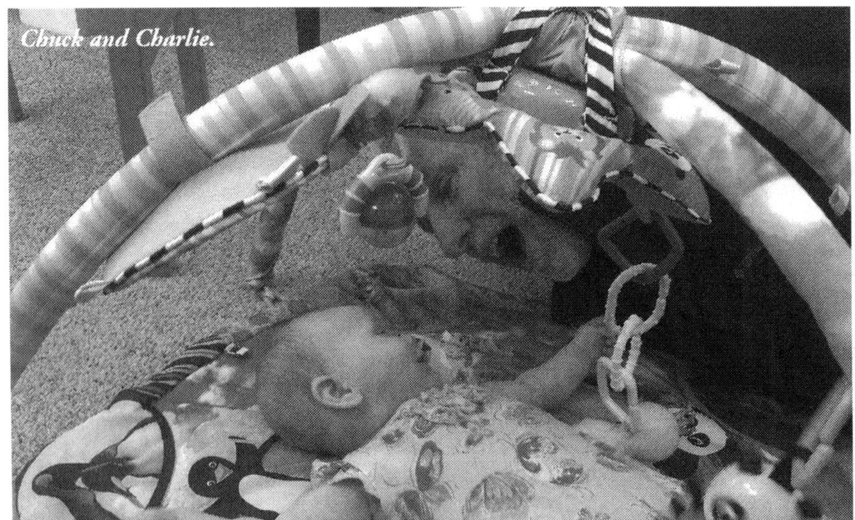

Chuck and Charlie.

Alicia with chicks.

BRINGING HOME LESSONS FROM COMMUNITY LIVING

(continued from p. 27)

Esther risking her life to save her people. We'll share our own stories of courage, and act these stories out for each other using "playback" theater.

Lesson #4: Create a generous social climate with a free flow of goods, services, and acknowledgment.

I've observed while living in intentional communities that a sense of obligation can kill joy and energy. Required assigned chores seem to create a climate of resentment, with essential tasks still not getting done. On the other hand, I've noticed that in communities with a more anarchistic approach, chores often fall to just a few people who notice what needs to be done, and who over time burn out on doing them. I wondered if there is a way to encourage folks in our new household to freely and energetically contribute to the good of the whole.

Recently Charles Eisenstein had come through town with his workshop on Sacred Economics, and an outcome of that has been the creation of *gift circles* in neighborhoods around Eugene. Folks show up for an evening to tell the whole group what they have to give and what they'd like to receive, and then they meet with each other individually to exchange promises of gifts. Once I asked to borrow a sewing machine, for example, and someone gave me one instead! How might this free and generous approach to life be sustained day by day amongst folks who live together?

To conduct an experiment in answering this question, I stocked our newly forming household with healthy bulk foods, and the garden shed with tools and seeds, so there would be a sense of abundance from the start. Then I committed to a practice of noticing and expressing gratitude to my housemates for work accomplished, household items contributed, meals offered, and stories told. At our house meetings we expand this practice when all of us offer specific appreciations to each other. We made a list of chores, and we each chose what we want to commit to doing based on our own sense of available time and what tasks we enjoy.

The results of this experiment in creating a space of freedom, service, beauty, and abundance are promising thus far. Our home is clean and orderly. The yard is becoming cultivated through love, with tender greens growing in our greenhouse. Here are some scenes from yesterday: All of us taking turns with a paintbrush to make one of our kitchen walls more colorful. Chuck and Alison making granola while Alicia creates a permaculture design for our homestead on her computer. All of us sharing a meal while telling our "stories of the day." Robert taking notes from our house-meeting while the dog soaks up affection. The baby smiling at us all. It feels like family.

At the same time that our own personal quality of life is improved through sharing a home together, we are contributing to solving a host of societal challenges. We reduce our per capita carbon footprint though sharing resources such as the energy needed to heat our common spaces. People who had been landless have access to gardens for growing organic fresh food, which improves their nutrition and health. It costs less to live in shared housing, which means those of us with small incomes can be housed rather than homeless. A single mom gets the support of an extended family, a young couple eager for parenthood get to help raise a small child, and middle-aged folks function as grandparents, reducing social isolation all around. For the benefit of people and the planet, I look forward to the day when it is normal for folks with shared interests and dreams to live together. ❧

Melanie Rios has lived in several intentional communities over the course of 40 years, most recently as cofounder of ALEA in Eugene, Oregon. Her passions are growing food on their half acre, singing and playing violin, nurturing a multigenerational household, and consciously transitioning towards eldership as a form of vital contribution to our world. Contact melanie@rios.org.

New Culture Perspectives for Everyday Life

By Sarah Taub with Michael Rios

It's 11 p.m. on a cool West Virginia night at New Culture Summer Camp East, where 90 cultural explorers have gathered for 10 days in the woods. Some are asleep in their tents, some are gathered in the big dome, others are chatting in the brightly lit main lodge. As I pass by the kitchen, the tension among the late-night prep crew is palpable. Judy comes over to me and says, "Could you talk to Steve? He thinks he's helping me out by being here, but he's really not!"

I tap Steve on the shoulder—"Looks like you're having a tough time. Let's talk." He is furious and resentful—two other shift members did not show up for the late-night prep for the morning's breakfast, and his partner Judy was trying to handle it by herself. "I don't know my way around a kitchen, but I couldn't leave her to do it alone," he says. I ask him to take a deep breath. "It's great that you want to help Judy out—but you don't really want to be there, and your resentment is making it harder for her."

He looks skeptical. "Let's think about this," I continue." You're forcing yourself to do something you don't want to do. Remember, you are always at choice, and only you are responsible for your own happiness—just like Judy is for hers. I bet I could find someone else who would love to step into the kitchen right now." I circle the building, putting out the request for good energy in the kitchen, and within minutes I get a volunteer—plus the original shift members, who have now arrived. Steve walks away, incredulous but relieved. No one is "made wrong" because they were late, and laughter and joking soon fill the night.

• • •

Being "at choice." Personal empowerment and responsibility for one's emotions. Flexibility and non-attachment. Asking for what you want. Contribution and service. No blame, no shame, no guilt. These are some of the values that have emerged over nearly 20 years of Network for a New Culture's experience as a community.

Most of us in New Culture don't live together, but we are part of an extended tribe that connects us in an intimate and powerful way. We have no gurus, no dogma, no guiding philosophy or established practices. Instead, our Summer Camp is always described as an experiment—we'll try anything that looks like it might work, and learn from that experience.

The vision of New Culture is to create a sustainable world based on love, freedom, and community. We explore this by creating gatherings where people explore the big questions about culture

Sharing tools for social change at New Culture Summer Camp East.

Photos courtesy of Sarah Taub

A spontaneous "backrub chain" at a New Culture Weekend.

A teenager and an adult camper hug at her community-created coming-of-age ceremony.

New Culture Summer Campers give and receive support for intense feelings in a "triad" format.

re-design—how do we get our food? how do we deal with money? how do we care for kids and elders? how do we handle relationships?—and practice living, loving, working, and having fun together.

At my first New Culture camp in Oregon in 2002, I experienced a depth of kindness, intimacy, and acceptance that I had never thought possible. I made meaningful connections with 100 people and felt a deep intimacy with many of them. My experience the next year was much the same. I felt profound changes in myself—I was more personally powerful, more self-accepting, more heartful and connected. Whatever was being created at New Culture Summer Camp, I wanted more of it!

So in 2004, Michael Rios and I, with four co-organizers, created our first East Coast Summer Camp. We copied the Oregon camp as best we could. With 40 attendees, only a few of whom had been to a New Culture camp before, we didn't know if we had "cultural critical mass." Three days later, we looked around at 40 people in a massive cuddle pile sharing from their hearts and gazing into each other's eyes and said, "It worked! This is New Culture camp!"

This experience taught us that certain perspectives seem to be at the heart of New Culture. We don't claim any originality for them—many of them have been taught for centuries. However, extended immersion in deep intimate relationships allows these perspectives to emerge in new and interesting ways.

Relationships of all kinds provide an opportunity for healing and personal growth. For instance, someone with a dependent personality who looks to others to meet their needs is likely to be disappointed in relationship. Yet that disappointment (or anger, or sadness, or fear), when explored insightfully, is the doorway to emotional independence; painful emotional reactions show us the places where we have not yet healed.

Without a skilled response, though, emotional reactivity can aggravate problems among people, and the more people involved, the more the reactivity can intensify and spread. Joe can't use the kitchen because Susie is cooking dinner—Joe gets mad, Susie gets offended, Lisa tries to intervene but is rebuffed and starts crying, and soon the whole community is in an uproar.

Our experiences over the years have shown us that certain attitudes and practices promote space around reactivity. Curiosity, transparency, gratitude, compassion—all of these require a person to take ownership of their inner reaction and create enough emotional space to think about it. If either Joe, Susie, or Lisa has the skills and empowerment to take an inner "step back" and witness their own process, they can break the cycle of reactivity. And the more skilled each person is in doing this, the more stable the community as a whole becomes.

With 90 people exploring intimacy and relationship, and living/working/playing together for 10 days or more, we can certainly count on a wide range of emotional reactions and growth opportunities to arise. At camp there are dozens of fellow travelers who have learned many ways of growing through these reactions, and who are happy to model and guide new ways of being. People often experience great leaps in personal power, freedom, and happiness during camp—and the strong extended community helps this continue all year long.

Over the years, we've noticed that the perspectives that we have gleaned from New Culture camps all seem to depend on one core practice: radical, compassionate acceptance of all parts of ourselves and of others. We have learned that every perspective and every voice has something of value to contribute and is beautiful when seen as one part of the great symphony of being human.

• • •

Walter walks up to me while I'm checking campers in. He's angry. "Why did I get assigned to work shifts on Tuesday? Can't they be on another day?" I immediately feel defensive; his bad teeth and strident manner put me off. "Well, I can't change your shifts—we have no one else to cover them." We go back and forth a few times; finally Walter walks away unhappy.

On the third day of camp, in our daily ZEGG Forum—where the community gathers and creates a "stage" for anyone to show themselves more deeply—Walter stands up to talk about his life. "I don't understand people," he says, pacing around in the middle of the circle of seated watchers. "I've never known how to get along with people—everyone seems to get it but I'm not in on the secret." It dawns on me that I have seen this before in people with Asperger's syndrome. Walter doesn't perceive social cues—he doesn't know how to tell when the person he's talking to is angry, bored, interested, or deeply moved. "I really wanted to go to tomorrow's workshop, because it's all about relationships and I thought I could finally learn something there." His anger makes sense now; he had wanted so much to tackle his lifelong problem. His sharing creates empathy in all of us, and several campers volunteer to be his replacement the next day.

Walter stays with us through camp takedown. On the first morning of takedown, a helper has an emotional meltdown and leaves camp angrily, creating emotional chaos for the rest of us. Walter, though, is an island of calm—the emotional interplay passes right through him. I spend the day with him taking down tents—his measured, objective approach is exactly what I need. Later that evening, six or seven of us sit with him and brainstorm ways he can employ his considerable intellect to connect better in social situations. My time with Walter is the highlight of this year's camp for me.

• • •

Listening to Walter opened up a space of curiosity and compassion, and helped me past my initial reactivity to an appreciation of the skills and needs of someone very different from myself.

One critical exercise of personal power is what we call "being at choice." This means that at every moment, you are making the choice to continue with what you are doing or to shift and choose something else. Many societies attempt to control their members through guilt and obligation—"You agreed to this, so you have to follow through!" Yet we often make agreements based on how we feel at a particular moment, and when the moment changes, our desires may change as well.

When people force themselves to continue on a no-longer-desired course, the inner conflict can lead to such negative feelings that the original intention is undermined, as with Steve's experience in the kitchen. Too often, people are afraid to re-negotiate their obligations, for a variety of reasons—and consequently, simple solutions to problems go unrecognized. In New Culture, we encourage people to acknowledge that their desires have shifted and to re-negotiate their commitments at any time. The result is that people are following their joy rather than their obligation. Work, relationships, and other undertakings flow without tension because everyone is there by choice, and can walk away if they wish. This creates a magical energy that draws people in, rather than pushing them away.

Even the concept of commitment, which in mainstream society is never allowed to be questioned, is subjected to critical exploration. One novel way to look at commitment is that it amounts to substituting a judgment made by our younger, less experienced, and possibly less wise self for the fully-informed judgment of our current, older, more experienced self.

• • •

I'm sitting next to Alice just before the start of Morning Circle. The sun is already hot and bright on the white tarps covering our geodesic dome. Her body is

A New Culture Summer Camper shares her truth with the community in the daily ZEGG Forum.

slumped in a chair. "I'm so exhausted...don't know how I'm going to handle my lunch prep shift this morning. Mark and I stayed up all night talking...what an amazing connection! But now I'm going to pay for it."

I can hear the self-blame in her voice. "Why don't you ask for someone to take your shift? Kevin did yesterday when he wasn't feeling well."

"Oh, I couldn't do that! Kevin was sick—I was just stupid!"

"Just give it a try—you chose to follow your excitement when you stayed up so late, and you may find that other folks support you in your choice."

At announcement time, Alice stands up and tentatively asks,"Could anyone take my kitchen shift this morning? I could trade for any other day...I'm just so exhausted today!" Three hands go up. Marie calls out, "I'd be glad to—Claire is cooking today and I want to spend time with her!" Despite Alice's protests, Marie refuses to assign one of her other shifts to Alice. "This is my gift—pass it along if you like." Gratefully, Alice heads off to her tent for a nap.

• • •

Rather than silently pushing herself to follow through on her work commitment, Alice reveals her feelings and needs to the group, and finds that her need creates a welcome opportunity for someone else. The experience of having her needs met creates a sense of abundance for Alice, and she will likely respond generously when others have needs that she could meet. Acceptance of oneself and one's own needs also makes it much easier to accept and respond empathetically to others.

Because of our practice of radical acceptance at camp, we have been able to include in our community people who have been forced to leave various other events and gatherings because of their behavior. What makes this possible is the community's empowered stance: clear communication, good personal boundary-setting, curiosity about others, and transparency about what we need and where we are struggling. And rather than being a strain on others, this radical acceptance becomes a benefit to the camp as a whole.

Two Summer Campers hug.

• • •

When Bruce shows up to help with camp setup, he's cheerful and willing to help, but his thinking is fuzzy, he doesn't get social cues, and he's impulsive. Three days into camp, we start getting complaints about him from other campers. "Bruce is stalking me. He followed me to my tent and hung around outside. I don't feel safe. Can someone escort me around camp?" Other women say the same thing, and report that he has touched them without permission. One man comes to us in fierce protective anger for his girlfriend's sake. Some are demanding that we kick him out.

We sit down with Bruce and try to explain how inappropriate his actions are. He is confused. "I was just trying to be friendly...other people were touching her, I thought it was OK." "Did she say 'no'?" "No, I don't think so...?" We realize that he is not getting the message that the women he has followed and touched did not want that contact with him—and we also realize that they did not deliver that message in a way that he could understand, with unambiguous direct words.

Bruce gets up in ZEGG Forum the next day and starts talking about what it's like to be him. "I've been kicked out of so many groups... Everyone else is connecting and touching, and I just don't know how to do it." Bruce's confusion and desire for intimacy shine through his words. When he sits down, Michael offers a reflection: "Bruce simply cannot get nonverbal cues. If we want to

A "pushing" exercise at New Culture Summer Camp East allows for physical expression of deep emotions.

help him stay here at camp, we need to give him clear verbal feedback about our boundaries. If he still breaks clear verbal boundaries, he's on notice that we'll ask him to leave. But let's see what happens if we give him clarity."

From that day on, there is a shift in camp. I watch as he approaches a woman in the main meeting space. "Can I sit next to you and hug you?" "You can sit next to me, but I don't want you to hug me." "OK." The women have stepped into their power and are giving him clear directions, and he is respecting their desires. Camp proceeds with no further incidents from him.

We allow the wisdom to arise from experience and practice, rather than starting with predetermined tactics and philosophies.

• • •

The understanding and compassion that arose during Forum inspired greater personal responsibility and clearer boundaries from the women. Initially, they saw themselves as victims of an abuser. As their understanding of Bruce shifted, their understanding of themselves shifted as well, from victims to powerful actors—they realized that in this situation, they could choose to act as mentors, providing clear, compassionate feedback on his actions. Bruce's difficulties became an opportunity for many women at camp to practice "being in charge" and speaking from their power.

Since New Culture is not primarily a residential community, it is our practices and insights that hold the New Culture community together and create our characteristically strong sense of *family*. They permeate and define all the different ways in which New Culture manifests itself: immersion camps, weekend gatherings, evening events, spontaneous informal get-togethers, and intentional communities that have built themselves on these insights.

We've found that these practices are effective in the rest of the world as well. For instance, my mother's strategy for getting needs met was to expect me to guess what she wanted. This led to disappointment for her, and guilt for me, because she wanted the sense of being valued that a surprise gift would bring—"If I have to tell you what I want, it doesn't count!" After long conversations about New Culture, my mother shifted her strategy. She told me, "I'm going to write a letter that explains what I want out of our relationship, and then I want to sit down and talk with you about it." That conversation, seven years ago, marked a turning point in our relationship. We have far less disappointment and guilt, and far more love and connection.

In the nine years since our first Summer Camp East, Michael Rios and I have developed a number of New Culture based programs—New Culture introductory courses, workshops on relationships, boundaries trainings, and other group transparency and connection processes. In 2011, we also began building a New Culture intentional community in West Virginia.

We regularly offer public New Culture programs in the Washington, DC area, as well as at conferences, festivals, and special events up and down the eastern United States. Over the years, Michael and I have trained over a thousand people in New Culture skills. We have also used these same insights to help other groups, social enterprises, and communities to increase their sense of connection, intimacy, and well-being.

We attribute the effectiveness of New Culture to a willingness to allow the wisdom to arise from experience and practice, rather than starting with predetermined tactics and philosophies. Even our systems of community decision-making evolve from year to year, and from one context to another. As we continue to grow and deepen our community processes, some of these insights will change, be added to, or be complemented by other perspectives. The willingness to hold lightly to all insights, to stay curious, and to let experience be our teacher, is the core insight that makes all the rest work so well. ❧

Sarah Taub, Ph.D. and Michael Rios are part of the Network for a New Culture (www.nfnc.org, www.cfnc.us). They live at Chrysalis, an intentional community in Arlington, Virginia (www.chrysalis-va.org), and are co-creating Allegheny Crest Intentional Village (aciv.cfnc.us), a new kind of entrepreneurial community in the West Virginia mountains associated with New Culture and the Abrams Creek Conference and Retreat Center (www.abramscreek-center.com). They regularly organize New Culture events aimed at creating a world based on awareness, compassion, and freedom rather than on fear and judgment.

Sarah is a cultural activist whose passion is creating events where people transform. She traded a tenured professorship in Cognitive Linguistics for a full-time focus on teaching the skills of peaceful, sustainable community—self-awareness, honesty, clear boundaries. Sarah's current koan: only when you let go of urgency can you be truly effective.

Michael is a social entrepreneur and practical visionary who has been creating living contexts for alternative lifestyles, social change, and personal growth for 45 years. He founded one of the first '60s communes, the first domestic violence hotline, and one of the first computer stores in the US. His favorite social organization principles include guerrilla capitalism and responsible anarchy.

For more information on New Culture, see ad on page 63.

CREATING THE IDEAL INTENTIONAL COMMUNITY
(OR REVITALIZING AN EXISTING ONE)

I, Sahmat, grew up in intentional communities and have lived in 10 of them. I have been so dedicated to Community with both humans and Nature that I've been called "The Community Guy". The communities I grew up in shared a fairly strong "sense of community". I call this deep and sustained sense of community "Common-unity" because it's a state of unity we share in common, with the unique individuality of each human and each species still honored. It's this state of Common-unity that I've found most valuable in life and to me it's the main reason for living in an intentional community. When a group is deep in Common-unity together, there's a shared sense of love, joy, and peace that tops any other group experience.

However, I've found that in all the communities I've lived in, the sense of community is not nearly as deep and sustained as it could be. It's precisely this lack of Common-unity that is the root cause of the catastrophic global suffering of racism, wars, child abuse, abuse of women, environmental and species destruction, etc. So the ultimate goal is ending global suffering through "Global Common-unity": the spreading of Common-unity throughout the world by forming a global network of Common-unity-dedicated Communities.

So I've spent my life learning how to create Common-unity-dedicated communities that share true Common-unity: a deeper and more sustained sense of community. There are two keys to starting a Common-unity community (or moving an existing community into deeper Common-unity):

1. The first key to Common-unity is for everyone to be "Common-unity-dedicated" as their top common priority. This doesn't seem to be the case in any existing community, which results in focus and energies being bled off into other priorities. So maintenance of Common-unity doesn't get enough time and energy.

2. The second key to Common-unity is to learn "Common-unity Skills", skills that must be practiced to maintain Common-unity: Speaking from the Heart, Empathetic Listening, Emptying of Ego-attachments, Conflict Resolution, Consensus, Heart Wound Healing, Cooperative Housing, and Cooperative Economics. Modern culture does not teach us these skills.

We at the Alliance for Global Community have developed free workshops that train you in these Common-unity Skills. The workshops contain the Sharing Circle process developed by M. Scott Peck, a Nature connection exercise developed by John Seed and Joanna Macy, healing exercises developed by Byron Katie and Richard Moss, and exercises in creating Cooperative Housing and Cooperative Economics. We've tested various versions of these Common-unity Skill Building workshops over the past 25 years, and we've found them to be quite effective in teaching Common-unity skills that can help maintain Common-unity. If you'd like to start a Common-unity-dedicated community, or if you'd like to bring more Common-unity into an existing community (perhaps through a Common-unity sub-community or "pod"), you need to learn or improve these Common-unity skills as soon as possible.

To find out how to sign up for a free public Common-unity Skills workshop or schedule a free workshop for an existing group or community, please go to my website thecommunityguy.org There you can also find out how to get a free copy of the book "Skill Building for Global Common-unity". You can contact Sahmat directly at info@thecommunityguy.org or at 434-305-4770.

COMMON-UNITY WITH HUMANITY AND NATURE

Quad-Parenting in Intentional Community

By Stephanie Powers

Like most summer days in Colorado, it was hot and sunny. You could see the heat waves pouring off the car as we stopped at a rest area shortly after entering Colorful Colorado. The heat is noticeably different out west from my hometown of Waterford, Michigan. It is a dry heat, so it doesn't have that same unbearably hot humidity as felt in the Midwest. We didn't know it yet, but we were moving to Sunrise Ranch, a spiritual intentional community set in the foothills of the Rocky Mountains. I still remember approaching the Ranch for the first time—the rolling hills of the countryside, farm animals strewn about the landscape. I thought to myself, "We could live here" as my two-year-old son Josiah sang songs in the backseat..."and on that farm he had a... door!" He has always been a creative little guy. "With a knock, knock here and a knock, knock there."

We pulled up to the Ranch and had lunch with the community in the Pavilion dining hall, where about 40 people, young and old, gathered for a communal meal. One table stood out to me, as there was a young woman wearing a brightly colored mumu, whose birthday it was that day. She was turning 18 and had lived at Sunrise since she was three years old. There was a strong sense of family and everyone was extremely welcoming. I felt as though we were long-lost family members and they had been waiting for us to arrive. After we met with the Spiritual Director and inquired about moving there, he simply told us, "If you feel called to be here, we'll work it out." Little did I know that this fateful lunch would prove to be a critical turning point in the unfolding book of my life story.

My *wasband* (an endearing term I use for my ex-husband) and I began our search for intentional community in 2002, with a shared vision of raising our children in community. We lived in Hawaii at the time and there weren't a whole lot of options

Step-dad Patrick (Dad-trick), Charlotte, Mama (Stephanie), and Josiah at the Pavilion Pond, Sunrise Ranch.

Photos courtesy of Stephanie Powers

Josiah with baby goats.

Halloween 2008 (day of the divorce) with the Sunrise kids.

Josiah painting brother's face.

on Oahu, where we lived. There were some forming permaculture communities on the Big Island, but they were really roughing it, living off the land and off the grid, something at the time I could not see myself happily doing. In 2004 we had saved enough money to leave the islands and go on a search for a community in which to raise our family. We visited several communities in the lower 48 over the next few years, including Ananda in Grass Valley, California; Dancing Rabbit in Missouri; Twin Oaks, Shannon Farm, and Acorn in Virginia; The Farm in Tennessee; Song of the Morning in Vanderbilt, Michigan; and the Center for Purposeful Living in North Carolina.

Each community was unique in their intention or reason for living communally. Some had shared income, whereas in others you had to have your own independent source of income. Some communities had a spiritual foundation; others did not. Some shared communal meals; some did not. Some grew their own food, while others did not. Through visiting the various communities we became clearer about what we were looking for. When we arrived at Sunrise, I was a bit leery and wondering if community was for me. I am so grateful that I found Sunrise when I did, because I was almost ready to give up the community search and my longtime dream.

Sunrise Ranch had so many aspects of what we in particular were looking for. First, a spiritual focus that was not dogmatic in its approach; instead it allows people to come into their own recognition of the truth of who they are as a divine being. A sustainable approach to agriculture that continues to expand and evolve—we grow and raise as much of our own food as possible, including annual vegetables, perennial fruit trees, and a host of native herbs. A thriving livestock program, including grass-fed cattle, laying hens, milking goats, and pigs. A childcare program where the parents and sometimes community members rotate in providing care for the children as part of their work pattern. A healthy balance of community time and private time—there are many communal meals throughout the week, and community-building days every other month or so.

The more time we spent there, the more it became clear that we were to be there on a longer-term basis. The feeling was mutual, and we were invited to stay and become a part of the Full Self Emergence program, an 18-month journey into learning and

Josiah (3 years old) and Mama.

Josiah, sister Charlotte, and Stepdad Patrick (Dad-trick).

living the teachings of Emissaries of Divine Light, the international organization of which Sunrise Ranch is the headquarters.

Everything was peachy; we were in love with the Ranch and all of what it has to offer. The only problem was that there was increasing tension in my relationship between my wasband and me. We had struggled for years to work through our interpersonal differences, which were becoming increasingly unhealthy. I came to a place inside of me where I was able to see that it is sometimes better to honor the completion of a cycle than to continue to live with something that is destructive and not allowing either of us to grow. By accepting that this cycle had come to a close, we could both move on to our next chapter.

We had a beautiful exchange, where we mutually removed our rings, allowing each other the freedom to move forward in our lives in a new way. We eventually held a private divorce ceremony led by a dear friend and community member, involving gift-giving and singing. We got divorced on Halloween, so we showed up to the court wearing a tutu, bunny ears, and an Afro. We went out for dessert afterward. When we got home we took our son trick-or-treating around the community with the other Sunrise kids and parents. My friends held a divorce shower for me, which included dozens of candles around the hot tub and a ritual of submerging ourselves under the water to release what we needed to let go of.

When we decided to part ways, we made an important agreement to continue to fulfill our mission of raising our child together in community. I strongly feel that we were divinely guided to Sunrise Ranch so that our family could continue to flourish in a beautiful and healthy way.

This morning, Josiah runs from my house to his Abba's (the Jewish name for Dad) house before school to get his bike, which he left there last night. His step-brother stopped by our house to pick him up and go to the bus stop together. It has been six years since I moved to Sunrise Ranch. Today, I am proudly raising my eight-year-old along "the quadrants," as we fondly refer to ourselves. Josiah has four parents now, two half siblings, and a step-brother. His step-dad and I also have a two-year-old daughter; and we live three doors down from his dad, step-mom, and their two other children. His step-mom and I take care of each other's children in our childcare program. Last night, both families sat together in the communal dining hall and shared a meal. Tomorrow we will all sing and have cake together to celebrate Josiah's step-dad's and step-brother's birthdays.

I am so proud of the way we continue to fulfill our original mission: we have persevered through thick and thin to actualize this commitment we have made to raise our child together in community. In many ways, I see us paving the way for so many other split families and providing a model for how to continue to raise children together after a divorce. Don't get me wrong—it is not all rainbows and roses. If raising a child with two parents with their own distinct viewpoints is challenging enough, try four people with four distinct viewpoints, all trying to get on the same page. Some days it is so hard; I feel discouraged and can't see how we are all going to work through an issue.

But those days are usually the exception rather than the rule. For the most part, we have the ideal situation for both the children and the adults. Living in a spiritually based intentional community encourages me to have faith in the creative process. I have done this long enough to have learned that everything is a cycle, and if I don't hold on to it, it will pass. Some of the best advice I received while attending the Opening Class was, "If you're going through hell, keep going." Don't stop there and stew in it—rather, allow the creative process to unfold. Another wonderful aspect of living in community is the support that our families receive. We have needed a mediator to help us work through issues. We have needed shoulders to cry on, as well as someone to believe in us and remind us that, above all, we need to do what's best for the children.

I am continually invited to stretch my capacity to love others and grow as a mother, a partner, and a friend.

It has not been an easy road, but one thing is for sure—it has all been worth it. All I've been through in the last six years has helped me evolve into who I am today. I am continually invited to stretch my capacity to love others and grow as a mother, a partner, and a friend. And I couldn't have done it without the support of the quadrants and my community, my family here at Sunrise Ranch. ❧

Stephanie Powers is a mother, partner, Youth Educator, and cook with a passion for nutrition, specifically food preservation and traditional foods for well-being. She has lived and served at Sunrise Ranch (sunriseranch.org) for the past six years, raising her two children along with the other children on the Ranch. She holds a Montessori teaching certification for Early Childhood, and has developed a summer camp, Camp Sunrise, which ran for the past four years. She is also a musician with a love for connecting people with each other and Spirit through song and dance.

Sunrise kids: Charlotte, Siri, Shemmesh, and Josiah.

Parenting in a Community of Friends: Happiness and Heartbreak

By Kristina Jansen

Orinda* is a community of about 100 individuals in California. We live in the hills above the city, on a ranch we own. There are roughly 20 children under the age of 13, and we have our own elementary school to educate them before they graduate to public high school in the larger community. While Orinda grew out of a shared ideal among a group of friends who were interested in a more honest and meaningful existence, it was not "intentional" in the beginning, but an organic outgrowth of a number of people with similar priorities: individual expression, emotional freedom, gender and age equality, honesty, harmonious households, psychological independence from early programming, personal growth, and a shared sense of adventure. That was nearly 40 years ago now, and to keep it going, it has evolved with intention, as well as affection and love and struggle and pain. It is more a very large extended family of friends than a purely functional intentional community, and it has been my home and my "family" since I was six years old, despite an eight-year stint in college and graduate school in the 1990s.

In 2006, my son Aaron was born. My choice to have a baby was a major departure from my earlier stance against procreating. But as I got l older, it became something that really mattered to me, and when I was 35, I gave my long-term boyfriend an ultimatum: "We start trying to have a baby by the time I turn 37, or I will leave you and find someone who will give me a child." It took him a few months to decide he wanted to share this with me, but he did, and I had Aaron four months before my 37th birthday. He turned seven in April. He calls me by my first name, shares a bedroom with two boys who are cousins with each other but unrelated to him, and besides me and his father, he has two other women and two other men who care for him as if he were their own. He's never lived in a nuclear family situation, and this is something I love about his world.

As for myself, I could just as naturally say "I'm a superhero" as I could say "I'm a mother." When it comes to identifying as a mother I feel like I'm playacting, just as I did as a little girl playing *Super friends* with the other kids I grew up with. It might be my temperamental allergy to labels and roles, or it could be that as a child of community, my relationships with my own parents and my own child are too complicated to fit into the stereotypical images that these labels invoke. In conventional society, I avoid the subject as much as possible, and when occasionally I find myself "checking-in" as a parent at my office with conventionally minded coworkers, I feel like a fraud. That said, I actually do perform a fair bit of "mothering"—just not usually with my own kid.

My friends Hugh and Jeannie have a daughter named Lucy, the same age as Aaron, and for whatever reason, she and I click. The same with the other girls around Aaron's age, and I have a strong attachment to all of them, as if they were my own kids. It turns out I'm a better "mother" to girls than I am for boys, and I spend more of my caretaking hours with the little chicks of my community than I do with the little clucks. When I am out and about in town, it is more likely to be a friend's daughter who accompanies me than it is my own son. People assume she is mine, and I don't correct them, for in many ways, she is just as much my child as my natural born son. Except sometimes things don't work out the way we expect.

When I am out and about in town, it is more likely to be a friend's daughter who accompanies me than it is my own son.

When I started writing this essay, it was April, and Aaron had just turned seven. The week after his birthday, two of the young people in our circle of friends got married in a big celebration on a farm in a different city. It was a big party, and nearly everyone we live with drove the five hours to join in. I brought two of the little girls to the wedding, and Aaron came with Joshua, who has been one of his primary caretakers since he was born. It was a joyous party, and one of the neatest parts of it to me was the easy flow of all the children and the adults, and the feeling of family among friends. I felt close to Lucy especially, and little details of our interaction that evening stand out to me now: reigning her in when she got hyper, removing a splinter from her finger, helping her find her discarded sweater when it got chilly, putting her to bed at the end of the night. Her father Hugh was at the party, but he had never been that involved in her day-to-day care, and she naturally came to me for what she needed as the "parental" adult in attendance. What I didn't know that weekend was that it was one of the last times I would get to put her to bed.

Hugh and Jeannie and I have been friends since I can remember. In fact they are both half a generation older than I am, so when I was a little girl, each of them were my sometimes caretakers. Hugh taught me how to drive. Jeannie used to mend my clothes. Their relationship was a more recent development than the years I have known them: a third marriage for Jeannie, and a second marriage for Hugh. It had ended four years ago, when Lucy was only two. Both Jeannie and Hugh, having been longtime members of the community, stayed around, and it seemed to me they would always be here.

This illusion was shattered for me the first week of May, when Jeannie and Lucy moved off the ranch unexpectedly. When I thought about how things had been going for Jeannie over the past few years, it was no surprise to me that she would make the decision to move out, but I was still unprepared for the emotional shock of losing the day-to-day contact with a child I had cared for since she was born. Jeannie was no longer happy living in a communal setting, and over the past few years, she had been isolating herself more and more from many people who had been her lifelong friends. Of course this was challenged by some of them, and more and more often, Jeannie would end up at odds with one or another person. So, when I put myself in Jeannie's shoes, it made sense for her to leave.

However, from Lucy's point of view, it seems a cruel choice to have made. Lucy has gone from being enmeshed in an ideal children's world—living with her friends on a ranch in mountains and having a rich set of adults to turn to for any of her needs—to living in a tiny two bedroom apartment with her mother. Her father has visitation rights, but Jeannie is controlling how much time he spends with her, and also where they can go, who else Lucy can spend time with, and every other aspect of Lucy's life. Anyone who was in conflict with Jeannie is off the approved list. I happen to be approved as a person to watch Lucy, but my boyfriend is not, so if I want to see her, I have to carve out an hour or two to spend in town, completely outside of my normal life. This is not something I can explain to Lucy. I have made the effort several times, but the whole experience is surreal and makes me feel awful. And there is nothing I can do about it.

I feel Lucy's absence in my life profoundly. I miss her. When I spend time with Lucy, she seems OK, though she complains to me about being bored in the apartment, and she keeps saying, "It's SO small!" when we talk about it. I can't imagine making the choice that Jeannie did. If I found myself unable to live within the context of my Orinda family, I might decide to move out. But from where I currently stand, I cannot imagine ripping Aaron away from the life he has known his whole existence, even if it meant being separate from him. Jeannie has her reasons and I know I shouldn't judge her, but it still makes me mad. ❧

When she is not "mothering" or spending time with her family of friends at Orinda, Kristina Jansen works in the renewable energy field, helping develop solar farms in California's San Joaquin valley.

*Orinda is a pseudonym, as are all the names in this story. Names have been changed to protect people's identities.

Healing Gender Issues through Community

By Marcus DeGauche

How could this be happening? For years I had prided myself on maintaining friendships with both women and men, not playing "favorites" (or so I thought), or at least not getting pulled into strong uncomfortable emotions that I often saw accompanying romantic relationships. I *could* accept strong emotions of attraction and love (which almost inevitably settled on women); but what about aversion and antipathy (which men more typically brought forth in me, especially if those men were linked to women I liked). I had maintained my equanimity partly by avoiding all situations where an "other" male might awaken such feelings. I had often steered away from possible romance because of this potential conflict. I hated holding someone else as an "enemy"; I hated feeling their antipathy toward me, and hated my own wish that they would disappear.

And yet, there they were: those skin-crawling emotions, accompanying the equally skin-tingling emotions I was much more fond of. For the first time in many years, I was in love! What's more, I was in love with a community-mate, who lived on the same beautiful piece of rural land as I did. So why was I also in such a yucky state of dislike? Why did I simultaneously consider a woman the most special person to me in the world, and an associated male as the one person who was most interfering with my unfettered happiness? If I were truly gender-blind, as I had attempted to be for decades, why was I now starting to want all males except me to vanish from the earth, or at least from my immediate vicinity?

While it would have been easy to blame intentional community for the situation that was causing me turmoil, the roots of my turmoil stretched significantly deeper than the topsoil of my current situation. Our polyamorous experiment in a small intentional community in rural Vermont seemed a long way from my mainstream upbringing on the opposite coast—but it brought up emotions I hadn't felt so strongly since childhood.

Photos accompanying this article are used by kind permission of Bread and Puppet Theater (Glover, Vermont; breadandpuppet.org) and the photographers. They depict scenes from the group's "Birdcatcher in Hell" production (pp. 45, 47) and the Bread and Puppet Museum (pp. 46, 48, 49).

Massimo Schuster

Relationship and Community as Mirrors

"A relationship is like a mirror. It reflects everything we have been avoiding. It has the power to reveal our divine potential as well as the darkest recesses of our shadow side. Loving, intimate relationship has a tendency to stir up all our old hurts, traumas, insecurities, fears, and control issues. Sooner or later, we must recognize and embrace the parts of ourselves and our loved ones that we've been avoiding, suppressing, and denying. When we use a loving relationship as a mirror to see who we truly are and what we have been hiding from, we enter the process of Self-discovery that moves us toward internal integration."

A friend recently sent me the wise words above, excerpted from Yogi Amrit Desai's article "The Yoga of Relationship" (www.amrityoga.org/more-teachings/yogarelationship.html). Substitute the word "community" for "relationship," and this statement may be just as true. When we combine the two—intimate relationship *and* community—the mirror can become impossible to deny, and the opportunities for awareness, acceptance, and healing doubly powerful as well.

Leaving It to Beaver

I grew up in a stereotypical '50s-era middle-class US family, as "wholesome" as they've probably ever come in human history. Although we resided just outside Hollywood, our lives were anything but dramatic. My parents obviously loved each other, my brother, and me, and took good care of us. We ate together every night, went to church together, vacationed together, and were the most important people in one another's lives. We were materially and emotionally secure—or should have been. Because of that "should," a fairly wide range of emotions were never accepted or acknowledged—and usually not even expressed.

Within my family, I grew to see the Female as my ally, and the Male as my enemy.

Part of me dwelt in that comfortable reality, in which my family and I lived in harmony and nothing was "wrong." Anger, resentment, rivalry, jealousy, and similar feelings had no place in this world. Beneath the placid surface, however, another emotional reality lurked. Because it was suppressed, it gained power. And it instilled a lot of shame in me, because I knew I had "no good reason" to feel some of the feelings I was *also* feeling (in addition to love and appreciation for my caring family, which could become dulled beyond recognition at times, because emotional suppression is not entirely selective).

What was the problem? Sometimes I've thought I had a combination of an Oedipal complex and a Cain complex. I never did kill my father, even in my imagination; and the only time I killed my brother was in a dream, and I immediately regretted it; but nevertheless part of my subconscious often wanted them to disappear so that I could have my mother to myself. In this region of my inner reality, my mother became my unwavering ally, and my father and brother my enemies. Even in "real life," I almost always felt more connected to my mother, and more distant from my father and brother, and noticed that my temperament more closely resembled hers than theirs. In my least happy years, that awareness of greater difference between us could easily morph into annoyance and even animosity. Within my family, I grew to see the Female as my ally, and the Male (of which I felt almost ashamed to be a representative, for reasons also extending far beyond my own family) as my enemy.

Strangely enough, these emotions, though strong, were not fixed or unchanging. When all four of us were together, I frequently found myself feeling close to my mother and estranged from or judgmental of my father and brother. (In hindsight, I came to believe that we three males were all acting as rivals for my mother's attention, in competition with one another—although somehow my father and brother had formed an apparent alliance in this.) But on those rare occasions when my mother would travel, leaving us three males alone for a week or so at a time, things changed markedly. As if miraculously, I and my father/brother would stop reacting negatively to one another, or being habitually silent with one another—we'd start to reach out and appreciate one another. We'd find a genuine comfort in each other's company that never was present in the same way when my mother was part of the equation. And as soon as my mother returned, my feeling of estrangement from them would return as well.

Jack Sumberg

No Words for the Shadow

We never discussed this dynamic. We didn't have words for it, nor did it fit into the image that others had of us, and that we had of ourselves, as a wholesome, trouble-free family. Wherever these very inconvenient emotions may have come from—and perhaps that didn't matter—there seemed no way out of them. In addition to the ongoing distress they caused me, they also instilled in me a sense of shame and a pattern of emotional suppression that extended to all areas of my life.

I think of this as the Shadow Reality of my childhood. The Sunny Reality of my childhood is one of many happy memories and genuine love among all of us. Especially when I talk with others about their often traumatic upbringings, I recognize that my relatively happy childhood was particularly blessed—making it is easy to push aside the Shadow Side as if it never existed. Yet that emotional underbelly did exist, gained power from my denial of it, and sometimes seemed like a terrible rut from which I'd never escape. I grew accustomed to living in those two emotional worlds, but only feeling good about one of them.

Independence and New Approaches

Eventually, the years brought independence and adulthood. With distance from my family, and more of my own life to live, I was able to loosen the ties of sometimes unhealthy emotional dependence and unspoken conflict. My relationships with the individuals in my family of birth matured. My feelings of competition, rivalry, and jealousy in relation to my brother and my father subsided and finally fell away. While I could still experience judgment or annoyance, they had lost much of their power. In fact, after awakening to some of the ways that I had distanced myself from them, and deeply regretting it, I made conscious efforts to rebuild bridges—efforts that eventually succeeded. I felt a great amount of relief as I found apparent freedom from the bondage of those uncomfortable and apparently-impossible-to-deal-with-or-even-talk-about family gender dynamics of my childhood.

Massimo Schuster

To achieve that independence, I had moved to the other side of the country. I found myself in rural New England, hotbed of conscious, back-to-the-land countercultural awakening—far from what I came to see as the artificiality and superficiality of Los Angeles County. I became involved with the intentional communities movement, lived in several communal settings, and finally found a long-term home in a community in the Northeast Kingdom of Vermont.

As a young adult and even into my 30s and 40s, I never tried to replicate a nuclear family—I focused on building my larger extended community family. I had few intimate relationships, believing that either they weren't important to me or that I wasn't cut out for them.

By constructing my life the way I did, I perhaps unconsciously steered away from situations that would have brought up the uncomfortable feelings of gender-related rivalry and conflict that had plagued the Shadow Side of my childhood. I'd sometimes have flashes of those feelings again: several times, I developed crushes and relatively close friendships with female community-mates who were already partnered with males from whom I felt much more distance. But those dynamics always resolved themselves without it becoming imperative to work through those deeper, lifelong issues they had started to bring up: dislike of a perceived rival for a favored female's attention, and by extension dislike on some level for men in general.

I succeeded for many years in avoiding the core issues that had shaped many of my choices and relationships throughout life.

I backed away from most potential intimate partners, largely because I had developed a story that I was unfit emotionally for a typical romantic relationship. I felt resigned to that story, without necessarily seeing its connection to unresolved gender-related issues from my childhood. I succeeded for many years, even decades, in avoiding the core issues that had shaped many of my choices and relationships throughout life.

Jolted into the Present

I might have sailed along fine this way, in avoidance, without the events of September 11, 2001. As it did for many, that day shook up my reality in multiple ways. It

Jack Sumberg

Northeast Kingdom, we don't have the fences or property lines that separate most "normal" modern households. In fact, we don't even have "normal" houses. Most of us live in small cabins or converted barns with minimal or no kitchen facilities; we share a communal kitchen/dining room and several other common buildings. We are in one another's lives all the time, partly as a result of architecture and physical layout, partly because of our desire to be a close-knit neighborhood and the ways we've designed our community's functioning and culture.

Age, class, educational background, sexual orientation, and other characteristics that often influence the formation of social circles and associations in the mainstream don't appear to matter much here in determining friendships. We are surprisingly diverse in these areas (though politically, we are all significantly left of center and/or green), yet our friendships seem to evolve from our connections on a heart/soul level, unimpeded by superficial differences. We are all dedicated to cultural experimentation, to shaking up assumptions, to supporting one another in finding individual and collective freedom from blind adherence to dominant paradigms.

In this open-hearted, convention-defying setting, the ground has always been fertile for polyamory and unconventional relationships. And after many years of steering clear of such entanglements, that's exactly where I found myself.

impacted me personally because some of my close friends' friends lost their lives. It also gave me more understanding than I'd ever had of the fleeting nature of my own physical existence—and my good fortune at being alive at all. (I myself was almost in lower Manhattan when the planes struck, on a very rare visit to New York City; only a delayed train kept me from being there.)

I didn't know immediately that everything had changed for me, but it had. Over the next year, newly aware of mortality and emboldened to live and stretch my boundaries while I still could, I opened up to others in ways I hadn't before. In particular, I found myself considering the first intimate relationship I'd had in years.

This relationship would not have happened, *could* not have happened, outside the context of intentional community. And it brought me face to face with my family-of-origin "gender issues" as nothing in the previous 30 years had done. Ultimately, it offered healing. It was extraordinarily complex—kind of like life in community. At the same time, it was one of the most simple, essential, basic experiences I'd ever had—also like life in community.

In this open-hearted, convention-defying setting, the ground has always been fertile for polyamory and unconventional relationships.

The Architecture of Intimacy

In our rural, land-based community on shared land in the

In the Stars, or Star-Crossed?

Cynthia and I had had a long courtship, though neither of us had been thinking of it that way at first (she was in an apparently committed monogamous relationship). Over the course of several years, we had grown closer, and I'd noticed significant attraction, which, I started to suspect, went both ways. More than a year into our friendship, she'd told me that she aspired to be polyamorous, and that she believed her partner would eventually be open to it—though we didn't discuss who might be involved in any new relationship she had. A number of months later, after he'd agreed "in principle" to polyamory, we found ourselves starting that experiment. Its allure had become irresistible, despite a significant age gap and many other differences that became increasingly obvious over time. And while physical attraction certainly played a role, I do believe it was also a genuine love that brought us together.

Unfortunately, her other partner, Rob, did not celebrate this new love. In fact, once polyamory moved from principle to practice, he reacted strongly against it. He and I had been friends, at least until he sensed where Cynthia's and my friendship was headed. Now, he was upset with both of us.

Without describing all the events of the next several months, I can say this: at times I was amazed that our experiment in unconventional relationships was going as well as it was—that Rob and I were inhabiting the same intentional community and being civil to each other, even sharing some meals together, rather than challenging each other to fights (as rivals for a woman's attention might have done in more conventional settings). And at times—especially when his reaction against our attempt at polyamory ended up solidifying rather than softening as Cynthia and I had hoped it would, and thus cast doubt on the long-term viability of our new relationship—the situation seemed miserable.

Rob and I had tried to "talk it out," and even seemed to be making progress, but eventually we reached a standstill. After a while he no longer even looked my direction, and there was apparently nothing I could do to change that. Theoretically (per our understanding of polyamory), love was limitless and each expression or experience of love was only going to create more love and happiness for everyone—but in real life, Rob felt extremely threatened by Cynthia's and my love for one another, even though it wasn't meant to exclude him, and he was in great distress, rather than being happy for us.

I had liked Rob once—but now, he was the archetypal male kill-joy. Why did men always ruin my happiness?

A Turn for the Worse

Cynthia realized that he wasn't going to "come around" any time soon. To try to achieve some peace in the household, and because of the general strain that the situation had brought about, she pulled back to a significant extent from our new relationship. Now, my discomfort with Rob morphed into a wish that he would just disappear from the scene. After all, he stood between me and happiness. I had liked him once—but now, he was the archetypal male kill-joy. Why did men always ruin my happiness? My world narrowed down, closed in on itself. Here I was, living in a place that was intended to be a model of healthy relationships, "living the dream"—and I felt like a fraud, with an inner emotional reality entirely out of sync with what my life was supposed to be about.

The feelings were so familiar—and they seemed to come from so long ago.

I realized that Rob had become indistinguishable, in my emotional world, from my father and my brother as I remembered them back in my childhood home. I found this profoundly disturbing. So much for having grown up and achieved freedom...

No longer could I deny that my family-of-origin gender issues still lurked in my psyche—and that they could still dominate it given the "right" conditions. Was there any way out this time, other than running away? I had invested a lot in my relationships within this community, especially with Cynthia and Rob. The prospect of fleeing seemed heartbreaking. While I didn't see a clear way out of the extremely distressing emotions I was experiencing, I knew by now to expect the unexpected, and that patience and trust can yield surprising outcomes. I didn't jump ship.

Recalibrations and New Beginnings

Fortunately, nothing in life is truly stagnant. Our experiment in polyamory was doomed to dissolve, and it did. (We came to realize that this had been inevitable—as we heard from multiple polyamorists, functional polyamory needs to be based on a strong foundation of consent and commitment to making it work among all involved.) Yet this dissolution led to further opportunities for growth. Cynthia, Rob, and I remained community-mates—in fact, we lived within sight of each other, and participated on some of the same work-teams. We couldn't have avoided each other if we'd tried.

Cynthia and I had gone through some ups and downs during our romantic relationship, even independent of Rob's influence on it. Post-relationship, in the absence of the affirmation of affection through sexual connection, we experienced some even stronger "downs" than we'd had as lovers, with fewer "ups" to balance them out. Simultaneously, the strain in Cynthia's

Jack Sumberg

relationship with Rob—a disharmony which had already been present and substantial before the polyamory experiment—continued to grow even with a return to monogamy. The iciness between Rob and me began to melt.

And soon it was Rob I felt much closer to, as we both were experiencing strain and hurt in our connections with Cynthia. Eventually, Rob and Cynthia separated romantically, and Rob and I discovered we probably had more in common with each other than we had with anyone else in the community, in terms of recent relationship experiences and even some core inner qualities (those same qualities that had bonded each of us with Cynthia, while also creating the dances of polarity we each had with her).

We talked with each other in moments of distress, when we needed someone to listen who would understand the pain we felt and the situation that had precipitated it. We offered each other perspectives that the two of us were in unique positions to have gathered. We found a level of trust with one another that I could never have anticipated during those times of intense rivalry for Cynthia's attention, when on some level we had each wanted—despite the desire to be a better, more enlightened person than that—for the other to disappear.

We even felt safe discussing the love and attraction we both still felt for Cynthia—though Rob, more than I, had concluded that he was "done for good" with any kind of romantic connection with her. We talked in a way that didn't seem to escalate our personal hurts, but helped release them; it never felt like "ganging up," but rather trying to achieve understanding. It opened the door to renewed appreciation in each of us of the person we had both loved, while also affirming the importance of our own self-care, respecting our own needs and boundaries in relating with her or with anyone else.

And More...

In fact, once this new landscape of trust and openness was firmly established between Rob and me, Cynthia and I also started spending more time together again. And, as I hadn't imagined in those dark days of apparently total separation from her, at times she and I even explored our connection physically again—developments I did not hide from Rob, but shared as I would with any good friend. My connections with Cynthia and Rob were obviously far from mutually exclusive, all-or-nothing propositions, as they'd once appeared—I came to understand they were complementary, and that I could value and cultivate both of them without imperiling either.

For perhaps the first time in my life, the Female and Male were not forces I needed to choose between. I could embrace them both, fully. I started to sense what "internal integration," as described by Yogi Amrit Desai, might mean—and to get an inkling that it might be happening to me.

What had seemed like a lifelong, subconscious schism in my world—both within and without—suddenly, miraculously, appeared to knit itself together. It seemed to not only bridge itself, but to join together as if one land mass—one with diverse terrain, rather like the Northeast Kingdom: some steep and challenging to traverse, other parts easy to enjoy and relax in, but all of it beautiful and worthy of wonder, and none of it cut off from the rest of it, or from me.

What had seemed like a lifelong, subconscious schism in my world suddenly, miraculously, appeared to knit itself together.

Appreciating a Perfect Storm

Though I'd eventually made peace with the males in my family of origin, I had obviously never successfully worked through the inner issues predisposing me toward estrangement from my own gender—the "Shadow Side" I had worked so hard to deny. It took the perfect storm of a relationship with an already-partnered woman in a close-knit intentional community, where there was no way to escape from or avoid the other people involved, to not only bring those issues to the forefront, but to present an opportunity to heal them.

And although difficult experiences in love often seem to lead to a callousing or shutting down, this experience seemed more to crack me open. It brought me to new experiences of honesty with a lover, with friends, and with community-mates alike—irrespective of gender. It revolutionized my inner emotional world. It expanded my capacity to love, and allowed me to fall permanently in love with those who contributed to this journey. It didn't make me permanently happy—I still experienced wants, desires, neediness, loneliness, a wishing-for-things-that-aren't—but it helped me see that my allies in life are everywhere (including within myself), regardless of anatomy, sexual orientation, or anything else. I'm thankful. ❧

Marcus DeGauche is a long-time communitarian, Bernie Sanders supporter (www.bernie.org), Bread and Puppet fan (breadandpuppet.org), Ben and Jerry's ex-customer (www.unilever.com/brands-in-action/view-brands.aspx), and pseudonymous contributor to Communities. *Some names and details have been changed to protect the innocent and well-intentioned (everyone in this story). The author thanks the editor for aid in wordsmithing, rearranging, and helping make head or tail of this tale.*

Deepening Community
The joy of togetherness

By Paul Born

"I really do not want more community than we already have at this church," shared a congregant during a Sunday morning adult Sunday school discussion. "What I like about this church is that no one judges you for not being more involved or attending regularly. If we had more community, people would expect too much from me."

I remember being dumbstruck when I heard these words, especially in this church context, having never considered that a Mennonite congregation—or any of its members—would not embrace community as one of its central organizing principles.

I need to admit, though, that my afterthought was, maybe he is right. If community means I am expected to be present every Sunday, give money, sit on at least one committee, join a smaller fellowship group, contribute to monthly potlucks, and provide meals and support to congregational members who are sick or in need, who has the time or energy for all that?

Maybe this is the same reason so many people do not know their neighbours. Do we really want to know when they are sick? Do we want to help them seed a new lawn or dig up one to plant a garden? Do we want to trust them enough to lend them a car or even our favourite kitchen tool?

Is It Worth the Investment?

Some days I think it would be so much easier to be anonymous in the crowd, to come and go as I like, to care only for those I choose and when I choose. I love this feeling of being free, anonymous, of living life on my terms. Besides, my days are so full, I am constantly with people and exhausted most days when I get home. I deserve that glass of wine by myself, in the backyard with that "keep your dog inside" and "only cut your lawn from 11-12 Saturday morning" kind-of-quiet all around.

Alone

I often feel alone and I do not like it. I find this feeling especially troublesome when I am in the midst of a crowd. You know that feeling you get when you go to a restaurant alone, or you are at a reception and there is an awkward moment when everyone is talking to someone other than you? You stand there alone, feeling left out, isolated, self-conscious...feeling like you want to hide or just walk away.

I am not talking about the introverted side of me that loves time alone to read, to re-energize, and to sit in the quiet of my own thoughts. I am talking about this deep-pitted feeling that it is all up to me. In the midst of the crowd—people all around, even people who love me—I get this anxious feeling and hear this recurring voice that reminds me to "take care of yourself because no one else will."

I recently had a conversation with a friend who reminded me that we die alone. Therefore,

Photos courtesy of Tamarack Institute

as we age, this pervasive sense of alone is an evolutionary preparation for death. That may be the most depressing thought anyone has ever shared with me.

What I find most curious is that this alone feeling I get is not related to the loneliness I feel at various times. Loneliness might happen when I am missing someone or wishing I was with others. I actually like the feeling of loneliness if for no other reason than that it indicates that I still love and want to be around those others who are dear to me. Viewing loneliness through this lens, it means I am very much alive. It is a part of living in community.

Community

During a recent interview, a young man just out of high school shared, "When I am in community, I do not feel alone." He was clearly an introvert, shy and self-conscious. But for him, this feeling of belonging was the antidote to feeling alone.

Community has many benefits, and feeling a sense of belonging is likely the most important. To feel a sense of belonging means that we feel we are in the right place; that we feel welcomed and embraced in a place or with a group. To belong is to be cared for and to reciprocate that caring, to know that "I am home." It is a willingness to extend our identity to a group of people or to an experience.

Having others in your life whom you know you can trust helps you make sense of who you are. It also can help shape your identity as you recognize the gifts you have to offer. The African term ubuntu, often used by Nelson Mandela, means "I am human because I belong. My humanity is caught up, is inextricably bound up in yours."

Community can better your economic prospects. Those in your community—family, friends, neighbours, fellow members of whatever communities you consider yourself a part of, faith-based or secular—can help you find a job, or lend you money for a business or to buy a house. They can also teach you to garden or help you learn a new skill. They can support you when you are unemployed and help you choose an educational direction. They can bind together to create a credit union, a school, or a community foundation, which all enhance your economic prospects.

Community makes us healthier. In his book *Love and Survival*, heart surgeon Dean Ornish shares his observations of patients with many supportive relationships and how they were more than twice as likely to recover well and live longer, compared to those who had fewer or no close relationships. The love, emotional support, and positive healing energy others bring to us during times of illness contribute to our healing just as much as medical science and procedures.

Perhaps the best reason to pursue more community in our lives is that it has proven to make us happier. A whole body of thinking is now catching on, known as the "economics of happiness." At its core is the argument that our gross domestic product is not a very good measure of human progress; instead, we should be measuring those things that enhance our collective quality of life.

One of the leading scholars advancing this idea, John Helliwell, a world-renowned professor at the University of British Columbia, concludes his talks by leading the audience in the song, "The More We Get Together, the Happier We'll Be."

A Missed Opportunity

My own community of faith, the Mennonite church, is struggling to maintain membership growth. Many individual churches are losing their young people to other denominations or they are stepping away from church altogether. Most Mennonite institutions have opened up to "non-Mennonite" membership, not so much to enhance their mission, but to survive.

Most blame this decline in church attendance to shifting priorities in the larger society and to people moving away from a faith identity.

My own Mennonite identity has been shaped both by a belief system that forms my faith and the historical Mennonite community I belong to. This identity certainly includes borscht and shoofly pie, but also peace and service. My Mennonite identity, and the people who have shaped it, make up an important core of my sense of community for me as it does for many others in our congregations.

Have we taken the importance of our identity as a community for granted? Have we downplayed the community aspect of our faith in order to emphasize the religious or spiritual dimension? I believe we have, and that this certainly must be considered when we look to determine the reason for struggling churches.

Deepening Community

At my home congregation, Stirling Avenue Mennonite Church in Kitchener, Ontario, we are taking four Sunday adult education hours to explore the role of community in our congregational life. The goal of this exploration is, first of all, to celebrate our communal life by sharing our stories, and, second, to consider the importance of and restore our commitment to a communal life together. We are exploring community by considering these four concepts:

• **Share Our Story:** The journey towards community begins as we share our stories, be they stories of fears or of joy. Sharing helps us to open up, to become vulnerable and to hear other people's stories. Thus do we begin to work together to distinguish truth from untruth and rational fear from irrational fear, to determine what we might do together. When we really hear one another, the bond of community is forged between us. We smile at each other; we feel warmth and joy as if we are home. In these times, we must make it a priority to take time for community. We need one another now, and we will need one another even more as times become more difficult.

• **Enjoy One Another:** As we continue to share our stories, and do so with the same

players over time, reciprocity and trust grow between us. This is an investment in deepening community, and the dividends this investment pays will be crucial to us in times of need. When we enjoy one another in a community we have invested in, we become a collective witness to the events around us. We can celebrate our achievements and those of our children together. How sweet are the victories and even failures that are experienced in community!

• **Take Care of One Another:** Reciprocity and trust have a wonderful effect when reaching out to help one another becomes as natural as breathing. We take care of one another not only because it is the right thing to do, and not only because people will help us if we help them, but primarily because the bond of love that has grown between us moves us to do so. Mutual acts of caring that happen often forge a sense of belonging. When we feel we belong, we feel safe and fulfilled; and when we feel safe and fulfilled, we can dare to develop hope and common purpose. Together, we have the strength to overcome almost any challenge that comes our way.

• **Build a Better World Together:** The first three acts of community give us energy for the fourth act of deepening community: building a better world together. In fact, we become a force for change that is unstoppable. The work of restoring our communities feels light and possible. We no longer feel alone in our fear or hopeless in our dreams; rather, we have the courage to see our dreams become real.

Each Sunday, we share a Bible verse and introduce the topic for exploration; then two members of the congregation share their experience of community. Next, we take time to share our own experiences in small groups.

During the four Sundays, we are able to answer these questions: How do we come to know each other's stories? When do we have fun together and why is this important for our congregational life? When have we felt cared for by this congregation, and when have we had the opportunity to give or express our caring to others in our community? What do we do together to make the world a better place and how has working together this way deepened our commitment to our congregational life?

Investing in Community

Like any investment, our community takes time and effort. We spend years investing for our retirement, setting aside dollars in order to live a good life in our old age. Our financial advisers tell us to start this process early, when we are young, in order to have enough when we're old, although they're always quick to add that it's never too late to start.

Investing in relationships to deepen community reaps a similar benefit. A strong family, a faith community or club, neighbours we can rely on, and friends who make the hours pass quickly, are equally worthy investments. Especially in times of loneliness, financial insecurity, or failing health, the skills we learn by seeking and living in community, and the network of relationships we build, will provide us with the joy and security we need. ❧

Paul Born is a community activist and best-selling author who has just released a new book, Deepening Community: Finding Joy Together in Chaotic Times. *He is also president of Tamarack—An Institute for Community Engagement; a faculty member of the Asset-Based Community Development Institute; and a senior global fellow of Ashoka, the world's largest network of social innovators. Learn more at www.deepeningcommunity.org. A different version of this article previously appeared in* Canadian Mennonite *magazine (canadianmennonite.org).*

A Community Conversation at Whole Village

By Sylvia Cheuy

I recently had the opportunity to host a conversation about community with a unique group of my neighbors: the residents of Whole Village (www.wholevillage.org)—an intentional community and ecovillage located in Caledon, Ontario—whose residents have a shared commitment to creating a community that is dedicated to sustainable living. The members of Whole Village own and operate a 190-acre organic farm. The farm's produce is sold through the Whole Village CSA as well as at several local area farmers markets.

About Whole Village

Greenhaven is the beautiful, cooperatively-owned home that sits at the heart of Whole Village. It includes 11 private apartments/suites that are all built around a common living, dining, and kitchen area. The home's design incorporates many eco-friendly design elements. In addition to making the space welcoming, comfortable, and functional, Greenhaven's design helps realize residents' shared commitment to shift to "living lightly on the earth" by incorporating renewable energy elements and encouraging less consumption by living together.

Whole Village residents share leadership, community responsibilities, housekeeping chores, and financial commitments. Decisions are made within the community using a consensus-based decision-making process that includes weekly house meetings and annual retreats where all aspects of community life are discussed.

For some, becoming a Whole Village member involved embracing a new mindset and an alternative way of living that requires considerable "un-learning."

Eating together is the norm at Whole Village and communal dinners are held most evenings. Most of the vegetables that are consumed are produced on the property. Responsibility for cooking and clean-up is shared by residents according to a rotating roster of cooks and clean-up crews.

Whole Village residents nurture connections with the broader Caledon community by hosting concerts, seasonal celebrations, and educational events—such as permaculture workshops—for school groups as well as the general public. They have also collaborated on specific environmental stewardship projects with the Credit Valley Conservation Authority, and community members also actively participate in local fairs and eco-educational events throughout the region.

Exploring the Meaning of Community at Whole Village

As the host and documenter of this conversation I was curious: how would the experience of being part of an intentional community and ecovillage lead to experiences of community that are similar or different from my own, more traditional, experience of community? Highlights from this rich conversation are shared below.

Community: A Sense of Belonging

After members recalled and shared powerful personal experiences of community with each other, we were able to identify several commonalities across this rich diversity of individual experiences. One dominant theme that quickly emerged was that of feeling connected and understood: a sense of belonging. People noted that this sense of belonging was a source of real inspiration which could be strengthened when it also included a commitment to a common goal that people were willing and able to work towards together.

Living Cooperatively: A New Paradigm for Happiness

Whole Village members noted that living in community creates different opportunities for happiness than what is often the norm. They felt that most people's experience of community is rooted in the dominant North American culture of consumerism and individualism. This paradigm suggests that personal happiness is something that can be purchased through material things or experiences. Whole Village members shared that being in community offers an alternative route to happiness. As one resident noted, "There is much more available to me when I'm living in community than when I am isolated," and another commented, "Being in community eliminates that sense of greed and encourages us to rely on others. Living with others returns us to the good. Happiness and fulfillment come from finding a shared way of being together."

Beyond the simple joy of being together, members stressed how happiness in community was also linked to working together to achieve shared goals, "not in a hierarchy, but united by a shared vision." The joy of discovering and benefiting from the knowledge and ability of others and appreciating the education that comes from sharing knowledge was also seen as one of the real benefits of living in community.

Community: Not Always Utopia

In spite of the benefits of community, living together is not always ideal or a utopia. Because the members of Whole Village farm together—which can be exhausting—*and* also live together, they noted that they can "bump up against each other" and that their diversity can lead to conflicts. This can make it challenging for "everyone to stay in heart." As one member noted, "We all join the community and bring our own baggage...and we can react to this. We also have to address these dynamics in the community."

Photos courtesy of Whole Village

Intentional Community's Unique Perspective on Community

Reflecting on the unique experience of community for Whole Village members, some noted that the decision to become part of an intentional community created specific challenges. For some, the move to Whole Village meant leaving an urban centre and adjusting to life within a rural setting. For others, becoming a Whole Village member involved embracing a new mindset and an alternative, more ecologically-friendly way of living that requires considerable "un-learning." As one member said, "I had to fight my own cultural programming in order to embrace living communally."

Another unique dimension of choosing to live in an intentional community, and adopting the alternative lifestyle of the Whole Village ecovillage, is explaining and managing the range of reactions that this decision generated within members' extended families.

Members also spoke about the multiple commitments that they each needed to juggle in terms of their obligations to living in intentional community. For those who were working outside the village, it was sometimes challenging to manage professional job responsibilities alongside their commitments to the community. One person explained, "There is a need to always find the balance between advancing community projects versus our own one-off projects." As well, the day-to-day complexities of maintaining Whole Village—as both an intentional community and an ecovillage—requires Whole Village members to pay attention to several important dimensions of work simultaneously. These include:

- **Commitment to a Shared Vision**—Members must share and maintain a commitment to living and working towards sustainability;
- **Assembling the Right Mix of Residents**—Having a shared vision is essential but not sufficient to sustain an ecovillage; it is also important that members have a diversity of skills, knowledge, and resources;
- **Tending to Interpersonal Dynamics**—Attention must be paid to how members are with one another, and learning how to work with each other's idiosyncrasies; and,
- **Ensuring Financial Viability**—Members must also pay attention to the economics of the community and ensure that adequate financing has been secured to sustain the community.

These complexities were articulated in a comment from one member who said, "As we learn more about permaculture it is difficult to reconcile the long-term plans this requires with the time and energy that goes into orienting new people about how we work and the rules we've set for how to work and live together."

In spite of the bigger commitment to relationship-building that living within an intentional community requires, members noted that living this way also creates opportunities for more in-depth learning. One member observed, "I've learned to talk more and I have been able to build relationships; before, I didn't really know anyone."

The Purpose of Community: Realizing that More Is Possible Together

As this conversation drew to a close, time was spent reflecting on what people discerned as the purpose and job of community. One point of consensus is that "we are happiest when we are altruistic" and that in community, "we have the ability to achieve a higher standard or quality of life." One person noted, "I believe that we are all interconnected, and so the more I help and care for others, the more I am contributing to a positive change and can 'get the ball rolling' towards a better life."

The group agreed that another central job of community is its unique role in supporting each of us to discover how to live more holistically and more authentically. One way that members observe this happens is that "living in community makes it harder to live behind masks." Several people shared that "in community, when people accept you as you truly are, it challenges you and holds you accountable to strive to be authentic." And "when you discover that people love you in your authenticity, it enables you to be more present." A metaphor offered some time ago by Laird Schaub was shared to illustrate this central role of community: "I remember him (Laird) saying that the work of community is the work of world peace. This reminds me that when we are able to create peace between us today, in our relationships with one other, we are making a contribution towards our deep hope for shared peace in the world." ❧

Sylvia Cheuy is a Director with Tamarack—An Institute for Community Engagement. She is a resident of Caledon, Ontario and a neighbor to the folks at Whole Village.

A Welcome Intimacy, or Too Little Privacy? Community Conversations at Lost Valley

By Macy Osborne

The most important elements in any community may be the relationships amongst individuals. The strong bonds needed to keep a community functioning well, and to create an atmosphere where members experience a sense of well-being, strengthen through conversation and constant communication. Each community has its own ways for members to keep in touch with one another and the group as a whole.

Residents at Lost Valley Education and Event Center/Meadowsong Ecovillage (Dexter, Oregon; www.lostvalley.org) take part in a host of meetings, announced via the community white board and email and attended by all who are able to be there and be present. These meetings include Community Petal (the residential community's biweekly logistical/policy meeting), Stewardship Council (which handles the activities of the nonprofit education/event center), and Well-Being meet-ups in the Sacred Yurt.

What do community members talk about that brings them close enough together in mind, body, and spirit so that they can function in unity as a productive, happy whole? The simple truth is, everything and anything. Meetings can center on specific topics or, especially in the case of Well-Beings, can simply be get-togethers where people check-in with feelings, what's going on in their lives, and if all needs are being met.

For the sake of writing this article a handful of Lost Valley members got together to talk. Those participating read over a list of questions and picked whichever they felt most comfortable and compelled to talk about. We scheduled two meet-ups, a week apart, each attended by different members who were drawn to different topics.

Conversation #1: What Brought Us Here?

At the first session we had Ananda, Anna, Catherine, Chris, Colin, Simon, and myself. A few children were also present. Anna and Simon were interested in listening but did not take part in conversing. I took notes. The first, most appealing question to this group was "What brought you to community?"

When you have a group of excited individuals who are more than satisfied with their situation and at peace with one another, a question such as this proves words, thoughts, and feelings can flow effortlessly, freely, and sometimes a little too quickly for the note taker. (With the participants' permission, I often paraphrase their words in this article.) With tougher topics people tend to talk more slowly and ponder more. Each person is given the chance to speak and the "conch" goes around in the circle.

Our gentle Ananda was the first to speak at our Well-Being meeting. "What brought me to community? A lot had to do with age and my family circumstances, and the conditions of the world. I'm 65, semi-retired; being in a community keeps me from becoming isolated. Now I'm with my family of choice on a daily basis. Being that I'm an empty nester, orphaned, and single, I could quickly be led to isolation. By living in this community I'm choosing not to settle for a community filled only with elders. Here I have a sense of belonging."

Next to speak was our sweet Catherine. "Coming from a small family meant I never felt part of a group. To me a family of choice means a family of understanding; I have a need to feel tribal. There is nothing about mainstream culture that I like. Everything about Lost Valley, I like! I spent years at the Lama Foundation and lived in three or four other communities, some of them more spiritually-focused and/or hierarchical than this one. Now, I believe we need to be equal among equals. If you just see the spiritual side of life, it's just one wing of the bird; the other wing is our human mental and emotional individual selves. There are basic reasons to evolve with other humans; we do that together. A certain level of truth comes up in community, revealing what our true needs are. This doesn't happen in mainstream competition. In a competitive environment, someone has to lose."

Then our hardworking Colin spoke up. "Lost Valley is the first intentional community I have lived in. The values of the community blend well and line up with my ethics and personal needs. Social and psychological health and more environmentally responsible ways of being belong together. I see us evolving beyond immature culture."

Our plant master and longest-standing member of the community, Chris had a lot of reasons for living in community. "Humans are social animals but some of us feel alienated from 'normal' life in the modern world. Our strong social needs can be suffocated within mainstream culture. I'm guessing in a community there is a larger proportion of introverts than one might expect. Some people may expect mostly extroverts in an intentional community, but extroverts

Chris Roth

may be more able to forge through mainstream life. Community provides a safer place for introverts and some people who are more sensitive.

"Here we are sharing with people in our day-to-day lives, instead of just encountering them. Encounters do not have the same feeling as, for example, cooking together. A big factor for me wishing to live in community is not having to drive a car so much to interact with others. I can meet more of my social, work, and other needs on foot, without boundaries created by street separation and traffic."

Colin agreed with this. "Here, things are also less commodified, with less money involved. We do not need to carry money on us at all times."

Catherine is an elder of the community and mentioned liking not having to do everything yourself and being able to rely on others for help or trade. "I find it tremendously relieving not having to do everything for survival, or to personally own everything I need to live. My equivalent of a suburban house is all over this campus."

Ananda, also an elder, agreed. "People jump in and are ready to help. There isn't always a need to ask; everyone has an 'of course' attitude. We are all valued and have our needs met. I don't feel alone or without help when I need it."

Colin stated a simple fact: "Community is a synonym for insurance." Chris agreed. "All sorts of fancy security systems aren't needed; we aren't worried about things being stolen."

Chris continued: "Another thing I value is the multigenerational aspect of community. Extended family that was normal throughout most of human evolution and in tribes has broken down on larger scales, so different generations are not living together anymore. It's rare that a grandpa lives with his kids and grandkids. People act like it's a burden and hassle to care for or even live with older generations. In community the young are not cut off from the elders. Children experience having many 'aunts' and 'uncles' around on site. This really enriches everyone's experiences of different decades of adulthood. Relationships with others change as age drops away and people experience each other simply as other human beings."

Colin added: "Age variation is important, as it is hard to be overserious when there is a one-year-old or a four-year-old around. Kids who grow up in community develop faster. They seem to be better adjusted and ahead of the curve."

Ananda laughed as she remembered her visit to a community for seniors: "They looked like they were at camp. Hanging out, spontaneous potlucks, but there was no diversity and I didn't want to be surrounded by people who were all just dying off at the same time. It did look like fun, but the reality was all of your new friends were just going to start dying off. The feeling around here is different, comfortable, and there is acceptance all across the spectrum. I'm accepted without makeup, in sweat suits. In cities and towns there is a feeling of not being accepted. In this community I can be myself without needing approval. There is no support for Maybelline."

Chris asked aloud what Maybelline was and a hearty chuckle went around the circle. [For those equally not in the know, it's a brand of cosmetics.]

Challenges of Moving to Community

We decided to switch the topic to challenges that people have after making the move from mainstream life to an intentional community. Catherine mentioned finding it difficult to lose her own personal agenda. "I had to learn to let go of my sense of control and need to clean everything. I came with expectations, and community for newcomers can include a process of ego softening that leaves one more patient and flexible in addressing both personal and community situations. This was the only aspect of community life that was difficult for me at first. Otherwise, my time here has been consistently meaningful and nurturing."

Colin continued: "Slowness to reach decisions can be difficult. At times I feel too much bureaucracy. I do understand slowness and am less critical than those who aren't 'plugged-in' to our community process. People who aren't as involved in the community are less patient and less understanding. Collective decision making versus individual decision making is what makes a community a community. I don't feel my voice is under-represented, because I am always involved from day one."

Macy Osborne

Chris spoke: "The patterns in outside culture bring in people who are used to the 'culture of complaint.' People are used to feeling powerless and complain and want to change things because they are used to feeling oppressed. Some have come in and said they can do better, and tried to take apart and replace policies and bylaws. In some cases they've done that, but not followed through with replacing them, or have left, dissatisfied, even after the change they said they wanted was made.

"Some people do not like consensus because it slows radical change. Group process can be a conservative process because we don't want to just throw things out. This is a paradox, because we are experimenting with different ways of doing things, and also trying to be cautious. People come in and sometimes inherently want to rebel, even against our alternative ways of doing things. Ultimately, though, I feel at home here and have confidence in the group process because people who live here have common sense."

Chris brought up another common community phenomenon: "It's also difficult for me when people I'm close to leave. There are times when rich connections I feel are lost. Ultimately, we have to deal with loss and change. Living in community can be like living many lifetimes because there is so much change. You really learn to live in the moment and deal with change and loss frequently, as people come and go. There is no escape."

Ananda spoke of the personal challenges she faced when coming into the Lost Valley community. "I used to be a teacher and took courses in leadership. I strove to be a good teacher when I entered community—a place where identity doesn't look the same as it does in the outside world. People here want to consult; they do not want a leader. I had to do a lot of adjusting when I first moved here. For me it was about learning to be a part of a collective and still have a voice. Leadership also looks different in community. I felt I needed to tame my passion, ambition, direction, and focus. That previous model doesn't seem appropriate. People here have watched me mellow out."

We all agreed that Lost Valley is not a place for those who wish to be led and that there is a collective here that makes the decisions. No one person can swoop in and change everything or "take over." We live in a safe community with level-headed individuals who mostly share the same values and enjoy sharing the same spaces. There is a desire to have even more of the community participate in decision making and be more involved in community meetings and activities. It is a blessing to get to see different sides of each other. Chris has appreciated seeing the various sides of people in the kitchen, the garden, community gatherings, and nonprofit business activities. "In a community," he observed, "it's hard to remain anonymous." Our first group seemed pleased with the idea of truly knowing what is going on with other community members—how they are feeling, and what is happening in their lives.

Chris Roth

Conversation #2: A Different Take

The new attendees in the second group were unaware of anything said in the first Well-Being meeting we hosted. Ironically, one of the first complaints was the idea of lack of privacy and others wanting to be in the know of the latest gossip. Concern about the rumor mill was expressed.

Our second group was much smaller. Chris was the only person other than myself from the first to attend the second Well-Being. Joining us was "bee" Steve, who has since moved out, and a lovely Anonymous.

Anonymous had a specific topic she wanted to bring to the circle. "It seems the general population in the Lost Valley community has real misconceptions about what the cause of mental illness is—the effects, the symptoms, the challenges—and what is mental health. As a mental health patient, I find it challenging to live among people who seem 'behind the times' to me in their concepts about mental health and things like schizophrenia, OCD, ADHD, ADD, bipolar, and schizo-affective to list a few.

"I feel I personally have a balanced view and approach to mental health. I see a lot of judgment here and the stigma of what comes along with mental health concerns. There is an imbalanced view at times. For instance, if someone takes over-the-counter or prescription medications there is a lot of judgment that I perceive others to have. Someone who may take these drugs and wish to remain open about it may experience shame, grief, loss, despair, and confusion. Many of those shadow emotions come up around the subject. It could lead someone to want to live in the city versus in community. In Eugene, Oregon it may feel safer to 'come out of the closet' about a mental health issue."

Chris asked: "Do you think this could be because in Eugene not everyone is so involved in everyone else's lives? I do think people have judgments here, maybe more than they do in the city, about the role pharmaceuticals play in people's lives (too great) and the role that natural remedies and more holistic approaches play (too small). At the same time, it is also easier to hide things from neighbors in a city than it is to hide things from each other here. If everyone in Eugene knew everyone as well as we know each other here, do you think you'd encounter the same thing?"

"We are so transparent in actions and words, and everything is so out in the open at Lost Valley," Anonymous responded. "I could see how someone dealing with a mental health concern would feel less despair, shame, and guilt in a city. Here I feel there are so many misconceptions surrounding mental health and mental health treatments that it would be difficult to find the love and support needed to deal with something as huge as being diagnosed with a mental health issue."

We heard from Steve for the first time: "Sometimes alcohol and drug abuse are indicative of a mental health issue. A person uses these to self-medicate." Anonymous: "Yes, and this self-medication can do a lot of harm, whereas the pharmaceuticals prescribed by a doctor may be healthier for the person. But I find people can be more judgmental about prescribed pharmaceuticals than they are about self-medication."

We observed that seeking alternative mental states through substances—whether natural or synthetic—is not part of our essential community culture. This is reflected in our Community Living Agreements, which ask residents to refrain from public intoxication, illegal drug use on site, etc. Permaculture, spirituality, and a desire for holistic living are widely-shared values here that make escaping via drugs or alcohol something that many people here don't even want to do. We also want to protect the land from any danger of illegal-drug-related seizure.

In general, plant-based medicines seem to be more accepted than any other kind in Lost Valley culture, but at the same time, "altering consciousness" in ways that interfere with our work as individuals, as a community, and as as nonprofit is not condoned at Lost Valley and can lead to a staff member's or resident's departure. Although the legal pharmaceuticals used by Anonymous are prescribed for her own well-being, she still feels the stigma of what she considers ill-informed "purer-than-thou" thinking from those who don't understand mental illness issues and treatments.

"Living in community can be like living many lifetimes because there is so much change."

More Challenges

Steve then talked about what he found to be challenging living at Lost Valley. This is the first community he has ever lived in. "No matter how hard you try to stay out the the rumor mill and gossip mill, everyone always seems to be exaggerating the facts. It causes me to want to withdraw at times. The result of this is people saying 'Oh no, what is wrong with Steve?' I find an imbalance: I want to interact, but I feel I am on stage and have to say the right things. It can be limiting and makes me feel that I can't be myself. I didn't come here to be gossiped about. I'd rather have someone come and check on me versus launching into gossip."

Chris, who's been in the community the longest, said that gossip has not always being a problem. "It used to be that if someone said something gossipy it would be talked about at Well-Being. In effect, there was no gossip, because we all knew each other well and talked directly with each other. We had established a level of trust and openness with each other that meant that we wouldn't talk behind backs—or if we did, we'd follow up by talking directly with the person involved. We were all accountable to each other for our communication patterns. I personally don't usually hear 'gossip' even now. But if people are experiencing it, then I'm not sure if the gossiping is due to the growth in the community's size or a loss of culture."

Steve suggested: "It has to do with our turnover rate. Trust is not developed right away and it becomes easier to gossip. Someone who has been here a long time may unload on an intern who is staying for three months, who may in turn unload on someone else."

Chris responded: "Even in those earlier days, people came for short periods—but if they acted that way, we told them that wasn't how we operated here—that we all needed to communicate with integrity, and speak directly with people we had issues with. Naka-Ima [a personal growth workshop that opened up communication among community members] was taken by everyone when they first arrived."

Steve again: "There are few people here I feel I can trust. I have said something to someone in confidence and found out they were not trustworthy. Some people understand confidentiality when there is a private conversation. When you ask to speak to someone in private, confidentiality is implied. But I heard about that private conversation later, from someone else.

"Another challenge I have found here," he continued, "is it is difficult to make a living so far from the city, and living here is expensive. You have to drive 20 miles to work at a menial job. People come here with great ideas, then can't afford to stay. I'm fortunate enough to have an onsite job, but if sales drop I won't be able to afford the meal plan."

Chris asked the group if they could end the conversation with what they loved about the community. Free hugs, the meal plan, and having children running about were all mentioned.

Variety: the Spice of Community Life

These two circles were excellent examples of how community conversations can vary so greatly depending on the week, the group, and the attitudes of those present. The first meeting had a much more positive, light tone, but that doesn't mean that anything at the second meeting could have been skipped. The tone of the gatherings always varies and the goal is for everyone to express themselves and be heard. While Steve has left the community since our conversations, the others who spoke all expect to stay.

Macy Osborne became the visitor coordinator at Lost Valley Education and Events Center in Oregon in May 2014. She is a permaculture student and full-time mom. Macy loves to spend all her time outdoors, whether it be biking, hiking, yoga, swimming, or rafting. She loves to read, write, study homeopathy and aromatherapy, and dance. Her motto is "don't worry, be happy!"

Macy Osborne

Transparency, Vulnerability, Interdependence, and Collaboration: An Intergenerational Perspective from a Boomer and a Millennial

By Melanie Rios and Skye Rios

Photo courtesy of Melanie Rios

I (Melanie) stepped out of the saddle shoes and plaid skirt that comprised my grade school uniform, adorned myself with a pair of faded blue jeans embellished with colorful patches, and began my four-decades-long journey to manifest the peace and love-based ideals of the '60s. But despite our best intentions, I've observed that it's not so easy to live and work together effectively in our intentional communities, social activist organizations, and workplaces. Dynamics that groups sometimes face include spending more hours trying to decide what to do than accomplishing tasks to support their goals, breaking into factions of people who judge and blame each other, becoming distracted from addressing what is needed in our deeply challenged world, and becoming bogged down in power struggles and resentments.

So what's holding us back from protecting our planet's ecosystem, reducing poverty and injustice, or peacefully addressing conflict? How can we interact with each other based on our authentic needs and offerings, rather than mask our needs with consumerism and violence?

Interacting authentically and tackling major world issues will require us to look critically at our history and challenges and improve our efficacy in collaboration. I propose that drastic improvements in our negotiations with each other will require us to break down our dominant social conditioning that was prevalent in the 1950s and continues today, which values individual achievement, identity, and intellect over the benefit of the collective. Instead, we will realize our collective power in the embrace of a new paradigm where we value interdependence over independence, transparency over confidentiality, and expressions of vulnerability over stoicism.

My perception is that many of the Millennial children who were raised in intentional communities and other alternative settings by boomer parents are capable of leading the way towards this shift in paradigm, standing on our shoulders with regards to communicating authentically, expressing vulnerability, and offering and accepting collaborative support.

Interdependence

Our mainstream culture teaches us to value being independent. As children we are expected to complete school assignments on our own, working in competition with fellow students for good grades. A sign of successful growing up is for us to get a job that pays enough for us to leave home and live on our own until it's time to marry and raise a family. Elders are considered to be in good shape if they qualify for "independent living" situations.

I question this value of independence that was inculcated in me as a child. My 23-year-old son Skye was raised with a different approach to education called "unschooling" that allowed him to create interdependent relationships with mentors he admired; he helped them out with their work in exchange for opportunities to learn from them. He reports that when he entered college, he felt discouraged to see so many of his peers not know what they wanted to learn or do with their life. Ironically, their upbringing, which compelled them to focus on accomplishing tasks on their own, led them to become less independent as authentic learners. Once free from their parents, many of his peers spent their time partying and feeling lost. Even those that find a passion are often weeded out of competitive career tracks because of enormous demands placed on individuals.

Now that Skye is in graduate school studying capture and storage of solar energy, collaboration is encouraged, but so is competition. Students feel pressured to become "first authors" on research projects in order to earn their Ph.D., while senior professors spend much of their time competing for grant funding rather than designing experiments or working in labs. We'd be more effective in accomplishing our goal of providing the world with clean energy, he says, if we focused more on doing research without worrying about who takes credit for the work. In his vision, motivation would come from curiosity and progress of the lab as a whole, rather than hyper-focus on individual contribution and the prize of first-authorship.

Transparency

Interdependent living is as important as working and studying interdependently, especially when there are children present. A Millennial friend of mine who was raised in intentional community currently lives in an urban community where three children are being raised by 10 adults living in two side-by-side houses. One community member is an apprentice midwife who leaves home to assist at home births while her two-year-old is cared for by other members of her community. One person works from his computer at home, earning enough money to subsidize the living expenses of several others. Another person grows food in their gardens, and distributes produce from the local health food store to neighbors in need. One person specializes in knowing the medicinal uses of plants, while someone else who enjoys negotiating bureaucracy has started a company which manages construction contracts to keep their network of carpenter friends legally employed.

This community seems pretty happy and relaxed raising young kids, especially in comparison to the couples and single parents I know who are raising children outside of intentional communities, hurriedly getting them off to daycare and schools in order to earn enough money to make ends meet. By increasing the ratio of adults to children and sharing resources, no one has to work too much, and their ecological footprint decreases along with their work load.

Some communities shy away from creating interdependence amongst members by requiring everyone to contribute the same amount of time and money to the whole, expecting everyone to participate in every decision, and rotating jobs amongst everyone. In my opinion, they are confusing egalitarianism with sameness. Embracing interdependence allows people to offer work and resources to their communities that match their interests, resources, and capabilities, while at the same time affirming that everyone is fundamentally of equal worth, and that each contribution is important. It may appear idealistic to think that everything that needs to get done will happen if there isn't a structure to fairly enforce contributions from each member, yet I've been continuously amazed to see how given enough people in a community and an attitude of respect and appreciation for each job, there is someone available to accomplish each necessary task who enjoys that kind of work.

Specializing in our work also encourages us to develop excellence in what we do. I appreciate living and working in communities where a few especially qualified people facilitate meetings, for example, as good facilitation requires skill. At the same time, it's important for there to be effective mentorship opportunities so that those without experience in an area of interest can gain skills in that area. Mentors and those being mentored have an interdependent need for each other, as it's natural for people with mastery to long to share what they've learned with others, and for those without skills to long for learning.

Transparency

Living interdependently effectively requires that people practice transparency, meaning that they share with each other what is true for them, and listen with deep respect for what others are saying. Those who have learned the art of transparency are good at asking for what they want, setting clear boundaries, sharing with gentle honesty their perceptions of others while those people are present, perceiving and acknowledging their own weaknesses and strengths, and deeply listening to each other without acting out on their emotional triggers.

The value of transparency contrasts with the values of personal privacy and confidentiality, which are both emphasized in mainstream culture, and are both important in settings in which there is a danger of violence. Clients need confidentiality to be honored in therapy sessions because they may have family members who might hurt them if they knew what was being said, for example. Many of us don't want the government or corporations to be violating our personal privacy by tracking our online activities and conversations because we don't trust them to use this information with our best interests in mind. Yet intentional communities, social activist groups, and workplaces operate best when there is trust amongst members. This trust is both a foundation for and created by transparent communication; they reinforce each other. Groups that want to function together effectively can use practices such as Sociocracy, Deep Democracy, Worldwork, or the Zegg forum to help them practice transparency if this sense of mutual trust doesn't emerge organically.

I witnessed a courageous form of effective transparency when some founders of an intentional community requested feedback from their community about how their actions as founders were perceived by others. Their boundary was a request for this feedback to be offered in the form of nonviolent communication if they found themselves triggered by what was said, and interpreters were available to assist with translation for speakers who weren't already skilled in using NVC. The community founders listened deeply to what others said, acknowledged mistakes they agreed they had made, and gently corrected what they perceived were misinformed rumors. This process of transparency helped to build increased trust between community members and these founders, and set a precedent for community members to graciously offer and accept feedback in other contexts.

The value of confidentiality, when misapplied, can contribute to communication breakdowns and broken relationships within workplaces and communities. Gossip is one form of confidentiality in which people talk about others in secret for the purpose of venting and/or for turning some people against others. In healthy communities, people sometimes discuss perceived weaknesses of someone when that person is not present, but it is done in a way in which it's clear that the person being discussed is cared for, and that the intention of the conversation is to improve relationships rather than to turn people against each other. In these contexts, it would be fine if the person walked in on the conversation and heard what was being said, and they are often gently informed about what was said if it is perceived they can make a difference in the dynamic. But when these expressions of concern about someone are gossip, the statements made secretly often get back to the person being discussed in ways they can't directly address because they don't know who said what. This secondhand communication often leaves people feeling upset, powerless, and depressed.

Illustrations by Kristen Reynolds

An example of when transparency would have been more helpful than confidentiality was when I invited a friend to stay with me at a community where I was living as a resident coach for several months. One community member let another community member know about her concern with my friend staying, and this sentiment was expressed to me, without telling me who held the concern, or why. I felt sad and resentful because I was living in a new town where I didn't have friends, and working too much to make new friends outside of the community. A month later the person who had spoken with me revealed the name of the person with the concern, and I was able to talk with her. Her concerns were alleviated once we had a personal, transparent conversation, and this went a long way towards healing my feelings about living and working with this community.

Vulnerability

One form of transparency is revealing our vulnerabilities to each other. In the world I grew up in we were not supposed to cry, shout, or admit our weaknesses; we pretended to feel "tough and cool" at all times. At 20 years old I felt hopeless regarding our planet's ecological crises and confused about my dad showing up for the first time in a dozen years. I didn't discuss my thoughts and feelings with friends or family members, but sang "I am a rock, I am an island" as I sat alone in my room for three months, emerging only to forage for food.

I witnessed stoicism recently when a man in his 50s came down with a life-threatening illness that required his full attention. He didn't tell anyone of this illness, and many of his fellow community members grew frustrated with his lack of follow-through on completing work he had promised to contribute. When I asked him why he hadn't revealed his health struggles, he replied that he didn't want to appear weak. He perceived that if people were to respect him in his field, he had to consistently show a strong face to the world.

My son Skye recently took a different approach to his own feelings of vulnerability. He was contemplating the more broken parts of our world: human trafficking; drone strikes on innocent people; the injustice in places like Ferguson, Missouri; and the causes of climate change. The burden he shouldered grew too heavy and he went public with his struggles, posting on Facebook a plea to crowd-source his mental health and request help in his recovery. Soon thereafter he flew from Denmark, where he was working, to Italy, to meet a friend with whom he felt he could share his concerns. He felt called to sit in a church in Venice, where he experienced an overload of insight about his role in addressing insanity in the world.

A confluence of factors resulted in a brief stay at the Psychiatric Hospital Ljubljana in Slovenia. When he shared this experience a few days later, friends, family, colleagues, and acquaintances showed up in droves to offer appreciation and support in person, by phone, and by email. I feel so grateful for this support, for without it, he may have ended up like many others who land in psych wards and are drugged into mental sluggishness for months or years. With continued assistance from others, he is channeling what he learned in the Venetian church to inform his choices going forward.

I've come to see that expressions of vulnerability, affirmation of our interdependence, and transparent communication are attributes that strengthen community. By sharing our fears, struggles, and great ideas with each other, we relieve our sense of isolation. Others naturally open up their compassionate hearts to us, and feel safe to talk of their own thoughts, feelings, and difficult experiences. This transparent communication helps us to become available for receiving gifts of help from each other, weaving webs of interdependent connections to bring to life the ideals we hold.

Melanie Rios has lived in intentional communities for 40 years, though she is currently living with just her partner in Portland, Oregon. She consults with communities, activist groups, and workplaces on conflict resolution, governance, and culture shift. As part of her role in cultivating community, she enjoys dancing, singing, and gardening.

Skye Rios is a National Science Foundation Graduate Research Fellow and works around the world to study new technologies for capturing and storing solar power. He is active as a dancer and activist. Among other pursuits, Skye serves as Board President for a nonprofit, Youth M.O.V.E Oregon, that is dedicated towards ending stigma surrounding issues of mental health.

HOW TO Live Together in Harmony

By Cedar Rose Selenite

I have to admit something about myself and it's very painful. For most of my adult life, I have not kept a clean house.

Sure, I can blame it on having three children close together in age, homeschooling them, often having several projects going on at a time that do not allow time for housekeeping...

But the truth is, there are dishes in the sink, sometimes even food left out on the counter.

Recently, I invited someone to live with me and my children with the intention of starting a small intentional community based in Nonviolent Communication. We are thinking of calling our house the Harmony Homestead. We shall call this person Joann. Joann has added such positivity and spiritual companionship to my life. She began helping around the house above and beyond what I would have expected. She could tell I was overwhelmed and struggling with so much on my plate.

But several weeks in, she sat me down to have a talk. I'm imagining it was difficult for her. I know it was intensely painful for me. "Cedar, there are ants in the kitchen, and food left out, and dishes in the sink. The yard needs work. I know you are a good, wonderful mother, but something's got to change around here! It's neglectful!"

I reflected back her concerns, said I understood, and wanted us to work together. But inside I was torn up. Time to face the reality of feedback. If I wanted to live with Joann, I would need to work with her and change my ways.

I tell this story because it really highlights what it takes to live in harmony together. **Joann was brave, honest, and willing to work together.** I was open to hearing feedback, and willing to find strategies to meet both of our needs.

There are five skills I believe we can learn and practice that make it more possible to live together in harmony, whether it's in a family, a roommate situation, an intentional community, or a working group.

1 Listen with curiosity. Take a deep breath, and breathe it out. Let go of all your own thoughts for just a moment. Hear what the other person is saying and be present. Guess at what the person is feeling and what is most important to them. Reflect back what you are hearing them say. This de-escalates tension, and helps the other person trust that what is going on with them is important to you. It also puts you into a more grounded state.

2 Share your needs too. Check in with yourself. Your needs are important too. To live together in harmony, everyone's needs need to be on the table. Solutions can come from looking at everyone's needs together.

3 Remember that relationships are nurtured by positivity. If you notice that you are giving and/or receiving mostly negative feedback, you will need to turn it around. Think of several things you are thankful for about the relationship or situation. Share these appreciations regularly. Relationship expert John Gottman recommends a ratio of five positive interactions for every one challenging interaction in order for a relationship to thrive.

4 Give your feedback carefully. In order for the other person or for your group to take in challenging feedback, you will need to remove blame from it. Use I-statements, state how you feel, and use no judgments. In order to get your concern across, say why it is important to you.

5 Be willing to collaborate. There are limits to getting people to do what we want them to by means of coercion or fear. When we do that we lose trust, and in some ways we lose the relationship. When we share power and collaborate, and when we are willing to hear what is most important to the other, we retain the relationship, the trust, and foster positivity and goodwill.

Things are looking up at Harmony Homestead. We've had a clean kitchen free of ants for weeks. I'm hopeful and grateful for having Joann in my life.

Cedar Rose Selenite teaches Nonviolent Communication and offers communication coaching and relationship healing mediations via skype. She is also an empathizer on EmpathyApp.com. Visit universalhumanneeds.org for more information on her offerings, and for more articles. She also offers a weekend workshop for intentional communities on how to live together in harmony. Email universalhumanneeds@yahoo.com to invite her to your community.

ECOSEXUALITY: Embracing a Force of Nature

By Lindsay Hagamen

Photos by Sheena Davis

It is only when we deal with the dis-eased character of modern sexuality and the ecological crisis as a single problem that is rooted in an erotic disorder that we can begin to discover ways to heal ourselves of our alienation from our bodies and from nature.[1] —Sam Keen

"Contact! Contact! Who are we? Where are we?"[2] Henry David Thoreau's words ring just as true now as they did when he wrote them up on the highest mountain in Maine over 150 years ago. Permaculture—rewilding—ecosexuality—these may be terms that resonate more strongly with today's crowd, but the urge is the same: a calling to immerse oneself in the raw forces of nature, to remember that being human means we are part of this Earth, and to relearn how to draw our sustenance and nourish our souls from the very places we call home.

In an age dominated by individual isolation, virtual reality, and the information economy, the hunger to partner with Life in its eternal dance and to experience the depth of real human connection is palpable. The primal energies of nature are as alluring as they are frightening, they invigorate us as much as they humble, they show us how fragile it is to be made of flesh and bone. Beneath the superficiality of the Twitter, Instagram, and Facebook posts, the soul of the millennial generation is crawling, naked and knowing, across the forest floor seeking the marrow that can nourish it back to life.

There is a movement underfoot. Alongside the software programmers and coffee-shop baristas, there are those who are returning to the forests, building with cob, practicing permaculture, creating community, sipping on bone broth, tanning hides, and fermenting everything from fruit and veggies to milk and grains. Thousands of young women across the country are meeting on the new moon to honor the cycles of their blood, others are embracing the wildness and sacredness of their sexuality, still others are practicing as herbalists, midwives, death doulas, and as practitioners of other traditional arts.

You could chalk this up to youthful exuberance or a primitive backlash against the sterility of cubicle life, but I think that this trend strikes at a vein that runs deep into the human psyche. Ever since the beginning of the industrial revolution, nature writers have grasped at words for our relationship with this Earth—a relationship they describe with increasing intimacy the further it slips out of our outstretched hands.

Standing amidst the towering trees and exalted rock faces of Yosemite in the early 1900s, John Muir exclaimed that "no holier temple has ever been consecrated by the heart of man."[3] For Aldo Leopold in the 1940s, the relationship focused on engaging with the land "as a community to which we belong."[4]

By the early 1990s, Wendell Berry described his experience with the land he called home in far more intimate terms: "bone of our bone, flesh of our flesh."[5] And it was Terry Tempest Williams who cut through any remaining artifice to urge activist, academic, and farmer alike to remove our masks and "admit we are lovers, engaged in an erotics of place." As if to give us permission to acknowledge what we already know in our bones to be true, she added, "There is nothing more legitimate and there is nothing more true...We love the land. It's a primal affair."[6]

• • •

As the spectrum and complexity of sexual expression becomes more readily accepted, the veil of shame that has cloaked sexuality since the dawn of agriculture is slowly beginning to lift. Sexuality finally has the opportunity to be understood on its own terms. Far from seeing the erotic as obscene or sexual desire as offensive, philosopher Sam Keen describes eros, or erotic energy, as the motivating principle of all life; it is eros that drives the acorn to become the oak. Erotic energy exists in all of nature, and it moves through us and around us, intertwining us with all Life. Sexuality is a potent and precious expression of this life energy, and it represents our primal desire to merge with Life itself.

This cosmetic-free and barefoot expression of sexuality is the adult child of the 1960s sexual revolution. Sobered by the prevalence of STIs and humbled by the rate of divorce and date-rape, intention and consent now take precedence over experimentation and drug use. Today's hunger is more for authenticity and community, holistic health and sustainability, and it translates into an acceptance that our bodies are born from this Earth. Gender norms slip away. Categories become cages. Nudity becomes nakedness. *Do not look away. This is who I am. I am of this Earth.*

• • •

The impulse to embrace the Earth—wildness, bodies, sex, death, food, community, each other—is simultaneously an act of love and instinct. The urge to protect the very things that give us life is a basic instinct of survival. The drive to extend ourselves to others with courage and compassion in a time of crisis is love. As a social movement, ecosexuality emerges out of the deep place in our bodies that is retching in the pain we are are inflicting on the world—on ourselves—and is grasping for the only thing that can bring it to an end: the rapture and pleasure of humbly submitting to intimacy so profound we begin to feel the Earth simultaneously as lover and as self.

Beneath the complexity and confusion of the ecological, economic, political, and erotic crises of our time lies one simple cause—disconnection. What more intuitive or logical response could there be to a crisis of disconnection than to once again hold the things that actually matter so close that we can feel their beating hearts—our bodies, the earth that sustains us, the places we call home, the people we call community? For in partnering with a place and its people, we draw strength and sustenance, purpose and meaning. Perhaps enough to even heal our self-inflicted alienation from this embodied world.

The search for reconnection with the natural, the embodied, and the authentic is what drives many branches of the ecological movement today. Permaculture seeks intimacy with the living systems that provide for our sustenance. Rewilding aims to reconnect the inner and outer wild landscape, to embrace it and live within it. Fostering communication, trust, and love with fellow humans so we can better live together is a focus of many intentional communities. Ecosexuality integrates all these elements with an explicit invitation to come back into our bodies and embrace the erotic energy that animates us and all of Life.

The path towards such profound intimacy with land and community requires time, knowledge, and ultimately love: we cannot love what we do not know, and we cannot know what we do not spend time with. It also requires skill, discipline, and patience. Whether it be with tree, rock, or person, letting another in, in their wholeness, requires that we suspend belief, let go of fantasy, and be exquisitely present.

• • •

Like wind, water, or any other force of nature, erotic energy moves through our communities, organizations, and landscapes. It can be empowering and invigorating, and it can be destructive and debilitating. Yet, rather than acknowledge sexuality as a force of nature that greatly influences every social endeavor, it is often cast aside as a private matter—as being of little relevance to efforts to live communally, share power, deepen knowledge, develop alternative economies, pass wisdom down through the generations, and create a culture that respects all of nature and all those who call Earth home.

Isolating sexuality is foolish at best. Wendell Berry offers far more condemning words: "the failure to imagine sex in all its power and sanctity is to prepare the ruin of family and community life." For sexual love lies at the heart of a community and ecological life, "it brings us into the dance that holds community together and joins it to its place."[7]

In embracing sexuality and erotic energy as an inherent part of our communities, and responding to the deep hunger we carry for intimacy in this time of such profound disconnection, ecosexuality offers a proactive approach that can heal and transform.

Imagine the world we will co-create together when we:

• Meet our needs through deep intimacy with Earth, self, and community, instead of goods and services;

• Design our relationship networks with as much care and intention as we design our permaculture gardens and community governance systems;

• Allow our love for this Earth to transform all aspects of our lives, including our intimate relationships;

• Channel erotic energy to benefit the ecosystems we love just as we might channel wind, water, and other energies of nature;

• Engage with the Earth as a lover and partner who we tend to, care for, and respect in a mutual relationship where we give more than we take;
• Be as intentional about sex as we are about what kind of foods we eat, which products we buy, and what plants we sow in the garden;
• Allow pleasure to be a guiding principle as we engage whole systems thinking within our communities;
• Allow ourselves to experience the sensual in nature and the nature in our sensuality;
• Give ourselves in service to the lands that feed us, the ecosystems that keep us healthy, and the communities that support us;
• Love our bodies as ecosystems and our ecosystems as bodies.

• • •

Every year, earth-lovers from all walks of life journey to the forests I call home on the plateau that descends off of Mount Adams in southern Washington for the EcoSex Convergence. Infused with a level of intentionality, sobriety, and intimacy unusual for a summer festival, the gathering aims to build a regional community of ecosexual practitioners who support each other in the transition to a love-based, sustainable culture.

For many, these five days in the forest are a time to reunite with old friends, develop new ones, and strengthen their personal relationship with the land. Others come drawn by the opportunity to teach and learn practical skills or to experience a place where sexuality is treated with intelligence and authenticity alongside conversations about food systems and gift economies. For some it's a rare opportunity to be able to make love in the forest under the night sky or feel the primal energies evoked by the rhythm of drums and the light of fire. But for all, it's a place where the wholeness of who they are is welcome and held by community, creating an all too rare experience where they are able to express their deepest longing, deepest sorrow, and deepest joy for the Earth we know as partner, lover, and self.

For, only when we create a container that is loving enough and strong enough to embrace the erotic, do we create a container that is loving enough and strong enough to embrace all of Life itself.

Can we really afford anything less?

Lindsay Hagamen is a steward of the Windward Community in southern Washington. She is coauthor of Ecosexuality: When Nature Inspires the Arts of Love *and co-creator of the annual EcoSex Convergence. Lindsay enjoys immersing her hands in rich garden soil, giving belly rubs to her pigs, and being a lover of the Wild.*

---

1. Sam Keen. *The Passionate Life.* 1992.
2. Henry David Thoreau. "Ktaadn." *The Maine Woods.* 1864.
3. John Muir. "The Hetch Hetchy Valley". Sierra Club Bulletin, Vol. VI, No. 4, January, 1908.
4. Aldo Leopold. *Sand County Almanac.* 1949.
5. Wendell Berry. "Conservation is Good Work." *Sex, Economy, Freedom & Community.* 1992.
6. Terry Tempest Williams. "The Erotics of Place: Yellowstone." 1991.
7. Wendell Berry. "Sex, Economy, Freedom & Community." *Sex, Economy, Freedom & Community.* 1992.

Review BY CHRIS ROTH

Remembering Zendik

Mating in Captivity [a memoir]

By Helen Zuman
She Writes Press, Berkeley, California, 2018, 240 pages
Available at ic.org/communities-bookstore

Helen Zuman's debut book describes in detail her six-year-long involvement with a radical intentional community that also fits many people's definition of "cult": Zendik Farm, which started in California in 1969 and then moved *en masse* to Texas, then Florida, then North Carolina (where Helen joined it in 1999), and finally West Virginia (around the time of her departure in late 2004). Helen arrived soon after the death of patriarch Wulf Zendik; Wulf's widow Arol and their daughter Swan were clearly "running the show," as they apparently had been for a while.

Helen came to Zendik at the age of 22 via the *Communities Directory* (pored over in her Harvard dorm room), inspired by its promise of reconnection to the body, to physical work, to earth, to community, to authenticity. It offered a sense of revolutionary belonging—a vibrant alternative to the soul-destroying "Deathculture" of modern America. Its members—numbering 60-plus at the time of her joining—tended to develop both an emotional and physical dependence on the group (especially once they had given it all their money and possessions, as nearly always happened when they progressed into more serious commitment—"give it up or leave" was the underlying expectation). Many believed they would experience "soul death" if they left the group.

As portrayed by Zuman, life at Zendik combined, on the one hand, the opportunity to test radical ideas about relationship and to align one's life with potentially transformative spiritual truths, with, on the other, the presence of what could easily be perceived as ongoing psychological and emotional abuse. Fear was a driving force—fear of reprimands from the leadership or others in the group, fear of humiliation or banishment, fear of life away from "the tribe." The Zendiks helped pioneer groundbreaking experiments in the "relationship revolution," including polyamory and non-possessiveness, and in open and honest talk about sex. Many of Wulf's teachings seem to align with those that people today (nearly 20 years after his death and 50 years after he cofounded Zendik) still (or again) find liberating—the basis of the inner and interpersonal revolutions necessary for any effective outer transformation. While the Zendik rhetoric about the "Deathculture" often seems extreme, human civilization does appear more and more to be courting self-destruction, fulfilling the darkest aspects of the Zendik analysis of a world-gone-wrong. No wonder 20-somethings looking for a world that made sense, a "tribe," flocked to the Zendik community—it seemed to embody a viable and deeply engaging alternative to what appeared to them as the isolating, meaningless, destructive path of mainstream American life.

Zendik leadership exerted control through a pattern of tearing down and rebuilding its members' self-esteem—then tearing it down again, boosting it back up, knocking it back down, *ad infinitum*. Members went to extreme lengths to gain and maintain Arol's fickle approval; in Helen's words, Zendik's hierarchy "lionized some, belittled many, and throttled dissent." (p. 207) While the leaders (Arol and Swan) were allowed to have steady "consorts," any other members whose relationships became too close would have their relationships broken up by the leadership's decree, as those kinds of exclusive, committed, dyadic relationships threatened loyalty to the group as a whole.

Moreover, the law of "psychic cause and effect" hung heavy over the group, as every misfortune was seen as the result of individuals' (or the group's) failings. Leaders blamed a kitchen-dining room fire on a rise of "square relationships"—romantic pairings that threatened the "Zendik first" philosophy. One's deepest intimacy must be with the whole group, not with an individual; the fire had been cosmic punishment for a lapse in that awareness. Arol also had a habit of separating children from their mothers, once she deemed the latter unfit to raise their own children.

Life at Zendik involved many opportunities for personal growth, whether it was becoming comfortable with "sex meetings," or receiving sometimes overwhelming amounts of personal feedback, or learning how to "sell"—which is how Zendik made most of its money (other than what its members gave it—often family inheritances). Groups of Zendiks took the Farm's merchandise, or "ammo"—self-produced music CDs, magazines, bumper stickers proclaiming "STOP BITCHING START A REVOLUTION"—to festivals, concerts, and other gatherings, and the seller's performance (success or lack thereof in gathering money, and sometimes in recruiting new Zendiks) was often the cause of either praise or excoriation upon their return home. Selling, too, was subject to the laws of psychic cause and effect. Those who truly believed in Zendik as the only place modeling the right way to be—the one tribe in which they belonged, and the one capable of outliving and transforming the "Deathculture"—would be able to translate that absolute belief in Zendik into sales/donations. Those who couldn't raise money were seen to be coming up short in their inner devotion or belief, and needed to redeem themselves or face grounding from selling trips (and/or possibly expulsion from the tribe itself). Other intentional communities could not measure up to what Zendik was doing—"Escapist hippie bullshit" is how one of Helen's lovers described East Wind, where he had lived for a few years. No other community got kinder treatment; Zendik was the only Real Deal.'

Helen herself went through major changes

(continued on p. 75)

REMEMBERING ZENDIK

(continued from p. 76)

and internal revolutions during the years she recounts. She entered Zendik as a virgin, uncomfortable and fearful in her own body, having felt increasingly detached from the world around her and ready to embrace a deep immersion in true experience and connection. She dove into life in a community where no subject of conversation, no matter how personal, was off-limits (although questioning the group's underlying assumptions and power structures was taboo); she struggled through hookups and breakups (some voluntary, some group-dictated), lost sight of her power, regained her power, left the group, returned to the group, went through conflicts and reconciliations, eventually liberated herself, and (spoiler alert) ended up married to someone she met while rebuilding her life after Zendik. Her tale is one of accelerated personal growth in a community context; there is no question that the person whom Zendik "spits out" at the end has been transformed, much more capable of manifesting her calling in life than the person who entered, despite and because of all the trials she has endured.

Helen is a riveting storyteller. This book, "sewn...from the frayed cloth of memory" (a remarkable achievement, considering its often journal-like detail and clarity) records her experiences, thoughts, and feelings throughout her Zendik years—interactions that reveal the nature of the group she was part of, but without the intrusion of constant analysis. The reader is immersed in her experience the same way she was, with the same questions—is this a disempowering cult? a unique opportunity to create social revolution? an unmatched opportunity for personal growth and transformation? none or all of these?—and the same shifting perspectives on the answers that Helen experienced. Only at the end do we learn her own ultimate conclusions, which are, essentially, that both can be true—an experience can be terrible and growthful at the same time.

By 2005, she had started describing Zendik as a cult, which helped her wrestle out from under its shadow. By 2017, her take has become more nuanced: "All groups fall along a continuum, from reverence to contempt for self-trust. I find no bright line dividing cult from culture—just stories jointly held, and questions invited or forced by crisis..." (p. 215)

And, after detailing the demise of Zendik Farm in the epilogue (the group dissolved in 2013, less than a year after Arol's death), Helen notes, "I count a number of ex-Zendiks among my dearest friends. Vining through the ruins, human ties remain." (p. 225)

• • •

I asked my friend Lawrence Siskind—who spent two years at Zendik Farm, leaving just months before Helen arrived (see his article "Relationships in the Crucible," COMMUNITIES #118, Summer 2003, pp. 40-42)—for his take on the book. After completing it in just a few days, he described it as a "compelling read" and said he concurred with "so much" in it; nothing in it rang untrue. The interpersonal dynamics Helen described all struck him as familiar, though he himself had managed to avoid being the brunt of as much "bullying" as Helen endured, likely partly because he'd found himself in a more advantageous position in the organizational hierarchy of relationships.

Was Zendik a cult, in his opinion? He was often asked that question on selling trips, and would always answer "yes—a good cult." Despite a post-residency money dispute with the group, he continues to believe that his experience there was beneficial in his own life, as it clearly was in Helen's—even as it was essential that each of them leave to continue their journeys. Lawrence admitted not believing in Wulf's philosophy, nor hating the "Deathculture," nor liking Zendik writings, art, or music (Helen had appreciated at least some of the writing, though she too disliked the music). But he loved the people there, loved living in that community, joining with "amazing people doing incredible things" in the interpersonal realm, giving and receiving feedback relentlessly. He says he has never seen that level of honesty within a daily lived culture—neither before nor since.

Although Arol was clearly a "bully"—one who usually didn't have to face feedback on her own behavior, because of her place in the hierarchy—she was also a preternaturally insightful person whose input helped others grow. She would "call bullshit when she saw bullshit," giving the kind of incisive feedback that we usually protect ourselves and each other from. "Everyone who stuck around hugely valued the experience and her insights," according to Lawrence. "If someone couldn't take Arol's input, they would leave, usually within a few months." Those who stayed knew that they had to deal with input they didn't want to hear (but that nevertheless often proved helpful), from Arol and from others—there are "not many places in society where you can get that."

In Lawrence's view, it is easy to dismiss a group as a "cult," but there is usually much more to the story—it's a label that shuts down curiosity and the capacity for understanding how the "cultish" group could actually have been beneficial to many people. "Zendik was good for me," Lawrence says. Helen would probably agree in her case too—it's an experience that liberated her from her old self and helped her become who she is today.

The communities movement would benefit from many more memoirs of this caliber—especially ones coming from communities with healthier power dynamics than Zendik. Even in light of the shortcomings of the group which spawned it, Helen's book can serve as an inspiration to future writers (whether of full-length books or of articles for this magazine) of what is possible in writing about intentional community life.

Chris Roth has detailed his own quasi-cult-like experiences in "Power and Disempowerment on the Ecobus" (COMMUNITIES #148) and "More Sustainable Than Thou" (COMMUNITIES #115).

Starting a Community
Finding a Community
Communication in Community
Sustainability in Community

V

POLITICS AND NEIGHBOR RELATIONS

ELEPHANTS OF A DIFFERENT STRIPE

Politics at Twin Oaks: Distinguishing "Acceptable" from "Combustible"

By Valerie Renwick-Porter

Here at Twin Oaks, we generally consider ourselves beyond conventional conversation restraints; this becomes immediately obvious by listening to a mealtime discussion of the lurid details of gruesome symptoms related to the latest sickness going around.

When it comes to talking about politics, it becomes a little more complicated. There are certain topics that we can all discuss with ease and generally agree upon. However, somehow there are others that are more like opening a can of worms while walking through a field of landmines...

ACCEPTABLE: Global warming and polar icecap melt
MORE DELICATE: What temperature to set the communal hot-water heater, and the ecological implications of using ice-cubes

ACCEPTABLE: Obama versus Hillary
A BIT TRICKIER: Organic versus Local

ACCEPTABLE: Increasing water shortages and the evils of the bottled-water industry
TREAD CAREFULLY: The fact that a certain communard-who-shall-remain-nameless replaced the low-flow shower head with one that delivers the approximate force and volume-per-minute of Niagara Falls, without any process

ACCEPTABLE: The discriminatory aspects of impending US immigration policy
WALKING ON EGGSHELLS: Our membership process about whether to accept that controversial visitor from the last visitor period

ACCEPTABLE: Gay marriage
CALL IN THE PROCESS TEAM: Your lover announces a desire to form a polyamorous triad with that statuesque blonde who arrived as a new member last week... ❉

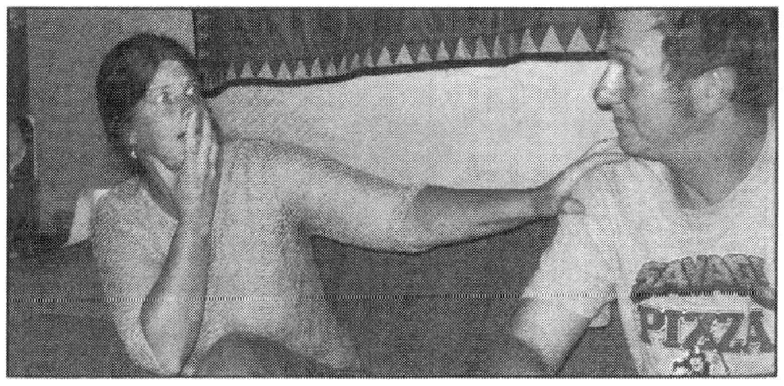

Valerie Renwick-Porter has weathered 16 years of politics at Twin Oaks community in Louisa, VA.

Thank you to Valerie and photographer Jay Paul (Woody) Kawatski and the enthusiastic thespians of Twin Oaks who so cheerfully staged these scenarios.

For more pictures, see page 62.

Finding no elephants in the living room, Twin Oakers search in the mail room and on the Opinions and Ideas board.

COMMUNITY CHALLENGES BY DOUG ALDERSON

Bursting the Bubble: The Challenges of Progressive Community Living in the Rural South

Many who live in progressive communities liken themselves to living in a bubble. Nearly everyone has an organic garden, enjoys natural foods and cooperative living, hates war, loves peace, and votes Democratic or Green Party. Except for the occasional pick-up truck to haul compost or firewood, gas guzzlers are nowhere to be seen, and there are a higher number of bicycles per capita.

In most progressive communities, there is little serious crime. Marijuana use is often tolerated, cigarette smoke is frowned upon, and what theft or vandalism occurs is usually from bored teens. But the bubble is often shaken or it bursts when the larger society presses in with its more serious afflictions, often stemming from oil and consumer addictions—a proposed new Wal-Mart, a dirty power plant, or a large-scale development. This often galvanizes a progressive community into unified action, and sometimes the culprit is defeated. This is easier done when the progressive community encapsulates most of a particular town, such as Brattleboro, Vermont, and entire regions of the Pacific Northwest. But small progressive communities often have it tough. In these enclaves, the dominant culture presses in on all sides, both in large and small ways.

Take the place where I live. It's a neighborhood community called Spiral Garden, tucked away in the piney woods south of Tallahassee, Florida in a largely low-income region. About 20 families and individuals intentionally purchased land adjacent to each other to form the community's nucleus. We have footpaths extending throughout the community, thick forested areas, sinkholes for swimming, berry patches, and numerous gardens. Community potlucks occur almost weekly at different homes and there are volleyball games, work parties, and times when people pitch in to help neighbors in need. Small town utopia!

Our challenges often stem from the folks who border our small community in all directions. Many are good people, but with different values. NASCAR and country music are popular.

Paul and Kristy Force's three-story yurt in Spiral Garden.

Photos by Doug Alderson

Author's home in Spiral Garden.

The popping of firecrackers at New Year's and Fourth of July can stretch across several days. Occasional guns are fired at all times of year. The aromas of roasting meat on grills, and of burning garbage, are commonplace. Litter and dumping is a chronic problem. We are constantly picking up beer containers, fast food wrappers, non-winning lottery tickets, and empty cigarette packs from our roads and yards. If a distant siren goes off, the "surround sound" howl of dogs resembles a Yellowstone wolf pack.

Everyone needs a bubble, whether it's the bubble of light created around one's self through meditation or the sense of security felt in one's home or community. But it can also be too rigid and confining.

Sometimes, petty theft occurs. At my family's self-built rustic house, situated on five wooded acres out of sight of other homes or the public road, we rarely locked our vehicles at night. Then, one night, a desperate young man wandered into our remote driveway and rummaged through our cars, taking CDs, loose change, and my daughter's checkbook. He was caught the next morning trying to cash checks made out to him, seeking his next crack cocaine fix.

Registered sex offenders settled in along our community's periphery. We learned about them through a public website. One friend inadvertently rented a house to one who had served five years in prison for repeatedly having sex with his 11-year-old stepdaughter. That caused consternation among community members. The disturbing part about viewing the website was that these offenders lived throughout the region, in rich and poor neighborhoods. It was a sickness that crossed boundaries, and permeated bubbles.

What really shook our sense of security, however, occurred on Tuesday, June 10th, 2008. That's when my road was closed off by police because my neighbor, Bo, had been murdered in his living room. He was found face down in a pool of blood amid signs of a struggle, and his 1988 Cadillac was missing. Forensics workers in protective suits searched his house and yard for evidence.

Bo was an elderly African American on disability who had cancer and a heart condition. He loved people—few people he met remained strangers for long—and his greatest vice was drinking beer or whiskey and playing cards with his peers. He rarely entertained guests inside his small wood-framed house. His front yard was his living room. On the grass beside a mountain of aluminum cans around a small fire, Bo would sit with friends or relatives. His lively voice would often drift through the pines. I liked to stop and talk to him as part of my daily walk. He was Old Florida. "I was out fishing the other day at the Wakulla River bridge," he told me one day,

Spiral Garden residents Paul Force and Lee Rigby (foreground) and Norma Skaggs and Pam Lightner (back row) share a laugh on Pam and Lee's porch.

"And I was catching 'em—some big ole' bream—and then this naked woman walked into the water at the landing and the fish stopped biting." Naked women change the mojo of fishing; everyone knows that.

My dog, Bear, liked Bo, too. He would visit him almost daily, and I suspected that Bo would give him meat scraps and bones that couldn't be found at our home. Sometimes, after a visit, Bear wouldn't be hungry for several hours. If Bear somehow missed his daily visit—usually on hot days when he didn't like to move much—Bo would ask me about him almost accusingly, as if I had mercilessly chained him up. He loved that dog.

Like generations of pets before him, Bear had come to us voluntarily. Bo said he had seen some people drop him off at the end of the road. He wandered to our driveway and wouldn't leave. While Bear was extremely gentle, we quickly learned that he would not tolerate confinement or being on a leash under any circumstance. He was an escape artist. So, we let him wander freely, and he mostly limited his rounds to Bo's house and ours.

After the police wrapped Bo's body in black plastic and transported him to the county morgue for an autopsy, the yellow tape was removed from across our road. The white tent that had been erected to protect workers from a violent thunderstorm that had erupted that afternoon was taken down, and all of the police and other vehicles eventually left. Bo's small house and yard was eerily quiet, suddenly empty of life. I sensed that Bo's spirit was unsettled. Given his health problems, I'm sure Bo knew his days were numbered, but he wouldn't want to go out like that. I said a prayer.

Three of the four people involved in Bo's murder were caught the next day. The perpetrators were a man and three women. Calvin Hills told police that when Bo answered the door, he hit him twice in the face and one of the women hit him repeatedly with a stick. After taking his wallet and car keys, they left Bo unconscious, not knowing if he was alive or dead. The four had previously done yard work for Bo, but they waited until nighttime to return and kill him. Hills said that he "knew what he was doing was wrong," but he was "just caught up in the moment and was just thinking about getting money so he could purchase more crack cocaine." Hills had a long record of previous arrests.

In reading about our area's history, I knew that roving bands of Civil War deserters were often the most desperate and dangerous men of their day. Now, it seemed to be drug addicts.

The day after Bo's body was removed, I heard voices and the sound of children's laughter at his house. I walked over. His daughter and grandkids had driven up from Tampa to clean out his place and prepare for the funeral. Bo's daughter was understandably hurt and angry. She appreciated my condolences, but she looked at me with pained eyes. "You didn't hear nothing

Some Spiral Garden community members in 2009. Author is in t-shirt in front row.

Author's road in Spiral Garden with Bo's former house, where murder occurred, on left.

Travel trailer home in Spiral Garden.

Paul and Kristy Force's sinkhole is often used for cooling off by community members.

that night?"

"No," I stammered. "I live a good ways up that driveway in the woods." Five acres separated our houses.

She nodded, understanding. "I think they surprised him," she said. "I think it was over real quick." She felt a need to give me the grisly details that the newspaper account had left out. I felt even worse.

I knew then that I couldn't help to protect my neighbor because of the bubble I had placed around my home in the form of acreage and natural beauty. I didn't hear the struggle, didn't hear the cries or gasps that may have occurred or the cranking of Bo's car as the perpetrators sped away into the darkness. Bo died alone. My dog slept through the whole thing, too, on our front porch.

A couple of days later, for the first time ever, my wife Cyndi said we should buy a gun. The bubble might need defending.

Interestingly, as timing goes, our annual neighborhood association meeting was the next Saturday. This was the best opportunity for neighbors inside and outside Spiral Garden to interact with each other. The main job of the neighborhood association was to maintain our unpaved roads so holes wouldn't grow into gaping pits that could swallow a front end. As expected, after the mandatory road discussion, Bo's murder was the main topic of discussion. The result? We agreed to work with local law enforcement to set up a neighborhood crime watch system of neighbors watching out for other neighbors and reporting anything suspicious. It was a start. Our community bubble was becoming more elastic, and as part of the ensuing dialogue, we began to talk about other issues, such as the carcinogens released when burning plastic garbage. Communication can lead to education and a change in behavior. Maybe the path will lead to a discussion about global warming and what we as a broader community can do about it.

Everyone needs a bubble, whether it's the bubble of light created around one's self through meditation or the sense of security felt in one's home or community. It helps us function without paranoia, a launching pad towards self-actualization. But it can also be too rigid and confining. The boundaries have to be carefully explored and allowed to expand if the need arises. There are no easy answers, only the opportunities each day presents.

A recipient of three national writing awards, Doug Alderson is the author of seven books, including The Vision Keepers: Walking for Native Americans and the Earth *(Quest Books). Additionally, his articles and photographs have been featured in magazines such as* Sea Kayaker, Wildlife Conservation, American Forests, Sierra, Mother Earth News, *and* Shaman's Drum. *For more information, log onto www.dougalderson.net.*

Problem: In the face of rampant greed and short-sighted self-interest, it's so easy to lose connection to the extraordinary creativity displayed around this planet.

Response: Establish a centralized access point to sources of social and environmental inspiration — enabling activists and organizers, students and citizens to identify and amplify what might help our own acts of creation.

EXEMPLARS!

a free, searchable, living library of what is hopeful, fascinating, and sustainable.

Visit **www.exemplars.world**

your portal to designing a sustainable future

Browse the 4 domains of **www.exemplars.world**
For each Exemplar, the initial insight, the organizing strategy, tools, outcomes, and a link to websites.

View relevant essays and videos.

Submit Exemplars you have created or know of, as we expand the data base.

1. Cities, towns & communities

2. Businesses and organizations

3. Systemic interventions

Sierra Club

Explore, Enjoy and Protect the Planet

4. **Cultural sustainability**

Curated by Paul Freundlich, pfreundlich@comcast.net

Founder, Green America

ZONING NIGHTMARE: Hartford's Scarborough Street House

By Dave Rozza, Hannah Simms, Josh Blanchfield, Julia Rosenblatt, Kevin Lamkins, Laura Rozza, Maureen Welch, and Simon Raahauge DeSantis

Somehow or another, our smallish urban intentional community of 11 has found itself at the center of a zoning brouhaha that none of us could have anticipated.

We are longtime friends who have been involved in community activism over the years. As our bonds deepened through our collective work and struggles, we developed a plan to live together as an intentional community in our city of Hartford, Connecticut. Over time, the concept of our extended family evolved and the core group solidified. Several of us lived first in an artist community, then in a purchased home together elsewhere in the city. We celebrated the births of our children and suffered the deeply painful loss of a community member to lung cancer.

When we began looking for a bigger house to fit all of us, we realized that we needed a total of nine bedrooms, a rare find in our city. We were committed to staying within Hartford city limits, and as we scouted for houses, there simply weren't many homes that fit the bill. In the spring of last year, we found the foreclosed mansion on Scarborough Street, a home with exactly nine bedrooms and two acres of land. It was still well outside our price range, but over the following three months, the price dropped $100,000. The stars aligned and we bought the house.

The house on Scarborough Street was, by far, the largest purchase any of us have ever made. We are "all in," both financially and emotionally, and it was important to us to make sure all *i*'s were dotted and *t*'s crossed, legally speaking. Though only two of us could be on the mortgage, we worked with a lawyer to draft a partnership agreement that makes us all legal owners of the home. We have a shared bank account and we make household purchases like food collectively.

As we moved forward, we were aware that the city's zoning codes could have been an issue for us. But any person who takes the time to really pore over the zoning regulations would find the exact same thing that we found: ambiguous zoning language that doesn't make any sense in a modern context. One of the main selling points of the house was that it resides on over two acres of land. This section of the city is designated as R-8, a "single family zone"; however, there is a density clause within the language that allots for 3.6 families per acre. Though we live and operate as a single family, we figured that if issues arose, we would be covered under that portion of the code.

The Hartford zoning regulations' definition of family reads:

"Family means, one (1) person; a group of two (2) or more persons living together and interrelated by consanguinity, marriage, civil union, or legal adoption; or a group of not more than two (2) persons who need not be so related, occupying the whole or part of a dwelling unit as a separate housekeeping unit with a common set of cooking facilities. The persons constituting a family may also include foster children; the number of which shall be in accordance with general statutes as amended and live-in domestic employees. For the purposes of determining density, a roomer, boarder or lodger shall not be considered a member of a family."

This definition allows for an unlimited number of domestic servants. So clearly, the code was not written with the sole purpose of controlling population density within the neighborhood. Dating from the late 1960s, its design seems to have been more about controlling who could afford to live there.

At no point in the buying process did we try to hide the makeup of our group and at no point did anybody advise us not to purchase this property because of the zoning ordinances.

Family photo.

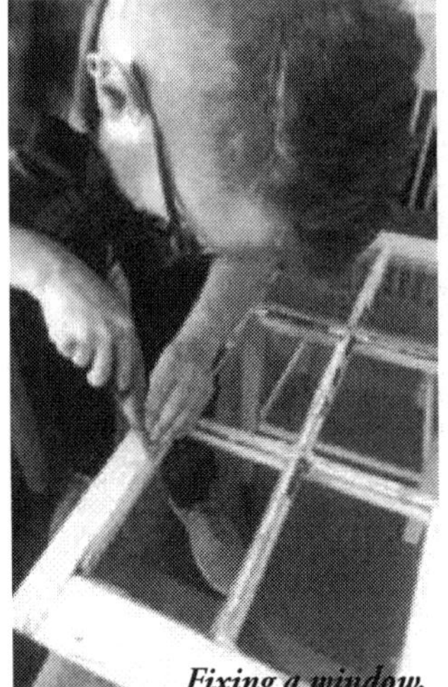
Fixing a window.

Kid committee game night.

Working in the back yard.

We moved in and began the difficult work of fixing the house up. Renovating a nine-bedroom historic home that had been empty for at least four years took all the time, energy, and money we had. We brought the electrical up to code and began to repair the plumbing. We went out of our way to consult with our neighbors about outdoor aesthetics and checked with them about the type of fencing we wanted to install for the dog. Studies demonstrate that empty houses contribute to neighborhood decline and reduced property values. We hoped that because we were purchasing and caring for an abandoned home, our neighbors would be happy to have us, even if our family structure isn't quite traditional. Interactions with the neighbors were very positive and we breathed a sigh of relief and let our guard down a little.

The first inkling we had that some of our neighbors were less than pleased with our arrival came about two months in, when a neighbor told us that there were "phone calls going up and down the street" about the number of cars we had. We had eight cars when we first moved in, one for each adult in the house. We had always planned to downsize and share vehicles but with the chaos of moving and renovation, we hadn't made it a top priority. Our driveway was small and we had been parking cars on the street (a call to Hartford Parking Authority confirmed that this is, in fact, legal, though apparently not the neighborhood norm). As soon as we were told this was an issue, we started parking only in our driveway. We sold two cars and moved driveway expansion to the top of the repair list. Although we remedied the situation, the damage had been done.

The neighbors convened a meeting to discuss our house (we were not invited). At this meeting, attended by 20 or so people, they decided to send a letter to the City of Hartford. Although we moved in wanting only to live quietly and happily, we are not ones to shy away at the first sign of trouble. We love each other, we love our home, and we will do anything we need to do to keep it.

We received a letter from the city stating that we "may be in violation of zoning." As requested, we contacted them right away to set up an inspection date. In the meantime, we drafted an email to our neighbors introducing ourselves and our living situation. We sent it to some neighbors who had been friendly towards us and asked them to forward it on to others on the street. This email was then forwarded to the city and we received a cease and desist order, stating that they had completed an "inspection via email."

Snow day.

Halloween.

Setting the Record Straight

A few things we've been wanting to share:

• It's not lost on us that we are fighting to stay in our beautiful mansion while others among us struggle each day for their lives, living under racism and other systems of oppression. White privilege plays a huge role in every aspect of our situation and we never forget that.

• Though some have drawn parallels and we are honored by the comparison, our struggle in no way compares to what our LGBTQIA brothers and sisters have endured and continue to endure. Marriage equality is only the first step on the long road to equality for all people.

• While we are not polyamorous, there are many poly families out there who have been forced to live in the shadows. Nobody should ever have to hide their consensual, loving relationships. Family is who you love, who you care for in your everyday life. If, collectively, we as humans stopped looking at the nuclear family as the point to strive toward and instead, began shaping our own definition of family and healthy relationships, what would the world look like?

• It is important to mention that a few of our neighbors have been absolutely wonderful to us, bringing us welcome baskets and inviting us over to their home for drinks. Their kindness means more than we could ever say.

• There are effective ways to allow for "functional families" while disallowing boarding houses, frat houses, and the other fears that our neighbors have. The Town of Bellevue, Washington just passed fantastic updates to their zoning ordinances that accomplish just that:

Bellevue, Washington's Definition of "Family":

Not more than four adult persons, unless all are related by blood, marriage, or legal adoption, living together as a single housekeeping unit. A group of related persons living in a household shall be considered a single housekeeping unit. Provided: a group of more than four unrelated adult persons living together in a dwelling unit may also be included within the definition of "family" if they demonstrate to the Director that they operate in a manner that is functionally equivalent to a family. Factors that shall be considered by the Director include whether the group of more than four unrelated persons:

A. Shares the entire dwelling unit or acts as separate roomers;

B. Includes minor, dependent children regularly residing in the household;

C. Can produce proof of sharing expenses for food, rent, or ownership costs, utilities, and other household expenses;

D. Shares common ownership of furniture and appliances among the members of the household;

E. Constitutes a permanent living arrangement, and is not a framework for transient living;

F. Maintains a stable composition that does not change from year to year or within the year;

G. Is not a society, fraternity, sorority, lodge, organization or other group of students or other individuals where the common living arrangement or basis for the establishment of the housekeeping unit is temporary; or

H. Can demonstrate any other factors reasonably related to whether or not the group of persons is the functional equivalent of a family.

The Director shall issue a written determination of whether a group of more than four unrelated adult persons are operating in a manner that is functionally equivalent to a family.

Bellevue's "Rooming House" Definition:

A non-owner-occupied dwelling that is subject to multiple leases or in which rooms are offered for rent or lease on an individual room basis.

—L.M.R.

We hired an accomplished attorney who is also a fellow activist and friend. We had a number of options before us:

• We could try to get a variance, which is essentially an exemption from the zoning law. Variances are difficult to obtain, at least in Hartford, and it wouldn't improve the situation for anybody else affected by outdated zoning regulations.

• Adult adoption is legal in Connecticut, but the judge who would decide the case lives in our neighborhood.

• We could have hired each other as servants, but we were worried about tax implications, not to mention that we don't want to hide behind a technicality.

Ultimately, the zoning regulations as they are currently written affect far more people than just us. We decided to challenge the definition of family within the city's zoning regulations.

There has been a great deal written about how zoning laws have been, and continue to be, used to oppress communities. There are many others in situations similar to ours who are forced to fly under the radar. In our city, which is one of the poorest in the country, many families are forced to remain silent while their landlords keep their homes in deplorable conditions, because the first question landlords ask is how many people are living within the dwelling and whether they are related by blood.

It is far past time to change Hartford's definition of family, not just for us, but for people in our city and beyond.

Simultaneous to the city's actions, our neighborhood civic association, WECA, convened a hearing to discuss our house. The WECA hearing kicked everything into high gear and made our situation very public. Op-eds and editorials starting appearing in the newspaper and local news stations took notice. From there, national news outlets picked up the story and it was shared widely on social media. We were, and continue to be, completely surprised and overwhelmed by all the attention our situation has received.

We then faced the zoning board of appeals. The board was able to rule only on whether the cease and desist order was issued appropriately, not whether the definition of family itself should be changed. All eight adults and one of the three children spoke at the hearing. We shared how we live as a family day to day, how we love and care for each other, how we support each other in happy times and hard times, how we live as more of a tight unit than most "typical" families do. At this hearing, many neighbors spoke against us, arguing that we are changing the character of the neighborhood and if they allow us, it will open the door to boarding houses which are—without question and for many reasons—a big problem in our city. These arguments are all easily addressed with well-written, thoughtful zoning language, and there have been attempts made by friendly folks within the city to do just that (attempts that were quickly shot down). Out of the five who heard our case, three board members were fully on our side and believe that the ordinance needs to be changed. They were saddened that they did not have the power to do so, and that they could not, in good faith, find the grounds to dismiss the cease and desist order. Two of those three were moved to tears that they couldn't help us.

With heavy hearts, we took the next step of filing a lawsuit in federal court against the city.

The day before we were set to announce our federal lawsuit against the city, the city, in turn, filed a preemptive lawsuit against us in state court.

Around this same time, the zoning board quietly changed the code to limit to three domestic servants, clearly an attempt by a few on the board to make our court case harder to pursue.

In a city where zoning violations are routinely ignored, where the blighted properties list is pages and pages long, and the slumlords who own properties in Hartford's low-income communities of color routinely get away with ongoing and repeated violations, why was a minor infraction to an unclear zoning ordinance enforced so heavily?

The case is currently in court, with our lawyer and the city's lawyer battling it out behind the scenes. We don't anticipate that there will be any significant progress made until the fall and in the meantime, we are not facing any mounting penalties and we are thrilled to have a little quiet time to simply enjoy family dinners, garden, celebrate birthdays, and play some epic games of hide and seek in our giant home.

We are worn out and exhausted. But at the same time, we are deeply hopeful. The amazing support we have received from friends, loved ones, and fantastic strangers gives us strength. We are sustained by the fact that our situation has allowed us to share with the world how joyful, fulfilling, practical, and sustainable intentional community life is. What keeps us going is the hope that we can change the definition of family for many more than just us. In the end, it's not the house that's the prize, it's our community. This is worth fighting for and we aren't going to let anyone tear us apart.

Dave Rozza, 37, likes things and stuff. Dave is super proud of his two awesome kids and adores his smart, beautiful, talented partner in crime, Laura...without her he would likely be lying in a ditch somewhere.

Hannah Simms, 31, is (as Tessa likes to remind her) the household's youngest grown-up. She works with Julia at theatre company HartBeat Ensemble, does a bunch of freelance theatre gigs and projects, and grows an overabundance of zucchini.

Josh Blanchfield, 37, is a social studies and history teacher, husband to Julia, and father to Tessa and Elijah. LOL is a literal term for Josh and his sense of humor keeps us snarfing our juice.

Julia Rosenblatt, 40, is (as Tessa likes to remind her) the household's oldest grown-up. She is the Artistic Director of HartBeat Ensemble, the mother of Tessa and Elijah, the wife of Josh, and a lover of sleep.

Kevin Lamkins, 38, is Associate Professor of English at Capital Community College in Hartford. He loves playing and listening to music, hockey, bikes, and zombie stuff. He also loves animals, especially his 13-year old calico, Rosa.

Laura Rozza, 37, works in the grants department for the Town of East Hartford. Things that make her happy include her partner Dave, who is amazing in every possible way, her son Milo, her step-son Joshua (not Josh Blanchfield), and her fluffy kitty Tater Tot.

Maureen Welch, 34, is a therapist and general feelings enthusiast. She enjoys drinking coffee with Simon, wearing rompers, and playing drums in the indie rock band The Lonesome While.

Simon Raahauge DeSantis is a 34-year-old Latin teacher originally from Massachusetts. His passions include rowing, bicycles, retired racing greyhounds, Mazda Miatas, and Maureen Welch. His loyal and lazy dog is Sofie.

NEIGHBOR NIGHTMARE in Northern California

By Chris Roth

Editor's Note: *Some details in the story below have been altered to preserve anonymity.*

Joan and Michael (not their actual names) have been cultivating community for most of their adult lives. A decade ago Joan moved to a rural intentional community in California's redwood country, where she met Michael, who'd been a long-term resident and facilitator of workshops focused on self-awareness, communication, and group connection. After a couple years of life together in community they moved into the nearest town to co-create a socially and ecologically responsible business, one of whose core values was also cultivating and giving back to their broader community. They eventually sold the business to another local couple and moved back to the country, finding a piece of rural land just outside of town where they started to host occasional gatherings and workshops at their house.

They soon decided to create a separate gathering space inside an old equipment barn. A core team created the design and did much of the work, and a series of work parties enlisted hundreds of people in helping build the earthen structure. Many artists, artisans, and eco-builders lent their touches to the central circular space and its outer rooms. It became a vibrant gathering place for an extended network of people interested in the offerings presented there—music, yoga, meditation, and workshops on communication, personal growth, and various forms of spirituality. Hundreds of people participated in events in the space during its first year of use, and it became an important force for "community" among those drawn there.

However, those golden days did not continue; use of Om Space (an initially half-facetious name which stuck) is now on indefinite hold.

I interviewed Joan over the phone recently. We hope her story will offer a cautionary tale and valuable lessons to others sharing similar visions who may aspire to enact them more easily.

• • •

What was your vision when you bought the land?

We wanted to go back to our roots of having a land-based lifestyle and being in community again. We had gotten very used to hosting and giving, because we developed a lot of abundance with the business in town. When we chose our place, we saw that it had a beautiful house that seemed great for hosting, and the land was also beautiful. We were feeling very confident and excited to be in the position to have a community and to host gatherings.

Our biggest priority was to be close to town, so distance would not be a barrier for most people to come. We went around to the neighbors before we bought it and said, "Hey, this is what we want to do: we are social, involved in the community, and we want to have some gatherings, house concerts, workshops, and things like that, but we recognize that could have an impact and we want to know how you feel about our hosting these kinds of things."

And the neighbors that we visited said, "I think it's great—thank you so much for talking to us." They also had some harsh things to say about the previous owners. At the time we were thinking, "Oh, wow, well of course we're not going to be like that." But now I understand more the phenomenon of when meeting somebody new and they start talking about other people and how things have been bad or hard, it's kind of a red flag—though it is easy to dismiss it as, "Wow, they just haven't had someone to talk to about this."

We had blinders at that point, we really did. We thought, "How could anything go wrong?" Things had been going so well in our lives and we're so steeped in the philosophy of open-hearted, honest, transparent communication, we must have been assuming unconsciously that if we're that way, and we're drawn to this land, it meant that things would go well. You could call it denial, or magical thinking, and in looking at it now it seems that way. But it did feel OK at the time.

We actually did not visit the one neighbor we're having the most difficulty with, because we couldn't even see his house; it was so far away and he has lots of land between it and us. We approached neighbors if we could see them. Looking back, we made some big mistakes in not understanding that a lot of people move out of town to the country because they want a particular way of life that usually involves having more control or more privacy—which is understandable.

Did you look into the legalities of what you were allowed to do on the land? Or how many people were allowed to live there, things like that?

We really did not look into that very much, to be totally honest.

Was that because of the general culture where people do a lot of things that aren't technically permitted? That was part of the culture of the intentional community you'd been in as well.

I think so, I think we had a lot of trust in ourselves for being caring and considerate, and our experience with that is with this bubble of community in which we all have a trusting understanding that even if something is difficult, we work it out. We didn't recognize that some people have no interest in doing that. And not only that, if they get rubbed the wrong way, they are going to be antagonistic, for reasons that don't make any sense to me.

We were also imagining being low-key. Then, when we started creating the gathering space, several people involved were masterful designers and builders and it became a really incredible community project. It created something for the community that was very beautiful. As we went along we got swept up in that and didn't pay attention to what could go wrong.

Had there been any problems before you built Om Space? And what was your vision for it? How did it come about?

No, there were no problems. We were having gatherings and workshops in the house. But when Michael's aging mom moved in with us, we considered her health concerns and how large groups of people in our house impacted her, and realized it would be much better to have some separation between the home space and these other things that we wanted to do. So we decided to have another space on the land—an Om Space.

We got involved with a friend who was a very dynamic designer, and our creative juices all started to merge in a fun and exciting way. In our minds we thought, "Well, you know, we talked to the neighbors before we bought the place, and everyone we talked to was supportive." We did a lot of research in terms of talking to designers, builders, architects, other community people, but we didn't actually research or understand all the laws, because we understood that there's a bunch of gray area. Everyone always said it's all about the neighbors, and so in our minds we thought, "Oh, we did that."

Looking back on all this recently, we have been grieving together about our naivete. Michael was afraid that our decision-making had come from a lot of arrogance in him, and maybe there is some, but overall I think it came from positivity, and trust, and naivete for sure.

Were there any problems as Om Space was being built?

One of the neighbors who is closest expressed concern that there were people driving by and not saying hi—they found that really offensive, and requested that we ask our guests to say hi when passing neighbors on the driveway. They also asked that people drive slowly, that we put a stop sign at the end of the driveway, and also that we plant a screen shielding their property from ours. So we had a friend come who is very experienced and skilled and we planted over 300 trees. No matter what happens, I'm so happy that we planted that forest.

I feel we had a good relationship at that point with that neighbor; that was a good communication.

Later, once the space was completed, that same neighbor told us there was a complaint. We don't know who it was from—we're pretty sure it was from this one neighbor who is going gangbusters on shutting everything that we do down in every way. Then the County got in touch with us and said, "Hey, it's been brought to

Illustrations by Anna Helena Jackson

our attention that you're having stuff going on here and that there's money being exchanged"—which there was; we had a couple of concerts and we collected money and paid the musicians. Apparently, to do that you need what is called a Home Occupation permit. We had not known that, and so we found this great guy who is a land use specialist and hired him to start applying for this permit. As part of that process, the permit application goes out to all the neighbors.

And the neighbors who complained about the stop sign and the driveway and all that stuff said that once it became formal, once it became a matter of its potentially being certified as legal, they stopped feeling good about it. If it had not become a legal issue, if they had not gotten a notice saying we were going to do this, they would have been totally fine with it. But they felt that they were in danger because if it became legal, and they agreed to anything, then we would not feel the same need to communicate with them any more.

We thought, "Oh my god, we're all about communication, we even lead workshops in it, and we want everything to be cool—but they don't know us or have that experience of us." And once they made their decision, it seemed set in stone. They became kind of unfriendly at that point.

That was the first indicator that we and our neighbors were operating in really different ways. A lot of neighbors were frightened when they got that application request, and wrote in opposition to us having a Home Occupation.

One problem, when we applied for the Home Occupation, was that the notice to neighbors from the County specified what we'd be *allowed* to do. We'd be allowed to have 70 people this many times a week and to have this many cars, and that was all spelled out. But that wasn't the level of activity that we intended; it was just the maximum that was allowed by law. We explained this afterwards to the neighbors but by then they already seemed to have made up their minds.

Feelings also started to be relayed to us about the nature of what we were doing. People were pretty careful about how they said it, but basically they reacted to the fact that we were doing yoga, and chanting, and that we had *murtis*, which are deity statues, and things like that.

I think we still were in this bubble of thinking, "God, there's just got to be a way to connect about all this," so we decided to have an open house and invite everybody over to our place to see it and talk about it. I tell you, that was so hard for me. I did not like that experience. I understood why were doing it, and Michael felt open to it. But all these people were looking at Om Space who had no understanding or appreciation, and it felt really strange to me.

Some of what we wanted to do was to open to all these people that we didn't know. So it became really ironic that our neighbors, our literal neighbors, were starting to dislike us and feel threatened by what we were doing. It was the opposite of what we wanted.

You were hoping to contribute to the neighborhood or build the neighborhood.

Yeah, and when we had the open house I was thinking, "*Yes*, we're doing this for our community." We invited them to have their own gatherings in it too. I feel stupid now in some ways. We were just so clueless as to how some people were really feeling about it—they were like, "God, I don't like this." There was a lot of judgment or just not being able to relate.

When you put in for the Home Occupation permit, you got all these objections. What was the next step?

Well, we tried addressing all the concerns, but it seemed like the feeling was not very good, so ultimately we withdrew the Home Occupation application and concluded that "Yeah, OK, we got excited about this because we have this incredible space, but people are really not wanting it. So let's just permit this beautiful building and we'll be able to use it and have gatherings and not have it be a business in any way. It'll just be something that we can still enjoy and do yoga and kirtan and some concerts in." So we started pursuing that route.

Our neighbors were starting to dislike us. It was the opposite of what we wanted.

When you built it, you built it without a permit, expecting that you would have to get a permit at some point?

Yes. The building that contains it, the old barn, already existed, so it was kind of a build-out situation. We decided that we would do it and then get it permitted after—but not before, because of the timing of the creative process. We asked a lot of people and it seems that the County does of course want you to do the permitting first, but that can take a really long time, and lots of people do something and then get the permit. So we paid very special attention to doing everything to code.

One of the things that this one very antagonistic neighbor is saying is, "You have to be punished, because you did something without a permit, and now there's just no way that this can happen." I mean we didn't know that we needed a Home Occupation permit. We were aware that when you do a building project you need some building permits, but we also thought, "This is an existing building and we're doing something inside the building."

And it was really only while it was happening that we started thinking of it as a possible business. We thought, "Wow, we're spending a lot of money on this, more than we expected, way, way more—and why not? It's a great resource for the community and it could help us reclaim some of the money we put into it." And actually the land use specialist told us that we're allowed to have a Home Occupation; the zoning is totally fine for having that. We just decided to withdraw it because it was becoming really intense.

So you withdrew it but that wasn't the end of the problems.

Nope. At that point I think whatever feathers were ruffled were still ruffled, especially in the case of one neighbor who, you know, the words that come out of his mouth are "This is not going to happen, I'm sorry, but this is not going to happen," whatever that means. I think he thinks that he has more power than he does, but he also has deep pockets and is willing to move forward in his opinion.

How did the other neighbors feel?

The other neighbors seemed a lot less willing to talk to us about what was OK or not OK. Our driveway has an easement on one of the neighbors' land, and actually that's a huge other piece... looking back, considering just even that alone, we would choose a different site. Basically we were advised that we had a 50/50 chance of getting the Home Occupation permit. It's allowed and legal in our zone, but the only reason it wouldn't be granted is because of the easement with the driveway, if that neighbor objected. My advice now is: if there's a driveway easement, don't have a community there.

So we decided to just go for getting the building permitted, and now this one especially antagonistic neighbor is hiring attorneys and filing appeals, which he has to pay for—because it seems like he does not want to us to be able to save and use the building at all, for anything. It really has become a power struggle at this point.

We're applying for the building to be permitted as an accessory structure to the house, and it's a little bit farther away from the house than is normally approved as an accessory structure. Before we can get the actual building permit, we need to get this accessory structure permit. An accessory structure can be a workshop space, a dance space, a studio, a play room, a place where people sleep over... It's not a residence, but you could think of it as another room of your house—it's just not attached to your house.

The neighbor is saying that it was an existing barn and that there's a law that says you cannot convert an existing barn to an accessory structure. But that is a new law that passed recently, and I think it's because people have been converting their barns into huge wedding venues and things like that. In any case, it turns out the building was never permitted at all, as a barn or anything else. So the land use permitting board recommended that they pass our application; they said yes, it's an accessory structure, and yes, it's farther away than normal but we see no good reason not to approve the application. But the neighbor is really going for it now with the lawyers and he showed up at the hearing and said because the board is not doing their job we all have to show up here and spend money and time doing this.

My advice now is: if there's a driveway easement, don't have a community there.

Has there been any pushback against this neighbor?

Well here's the thing. I have a little studio that happens to be 204 square feet, where I play my music and prepare for teaching. The legal limit of a studio is 200 square feet. He decided that this space is a schoolhouse, and he reported it, and said there's a schoolhouse here that's being operated. He also reported the other storage building that is near Om Space, that our friend uses as a studio—he claimed it was a residence. So he's really reporting us, and every structure...it's like a nightmare.

It's true that our friend was sleeping in the storage building, but not very often. And it's OK for someone to sleep in there occasionally; it just can't be a residence, which means it can't have a bathroom and other things like that, and it doesn't. The point is that he's looking at these structures and he's turning them in. And meanwhile the other neighbors all have structures that are being used as residences but not legal ones. My opinion is that he's in a position where he's being a bully, and these other neighbors are thinking, "Whoa, he's turning them in, he sees our places too, he has a perfectly good view." And now they don't want to say anything...they're scared.

They're afraid of opposing what he's saying and doing.

Exactly, why would they oppose him? They will sort of go along with him so that he doesn't report them.

It's gotten into the realm of harassment, for me, to have this person who is watching, and keeping track, and then saying these things about us that aren't true. I talked to our lawyer about it, and he said it is harassment: he's slandering you and making things up about you, and I can send him a letter.

So you have a lawyer who is attempting to stop him?

Yes, we have a lawyer and a land use specialist who work really well together, and we like them and trust them. They keep reassuring us that what this neighbor is claiming and how he's going about it don't have much to stand on. At the hearing this neighbor and his lawyer presented a really, really thick—like phonebook-sized—document about us, and I think part of his claim is that we had a business in town, and so our intentions are...well, what they kept murmuring and muttering behind us was "bait and switch, bait and switch." They think that we are just trying to get away with something surreptitiously. It's a complete lack of trust, and I don't see how we could gain that trust at this point. So it's been a lot of emotional stress and grief and regret, really. I feel like if we could do it all over again we wouldn't have done this.

You would have chosen a different place.

Yes. And then we would have done it a different way too.

What would you say to someone who doesn't want to end up in this situation? One is: don't get a property with an easement through someone else's land.

Right. And I think we would buy land where the neighbor presence is pretty much nonexistent—where you don't really see the neighbors or interact with them or share a driveway with them. And then we would do things low-key. Maybe we would still make a building like this but I think we wouldn't be as trusting; we wouldn't think that we could just put this out to all the neighbors out of town and they'd all be like, "Great, this is great, yea!" It's sobering that a lot of people don't want change, they don't want something new, and they don't care about the same things that we do. That's just part of how it is.

Have there been any complaints about noise?

No, you can't hear anything coming from inside the space; it's totally sound-insulated with earthen walls. The biggest effect, and it is a real effect, is cars, coming and then parking when we have an event or gathering. We totally understand that. I wish there was a way that we could say, "Hey we're really sorry, we get it that you don't want this here, but what *would* be fine?" But we've basically tried that, and so far the neighbors aren't willing to say they're fine with *anything*. So now we're in a position where our neighbors are dictating our lifestyle. Because the issues got raised and it has gone through the permitting and the County, everyone has a say now in the lifestyle that we're living. That feels really weird to me. If we lived in town, we could hold parties and have people over and do yoga and not worry about the neighbors stopping that.

I've heard that you have a couple neighbors who blast really loud music for long periods of time...

Yes, and there's absolutely nothing to say about that, legally. They blast very loud music, just broadcasting it out to the whole valley, and those same neighbors and others nearby have dogs that bark incessantly, and some other neighbors recently cut down the whole forest of trees on their land—and they are all allowed to do those things. Meanwhile, it feels like our activities are open to total scrutiny, and that feels terrible; I hate it. It's definitely not what I was imagining.

Because the issues got raised, everyone has a say now in how we're living.

My hope at this point is that we'll keep slogging through and we'll get the accessory building permit and we'll be in a position where there's not this constant attack; that we'll just be able to use the space again and then hopefully the issue will just kind of fade away.

Do you still see any possibilities for cultivating residential community on your land?

We are allowed to have five unrelated adults living in the house, and we also have another lot on the same land and are allowed to build another house. We spent so much money on this project I'm not sure how we'd go about that, but there probably still is a way to have community and to grow more food and do more permaculture projects. My sights have been turning more towards the land and how we can use the land, because I'm just not interested in living in a big house out in the country with my small family—that was never my intention. I want to have community in some way, but I've been told that using that word isn't always so good, it's like a red flag a little bit...

"Community"?

Yeah...that's just incredible.

So that's a red flag among the kind of neighbors you have?

Yes. I just didn't think that this would happen. ❧

Chris Roth has been witnessing, navigating, and occasionally running smack up against the legal obstacles to living in community (especially ecologically responsible community) for nearly three decades now.

Public vs. Private: GROUP DILEMMA LAID BARE!

By M. Broiling and T. Shirtless

Among the perennial questions our community grapples with: how "exposed" do we want to be?

We operate a conference center, hold courses and workshops, host visitors, and receive frequent postal and freight deliveries. More often than not, our conference guests, students, and visitors fall on the socially progressive side of the spectrum, but most are not unreconstructed hippies or obviously enlightened indigo, crystal, or rainbow children. Nor are the relatives of everyone who lives here. Nor, indeed, are all of us.

Our neighbors aren't either, and have a tendency to leap to quick conclusions on seemingly scant evidence. A drumming and chanting ceremony at the fire circle years ago precipitated a persistent rumor that we were a satanic cult. The logical leap from "glimpse of skin" to "nudist colony" is a surprisingly short one to make, within some neighbors' mentality.

We've defined "clothing required" and "clothing optional" zones in our community, but few community members are fully satisfied with these. Clothing is required in areas that are visible from our main drive, and that are in or around our main dining area, kitchens, offices, and classrooms. It is generally required in any areas used by conference guests, when they are here, even in those that are normally clothing-optional. It is optional in most places that are generally used only by the community, as long as they are not in sight of our main drive, a neighbor's property, or a road.

We generally agree on the meaning and application of "clothing optional": complete nudity is acceptable. "Clothing required" is more tricky to define.

In most places other than our certified kitchen, male toplessness is accepted and practiced in hot weather. However, female toplessness is not accorded the same status. Every few years, this becomes a topic of discussion at a community meeting. We all agree that the distinction is patently unfair to women, who are required to endure discomfort that men are not. But the "public" part of our identity—and our economic reliance on it—always lead to the same conclusion: we can't change the policy by which required clothing includes tops for women, but not for men.

Some men and women have lobbied for a ban on male toplessness wherever female toplessness is not allowed. Others have suggested that men can show support for women by voluntarily resisting the urge to take off their shirts in these circumstances. Others have said that male toplessness is the first step toward liberation, and that one step is better than none. Others have suggested that we change the policy to allow both male and female toplessness, and let the chips fall where they may in terms of impact on our reputation and businesses. And still others have suggested that in the absence of an immediate policy change, civil disobedience is the appropriate response: breaking our own rules to force the issue, and as a step toward getting comfortable enough to overturn them officially.

Ironically, toplessness is totally legal in our area for women as well as men—including on the streets of the nearest city. But a combination of conservative rural neighbors and a diverse clientele has kept our community—which fashions itself "ahead of the times" in most realms—behind the times here.

Although this gets under many community members' skin—at the same time that it keeps many community members' skin under clothing—the compromise endures. ❧

On hot days, M. Broiling and T. Shirtless are (respectively) sweltering, and comfortable, around the community picnic tables at lunchtime.

Lessons in Participatory Democracy

By Sylvan Bonin

While I write, trees are falling next door. Every time I go near the Common House I can hear their trunks cracking and the earth-shaking crash when they fall. My heart is breaking and my stomach is in knots. Members of our community stand at the edge of the property to drum and bear witness. I wonder if that makes the developer and the workers uncomfortable? They don't understand why we are crying: to them it's just progress, just profit, just a job. To us, it's the loss of the character of the place we live, the loss of habitat, the loss of cooling and filtering for the air, the loss of the 200-year old life-forms that were here before us.

There used to be a law that would have protected many of those trees. Snohomish County has a Tree Ordinance, but several years ago developers lobbied to have it changed. The law was gutted: exceptions made easier, fines made smaller, the number of trees to be protected was reduced.

I live at Songaia Cohousing, in Bothell, Washington, just outside of Seattle and half an hour from the tech centers of Bellevue and Redmond. In King County, where those cities are located, there is a very public debate over population growth and the challenges that brings. Snohomish County, where I live, has long been a rural area, a patchwork of farms and forests and a few small developments. Discussions about growth in Snohomish County have been mostly out of the news, but recently that is changing.

Songaia was surrounded by woods when I first came here. Now the road we live on is mostly giant suburban homes, and large developments are going in on three sides of us this year. Two of those developments threaten wetlands, forests on our own property, and create public safety concerns. Part of the problem is that the county isn't enforcing their own Long Term Plan. The Long Term Plan (LTP) is the document that guides development. It specifies how dense various areas can be, how many trees must be left, how wetlands are to be protected, and how traffic is expected to be impacted. Developers can ask the county to waive or change parts of the LTP for their particular project, and since the county nearly always does so, the developer has no reason not to ask!

We are wrestling with how much of our resources we should devote to fighting the developers, to making the county stick to its own LTP, and if we should get involved in the much bigger issue of how development is being handled throughout the county. While we are taking this developer to court over these two projects, we recognize that this fight is a microcosm, a reflection of another level. Do we have the time, money, and energy to become involved in protecting land beyond our neighborhood? Already some members of Songaia are nervous about the existing monthly tours and occasional open-to-the-public events. As we push back, make a lot of noise, get a lot of press, there are more strangers visiting here, including news crews with cameras and microphones. This week we had a radio spot, last week the county newspaper crew was here. Next week we host the developers for a tour, and we've invited the Hearing Examiner to come visit. We will continue to connect with nonprofit groups and other threatened neighborhoods. Our local County Council member was the only dissenting vote when the Council supported the developers, so we've invited him to meet with us to discuss the directions Snohomish County is going. All of this press is getting a lot of attention, and with it, a lot more visitors. Even the residents who can see the necessity of all the visitors aren't always comfortable with it. Some retreat to their private home and shut the door, others plan to be off the property when the news crews are here.

Songaia was surrounded by woods when I first came here; now large developments are going in on three sides.

We are getting a painful lesson in Democracy: if you don't want it to go to the highest bidder, you have to get involved early, stay informed, connect with others who share your interests. When the county's Long Term Plan was made, guiding development over the next few decades, the broad strokes seemed fine. No one here had time to get involved at the level of detail it would have taken to notice the loopholes, because they were busy trying to plan and build an intentional community, run nonprofit groups, raise children. When the Tree Ordinance was changed, no one here noticed because they weren't involved with county planning. When the Urban Growth Boundary was changed, expanding to cover more area, everyone was too busy growing a garden, holding workshops, running businesses, and why wouldn't we be? We live in a progressive area with elected officials who care about the environment. Songaia was founded by people who wanted to make the world better, but for a long time that energy has been focused inward, on turning our 15 acres into a paradise. Now we are realizing that if we don't focus some of our energy outwards, to the rest of the county, we might become an island oasis instead.

We aren't the only neighborhood where this sort of "dumb growth" is happening. On the other side of the county is a development called Frognal Estates, 112 proposed houses on 22 acres of heavily wooded steep ravine, draining into Picnic Point Park and Picnic Point Creek. Here again the county Planning Commission overrode its own rules for density, buffers, and protection of wetlands and steep slopes. They ignored the public comment process, which appears to be a routine joke. They ignored inadequate roads, schools, and other infrastructure. In recent months Songaia has connected with the Picnic Point Preservation Committee. We've been to the hearings for their appeals, and they've been to ours. While both appeals have been lost, the connections we've made with those neighbors might turn into something bigger scale and longer term.

Recently we've become aware of another inappropriate development nearby. Wellington Park, a proposed sports complex, would replace a wooded park full of trails, habitat, and wetlands. Developers who would benefit financially have again pushed the Planning Commission to grant them exceptions and override public outcry. It is too late to save the patch of forest next door to us, but can "Neighbors to Save Wellington Park" benefit from what we have learned?

Both Songaia and Picnic Point residents have been talking to the Livable Snohomish County Coalition. LSCC, formed by Snohomish County Audobon Society director Kristin Kelly, aims

Songaia residents and interns stand witness, with drums and songs, while the trees fall 10' from our driveway.

to bring the region's residents together to make progressive, win-win plans that protect our environment and encourage good land use and development practices. LSCC networks groups together, so that instead of fighting separate fights we can support each other, learn from each others' processes, possibly even raise money jointly. Separately we can be dismissed as just NIMBY neighbors, together we are a movement for smarter development.

Some Songaia residents love the activism. Others support their neighbors but want to stay as private as possible themselves. Still others aren't so sure we should be putting ourselves in the spotlight this much. Some are feeling the beginnings of the "fishbowl" effect and wondering if their home will still be their sanctuary. We are debating proper use of community funds: should they be used only for maintaining our buildings and gardens, or should they be used to help maintain our beautiful Pacific Northwest region? How far does that responsibility extend? Our street? As far as we can see? The Urban Growth Boundary Area? The whole county?

Every community has an obligation to work to define their borders, the space in which they live and thrive, and the space they feel responsible for helping to maintain. How far does our reach go? ❧

Sylvan Bonin lives at Songaia Cohousing, near Seattle, Washington. She spends most of her time gardening, cooking for the community, putting up the abundance of the garden and orchards, building and fixing things, and teaching edible wild foods and mushroom foraging. Between "suburban homesteading" and raising a son, she makes as much time as possible for art and dancing.

This was a forest on Monday. After four appeals and $60,000, we won concessions including no fence and the right to choose the trees to be planted in the landscape buffer.

County Code specifies a 15' tree protection buffer, but the county allowed the developer to reduce this to 10'.

Photos courtesy of Sylvan Bonin

Kids at play at Sunward.

WHITE BIAS, BLACK LIVES:
When Unconscious Bias Affects Your Community

By Katy Mattingly

No one thinks they are racist. None of us believes we have a bias against an entire group of humans for no other reason than the color of their skin or the nationality of their ancestors. No one thinks—I'm a bad person, I'm unfair, I'm hateful.

Instead, we believe we are behaving rationally. We think we understand a thing or two about human nature, about who is safe and who is unsafe. We say to ourselves, "I may not be able to say it out loud in this meeting, because of these politically correct types, but they are fooling themselves. I'm a good judge of strangers, of who is good and who is bad." Everyone has a gut instinct. Everyone is driven to follow that instinct—right or wrong.

But of course, racism has affected everyone in America—me, you, and all our neighbors. It's *in* our gut instincts. We don't have to look far into the nation's history, politics, media, or current affairs before we see racism all around us. No one thinks "I am racist" but every child of color in America must face racism—it's everywhere. Even in our liberal intentional communities.

In my community, it's been showing up when children play on our property. Do you see a neighborhood kid, a visitor, a boy you know playing basketball with his little brother? Or do you see a stranger, a trespasser, a young man threatening your family's safety and peace of mind? How do you decide?

Unconscious Bias

Unconscious bias is the idea that stereotypes common in American culture get under our skin, past our mental constructs, and have a way of informing our behavior without our conscious mind's approval. Sometimes called implicit bias, implicit associations, or microaggressions, the concept has been proven scientifically in the psychological literature.[1] If you're willing to have some uncomfortably fascinating moments with yourself, take a few brief online assessments of your own bias at implicit.harvard.edu/implicit/takeatest.html.

Maybe you've noticed unconscious bias in your own life when you accidentally associated a southern accent with stupidity, when you assumed the Latina you didn't recognize at work was there to empty your trash, when a black man got on your bus and you pulled your purse closer, then wondered why you were afraid.

Maybe you've noticed unconscious bias in your intentional community. It may be there when someone on the membership committee asks: "Is this family really *a good fit* for us?" Or when there are more women than men in your neighborhood but somehow meetings are mostly filled with male voices. It may be functioning when some visitors are asked questions, and others are left alone.

Is It Really Happening Here?

Sunward Cohousing, just outside of Ann Arbor, Michigan has been struggling with unconscious bias for a long time. Founded in 1998, we built our beautiful community of 40 homes from the ground up on an old gravel pit, just around the corner from a low-income, subsidized apartment complex. Later, two other cohousing communities formed next door. About 500 people live within a mile of each other in these four separate communities.

Many, though not all, of the cohousing residents are white, wealthy, and older. Many, though not all, of the apartment complex neighbors are African American, working class, and younger. Often, though not always, you can make a good guess about where a neighbor lives from a quick glance.

Decisions based on unconscious bias happen in split seconds. In group or out group? Friend or stranger? Safe or unsafe? And because adults in our extended neighborhood tend to stay near their own homes, it's the *children* who cross lines and show up as visitors or trespassers.

Take a look at that kid at the basketball hoop. Do you recognize him? Does he belong here? Is he a problem? Should you notify someone? Should you ignore him? Do you have time to go chat with him? Are you happy to see him? Do you feel worried for him? Are you afraid of him?

Are you willing to add "why?" to the end of every one of those questions?

Over the past two years my community has had some great interactions with neighborhood kids who visit our playground, our woods, our pond, and our common house. Our kids are friends and classmates and campmates with kids from the other three communities. Some of us from Sunward canvassed the low-income neighborhood before last year's presidential election and talked to teens there about registering to vote. Some charming and hard-working neighborhood kids showed up for our work day and worked long and hard beside us in the gardens.

And we've also had some terrible experiences with each other. One kid was accused of stealing something after being seen inside our common house. One damaged a garden and was verbally threatened with violence by a member. Some kids playing basketball refused to leave after they were asked nicely, and it devolved into curses and shouting on both sides.

The terrible experiences are the ones that get talked about in community meetings. We've tried many approaches. We started keeping the common house locked. We hung a "members and their guests only" sign at the basketball hoop. We encouraged visiting kids to stay and play but only if a Sunward adult was present. We asked kids to leave. We threatened to call 911 if they didn't.

And because we're home to about 100 people with different beliefs and experiences and free will, we've never responded consistently or agreed on the "right" way to behave. Some of us have invited kids inside for a snack. Some of us have physically dragged them off the property. Some of us have stopped reading emails about the issue or coming to meetings where it is discussed. The police have been called to deal with children. More than once.

It is painful *but essential* to note that children who are dark-skinned are treated differently than children who are white-skinned. I am unaware of a single instance of the police being called on white kids who trespass. Including the white girls who lit a fire in our woods, got drunk, threw up, and slept out there overnight. Or the white boys who rode their mopeds up and down our delicate trails.

When we try to talk about the issue in community meetings, it often feels as if we're speaking different languages. When someone feels afraid, it's difficult to communicate to that person that her fear might be more about unconscious bias than it is about actual risk. We hear: "I'm just sensitive to the sound of loud voices." We hear: "It's just that I was hurt once and I don't want to talk about it." We hear: "I prefer not to have to see strangers and those kids look like they don't belong here."

Mostly we hear: "This isn't about race, it's about something else."

But it is about race. We are mostly Americans here in my neighborhood. We are mostly white Americans. And we are unconsciously biased against people of color in general and black boys in particular.

The Process

Unconscious bias can be tricky to address. It's *unconscious.* Have you ever tried to change something about yourself you're barely aware of? Have you ever tried to get someone else to change a behavior she doesn't even know she's participating in? Have you ever been told something about yourself you were loath to believe?

We formed a small group to help the community walk through a Consensus-Oriented Decision-Making[2] process (CODM, for short) designed to answer the following question: *What should we do when random, uninvited kids show up on our property?*

CODM invites participants to generate a list of concerns which should be addressed in any eventual proposal; ours fell into five main categories:

Safety of People	We affirm the right of adults and children, members and residents of neighboring communities, to *feel* safe and to *be* safe.
Safety of Property	We may face legal and financial liability if a child is injured here; we wish to prevent harm to our buildings and property.
Relationships	We wish to build, nurture, and sustain relationships with our neighbors. This includes helping our kids befriend neighbor kids, and getting to know the parents of visiting kids.
Fairness	We are concerned with fairness, and desire a consistent response across incidents whether the kids visiting/trespassing are from the other cohousing communities or from the apartment neighborhood.
Effectiveness	The chosen approach should be actionable, sustainable, flexible, and evaluated for effectiveness.

Next in the CODM process, we're invited to choose a general approach. Over several meetings, two different ways of responding to the issue emerged: *protective* and *welcoming.* We named these intentionally. The CODM team included proponents of both approaches, as well as a facilitator experienced with remaining neutral. Clearly, we couldn't label one approach *safety* any more than we could label the other *anti-racist.* Instead we identified positive language for both broad strategies.

Next, across multiple meetings, we hung large sheets of newsprint and brainstormed about each of the basic, shared concerns listed above. How could we address people's safety with a welcoming approach? How could we address it with a protective approach? Here are some samples from the brainstorming sessions:

CONCERN Safety of People	APPROACH Welcoming	APPROACH Protective
Physical violence between residents and visitors Unpleasant verbal interactions Harm to kids by unnecessary use of law enforcement Using law enforcement when needed	De-escalate conflicts, use a respectful tone Trained team of responders who volunteer to interact with kids Written definition of when law enforcement is necessary, save it for emergencies, not damage to property, not trespassing Post-incident debriefs led by mediation committee	Install/improve common house locks Resident responders who are trained by the police Ask the police for proactive help Improve signage stating our trespassing policies Sign-in sheets for all guests

Ultimately, the community expressed a clear preference for the welcoming approach. At this point, CODM guided us to return to the minority preference—the protective approach—to select aspects which should be included in the draft proposal.

The Proposal

You may have noticed that the concept of a team of trained responders appears under both approaches above. The idea of a team of willing volunteers who feel comfortable interacting with neighbor kids and could be on call for incidents arose again and again as Sunward discussed these challenges. This text is from the current draft proposal:

All residents are encouraged to contact the response team (trained Sunward adults) if they are uncomfortable about uninvited children on the property. Members of the response team converse with kids and youth and, in most cases, ask them to leave. They treat everyone fairly and consistently. Team members are trained to use a relationship-centered approach, are sensitive to unconscious bias, and committed to communication that is fair, safe, and effectively sets boundaries. Calling 911 is an option of last resort used only in emergencies. Trespassing in and of itself is not considered an emergency.

Addressing Unconscious Bias

The proposal on the table attempts to address the challenges of unconscious racial, gender, and socioeconomic status bias in multiple ways.

Separate Crime Prevention from Kid Visits. It has been difficult to decouple the concept of crime prevention from interactions with neighborhood children. The team affirmed repeatedly that this proposal does not address security cameras, or neighborhood watch, or trespassing by adults, or recent petty property crimes committed or suspected in the neighborhood. This process is only to identify what we should do (and not do) when random, uninvited kids show up.

Provide Multiple Roles. By volunteering to be available, response team members could benefit those who feel unsafe or uncomfortable interacting directly with the kids. Sunward could develop a process by which those who have lost their temper or threatened children are excluded from the team and relieved from feeling responsible for enforcement. Responders can be trained to look for unconscious bias and discuss it during incident debriefs.

Limit Calls to Law Enforcement in Non-Emergencies. Decision points in this area have been particularly fraught. Unconscious bias for or against the police runs deep. For many white people, it's shocking news to realize that many people of color and poor people feel the most unsafe when police are present. The current proposal aims to protect black kids from unnecessary contact with the police by providing a written definition of their role—while of course leaving every member free to make their own choices about calling 911.

Address Age Bias. "People of all races see black children as less innocent, more adultlike and more responsible for their actions than their white peers."[3] White people also tend to guess black children as older than they are. By suggesting that the policy applies to older teens and young adults, Sunward is attempting to counteract this potentially dangerous misperception and limit calls to 911.

Fairness. The draft proposal emphasizes consistency, fairness, and application to kids from all nearby neighborhoods, including the other cohousing kids. If black children are not allowed to trespass on community property, then white children aren't allowed to either.

Know the Impact of Language. Most people are unlikely to warm to being labeled as *racist*. Referencing *unconscious bias* instead can welcome white people to these discussions. At the same time, know the phrase can sound to some like an ineffective synonym for *racism*. According to African American comedian and activist W. Kamau Bell, microaggression and unconscious bias are just "fancy ways for describing racism that isn't necessarily fatal. Racism that makes our so-called white friends ask 'How do you know it was racism?'...the kind of racism that drives you crazy. Death by a thousand racist cuts."[4]

Conclusion

Probably no one is surprised that a midwestern cohousing community of mostly white baby boomers has not solved American racism in 2018. Despite the expressed desire of many to feel more *comfortable*—for example by excluding non-member kids—I think it's fair to say that *no one feels better* yet. In fact, those of us who are committed to unlearning our unconscious bias would suggest that feeling *uncomfortable* is one marker of progress!

We're not done. But the Consensus-Oriented Decision-Making process has shown us a way forward that hasn't required 100 percent agreement or even a shared definition of the problem. We hosted multiple uncomfortable conversations about race, class, gender, and age. We held listening circles which took our neighbors' fears and experiences seriously. We will continue to ask if our behavior is consistent with our values, and if our impact on neighborhood children matches our intentions. All of which has demonstrated a key benefit of living in community—working through hard issues, holding each other accountable, and taking shared action for the highest good.

Katy Mattingly is a member of the Consensus-Oriented Decision-Making Kids team at Sunward Cohousing in Ann Arbor, Michigan. This article was read and edited for accuracy and clarity by the entire team, but not co-written, and reflects Katy's own opinions and experiences of the community process. Notably, zero child visitors were consulted in the writing of this article.

---

1. For more information check out *Blind Spot: Hidden Biases of good people.* (2013.) Banaji, M.R. and Greenwald, A.G. Or *Everyday Bias: Identifying and navigating unconscious judgments in our daily lives.* (2014). Ross, H.J.
2. See *Consensus-Oriented Decision-Making: The CODM model for facilitating groups to widespread agreement.* (2010.) Hartnett, T.
3. www.nytimes.com/2017/07/26/opinion/black-kids-discrimination.html
4. *The Awkward Thoughts of W. Kamau Bell.* (2017.) Bell, W.K.

Printed in Great Britain
by Amazon

66271100R00237